TRIBAL AN1  ꞮS

George Dalton
is professor of economics and anthropology at Northwestern
University and a staff member of its Program of African Studies.
He received his B.A. degree from Indiana University, his M.A.
from Columbia University, and, in 1959, his Ph.D. from the
University of Oregon. He has taught at Boston University and
Bard College.

In 1961–1962 he spent fifteen months in West Africa as
deputy director of Northwestern University's Economic Survey
of Liberia and is co-author of a volume on Liberian economic
development. He is the author of *Economic Anthropology and
Development* and *Economic Systems and Society*, and, with
Paul Bohannan, he edited *Markets in Africa*. He has published
articles on economic anthropology, comparative economy, and
economic development.

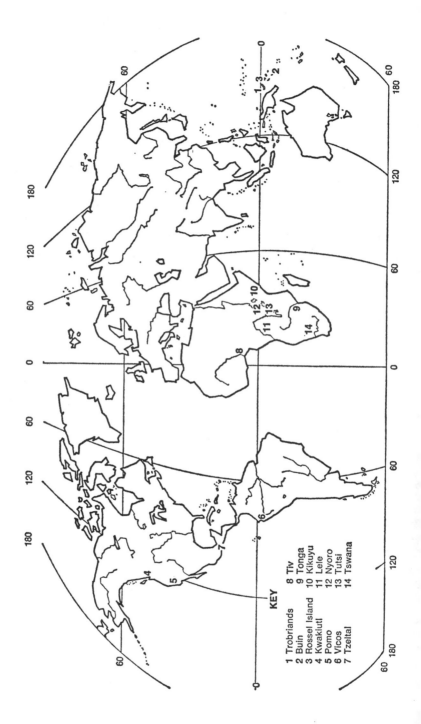

KEY

1 Trobriands   8 Tiv
2 Buin   9 Tonga
3 Rossel Island   10 Kikuyu
4 Kwakiutl   11 Lele
5 Pomo   12 Nyoro
6 Vicos   13 Tutsi
7 Tzeltal   14 Tswana

Texas Press Sourcebooks in Anthropology
were originally published by the Natural History Press, a division of Doubleday and Company, Inc. Responsibility for the series now resides with the University of Texas Press, Box 7819, Austin, Texas 78712. Whereas the series has been a joint effort between the American Museum of Natural History and the Natural History Press, future volumes in the series will be selected through the auspices of the editorial offices of the University of Texas Press.

The purpose of the series will remain unchanged in its effort to make available inexpensive, up-to-date, and authoritative volumes for the student and the general reader in the field of anthropology.

Tribal
and
Peasant Economies

Readings in Economic Anthropology

Edited by George Dalton

University of Texas Press

Austin

Library of Congress Cataloging in Publication Data

Dalton, George, ed.
  Tribal and peasant economies.

  (Texas Press sourcebooks in anthropology)
  Reprint of the ed. published for the American Museum of Natural
History by the Natural History Press, Garden City, N.Y., in series:
American Museum sourcebooks in anthropology.
  Bibliography: p.
  Includes index.
  1. Economics, Primitive—Addresses, essays, lectures. I. Title II. Series.
III. Series: American Museum sourcebooks in anthropology.
  [GN448.D34 1976]   330.9   75-44040
  ISBN 0-292-78015-X

*Published by arrangement with Doubleday & Company, Inc. Previously
published by the Natural History Press in cooperation with Doubleday
& Company, Inc.*

ACKNOWLEDGMENTS

I should like to thank Conrad M. Arensberg, Saul Benison, Gerald D. Berreman, David Brokensha, Clifford Geertz, Everett E. Hagen, Manning Nash, Walter Neale, Hans Panofsky, and Andrew Vayda for giving me suggestions on what to include in this volume. I am grateful also to my secretary, Ruth Curtis, for her work in preparing the manuscripts for the press, and to the authors and publishers of the articles and chapters reprinted in this volume for their permission to do so. The original place of publication is cited on the first page of each of the essays.

CONTENTS

INTRODUCTION

George Dalton

An anthology is a selection of writings from a much larger body of literature. In this introduction I will explain why the selection I have chosen seems to me a useful one by relating the writings included to the principal concerns of economic anthropology.

One of several reasons for the marked increase of interest in the economic aspects of subsistence and peasant communities in recent years is the Colonial Revolution in Africa, Asia, and Latin America. The achievement of political independence and the new nations' striving for economic development makes systematic knowledge of the economies and societies of underdeveloped communities very important. Such knowledge is the stock in trade of anthropologists. Understanding the structure of what is and what has been is necessary to those people charged with formulating intelligent policy on what ought to be. For societies without literacy and written records, economic anthropology can serve as a kind of economic history—an ethnographic record of economic organization before industrialization and development take place.

A related reason for the growth of interest in economic anthropology is that all social scientists now poach on areas that used to be the exclusive preserve of anthropologists. In this volume the sociologist Neil Smelser gives us valuable theoretical insights into processes of socio-economic change (3). And economists in their concern with transforming traditional economies are creating a political economy of development which takes account of social and cultural institutions vastly different from those of contemporary Europe and America (Hagen 1962; Myrdal 1957; Lewis 1955; Adelman and Morris 1965). The common concern with economic development has brought about a shotgun wedding of the social sciences. We are all developers now. Eight of the contributors to this volume are not anthropologists, and almost half the essays touch on aspects of social and economic change.

Another reason for the growth of interest in economic anthropology is the work of the economic historian Karl Polanyi (1944: Chapter 4; Polanyi, Arensberg, and Pearson 1957), which provides a useful theoretical framework for analyzing primitive and archaic economies.[1] Polanyi's work on the nature of transactional modes, petty markets, and primitive money is made use of in this volume in the essays of Bohannan (9), Finley (21), and Dalton (5, 16).

Anthropologists who study the economies of the peoples among whom they do fieldwork concern themselves with two broad themes: how economic organization, ecology, and technology relate to the rest of social organization and culture; and the causes and consequences of economic, technological, social, and cultural change in the small communities of the underdeveloped world. Which of the themes a writer emphasizes depends on the condition of the people at the time of his fieldwork. The older generation of anthropologists—Malinowski is the best example in this book—are likely to present a static picture of the structured relationships between economy and society in a traditional setting. Those who did their fieldwork more recently—Bohannan, Douglas, Geertz—consider socio-economic change because the peoples they study (and their small societies and economies) are changing.

For any matter relating to economy that concerns anthropologists, there is an important literature outside of anthropology. The point requires emphasis because anthropologists sometimes do not bring to their economic analyses the same comparative base they bring to kinship, law, politics, and religion. I illustrate the point in this volume by including writings on European and Japanese pre-industrial economic history: on the nature of gift-giving and treasure items in economies in which market exchange is absent or unimportant, compare Finley on archaic Greece (21) with

[1] For an expository account of Polanyi's work, see Dalton (1965a). Those of Polanyi's essays of most interest to anthropologists are in George Dalton, editor, *Primitive, Archaic, and Modern Economies: Essays of Karl Polanyi*, Anchor Books, 1967.

Malinowski on the Trobriands (13). On land tenure, and on economic obligations of political inferiors toward superiors in sharply stratified societies, compare Pirenne on medieval Europe (22) with Maquet on the Tutsi (6) and Beattie on the Bunyoro (7). On peasantry, compare the extraordinarily sensitive account of European peasants by the historian Handlin (25) with the descriptions of Latin American peasantry by Wolf (28) and Nash (29), and Chinese peasants by Yang (18).

It is not only on the organization of subsistence and peasant economies and how these relate to social organization, culture, and folk-views that the historical accounts complement the anthropological. On the extremely complicated issues of social and economic change, growth, and development (processes of urbanization, industrialization, commercialization, and national integration) that increasingly absorb anthropological analysis, the historians give us a rich literature well worth the consideration of any anthropologist who would rather be well informed than needlessly original. Anthropologists are aware of the relevance of European history to anthropology when the lesson is taught by a Durkheim or a Weber. But note that Max Weber teaches us not only the connections between religion and economy (24), but also—and with rare insight—that the national European economies integrated by market exchange were historically unique: that market dependence for livelihood was a presupposition of modern industrial capitalism (23). On related matters, such as sequences of socio-economic change, and the social consequences of growth in production for market sale, compare also Takizawa's description of the Japanese experience (19) with Schapera's (10) and Bohannan's (9) accounts of African peoples.

Several of the writings are summary articles each of which gives the reader analytical conclusions drawn from empirical literature on a specific topic: Nash (1) and Forde and Douglas (2) give concise accounts of the salient characteristics of tribal and peasant economies. Kolenda (17) summarizes the principal writings on reciprocal *jajmani* relationships in village India. Wolf (28) draws from a large literature to classify several types of Latin American peasantry. Dalton (5) describes typical modes of resource allocation, work organization, and produce disposition in indigenous African economies and contrasts these to industrialized market economies of Europe and America, and surveys a number of writings on rural Africa to point up the frequent case of social malaise caused by piecemeal change, and by economic growth without development (11).

Finally, some of the writings consider contentious issues in economic anthropology. On one such issue, the nature of primitive money, I have included several articles because the issue involves important matters of methodology as well as substance. Reading Douglas (8), Thurnwald (14), Bohannan (9), Armstrong (15), and Dalton (16), will help answer the question of the relevance of conventional economic concepts (in this case, the model of money as it is used in capitalism), to the analysis of subsistence economies; moreover, the discussions contrast primitive money-stuff used in status payments and reciprocal exchanges (e.g., bridewealth) with money used in commercial purchases. Drucker (26) shows that the notorious case of the aggressive Kwakiutl potlatch was a very late development, after the Kwakiutl became importantly enmeshed in cash-earning, and not at all what the potlatch was indigenously. Vayda (27) describes one form of noncommercial external trade and suggests it has latent functions of ensuring material access in times of dearth, as well as prestige functions.

SUMMARY

The writings chosen for this volume describe what economic anthropology is, what it is becoming, and what the editor, at least, thinks it ought to be. There are writings on relatively static, traditional economies of two principal sorts: subsistence (primitive, tribal) economies, and peasant economies; and on economies undergoing social and economic change and development. There are writings which show how the work of economists, historians, and sociologists provide analytical insights into matters of interest to anthropologists. There are writings which consider contentious theoretical and conceptual issues: what is primitive money? Do the similarities between stratified societies in Africa and those of medieval Europe justify the use of the term "feudalism"? What are the differences between peasant economies and societies on the one hand, and those called primitive and modern on the other? What was the potlatch? How transferable is conventional economics to economic anthropology?

The arrangement of the readings in this volume is by geographical area, with articles relating to social and economic change appearing at the end of each section. To have arranged the articles according to some other format would either have suggested a uniformity among primitive and peasant economies that I think spurious and misleading, or have created other difficulties.

There are three other principles of classification I considered using. The first is the oldest set of distinctions used by anthropologists, which is according to technology, ecology, and principal source of subsistence: gathering, hunting and fishing, agricultural, and pastoral economies. However, these distinctions tell us almost nothing about economic organization. To use a familiar example, according to this kind of classification, the U.S. and the U.S.S.R. would appear in the same category (manufacturing and agricultural) because the criteria for classification ignore economic characteristics.

A second possibility is to use a system of classification based on the structural characteristics of large-scale industrial capitalism, as Herskovits does in his *Economic Anthropology:* production, exchange and distribution, property, the economic surplus. However, I find some of these categories too broad and ill-fitting for economic anthropology. The dozen or so large, developed, rather similar national economies of Western Europe and North America that these categories were designed to fit are in a number of important ways systematically different as a group from the hundreds of small subsistence and peasant economies and societies that are the concern of economic anthropology.

My own articles reprinted in this volume contain classifications that I find useful to analyze primitive and peasant economies: resource allocation, work organization, product disposition, internal and external transactional modes (reciprocity, redistribution, market exchange; administered trade), money uses (commercial and noncommercial), subsistence spheres, prestige spheres, conversions, peripheral markets, etc. But to have used these as the basis for choosing or arranging articles would have made my theoretical approach to the subject more prominent than I think proper in a book such as this. Therefore I chose a more neutral format, arrangement by geographical area, and chose articles of high quality that give both ethnographic description and theoretical analysis.

I GENERAL VIEWS

1 THE ORGANIZATION OF ECONOMIC LIFE

Manning Nash

The economic life of man shows a great variety over time and space. In the New Hebrides islands, the main economic concern is the accumulation of pigs. Men raise pigs, exchange pigs, lend out pigs at interest, and finally in a large ceremonial feast destroy the pig holdings of a lifetime. Among the Bushmen of the Kalahari desert there is no private property in productive goods, and whatever the hunting band manages to kill is shared out among the members of the group. In the Melanesian islands every gardener brings some of the yams from his plot to the chief's house. There the pile of yams grows and grows, and eventually rots, to the greater glory of the tribe. The Indians of Guatemala and Mexico live in communities each with its own economic specialty. One group produces pottery, another blankets, another lumber and wood, and the next exports its surplus maize. These communities are tied together in a complex system of markets and exchange.

How are these economic activities to be interpreted and explained? What body of ideas can make sense of the gift-giving of the Plains Indians, the personalized markets of Haiti, the elaborate ceremonial of exchange in the Trobriand Islands (Malinowski 1922)? Less than half a century ago the differences among economic systems were explained by the hypothesis of social evolution. Different economic systems were assigned to levels or stages of the evolution of human society and culture. It was assumed that there had been an evolution from simple hunting

FROM Manning Nash, "The Organization of Economic Life," in Sol Tax, ed., *Horizons of Anthropology* (Chicago, Aldine Publishing Company, 1964), pp. 171–180. Reprinted by permission of the author and publisher.

bands, with communal property rules, to villages with settled
agriculture and clan or family property, and that was followed
by a stage of political units with advanced technology and private
or state property. This view of economic evolution has not fared
well in the face of modern field research. Two chief things have
made this mode of explanation lose its force. First, the rising
tide of field investigation of economic systems revealed a whole
host of economic arrangements which this crude classification by
stages could not contain. And second, the idea of stages of
evolution shed very little light on the actual processes of economic
change. A new model of the variables to explain economic systems and their changes over time is now being fashioned. This
model rests on about four decades of accumulated information,
and on methods and theories developed in the act of gathering
and interpreting that data.

Method in studying economic systems is basically the same
as in the rest of social and cultural anthropology. Method is a
device to study social regularities, and to give meaning to those
regularities. In the study of nonmonetary, or partially monetized
economies, getting the basic facts is often a test of the observer's
ingenuity. Many new ways of getting measurable or nearly
measured data have been invented, and recent research is marked
by an emphasis on quantities or relative magnitudes of economic
activities.

The distinguishing features of peasant and primitive economic
systems fall along four axes. The first is *technological complexity
and the division of labor*. These are relatively simple societies,
technologically. A simple technology means that the number of
different tasks involved in any productive act are few. Usually
it is the skill of a single or a few producers which carries production from beginning to end. Many primitive and peasant technologies are ingenious, marvelously fitted to a particular environment, requiring high levels of skill and performance, but still very
simple. The Bemba of Rhodesia (Gluckman 1945) wrest a living
from poor soil with uncertain water supply by an intricate method
of cultivation. With good rains and luck they harvest their crop
of finger millet. The system is one of balance in a precarious
ecological niche, but the task structure is simple, and the tools
involved require only human energy to operate. The specialized
operations involved are not the kind which make an interrelated

web of occupations. Men do most of the agricultural work among the Bemba, and one man is virtually as good as another in his agricultural skills. The division of labor follows the natural axes of sex and age. An occupational list in a peasant or primitive society is not a long one. Persons tend to learn their productive skills in the ordinary business of growing up, and within age and sex categories there is high interchangeability among productive workers. Work and tasks are apportioned to the appropriate persons, without much regard to differences in skill or productivity. The technology also sets the limits of the size of combined working parties. Except at peak periods—planting or harvesting in agricultural communities, an organized hunt at the height of the animal running season—large working parties are not found. Effort and work are closely tied to a pattern fitted to the annual and ceremonial cycle, not to the continuous demands of a highly organized economy with a wide social division of labor.

The second feature of peasant and primitive economy is the *structure and membership of productive units*. The unit of production, the social organization carrying out the making of goods, is dependent on, and derived from, other forms of social life. Peasant and primitive societies do not have organizations whose only tasks are those of production, and there are no durable social units based solely on productive activities. The bonds of kinship which structure families, clans, and kindreds are often the bonds which organize economic activities. Territorial bonds may serve to create local producing organizations. And the political structure, especially in societies with hereditary nobilities, is often used as a mechanism for forming productive units. This dependence of economic units on prior kinds of social relations has a typical series of consequences. Productive units tend to be multipurposed. Their economic activities are only one aspect of the things they do. The economic aspect of a family, a local group, or a compound composed of patrons and clients, is just one area where the maintenance needs of the group are being met. Therefore, in these societies there tend to be many productive units, similarly structured, all doing the same sort of work. These productive units are limited in the sorts of personnel they are able to recruit, the capital they are able to command, and the ways in which they may distribute their product. There does not exist a labor market, nor a capital market, nor a system of distribution to factors of production. A striking example of productive units based on relations derived from the organization of social groups only partially oriented to economic activity is the Indian pottery-making community in southeastern Mexico. This community is composed of 278 households. Each household is engaged in the production of pottery for sale, with virtually the same technology (Nash 1961). Every household looks like every other in its productive organization. Or again, from Mexico, among the people of Tepoztlan (Lewis 1951) many make their living by the sale of services at a wage. Yet people must be sought out for employment, and hiring a fellow member of the community is a delicate social job. The transaction cannot appear as a strictly economic one.

The third distinguishing feature of peasant and primitive economies is the *systems and media of exchange*. In an economy with a simple technology, productive units which are multipurposed and derived from other forms of social organization, and with a division of labor based chiefly on sex and age, a close calculation of the costs of doing one thing or another is often impossible, or merely irrelevant. The advantages of a change in the use of time, resources, and personnel are arrived at through the logic of social structure, through a calculus of relative values, not in terms of the increase of a single magnitude such as productivity. This inability to estimate closely the costs and benefits of economic activity is aggravated by the absence of money as *the* medium of exchange. Most of the world now has some familiarity with the use of money. In fact, some societies developed full, all purpose money prior to contact with the industrial and commercial West (Davenport 1961). And many societies have standards of exchange like the Polynesian shell currencies, or the tusked pigs of Melanesia, the salt currency of the horn of Africa, or the cocoa beans of the Aztecs. But this is quasi-money, or special purpose money; it is merely the standard with the widest sphere of exchange. Special purpose money is confined to a particular circuit of exchange, and the circuits of exchange in the economy are only partially tied together. Among the Siane of New Guinea (Salisbury 1962) there are different kinds of exchange of goods, and each kind of goods is limited to its particular circuit. Some goods can be exchanged only for subsistence items, others only for luxury items, and others only for items which confer status and prestige. The Tiv of Nigeria (Bohannan 1955) have similar multicentered exchange systems with media appropriate to each sphere of exchange. Food is exchanged for food, and can be exchanged for brass rods; brass rods exchange for the highest valued goods, women and slaves. And a reverse or downward movement of exchange items was severely resisted and considered illogical and unfortunate among the Tiv.

The media of exchange and the circuits of exchange are set into various kinds of systems of exchange. The most common systems of exchange are markets, redistributive system, reciprocal exchange, and mobilization exchange. The market system is widespread among peasants, and in Meso-America tends to be free, open, and self-regulating (Tax 1952). In Haiti (Mintz 1961) the market is competitive, free, and open, but special bonds of personal attachment grow up between some buyers and some sellers which cut down some of the risk and uncertainty involved in small peasant trading. Rotating market centers, with a central market and several subsidiary markets, are a fairly common feature in Burma among the Shans, in several parts of Africa, north and south of the Sahara, and in many places in the Near and Far East. These market systems usually operate without the presence of firms, and lack investment in expensive facilities of exchange, including the spread of information. The single complex of markets, firms, capital investments, entrepreneurs, deliberate technical investment, and property rules to facilitate accumulation and exchange is apparently a historical precipitate peculiar to the West. In the ethnographic record it does not appear as a necessary bundle or sequence of events.

Reciprocity of exchanges is exemplified by the practices of gift-giving (Mauss 1925) or kula exchange of the Trobriand Islands and tends to lack much bargaining between, to rest on fixed sets of trading partners, and to occur between equivalent units of the social structure. Thus clans exchange with clans; barrios or wards with wards; households with households; tribes with tribes; or communities with communities. The reciprocal exchange is for near equivalences in goods and services. The rates of exchange tend to be fixed. Redistributive trade takes place in societies with some systems of social stratification, but not organized for market exchange. An African paramount chief may collect tribute in the form of goods and redistribute it down the social hierarchy through his clients and kinsmen. Or administered trade at fixed prices, with a political center exchanging with its peripheries is another common example (Polanyi 1957b). Redistributive exchange keeps a political and status system operating without great gaps in wealth between the different classes of status groups. A system of mobilization for exchange (Smelser 1959) collects goods and services into the hands of an elite for the broad political aims of the society. The irrigation empires of the early civilizations apparently had these sorts of exchange systems, and some of the new nations of Asia and Africa have systems like this in conjunction with some aspects of market, redistribution, and reciprocal exchange.

The fourth dimension of variation in economic systems is in the *control of wealth and capital*. Generally, investment takes the form of using resources and services to buttress or expand existing sets of social relations. The chief capital goods in peasant and primitive societies are land and men. Tools, machines, terraces, livestock, and other improvements in productive resources are controlled in a manner derived from the conventions of control and allocation of land and human beings. Land tenure is an expression of the social structure of a peasant and primitive society, and the allocation of land results from the operation of the system of kinship, inheritance, and marriage, rather than through contracts or transactions between economic units. Even in those societies where corporate kin groups like clans do not exist as landholding bodies, special devices like the establishment of titles, or kindred-based landholding corporations may be invented as on Truk (Goodenough 1951). Manpower, like land, is also organized to flow in terms of given social forms, not to abstract best uses.

For peasants and primitives to maintain their societies, capital, or property rules, or economic chance may not be permitted to work in ways disruptive of the values and norms of the society. A fairly common device for insuring that accumulated resources are used for social ends is the leveling mechanism. The leveling mechanism is a means of forcing the expenditure of accumulated resources or capital in ways that are not necessarily economic or productive. Leveling mechanisms may take the form of forced loans to relatives or coresidents; a large feast following economic success; a rivalry of expenditure like the potlatch of the Northwest Coast Indians in which large amounts of valuable goods were destroyed; or the ritual levies consequent on office holding in civil and religious hierarchies as in Meso-America; or the giveaways of horses and goods of the Plains Indian. At any rate most peasant and primitive societies have a way of scrambling wealth to inhibit reinvestment in technical advance, and this prevents crystallization of class lines on an economic base.

This schematic presentation of the major features of peasant and primitive economies serves to place them in a comparative series of economic organizations and to extend the range of social contexts for economic analysis. But charting the range and diversity of economic systems is only a part of the task of anthropology. How economic systems relate to the total social system is a question of major theoretical importance. Economic action is only a part of the system of social action. It is tied to the whole social system in three ways: first by normative integration, second by functional interdependence, and third by causal interaction. The ends sought in the economic sphere must be consonant, or complementary, with goals in other spheres. Economic activity derives its meaning from the general values of the society, and people engage in economic activity for rewards often extrinsic to the economy itself. From this point of view, there are no economic motives, but only motives appropriate to the economic sphere. In peasant and primitive societies the norms and values used to define a resource, a commodity, control over goods and services, the distributive process, and standards of economic behavior, are the norms governing most social interaction. The economy is not so different from the rest of society so that one set of values holds there, and other values hold in other contexts. The economic system does not exhibit an ethic counterposed to the regnant value system.

The functional interdependence of economy and society (Parsons and Smelser 1957) stems from the fact that the same persons are actors in the economic, the kinship, the political, and the religious spheres. The role of father must fit in some way with the role of farmer, and these must fit with the role of believer in the ancestor cult, and these must fit with authority position in the lineage, to take an example from the Tallensi (Fortes 1949). The interdependence of parts of a society means that there are limits to the sorts of economies and societies that may coexist in one time and space continuum. These limits only now are being charted. But it is plain that a system of reciprocal exchange rests on social units that are nearly equivalent in status, power, and size. The marriage and descent system of the Nayar (where husbands were warriors who lived away from wives and where descent was matrilineal) is an instance of the functional compatibility of an occupational and status system with a marriage and descent system.

The causal interaction of economy and society turns on the pivot of the provision of facilities. For given forms of social structure a given variety and volume of goods and services are required, and if there are shifts in facilities available, there will be shifts in the rest of society. Conversely, shifts in the social structure will change the volume and variety of goods and services a society produces. The empirical way of finding these causal interactions is to study peasant and primitive societies undergoing change. The facts of change are the only sure guides to generalizing on the sequences, forms, and processes of economic and social interaction. Much of the change in the economic life of peasants and primitives comes from the expansion and spread of the Western forms of economic activity.

The expansion of the economic frontier can be seen in places like Orissa, the hilly tribal region of India (Bailey 1957). Here economic opportunity in the wake of the spread of the money economy has allowed some castes to move quickly up the status ladder and forced some traditional high status castes downward. The economic frontier in the form of money and new opportunities tends to change the role of corporate kin groups and place more emphasis on smaller familial units (Worsley 1956), to introduce a re-evaluation of the goods of a society (Bohannan 1959), and to put pressures on traditional authority systems.

The chief way that peasants and primitives get involved in the world economy is through entering a wage-labor force, or by producing something that can sell in international trade. The effects of entering a wage-labor force (Watson 1958) often start conflicts between generations, raise problems about the control of income, and sometimes depopulate the society so that its social structure collapses. A rural proletariat may replace a tribal society. Income from entrepreneurial activity by peasants poses larger problems for the social system (Firth 1954). It may result in greater wealth differences, in modifications of the use of capital, in loosening the integration of the society, and in changing the authority patterns. The boom involved in peasant agriculture (Belshaw 1955) often involves a change in religious and ethnical concepts, and an increase in the importance of economic activity relative to other forms of social activity.

The introduction of factories to peasant and primitive societies (Nash 1958) provides, in theory, the widest possibilities for transformation. The change induced by a factory may be akin to that from the increased use of money from wage labor, or the expansion of the economic frontier, but it tends to tie the community more closely to a national and international economic network, to provide a new context for political change, to give a base for new voluntary groupings, and to exert great pressures on extended familial networks, and above all to demand a sort of flexibility and mobility of persons and institutions usually not found in traditional societies (Moore and Feldman 1960).

What the studies of economic change have taught is that modifications in economic activity set up a series of pressures and tensions in the society and culture and that there are limited possibilities for their resolution. There is no generally agreed upon sequence of change, and hardly more consensus on final forms, but the evidence seems to indicate that economic systems are among the most dynamic parts of a society, and that economic activity, in the sense of the provision of facilities for the organization of the rest of society, is one of the most pervasive and determinative aspects of social life. It sets the limits within which social structures and cultural patterns may fall.

The field of economic anthropology has mainly, thus far, worked on the description and interpretation of small-scale societies, but by principle and method it is not limited to them (Berliner 1962). It is moving into problems of economic and social change, and illuminating the relations of economy and society, and the causal interaction of economic variables and other parts of society and culture. Its greatest challenge and potential is the fashioning of a theory encompassing both economic and noneconomic variables in a single explanatory system. It may then provide a framework for a truly comparative study of the form, function, and dynamics of economic systems (Dalton 1961).

BIBLIOGRAPHICAL NOTE

Modern studies in economic anthropology stem from Malinowski's *Argonauts of the Western Pacific* (1922). Raymond Firth's *Primitive Polynesian Economy* (1939) is a landmark in field studies. Melville Herskovits' *Economic Anthropology* (1952) is a good catalog of the empirical work to date. Sol Tax's *Penny Capitalism* (1953) is probably the most complete and detailed description of a small scale non-Western economy. Specialized studies like Bohannan and Dalton (1962) and a growing interest in economic and social change (Salisbury 1962 and Epstein 1962) now dominate research and theory.

2 PRIMITIVE ECONOMICS

Daryll Forde and Mary Douglas

The economies of primitive peoples differ widely. The Australian aborigines, for example, or the Californian Indians live solely by hunting and foraging, without any knowledge of plant cultivation or stock raising. The Fula of the west Sudan or the Bedouin Arabs are herders and depend on cultivation only to a minor degree, or may themselves not grow any crops at all. There are hand-cultivators with no large livestock as in tsetse infested districts in central Africa. There are stock raisers who grow cereals and supplement their larders by hunting, as do the Southern Bantu of Africa.

Agriculture appeared late in human history, and afforded a means of greatly increased production. But the food-gatherers do not necessarily all live at a lower level of subsistence than the cultivators. Some nonagricultural peoples developed elaborate techniques for exploiting the wild products of their environment. The fishing and hunting tribes of the Northwest Coast of North America not only made huge catches; they knew how to split trees into planks for their solidly built loghouses, how to construct ingenious dams and fishtraps, and even how to organize successful whaling expeditions. Technically they were more advanced than many cultivating peoples. Pastoral nomadism which is popularly believed to have preceded the development of agriculture actually appeared at a later stage in the Old World on the

FROM Daryll Forde and Mary Douglas, "Primitive Economics," in *Man, Culture and Society*, Harry L. Shapiro, ed. Copyright © 1956 by Oxford University Press, Inc., pp. 330–344. Reprinted by permission of the authors and publisher.

fringes of settled populations used to cultivation with the rearing of livestock.

The distinguishing features of a primitive economy are not to be found in any particular mode of securing a livelihood. The basic condition is a low degree of technical knowledge. However favorable the climate, and rich the natural vegetation and animal life, peoples equipped with only simple techniques are limited in their exploitation of their country's resources.

The level of production of food supplies and the tools by which they are secured is everywhere vitally dependent on the amount of energy that can be harnessed for productive tasks, and it is important to realize the limited capacity for production of peoples lacking power-driven machines. An adult human being can directly exert energy equivalent to only about one tenth of a unit of horsepower and many primitive peoples have lacked any other prime source of power, apart from a limited use of fire. Without animal or water power for lifting and traction, their productive capacity is severely limited by their restriction to hand-tools such as the bow, the hoe, and the fishnet. These must remain mechanically simple and accordingly require little specialization in their manufacture and use. At the same time the level of output per man that they make possible is not great enough to release any significant proportion of the population from the common task of food production, so that there is little scope for any considerable division of labor.

Advanced civilizations have tended to spread into the most favorable lands, so that there is also a tendency for the least well-equipped peoples to be found living in the most harsh and intractable regions.[1] To these they have adapted themselves as best they can—the Eskimos to snow and ice, the marsh-dwellers of the Euphrates to swamplands and flood, Bushmen and Bedouin Arabs to drought and desert. In many tropical lands, rapid exhaustion of the soil sets a basic limitation on cultivation by primitive methods.

Natural conditions restrict certain kinds of development and permit others, but they do not dictate in any precise way the lines on which an economy shall develop. Man by his skill and labor

---

[1] On the other hand, some of the richest lands, the western forest and central plains of North America, were still occupied by primitives until the opening of the nineteenth century.

produces a kind of secondary environment, which is a function of techniques as well as of resources. This ecological framework, product of man's skill and his environment, varies widely from one people and region to the next, according to the different materials at hand and the individual bent of their interests and skills.

Preoccupation with the daily or seasonal food supply, the frequency of hardship, and the risks of hunger are obvious characteristics of a primitive economy. So also are the limitations of transport, though this applies, of course, with less force to the livestock breeders such as the horse and camel nomads. Less obvious, but just as fundamental, are the difficulties of storage, which restrict the accumulation of food and other goods. Heat, damp, and the white ant effectively destroy any possessions which the Bemba of North Rhodesia or the Nambikwara of the South American Mato Grosso may succeed in amassing. In Polynesia the people of Tikopia did not know how to cure fish, and only one of their crops had good keeping properties. The Eskimo, admittedly, can freeze his meat, and keep it for indefinite periods, but the ice which makes food storage possible for him causes other shortages, of vegetable foods, of wood for fuel and shelter. Pastoralists are better off in this respect, as herds provide a natural store of wealth, but cattle are vulnerable to disease, the onset of which may disrupt the whole economy.

Productive equipment is relatively simple and few durable goods of any kind are made. In short, the productive effort of a primitive economy is capable of anticipating its future needs only for a very brief span. Accumulation is difficult, long-term planning impossible.

Insecurity, then, is frequently the mark of a primitive economy. But on this score there is considerable variation from one primitive economy to another. Some food-gathering peoples, for example, the acorn-eating Yokuts of California, and the Kwakiutl fishers of British Columbia, were blessed with a natural abundance of basic resources.

Another common characteristic of a primitive economy, though also not a universal one, is a lack of diversity in the major resources. Some peoples are heavily dependent on a few products, which are processed so as to provide food, shelter, weapons, tools, and nearly all the main needs of the people. This tendency is particularly noticeable among hunters and herders. The Eskimo takes from the seals he kills meat to eat, fat for fuel and for lighting, fat for anointing himself, skins for covering, sinews for thongs, bones for harpoons and arrow heads. There is an economy of effort, but the risks are high. If, during a stormy winter, seals are absent from a usually sheltered bay, starvation and death for the whole community may result. The cattle-keeping Nuer of the southern Sudan turn the products of their cattle to meet most of their essential requirements: blood, milk, cheese, and meat for sustenance; horn and bone for weapons; dried dung for fuel; hides for covering and thongs and bags. But during the rinderpest epidemic at the end of the last century, when their cattle died wholesale, they were in desperate straits. Among such peoples enormous stress is placed on the value of their main resource, which tends to become the focus of their religious symbolism. For the Nuer, cattle play a central role in their religious life, being used for every ceremonial and sacrifice. Such a tendency to place exceptionally high value on a few vital resources may distort the development of an economy. Nuer country abounds in game and wild birds, yet they seldom exploit them, despising wild game as food if they can get milk and beef. Conversely hunting peoples often disdain the meat of domesticated animals. One effect is that the full range of resources actually available with existing techniques are not exploited. Another is to inhibit internal and external exchanges. Thus the Nuer were averse to dealing with Arab traders, as these had no cattle and cattle were the only form of wealth which interested the Nuer.

We may sum up the basic characteristics of primitive economies as follows: preoccupation with the daily and seasonal food supply, limitation of transport, difficulties of storage, overdependence on one or two major resources. These restrictions derive mainly from a low level of technical knowledge, which severely limits productive capacity. Wherever these characteristics are found, certain consequences flow from them. The economic unit is small and, save for occasionally bartered specialities, does not transcend the population of a small village. Social relations are of the personal, face-to-face kind. Everyone has known everyone else from childhood, everyone is related to everyone else. The sick and unfortunate are able to depend on the kindliness of immediate neighbors. The sharing of tools and of supplies to meet individual shortages are matters of moral obligation between kinsfolk and neighbors. Impersonal commercial relations hardly exist. The group which lives and works together has strong feelings of solidarity, partly because they are isolated from other groups by poor communications.

The small size of the social group within which production is organized and exchange effected also reduces the opportunity for specialization. Such skills as are practiced are known to everyone of the appropriate age and sex (Redfield 1960:346) in the community. Certain kinds of work are traditionally assigned to men, others to women, but full-time specialists are very rare. The work of the potter, boatbuilder, smith, or magician is a voluntary spare-time task.

In such a setting economic relations have not been separated out from other social relations. There is no question of one man working for another whom he knows only as an employer. Men work together because they are related to each other, or have other social obligations to one another. Important economic processes are thus embedded in wider social needs, and are inextricably mixed with politics, ceremonial, and general festivity. When the Blackfoot Indians of the Plains used to congregate in the summer for tribal buffalo drives, which were their main economic activity, a short period of intensive hunting was followed by feasts and dances, and the social life of the tribe reached its peak. The great annual ceremony of the Sun Dance brought not only the economic, but also the political and religious activities of the year to a grand climax.

In an economy for which these general conditions hold true, economic exchange is necessarily limited. Markets remain undeveloped because the advantages of internal exchange are slight. The household provides for its daily needs from its own production. Surpluses cannot speedily be sent to areas of scarcity because of the difficulties of transport. On the other hand, if the surplus is to be used at all, it must somehow be distributed at once, because of the technical difficulty of storage. As everyone produces much the same range of articles as everyone else, there will be little demand locally for any excess production. Often the only way an individual can dispose of a surplus is by holding a lavish feast or simply by giving it to kinsmen and neighbors who will feel bound to repay one day.

But primitive economics are not, as a rule, completely closed. Some external trade, however sporadic, is usually possible. Hunters may be in contact with cultivators and exchange meat for cereals, as did the Congo forest pygmies with their Negro neighbors in a silent trade in which the two parties to the exchange never came face to face. Shore-dwelling people may exchange fish for crops with inland cultivators. One community may produce a surplus of one speciality, a local delicacy, a raw material, or a prized ornament, and trade it with another speciality of another tribe. Among the Kalahari Bushmen there was a system of trade relations, both with their Bantu neighbors and between the different tribes. Centrally placed groups played the part of intermediaries, obtaining from their northern neighbors supplies which they bartered further south, and vice versa. In this trade eggshell beads and tobacco, because there was always a steady demand for them, had a fixed value according to which other goods could be "priced."

Internal exchange is also possible, as when four or five little communities meet regularly in a local market and cancel out small inequalities of output by exchanges. The difference between this kind of market and the markets of developed economies is that goods which are offered for exchange have not been produced primarily for sale, but are the fortuitous surplus of subsistence production. This is an essential difference between production in the primitive and in the developed economy. For these economies, instead of "primitive," the word "subsistence" is often used, to emphasize the contrast with complex modern exchange economies.

The production unit does not necessarily correspond to the unit of consumption; the size of the former is generally determined by technical considerations, while the size of the consumption unit may vary from a group of households to include the whole of the local community.

For production people cooperate in different groups at different seasons, according to the nature of the work. For some tasks the most efficient unit may be only one man: the Eskimo hunter waiting at his seal hole is better alone. The success of Bushman hunting often depends on fleetness of foot; in the wet season the sodden ground impedes the animals and even in the dry season the young buck can often be chased and run down, as the hot sand causes their hoofs to come off. For this kind of hunting, one man and a dog is the best team. At other times the whole male force of a large band may set barricades and pit-falls across a valley, and then drive a herd of wild animals into the great trap.

Other kinds of production can be broken up into a number of tasks performed by separate individuals. Only one man at a time can operate a Congolese handloom for weaving raffia. But the various processes for preparing raffia and the loom can be farmed out to different individuals to do in their own time: an old man may be the most suitable person for the intricate sorting of the strands, and a young man for the heavy work of actual weaving.

In agricultural work the pressure of the changing seasons may make it urgent for each farmer to get help in clearing the fields. In bush clearing a team is more efficient than a series of sepa-rate workers. According to local custom, a man may be able to call out a labor gang composed of his age-mates, his kinsmen, or all the able-bodied men of the district. The nature of the work tends to determine the size of the working unit, but because most tasks are not very complex, and because those few that do in-volve large-scale collaboration are of short duration, large work-ing units are rare.

As to the reward of labor, there is little attempt to calculate the contribution of each unit, and to give it a corresponding share of the product. Among Bushmen, whether the game brought to the camp has been run down by an individual hunter, or killed in a communal battle, the rules for distributing the meat are still the same: all members of the camp are entitled to their share. A man who has killed a buck on his own, still has to hand it in to be divided by the camp leader according to fixed rules which set aside certain parts for the married men, others for the young men, others for women, according to their several status. The women of the band who collect the vegetables daily keep for their families the product of their own foraging, but meat repre-sents an irregular supply of an important food, and the system of even distribution of game insures a share for all families of the community.

Where labor gangs are formed to clear land, each member in turn gets the benefit of the work of the whole group. In some cases a feast is offered as inducement to the workers, but the ultimate incentive is the maintenance of good will, which insures to each worker similar help in his need. In a primitive economy there are no wages (except for specialists' fees to healers, magicians, and smiths). A man does not normally earn his right to a particular share of output by contributing a particular piece of work. His claim to a share is based on his membership and on his status in the social group, household, camp, club, et cetera for which the work is being done. He works in order to fulfill his social obligations, to maintain his prestige and the status to which his sex, age, rank, et cetera may entitle him.[2]

It is as difficult to distinguish a regular unit of consumption as a regular unit of production. Rights to enjoy certain things may be vested in individuals, in families, or in the community as a whole. Different kinds of sharing situations may be set in the framework of different social groups, so that it is impossible to consider the society as divided into a fixed series of units of consumption such as the family. Food may be cooked by wives at their domestic hearths, but part of it is carried out to contribute to a general supply which the men share among themselves.

Among the Nuer, for example, the extended family is the cattle-holding unit, and each family's rights to cattle in payment of fines or at marriages are jealously guarded. But where the food products of cattle are concerned, men habitually eat in each other's homes to such an extent that the whole village seems to draw on a common stock. In agricultural communities, the land rights of individuals are generally restricted by overriding rights vested in the village as a whole. A Bemba village, under its headman, owns its land by right of occupation; each male member has rights in the land he has cleared, by virtue of accepted residence. Each wife has her granary for storing the crop she has raised on the fields provided by her husband. But the whole village, with its fields, and granaries, is at the same time a kind of joint housekeeping concern, for the rules of hospitality and the habit of food-sharing distribute the product of the year's work over the whole village.

Such customs are common in most primitive economies, and tend to even out the inequalities of income that result from

[2] See the analogy drawn by Professor Redfield with work and consumption within the family (Redfield 1960: Chapter 16).

primitive techniques. Public opinion forces a household whose harvest has prospered more than those of the neighbors to share its advantages with them. Equality of distribution, then, according to status rather than reward allocated according to work, is another characteristic feature of a primitive economy. This does not mean that some economic privilege is not accorded to those who have high status.

The obligation to distribute income is supported by two factors. One, which brings home to all the importance of generosity, is the constant menace of want. Everyone is aware of his own insecurity and consequent dependence on his neighbors. The second, as we have already seen, is the technical difficulty of conserving goods for future consumption. Perishable goods constitute a major part of the wealth of these economies, and enjoyment cannot be postponed to an indefinite future. The man who distributes his surplus to his neighbors has the satisfaction of gaining prestige. And since the obligation to repay gift for gift is fully recognized, he is even laying up some security for himself for the future. By giving away his own surplus he is making a number of people beholden to him. This is an elementary form of credit. The recipients of his gifts will be expected to treat him likewise when occasion arises. They also accept his influence, and help to build up his standing in the community.

In a primitive economy political power is not related to economic control in the same way as in a highly developed economy. Since, as we have seen, the system of production is based on small independent units, it does not offer means for concentrating power through control of resources or productive equipment. A man can best satisfy the drive for power and prestige by attaching to himself a group of adherents: to them he affords protection and a lavish board; they give him status and authority. Competition, in a primitive economy, is not specifically economic, but social. On the other hand, economic advantages do often follow from high social status. Only a chief or a shaman among the Nambikwara can have more than one wife, and this is regarded as a reward for his responsibility. The chief of a district among the Bemba needs many wives, simply in order to organize the catering for councilors and visitors to the court. The payment of tribute to the chief, and the distribution by him of hospitality and largess are complementary aspects of his status.

He needs the contributions of his subjects in order to fulfill his obligation to give lavishly to them. Thereby he also maintains his position. Although loyal villages send teams to cultivate his fields, and so ensure a grain supply commensurate with his responsibilities, the Bemba chief does not try to organize maximum production. He prefers to fill his granaries from windfall payments of tribute in kind. This illustrates a bias in the relation between economic and political organization in a primitive economy. It is not through control of production that political advantages and privileges in consumption can be acquired; rather it is that distribution can be controlled only by building up social status and gaining political authority.

The dominant institutions in a primitive economy, while predominantly political or religious, are nevertheless important channels for the redistribution of wealth. Where there is powerful chieftainship, what is brought in as tribute is quickly given out again as rewards and gifts: local inequalities of production over the chiefdom are thus evened out. It is usual for those who have met with disaster to ask for help from the chief, and he can call on his prosperous subjects to provide emergency supplies. In some societies one important channel of economic redistribution may be through associations of leading men, in the so-called "secret societies." As entrance to them is gained by payment of fees, which are shared by all members, the accumulated wealth transferred in fees receives wide redistribution.

Marriage, too, often has a prominent economic function as a distributing agency. Where descent is patrilineal, marriage transfers rights over a woman and her children from her father to her husband. As in many societies this transfer is secured by substantial gifts to the bride's kinsfolk, so through the constant succession of marriages redistribution of wealth takes place. A man may build up his herd of cattle until he has enough to acquire a new wife, for himself or for one of his sons. Negotiations are opened, and shortly his herd is reduced again to a few beasts.

Since all regular social obligations are channels of economic distribution in these ways, it is not exaggerating to say that social ties perform the function of rudimentary credit institutions in primitive economies. One tribe in South Africa has recognized this in their saying: "A man is the bank of his father-in-law."

Although labor is given for the sake of fulfilling social obligations, and although distribution similarly follows the same lines, this is not to say that there is not a keen sense of *quid pro quo* in particular transactions. A meanness is well remembered and paid off at an early opportunity. A man who consistently fails to turn up at working parties is forfeiting his title to membership in the group in question, and losing any right to a share in its product. The idea of equivalence in giving and receiving is clearly recognized. There is no such thing as a free gift. Every act of generosity is expected to be repaid by an equivalent deed at some later date. Under this convention of strict reciprocity, what may seem at first sight to be reckless squandering can often be a prudent outlay of resources.

The crucial difference between gift and sale is that the first object of gift exchange is the building up of a social relationship, whereas in buying and selling, any continuous social relation between the parties is merely incidental. Even in a modern economy, a significant part of the distribution of wealth is by gift exchange, although the main part is by commercial trade. In a primitive economy there may be no commercial trade, or it may account for very few of the transactions which take place, but there will certainly be a well-developed system of exchange through gifts, which distribute supplies at the same time as they cement social relations.

Most of the concepts devised for analysis in economic science, such as capital, investment, saving, interest, et cetera have been developed for the study of complex exchange economies. Entities and processes corresponding to these basic categories can be recognized in embryonic form in a primitive economy. But they are not necessarily significant for describing the economy of peoples who have few durable goods, no money, and few commercial exchanges. How, for example, should the distinction between liquid and fixed resources be applied to an economy where nearly all goods can be used in all kinds of transactions? Should cows be classified as producer or as consumption goods? Is any insight gained by describing a polygamist's wives in one context as capital investment for him, as his labor force in another, as the principal consumers in another? Conditions in these simple undifferentiated economies seem to make nonsense of fine distinctions elaborated for highly specialized modern economies. On the other hand, these fine distinctions apply to economic realities which have developed out of the less specialized economic relations of the primitive societies. In the latter one can, as it were, trace them back to their more generalized roots.

The simplest definition of capital, and one which is significant for any primitive economy, concentrates on the tools and equipment for production. A man, or a group, who gives up time and energy to make a special tool for a special task, be it a digging stick, or a fish weir, or canoe, expects to be able to use it for a considerable period. In a wider sense, not only tools, but any of the things which are produced in order to yield future services over a stretch of time such as houses, bridges, or granaries, are capital.

Primitive economies are, by definition, poor in capital equipment. The quantity, effectiveness, and variety of their tools and weapons, the durability of their houses, the serviceability of their roads and paths, are strictly limited by the low level of technical knowledge. Cultivators have their hoes and granaries, knives and baskets; hunters have their spear-throwers, harpoons, bows, hunting poisons, implements for curing hides and skins. Some fishing communities, and especially ocean-going peoples, maintain a greater amount of capital equipment for their exploitation of the sea. They have different kinds of canoes, elaborate fishtraps, nets, and lines, which all represent considerable outlay of labor in their manufacture, and which give valuable services over many years.

The fact that fishing communities invest in more capital equipment than cultivators, herders, or hunters, might be expected to put them in a class apart from other primitive economies, were it not for two things. First, all their equipment is directed to one kind of production only, the harvest of the sea. An economy which is heavily dependent on one main resource cannot develop the complexity and high degree of internal differentiation of the modern economy. For another, this main resource of a fishing economy is essentially perishable. Drying or smoking only preserves fish for a very limited period in all but the coolest climates. A community is incapable of developing a complex exchange economy so long as the greater part of its production is devoted to perishable goods. Only by mastering the technical difficulties of storage, and so being able to accumulate a variety of goods, can a community save. Saving is abstaining from consuming in the present, in order to consume in the future. If its wealth is in the form of perishable goods, a community cannot save. Thus low capacity to postpone consumption is the mark of a primitive economy.

In such an economy there can be little specialization of production and correspondingly little exchange. From this follows the absence or very limited development of money, which is essentially a medium of exchange. But primitive economies are not necessarily entirely without money. Some kind of currency, accepted for certain exchanges, was long in use in Melanesia, western North America, and parts of tropical Africa.

Almost anything, from pigs, cowries, iron rods to strings of shells or tobacco, can be used as a standard for measuring relative values and as a medium of exchange. When some such object is used as money in a primitive economy, it is usually employed only for a restricted range of transactions. We find that by convention only certain kinds of goods or services can be bought and sold, or that only between certain categories of persons can there be a buying and selling relationship. Between other persons, or where other essential commodities are concerned, there are conventions of giving or sharing, not of buying and selling.

The existence of a monetary system, however rudimentary, gives the individual member of the economy an opportunity of saving. He accepts money in exchange for his products because it gives him a title to buy something else, at once, or in the future. So it enables him to postpone consumption to a time of his own choosing. It provides him with a link between the present and the future, extending the period during which his present wealth can be enjoyed. If an individual puts a store of money aside, he builds up a right to spend it in the future. Even if the borrower spends it all, the lender is still saving, so long, of course, as the borrower can be trusted to repay. When the debt is later repaid, the lender can enjoy the benefit of having refrained earlier from consuming his wealth. He will have saved for his own future, but as far as the economy as a whole is concerned there will have been no saving at all. The saving of one individual has been canceled by the spending of the other. Monetary savings of individuals do not imply that the total community will necessarily be saving anything. In a modern economy, savings correspond in this way to one type of spending, investment,

or spending on durable goods. But where the economy is capable
only of producing perishable goods, this cannot be so. Even if it
has some kind of monetary system, the money saved by all the
individuals is equivalent only to so much chalking up of claims
against each other. Where the goods which can be acquired with
the money are of a perishable kind, the people would, for all
their individual saving of money, be no more secure against
death or famine than if, without any monetary system, the rotting
away of food were anticipated by great feasts. Money of itself
does not give a closed economy any link between the present
and the future. It does not enable the community to save, even
though it makes individual saving possible. As saving simply
means laying by wealth which is not immediately consumed, a
community can only be said to save to the extent that durable
goods are produced, houses, carved cups and bowls, well-tilled
fields, canoes, fishing nets, spears, knives, et cetera. Such production in primitive economies is restricted in amount by the limited
techniques available.

In a primitive economy the character of the distributive system
can have adverse effects on the incentives to labor, and so on
production. The incentive to work is derived not only from the
simple need to provide subsistence, but largely from the drive for
prestige, the satisfactions of working together, the pleasures of
conviviality, and the common interest in the product of the work.
The sum of these incentives may not necessarily secure maximum
production. The obligation to share with neighbors any private
windfall or surplus may have a deterrent effect on production.
In the rural economy of Java, if a man wishes to become rich,
it may be necessary for him to leave his home and settle in another village, as a stranger on whom the usual obligations of village membership do not fall. Otherwise every improvement in
his own condition must be shared with all the village. A rank
system may have a similar deterrent effect if a certain standard
of living is considered suitable for a chief and another lower one
right for a commoner. An ordinary man may be afraid of amassing riches for fear of seeming to aspire beyond his station, or be
deterred by knowing that he will have to hand over a great part
of his gains to the chief.

Many economies today lie at an intermediate stage between
primitive and developed. There are still in Europe rural com-

munities of farmers who mainly produce for their own needs, but send their surplus products to markets which link them with the world markets of modern capitalism. Through this link they are able to acquire tools, machinery, clothing, which they do not produce for themselves. Such dependent economies are found, for example, in rural Ireland, in Poland, and in the Balkans.

Other economies of an intermediate type are those which, though characterized by a simple technical knowledge, are only partly self-subsistent as a result to their access to the world market. They are able to produce some crop or offer their labor for sale in a modern market, and can satisfy many of their wants from that market. The fishing villages on the coast of Malaya are linked by Chinese middlemen with markets in Singapore or Indonesia. Cocoa farmers in the Gold Coast, or cotton growers in Uganda, are intimately affected by changes in world prices for their produce. These are economies that combine an important element of subsistence production with an important element of external exchange. They are not a new development. Coastal West Africa, for example, has had cash-crop economies of this type for over three hundred years.

The essential difference between the way affairs are run in a primitive economy and the working of a developed economy cannot be summed up by the absence or presence of the profit motive. Primitive peoples are as alive to the furthering of their own advantage as anyone in a capitalist economy. It is not true that they are devoid of economic sense. The most striking difference is the personal nature of all relations in a primitive economy, compared with the impersonal nature of most economic relations in modern society.

In the intermediate dependent economies, as in the truly primitive economies, all social relations are of the personal kind, but the people will also have some impersonal relationships with traders, moneylenders, and middlemen from the external economy. Such contacts give them access to valuables and capital goods produced by techniques that are far beyond their capacity. The technical difficulty of storing wealth may be overcome, partly by importing durable goods, partly by financial means. A banking system, or the mere circulation of money which has value in a nearby advanced economy, creates possibilities of postponing consumption, not only for the individual, but for the community as a whole. In these cases money put by can mean real saving, because at any time it can be used to import goods into the community.

Every contact which a primitive economy comes to have with a complex economy modifies its primitive characteristics. The feelings of village solidarity, the obligations of mutual aid and hospitality, will be present, but diluted. Family ties will still regulate production and distribution to a considerable extent, but the subsistence unit which shares a common board and common purse will be relatively smaller than in the primitive economy. It will be possible to distinguish within the total residential group regular units of consumption corresponding to family units. The social pressure forcing a man to share his gains with the whole community will still be there, but less pronounced, and the conflict between his economic ambitions and his responsibilities to the community will generate social friction. Inequalities of wealth will be tolerated. Some equivalence between the unit of labor and the amount of its reward will be increasingly aimed at. Wages will begin to be paid as one of the incentives to labor. These intermediate economies are not to be classed with modern capitalist economies, but they owe to their contact with them those features which distinguish them from the truly primitive.

3 TOWARD A THEORY OF
MODERNIZATION

Neil J. Smelser

A thorough analysis of the social changes accompanying economic development would require an ambitious theoretical scheme and a vast quantity of comparative data. Because I lack both ingredients—and the space to use them if I possessed them —I shall restrict this exploratory statement in two ways: (1) Methodologically, I shall deal only with ideal-type constructs in the Weberian sense; I shall omit discussion of any individual cases of development, as well as discussion of the comparative applicability of particular historical generalizations; (2) Substantively, I shall consider only modifications of the social structure; I shall omit discussion of factor allocation, savings and investment, inflation, balance of payments, foreign aid, size of population, and rate of population change, even though these variables naturally affect and are affected by structural changes. These restrictions call for brief comment.

Max Weber defined an ideal-type construct as a "one-sided accentuation . . . by the synthesis of a great many diffuse, discrete, more or less present and occasionally absent *concrete individual* phenomena, which are arranged . . . into a unified *analytical* construct. In its conceptual purity, this mental construct cannot be found anywhere in reality" (Weber 1949:90, 93). The analyst utilizes such ideal constructs to unravel and explain a variety of actual historical situations. Weber mentioned explicitly two kinds of ideal-type constructs—first, "historically unique configurations"

FROM Neil J. Smelser, "Mechanisms of Change and Adjustment of Changes," in Wilbert E. Moore and Bert F. Hoselitz, eds., *The Impact of Industry*. Paris: International Social Science Council, 1963. Reprinted by permission of the author and publisher.

such as "rational bourgeois capitalism," "medieval Christianity," etc., and second, statements concerning historical evolution, such as the Marxist laws of capitalist development (Weber 1949:93, 101–103). While the second type presupposes some version of the first, I shall concentrate on the dynamic constructs.

Economic development generally refers to the "growth of output per head of population" (Lewis 1955:1). For purposes of analyzing the relationships between economic growth and the social structure, it is possible to isolate the effects of several interrelated technical, economic, and ecological processes frequently accompanying development: (1) In the realm of technology, the change *from* simple and traditionalized techniques *toward* the application of scientific knowledge. (2) In agriculture, the evolution *from* subsistence farming *toward* commercial production of agricultural goods. This means specialization in cash crops, purchase of nonagricultural products in the market, and frequently agricultural wage-labor. (3) In industry, the transition *from* the use of human and animal power *toward* industrialization proper or "men aggregated at power-driven machines working for monetary return with the products of the manufacturing process, entering into a market based on a network of exchange relations" (Nash 1954:271). (4) In ecological arrangements, the movement *from* the farm and village *toward* urban centers. These several processes often occur simultaneously; this is not, however, necessarily the case. Certain technological improvements—*e.g.*, the use of improved seeds—can be introduced without automatically and instantaneously producing organizational changes; agriculture may be commercialized without accompanying industrialization, as in many colonial countries; industrialization may occur in villages; and cities may proliferate in the absence of significant industrialization. Furthermore, the specific social consequences of technological advance, commercialized agriculture, the factory, and the city, respectively, are not in any sense reducible to each other.

Despite such differences, all four processes tend to affect the social structure in similar ways. All give rise to the following ideal-type structural changes which ramify throughout society: (1) Structural differentiation, or the establishment of more specialized and more autonomous social units. I shall illustrate this process in several different spheres—economy, family, religion, and stratification. (2) Integration, which changes its character as the old social order is made obsolete by the process of differentiation. The state, the law, political groupings, and other associations are particularly salient in this integration. (3) Social disturbances—mass hysteria, outbursts of violence, religious and political movements, etc.—which reflect the uneven march of differentiation and integration.

Obviously, the implications of technological advance, agricultural reorganization, industrialization, and urbanization differ from society to society, as do the resulting structural realignments. Some of the sources of variation in these ideal patterns of pressure and change follow:

(1) Variations in pre-modern conditions. Is the society's value system congenial or antipathetic to industrial values? How well integrated is the society? How "backward" is it? What is its level of wealth? How is the wealth distributed? Is the country "young and empty" or "old and crowded"? Is the country politically dependent, recently independent, or altogether autonomous? Such pre-existing conditions shape the impact of the forces of economic development.

(2) Variations in the impetus to change. Do pressures to modernize come from the internal implications of a value system, from a desire for national security and prestige, from a desire for material prosperity, or from a combination of these? Is political coercion used to form a labor force? Or are the pressures economic, as in the case of population pressure on the land or loss of handicraft markets to cheap imported products? Or do economic and political pressures combine, as in the case of a tax on peasants payable only in money? Or are the pressures social, as in the case of the desire to escape burdensome aspects of the old order? Such differences influence the adjustment to modernization greatly.

(3) Variations in the path toward modernization. Does the sequence begin with light consumer industries? Or is there an attempt to introduce heavy, capital-intensive industries first? What is the role of government in shaping the pattern of investment? What is the rate of accumulation of technological knowledge and skills? What is the general tempo of industrialization? All these affect the nature of structural change and the degree of discomfort created by this change.

(4) Variations in the advanced stages of modernization. What is the emergent distribution of industries in developed economies? What are the emergent relations between state and economy, religion and economy, state and religion, etc.? While all advanced industrialized societies have their "industrialization" in common, unique national differences remain. For instance, social class differs in its social significance in the United States and the United Kingdom, even though both are highly developed countries.

(5) Variations in the content and timing of dramatic events during modernization. What is the significance of wars, revolutions, rapid migrations, natural catastrophes, etc., for the course of economic and social development?

Because of these sources of variation, it is virtually impossible to discover hard and fast empirical generalizations concerning the evolution of social structures during economic and social development. My purpose, therefore, in this paper, is not to search for such generalizations, but rather to outline certain ideal-type directions of structural change which modernization involves. On the basis of these ideal types we may classify, describe, and analyze varying national experiences. Factors such as those just described determine in part the distinctive national response to these universal aspects of modernization, but this in no way detracts from their "universality." While I shall base my remarks on the vast literature of economic development, I can in no sense attempt an exhaustive comparative study.

STRUCTURAL DIFFERENTIATION IN PERIODS OF DEVELOPMENT

The concept of structural differentiation can be used to analyze what is frequently referred to as the "marked break in established patterns of social and economic life" in periods of development (Kuznets 1955:23). Simply defined, differentiation refers to the evolution from a multifunctional role structure to several more specialized structures. The following are typical examples: (1) In the transition from domestic to factory industry, the division of labor increases, and the economic activities previously lodged in the family move to the firm. (2) With the rise of a formal educational system, the training functions previously performed by the family and church are established in a more specialized unit—the school. (3) The modern political party has a more complex structure than tribal factions and is less likely to be fettered with kinship loyalties, competition for religious leadership, etc. Formally defined, then, structural differentiation is a process whereby *"one* social role or organization . . . differentiates into *two or more* roles or organizations which function more effectively in the new historical circumstances. The new social units are structurally distinct from each other, but taken together are functionally equivalent to the original unit" (Smelser 1959:2).

Differentiation concerns only changes in role structure. We should not, therefore, confuse differentiation with two closely related concepts: (1) The cause or motivation for entering the differentiated role. Wage-labor, for instance, may result from a desire for economic improvement, from political coercion, or indeed from a desire to fulfill traditional obligations (*e.g.*, to use wages to supply a dowry). These "reasons" should be kept conceptually distinct from differentiation itself. (2) The integration of differentiated roles. As differentiated wage-labor begins to appear, for instance, there also appear legal norms, labor exchanges, trade unions, and so on, which regulate—with varying degrees of success—the relations between labor and management. Such readjustments, even though they sometimes produce a new social unit, should be considered separately from role specialization in other functions.

Let us now inquire into the process of differentiation in several different social realms.

DIFFERENTIATION OF ECONOMIC ACTIVITIES

Typically, in underdeveloped countries, production is located in kinship units. Subsistence farming predominates; other industry is supplementary but still attached to kin and village. In some cases occupational position is determined largely by an extended group such as the caste.

Similarly, exchange and consumption are deeply embedded in family and village. In subsistence agriculture there is a limited amount of independent exchange outside the family; this means that production and consumption occur in the same social context. Exchange systems proper are still lodged in kinship and community (*e.g.,* reciprocal exchange), in stratification systems (*e.g.,* redistribution according to caste membership), and in political systems (*e.g.,* taxes, tributes, payments in kind, forced labor). Under such conditions market systems are underdeveloped, and the independent power of money to command the movement of goods and services is minimal.

As the economy develops, several kinds of economic activity are removed from this family-community complex. In agriculture, the introduction of money crops marks a differentiation between the social contexts of production and consumption. Agricultural wage-labor sometimes undermines the family production unit. In industry it is possible to identify several levels of differentiation. Household industry, the simplest form, parallels subsistence agriculture in that it supplies "the worker's own needs, unconnected with trade." "Handicraft production" splits production and consumption, though frequently consumption takes place in the local community. "Cottage industry," on the other hand, frequently involves a differentiation between consumption and community, since production is "for the market, for an unknown consumer, sold to a wholesaler who accumulates a stock."[1] Finally, manufacturing and factory systems segregate the worker from his capital and frequently from his family.

Similar differentiations appear simultaneously in the exchange system. Goods and services, previously exchanged on a non-economic basis, are pulled more and more into the market. Money now commands the movement of more and more goods and services and thus begins to supplant—and sometimes undermine —the religious, political, familial, or caste sanctions which previously had governed economic activity. Such is the setting for the institutionalization of relatively autonomous economic systems which show a greater emphasis on values as universalism, functional specificity, and rationality.

Empirically we may classify underdeveloped economies according to how far they have moved along this line of differentiation. Migratory labor, for instance, may be a kind of compromise between full membership in a wage-labor force and attachment to an old community life; cottage industry introduces

[1] These "levels," which represent points on the continuum from structural fusion to structural differentiation, are taken from Boeke (1942:90).

extended markets but retains the family-production fusion; the hiring of families in factories maintains a version of family production; the expenditure of wages on traditional items such as dowries also shows this half-entry into the more differentiated industrial-urban structure. The reasons for these partial cases of differentiation may lie in resistances on the part of the populace to give up traditional modes, in the economics of demand for handmade products, in systems of racial discrimination against native labor, or elsewhere. In any case, the concept of structural differentiation provides a yardstick to indicate the distance which the economic structure has evolved toward modernization.

DIFFERENTIATION OF FAMILY ACTIVITIES

One implication of the removal of economic activities from the kinship nexus is that the family loses some of its previous functions and thereby itself becomes a more specialized agency. The family ceases to be an economic unit of production; one or more members now leave the household to seek employment in the labor market. The family's activities become more concentrated on emotional gratification and socialization. While many halfway houses such as family hiring and migratory systems persist, the tendency is toward the segregation of family functions and economic functions.

Several related processes accompany this differentiation of the family from its other involvements: (1) Apprenticeship within the family declines. (2) Pressures develop against the intervention of family favoritism in the recruitment of labor and management. These pressures often lie in the demands of economic rationality. The intervention often persists, however, especially at the managerial levels, and in some cases (*e.g.*, Japan) family ties continue as a major basis for labor recruitment. (3) The direct control of elders and collateral kinsmen over the nuclear family weakens. This marks, in structural terms, the differentiation of the nuclear family from the extended family. (4) One aspect of this loss of control is the growth of personal choice, love, and related criteria as the basis for courtship and marriage. Structurally this is the differentiation of courtship from extended kinship. (5) One result of this complex of processes is the changing status of women, who become generally less subordinated economically, politically, and socially to their husbands than under earlier conditions.

In such ways structural differentiation undermines the old modes of integration in society. The controls of extended family and village begin to dissolve in the enlarged and complicated social setting which differentiation creates. New integrative problems are posed by this growing obsolescence. We shall inquire presently into some of the lines of integration.

DIFFERENTIATION OF VALUE SYSTEMS

The concept of differentiation can also elucidate the delicate problem of the role of values in economic development. It is clear that values affect development significantly, though in many different ways. Max Weber's analysis of Protestantism is an illustration of the force of religious values in encouraging development. In addition, secular nationalism plays an important role in the industrial "takeoff."

> . . . with the world organized as it is, nationalism is a *sine qua non* of industrialization, because it provides people with an overriding, easily acquired, secular motivation for making painful changes. National strength or prestige becomes the supreme goal, industrialization the chief means. The costs, inconveniences, sacrifices, and loss of traditional values can be justified in terms of this transcending, collective ambition. The new collective entity, the nation-state, that sponsors and grows from this aspiration is equal to the exigencies of industrial complexity; it draws directly the allegiance of every citizen, organizing the population as one community; it controls the passage of persons, goods, and news across the borders; it regulates economic and social life in detail. To the degree that the obstacles to industrialization are strong, nationalism must be intense to overcome them. (Davis 1955:294)

In fact, nationalism seems in many cases to be the very instrument designed to smash those traditional religious systems—such as the classical Chinese or Indian—which Weber himself found to be less permissive than Protestantism for economic modernization. Yet nationalism too, like many traditionalistic religious systems, may hinder economic advancement by "reaffirmation of traditionally honored ways of acting and thinking" (Hoselitz 1952a:9), by fostering anticolonial attitudes after they are no longer relevant, and, more indirectly, by encouraging passive expectations of "ready-made prosperity" (van der Kroef 1955). It seems possible to distinguish between these contrasting forces of "stimulus" and "drag" that value-systems have on economic development by using the logic of differentiation. . . .

In the early phases of modernization, many traditional attachments must be modified in order to set up more differentiated institutional structures. Because these established commitments and methods of integration are deeply rooted in the organization of traditional society, a very generalized and powerful commitment is required, in the nature of the case, to "pry" individuals from these attachments. The values of ascetic and this-worldly religious beliefs, xenophobic national aspirations, and political ideologies such as socialism provide such a lever. Sometimes these various types of values combine into a single system of legitimacy. In any case, all three have an "ultimacy" of commitment in the name of which a wide range of sacrifices can be demanded and procured.

The very success of these value-systems, however, breeds the conditions for their own weakening. In a perceptive statement, Weber noted that by the beginning of the twentieth century, when the capitalistic system was already highly developed, it no longer needed the impetus of ascetic Protestantism. Capitalism had, by virtue of its conquest of much of Western society, solidly established an institutional base and a secular value-system of its own—"economic rationality." These secular economic values no longer needed the "ultimate" justification required in the newer, unsteadier days of economic revolution.

Such lines of differentiation, we might add, constitute the secularization of religious values. In this process, other institutional spheres—economic, political, scientific, etc.—come to be established more nearly on their own. The values governing these spheres are no longer sanctioned directly by religious beliefs, but by an autonomous rationality. Insofar as such rationalities replace religious sanctions in these spheres, secularization occurs.

Similarly, nationalistic and related value-systems undergo a process of secularization as differentiation proceeds. As a society moves toward more and more complex social organization, the encompassing demands of nationalistic commitment give way to more autonomous systems of rationality. The Soviet Union, for instance, as its social structure grows more differentiated, seems to be introducing more "independent" market mechanisms, "freer" social scientific investigation in some spheres, and so on. These measures are not, moreover, directly sanctioned by an appeal to nationalistic or communistic values. Finally, it seems a reasonable historical generalization that in the early stages of development nationalism is heady, muscular, and aggressive; as the society evolves to an advanced state, however, nationalism tends to settle into a more remote and complacent condition, rising to fury only in times of national crisis.

Thus the paradoxical element in the role of religious or nationalistic belief-systems; insofar as they encourage the breakup of old patterns, they may stimulate economic modernization; insofar as they resist their own subsequent secularization, however, the very same value-systems may become a drag on economic advance and structural change.

DIFFERENTIATION OF SYSTEMS OF STRATIFICATION

In analyzing systems of stratification, we concentrate on two kinds of issues:

(1) To what extent are ascribed qualities subject to ranking? Some ascription exists in all societies, since the infant in the nuclear family always and everywhere begins with the status of his parents. The degree to which this ascribed ranking extends beyond the family to race, ethnic membership, etc., varies from society to society. In our own ideology we minimize the ascriptive elements of class and ethnic membership, but in practice these matter greatly, especially for Negroes.

(2) To what extent do ascribed qualities determine membership in occupational, political, religious, and other positions in society? In theory, again, the American egalitarian ideology places a premium on the maximum separation of such positions from ascribed categories, but in fact family membership, minority group membership, etc., impinge on the ultimate "placing" of persons. In many nonindustrialized societies this link between ascription and position is much closer. Such criteria as these reveal the degree of "openness," or social mobility, in a system.

Under conditions of economic modernization, structural differentiation increases along both these dimensions:

(1) Other evaluative standards intrude on ascribed memberships. For instance, McKim Marriott has noted that in the village of Paril in India:

> . . . Personal wealth, influence, and morality have surpassed the traditional caste-and-order alignment of kind groups as the effective bases of ranking. Since such new bases of ranking can no longer be clearly tied to any inclusive system of large solidary groupings, judgments must be made according to the characteristics of individual or family units. This individualization of judgments leads to greater dissensus (*sic*). (Marriott 1964: Chapter 35; Coleman 1958:70–73)

Of course, castes, ethnic groups, and traditional religious groupings do not necessarily decline in importance *in every respect* during periods of modernization. As political interest groups or reference groups for diffuse loyalty, they may even increase in salience. As the sole bases of ranking, however, ascriptive standards become more differentiated from economic, political, and other standards.

(2) Individual mobility through the occupational hierarchies increases. This signifies the differentiation of the adult's functional position from his point of origin. In addition, individual mobility is frequently substituted for collective mobility. Individuals, not whole castes or tribes, compete for higher standing in society. This phenomenon of increasing individual mobility seems to be one of the universal consequences of industrialization. After assembling extensive empirical evidence on patterns of mobility in industrialized nations, Lipset and Bendix concluded that "the overall pattern of [individual] social mobility appears to be much the same in the industrial societies of various Western countries" (Lipset and Bendix 1959:13ff.). Patterns of class symbolization and class ideology may, however, continue to differ among industrialized countries.

THE INTEGRATION OF DIFFERENTIATED ACTIVITIES

One of Emile Durkheim's remarkable insights concerned the role of integrative mechanisms under conditions of growing social heterogeneity. Launching his attack against the utilitarian view that the division of labor would flourish best without regulation,

Durkheim demonstrated that one of the concomitants of a growing division of labor is an *increase* in mechanisms to coordinate
and solidify the interaction among individuals with increasingly
diversified interests (Durkheim 1949: Chapters 3–8).[2] Durkheim
found this integration mainly in the legal structure, but one can
locate similar kinds of integrative forces elsewhere in society.

Differentiation alone, therefore, is not sufficient for modernization. Development proceeds as a contrapuntal interplay between differentiation (which is divisive of established society)
and integration (which unites differentiated structures on a new
basis). Paradoxically, however, the process of integration itself
produces more *differentiated* structures—*e.g.,* trade unions, associations, political parties, and a mushrooming state apparatus.
Let us illustrate this complex process of integration in several
institutional spheres.

ECONOMY AND FAMILY

Under a simple kind of economic organization—subsistence
agriculture or household industry—there is little differentiation
between economic roles and family roles. All reside in the kinship structure. The *integration* of these diverse but unspe-
cialized activities also rests in the local family and community
structures and in the religious traditions which fortify both of
these.

Under conditions of differentiation, the social setting for production is separated from that for consumption, and productive
roles of family members are isolated geographically, temporally,
and structurally from their distinctively familial roles. Such differentiation immediately creates integrative problems. How is
information concerning employment opportunities to be conveyed
to workpeople? How are the interests of families to be integrated with the interests of firms? How are families to be protected from market fluctuation? Whereas such integrative exigencies were faced by kinsmen, neighbors, and local largesse in
pre-modern settings, modernization gives birth to dozens of in-

---

[2] A recent formulation of the relationship between differentiation and
integration may be found in Bales (1950).

stitutions and organizations geared to these new integrative problems—labor recruitment agencies and exchanges; labor unions; government regulation of labor allocation; welfare and relief arrangements; cooperative societies; savings institutions. All these involve agencies which specialize in integration.

COMMUNITY

If industrialization occurs only in villages or if villages are "built around" paternalistic industrial enterprises, many ties of community and kinship can be maintained under industrial conditions. Urbanization, however, frequently creates more anonymity. As a result, one finds frequently in expanding cities a growth of voluntary associations—churches and chapels, unions, schools, halls, athletic clubs, bars, shops, mutual aid groups, etc. In some cases this growth of integrative groupings may be retarded because of the back-and-forth movement of migratory workers, who "come to the city for their differentiation" and "return to the village for their integration." In cities themselves the original criterion for associating may be common tribe, caste, or village; this criterion may persist or give way gradually to more "functional" groupings based on economic or political interests.

POLITICAL STRUCTURE

In a typical pre-modern setting, political integration is closely fused with kinship position, tribal membership, control of the land or control of the unknown. Political forms include chieftainships, kingships, councils of elders, powerful landlords, powerful magicians and oracles, etc.

As social systems grow more complex, political systems are modified accordingly. Fortes and Evans-Pritchard have specified three types of native African political systems, which can be listed according to their degree of differentiation from kinship lineages: (1) small societies in which the largest political unit embraces only those united by kinship; thus political authority is coterminous with kinship relations; (2) societies in which the political framework is the integrative core for a number of kinship lineages; (3) societies with an "administrative organization" of a more formal nature. Such systems move toward greater differentiation as population grows and economic and cultural heterogeneity increases (Fortes and Evans-Pritchard 1940:1–25). In colonial and recently freed African societies, political systems have evolved much further, with the appearance of parties, congresses, pressure groups, and even "parliamentary" systems (Apter 1956; Hodgkin 1957:115–139; Almond and Coleman 1960). In describing the Indian village, Marriott speaks of the "wider integration of local groups with outside groups" (Marriott 1958). Sometimes this wider political integration, like community integration, is based on an extension and modification of an old integrative principle. Harrison has argued that modern developments in India have changed the significance of caste from the "traditional village extension of the joint family" to "regional alliances of kindred local units." This modification has led to the formation of "new caste lobbies" which constitute some of the strongest and most explosive political forces in modern India (Harrison 1960:100ff.). We shall mention some of the possible political consequences of this persistence of old integrative forms later.

These examples illustrate how differentiation in society impinges on the integrative sphere. The resulting integrative structures coordinate and solidify—with varying success—the social structure which the forces of differentiation threaten to fragment. In many cases the integrative associations and parties display tremendous instability—labor unions turn into political or nationalistic parties; religious sects become political clubs; football clubs become religious sects, and so on (Hodgkin 1957:85ff.). The resultant fluidity points up the extremely pressing needs for reintegration under conditions of rapid, irregular, and disruptive processes of differentiation. The initial response is a kind of trial-and-error floundering for many kinds of integration at once.

We have sketched some structural consequences of modernization and integration. These changes are not, it should be remembered, a simple function of "industrialization." Some of the most far-reaching structural changes have occurred in countries which have scarcely experienced the beginnings of industrialization. For instance, colonialism—or related forms of economic dominance—creates not only an extensive differentiation of cash products and wage-labor but also a vulnerability to world price fluctuations in commodities. Hence many of the structural changes described above—and the resulting social disturbances to be described presently—characterize both societies which are industrializing and some that are still "pre-industrial."

DISCONTINUITIES IN DIFFERENTIATION AND INTEGRATION: SOCIAL DISTURBANCES

The structural changes associated with modernization are disruptive to the social order for the following reasons:

(1) Differentiation demands the creation of new activities, norms, rewards and sanctions—money, political position, prestige based on occupation, and so on. These often conflict with old modes of social action, which are frequently dominated by traditional religious, tribal, and kinship systems. These traditional standards are among the most intransigent of obstacles to modernization, and when they are threatened, serious dissatisfaction and opposition arise.

(2) Structural change is, above all, *uneven* in periods of modernization. In colonial societies, for instance, the European powers frequently revolutionized the economic, political, and educational frameworks, but simultaneously encouraged or imposed a conservatism in traditional religious, class, and family systems.

> . . . the basic problem in these [colonial] societies was the expectation that the native population would accept certain broad, modern institutional settings . . . and would perform within them various roles—especially economic and administrative roles—while at the same time, they were denied some of the basic rewards inherent in these settings . . . they were expected to act on the basis of a motivational system derived from a different social structure which the colonial powers and indigenous rulers tried to maintain. (Eisenstadt 1957:298)

Under noncolonial conditions of modernization similar discontinuities appear. Within the economy itself, rapid industrialization, no matter how coordinated, bites unevenly into the established social and economic structure. And throughout the society, the differentiation occasioned by agricultural, industrial, and urban changes always proceeds in a seesaw relationship with integration; the two forces continuously breed lags and bottlenecks. The faster the tempo of modernization, the more severe are the discontinuities. This unevenness creates *anomie* in the classical sense, for it generates disharmony between life experiences and the normative framework by which these experiences are regulated.

(3) Dissatisfactions arising from conflict with traditional ways and those arising from *anomie* sometimes aggravate one another when they come into contact. *Anomie* may be relieved in part by new integrative devices such as unions, associations, clubs, and government regulations. Such innovations are often opposed, however, by traditional vested interests because the new forms of integration compete with the older undifferentiated systems of solidarity. The new result is a three-way tug-of-war among the forces of tradition, the forces of differentiation, and the new forces of integration. Such conditions create virtually unlimited potentialities for group conflict.

Three classic responses to these discontinuities are anxiety, hostility, and fantasy. These responses, if and when they become collective, crystallize into a variety of social movements—peaceful agitation, political violence, millenarianism, nationalism, revolution, underground subversion, etc. There is plausible—though not entirely convincing—evidence that those drawn most readily into such movements are those suffering most severely the pains of displacements created by structural change. For example,

> [Nationalism appeared] as a permanent force in Southeast Asia at the moment when the peasants were forced to give up subsistence farming for the cultivation of cash crops or when (as in highly colonized Java) subsistence farming ceased to yield a subsistence. The introduction of a money economy and the withering away of the village as the unit of life accompanied this development and finally established the period of economic dependence. (Jacoby 1949:246)

Other theoretical and empirical evidence suggests that social movements appeal most to those who have been dislodged from old social ties by differentiation but who have not been integrated into the new social order.

Many belief-systems associated with these movements envision the grand and almost instantaneous integration of society. In many cases the beliefs are highly emotional and unconcerned with realistic policies. In nationalistic colonial movements, for instance, "the political symbols were intended to develop new, ultimate, common values and basic loyalties, rather than relate to current policy issues within the colonial society" (Eisenstadt 1957:294). Furthermore, such belief-systems reflect the ambivalence resulting from the conflict between traditionalism and modernization. Nationalists alternate between xenophobia and xenophilia; they predict that they will "outmodernize" the West in the future and simultaneously "restore" the true values of the ancient civilization; they argue for egalitarian and hierarchical principles of social organization at the same time (Matossian 1957). Nationalistic and related ideologies unite these contradictory tendencies in a society under one large symbol; then, if these ideologies are successful, they are often used as a means to modernize and thus erase those kinds of social discontinuity which gave rise to the original nationalistic outburst.

Naturally not all the cases of early modernization produce violent nationalistic or other social movements. When such movements do arise, furthermore, they take many different forms. I shall merely list what seem to be the five most decisive factors in the genesis and molding of social disturbances:

(1) The scope and intensity of the social dislocation created by structural changes. "The greater the tempo of these changes . . . the greater the problems of acute malintegration the society has to face" (Eisenstadt 1957:294; Coleman 1957:42ff.; Hodgkin 1957:56).

(2) The structural complexity of the society at the time when modernization begins. In the least developed societies, where "the language of politics is at the same time the language of religion," protest movements more or less immediately take on a religious cast. In Africa, for instance, utopian religious movements seem to have relatively greater appeal in the less developed regions, whereas the more secular types of political protest such as trade union movements and party agitations have tended to cluster in the more developed areas. The secularization of protest increases, of course, as modernization and differentiation proceed.

(3) The access of disturbed groups to channels of influencing social policy. If dislocated groups have access to those responsible for introducing reforms, agitation tends to be relatively peaceful and orderly. If this access is blocked, either because of the isolation of the groups or the intransigence of the ruling au-

thorities, demands for reform tend to take more violent, utopian, and bizarre forms. Hence the tendency for fantasy and unorganized violence to cluster among the disinherited, the colonized, and the socially isolated migrants.

(4) The overlap of interests and lines of cleavage. In many colonial societies, the social order broke more-or-less imperfectly into three groupings: first, the Western representatives who held control of economic enterprises and political administration, and who frequently were allied with large local landowners; second, a large native population who—when drawn into the colonial economy—entered as tenant farmers, wage laborers, etc.; and third, a group of foreigners—Chinese, Indians, Syrians, Goans, Lebanese, etc.—who fitted "in between" the first two as traders, moneylenders, merchants, creditors, etc. This view is oversimplified, of course, but many colonial societies approximated this arrangement. The important structural feature of such a system is that economic, political, and racial-ethnic memberships *coincide* with each other. Hence *any* kind of conflict is likely to assume racial overtones and arouse the more diffuse loyalties and prejudices of the warring parties. Many colonial outbursts did in fact follow racial lines. Insofar as such "earthquake faults" persist after independence, these societies are likely to be plagued by similar outbursts. If, on the other hand, the various lines of cleavage crisscross, it is more nearly possible to insulate and manage specific economic and political grievances peacefully.

(5) The kind and extent of foreign infiltration and intervention on behalf of protest groups.

STRUCTURAL BASES FOR THE ROLE OF GOVERNMENT

Many have argued on economic grounds for the presence of a strong, centralized government in rapidly modernizing societies. Governmental planning and activity are required, for instance, to direct saving and investment, to regulate incentives, to encourage entrepreneurship, to control trade and prices, and so on. To such arguments I should like to add several considerations arising out of the analysis of structural change in periods of rapid development:

(1) Undifferentiated institutional structures frequently constitute the primary social barriers to modernization. Individuals refuse to work for wages because of traditional kinship, village, tribal, and other ties. Invariably a certain amount of political pressure is required to pry individuals loose from these ties. The need for such pressure increases, of course, with the rate of modernization desired.

(2) The process of differentiation itself creates those conditions which demand a larger, more formal type of political administration. A further argument for the importance of government in periods of rapid and uneven modernization lies, then, in the need to accommodate the growing cultural, economic, and social heterogeneity, and to control the political repercussions from the constantly shifting distribution of power which accompanies extensive social reorganization.

(3) The apparent propensity for periods of early modernization to erupt into explosive outbursts creates delicate political problems for the leaders of developing nations. We might conclude this essay on the major social forces of modernization by suggesting what kinds of government are likely to be most effective in such troubled areas. First, political leaders will increase their effectiveness by open and vigorous commitment to utopian and xenophobic nationalism. This commitment serves as a powerful instrument for attaining three of their most important ends: (a) the enhancement of their own claim to legitimacy by endowing themselves with the mission for creating the nation-state; (b) the procurement of otherwise impossible sacrifices from a populace which may be committed to modernization in the abstract but which resists the concrete breaks with traditional ways; (c) the use of their claim to legitimacy to hold down protests and to prevent generalized symbols such as communism from spreading to all sorts of particular grievances. These same political leaders should not, however, take their enthusiasm for this claim to legitimacy too literally. They should not rely on the strength of their nationalistic commitment to ignore or smother grievances altogether. They should play politics in the usual sense with aggrieved groups in order to give these groups an access to responsible political agencies and thereby reduce those conditions which give rise to counterclaims to legiti-

macy. One key to political stability would seem to be, therefore, the practice of flexible politics behind the façade of an inflexible commitment to a national mission.

In this essay I have attempted to sketch, in ideal-type terms, the ways in which economic and social development are related to the social structure. I have organized the discussion around three major categories—differentiation, which characterizes a social structure moving toward greater complexity; integration, which in certain respects balances the divisive character of differentiation; and social disturbances, which result from the discontinuities between differentiation and integration.

To this analysis must be added four qualifications: (1) I have not attempted to account for the determinants of economic development itself. In fact, the discussion of differentiation, integration, and social disturbance takes as given a certain attempt to develop economically. These three forces condition the *course* of development, however, once it has started. (2) For purposes of exposition I have presented the three major categories in a certain order—differentiation, integration, social disturbances. We should not assume from this, however, that any one of them assumes causal precedence in the analysis of social change. Rather they form an interactive system. Disturbances, for instance, may arise from discontinuities created by structural differentiation, but these very disturbances may shape the course of future processes of differentiation. Likewise, integrative developments may be set in motion by differentiation, but in their turn they may initiate new lines of differentiation. (3) Even though the forces of differentiation, integration, and disturbance are closely linked empirically, we should not "close" the "system" composed of the relationship among the three forces. Differentiation may arise from sources other than economic development; the requirement of integration may arise from conditions other than differentiation; and the sources of social disturbance are not exhausted by the discontinuities between differentiation and integration. (4) The "all-at-once" character of the transition from less differentiated to more differentiated societies should not be exaggerated. Empirically the process evolves gradually and influences the social structure selectively. The emphasis on various halfway arrangements and compromises throughout the essay illustrates this gradualness and irregularity.

II AFRICA

4 AFRICA'S LAND

Paul Bohannan

The most compelling issues in Negro Africa today are freedom and land. Land, like freedom, must be subject to some controls if it is to be usable and valuable. Again, land, like freedom, is subject to endless interpretations and disputes. Finally, with land, like freedom, the scarcer it is or the more uses that a civilization may have for it, the more vital and the more desirable it becomes.

The land-base of any society is one of the most fundamental considerations about it. The land-base of any rapidly changing society is, therefore, crucial, for the man-land relationship differs vastly from one kind of society to the next. This man-land relationship was the subject of detailed investigation by the original, inquiring mind of Sir Henry Sumner Maine in the late nineteenth century. No man of equal range or equivalent perception has inquired into the matter since, though we now know enough to provide the basis for a new, wide, and searching view of the whole issue of land and its place in society.

Sir Henry Maine was concerned specifically with problems of man-land relationships in rapidly changing societies. Since he was a jurist, he worked with the material most readily available to him—the codes of ancient and exotic peoples. His investigation of the changes in land law which must come about when a society changes from a tribal or kinship to a village or locality-dominated form of government, or from a village form to a state form of government, are today about the only usable models

FROM Paul Bohannan, "Africa's Land," *The Centennial Review*, IV (1960), No. 4, pp. 439–449. Reprinted by permission of the author and publisher.

which can be found in the tremendous literature on land in societies in flux.

The task before students of African land is a fairly easy one to outline, but will be extremely difficult to carry out. In short, the problem is this: the largest portions of Africa are proceeding from tribal forms of social organization to nation states and impersonal markets: colonialism has been, for the most part, merely a boost in that direction, a phase. Now, what are the changes in land tenure rules, in attitudes toward land, in economy, and all the other factors which such changes entail, and how are Africans managing them and responding to them?

I

In order to answer such questions, it is necessary, first, for us to look into just what is demanded in the way of land law by the twentieth-century, Western type of national state and by the relatively free market economy which Westerners have con-joined with it. That the junction of state and free market is not a necessary one we can see by looking at the Communist world. Yet the linking of these two features in the West has brought about a peculiar notion of land which we must examine if we are ever really to understand what other people with their completely different conceptions think and do about it.

Just what is it that Westerners mean by "land tenure"? To break the question down even further, what do we Westerners mean by "land," and what do we mean by "tenure"?

Every people, including ourselves, must have some view of the physical milieu—the "folk geography"—of the world and their part of it. It is instructive to pursue the Western ethnographic situation in the matter of conceptualization of "land." Westerners divided the earth's surface by use of an imaginary grid, itself subject to manipulations and re-definitions. We then plot the grid on paper or on a sphere, and the problem becomes one of correlating the physical features of the land and sea to this grid. We have developed instruments for locating ourselves on the earth's surface in relation to the position of the stars. There are precise rules for symbolizing the information from the instruments with which we do so and for transferring it to the gridded map. We have, for this and other purposes, perfected a system of measurement which allows us to repeat precisely operations which have been carried out in the past; thus we have been able to locate and measure pieces of the earth's surface, and to record our computations on maps. These measured pieces become, for some purposes at least, identifiable "things."

Land, whatever else it may also be, is for Westerners a measurable entity divisible into thing-like "parcels" by means of mathematical and technical processes of surveying and cartography based ultimately on astral position. This complex notion of "land," with its accompanying technology, is an absolute essential to the Western system of land tenure, as well as to the Western market-oriented economy.

When we come to the notion of "tenure" in our own system, we must unravel an even more tangled ambiguity. First of all, the notion of "tenure" assumes an idea of "land" of the sort we have already described. Only if it is divisible and the divisions precisely calculable and measurable can "land" be "held." Only if land is cut up into definable units can it enter the market or, as the jurist sees the same phenomenon, be subject to contract. Contract and a land market create specific types of relationship between men and land.

However, holding a piece of landed "property" in a society marked by a free market is more than a mere relationship between a man and a thing-like piece of land. As the best jurisprudential opinion has long told us, it is a relationship among persons. "Tenure" has to do with rights *in* land *against* or *with* other persons. Thus, in addition to the man-land unit, usually called a "property system" by Westerners, we have a man-man unit, usually referred to as part of the social system.

When we discuss the land question in terms of the social system, we do so in terms of the word "rights." "Rights" are attributes of persons against other persons. But in European languages, with the particular notions of land they reflect, "rights in land" can become attributes *of the land*. This "land right" links a person and a piece of land. But the equation of rights of people with rights in land, making one the obverse of the other, does not happen in most African societies. Therefore, when we return from the Western to the African situation, we must ask how we can classify African attitudes to "land" and African versions of "tenure" in order to know just what sort of a revolution is taking place today.

II

This question can be answered by generalizing the factors we have found so that they can guide us in working with several cultures at once. Three factors are involved: a concept of geography, a mode of correlating a man with his physical environment, and a social system with a spatial dimension. These factors can then be restated as axioms: (1) A people will have a representation of the country in which they live; that representation can be seen by the analyst in analogy to the Western map. (2) Members of any society have a set of concepts for speaking about and dealing with the relationships between themselves and the earth they exploit. (3) The spatial aspect of any social organization has some sort of overt expression in word and deed. The study of land in society is the way in which any people associates map, property, and spatial relationships.

It is, I believe, a fact that no African societies used indigenously an astrally based map such as our own, although a few peoples elsewhere, notably the Polynesians, did do so. Astral maps are, of course, sea-farers' maps. In the absence of a developed land market or of an aviation industry, there is seldom any need to apply sea-farers' maps to land masses.

However, a few African peoples did divide up the earth's surface into pieces by using terrestrial landmarks. The Kikuyu of Kenya are a notable example; the Bahaya of Tanganyika are another. In spite of the differences in map and in social organization, the Kikuyu had a man-land unit which was more or less immediately translatable into Western property terms. The Kikuyu struggle has not been with changing types of property notions— although they have had that too with reference to land that Europeans considered empty—so much as it has been with ensuring stability of tenure by getting their land surveyed and recorded. The task of putting it onto an astral map so that English property law and the land market can be made precisely to apply to it was a relatively minor change from the standpoint of perception.

Far greater numbers of African societies, however, did not split land up into pieces at all. Here we shall mention only two other methods by which an area can be made into a socially recognizable "map." One of these is by a series of specific terrestrial points which are given particular recognition and either economic or ritual meaning by the people concerned. To quote two examples hurriedly, the Plateau Tonga of Northern Rhodesia, studied by Dr. Elizabeth Colson, hook their social organization to the earth *not* by means of anything we would ourselves consider land tenure, but by means of a set of rain shrines, each of which is associated with surrounding villages, and each of which is specifically placed on the earth—possibly but rarely subject to move on ritual authority. Opportunity to move from one village to another is very wide, and acceptance as a resident in a village automatically carries with it not only fealty to the shrine but a right to make a farm nearby on any land not farmed at the moment nor claimed as fallow by another resident. Tonga farms can be cultivated for five or six years before the soil is exhausted. Given this placement, Tonga can be seen to have short-term "farm tenure," as it were, in the village area near the shrine.

The Bedouin Arabs of Cyrenaica, studied by E. E. Evans-Pritchard, are another well-documented example in which the tribal lands are attached to saints' graves or wells. Many pastoral societies and most of those who practice shifting cultivation see the land in this sort of association with society. The pastoral Fulani, with their long, sweeping cycles of movement, and the slash-and-burn peoples of the Congo forests, with their relatively short moves, can all be included in this classification.

In the other mode of connecting society to space, the social organization is conceived in terms of pure space, and is only incidentally linked with the physical environment by vicissitudes of farming or other land uses for very short periods of time. The Tiv of central Nigeria are an example of a farming people who are characteristic of this type. They see geography in the same image as they see social organization. The idiom of descent and genealogy provides not only the basis for lineage grouping, but also of territorial grouping. The Tiv group themselves according to a lineage system based on the principle of segmental opposition. Every "minimal lineage" is associated with a territory. This minimal lineage, two or three hundred men derived from a single ancestor, with their wives and daughters, is located spatially beside another of precisely the same sort—that is, descent from the brother of the ancestor of the first. In reference to the father of the two apical ancestors of the two minimal lineages, they form an inclusive lineage, and their territories form a spatial unit. This process continues genealogically for several generations, until all Tiv are included; it continues spatially until the entirety of Tivland is seen as a lineage area, segmenting into increasingly smaller lineage areas.

This "genealogical map" of Tivland moves about the surface of the earth in sensitive response to the demands of individual farmers as those demands change from year to year. The "map" in terms of which Tiv see their land is a genealogical map, and its association with specific pieces of ground is of only very brief duration—a man or woman has precise rights to a farm during the time it is in cultivation, but once the farm returns to fallow, the rights lapse. However, a man always has rights in the "genealogical map" of his agnatic lineage, wherever that lineage may happen to be in space. These rights, which are part of his birthright, can never lapse. A mathematician friend has suggested to me that whereas the Western map, based on surveys, resembles geometry, the Tiv notions resemble topology, which has been described as "geometry on a rubber sheet." The Western map is necessarily rigid and precise if the principle of contract is to work; the Tiv map is constantly changing both in reference to itself and in its correlation with the earth, thus allowing the principle of kinship grouping to work. For the Tiv, the position of a man's farm varies from one crop rotation to the next, but neither his juxtaposition with his agnatic kinsmen nor his rights change in the least. Tiv, like Tonga, might be said to have "farm tenure" but they do not have "land tenure."

Thus, instead of seeing their maps primarily in terms of man-thing units such as property, many Africans at least saw something like a map in terms of social relationships in space. They thus axiomized, so to speak, the spatial aspect of their social groups and provided themselves with a social map, so that they were left free to question the ways in which they attached either social groups or individuals to exploitational rights in the earth. Usually they were imprecise, group membership being the valued quality. Westerners, on the other hand, axiomize their map in terms of their property norms and values, and see the social system which results as fundamentally a series of contracts and hence open to question. As a result, Westerners question the social system that lies behind land usage, while Africans question the property ideas associated with it.

III

This relative inability on the part of Westerners to question whether or not a land system is in fact a property system— that is, the assumption that it always is, even if land does not enter the market—has led to the continued life of a silly concept called "communal ownership." Now, in a fully developed, contractually oriented society like our own, communal ownership can and does exist. That is to say, the commune, whatever its nature, can be viewed as a jural person. As a corporation aggregate, it is capable of owning property under the law. The difficulty arises because this fiction has been used by many Westerners to make sense out of most African land systems. A more farcical situation is difficult to imagine.

Sir Henry Maine pointed out long ago that in a community based on kinship, the land is an aspect of the group, but *not* the basis of grouping. Notions of "communal ownership," manipulated by people who assume property and market as the basis of society, have made the land the basis of grouping in a system in which spatial extension and concomitant rights to exploit the environment are mere aspects of the social group. The indigenous basis of grouping is kinship in some parts of Africa, while in others it is a village community similar to those Maine studied in India and Europe. In *no* place in Africa did the basis of grouping depend indigenously on contract.

Property, in the Western sense, and its resultant contractual relationships, are the fundamental basis of grouping in the Western type of national state. In a developed market economy, a land market emerges—with whatever agony to the people who must see it to fruition. Therefore, as African societies become

Western type national states, as they come to have more fully evolved market economies, the problem before them is how to preserve certain of their valued kinship groups. Their answer is the same as the one found by some of the more prosperous of American Indian tribes such as the Osage. They are turning their kinship groups into corporations aggregate before the law. This means that they can both maintain at least some of the valued qualities of the kinship group at the same time that they are making themselves into corporations—sole or aggregate— which are the units of "modern societies," based on contract and on the open market.

The Osage, when they struck oil, turned their tribe into a limited corporation under the laws of the State of Oklahoma. The Yoruba people in the Western Region of Nigeria are turning their extended-family compounds into landholding units before the law, under the "Communal Land Rights (Vesting in Trustees) Law" of 1958.

This law, in brief, makes a matter of legal record the change in the nature of the Yoruba lineage group called the *ebi*, though it does so in legal language which eschews mention of the *ebi*. The *ebi* in traditional terms was an agnatic descent group which shared a common residence. Every quarter of every Yoruba town had several *ebi*, and on some occasions an *ebi* could split into two or more *ebi*. This body of agnatic kinsmen, with their wives, also had an estate—a more or less precisely determinable area within which they traditionally farmed, and which they protected from encroachment by others. Within the *ebi*, the members farmed not in specific places which they considered their own, but the group moved its farms about within the area so that they could remain as a unit to take advantage of the best soils and to control the system of fallowing. Nobody "owned" anything, but every member had a right to a farm sufficient to support his immediate dependents. These rights to a farm were inalienable. The *ebi* had a head and a council which ran the agricultural affairs of the *ebi* in a kind of committee.

This mode of spatial distribution and concomitant exploitation of the environment leaves several things to be desired in the new society which has developed under colonialism and is fast breaking away from it. In the first place, it grants a man land rights *only* insofar as he is a part of a lineage. The mo-

ment he ceases to be an effective member of his lineage, he
foregoes his land rights until he again becomes an effective
member. Under modern conditions, Yoruba often want to remain
members of their lineages, but also want to have land rights
of a different sort. Sale of land, which was impossible in the
old system because land was the spatial dimension of the *ebi*
rather than a commodity which could be considered "property"
and sold in the market, became desirable when the economic
system changed in such a way as to make it feasible. Immediately, a sort of pull or pressure was set up between the
ebi land unit and the individual. Either a man must cease being
an individual in the new system, or the *ebi* land unit, as an
institution, had to go.

The "Communal Land Rights (Vesting in Trustees) Law"
is a legal mechanism by means of which this particular difficulty
has been solved. European analysis of Yoruba land tenure has,
from the beginning, classed the *ebi*'s spatial dimension as "land
owned in communal tenure." The *ebi* is certainly a community
of sorts, and since it was associated with land, the European
notion of "tenure" was automatically applied without question
as to whether it applied or not. This assumption had the result
of turning the *ebi,* in European eyes, into a corporation aggregate before the law. With this European analysis in terms
of legal corporations, a subtle change was introduced. The Europeans, in the legal system they fostered, gave the *ebi* a legal reality
which it formerly had not possessed. From being only a social
group, it now became a legal entity. Yoruba were a bit late
in recognizing what had happened. But since they did recognize
it, they and their legislators have seen in it a means of preserving
the *ebi* as a social group fulfilling the basic needs of what we
would call social insurance and community center at the same
time that they have strengthened the modern institution of private property.

Thus, in the indigenous system, the *ebi* did not "own" land
communally or any other way. Rather, it was a social group
with a spatial dimension. This vital difference was recognized
by Sir Henry Maine and was vividly described by him. Later
scholars have usually forgotten it. In the modern system the
ebi of the Yoruba has been turned into a legal entity, before
the laws of Nigeria, and can *therefore* "own" land. "Communal

land ownership" assumes that the commune is, before the law, the same sort of unit as the individual. That idea has penetrated Yoruba cultural values and, indeed, communal land ownership under the law is actually taking place.

The legal mechanisms of the West have for centuries been the device by means of which Westerners have had their cake at the same time they have eaten it. Therein lies its strength. The peoples of the Western Region of Nigeria are now, in fact, preserving at least a part of their traditional culture by means of this Western legal form. I think it likely that we can find a great many more instances in which fragmented values which have resulted from the flooding of African society with new ideas have been reconsolidated by a legal device. The Western genius today is a legal one. A legal context is also one that is, by cultural tradition, congenial to most Africans. The result is that we see before us the spread of Western law with the concomitant salvation of many of the indigenous institutions which Africans find valuable.

5 TRADITIONAL PRODUCTION
IN PRIMITIVE AFRICAN ECONOMIES

George Dalton

Economic historians often stress the role played by the traditional institutions of pre-industrial European countries in shaping their sequential patterns of development: that the costs, speed,
and specific lines of development were influenced by what existed before industrialization (Gerschenkron 1952; Rostow 1960).
However, we seem not to apply the lesson to exotic areas such as
Africa. Economists rarely show interest in the voluminous anthropological literature concerned with the economic organization
of primitive societies before Western impact. Yet it is these same
primitive societies in Africa, Asia, and Latin America which are
now so much the concern of the economics of development.

Although Western impact in the form of wage employment
and dependence upon cash cropping have become widespread in
Africa, it is probably still true (as it was in the early 1950s), that
most Africans get the bulk of their livelihood from traditional
modes of production within the framework of tribal societies.[1]
It is with such relatively unchanged, primitive economies in
Africa that this paper is concerned.

There are at least two kinds of development problems for the
solution of which knowledge of primitive economic structure is
useful: (1) What accounts for the marked difference in receptivity to economic and technological change among primi-

FROM George Dalton, "Traditional Production in Primitive African
Economies," *Quarterly Journal of Economics,* LXXVI, pp. 360–378. Copyright © by the President and Fellows of Harvard College.

[1] ". . . between 65 percent and 75 percent of the total cultivated land
area of tropical Africa is devoted to subsistence production." United Nations (1954:13).

tive societies? Why do some adopt Western institutions and techniques with ease and alacrity while others resist the changes necessary to generate growth? (2) Why is economic development often accompanied by traumatic social change? Is it possible to reduce the social costs and dislocations by building compensators into the new economic forms?[2]

The point of this paper is to show how primitive economies in Africa differ structurally from developed economies in the West. Our concern is not so much with technological differences as with differences in the organization of production. And for either the West or primitive Africa it is convenient to regard production of any kind as consisting of three component sub-processes: the allocation of labor and other factors; the work process of arranging and transforming resources into products; the disposition of what is produced.

THE ABSENCE OF MARKET DEPENDENCE

At the outset, we may summarize our main theme as follows. The absence of market exchange as the *dominant*[3] economic organization allows indigenous African production to take forms different from those in Western economy. These forms invariably entail social control of production by kinship, religion, and political organization. Therefore, change in primitive economic processes means inevitable change in social organization.

> In primitive communities, the individual as an economic factor is personalized, not anonymous. He tends to hold his economic position in virtue of his social position. Hence to displace him economically means a social disturbance. (Firth 1951:137)

It is necessary to emphasize the economic importance of indigenous social organization because production in tribal Africa

[2] On social aspects of economic development see Bohannan (1959:491–503); Keyfitz (1959:34–46); Douglas (1962); Moore (1955:156–65).

[3] By dominant is meant that source which provides the bulk of material livelihood. Market-place exchange occurs frequently in indigenous Africa, but may provide sellers with only a minor portion of their income. The point is considered at length later in the paper. It should be emphasized that market-place exchange does *not* refer to long-distance trade, usually in prestige goods (gold, cattle, ivory), sometimes carried on by professional traders, sometimes under government commission. On such trade, see the writings of Karl Polanyi referred to throughout the paper.

is most frequently a community activity in MacIver's sense, and only rarely associational:

> Association is a group specifically organized for the purpose of an interest or group of interests which its members have in common. . . . Community is a circle of people who live together, who belong together, so that they share not this or that particular interest, but a whole set of interests wide enough and comprehensive enough to include their lives.[4]

We are used to thinking in terms of "production units" because the Western firm is an association, not importantly affected by kinship, religious, or political affiliation of participants. In Africa, however, production is often undertaken by intimate communities of persons sharing a multitude of social ties and functions, one of which happens to be the production of material goods. If we are not to prejudge the nature of production organization in African economy, it must be understood that none of those special characteristics of Western production due to the use of machines and reliance upon factor and output markets, need be found. The component processes exist: the allocation of factors; the arrangement of work; and the disposition of produce. How they are organized in the absence of market integration must be a matter for investigation. In a word, every society has production processes, but not necessarily production "units."

Indigenously, the most important production lines in Africa are agricultural, carried on without machine technology, and for subsistence purposes rather than primarily for market sale (United Nations 1954).[5] Unlike his counterpart in the American Midwest, the African farmer typically is not enmeshed in that kind of larger economy from which he extracts his livelihood as a specialist producer of cash crops, the money proceeds of which are used to recoup his costs of production, and the residual

[4] MacIver (1933:9, 10, 12) quoted in Nadel (1942:xi). The distinction goes back to Tönnies' *Gemeinschaft und Gesellschaft*, and to Weber (1947:136–37). Association and community are not to be regarded as mutually exclusive, but as opposite ends of a range describing degrees of emphasis. What is here meant by community is characterized, in a recent work, as diffuse, ascription-centered, and socially recruited. See Udy (1959:39, 53).

[5] The literature on indigenous nonagricultural production in Africa is fragmentary. A good study of handicraft production is contained in Nadel (1942).

(his income proper), used to buy daily-used material items and services.

The absence of machines and of market dependence are related: as with hired labor or any other *purchased* factor, a machine represents a money cost which can be incurred only if the purchaser uses the machine to enlarge his money sales revenue from which he recovers its cost. The analytical point to be stressed is that without purchased ingredients of production, and without reliance upon market disposition of output, input and output decisions of producers cannot be based on factor and output prices as guiding parameters. That neither factor nor product prices exist to constrain the indigenous African agriculturalist (as they do the Western) is crucial to understanding why it is that Africans can organize production in such seemingly bizarre "social" ways.

The absence of Western technological and market constraints means also the absence of the Western kind of material insecurity. It is not technological unemployment and depression which are the threats to the continuity of production and income, but rather physical environment—weather, plant disease. That there is no counterpart to depression-born unemployment is simply a reflection of the absence of dependence on market sale.

A related point of contrast is that unlike the Western worker, the African is rarely a full-time specialist in one occupation or in one production group (Schapera and Goodwin 1937:153; Herskovits 1952a:94, 106). Not only is it typical for him to produce for himself a wide range of the items he uses—his own house and tools as well as his food—but during the course of a year he is frequently a part-time participant in several production activities: he may join sporadic work-parties to do specific tasks such as clearing fields for friends, kin, and chief; he may be of an age set which is obliged to perform community services such as repairing roads (Nadel 1942:248; Herskovits 1952:113; Kluckhohn 1962); he may go on seasonal expeditions to extract ore for metals (Cline 1937:56). In sum, it is frequently the case that during the year an African will work in several production groups, no one of which is crucial to his own livelihood. It is also common for an African to receive substantial amounts of factors, goods, and services as gifts, or in forms other than remuneration for work performed.

Production and Social Organization

The negative point stressed above, that the absence of machines and market dependence means the absence of those kinds of constraints on production organization in the West, clears the way to examine two positive points stressed repeatedly in the literature of primitive Africa: (1) That neighboring societies sharing the same physical environment often produce markedly different ranges of output (Winter 1962), with different technologies (Douglas 1962) used within differently organized production groups (Mead 1937; Udy 1959). (2) That such economic and technological differences are largely attributable to differences in social organization: that kinship, political, and religious institutions constrain and direct all phases of production, in the same sense that market structure and machine technology constrain and direct production in Western economy.

The connections between indigenous African production and social organization may be described in three ways: (1) In terms of the MacIver-Nadel distinction, production groups typically are not separate associations but rather are integral parts of a community:

> . . . obligations to participate tend to be obligations to associate with the group involved rather than specifically engage in production. (Udy 1959:104)

> The ties between producers tend to reach out beyond this common interest in the act of production and its rewards alone. A production relationship is often only one facet of a social relationship. . . . economic relations can be understood only as a part of a scheme of social relations. . . . Economic anthropology deals primarily with the economic aspects of the social relations of persons. (Firth 1951:136–38)

> . . . special organizations to carry out cultivation or manufacture need not be expected among the Bantu; the functions are always actively carried out, but often by organizations of which the family or household is the most important, which exist to carry out almost all necessary functions, including the religious, the legal, the political, and the educational, and which conduct manufacture and agriculture alongside of these other activities. (Goodfellow 1939:7–8)

(2) The same point is generalized by Karl Polanyi in saying that primitive economy is "embedded" in society, in the sense that the economic system functions as a by-product of noneconomic institutions: that economy as a cohesive entity, a separate set of practices and relationships apart from social organization, does not exist in primitive life (Polanyi 1944: Chapter 4; 1947; 1957).

(3) If the organization of production in African economies is indeed an inextricable part of social community, it should be possible to show how *each* component subprocess of production —the allocation of factor resources, the arrangement of work, and the disposition of produce—is related to social structure.

ALLOCATION OF FACTORS OF PRODUCTION

Production in all economies requires organizational devices and rules to direct labor, land, and other resources to specific uses. Resource allocation is never unstructured because continuity in the production of basic goods is never unimportant. One may gain insight into the special rules which mark off types of economy—say, the United States compared with the Soviet Union compared with the Bantu of South Africa—by asking which transactional procedures channel resources to production lines: how are land, labor, and other resources allocated; how do they change hands or usage?

In our own economy, factors as well as products are marketable commodities. In tribal Africa, products are frequently marketed, but factors almost never. A distinguishing characteristic of such economies is that labor and natural resources have no separate "economic" organization: factor movements and appropriations are expressions of social obligation, social affiliation, and social right. A second characteristic is that typically, land utilization is organized differently from labor utilization. Unlike Western market economy *each* of the factor ingredients may enter production lines through *different* institutional channels, the channels being structured social relationships. Both points are illustrated by the following examples.

In much of agricultural Africa, land for homesteads and farms is acquired through tribal affiliation or kinship right. One receives land as a matter of status prerogative; only rarely is land acquired or disposed of through purchase and sale (Bohannan 1960; Herskovits 1952:364–65). The Bantu are typical in this regard:

> Every household-head has an exclusive right to land for building his home and for cultivation. Generally he can take up such land for himself within the area controlled by his sub-chief or headman, provided that he does not encroach upon land already occupied or cultivated by others. Failing this, it is the duty of his headman to provide him gratuitously with as much land as he needs. . . . He also has the right, subject to the approval of his headman, to give away part of it to a relative or friend, or to lend it to someone else. But he can never sell it or dispose of it in any other way in return for material considerations. Should he finally abandon the spot, his land reverts to the tribe as a whole and can subsequently be assigned to someone else. The only other way in which he can lose his right to the land is by confiscation, if he is found guilty of some serious crime. (Schapera and Goodwin 1937:157)[6]

So, too, with the Tiv (Bohannan 1954), the Dahomeans (Herskovits 1938), the Nupe (Nadel 1942), and the Kikuyu.[7]

What makes the African social integument so important for factor allocation (and therefore production) is that land may be acquired through one set of social relationships, while labor to work the land is acquired through others. In the same Bantu societies in which land is acquired from chiefs by all family heads as a matter of tribal affiliation, labor to work the land is acquired by marriage rights (wives do the sustained cultivation), and by kinship and friendship reciprocity (work parties to do specific tasks such as clearing fields and harvesting). Put another way, the "labor" to perform different tasks in growing the same crop —clearing the field, planting, harvesting—may be acquired through different social relationships (Schapera and Goodwin 1937:149, 151–52).

The extent to which various community relationships allocate factors to production lines is even greater than indicated above. Each separate production line—farming, cattle-raising, house construction, road construction—may use somewhat differently institutionalized procedures for recruiting the labor and acquiring

[6] See also Sadie (1960:297).
[7] The Kikuyu came closest to Western concepts of land tenure, and land was sold on rare occasions. See Kenyatta (1938); Bohannan (1960).

the land and material resources used in each; that is to say, labor for agriculture may be acquired in several ways, each different from labor used in producing other goods.

As will be pointed out below, such factor diversity born of multiple social obligations is also the case with the disposition of the goods produced. African economies are "multicentric" (Bohannan and Dalton 1962) in the allocation of both factors and produce. This multicentricity is expressed in two ways, both extremely common in primitive economy: (1) Resources and products are arranged in groups, the items in one group exchangeable with each other, but not with items in other groups (Firth 1958:69); indeed, there may be items which are not exchangeable at all. Typically, "subsistence" items form one or more exchangeable groups, and "prestige" items, others. (2) Each commensurable group of factors and products may be transacted by an essentially different socio-economic device or procedure (reciprocity or redistribution); each socio-economic procedure expressing the special social obligation which induces the material transaction and, where relevant, dictating the permissible ratios at which commensurable goods may change hands (Polanyi 1957b; Dalton 1961).

Market exchange is also a common transactional procedure in tribal Africa, but differs sharply from reciprocity and redistribution in the permissible range of goods transacted in markets, the forces which determine exchange ratios, and in the absence of a social imperative connected with market transactions.

In summary, an African's role in each production process is usually defined by some aspect of his social status—tribal member, husband, cousin, friend, elder. The question, what forces, institutions, or rules direct labor, land, and other resources to specific lines of production, can be answered only with reference to community social organization.

Work Arrangement

The specific arrangement of work in any production line is the combined result of physical environment, technology, economic structure, and social organization. But the relative importance of each may differ between different production lines and between different types of economy. Here we will be concerned with one primary point of difference between Western and primitive subsistence economies: in our own system, the constraints imposed by economy-wide market integration and by machine technology are far more important in determining work organization than those imposed by physical environment and social structure. In tribal Africa just the opposite is the case: physical environment and social structure are all-important because of the absence of machine technology and of a larger market economy to enforce economizing decisions on local producers.

That physical environment imposes sharp constraints on African work organization is due to the great reliance by the Africans on production lines entailing little fabrication, such as agriculture and herding. Compared with their Western counterparts, the African agriculturalist and herder lack those devices of applied science (irrigation equipment, disease-resistant seeds, scientific stock breeding) which reduce ecological risks in the West (Forde and Douglas 1956:337). Indeed, technology and science have allowed some Western farmers to organize farm work on something like a factory basis. However, the economic as distinct from the technological differences between Western and primitive production, deserve emphasis. Dependence on market sale for income together with reliance on purchased factors, force Western farmers into the same economizing choices of weighing costs against sales revenues that typify manufacturing processes. With us, farm production too is sensitive to market prices, which of necessity serve as guiding parameters for production decisions including efficient work organization as measured by least cost.

Where African producers do not use purchased factors and do not depend on market sale, economizing least-cost choices in work arrangement are not enforced by technological or economic necessity, as in the West. We are told frequently that in primitive economy social relationships and values are important determinants of work organization (Lloyd 1953:31; Mead 1937; Udy 1959): that sexual division of labor is maintained, that magic and religion impinge on work schedules, that there is often a festive aspect to work parties, and that it is not uncommon for more labor to be lavished on a task than is strictly necessary. It is because of the absence of Western market and technological constraints that work *can be* arranged to express social relationships. The tribal producer does not have a payroll to meet. It is *not* that he is indifferent to material abundance or efficiency; rather, unlike the West, there is no larger economy to compel producers to seek cost minimization, or provide them with economic directives (factor and output prices) to make economizing decisions in work arrangement. It is important to understand this point in order to understand why economic development or Western "impact" induces such deep and wide social dislocation. When Western market economy comes to dominate some area of Africa—typically, through a land shortage forcing changeover to production of cash crops—there are socio-economic repercussions because of the need to reorganize factor allocation, work arrangement, and the range of items to be produced, in accordance with market criteria (Gulliver 1962).

DISPOSITION OF PRODUCTS

The apportionment of outputs is a concept familiar to Westerners. We are used to tracing through the yearly flow of goods to their final recipients as is done in national income accounting and input-output analysis. But as one economist who tried to measure product and income flows in primitive African economy points out, our Western categories of analysis are derived from our own very special market-integrated structure.

> An attempt to examine the structure and problems of a primitive community in the light of the existing body of economic thought raises fundamental conceptual issues. Economic analysis and its framework of generalizations are characteristically described in terms appropriate to the modern exchange economy. It is by no means certain that the existing tools of analysis can usefully be applied to material other than that for which they have been developed. In particular it is not clear what light, if any, is thrown on subsistence economies by a science which seems to regard the use of money and specialization of labor as axiomatic. The jargon of the market place seems remote, on the face of it, from the problems of an African village where most individuals spend the greater part of their lives in satisfying their own or their families' needs and desires, where money and trade play a subordinate role in motivating productive activity. (Deane 1953: 115–16)[8]

[8] The same point is made by Firth (1951:121).

The absence of purchased factors (including machinery) and the lack of dependence on market sale for livelihood, together with the pervasive influence of the social integument, are reflected in the disposition of produce as well as in the allocation of factors and the organization of work:

> The income-creating process is itself part and parcel of the income it yields, and the results of the process cannot be abstracted from the process itself. (Frankel 1955:41)

If the categories we use to describe output disposition are to be analytically revealing they must be derived from the special structural characteristics of indigenous African economies. We follow therefore the African emphasis on the social obligations to pay and to give, and the rights to receive goods and services, built into social situations. In the succinct statement of Firth, "From each according to his status obligations in the social system, to each according to his rights in that system" (Firth 1951: 142).

In primitive economy, transactions of products are like those of factors in four ways: (1) Factors and products both may be transacted by different rules or mechanisms within the same economy. (2) Both may enter different transactional spheres, in the sense that the items in each sphere are commensurable and exchangeable only with other items in the same sphere, and not with items in different spheres. (3) The dispositions of factors and products cannot be understood outside the social situations which provide the impetus for their movement, i.e., transactions of both express underlying social relationships. (4) What might be called "socially guaranteed subsistence" is arranged both through factor resource and product disposition. Illustration of each point is given below.

RECIPROCITY

Factors and products are transacted by any of three socioeconomic rules or principles: reciprocity, redistribution, and market exchange (Polanyi 1957b). Reciprocity is obligatory gift- and counter gift-giving between persons who stand in some socially defined relationship to one another. Indigenously, gifts of produced items and factors are regarded simply as one form—material, or economic—of expressing such social relationships. (In our own society, a birthday gift from father to son is just one among many ways of expressing their kinship relation.)

Reciprocity plays a much more important part in primitive African economies than in our own: the frequency and amount of such gifts are greater; the number of different people with whom one person may engage in gift exchange is larger; the social obligations (and sanctions) to do so are stronger; and, above all, such gift reciprocity may play an important part in production (especially in labor allocation), which is rarely the case in our own economy outside the family farm.

After describing the network of obligatory gift transfers of labor and material products among kin and friends, at ordinary times as well as during festive occasions, Schapera and Goodwin explain the importance of reciprocal flows in Bantu societies:

> The main incentive to conformity with these obligations is reciprocity. In the relative absence of industrial specialization and consequent economic interdependence, kinship serves to establish greater social cohesion within the community, and to integrate its activities into a wider co-operation than obtains within the restricted limits of the household. The so-called "communal system" of the Bantu is largely a manifestation of this close bond of solidarity and reciprocity arising out of kinship and affecting well-nigh every aspect of daily life. (Schapera and Goodwin 1937:166)

The great variety of items and services transacted reciprocally helps to explain why "production" is invisible, so to speak, in primitive economies: from the viewpoint of the participants, the movement of resources and products is not regarded as an activity distinct from other social activities. A gift of labor to help a kinsman clear his land (part of production) may not be distinguished from a gift of cattle to help him acquire a bride; or, indeed, a gift of a song or a name. The pivotal matter is the social relationship between the persons which induces gifts of labor, cattle, songs, and names. When the source of the gift obligation is the same, there is no reason for the participants to mark off the labor gift as part of production. *It is only when production activities become divorced from activities expressing social obligation* that production becomes marked off as a peculiarly *economic* activity, apart from other activities (as, of course, occurs in market economy).

REDISTRIBUTION

Redistribution entails obligatory payments of material items, money objects, or labor services to some socially recognized center, usually king, chief, or priest, who reallocates portions of what he receives to provide community services (such as defense or feasts), and to reward specific persons. Typically, but not invariably, the central figure is also endowed with the right to distribute unused land or hunting sites; these allocation rights are vested in him in the name of the community by virtue of his high political, juridical, military, or religious authority. As with reciprocity between friends or kin, the obligation to give over factors, such as labor for the chief's garden or new house, may not be distinguished from the obligation to pay over items such as food. Indeed, what appear to us as economic transactions of resources and products need not be distinguished indigenously from such as express the obligation to perform military service.

Among the Bantu the chief receives payments of specific goods and services from all his people, and payments of fines and bloodwealth. Such tribute payments are partly in recognition of his position as the steward of tribal landholdings, and of his juridical authority. The word "tribute" is important here in both its economic and social meanings: the goods and labor paid over are tribute, and the social recognition of authority is a tribute:

> By virtue of his official status as head of the tribe he also played an important part in the economic organization. . . . He received tribute from his people, both in kind and in labor. He was given a portion of every animal slaughtered or killed in the chase; the *lobola* [bridewealth] for his chief wife was paid by the members of his tribe; he had the right to call upon his subjects to perform certain tasks for him, such as building his huts or clearing the land for his wives' gardens; above all, he received fees for hearing cases and fines for misdemeanors, and, in cases of homicide the culprit paid compensation not to the relatives of the deceased but to him. (Schapera 1928:175)[9]

His material receipts cannot be regarded apart from the chief's

[9] See also Herskovits (1938:78–80).

material obligations to his people. He uses the payments and fines for his own maintenance, but also to provide community services and to reward special service of his subjects:

> . . . all this accumulation of wealth by the chief was really made on behalf of the tribe. One quality which was always required of the chief was that he should be generous. He had to provide for the members of his tribe in times of necessity. If a man's crops failed he would look to the chief for assistance; the chief gave out his cattle to the poorer members of his tribe to herd for him, and allowed them to use the milk; he rewarded the services of his warriors by gifts of cattle; his subjects frequently visited him in his kraal and during their stay he fed and entertained them. (Schapera 1928:175)[10]

Just as an individual receives land from his chief and labor from his wives, kin, and friends as a matter of right, so too does he receive material aid in time of need as a matter of social right. Rarely in African societies are there special institutions to care for the disabled or the destitute (Sadie 1960:297). Subsistence is guaranteed among the Bantu—as is the case widely in primitive Africa—in two ways: through socially structured rights to receive factors of production, and through emergency allotments of food from the chief and gifts from kin. It is these socially assured rights to labor and land, and to emergency subsistence, which has sometimes been mistaken for "primitive communism."[11]

MARKET EXCHANGE

As with reciprocity and redistribution, market exchange is a common transactional procedure, especially in West Africa. However, indigenous market transactions differ sharply from those la-

---

[10] See also Fortes and Evans-Pritchard (1940:8–9).

[11] See Polanyi (1947:112); also Firth (1951:145–46). It should be added that the material insecurity which results from dependence on favorable weather and other aspects of physical environment, together with low productivity techniques and the lack of storage and processing facilities, also work in the direction of mutual aid and sharing. See Forde and Douglas (1956:337).

beled reciprocity and redistribution, and differ also in important respects from market transactions in developed economies.[12]

Purchase and sale seem to us peculiarly *economic*—permeated by utility and material gain—precisely because market transactions are neither induced by nor express social obligations or relationships. Unlike the partners to reciprocal and redistributive transactions, buyers and sellers in the market share no social tie which *obliges* them to engage in the market transactions. Therefore terms of trade may be haggled out without social disruption, both parties to the exchange being socially free to seek their own maximum material advantage.

Indigenous market exchange in Africa might better be called market-place exchange to point up the absence of labor and land markets. In primitive Africa, market exchange is usually confined to a limited range of produced items transacted by face-to-face buyers and sellers in market places. Moreover, the market exchanges are usually peripheral, in the sense that most sellers do not acquire the bulk of their livelihood, and buyers the bulk of their daily used goods and services, via the market-place sales and purchases. Although the market prices are determined by familiar supply and demand forces, there is absent that crucial feedback effect which links change in market price to production decisions. Unlike the price mechanism in a market-integrated economy like the United States, prices formed in African market places do not serve to reallocate factors among production lines, because labor and land do not enter the market and basic livelihood is acquired in non-market spheres. Market-place exchange is found widely in Africa as a peripheral pattern in the same societies in which all important output and factor flows are carried on via reciprocity and redistribution.[13]

[12] For an extended treatment of markets in primitive compared with developed economies, see Bohannan and Dalton (1962).

[13] Soviet economy provides an analogy: peasant market-place exchange of a few food and craft items which are bartered at freely fluctuating prices, is a peripheral pattern compared with the dominant central planning complex through which most goods are produced and almost all factors allocated. There are in Africa peasant economies such as cocoa farming in Ghana, in which market exchange is dominant.

COLONIAL IMPACT AND THE NEW NATIONAL ECONOMIES

It is necessary to consider the socio-economic impact of colonialism to understand the present situation in much of Africa. Two points especially must be made clear.

The destructive aspect of colonialism was not *economic* exploitation of Africans in the conventional Marxist sense; it could hardly be so considering that material poverty was already the common lot before the Europeans arrived. It is, perhaps, our own cultural emphasis which makes us focus on the real-income component of welfare and regard it as the sole component. Typically, colonialism did not make Africans worse off *materially;* it destroyed culture and society of which the indigenous economy was an inextricable part.[14] It destroyed materially poor but unusually integrated ways of life, wherein economic and social processes were mutually dependent and reinforcing. This is something on a different plane from simple material betterment or worsening. The destructive colonial impact consisted in forcing socio-economic change which was not meaningful to Africans in terms of their traditional societies:

> For the sting of change lies not in change itself but in change which is devoid of social meaning. (Frankel 1955:27)

Despite any real income increases which may have resulted, European enterprise was devoid of social meaning for Africans because it required work which was not part of social obligation to kin, friends, or rulers. Work for Europeans was not done as a by-product of traditional social relationships, and work for Europeans meant not working at those traditional tasks which were expressive of social rights and obligations:

[14] There is a familiar parallel situation worth mentioning. Some literature of the British industrial revolution addresses itself to the question, "Did the English workers get better or worse off during the period of rapid industrialization?" The writers then attempt to measure real income changes to find an answer. The ambiguity lies in implicitly defining better or worse off solely in terms of real income, despite the massive social dislocations involved in movement from a rural peasant to an urban industrial way of life. See Ashton (1949).

> Of [indigenous] labor itself, we can say . . . that it is a socially integrative activity. . . . Nor must we forget that wherever European and other more complex societies have encouraged primitive man, the carrot has been a bribe (and a pitiful indemnity) for those who must willingly neglect the performance of what are to them socially important functions so that they can perform during that time activities which are not integrative in their own society. (Steiner 1957:118–19)

Material income is important to Africans not only because it sustains life, but also—in Steiner's phrase—because the work processes which yield income and the transactional disposition of the labor, resources, and products are so organized as to express and strengthen social relationships and purpose: kinship, tribal affiliation, friendship and religious duty. It is noteworthy that in the few cases in which Africans have been able to work for Europeans without giving up most of their usual activities, traditional social life has remained intact (Watson 1958). Most frequently however, entering the newly created market economy as laborer, specialist producer of cash crops, or commercial trader buying for resale, has meant enlarged material income at the sacrifice of work activities which were necessary to traditional social organization, and so the latter deteriorated.

What has been called the "demonstration effect"—increased willingness to enter commercial activities in order to acquire Western material items—works in the same direction. In traditional society material wealth acquisition was largely a by-product of social status (Douglas 1962; Herskovits 1938:73). Typically, only those of higher social rank were permitted to acquire certain wealth items or an unusual amount of wealth. In the kingdom of Dahomey, for example, "The accumulation of wealth, except by those whose status entitled them to wealth, was deemed treason to the state" (Polanyi 1966). A socially divisive impact of Western economy in Africa has been the democratization of wealth. Neither market organization nor industrialism impose status criteria on wealth acquisition. Rather the opposite is the case (as Sir Henry Maine has long since told us).

It should be added that the force of socio-economic change in Africa cannot be explained in the simple terms of changed ownership of property. To the extent that Africans sell their labor to European firms (and other Africans), they become proletarians.

What strikes the Marxists is that the wage laborers engage in production processes the capital instruments of which they do not own. This is true, of course, but the crucial point is not that the workers do not own the buildings and machines, but that they come to depend for their livelihood on the impersonal market sale of their labor. Material income thereby depends upon forces, people, and institutions outside of and not controlled by the indigenous social community. Work becomes a thing apart from the other aspects of life, organized as a separate association, and not merely one facet of community life.

What is important for our purpose is that the same is true where Africans do *not* become proletarians, but enter market economy by producing cash crops on their own land. Here they own the instruments of production, but like the wage laborers also come to depend for their livelihood on market sale for a money income. The latter mode of entering the exchange economy can be as disruptive to indigenous social and economic organization as wage labor, and for the same reasons. It is not alienation from the means of production which is socially divisive, but rather the dependence upon impersonal market forces unrelated to indigenous social control; the separating of economy from society by divorcing resource allocation, work arrangement, and product disposition from expressions of social obligation. And, to be sure, the consequent loss of socially guaranteed subsistence, as well.

In advocating policy measures for developing African economies one must avoid the vice of utopianism: to create a blueprint of what ought to be which bears no relation to what is, and so is unachievable. However, to retain indigenous social organization in the new economies of markets and machines is obviously impossible. What is not impossible is to frame local economic organization and national policies which allow the expression of traditional values of reciprocity and redistribution within the new economic and technological context. As we are learning from our own welfare state experience, even within efficiency constraints, economic organization is capable of contrived flexibility to accommodate social values (Mvrdal 1960). The extent of diversity among the already developed nations indicates the possibility of creating distinctive African forms viable economically and socially.

The real task is not to force change but to induce it in a manner which will be meaningful to the members of the societies it affects. (Frankel 1955:78–79)[15]

The institutions being fashioned in the newly independent countries of Africa may appear somewhat suspect in the West. They include strong central controls, unions, producer's and consumer's co-operatives, and much else of the paraphernalia of welfare and socialist states, even at the very beginnings of development; indeed, even in countries without industrialization.

What deserves emphasis is that political and economic structures transplanted to Africa from the West are being adopted with major changes to suit African needs and traditions. Neither democracy nor the welfare state mean to Africans what they do to Westerners because Africans did not share those Western political and economic experiences, in reaction to which democracy and the welfare state came into being in the West.[16] To us, the welfare state is a reaction against the social and economic experiences of squalor, depression, and war resulting from industrialism within the economic context of the relatively uncontrolled market system. The Africans neither shared our experiences of the pre-1930 system, nor committed themselves to our laissez-faire ideology (which we so painfully had to unlearn).

We should not be overly eager to create in Africa an uncontrolled market idyll the blessings of which we so insistently deny

---

[15] Herskovits points out that the successful transition to market-oriented production in Ghana is characterized by ". . . inner developments based on pre-existing patterns rather than development induced by the direct application of forces impinging from outside and cast in terms foreign to native practices. Here there is no lack of incentive to expand production." Hoselitz (1952:102). See also Moore (1955:164); also Kenyatta (1938:317–18).

[16] In much of Africa, creating conditions necessary for the success of democratic political institutions is likely to be even more difficult than creating the economic and technological bases for growth. Tribal instead of national identification, widespread illiteracy, and the initial power assumed by the single parties and leaders who brought political independence, all militate against democracy as it is known in the West. Moreover, unlike economic development, political democracy must be fashioned almost wholly from within; there are really no equivalents in the political sphere to the economic aid and technical assistance to be had from abroad. However, the existence of single political parties should not be taken as *ipso facto* evidence of dictatorship. Diversity, and dissenting views within unified political and judicial structures, are not uncommon African traditions. One must hope for the substance of democracy, but not for the familiar forms.

ourselves. To Africans, the welfare state and policies of strong central control mean techniques for rapid economic development and political unification, which, at the same time, express social responsibility in accord with traditional usages. It would be unseemly to deny the Africans material aid or sympathy because—like us—they insist upon having institutions shaped by historical experience and current needs.[17]

[17] Africa has two kinds of history: the conventional kind to be studied through European accounts of exploration, settlement, and colonial rule, and an unconventional kind to be studied through anthropological accounts of indigenous economic and social organization.

6 THE PROBLEM OF TUTSI DOMINATION

Jacques Maquet

Ruanda at the beginning of this century could be characterized as a caste society if by that is meant a collectivity composed of several hierarchical groups, each predominantly endogamous, with its own traditional occupations, and made up almost exclusively of individuals born of parents themselves belonging to the group. The two principal castes were the Hutu agriculturalists and the Tutsi herders. The latter enjoyed a dominant position that permitted them to exploit the farmers in the sense that they obtained a proportionately greater quantity of consumption goods without furnishing the counterpart in labor.

How had they succeeded in maintaining this system of domination that fifty years ago appeared quite stable? Two categories of factors are significant in this respect: first, external circumstances in regard to the social system that were actually beyond Tutsi control; then, the social organization through which the noble caste had assured its superiority. This article is principally devoted to the social factors, but we must first very briefly indicate what elements of the physical, biological, and cultural environment were important from the point of view of Tutsi supremacy. However, not all were favorable to it, as we shall presently see.

The demographic proportion between the two castes and their physical characteristics certainly constituted factors favorable to domination. It seems indeed that the proportion of Tutsi in relation to the total population never varied greatly from 10 percent. This is extremely important. If the Tutsi had, for example, con-

FROM Jacques Maquet, "Le Problème de la Domination Tutsi," *Zaïre, revue congolaise* (1952) 6:1011–16. Reprinted by permission of the author.

stituted 50 percent of the population, the Hutu would never have been able to supply them the labor force and products of the soil necessary to assure them a comfortable existence. Also, the different physical appearances included in the stereotype of each caste have been cleverly exploited by the Tutsi. They have used their slender figure and their light skin in order to affirm the idea of a natural superiority over the Hutu, who are of ordinary stature and with coarse features.

Three other external factors seem rather to have constituted obstacles that the Tutsi had to overcome. The orographic configuration of the country (hills with abrupt slopes, a mountainous range separating the Congo basin from that of the Nile) were not favorable to the rapid communication necessary to a centralized government. Then, the agricultural surplus was very limited. This resulted from the poverty of the soil, the irregularity of rainfall, and the methods of cultivation. A centralized government needs a large body of officials and warriors whose subsistence must be assured. Finally, with the very important exception of cattle, the material culture of the Tutsi did not present essential differences from that of the Hutu. By "essential differences" we mean that Tutsi equipment did not include elements like gunpowder, the combustion engine, or electricity, which when they are exclusively possessed by a group suffice to assure it an easy domination.

The problem that the Tutsi had to solve within the limits imposed by this framework can be formulated in three questions: how to maintain a caste system while safeguarding the cohesion of the total collectivity, how to exploit and at the same time to protect the inferior group, how to establish a centralized and absolute government while delegating power to some subordinate authorities.

To begin with let us consider the first of these three apparent contradictions: caste society and social cohesion. For the members of the dominant hereditary group to be able to keep their privileges, the instruments of prestige and power must remain under their exclusive control. In Ruanda social power and prestige rest on the effective disposition of the cattle that the Tutsi invaders brought with them in the past. The distribution of the livestock was made almost exclusively through *ubuhake,* an institution of clientship by which an individual inferior in prestige and wealth offered his services to another, who in return gave him the usufruct of one or several cows. Through this institution, which could be called feudal, the Tutsi retained the final control over all Ruanda cattle. The Tutsi lord, by reserving for himself the ownership without usufruct of the cows he granted to his client, could always take them back again.

Another condition necessary for the maintenance of the superiority of a caste is that its members should enjoy, if possible without effort, a higher standard of living than the common people. Once more the institution of clientship permitted Tutsi possessing a few head of cattle to live well without having to participate manually in the process of production.

For a caste to keep its identity it is necessary for its *esprit de corps* to be preserved and for its traditions to be transmitted from one generation to another. These functions were fulfilled by the military structure. Young Tutsi, and they exclusively, spent several years at the court of the king or of an important chief in military companies where, in addition to training in the use of weapons, they received the full education of young noblemen.

In order that the dogma of innate superiority of the noble caste should not be questioned, it is necessary to prevent the degradation of any member of the race of noblemen. Clientship was an institutionalized way of avoiding such a disgrace. The Tutsi who was threatened with loss of class through impoverishment became the client of another who was wealthier. In return for his counsel and his presence as a courtier, he received several cows which he gave in turn to Hutu clients; this allowed him to live according to his rank.

But if a caste puts too much stress on the characteristics that make it a socially self-contained group—if it isolates itself within the collectivity of which it is but one element—the cohesion of that society can be destroyed. Consequently, powerful factors of solidarity are necessary in order to counterbalance the tendency toward disintegration that exists in any caste structure.

It is again the institution of clientship that most effectively fulfills this function of social integration. Through it a great many Hutu shared in the social power of the superior class by identifying themselves with a protector, a member of the dominant group. They obtained the use of several cows symbolizing the system of pastoral aristocratic values, and they entered into a system of relations through which agricultural and pastoral products were distributed to the whole of the population. The personal tie with a member of the privileged caste and the access to the possession, even though uncertain, of cattle seem to have been essential from the point of view of national solidarity.

Another unifying factor was the plurality of the social structures with which every Nyarwanda was affiliated. Almost every individual participated in three hierarchies and was thus bound to his rulers, and especially to the king, by more than one channel by virtue of dwelling on a certain hill. The Nyarwanda was subject to a territorial chief who was charged with collecting duties and payment in kind from the subjects and with transmitting them to the king through the intermediary of several officials. In the second place, each Nyarwanda formed part of an army. Only the Tutsi were warriors, but the other members of the army were liable to the military chief for certain payments in labor and in kind. They received from the latter certain advantages such as the usufruct of livestock. Finally, the feudal structure integrated almost every individual in a network of loyalty relations such that the person occupying the superior position in one of these relations occupied at the same time the inferior position in another (the great chiefs were in reality vassals of the king).

A third integrating factor was the ideology developed about the institution of monarchy. The *mwami* was regarded not only as the king of the Tutsi but of all Nyarwanda. His divine origin separated him from men and conferred upon him an authority that the mass of his subjects would not dream of doubting. In Ruanda, as in many cultures, the king was a divine and paternal figure. This association helped create a feeling among the inhabitants of the country of belonging to an entirety that offered certain analogies to the family.

The second apparent contradiction sets off the necessity of the exploitation of the Hutu against that of their protection. The dilemma of all conquerors establishing themselves firmly in a new territory is whether they themselves will extract the natural wealth of the country or whether they will do it through the natives. The Tutsi have solved this problem by choosing the second alternative. Various tributes have been imposed on the Hutu: forced labor and contributions in products of the soil. The governors obtained them through the channels of the administrative and military structures, the ordinary Tutsi through the system of clientship. When a group has imposed itself as firmly as the Tutsi its problem is not so much to exploit as to limit exploitation so that the tribute payer neither flees the country nor dies. It is therefore necessary to protect him against excessive assessments and against individual exactions.

The universality and the organization of the obligations contributed to keeping the assessment level bearable, for they assured sufficient and regular revenues to the rulers. Protection against the exactions of avaricious chiefs and lords was assured first of all by the existence of traditionally accepted rules. These rules were not so precise or so severely sanctioned as in Western fiscal law, but they nevertheless established standards beyond which public opinion felt that abuse began. When a lord appeared to be too demanding of his clients he no longer found new ones, and those he had would try to leave him.

This leads us to mention another protection more effective than customary law: the possibility for every man of some capability of assuring himself a defender and a protector. This possibility resulted from the plural character of the political structure. When one has but a single superior, all must be obtained from him and there is no appeal. In a plural system there are several immediate superiors who are approximately equal in rank and are interdependent. It is then possible to obtain the support (or even complicity) of one chief while resisting another.

The third apparent contradiction, which contrasts the necessities of a centralized and absolute power with the dangers of delegation of power to subordinate local authorities, was felt particularly strongly in a feudal and mountainous country. Clientship creates personal ties of fidelity between the client and his lord, but this loyalty does not extend beyond the lord. One obeys his lord because he is his lord and not because he is a representative of the king. Now all the local Tutsi chiefs had clients. The mountainous nature of the country, by rendering communications difficult, also favored the formation of local, independent lordships. Moreover, in a nonliterate culture, to administer the country and to collect the taxes in an efficient manner required that the subject and the authority should know each other personally. Since the population was about 1,700,000 persons. it was indeed necessary to delegate power.

Despite these difficulties the Tutsi governors of the Ruanda were able to prevent the fragmentation of the political unity of their country. The ritual and divine character of royalty did certainly contribute to the chiefs' submission, but, we think, to a very limited degree. History tells us that when a *mwami* appeared weak one or another great chief did not hesitate to revolt and to assassinate him even though he was divine. Besides the strength of armies, the most effective mechanism of submission to the central power seems to have been the multiplicity of chiefs independent of one another. Not only were there chiefs of the same rank belonging to different hierarchies and ruling the same individuals, but in the same administrative structure there were two chiefs who had the same territorial jurisdiction: one who was concerned with food revenues, the other with taxes on livestock. Such a situation successfully maintained distrust, hostility, and jealousy among the chiefs. Thus any one of them was quick to warn the *mwami* if one of his colleagues was plotting treason. Moreover, the inevitable conflicts of jurisdiction permitted the superior authority to meddle in quarrels and to inflame them.

It is in this way that the political organization of the Ruanda, constituted by the administrative, military, and feudal structures, allowed the Tutsi to keep alive the society of Ruanda while profitably monopolizing social, political, and economic power.[1]

For Further Reading

Maquet, Jacques J., *Le système des Relations sociales dans le Ruanda ancien,* Tervuren: Musée Royal du Congo Belge, Annales, Sciences de l'Homme, Série in 8°, Ethnologie, 1, 1954. The basic work on Ruanda political organization.

Maquet, Jacques J., *Ruanda; essai photographique sur une société africaine en transition,* Brussels: Elsevier, 1957; Maquet, J. J., "The Kingdom of Ruanda," in Forde, Daryll (ed.), *African Worlds: Studies in the Cosmological Ideas and Social Values of African Peoples,* London: Oxford University Press for the International African Institute, 1954, pp. 164–89. Both contain valuable background material on the Ruanda.

Oberg, K., "The Kingdom of Ankole in Uganda," in Fortes,

[1] Paper presented at the International Congress of Anthropological and Ethnological Sciences in Vienna, September 1–8, 1952.

M., and Evans-Pritchard, E. E. (eds.), *African Political Systems,*
London: Oxford University Press for the International African
Institute, 1940, pp. 121–62. A brief description of a state system
based on two caste groups.

7 BUNYORO: AN AFRICAN FEUDALITY?

J. H. M. Beattie

In a recent article in this *Journal,* Dr. Jack Goody discussed the utility of applying the concepts and vocabulary of Western feudalism to traditional African states (Goody 1963:1–18). He pointed out that the term "feudalism" has been used in many senses even by European historians, and he concluded that although the specific institutions into which feudalism (however defined) may be broken down may often usefully be compared, the kind of overall comparison that is invited by words like "feudalism" is best avoided at this stage.

In this paper I adduce corroborative evidence for Goody's thesis from my own study of a traditional African kingdom.[1] I give a brief account of some of the main structural features of the interlacustrine Bantu state of Bunyoro, in western Uganda, as they existed in pre-European times. And in doing so I consider the usefulness, in the context of the Nyoro polity, of feudal ideas.

First, for the purposes of this essay, at least some content must be given to the general concept of feudalism. As Goody noted, some authors, though not as a rule professional historians, have written as though any society with a ruler, a rough hierarchy of chiefs, and a subordinated peasantry were *ipso facto* feudal. Some of the earlier anthropologists, and Potekhin in his paper on

FROM J. H. M. Beattie, "Bunyoro: An African Feudality?" *Journal of African History* V, I (1964), pp. 25–36. Reprinted by permission of the author, the editor of the *Journal of African History,* and the Cambridge University Press.

[1] I carried out fieldwork in Bunyoro in 1951–53, and again in 1955, mostly under the auspices of the Treasury Committee for Studentships in Foreign Languages and Cultures whose support I gratefully acknowledge.

Ashanti Feudalism, took such a view (Potekhin 1960). On it, a vast number of past and present states in Africa and elsewhere throughout the world are feudal; the difficulty is, of course, that so vague and all-inclusive a formulation is analytically useless. Unless the feudal analogy can provide some clear criteria for distinguishing some kinds of "traditional" states from others, there is little point in adopting it. The view of feudalism which stresses specifically a particular kind of land-holding is somewhat more useful. On this view feudalism is a form of polity based on the relation of vassal and superior arising from the holding of land "in feud," that is, in consideration of service and homage from vassal to lord.[2] This formulation selects only one element in the complex of medieval European feudal institutions, and that one not always considered essential. But it does point to the reciprocating, contractual element in feudalism, and so to the personal nature of the relationships involved and the stress on personal loyalty between inferior and superior. Thus Maquet stresses the personal bond between two persons unequal in power, involving protection on one hand, fealty and service on the other (Maquet 1961: Chapter VI and *passim.*). These criteria do conveniently, if broadly, distinguish such polities from those in which specialized political authority either is altogether lacking or is distributed on an impersonal, bureaucratic basis. But although such simple characterizations may have some descriptive value, they omit reference to certain important features of European feudalism which are lacking in states like Bunyoro. So unless what is and what is not implicit in the notion of feudalism is carefully specified, they too may lead to misunderstanding.

Probably the clearest summary of what are most usefully regarded as the essential characteristics of feudalism is Marc Bloch's, quoted by Goody in his article (Bloch 1961:466). Bloch, it will be remembered, specified five fundamentals. These were: (1) the fief, usually but not essentially land; (2) the personal nature of the bond of political dependence; (3) the dispersal of authority—rulers have to delegate and they have to make loyalty worth while. These criteria fit many African kingdoms, including Bunyoro, well enough. But then he has also: (4) a reference to a specialized military class, something that is not found in Bunyoro or in many of the African polities which have been

2 See the *Shorter Oxford English Dictionary* definition.

described as feudal; and (5) the reference to the survival in some form of the idea of the state.

This last point is important: if European feudalism in its beginnings implied the weakening, even the breakdown, of the state, and the distribution of powers formerly held by it among private individuals, in most African states there has been no such breakdown. In fact, as Goody remarks, many if not most of the polities which have been described in feudal terms represent a trend towards rather than away from centralization (Goody 1963:8). Far from expressing the breakdown of a formerly more strongly centralized authority, they represent, in many cases, what appear to be the first beginnings of such authority. Thus among the Alur, described by Southall, hitherto chiefless communities have in historical times come voluntarily under the dominion of chiefly lines (Southall 1956), and the evidence suggests that in the case of at least some of the interlacustrine Bantu kingdoms intrusive minorities imposed centralized forms of government on pre-existing segmentary societies.

A further important point of difference between European feudalism and some types of "African feudalism" relates to the question of which categories of persons were linked as subordinate and super-ordinate. In Europe the characteristic feudal bond was between the tenant or fief-holder and a nearby chief or lord, from whom he held his fief and to whom he looked for protection (Bloch 1961:444); there was no direct link between the fief-holder and the king. Thus the king's links with his subjects were only indirect, and for the most part they were only of secondary importance. In Bunyoro and kingdoms like it, however, the case was very different. Although subordinate chiefs were sometimes powerful and revolt was by no means unknown, loyalty to and dependence upon the person of the king himself were explicit and universal values at all levels, and these values were constantly expressed and reinforced in service, homage and ritual (Beattie 1960: Chapter 4). Virtually all political rights in the kingdom were held, and were seen as being held, directly of the king, and at his pleasure. Although he was by no means an "absolute" ruler, he was regarded by all as the sole original source of political authority. In Bunyoro, as in some other African kingdoms, the polity sometimes called "feudal" was really a means to achieving and sustaining a system of centralized administration; in no sense was it a symptom of the breakdown of such a system.

A brief examination of some of the typical political institutions of traditional Bunyoro, and some consideration of how the system worked, may enable us to decide whether, and how far, the basic categories of feudalism are helpful in understanding it. For these purposes, it is useful to regard the Nyoro state as entailing a balance of opposing forces: those of centralization on the one hand, which have the effect of expressing and reinforcing the king's power; and those of decentralization on the other hand, the effect of which is to strengthen the power of chiefs and subjects as against the central authority. In this equation, the chiefs inevitably played a double role, being at the same time an intrinsic part of and a potential threat to the kingship. Traditional Bunyoro was a centralized polity of some stability (though it was less centralized and less stable than the neighbouring and territorially more compact kingdom of Buganda), so centripetal forces will demand more attention than centrifugal ones.

The latter can be dealt with fairly briefly. They comprise, first, the degree of independence exercised by the chiefs and, second, the effectiveness of the indigenous regional groupings at the community level; families, lineages, clans, and neighbourhoods. I deal first with the chiefs. Like other traditional rulers, the king (*Mukama*) of Bunyoro could only retain his power by giving some of it away. Some writers, such as Murdock, have regarded kingdoms like Bunyoro as "African despotisms," African despotism being a sort of counterpart of Oriental despotism, even though not hydraulic (Murdock 1959: Chapter 6). Certainly some African rulers have at some times acted despotically; but with a widely dispersed population, poor communications and a simple technology (especially in regard to weapons), it is difficult to maintain for long, if at all, any very high concentration of political power. Always there were some institutionalized checks on the abuse of power by the central authority. In Bunyoro the great territorial chiefs, of whom in historical times there were a dozen or more,[3] enjoyed a good deal of autonomy, governing

[3] Roscoe lists ten, without specifying the period to which he is referring (Roscoe 1923:53). The present Mukama of Bunyoro listed twenty-eight countries as having been "arranged" by his father, Mukama Kabarega, during the second half of the last century (K.W. 1937:67) but many of these are outside the present boundaries of the kingdom.

their areas rather like private estates. Their rights over these
territories and their inhabitants, which they held from the king
as his subordinates and on condition of tribute payment and
homage to him, were subject to restrictions, but within their areas
these chiefs were accorded high prestige, and received homage
and tribute similar to, but on a much smaller scale than that
paid to the king, whose representatives they were. But they did
not possess these powers in their own right. They enjoyed them
only because they were the king's nominees, "the Mukama's
spears." Nevertheless they could and did claim a considerable
measure of independence, especially if they were remote from
the capital. In several recorded instances this extended to actual
revolt, and to the setting up of independent units. The neighbouring kingdom of Toro originated early in the nineteenth century in rebellion by the dissident Nyoro prince Kaboyo (K.W.
1937:67; Fisher 1911:149), and in Baker's time and later one
of the king's agnates, Ruyonga, maintained (with some European
support) virtual independence in the north of Bunyoro for many
years (Baker 1895: Chapter 23 and *passim*.). So although the
chiefs were indispensable to the effective functioning of the centralized Nyoro political system, at the same time they were, and
were recognized to be, a constant threat to it. I show below
how this threat was met.

The chiefs were an essential component of the Nyoro administrative system; the localized groups of clansmen and neighbours
who made up the Nyoro community were not; rather they stood
in opposition to it. There is no clear evidence that Nyoro society
was ever of the acephalous, segmentary kinship-based type described for many other parts of Africa (including some neighbouring areas) but for what it is worth it may be speculated that
it may well have been so in the remote period before the present
ruling line or its predecessors had appeared on the scene. At any
rate, what is certain is that while there can be no centralized state
without subordinate political authorities and subjects, it is perfectly possible for a segmentary society to exist without chiefs or
specifically political functionaries at all. African peoples like the
Nuer and the Tallensi have done so up to very recent times.
Where, as in Bunyoro, a centralized government is super-imposed
on a community which retains many of the "segmentary" characteristics of a clan and lineage system (for example, a hundred

or more exogamous "totemic" clans with a tradition of former localization, and many of the social usages and values appropriate to such a system), there must be some kind of adaptation between the two elements; the state must somehow come to terms with the community. I consider below some of the means traditionally adapted to this end in Bunyoro. Here I wish to stress that Nyoro themselves are well aware of the difference, even the opposition, between the state and the central government on the one hand, and the local community or neighbourhood on the other. For the first they use the terms *obukama* (kingship) and *obulemi* (rule or government); the second they refer to by such terms as *obunyaruganda* (clanship), *obuzaranwa* (kinship) and *obutahi* (neighbourhood). Often they consciously oppose these two fields of social interaction. From the Nyoro peasant's viewpoint, the first is something external, even oppressive—the root *lema* means "to bear down upon," "to be too heavy for," as well as "to rule" —the second provides the intimate and familiar context of every-day village life. And in fact the demands of the king and his chiefs on the one hand, and of clansfolk, kin and neighbours on the other, may and often do conflict. Nyoro see their social structure as dual, not monolithic, and the problem of reconciling its two components is quite explicit in Nyoro culture.

These, in brief, are the major divisive forces in Nyoro political structure, opposing the king to his chiefs on the one hand, and the kingship or state to the local community on the other. How are these gaps bridged? I consider, rather arbitrarily, those institutions which I call centripetal under two heads: first, those which relate to the king's (and the chiefs', so far as they are, as it were, political extensions of the king) relations with the people as a whole, and second, those concerned more specifically with the king's relations with his territorial chiefs. Again rather arbitrarily, I list five institutions under the first head and five under the second. Other institutions could no doubt be identified, and some of the ones here recorded could probably be further broken down. However, the ten listed are of key functional importance, and also they are particularly characteristic of Bunyoro, and in some degree of other similar states.

I begin with those institutions which relate the kingship with the people as a whole. First, the kingship is hereditary in the male line; only the son of a king can become a king. But not the eldest son; we shall see the point of this below. Thus the institution of kingship is (I am using the historical present here and elsewhere) the enduring focus and centre of Nyoro society; it provides a central political value and a symbol of national identity for all Nyoro. Succession is not predetermined; any son of a king except the eldest may inherit: which one does so depends on the support he can command. Often two, sometimes three or more, eligible princes have competed for the succession after their father's death. So, in Bunyoro as in some other kingdoms, there was a period of lawlessness and anarchy between reigns, an interregnum during which warring factions made life for ordinary people dangerous and uncertain. To them, it was plain that the maintenance of the kingship was a condition of security and of national well-being, for when it was suspended the country was reduced to chaos and confusion.

It has just been noted that the king's first-born son could not succeed him, and this provides the second institutional means of integrating king and people. The eldest son automatically assumed the office of *Okwiri,* the headship of the Bito, that is, of the numerous and powerful clan (or perhaps congeries of clans) of which the king was a member. In strongly stratified Bunyoro, where the gap between the ruling Bito and the ordinary peasants (Iru) was universally recognized and strongly marked, an effect of this institution was, as it were, to detach the king from his identity with his own agnatic group, and so to free him for his role as ruler and leader of all Nyoro, not just of his own group, the Bito. The gap is one which must be bridged wherever a ruling clan or other group achieves dominance over a subordinated majority of supposedly different stock, and Bunyoro's office of *Okwiri* provides one means of rendering the kingship acceptable to the mass of the governed.[4]

Third, the value of the kingship is stressed in tradition, myth, ritual and ceremonial. Tradition links the ruling Bito dynasty, through the two earlier Cwezi and Batembuzi dynasties, with the

[4] In the neighbouring interlacustrine kingdom of Ankole, the same gap (there between the ruling Hima and the Iru) is differently bridged. There the cult of a drum, Bagyendanwa, which is thought to be "above" the king and accessible to Hima and Iru alike, provides a focus for national unity transcending the wide social division between the pastoral Hima minority and the peasant Iru (Oberg 1940:155).

very beginnings of the world. Although there is strong evidence that the present Bito rulers are Nilotic intruders who have been in Bunyoro for two or three centuries at most (Crazzolara 1950: Chapter 21), they claim, and Nyoro do not dispute the claim, that they are descended in an unbroken paternal line from the earliest rulers. This "mythical charter" effectively makes the kingship an acceptable, even unquestioned, institution. The king's importance to the country as a whole is further expressed in the familiar idiom of "divine kingship": he is mystically identified with his kingdom, and his well-being is as indispensable to it as it is to him. His importance and uniqueness are stressed in numerous usages, of most of which accounts are available elsewhere (Beattie 1959:134–45). He has his special drums, spears and other regalia; distinctive forms of greeting are reserved for him and may not be used to anyone else; his more important doings are described in a court vocabulary applicable only to him; his accession and death are marked by elaborate and special ceremony. Everybody approaches him humbly and submissively; even today his senior chiefs kneel to hand him anything or to receive anything from his hands. All these usages impress on everybody's minds the paramountcy of the kingship and its absolute superiority over every other force or faction in the state. In an almost literal sense, everything is seen as depending on or derived from it. To traditionally minded Nyoro, the kingship is indispensable.

Fourthly, as in other African kingdoms, the king's economic role was an important centripetal or integrating force in the Nyoro state. Mauss has classically demonstrated the ubiquity of prestation or gift exchange as a means to social integration (Mauss 1954), and the Nyoro king was the centre of such an exchange system. Not only the chiefs but any Nyoro could visit the king, and he would not come empty-handed: women, cattle, beer and grain were continually passing into his hands. Reciprocally, as well as presenting cattle or women to persons to whom he was obliged or who were in need, the king gave feasts at frequent intervals. Some of his special praise-names stress his openhandedness. Thus he is called *Agutamba* (he who relieves distress), and *Mwebingwa* (he to whom people run for help); the first name is part of his official title. The Mukama's role as the greatest giver and receiver in the country played a major part in

binding his people to him in mutual interdependence. It should
be stressed that the obligation to give to, and the right to receive
from, the king extended (in theory at least) to all his subjects; it
was not restricted to his chiefs. Although, as the Mukama's representatives, the chiefs were themselves the centres of similar but
very much smaller-scale systems of exchange, every man, and
especially every man who held any kind of authority above the
family level, stood potentially if not actually in a direct personal
relationship with the king. Even the lowest grades of chiefs were
not appointed by the senior chiefs but by the king himself: this
might sometimes amount to little more than the confirmation of a
chief's nomination, but this confirmation was indispensable. In
the case of important chiefs, a formal ceremony of installation
had to be performed by a special agent of the king, and all
recipients of political authority were, in theory, required to bind
themselves to the Mukama by a ceremony of "drinking milk"
with him. In former times even succession to a clan headship
had to be validated by the king. All of these appointments and
confirmations required that the recipients of authority should
make gifts to the king: since authority itself was a gift no less
than material goods, there was a reciprocal element in these
transactions. The continuing network of exchanges thus involved
must have served as a powerful integrative force in the traditional
kingdom.

Finally, the constitution of the royal household itself provides
a significant means of bringing people and kingship together. The
king maintained, and maintains to the present day, a great number of palace officials, including ritual experts, keepers of the
various regalia, musicians, cooks, bath attendants, herdsmen, and
many others. These far exceed the numbers needed for practical
purposes. Among them are representatives of all of the few
specialist occupations in the country, such as pottery, barkcloth
making and iron-working. Even more important, these officials
also represent many of the hundred or more clans to one or
other of which every Nyoro belongs. Many of the palace offices
are traditionally tied to particular clans, and each is jealously
guarded as the exclusive prerogative of that clan; in this way the
kingship absorbed the clan system, to which it stood in opposition,
into itself. Even today, the hereditary tenure of such an appoint-
ment (which is far from onerous, involving perhaps attendance at

the palace for a few days each month) is highly valued. When I was in Bunyoro a young man of good education holding such a post, which required him to live near the palace, turned down an offer of lucrative employment outside the kingdom rather than give up his hereditary position at the palace.

Even the king's selection of his "wives" may be regarded as serving a similar end. Nyoro kings were traditionally polygynous, often extremely so. It is not recorded how many wives Kabarega, the last independent Nyoro king, had, but the names of 140 children begotten by him are on record (Bikunya 1927:75–6). The Mukama could take his women from any of the clans, with one or two exceptions, and a son of any of these women was eligible to succeed him. Thus not only was the whole clan honoured (and many clans have been so honoured) by having given a "wife" to the Mukama, but a girl so given might conceivably become the mother of the next king. If she did, the whole of her clan would become "mothers" and "mother's brothers" to the new king, and would acquire extremely high status in the kingdom, as well as being rewarded by offices and estates.

These are some of the institutions through which the Nyoro people as a whole were bound to the kingship in common recognition of its importance and indispensability. I now go on to consider some of the ways in which the king's chiefs themselves were bound to the king in a relationship, more or less stable, of subordination and personal obligation.

First, Nyoro chiefs are not hereditary. At all levels, as was noted earlier, they are individually appointed, or their appointments are confirmed, by the king. Traditionally, proprietary rights over particular areas and their peasant occupants were allotted as a mark of royal favour, often as a reward for service. In the pre-European era this service might have been military; in more recent times it is more likely to have been economic or domestic. Even a few years ago loyal service in the royal household, for example, as cook or regalia-keeper, was sometimes rewarded with a minor chiefship. In Bunyoro, as in medieval England, "personal service to the king brought a rich reward" (Stenton 1955, Vol. 3:19). Obviously such appointments are less appropriate in the conditions of the twentieth century (modern administration calls for learned skills not taught in the Mukama's kitchen or bathroom) than they were in traditional times, and in the 1950s they

were giving rise to some resentment among educated Nyoro.[5]
But what they stressed was the fact that political authority was
traditionally thought of as being in the last resort the personal
property of the Mukama. The very word Mukama means the
master or owner of anything—or everything. Subordinate authority is accordingly his gift, and like most gifts it is not given
unconditionally. Chiefs retained their rights over the territories
allotted to them and their inhabitants only on condition of service
and homage to the king, and he could and sometimes did dismiss
them summarily.

Second, the importance of the allocation of authority, and its
origin in the person of the Mukama, are emphasized by ritual.
The delegation of authority is not a purely administrative, secular
affair; it is also a rite. The king, like other persons and events
which have the quality of being both extraordinary and potentially dangerous, is believed to possess a special ritual potency,
called *mahano,* and when he delegates his authority he gives
away at the same time some of his own *mahano* or essence.[6]
This is expressed in the traditional rite, already referred to, of
"drinking milk" with the Mukama, in recent times replaced by
the ceremonial handing of a roasted coffee berry by the king to
the person who is being vested with subordinate authority. The
symbolism involved is plain. The king's sacred herd of cattle and
the milk from it were traditionally most intimately linked with
both his and the country's well-being, and roasted coffee berries,
often handed round in Nyoro homes when specially favoured or
distinguished guests are entertained, are associated also with the
institution of blood partnership, the closest bond conceivable between men. Coffee berries, the two segments of which are closely
united in the same husk, aptly symbolize a particularly close
attachment. If ritual is a language, a way of saying something
held to be important, then these usages express, and so tend to
reinforce, the value attached to the central political power in
Bunyoro and to its delegation.

[5] A new Agreement (to replace the original Bunyoro Agreement of
1933) between the Governor and the Mukama deprived the Mukama of
the power which he had held under the first Agreement to appoint and
dismiss his chiefs without consultation with his Native Government. For a
brief account of the "democratizing" of the Nyoro kingdom in recent
years, see Beattie (1961:8–20).

[6] For a discussion of this concept see Beattie (1960:145–50).

A third way in which senior chiefs and other eminent persons (these categories were traditionally hardly distinguishable) might be bound to the king and the kingship was through a system of what may be called "ennoblement." Traditionally the king might award elaborate beaded "crowns" or headdresses, decorated with coloured beads and cowrie shells and bearded with colobus monkey skins, to senior chiefs or other persons whom he wished particularly to distinguish. This was the highest gift which the king could bestow, and was awarded only to persons who had served with particular distinction, or who had achieved conspicuous military success. It was also traditionally awarded to the king's "mother's brother," that is, to the head of his mother's clan. As well as his crown (*kondo*), the person thus ennobled received extensive proprietary territorial rights over some part of the country, so that if he was not already a chief, as he most likely was, he was made one by the award.[7]

Even more than the grant of political authority, the grant of a crown implied the bestowal, so to speak, of some part of the potency of the kingship itself. This is clear from the rigorous ritual prohibitions which possession of a crown implied. Thus crown-wearers were subject to ritual food prohibitions (they were debarred from eating low-status foodstuffs like sweet potatoes or cassava) similar to those observed by the king himself. Unlike ordinary political office, crowns were hereditary in the male line, though an heir would have to be confirmed in his succession by the king himself. The institution is now dying out; no crown has been awarded for many years. This is not surprising. The king has not been the ultimate source of political power in Bunyoro since the last century; the territorial rights that formerly accompanied the award no longer exist in their traditional form, and in any case they are no longer at the Mukama's personal disposal.

Fourthly, the major chiefs were required to maintain houses at or near the capital as well as in the territories allotted to them, and they had to attend the king's court constantly (Roscoe 1923: 53). Failure to do so was noticed, and laid the negligent chief open to suspicion of rebellious intentions. When a chief left the capital, he had to leave behind him a deputy (*mukwenda* or

---

[7] The persons thus favoured were the men referred to by Roscoe as the "Sacred Guild" (Roscoe 1923:51).

musigire), who assumed all his titles and represented him at court during his absence. In the same way the chief would be represented in his own area by a *musigire* while he was absent at court. When the chief is absent from the royal court, his deputy in a real sense *is* the chief. So in theory the senior chiefs were always in attendance upon the king, while at the same time they were always engaged in the discharge of their duties as the king's territorial administrators. In this way the *musigire* system enabled the senior chiefs to sustain at the same time two scarcely compatible roles. A chief is essentially a "king's man," and must, by constant attendance, continually express his personal devotion to and dependence upon the Mukama. At the same time he is also a territorial ruler, personally responsible for the good government of the region allotted to him. The importance of the requirement of constant attendance at the palace as a check to centrifugal tendencies is obvious. It is worth noting, also, that it also provided the king with a more or less permanent group of advisers: in systems of this kind there is no need for a separate royal council or "secretariat"; the same people can serve both as councillors and administrators.

Fifthly and finally, the king himself did not reside permanently at his capital, which itself was frequently changed in traditional times. Like William I of England, he frequently undertook protracted tours around his kingdom, accompanied by numerous retainers, staying for days and even weeks at the headquarters of one or other of his chiefs. It fell upon the local population to build, on the model of the palace itself, the necessary accommodation for him and his entourage, and to provide ample supplies of food and drink for the royal party. In return, the king provided feasts of meat and beer for the local people. These frequent tours (which were carried out in considerable state even when I was in Bunyoro ten years ago) enabled the Mukama to keep an eye on the local activities of his chiefs of all ranks, and also to keep a finger on the pulse of public opinion.

On the basis of this summary account of some of Bunyoro's most important traditional political institutions, can we say whether Bunyoro is "feudal" or not? Indeed, is there any point in asking such a question? If, with Maquet, we regard as feudal any political system centred on face-to-face relations between persons of unequal power, one offering protection, the other service and loyalty (Maquet 1961a), then Bunyoro is indeed feudal. But so, it might seem, are most, if not all, small-scale, pre-industrial states. For political relations are by definition between persons of unequal power, of whom one gives orders and the other obeys; they must offer some mutual advantage if they are to persist; and in societies lacking writing, post offices and telephones, political relations, like all other relations, must be face-to-face ones. If, alternatively, with the *Shorter Oxford English Dictionary* (and perhaps with more etymological propriety) we hold feudalism to consist essentially in the holding of land, and of the authority associated with such tenure, by an inferior from a superior "in feud," on conditions or service and homage, then, also, Bunyoro is a feudal state. But even here, it is evidently clearer and more helpful to say that in Bunyoro the allocation of land and of territorial authority is of a type similar to that found in the feudal polities of medieval Europe, than it is to say roundly that Bunyoro is a feudal state. For if (say) Norman England was a feudal state, then Bunyoro resembles it—and quite strikingly—in some respects, and differs from it—perhaps a little less obviously—in others.

Like Goody, I consider it to be more useful and illuminating to retain the term "feudalism" and its associated vocabulary for the complex European polities to which they were first applied (and perhaps to such other systems, like the Japanese one, which can be shown to resemble it in all or most of its essential features), and to describe the political institutions of traditional Bunyoro and of other African kingdoms as far as possible in their own terms. This of course is not to deny the usefulness of drawing attention to analogies with European feudalism where these are found, or the importance for fieldwork of knowing, from historical sources, how other peoples, at other times and in other conditions, have dealt with the problems of government in small-scale societies. But although traditional Bunyoro had much in common with the feudal states of medieval Europe, it also differed from them in very important respects. If we are to describe it as a feudal state, however we restrict or modify our definition of feudalism, we shall, in underlining the similarities, inevitably tend to ignore or at best to understress the differences.

102

J. H. M. Beattie

SUMMARY

In terms of Marc Bloch's celebrated definition, the traditional interlacustrine Bantu kingdom of Bunyoro, in western Uganda, is "feudal" in some respects but not in others. This is shown by a survey of Bunyoro's traditional political institutions, some of which tended to decentralize, others to centralize, political power and authority. Of the first, the most important were the considerable degree of independence enjoyed by the chiefs, and the largely self-sufficient community relationships of neighbourhood and kinship. Of the centripetal institutions, some linked the people to the kingship, others bound the chiefs to the king. Examples of both types are described. It is concluded that although traditional Bunyoro shared some features with European "feudal" states, it also differed from them in important respects. Thus it would be misleading to refer to it, without a good deal of qualification, as a "feudality."

8 RAFFIA CLOTH DISTRIBUTION IN THE LELE ECONOMY

Mary Douglas

The distribution of raffia cloth among the Lele[1] raises two questions. One, mainly ethnographic, is that of the various functions served in the course of its circulation from hand to hand. In answering this, the second question arises. In some aspects raffia cloth seems to perform monetary roles. Is it to be classed as a type of primitive money? In the widest sense it seems to be an imperfect type of money, performing in a restricted manner some of the main functions of money: it acts as a store and a standard of value; it is given as payment for services and sometimes used as a medium of exchange. It is not, however, the principal, or usual, means of distribution in the economy. I hope that a discussion of the shortcomings of Lele raffia as a form of money may be interesting to others working in societies which are similarly on the verge of a market economy.

DISTRIBUTION OF GOODS

Little in the environment or productive system of the Lele encourages large-scale collaboration. They live at a density of about 4 persons to the square mile (the figure excludes recent alien immigrants). There are no markets. Each village (Douglas

FROM Mary Douglas, "Raffia Cloth Distribution in the Lele Economy," *Africa* (1958), No. 28, pp. 109–22. Reprinted by permission of the author and the publisher.

[1] The Lele inhabit the region between the Loange and the Kasai rivers, in the Kasai District of the Belgian Congo. My fieldwork among them in 1949–50, and in four months in 1953, was made possible by a fellowship of the International African Institute and with help from the Belgian Institut pour la Recherche Scientifique en Afrique Centrale.

TABLE I. DISTRIBUTION OF GOODS

Productive work	Range of collaboration	Product	Range of distribution
MEN			
Hunting:			
(a) Communal	Village-wide	} Meat	Village-wide, according to membership of cults, and according to kinship obligations of hunters
(b) Bow, snares, or pit-traps	Individual		
Clearing land for cultivation	Individual or 2 age-mates or brothers		
Raffia-palm cultivation	Individually owned and worked, except for sending junior for wine	Wine	Village-wide, at nightly men's club; father, mother, and mother's brother of tapper and his age-mates
Weaving	Individual	Cloth	Distribution detailed below
Oil-palms	Individual cuts fruit from wild palm for wife to process and use or sell	Oil and Cash	Man keeps cash, woman uses oil
House-building	Sons, brothers, age-mates, son-in-law may occasionally help	House	Man, wife, small children
Smithing	Individual leisure-time specialists, collaborating with charcoal burner/bellows boy	Hoes, knives, arrowheads, gouges, &c.; maintenance of these	By gift with small acknowledgement fee to kinsmen of smith; or sale to strangers
Wood-carving	Individual leisure-time specialists, with occasional junior help	Drinking-cups, bellows, bows, plates, pestle, loom, shuttle, combs, drums	As for smiths
WOMEN			
Sowing, hoeing, harvesting	Wife alone, with occasional help from mother or sister	Maize, manioc, bananas, peppers, ground-nuts, calabashes	If stored, crops under wife's control; if sold, cash jointly owned by husband and wife
Cooking	" "	Cooked food	Wife gives to husband and his age-mates, to son and his age-mates; children and sisters and wifeless fellow clansmen

		Fish	As for cooked food
Fishing			For household use
Firewood and water			" " "
Salt-making		Salt	or given to kinsmen for small acknowledgement fee
Gathering relish, vegetable or insect	or parties of children		As for cooked food
Basketry	Individual leisure-time specialists	Baskets for storage, transport, fishing, sifting, &c.	By gift with small acknowledgement fee to kinsmen of craftswoman, or sold to strangers
Pottery		Cooking-pots	As for baskets

TABLE II. INHERITANCE

	Heirs
(A) Goods	
Crops	Matrilineal inheritance group. Crops used for maintenance of children in year of mourning.
Raffia palms	" " "
House	Generally destroyed if death took place at home; otherwise kept by widow, or allocated according to village needs.
Personal belongings, weapons, tools, drum, containers, &c.	Matrilineal inheritance group distributes to sons or sisters' sons.
Stocks of raffia, camwood, or money	Matrilineal inheritance group, entrusted to eldest man to be administered on behalf of group as a whole, after claims on dead man's estate have been settled.
(B) Widows	Matrilineal inheritance group; after year of mourning widows allocated to members, according to seniority, need, and incest regulations.
(C) Rights over Clients (i.e. descendants of women paid in blood compensation)	Matrilineal inheritance group; administered on behalf of group as a whole by eldest men.

1957a) (average population 190) is largely self-sufficient in producing for its needs, and with one exception there is no teamwork
or long-term collaboration within it. The exception is the communal hunt, in which most of the able-bodied men of the village
combine. Normally work is individually performed, and the basic
unit of collaboration consists of husband and wife, each performing the tasks traditionally allotted to their sex. The division of
labour has the characteristic—common enough, but worth noting
for its consequences—of reserving physically exacting work for
the men. This puts the older men at a relative disadvantage,
which is partially adjusted by raffia-cloth distribution, as I shall
show.

As Table I shows, units of labour do not correspond to units
of consumption, and, though for most goods the range of distribution is wider than the producing unit, it is still not very wide. For
most things, the kin of individual producers living locally are the
widest group claiming a share in the product. Only for meat
and wine is the whole village the sharing group. It would not be
difficult for the Lele to lead their whole economic life within the
bounds of each individual village.

Inheritance is another way of claiming goods. A new group
emerges here, the matrilineal heirs of the dead.

The inheritance group does not appear as a unit in the first
table, as they never work together, neither feed nor live together.
It consists of fellow clansmen of the dead living in the same
village or in villages near by. The members coalesce as a group
through their common interest in the distribution, not of goods,
but of rights over women. None of the goods (detailed in (A) of
Table II) are as interesting as the rights over women ((B) and
(C) in the table) that a man may leave, excepting such small
stocks of camwood and raffia or money as may be left which can
be used to acquire such rights.

As may be seen from these tables, goods are distributed mostly
on the basis of status, and not by purchase. A man's claims to a
share in the product of anyone's labour, including his own, depends directly on who he is (boy, husband, father, &c., i.e. his
relation to others) and not on his purchasing power, or on his
work. Ultimately, of course, his status is something which he
builds up by his own efforts, i.e. by generously and effectively
interpreting his obligations. But at any one moment his status is
known, and determines his share of what is going. This means

that, although many things appear to have a traditional price, in raffia cloth, there is no real price system or level of prices, since it is not offer of the traditional price, but the status of the recipient, which entitles him to the goods.

USES OF RAFFIA

Every man and boy can weave. The preparation of materials for weaving is long and the actual work of weaving is more arduous than might be supposed (Douglas 1962). After the loom is set up, a man has to work steadily to weave two or three lengths in a day. Five lengths is supposed to be very fast working, and most men make one in an afternoon.

Two lengths sewn together, with stitched, embroidered, or fringed hems, make a skirt for a woman or a man. Five to ten sewn lengths, without embroidery, make a semi-ceremonial man's skirt, *lupungu*. Ten lengths, with a richly appliqué border, is a dance-skirt, *mapel mahangi*. This is the joint property of the matrilineal clan section, the group of matrilineal heirs, and a highly prized heirloom. Worn in everyday use, for hunting and working, a raffia skirt lasts only about four months. They are often carefully darned and patched. Shabby dress is much despised. Lele love the sight of well-woven cloth, correctly folded and tied for presentation.

Informal gifts of raffia cloth smooth all social relations: husband to wife, son to mother, son to father. They resolve occasions of tension, as peace-offerings; they make parting gifts, or convey congratulations. There are also formal gifts of raffia which are neglected only at risk of rupture of the social ties involved. A man, on reaching adulthood, should give 20 cloths to his father. Otherwise he would be ashamed to ask his father's help for raising his marriage dues. A man should give 20 cloths to his wife on each delivery of a child which qualifies him for entry into a cult group (Douglas 1957) or she may repudiate the marriage. He should bury each of her parents with a mortuary gift of 20 cloths; if she reports a would-be seducer, he should reward her virtue with 20 cloths.

Certain dues must be paid before a relationship or status is entered. Among these are age-set dues, which may vary from 6 to

10 or so, according to the local rule; marriage dues, 50 to the father, 40 to the mother; entrance fees to cult groups: Begetters, 100, Diviners, 100, Twin Diviners, 40, Pangolin cult, 20. Then there are fees for ritual officiants who perform healing rites or give oracular consultations: these may mount from one or two for a divination to 100 for a major cure.

Fines are paid to restore status after an offence has been committed. Adultery damages are usually 100 cloths; fines to the village for ritually spoiling it by fighting may be from 2 upwards, according to the occasion. Finally, tribute to chiefs is paid in raffia cloths.

This list, though abbreviated, shows that raffia is used extensively for the payment of services and the acquisition of status. The high demand for it for these purposes probably creates a value apart from its intrinsic value as a textile. The heaviest charges fall in the early part of a man's life, and the raffia paid on most of these occasions goes from young men to old men. A man who has entered an age-set, married, entered the Begetters' cult, and become a diviner, will have disbursed a minimum of 300 raffia cloths, and probably spent many more in maintaining good relations with his wife, in-laws, his father and mother, and settling adultery damages. Cloths paid for admission to cults are distributed between existing members, so that a man, once he has joined a cult, can regard his own fee as an investment which will bring in a regular return when each new initiate pays for entrance. Similarly, a man with several daughters enjoys an income of raffia cloths from his sons-in-law.

The effect is that young men are constantly in need of large quantities of raffia cloth, and older men are constantly receiving it. Young men do not expect to weave enough to pay for their own needs, in fact, old men are said to have more time for weaving. So young men go to old men to ask for help in raising their fees and fines. Thus there is asymmetry in raffia indebtedness between young and old, which goes some way to redress the disequilibrium between the generations created by the division of labour. Old men have a fund of raffia from which they can reward juniors, bolster up their own prestige, and make up for their declining effectiveness in cultivation and in the hunt.

A man trying to raise large sums of raffia draws on maternal and paternal ties of kinship, but more heavily on the former.

Investigation of this is difficult, for people tend to forget the help of men with whom they have later quarrelled. Raffia loans and debts have a *prima facie* suitability for quantitative treatment, but I found I could not rely on information about transactions I had not witnessed, and here I confine myself to reporting a few such cases.

A man may be able to collect raffia from several quarters: from his own clan, his father, and affines, from his lord if he is a clan-client,[2] and from his clients if he is a lord. This is obviously more relevant to a study of kinship behaviour, but here it is worth noting that one of the characteristics of raffia, divisibility into small units, makes it a suitable form of wealth to reflect certain characteristics of the kinship pattern: division of responsibility between maternal and paternal kin, and the freedom of the individual to affiliate to the kin group of his choice.

Examples

I describe here how a man and his two sons raised large sums for marriage dues and adultery compensation. I shall refer to them by letters, indicating clan membership, and numbers, indicating age-position in their local clan section. Both sons of B7 needed to raise their marriage payments at the same time. For the elder, A13, his father gave one she-goat worth 40 cloths, and 10 raffia cloths, and the boy's clan accepted responsibility for the rest of his dues. The boy himself was ill and was not expected to make a contribution.

A14 raised his marriage dues in instalments. For the first payment of 10 cloths, he wove 6 himself, and his father gave him 4. For the next payment of 10 cloths, he wove 3, his mother gave 3, three of his senior clansmen contributed one each, and E3, a client of his clan, gave one, saying that his own mother's mother had been married to A14's mother's mother's brother. Then he raised 300 francs, the equivalent of 30 raffia cloths.

[2] I use the word "client" for the status of men and women descended from a woman over whom certain rights have been transferred to settle a blood debt, and the word "lord" for the status of the representative of the clan to whom these rights have been transferred. As the institution is complicated, with far-reaching effects on Lele social organization, it must be described in a special article.

One hundred francs were given by A5 who obtained them from a man of E clan on a promise of 10 raffia cloths. It is noteworthy that the money was "bought" on a promise of raffia, but it was eventually returned when A1 trapped a pig and sold the meat, so if the supplier of 100 francs hoped to get raffia for 10 francs a piece, he was disappointed. Another 100 francs were given to A14 by his father, who had borrowed the money from a friend in the next village. Another 100 francs were given by the three men of clan C living in the village, on the grounds that their father had been A14's mother's brother. A14 also earned another 250 francs himself. The equivalent of 75 raffia cloths had been raised, but the full amount of 100 cloths would have to be raised before he could marry the girl, as she came from another village, and no existing ties facilitated the negotiations. His brother, by contrast, marrying a girl of the same village, had already been able to set up house, though only half the payment had been completed. His father was hoping to be able to raise another 200 francs for A14 by demanding a refund of the purchase price of a worthless dog he had bought from another village.

In this case, the wide range of kinsmen from whom contributions were taken is significant. A14 had great difficulty in levying anything substantial from his own clansmen, of whom there were 17 in the village. Men in smaller, more compact clan sections generally had more support from their clansmen. A5 had been on begging rounds for him, and reported that all but two had refused: the older men made difficulties because A14 had been fighting and was a disturbing element in the village; the boys junior to himself replied that they were young and had nothing to give. Refusals to help the young man with his marriage dues were intended as sanctions on his past behaviour, but the effect was to weaken bonds of clanship, not to strengthen them. The same old men later felt unable to ask A14 for services which they would have liked to command.

While these negotiations were proceeding, B7, the boy's father, was caught in adultery with the wife of their mother's brother, A5, who demanded immediate payment of 100 raffia cloths. B7 was not in real straits, because his own clansmen were involved in a factional quarrel, so they were unusually slow to co-operate with each other. He produced the equivalent of 40 raffia cloths, as follows: a fellow clansman lent him a small bar of camwood, valued at 20 cloths; a man of clan C, not a kinsman, advanced to him, against a promise of payment, a smaller bar worth 10 cloths; a man gave him 100 francs as an outright gift because his brother had married B7's sister's daughter. He was given time to find the rest.

It emerges from these examples that certain goods and Congo francs are acceptable in lieu of raffia. No doubt, as the economy becomes more commercialized, the range of these alternatives to raffia will increase, but at the time of my fieldwork they were limited to camwood, Belgian Congo francs, and goats. Certain objects, traditionally acceptable, had gone out of circulation: iron bells worth 50 cloths, copper bars worth 100 cloths, and slaves.

The adoption of goats in recent years, as a substitute for large raffia payments, is interesting, as their role is also almost purely monetary in the Lele economy. The Lele do not eat goat-flesh[3] but accept goats as a store of value which can always be converted into francs by sale to Luba lorry drivers and plantation workers.

The following is a list of the main units and equivalences used in raffia negotiations:

TABLE III. RAFFIA VALUES

Unit of raffia	Name	Equivalent goods
9 or 10 cloths	*ibok la bipolo* (bundle of cloth) or *ihangi la bipolo* (10 cloths)	Axe
	mabok ma pe (2 bundles) or	a 3-foot bar of camwood
18 or 20 cloths	1 *nghei* (trade salt)	a he-goat
	2 *mihei* (trade salt)	2 *mihei* or one she-goat or a 5-foot bar of camwood
40 cloths	3 *mihei*	3 *mihei* or she-goat with young
60 cloths	*lutuku*	*ikoko* (copper bar)
90 or 100 cloths		*ibondo* (slave)

The peculiarity of these units is the 10 percent margin allowed in making up a standard amount of raffia. *Ibok* is supposed to consist of 10 cloths, and *lutuku* of 100, yet no one can haggle or complain if the exact number is not reached when the payment is in raffia cloths. But this latitude is not extended to the goods

[3] See chapter on the Lele in Douglas (1954), in which their repugnance for the flesh of domestic animals in discussed.

accepted as substitutes for raffia. If a bar of camwood does not come up to 2 *mihei* in quality or size, it is treated as a 1 *nghei* unit; the goat is always the number of *ibok* indicated by its sex, neither more nor less. The full money equivalent is always required. For example, if raffia is valued at 10 francs a piece, for a payment of 100 cloths the full 1,000 francs must be paid, though if it is made in raffia cloth, 90 cloths will be accepted. Whatever the origin of this convention, it usefully expresses the higher value of raffia over any of the conventional substitutes.

MONETARY ROLE OF RAFFIA

Raffia cloth is bartered for the goods which are imported from foreign tribes. The Lele see themselves in their foreign relations as the great clothiers of the Kasai region. The Njembe from the south come with large calabashes, arrow-heads, hoes and knives, bells and other iron work; the Dinga on the river bank sell pottery and fish; the Pende to the east sell baskets, and camwood which they have obtained from the north, and the Nkutu sell camwood, all in exchange for raffia cloth. The Cokwe hunters accept it in payment for game, though they do not wear it, and intend to sell it.

Apart from its export as a barter commodity, raffia cloth is used in internal trade, whenever anything is bought from a skilled specialist with whom the buyer has no close kinship ties. In these cases raffia has a real monetary role, as a medium of exchange, for the seller accepts it in order to use it as payment for other exchanges.

This range of goods is very narrow, as people tend to go without, if they cannot obtain what they need from a kinsman. However, skilled craftsmen sometimes gain a great reputation for carving, and may supply drums, bellows, or drinking-cups to strangers from afar off. They will charge as much as 50 raffia cloths for a big item. These charges are real prices, to be distinguished from the gifts made to a craftsman who furnishes objects to kinsmen. Baskets, fish-traps, fur hats, carved cosmetic-bowls, dishes, cups, loom, mortar—the producer of these things is likely to receive no more than one or two cloths from a kinsman, in recognition that both parties acknowledge their relationship.

I had great difficulty trying to buy ordinary domestic objects with francs. They had no traditional price, as they usually changed hands on kinship lines, with an "acknowledgement fee" of one or two cloths. My friends, mistaking this fee for a price equivalent to the value of the goods, tried to persuade reluctant sellers that they ought to part with their things for 10 or 20 francs, the official equivalent of one or two raffia cloths. However, even if I doubled the number of francs, they were still not willing to sell. For raffia cloth they would have sold willingly, but my ethnographic collection seemed doomed, since I could not buy raffia cloth for francs.

RELATION TO CONGO FRANCS

Although raffia cloth is only used as currency in a limited range of transactions, the analogy with money is the simplest way of describing its behaviour. In one sense the Lele were trying to work with a raffia currency convertible into Belgian Congo francs at a rate which undervalued raffia. The conversion of raffia into francs applied only to a few rare purchases (such as buying a drum from a distant craftsman), but it applied extensively in all payment of compensation, dues and cult fees, and fines. The older men, who were not wage-earners, needed francs for payment for taxes and fines, while many young men found it easier to earn money than to obtain raffia, so this arrangement suited all parties. Even at the Native Tribunal fines and taxes could be paid in raffia in lieu of francs, and an official rate of exchange was therefore recognized. In 1924 this was 2 raffia cloths to the franc (Registre Ethnographique 1924), and since that date the value of raffia has gone up by leaps and bounds, expressing the greatly increased circulation of francs in the region, the opportunities for wage-earning, and the development of retail shops. On my first visit in 1949, one cloth was valued at 5 francs; in 1953 it was worth 10 francs. Even then these prices, fixed for the payment of fines at the Tribunal, did not at all reflect what raffia would have earned in a free market. The Lele adopted the official rates of exchange for all their dealings in raffia among themselves; they knew it was undervalued, but felt obscurely that a devaluing of the Congo franc would be against their interests. The result was that it was impossible to buy raffia for francs at the official rate, but to offer a higher unofficial rate was disapproved. Once I had acquired raffia I could easily buy goods which had been refused for the equivalent value in francs, but I could only obtain raffia by applying to the Tribunal, and even there the native clerks were reluctant to sell large quantities.

In their reluctance to sell for francs, and the readiness to sell for raffia, there is an element of what I can only call "irrational producer's preference," which I believe may attach to goods produced for subsistence in any economy. For instance, in our own economy, the producer of garden flowers or home-made jam would similarly be unwilling to sell his goods for cash at the retail price, though he would be happy to give them away to a neighbour for nothing. Some things are classed as more suitable for gift or friendly barter than for sale, and the ordinary market price would not compensate the producer for his work in the same way as he would be rewarded by the prestige and satisfaction of making a gift.

This attitude is exactly the reverse of the producer whose goods are intended primarily for sale. To him money seems scarcer than the products of his daily labour, and he will cheerfully barter away the goods at less than the usual price, if by doing so he can avoid parting with hard-earned cash. This difference was suggested to me by Dr. Salim's study of mat-weavers in Iraq,[4] and I suggest that the contrast between the attitudes of subsistence producers and exchange producers to the money value of their products may be widespread.

Although the Lele would sell small objects to me for raffia, but not for francs, this was not simply a preference for one kind of currency over another. The situation was, for them, redolent of the atmosphere of gift-exchange, not of trade, and the conventions of the former make one kind of exchange more acceptable than the other.[5] It is none the less true that the official rate undervalued raffia cloth. Why did a black market in raffia

---

[4] Doctoral thesis, now being prepared for publication.

[5] Many instances of similar conventions restricting exchanges could be cited, cf. Bohannan (1955); Leach (1951). See also many examples cited by Hoyt (1924:84–85).

not develop? Or at least, why did the production of raffia not increase to keep pace with the demand for it?

Social pressures inhibited men from buying and selling raffia. I heard of men obtaining francs with the promise of raffia, but I rarely heard of the eventual repayment being made in anything other than francs. Wage-earners in the north would sometimes carry their money to the south where opportunities of wage-earning were few, and the demand for francs consequently so much higher that the official rate was probably satisfactory to all parties. In these cases kin ties between the parties were not likely to inhibit the sale. Normally, for a man to be obliged to buy raffia with money would be felt as a failure of all the social bonds by which he could be expected to raise raffia cloth. It would be as absurd as the imaginary case of an Englishman reduced to buying Christmas cards to adorn his mantelshelf. In other words, there was no market in raffia, so there could not easily be a black market.

Men would never admit that the difficulty of raising fees deterred them from applying for cult initiation. On the contrary, they would boast of the sources they could hope to tap. For example, one man, who was the son of a village-wife,[6] said that his fathers (meaning the men of that village) would be delighted if he were accepted as a candidate for pangolin initiation, as it would give them an opportunity for contributing the whole of his raffia fees. Another man, who married the daughter of a village-wife, said that of course he had been obliged to undergo initiation into the Begetters' cult in her village, so that his fathers-in-law could stand the whole of the costs for him, and they would have been very hurt if he had been initiated in his own village. The very costliness of marriage with a daughter of a village-wife is an attraction, as it gives scope for proving social solvency. Less successful individuals, like B7 above, who have to weave, earn, and somehow scrape together their raffia payments by themselves, are assiduous in excusing their various kinsmen, or, if they criticize the living for meanness, it is because they compare them with some dead uncle or father whom they could have touched for as much raffia as they required.

[6] "Village-wife" is a woman whose marriage dues have been paid by an age-set of the village, and who is for all practical purposes regarded as the communal wife of the men of the village. See Douglas (1951).

Shortage of Raffia

Every man and boy can weave, and every man and boy would like to possess more raffia than he does. But they do not try to satisfy their own demand by sitting down to produce it. The Lele would explain that they are short of raffia now because they have so many competing demands on their time, especially earning money for taxes, that they cannot weave as much as their ancestors used to. This may be true, but, if so, I believe it only aggravates a shortage of raffia which is inherent in a quasi-inflationary situation.

In capital investment Lele economy is as stationary as any other primitive economy. But from the point of view of an individual who starts lending and borrowing raffia, it appears as a temptingly expanding financial system. The "enterprises" into which a man is asked to put his available raffia cloths are productive, not of material goods, but of prestige: helping a kinsman with marriage dues, compensation for offences, medical fees, fines, entrance fees. Ever since boyhood he has been drawing on the stock of his elders, and has been made aware of a sense of obligation when they helped him. As soon as he acquires any surplus stock of his own, he starts to create obligations towards himself by lending. He gets drawn into a social game in which, if he cannot give the impression of generosity, he loses not only prestige but the opportunities of obtaining credit when he needs it. A man's dignity as a member of a village, able to pay his way and help his kin, depends on credit, for the contributions of clansmen to one another's raffia needs are largely a matter of gifts made in the expectation that the recipient will be equally generous when their turn comes to ask his help.

Since it is desired, not as purchasing power, present or future, but for the sake of the prestige gained by parting with it, there is no point in hoarding raffia. Raffia cloths stored away are buried talents. The Lele would agree with the millionaire industrialist who said that the ultimate failure of a rich man was to die rich. The more famous and the more generous a man has been, the greater the number who expect to share in the division of his estate, but in practice, reputedly rich men tend to leave paltry possessions. The heirs are often disappointed to find that they are burdened with the debts of the departed. Needless to say, the men who had died after extracting the last jot of credit out of their acquaintance are those who are considered to have lived most successfully.

Lele are constantly turning over in their minds ways of meeting their financial commitments, counting their assets, and possible future expectations. Among the young especially there is a feeling like financial pressure. A man will make promises on the strength of his unborn daughter's future bridewealth; any insult or injury will be almost welcomed as possible subject for a claim. In the frequent conversations about the need to raise raffia cloth, it is a striking fact that men think first, not of sitting down to weave, but of pursuing any debts or claims outstanding. They hope to meet their demand for raffia by increasing the velocity of circulation rather than by increasing supplies. No one is expected to be anything but quick in making claims, or ruthless in pursuing debtors. The result is an inflationary pressure on the available supplies of raffia. It is a situation in which too few raffia cloths are circulating after too many debts and promises. Raffia is no sooner paid over than it is transferred again to liquidate debts of ten or twenty years' standing.

I cite one example to show how easily an I-owe-you situation can be transformed into a you-owe-me one. A diviner in South Homb was temporarily cured of his leprosy by another diviner from afar, who charged him 100 raffia cloths. It is held that a cured man will relapse if he does not promptly pay his doctor. The patient had raised the equivalent of 30 cloths by borrowing from a colleague, and was casting about for more credit when his healer fell ill with intestinal trouble. The former patient quickly dispatched a powerful remedy, and reckoned that if he obtained a cure he would charge 70 cloths, thus exactly discharging his own debt. In other cases, when there is not so much urgency, payments can generally be delayed for years, so that when the final reckoning comes, both parties have scores to settle with each other.

The Village Treasury

From what has been said, it will be obvious that no one keeps large stores of raffia, and also obvious that this was too delicate a subject to investigate. Individuals like to store a few surplus cloths with one of their sisters, so as to evade the demands of wives and children. A woman trusted in this way would generally justify her brother's regard for her discretion. A much easier insight into raffia distribution came to me through watching the public affairs of the village.

Each village has an official, named *itembangu la bola,* whose post combines the duties of spokesman and treasurer. He is a young man, chosen because of his *lutot* (eloquence) and because of his trustworthiness for keeping the *bikete bia bola* (things of the village). As the village budget is run on a deficit, the last responsibility is a matter of accountancy, not of keeping valuables under his hand.

The village has a corporate personality. Like a man it can acquire wives, slaves and clients, sue for compensation for injury to these, and receive payments for a transfer of rights over them or their children. Corresponding to these abilities, it has liabilities to make all the usual payments a man is liable to make in acquiring wives, or in compensating for offences committed by their children, paying son's marriage fees, and so on. Whenever something is paid to the village, a meeting is called, and decisions are taken about how the new funds are to be disposed of.

Five daughters of village-wives of South Homb were married within a few years of each other. Three of them married within the same village, and their husbands were therefore required to pay over only half the amount that would have been asked if they had come from outside, i.e. 2 *mihei* instead of 4. One man was blind, and though now married for 8 or 9 years, he had never been pressed to give more than the first instalment, one bar of camwood. This the village had put with 2 other bars raised from another source, and used to make the first repayment of a debt of 10 bars of camwood (200 raffia cloths), owed to a man of North Homb who had died unpaid, and whose heirs were pressing for payment. Two other girls were married to a man of

Bushongo, as a kind of gesture of welcome when he came to settle permanently in the village. He was subsequently installed as junior official diviner of the village, and the 4 *mihei* which he paid to the village for both girls exactly covered the fee which the village owed to the outside officiant who had performed the rite of installing him.

For one of the two girls who married outsiders, the groom paid up 5 bars of camwood. On receiving these, the village ignored outstanding claims against itself *qua* village, and quietly divided them amongst each of its 5 constituent clan sections.

For the youngest girl the prospective son-in-law paid up 3 *mihei* while I was there. The fourth was still outstanding. Of the 60 cloths paid up, it was agreed that 40 should be given at once to the grandfathers of the girl herself as marriage dues for her mother. As the latter had been herself a daughter of a village-wife, 4 *mihei* or 80 cloths should have been given. At first the representative of the grandfathers refused to accept the half payment, pointing out with some justice that it was already long overdue. The men of South Homb rallied him by asking why he had not brought the 10 chickens with which it is proper for a father-in-law to acknowledge the receipt of marriage dues, and he finally agreed good-humouredly to take what was offered, and to go home to collect the chickens, giving South Homb time to collect the remaining cloths.

South Homb actually had an additional 20 cloths in hand, for their son-in-law had paid 60, but it had been decided that this last *nghei* should be devoted to settling an equally long-overdue debt with the head man of the next village, Middle Homb. He required 30 cloths in damages for a charge of sorcery made against one of his wives, who had been cleared after submission to the poison ordeal. It was agreed at the meeting that 100 francs should be raised by levies on each of the clans of the village, and that these should be added to the 20 cloths, so that this claim of twenty years' standing could be settled outright.

At the same meeting, the old head of the village of South Homb put in a rather hopeless claim for at least 30 cloths as part repayment of the copper bar he had advanced to the village for the marriage dues of one of its (now quite elderly) village-wives. The claim was brushed aside, on the grounds that many big debts had to be written off now that it was no longer possible to

settle accounts by the transfer of women. On this point I shall
have more to say.

These examples illustrate clearly the importance of raffia in its
social role, creating ties of mutual obligation, between individuals and their fellow clansmen, between young and old, between
clans and villages, and between villages. If we recall that the
scale of their economy is so small that each village could almost
produce and consume its whole wealth in isolation, we can see
that raffia circulation immensely enlarges and enriches their
social life.

RIGHTS OVER WOMEN

To take the monetary metaphor too literally would lead us to
doubt the whole analysis of raffia distribution, for in a monetary economy the shortage of raffia would eventually stimulate
an increase in supply. It is not enough to explain the continued
shortage of raffia by the imperfections of the market, or the undeveloped mercantile spirit of the people. It has also to be appreciated that until recently any Lele man had always the means
of liquidating at one stroke an excessive pile of raffia debts.

One hundred cloths were equivalent to rights over a slave or a
woman. Slavery (following capture in war) had ended in the
early 1930's. Rights over women, creating a form of clientship
which was used to settle blood debts, could still be transferred,
but the Belgian administration was trying to end the system.
Anyone wishing to repudiate his status of client can now take the
matter to court, and end the relation with a cash payment. This
is a subject for a separate study. But it is essential here to know
that the Lele think of raffia primarily as a means to acquire rights
over women, and therefore, if they could not repay loans in raffia,
could settle by a direct transfer of rights over a woman or a
slave.

Raffia is indeed paid out for all the various purposes I have
listed, but when a man receives raffia, he hopes to use it to acquire
a wife, or to sweeten relations with his wife and her kin, or to
help a sister's son to acquire a wife. It may be diverted into
other directions before he can put it to these ends, but this is
simply because other men have made successful claims on his

stocks, which they also intend to use for acquiring and maintaining wives.

In a sense, raffia keeps its high value, not because of its use as a textile, but because it gives command over women, and, in a polygamous society, women are always scarce. Consistently, then, if a man's debts of raffia threaten to overwhelm him, he can cancel them by relinquishing rights over women in favour of his creditor. When this happens, no comparison with bankruptcy could be apposite, for the social bonds of creditor and debtor have been replaced by kinship ties. Formerly, the "inflation" which I have mentioned was not controlled merely by the limits of lenders' credulity. Under the old system, the man who advanced 100 raffia cloths to a friend did so against the security of the sisters and clanswomen of the borrower. If repayment were refused, public opinion would applaud him for taking one of them by force. It follows that the inflationary trend was transferred to rights over women, who were, even before their birth, pledged as backing for loans.

It is this final equation of 100 raffia cloths for rights over a woman which clarifies the difference between the system of raffia distribution as it used to be, and the quasi-monetary system it is becoming, and which also explains some apparent anomalies in the Lele attitudes to raffia values.

CONCLUSION

What has become of the view that raffia might be classed as a primitive type of money? The essential quality of money is that it gives its possessor purchasing power. Lele use raffia principally for payment of marriage dues, fines, blood-compensation, and cult entrance fees, which may be collectively called "status-payments," not purchases. As a medium of exchange it functions only rarely, as this is not a market economy. A very great number of other forms of so-called "primitive money" are used in these ways, in Melanesia and North America, as well as in other parts of Africa.

Primitive money is often discussed without reference to the degree of commercial development. To correct this tendency, I find the most useful theory of money is Menger's (Menger 1892), which starts from the different degrees of saleability of commodities in general. Those which are most highly saleable tend, with the development of markets, to become generally acceptable media of exchange—"money." Improved market conditions increase the superior saleability of such goods, so that when such goods as are relatively most saleable become money, there results "an increasing differentiation between their degree of saleableness and that of all other goods. And this difference in saleableness ceases altogether to be gradual, and must be regarded as something absolute . . . hence the difference of meaning attaching to 'money' and 'wares,' to 'purchase' and 'exchange' " (Menger 1892:250).

At first sight, Lele raffia seems to have a high degree of saleability. If markets were to have developed without European contact or the introduction of francs, it would have been likely to have become a medium of exchange. But its saleability, on closer inspection, is not something inherent in the internal working of the economy, but something which strikes the outsider arriving to do business. If the outsider can acquire raffia, he can buy everything with it, so it seems to him pre-eminently saleable. But it turns out to be not buyable, and this is because it is not strictly saleable between members of the community, because of what Menger calls "limitations imposed socially and politically upon exchanges and consumption of that commodity." On the criterion of saleability Lele raffia has evidently not developed into a form of primitive money, because most of their goods are distributed without buying or selling.

This approach suggests why travellers in other societies have so readily reported that a favourite commodity, wampum, shells, or iron bars, is the native money: they observe that when it comes into their hands it has an altogether superior degree of saleability, and if they stay to trade they may never remark that between natives it was originally scarcely saleable at all, though with the introduction of markets it soon becomes so. The advantage of following Menger is that we can avoid the paradox of money without commerce, and the study of primitive money can be confined to its appropriate sphere, the emergence of market economies.

9 THE IMPACT OF MONEY
ON AN AFRICAN SUBSISTENCE ECONOMY

Paul Bohannan

It has often been claimed that money was to be found in much of
the African continent before the impact of the European world
and the extension of trade made coinage general. When we
examine these claims, however, they tend to evaporate or to
emerge as tricks of definition. It is an astounding fact that
economists have, for decades, been assigning three or four
qualities to money when they discuss it with reference to our own
society or to those of the medieval and modern world, yet the
moment they have gone to ancient history or to the societies and
economies studied by anthropologists they have sought the "real"
nature of money by allowing only one of these defining characteristics to dominate their definitions.

All economists learned as students that money serves at least
three purposes. It is a means of exchange, it is a mode of payment, it is a standard of value. Depending on the vintage and
persuasion of the author of the book one consults, one may
find another money use—storage of wealth. In newer books,
money is defined as merely the means of unitizing purchasing
power, yet behind that definition still lie the standard, the payment, and the exchange uses of money.

It is interesting that on the fairly rare occasions that economists discuss primitive money at all—or at least when they discuss it with any empirical referrent—they had discarded one or
more of the money uses in framing their definitions. Paul Ein-

FROM Paul Bohannan, "The Impact of Money on an African Subsistence
Economy," *The Journal of Economic History*, XIX (1959), No. 4, pp.
491–503. Reprinted by permission of the author and the Economic History
Association.

zig (1949:319–26), to take one example for many, first makes a plea for "elastic definitions," and goes on to point out that different economists have utilized different criteria in their definitions; he then falls into the trap he has been exposing: he excoriates Menger for utilizing only the "medium of exchange" criterion and then himself omits it, utilizing only the standard and payment criteria, thus taking sides in an argument in which there was no real issue.

The answer to these difficulties should be apparent. If we take no more than the three major money uses—payment, standard, and means of exchange—we will find that in many primitive societies as well as in some of the ancient empires, one object may serve one money use while quite another object serves another money use. In order to deal with this situation, and to avoid the trap of choosing one of these uses to define "real" money, Karl Polanyi (1957:264–66) and his associates have labeled as "general-purpose money" any item which serves all three of these primary money uses, while an item which serves only one or two is "special-purpose money." With this distinction in mind, we can see that special-purpose money was very common in pre-contact Africa, but that general-purpose money was rare.

This paper is a brief analysis of the impact of general-purpose money and increase in [external] trade in an African economy which had known only local trade and had used only special-purpose money.

The Tiv are a people, still largely pagan, who live in the Benue Valley in central Nigeria, among whom I had the good fortune to live and work for well over two years. They are prosperous subsistence farmers and have a highly developed indigenous market in which they exchanged their produce and handicrafts, and through which they carried on local trade. The most distinctive feature about the economy of the Tiv—and it is a feature they share with many, perhaps most, of the pre-monetary peoples— is what can be called a multi-centric economy. Briefly, a multi-centric economy is an economy in which a society's exchangeable goods fall into two or more mutually exclusive spheres, each marked by different institutionalization and different moral values. In some multi-centric economies these spheres remain distinct, though in most there are more or less institutionalized means of converting wealth from one into wealth in another.

Indigenously there were three spheres in the multi-centric economy of the Tiv. The first of these spheres is that associated with subsistence, which the Tiv call *yiagh*. The commodities in it include all locally produced foodstuffs: the staple yams and cereals, plus all the condiments, vegetable side-dishes and seasonings, as well as small livestock—chickens, goats, and sheep. It also includes household utensils (mortars, grindstones, calabashes, baskets, and pots), some tools (particularly those used in agriculture), and raw materials for producing any items in the category.

Within this sphere, goods are distributed either by gift giving or through marketing. Traditionally, there was no money of any sort in this sphere—all goods changed hands by barter. There was a highly developed market organization at which people exchanged their produce for their requirements, and in which today traders buy produce in cheap markets and transport it to sell in dearer markets. The morality of this sphere of the economy is the morality of the free and uncontrolled market.

The second sphere of the Tiv economy is one which is in no way associated with markets. The category of goods within this sphere is slaves, cattle, ritual "offices" purchased from the Jukun, that type of large white cloth known as *tugudu,* medicines and magic, and metal rods. One is still entitled to use the present tense in this case, for ideally the category still exists in spite of the fact that metal rods are today very rare, that slavery has been abolished, that European "offices" have replaced Jukun offices and cannot be bought, and that much European medicine has been accepted. Tiv still quote prices of slaves in cows and brass rods, and of cattle in brass rods and *tugudu* cloth. The price of magical rites, as it has been described in the literature, was in terms of *tugudu* cloth or brass rods (though payment might be made in other items); payment for Jukun titles was in cows and slaves, *tugudu* cloths and metal rods (Akiga 1939:382).

None of these goods ever entered the market as it was institutionalized in Tivland, even though it might be possible for an economist to find the principle of supply and demand at work in the exchanges which characterized it. The actual shifts of goods took place at ceremonies, at more or less ritualized wealth displays, and on occasions when "doctors" performed rites and prescribed medicines. Tiv refer to the items and the activities within this sphere by the word *shagba,* which can be roughly translated as prestige.

Within the prestige sphere there was one item which took on all of the money uses and hence can be called a general-purpose currency, though it must be remembered that it was of only a *very limited range.* Brass rods were used as means of exchange *within the sphere;* they also served as a standard of value within it (though not the only one), and as a means of payment. However, this sphere of the economy was tightly sealed off from the subsistence goods and its market. After European contact, brass rods occasionally entered the market, but they did so only as means of payment, not as medium of exchange or as standard of valuation. Because of the complex institutionalization and morality, no one ever sold a slave for food; no one, save in the depths of extremity, ever paid brass rods for domestic goods.

The supreme and unique sphere of exchangeable values for the Tiv contains a single item: rights in human beings other than slaves, particularly rights in women. Even twenty-five years after official abolition of exchange marriage, it is the category of exchange in which Tiv are emotionally most entangled. All exchanges within this category are exchanges of rights in human beings, usually dependent women and children. Its values are expressed in terms of kinship and marriage.

Tiv marriage is an extremely complex subject (Akiga 1939: 120–27; and L. and P. Bohannan 1953:69–78; 1958:384–444). Again, economists might find supply and demand principles at work, but Tiv adamantly separate marriage and market. Before the coming of the Europeans all "real" marriages were exchange marriages. In its simplest form, an exchange marriage involves two men exchanging sisters. Actually, this simple form seldom or never occurred. In order for every man to have a ward (*ingol*) to exchange for a wife, small localized agnatic lineages formed ward-sharing groups ("those who eat one Ingol"—*mbaye ingol i mom*). There was an initial "exchange"—or at least, distribution —of wards among the men of this group, so that each man became the guardian (*tien*) of one or more wards. The guardian, then, saw to the marriage of his ward, exchanging her with outsiders for another woman (her "partner" or *ikyar*) who becomes the bride of the guardian or one of his close agnatic kinsmen, or—in some situations—becomes a ward in the ward-sharing group and is exchanged for yet another woman who becomes a wife.

Tiv are, however, extremely practical and sensible people, and they know that successful marriages cannot be made if women are not consulted and if they are not happy. Elopements occurred, and sometimes a woman in exchange was not forthcoming. Therefore, a debt existed from the ward-sharing group of the husband to that of the guardian.

These debts sometimes lagged two or even three generations behind actual exchanges. The simplest way of paying them off was for the eldest daughter of the marriage to return to the ward-sharing group of her mother, as ward, thus cancelling the debt.

Because of its many impracticalities, the system had to be buttressed in several ways in order to work: one way was a provision for "earnest" during the time of the lag, another was to recognize other types of marriage as binding to limited extents. These two elements are somewhat confused with one another, because of the fact that right up until the abolition of exchange marriage in 1927, the inclination was always to treat all non-exchange marriages as if they were "lags" in the completion of exchange marriages.

When lags in exchange occurred, they were usually filled with "earnests" of brass rods or, occasionally, it would seem, of cattle. The brass rods or cattle in such situations were *never* exchange equivalents (*ishe*) for the woman. The only "price" of one woman is another woman.

Although Tiv decline to grant it antiquity, another type of marriage occurred at the time Europeans first met them—it was called "accumulating a woman/wife" (*kem kwase*). It is difficult to tell today just exactly what it consisted in, because the terminology of this union has been adapted to describe the bride-wealth marriage that was declared by an administrative fiat of 1927 to be the only legal form.

Kem marriage consisted in acquisition of sexual, domestic, and economic rights in a woman—but not the rights to filiate her children to the social group of the husband. Put in another way, in exchange marriage, both rights *in genetricem* (rights to filiate a woman's children) and rights *in uxorem* (sexual, domestic, and economic rights in a woman) automatically were acquired by husbands and their lineages (L. Bohannan 1949). In *kem* marriage, only rights *in uxorem* were acquired. In order to affiliate the *kem* wife's children, additional payments had to be made to the woman's guardians. These payments were for the children, not for the rights *in genetricem* in their mother, which could be acquired only by exchange of equivalent rights in another woman. *Kem* payments were paid in brass rods. However, rights in women had no equivalent or "price" in brass rods or in any other item—save, of course, identical rights in another woman. *Kem* marriage was similar to but showed important differences from bridewealth marriage as it is known in South and East Africa. There rights in women and rights in cattle form a single economic sphere, and could be exchanged directly for one another. Among Tiv, however, conveyance of rights in women necessarily involved direct exchange of another woman. The Tiv custom that approached bridewealth was not an exchange of equivalents, but payment in a medium that was specifically not equivalent.

Thus, within the sphere of exchange marriage there was no item that fulfilled any of the uses of money; when second-best types of marriage were made, payment was in an item which was specifically not used as a standard of value.

That Tiv do conceptualize exchange articles as belonging to different categories, and that they rank the categories on a moral basis, and that most but not all exchanges are limited to one sphere, gives rise to the fact that two different kinds of exchanges may be recognized: exchange of items contained within a single category, and exchanges of items belonging to different categories. For Tiv, these two different types of exchange are marked by separate and distinct moral attitudes.

To maintain this distinction between the two types of exchanges which Tiv mark by different behavior and different values, I shall use separate words. I shall call those exchanges of items within a single category "conveyances" and those exchanges of items from one category to another "conversions" (Steiner 1954). Roughly, conveyances are morally neutral; conversions have a strong moral quality in their rationalization.

Exchanges within a category—particularly that of subsistence, the only one intact today—excite no moral judgments. Exchanges between categories, however, do excite a moral reaction: the man who exchanges lower category goods for higher category goods does not brag about his market luck but about his "strong heart" and his success in life. The man who exchanges high category goods for lower rationalizes his action in terms of high-valued motivation (most often the needs of his kinsmen).

The two institutions most intimately connected with conveyance are markets and marriage. Conveyance in the prestige sphere seems (to the latter-day investigator, at least) to have been less highly institutionalized. It centered on slave dealing, on curing, and on the acquisition of status.

Conversion is a much more complex matter. Conversion depends on the fact that some items of every sphere could, on certain occasions, be used in exchanges in which the return was *not* considered equivalent (*ishe*). Obviously, given the moral ranking of the spheres, such a situation leaves one party to the exchange in a good position, and the other in a bad one. Tiv say that it is "good" to trade food for brass rods, but that it is "bad" to trade brass rods for food, that it is good to trade your cows or brass rods for a wife, but very bad to trade your marriage ward for cows or brass rods.

Seen from the individual's point of view, it is profitable and possible to invest one's wealth if one converts it into a morally superior category: to convert subsistence wealth into prestige wealth and both into women is the aim of the economic endeavor or individual Tiv. To put it into economists' terms: conversion is the ultimate type of maximization.

We have already examined the marriage system by which a man could convert his brass rods to a wife: he could get a *kem* wife and *kem* her children as they were born. Her daughters, then, could be used as wards in his exchange marriages. It is the desire of every Tiv to "acquire a woman" (*ngoho kwase*) either as wife or ward in some way other than sharing in the ward-sharing group. A wife whom one acquires in any other way is not the concern of one's marriage-ward sharing group because the woman or other property exchanged for her did not belong to the marriage-ward group. The daughters of such a wife are not divided among the members of a man's marriage-ward group, but only among his sons. Such a wife is not only indicative of a man's ability and success financially and personally, but rights in her are the only form of property which is not ethically subject to the demands of his kinsmen.

Conversion from the prestige sphere to the kinship sphere was, thus, fairly common; it consisted in all the forms of marriage save exchange marriage, usually in terms of brass rods.

Conversion from the subsistence sphere to the prestige sphere was also usually in terms of metal rods. They, on occasion, entered the market place as payment. If the owner of the brass rods required an unusually large amount of staples to give a feast, making too heavy a drain on his wives' food supplies, he might buy it with brass rods.

However, brass rods could not possibly have been a general currency. They were not divisible. One could not receive "change" from a brass rod. Moreover, a single rod was worth much more than the usual market purchases for any given day of most Tiv subsistence traders. Although it might be possible to buy chickens with brass rods, one would have to have bought a very large quantity of yams to equal one rod, and to buy an item like pepper with rods would be laughable.

Brass rods, thus, overlapped from the prestige to the subsistence sphere on some occasions, but only on special occasions and for large purchases.

Not only is conversion possible, but it is encouraged—it is, in fact, the behavior which proves a man's worth. Tiv are scornful of a man who is merely rich in subsistence goods (or, today, in money). If, having adequate subsistence, he does not seek prestige in accordance with the old counters, or if he does not strive for more wives, and hence more children, the fault must be personal inadequacy. They also note that they all try to keep a man from making conversions; jealous kinsmen of a rich man will bewitch him and his people by fetishes, in order to make him expend his wealth on sacrifices to repair the fetishes, thus maintaining economic equality. However, once a conversion has been made, demands of kinsmen are not effective—at least, they take a new form.

Therefore, the man who successfully converts his wealth into higher categories is successful—he has a "strong heart." He is both feared and respected.

In this entire process, metal rods hold a pivotal position, and it is not surprising that early administrators considered them money. Originally imported from Europe, they were used as "currency" in some part of southern Nigeria in the slave trade. They are dowels about a quarter of an inch in diameter and some three feet long; they can be made into jewelry, and were used as a source of metal for castings.

Whatever their use elsewhere, brass rods in Tivland had some but not all of the attributes of money. Within the prestige sphere, they were used as a standard of equivalence, and they were a medium of exchange; they were also a mode for storage of wealth, and were used as payment. In short, brass rods were a general purpose currency *within the prestige sphere*. However, outside of the prestige sphere—markets and marriage were the most active institutions of exchange outside it—brass rods fulfilled only one of these functions of money: payment. We have examined in detail the reasons why equivalency could not exist between brass rods and rights in women, between brass rods and food.

We have, thus, in Tivland, a multi-centric economy of three spheres, and we have a sort of money which was a general-purpose money within the limited range of the prestige sphere, and a special-purpose money in the special transactions in which the other spheres overlapped it.

The next question is: what happened to this multi-centric economy and to the morality accompanying it when it felt the impact of the expanding European economy in the nineteenth and early twentieth centuries, and when an all-purpose money of very much greater range was introduced?

The Western impact is not, of course, limited to economic institutions. Administrative organizations, missions and others have been as effective instruments of change as any other.

One of the most startling innovations of the British administration was a general peace. Before the arrival of the British, one did not venture far beyond the area of one's kinsmen or special friends. To do so was to court death or enslavement.

With government police systems and safety, road building was also begun. Moving about the country has been made both safe and comparatively easy. Peace and the new road network led to both increased trade and a greater number of markets.

Not only has the internal marketing system been perturbed by the introduction of alien institutions, but the economic institutions of the Tiv have in fact been put into touch with world economy. Northern Nigeria, like much of the rest of the colonial world, was originally taken over by trading companies with governing powers. The close linkage of government and trade was evident when taxation was introduced into Tivland. Tax was originally paid in produce, which was transported and sold through Hausa traders, who were government contractors. A few years later, coinage was introduced; taxes were demanded in that medium. It became necessary for Tiv to go into trade or to make their own contract with foreign traders in order to get cash. The trading companies, which had had "canteens" on the Benue for some decades, were quick to cooperate with the government in introducing a "cash crop" which could be bought by the traders in return for cash to pay taxes, and incidentally to buy imported goods. The crop which proved best adapted for this purpose in Tivland was beniseed (*sesamum indicum*), a crop Tiv already grew in small quantities. Acreage need only be increased and facilities for sale established.

There is still another way in which Tiv economy is linked, through the trading companies, to the economy of the outside world. Not only do the companies buy their cash crops, they also "stake" African traders with imported goods. There is, on the part both of the companies and the government, a desire to build up "native entrepreneurial classes." Imported cloth, enamelware, and ironmongery are generally sold through a network of dependent African traders. Thus, African traders are linked to the companies, and hence into international trade.

Probably no single factor has been so important, however, as the introduction of all-purpose money. Neither introduction of cash crops and taxes nor extended trading has affected the basic congruence between Tiv ideas and their institutionalization to the same extent as has money. With the introduction of money the indigenous ideas of maximization—that is, conversion of all forms of wealth into women and children—no longer leads to the result it once did.

General-purpose money provides a common denominator among all the spheres, thus making the commodities within each expressible in terms of a single standard and hence immediately exchangeable. This new money is misunderstood by Tiv. They use it as a standard of value in the subsistence category, even when—as is often the case—the exchange is direct barter. They use it as a means of payment of bridewealth under the new system, but still refuse to admit that a woman has a "price" or can be valued in the same terms as food. At the same time, it has become something formerly lacking in all save the prestige sphere of Tiv economy—a means of exchange. Tiv have tried to categorize money with the other new imported goods and place them all in a fourth economic sphere, to be ranked morally below subsistence. They have, of course, not been successful in so doing.

What in fact happened was that general-purpose money was introduced to Tivland, where formerly only special-purpose money had been known.

It is in the nature of a general-purpose money that it standardizes the exchangeability value of every item to a common scale. It is precisely this function which brass rods, a "limited-purpose money" in the old system, did not perform. As we have seen, brass rods were used as a standard in some situations of conveyance in the intermediate or "prestige" category. They were also used as a means of payment (but specifically not as a standard) in some instances of conversion.

In this situation, the early Administrative officers interpreted brass rods as "money," by which they meant a general-purpose money. It became a fairly easy process, in their view, to establish by fiat an exchange rate between brass rods and a new coinage, "withdraw" the rods, and hence "replace" one currency with another. The actual effect, as we have seen, was to introduce a general-purpose currency in place of a limited-purpose money. Today all conversions and most conveyances are made in terms of coinage. Yet Tiv constantly express their distrust of money. This fact, and another—that a single means of exchange has entered all the economic spheres—has broken down the major distinctions among the spheres. Money has created in Tivland a unicentric economy. Not only is the money a general-purpose money, but it applies to the full range of exchangeable goods.

Thus, when semi-professional traders, using money, began trading in the foodstuffs marketed by women and formerly solely the province of women, the range of the market was very greatly increased and hence the price in Tiv markets is determined by supply and demand far distant from the local producer and consumer. Tiv react to this situation by saying that foreign traders "spoil" their markets. The overlap of marketing and men's long-distance trade in staples also results in truckload after truckload of foodstuffs exported from major Tiv markets every day they meet. Tiv say that food is less plentiful today than it was in the past, though more land is being farmed. Tiv elders deplore this situation and know what is happening, but they do not know just where to fix the blame. In attempts to do something about it, they sometimes announce that no women are to sell any food at all. But when their wives disobey them, men do not really feel that they were wrong to have done so. Tiv sometimes discriminate against non-Tiv traders in attempts to stop export of food. In their condemnation of the situation which is depriving them of their food faster than they are able to increase production, Tiv elders always curse money itself. It is money which, as the instrument for selling one's life subsistence, is responsible for the worsened situation—money and the Europeans who brought it.

Of even greater concern to Tiv is the influence money has had on marriage institutions. Today every woman's guardian, in accepting money as bridewealth, feels that he is converting down. Although attempts are made to spend money which is received in bridewealth to acquire brides for one's self and one's sons, it is in the nature of money, Tiv insist, that it is most difficult to accomplish. The good man still spends his bridewealth receipts for brides—but good men are not so numerous as would be desirable. Tiv deplore the fact that they are required to "sell" (*te*) their daughters and "buy" (*yam*) wives. There is no dignity in it since the possibility of making a bridewealth marriage into an exchange marriage has been removed.

With money, thus, the institutionalization of Tiv economy has become unicentric, even though Tiv still see it with multicentric values. The single sphere takes many of its characteristics from the market, so that the new situation can be considered a spread of the market. But throughout these changes in institutionalization, the basic Tiv value of maximization—converting one's wealth into the highest category, women and children—has remained. And in this discrepancy between values and institutions, Tiv have come upon what is to them a paradox, for all that Westerners understand it and are familiar with it. Today it is easy to sell subsistence goods for money to buy prestige articles and women, thereby aggrandizing oneself at a rapid rate. The food so sold is exported, decreasing the amount of subsistence goods available for consumption. On the other hand, the number of women is limited. The result is that bridewealth gets higher: rights in women have entered the market, and since the supply is fixed, the price of women has become inflated.

The frame of reference given me by the organizer of this symposium asked for comments on the effects of increased monetization on trade, on the distribution of wealth and indebtedness. To sum up the situation in these terms, trade has vastly increased with the introduction of general-purpose money but also with the other factors brought by a colonial form of government. At the same time, the market has expanded its range of applicability in the society. The Tiv are, indigenously, a people who valued egalitarian distribution of wealth to the extent that they believed they bewitched one another to whittle down the wealth of one man to the size of that of another. With money, the degree and extent of differentiation by wealth has greatly increased and will probably continue to increase. Finally, money has brought a new form of indebtedness—one which we know, only too well. In the indigenous system, debt took either the form of owing marriage wards and was hence congruent with the kinship system, or else took the form of decreased prestige. There was no debt in the sphere of subsistence because there was no credit there save among kinsmen and neighbors whose activities were aspects of family status, not acts of money-lenders. The introduction of general-purpose money and the concomitant spread of the market has divorced debt from kinship and status and has created the notion of debt in the subsistence sphere divorced from the activities of kinsmen and neighbors.

In short, because of the spread of the market and the introduction of general-purpose money, Tiv economy has become a part of the world economy. It has brought about profound changes in the institutionalization of Tiv society. Money is one of the shatteringly simplifying ideas of all time, and like any other new and compelling idea, it creates its own revolution. The monetary revolution, at least in this part of Africa, is the turn away from the multicentric economy. Its course may be painful, but there is very little doubt about its outcome.

10 ECONOMIC CHANGES
IN SOUTH AFRICAN NATIVE LIFE

I. Schapera

The native problem as it exists to-day [1928] in South Africa is not a phenomenon of recent growth. The issues which confront the country are the product of many decades of inter-racial contact and adjustment, during which Europeans and Natives have exercised a steadily growing influence upon each others' lives. Under the influence of European culture many of the Natives have abandoned their original tribal customs, and their social life is being reorganized on a new basis by the adoption of European habits and ideas. On the other hand, the presence of the Natives has so profoundly affected the social and economic development of the Europeans as to have become almost an integral part of the whole structure of civilization in South Africa. It is no longer possible for the two races to develop apart from each other. The future welfare of the country now depends upon the finding of some social and political system in which both may live together in close contact, without that increasing unrest and disturbance that seems to develop as the inevitable result of the lack of stability and unity in any society.

For the successful solution of this great problem of inter-racial adjustment, it is necessary to have a thorough knowledge and understanding not only of the existing situation, but also of the processes which have led to its creation. Until we have investigated carefully the story of their relations in the past, we can neither appreciate the many sources of friction and even conflict between the two races, nor establish any sort of harmonious rela-

FROM I. Schapera, "Economic Changes in South African Native Life," *Africa*, Vol. I, (1928), pp. 170–188. Reprinted by permission of the author and publisher.

tionship between them. We must be willing to seek guidance from the experiences of our predecessors and to apply with discrimination the lessons which they teach us. The historical study of the native problem is thus a subject not merely of scientific or academic interest, but of immense practical importance.

In the present paper[1] an attempt is made to trace out the main changes that have taken place in the economic life of the Natives of South Africa as a result of their contact with the Europeans. It is no exaggeration to say that the economic interdependence of the two peoples to-day constitutes the most vital and controversial aspect of the native problem; and it is of considerable importance therefore to have some indication of the development of this interdependence. Owing to the limitations that necessarily impose themselves upon a short preliminary survey such as this, it has been thought advisable to deal only with the so-called "Kafir" tribes[2] of the eastern districts of the Cape. This is not altogether a disadvantage. The Eastern Province with the Transkei is the native area where European influence has longest been felt; and as it is also justifiably regarded as the scene of the most successful native policy yet pursued in South Africa, it offers an excellent field for an investigation of this type.

II

At the time of their first contact with the Europeans, the native peoples of this region were divided into many small tribes.[3] Each

[1] In the preparation of this paper I have been greatly helped by a course of lectures on *The Native Problem from the Economic Point of View*, delivered at the University of Capetown in 1924 by Professor A. R. Radcliffe-Brown, who has kindly permitted me to draw upon my notes of these lectures.

[2] Under the term "Kafir" are generally included the AmaXosa, AmaMpondo, AmaMpondomisi, and AmaTembu of the Transkei (each of which groups is subdivided into a number of autonomous tribes), as well as the "Fingoes" of the Ciskei, who are the fugitve remnants of tribes from Natal broken up during the great inter-tribal wars at the beginning of the last century.

[3] For descriptive accounts of these Natives and their economic organization see G. M. Theal, *Ethnography and Condition of South Africa before 1505;* A. Kropf, *Das Volk der Xosa-Kaffern; Report of the Commission of Native Laws and Customs* (Cape Parliamentary Papers, G 4, '83); G. Fritsch, *Die Eingeborenen Südafrikas;* M. Richter, *Die Wirtschaft der südafrikanischen Bantuneger.*

tribe occupied its own territory, and lived independently under its own chief, who held his position by virtue of inheritance. His authority was generally considerable, but his actual power was somewhat restricted by a council drawn from his relatives and the more influential heads of families. Within the tribe the outstanding social unit was the household, i.e. the group of people who clustered about a headman. The headman (*umnumzana*) was usually more than the head of a single family—he was the responsible head of a group of families who lived together in a single settlement or kraal (*umuzi*). Such a group might consist, e.g. of a man with three wives and their dependent children, a married son or two, a younger brother, also married, and perhaps a few dependants not related by blood. The settlement was arranged in what tended to be a circle of huts, with an inner circle for the cattle, and was clearly marked off from other settlements. Each wife had her own hut. Opposite the main entrance was the hut of the headman's chief wife, then came the huts of the other wives in order of importance, and then the huts of the married sons, relations, and dependants. The whole household and everything associated with it was under the control of the headman, who was responsible to the chief for the behaviour of its inmates. These households were scattered over the tribal territory at irregular intervals, say a quarter of a mile or so apart; and were not only the local units but also constituted the larger economic units in the tribe. They were the primary groups for the production and consumption of food.

For their subsistence the Natives depended mainly upon pastoralism and hoe-culture. They kept cattle and goats, which supplied them with much of their food, in the form of milk, which was drunk sour, and with the raw material (leather) for some of their industries. The cattle were rarely killed for food, save on ceremonial occasions, meat being obtained chiefly by hunting. In addition crops were cultivated, chiefly of millet and maize, but supplemented by vegetables such as pumpkins, peas, and beans. The cattle were herded and milked by the men, while the care of the fields was in the hands of the women, who were prohibited by religious sanction from having anything to do with the cattle.

The subsistence of the people was intimately bound up with their system of land tenure. In theory all the land occupied by the tribe belonged to the chief, not, however, in the sense of a personal possession of which he could dispose freely, but vested in him and administered by him as the representative and head of the tribe. He parcelled it out in large areas to various powerful headmen, and by these the other headmen were granted land to cultivate and upon which to build their kraals. Once a man had his lands granted to him, he was secure in his possession of them so long as he continued to live at the spot and his fields were cultivated. The only way in which he could be dispossessed was if the chief turned him out of the tribe. If he left his land it reverted to the people as a whole, and could be reallotted subsequently. Only a small portion of the tribal land, however, was allotted for cultivation and residence. The greater portion, especially the open grass-lands, was reserved for pasturage, while much of the land was used as hunting-ground. Pasture-land was used in common, but its use was regulated by the chief, who decided which portions were to be thrown open to the cattle and which were to be set aside for future needs.

Only a headman would have land allocated to him, and he was at liberty to divide his land for cultivation among his dependants as he pleased. Usually each wife had her own field or fields, and these belonged to her and her descendants as long as she liked to use them. No one else had the right to use them without her permission. The ground was broken up and cleared by the men, and the women then had to hoe, sow, weed, gather up, and thresh the crops. They generally endeavoured to grow enough to last them from one season to another; and each wife had her own granary into which her harvest was put. From this granary she took each day what she needed for her supplies, and with this she fed her husband and her children, besides sending to each of the other women in the kraal a little of whatever dishes she had prepared. Each hut that contained a married woman was thus the centre of an independent economic group. At the same time all the people recognizing a common family head shared, as it were, in the produce of the whole settlement.

The same principle was found in connexion with the cattle. Every man who was the head of a household owned some cattle, but these were not used by the group as a whole. They were almost all distributed among the different huts. When a man married he set aside certain cattle from his general herd for the use of his wife, and these cattle with their increase henceforth belonged to her hut, and could not be alienated without her consent. Their milk belonged to her particular hut, and the *lobola* (bride-price) for her son was taken from them. On the death of a headman the cattle attached to each hut was inherited by the eldest son of that hut, who would then become responsible for all the juniors under him. The general herd which had never been distributed went to the principal heir, the eldest son of the headman's chief wife.

In addition to thus providing its own food-supply, each household also constituted an independent industrial unit. In the main all the articles of domestic use were made within the household. Each household built its own huts, the men erecting the framework and the women thatching the covering. Clothing was made of leather prepared in the household by the men, a woman's clothes being provided by her husband. Wooden utensils, such as milk pots, stools, and head-rests, were made by every man for himself, and similarly every woman made her own baskets and clay pots. Thus practically everything required within the household was made by its members. The one exception to their self-sufficiency was in the case of iron implements, for the making of which there were special smiths.

The division of labour was thus at a minimum, and was chiefly as between the sexes. This absence of specialization meant that there was a general even level of skill, and that not of a very high standard, although occasionally people would be found prepared to expend much trouble and care over the making of their utensils. It also meant that trade and exchange were of little importance, since each household produced what it required for its own use and consumption. There was, however, a certain amount of barter, as in the case of iron, for the smith exchanged the implements he made for grain and cattle. Sometimes, too, a woman who made better pots than others would exchange a pot for the value of the grain it held, if it were maize, or for half its contents if the grain were small; but there was no regular industry of making pots for exchange.

Once the Native had his huts, his utensils, and so on, the only form in which he could accumulate wealth was cattle. The wealth of a household consisted in its herds of cattle; and to a certain extent, indeed, cattle may be regarded as a standard of value in native life—*lobola* was paid in cattle, the chief levied fines in the form of cattle, and so on. But there was, however, a limit to the accumulation of cattle by the ordinary Native. There was no motive in native life which would lead to a man's accumulating cattle beyond a definite point; once he had enough cattle to maintain his household, there was nothing more which he could hope to gain by their possession. He could not even contemplate—what we are able to do—a rise in rank or social status due to the accumulation of wealth.

In the native social system rank was confined to the chief and his family, and was dependent entirely upon birth. The chief occupied a very prominent position in native life. He was the head of the government and regulated the affairs of the tribe; he was the leader in war and the chief magician of his people; he settled disputes and tried misdemeanours. By virtue of his official status as head of the tribe, he also played an important part in the economic organization. He was, as it were, the only capitalist—the only person who was really permitted to accumulate wealth. He received tribute from his people, both in kind and in labour. He was given a portion of every animal slaughtered or killed in the chase; the *lobola* for his chief wife was paid by the members of his tribe; he had the right to call upon his subjects to perform certain tasks for him, such as building his huts or clearing the land for his wives' gardens; above all, he received fees for hearing cases and fines for misdemeanour, and in cases of homicide the culprit paid compensation not to the relatives of the deceased but to him. As all fines and compensations were paid in cattle, he usually became very rich in consequence.

At the same time all this accumulation of wealth by the chief was really made on behalf of the tribe. One quality which was always required of the chief was that he should be generous. He had to provide for the members of his tribe in times of necessity. If a man's crops failed, he would look to the chief for assistance; the chief gave out his cattle to the poorer members of his tribe to herd for him, and allowed them to use the milk; he rewarded the services of his warriors by gifts of cattle; his subjects frequently visited him at his kraal, and during their stay he fed and entertained them. A chief who was poor or niggardly in providing for his subjects soon found them deserting him for some wealthier or more liberal rival. The chief, then, while accumulating wealth was also expected to distribute it. He had thus a very definite and important role in native economic life —it was he who scattered any surplus wealth there might be, when that surplus wealth was needed.

It was owing to this important economic function of the chieftainship that there was a limit to the accumulation of wealth by the commoner. A tribe was wealthy if its chief was wealthy, and important if its chief was important; but the commoner had no right to become a rich man—the social scheme did not permit of it. Moreover the chiefs were usually very jealous of their economic position, and looked with suspicious eyes upon any of their subjects who became too rich. The wealth of the chief was intimately associated with his office and economic functions, and any member of the tribe who showed signs of growing too wealthy was feared as a possible rival. An accusation of witchcraft would follow, and all the man's herds would be confiscated by the chief. There was thus no inducement for the Native to accumulate wealth either for its own sake or for the prestige it would bring him. Instead he used all the cattle he could afford for obtaining wives and thus increasing his household. The desire for children was, and still is, the fundamental motive in native life; and the larger a man's household was, and consequently the greater the number of his adherents, the more influential was his position. Hence the Native utilized his cattle both in order to obtain wives and to have the means of supporting them; and the desire for cattle, so important a feature of native life, was largely determined by this consideration.

III

Under the influence of European civilization this economic system has been very largely destroyed. The first contact of Europeans with the Natives took place at the beginning of the eighteenth century, in the course of eastward expeditions from the settlement at the Cape in search of cattle, ivory, or any other valuables which could be purchased for useful articles of barter. Generally speaking, this was the nature of the relations which existed between the Europeans and the Natives until early in the nineteenth century. Parties, authorized and unauthorized, made expeditions into native territory, some with the object of elephant hunting as well as to procure ivory which had already been obtained by the Natives, others to trade in cattle and perhaps to endeavour to recover their own cattle.

For a long time the intercourse between the two peoples was marked by conflict. Under the old native system there was no effective check on territorial expansion, and during the eighteenth century the native tribes were rapidly pushing to the west along the coastal belt. The first real suggestion of limitation came with their impact against the eastern tide of European migration, when in 1778 the Fish River was declared the official boundary between the two peoples. For many years the eastern border of the Colony was in a state of the utmost confusion due to the constant inroads of the Natives. The European population on the eastern frontier at this time was small and not very powerful, and consisted mainly of cattle farmers. To the Native, accustomed to raiding his enemies, the opportunities for cattle-lifting were too good to miss. Time and again the Natives returned to drive off the cattle of the farmers, thousands being secured in this way. Various expedients were tried without success to prevent raids, until in 1812, after a short war, a line of military posts, especially Grahamstown, was established along the frontier. This enforcing of the Fish River boundary emphasized the fact of territorial enclosure to the Native. Before 1812 the question had been which of the two races, each advancing in face of the other, should give way; and the native intruders into European territory had been far more numerous than European intruders into native territory. This campaign effected a real clearance within the Colonial borders, and the later war of 1819 marked the turning-point when, strengthened and almost forced to move by trouble with the Natives, the Europeans began to annex territory the native claim to which had hitherto not been disputed. The long and troubled history of the political relations between the two races in the years that followed need not concern us here.[4] There was a series of wars, each followed by the further extension of European control over the Natives, until with the annexation of Pondoland

---

[4] The political aspect of contact is best summarized in E. A. Walker, *A History of South Africa.* The economic aspect is dealt with to some extent by E. H. Brookes, *A History of Native Policy in South Africa,* and J. R. L. Kingon, *L'Éducation des Primitifs.*

in 1894 the last of the independent native areas between the Cape and Natal was brought under the direct rule of Europeans.

During the early years of contact the economic relations between the two peoples consisted entirely in trade. In spite of proclamations forbidding all intercourse with the Natives, in the hope that border quarrels might be avoided, a good deal of clandestine trade was still carried on with them, for the country in those days abounded in ivory. Even the soldiers on garrison duty in the forts along the frontier seem to have participated in what soon became a fairly extensive trade. Eventually it was decided to institute periodical fairs, where trading could be done under strict supervision, Fort Willshire being chosen for this purpose in 1824. Here licensed traders took their goods, and the Natives brought ivory, cattle, hides, and gum, desiring in exchange such things as copper-wire, hatchets, beads, buttons, and knives. It is an interesting illustration of the economic privileges of the chiefs to find that they usually took half of whatever the commoners obtained, as a right which was their due. The traffic was carried on under the supervision of the commander of the fort, who was careful to prevent arms or liquor from being sold to the Natives.

These fairs, however, did not last very long. Many traders, tempted by the profitable nature of clandestine trade, began to seek permission to go into the interior for trading purposes. The granting of licences in response to these appeals amounted to a reversal of the policy which had led to the institution of the Willshire fairs, and the adventurers were so successful that licences came in time to be freely granted for trading expeditions into the native territories. But once itinerant traders moved throughout the country there was no longer any need for the Natives to make their way with their goods to the Fort, and in consequence fairs there came automatically to an end. By 1830 trading stations were scattered thickly over the Ciskei, and by 1834 the native trade in ivory, hides, and gum had risen to about £40,000 per annum. As time went on, and with the extension of European control over the native territories, trading stations became more and more numerous, until to-day the trading station is one of the most frequent sights in the Transkei. The volume of native trade has swollen enormously since the early days, and to a large extent now forms one of the main sources of prosperity in the Eastern Province.

The first effect of contact on the economic life of the Native was thus the substitution of European goods for native products. The white man brought with him new articles of various kinds, many of which appealed to the Native. At first personal ornaments, such as beads, copper-wire, and brass buttons, were most in demand, but gradually the skin clothing of the Native was replaced by blankets, the implements made by the smith were superseded by imported metal goods, the wooden utensils and clay pots by the tin mugs and iron pots of the trader. In this way began a process by which the native products have disappeared to have their place taken by European wares, brought in and sold by trade. The productive work of the native household has been completely changed. The Natives no longer devote themselves to the same tasks as before. The home industries, the only industries there were, are dying out more and more, even in the least affected parts of the native areas; all the kraal handicrafts have suffered, and some have completely disappeared. Moreover new tastes have been created in the Native. The beads and buttons of the early traders have long been superseded by cloth, blankets, iron pots, axes, picks, and knives. Many articles, such as European clothing, groceries, crockery, and in many cases furniture, saddlery, and so on, which were quite recently luxuries, he is now beginning to regard as necessaries; and with the spread of educational influences the demand for them has grown. In progressive districts even the huts are being abandoned, and stone buildings on the European model erected, with corresponding innovations in the form of beds, tables and chairs, table-linen, and crockery. The range of individual possessions is increasing, and in material objects at least the Native is adopting more and more from European culture.

Even more far-reaching in its effect upon the economic life of the Native was the fact that he had to enter into a system of exchange with the traders. In order to obtain European goods he had to exchange something for them. He had to learn how to buy and sell, to familiarize himself with the use of money. In the early days ivory, hides, and gum formed the main articles of exchange, but as the supply of these fell away, and as the wants of the Native increased, he was forced to find some other means of satisfying them. His land he could not part with, as it was vested in the chief, so the three main things he had to offer were his cattle, crops, and labour.

At first cattle were an important article of trade, but it was not long before their importance declined. There were several reasons for this. Under the tribal system the Natives had been in the habit of procuring cattle which they could not acquire in any other way by making plundering forays into their neighbours' territory; and in the earlier years of contact native thefts of European cattle formed an everlasting source of conflict. The herds of the European farmers lay at the mercy of the Native, and if there was any trade in cattle more often than not it was cattle stolen from the Europeans which was traded back to them, or if the Native did part with his own herds, it was only in order to steal them back at the first opportunity. But with the strengthening of the European population on the eastern frontier, and with the establishment of law and order in the native territories, this method of obtaining food and the means with which to pay *lobola* for their wives disappeared. Very shortly, therefore, after the Europeans had asserted their rule, the increase in the native population and the contraction of the sources from which they had derived a livelihood began to show their effects. Then came the famous "cattle-killing delusion" of 1857, when it is estimated that the Natives slaughtered over 150,000 of their cattle; and the trade in cattle completely fell away. This was followed in later years by the spread of rinderpest to the native territories, which decimated the native herds, and, shortly after Union, East Coast fever and drought still further reduced the native stock. To-day the Native is in need of cattle. To him they still are of the greatest value, both as a source of food and especially as the means of obtaining a wife; he will not readily part with his stock, and it may even be said that the desire for cattle has become one of the most powerful motives driving the Native to enter more and more into the economic system of the Europeans.

It is only within recent years that native crops have become of any importance as an article of trade. At the same time the character and scope of native agriculture have improved considerably. Under the tribal system, as we have seen, all the cultivation was done by the women. The crops raised were few in number, and the methods employed wasteful and unproductive.

The most important change here was brought about by the introduction of the plough. This was directly due in the first place to missionary effort early in the nineteenth century, but it was afterwards actively and deliberately supported by the administration. The use of the plough has now spread very widely, carrying with it improved agricultural methods, and, what is far more significant, a reconstruction of society. The use of the plough involved the harnessing of cattle; and as the native social and religious system prohibited women from having anything to do with cattle, the men now had to do the ploughing. The change in the native division of labour was profound, although the other agricultural work, such as hoeing and reaping, still remains to a large extent in the hands of the women.

Accompanying this revolution in the character of native agriculture, there has been a considerable extension in the range of agricultural activity. As a result partly of missionary influence, partly of imitation of European neighbours, landlords or masters, but due mainly to a policy deliberately carried out by the administration, native methods of agriculture have improved immensely. The Native has begun to grow in quantity for exchange as well as for subsistence; new crops have been introduced with some measure of success, such as wheat, barley and oats, fruit and vegetables, and tobacco; while associations are rapidly springing up among the Natives for the encouragement and training of their agricultural production. Irrigation, agricultural education, and individual land tenure, combined with the relative shortage of cattle, are tending to make the Native pre-eminently an agriculturist. The trade in native crops is still proportionately slight, but there seems no doubt that in the course of time it will increase considerably.

The most important factor of change, however, has been the selling of his labour by the Native. From the outset there was the demand by the Europeans for native labour, for cheap unskilled labour, and the Natives have not been slow in responding. This was the case especially after the "cattle-killing delusion" of 1857, when under the impulse of religious enthusiasm all their existing cattle and crops were destroyed by the Natives at the instigation of the notorious "prophet" Umhlakaza. As a result nearly 100,000 Natives wandered forth to find some means of living. Relief works were multiplied in the Colony to meet the crisis, and more than 40,000 Natives were taken into service in various parts of the country. From this time on there has been an increasing flow of Natives to the labour market. Domestic service, farm labour, and industrial tasks all called for native employment, and the opening of the great mining industries greatly stimulated the demand. The primary motive which urged the Natives to sell their labour in this way was their need of the money with which to purchase their new requirements. As they became more civilized their wants increased, and in order to satisfy these wants they had to go out to seek remunerative employment. Then also the imposition of the hut-tax by the European government formed an additional stimulus, for the Native had to earn the money with which to pay his tax.

Although in many respects the kraal life of the Natives often remains but slightly altered, the demand for labour has already led to significant changes in their habits and customs. They are still primarily agriculturists or herdsmen working on their own account, but a very large proportion of them have now also become temporary wage-earners. It is a common practice for able-bodied men to leave their homes from time to time to enter the service of white employers, and for this purpose they often travel great distances. As a rule they do not remain employed for more than about six months. In this time they can often, without much difficulty, save a fair amount out of their earnings, and with this money they generally return to their kraals and resume their normal occupations. While this practice takes them into many other employments, it has greatly strengthened their position as agriculturists. With the savings which they bring home they are able to make good the ravages of rinderpest among their cattle and to buy the implements which they need for the cultivation of their fields. In many districts large numbers of European ploughs have in this way been purchased by the Natives. To-day this going out to labour has become a regular feature in native life, the principal method by which they can obtain the means to satisfy their new needs and tastes.

The chief result of this demand for labour has been to turn the native population into a class of unskilled labourers, moving about from place to place in search of work. The aim of the Native for the most part still remains to work for a short period only, and then to return home when he has saved some money.

But there is now a growing tendency for the Natives to stay at work in the towns for longer periods. They are also beginning to acquire some degree of skill in certain classes of employment, and with this may be associated the fact that a growing proportion of the native population are drifting away from their own districts and living in or near the towns in which they work. These Natives are beginning to look for permanent rather than temporary labour, and are becoming urban dwellers who do not return to their kraals at all. They are becoming detribalized, in other words, and many of them have ceased to be agriculturists and herdsmen, and are now primarily industrial labourers.

It is not difficult to appreciate the effect this has upon the life of the people. The many thousands of Natives constantly employed on farms, railways, and public works, and in mines and workshops, are inevitably being brought into more intimate contact with European civilization and all that it means to them. In the towns they acquire new tastes, new habits, and new vices; they return to their kraals profoundly altered, and with an increasing detachment from the old tribal system. They cannot come into contact with the relative freedom of civilized life, enter into individual contracts, and secure earnings formerly undreamt of, and yet retain their old communal ideas and submit to the caprice and exactions of their tribal superiors. In the kraals also these economic changes are slowly but surely undermining the tribal system. The regular absence at work of the younger men is beginning to leave its mark upon the social life. As long as the period of work away from the kraal was short, the effect was not so serious; but when the intervals began to lengthen the old routine of life had perforce to suffer. Social ties are being weakened, and the families broken up by the long absence of the bread-winners.

The breakdown of the tribal system has been further stimulated by other factors. Of these not the least significant was the decay of the chief's economic functions. This is partly the result of a policy deliberately carried out by the administration since the middle of last century. The chiefs were still recognized by the Europeans as a means of government, but their jurisdiction, more particularly in criminal matters, was gradually transferred to European magistrates and commissioners. They were induced to accept fixed salaries from the government, in return for which they had to surrender their right to fines imposed on their people. They were also deprived of the power of making war against rival tribes, and were thus discredited in the eyes of their people, who looked to war as one of their principal means of acquiring cattle. In this way the chiefs were deprived both of their most important functions in native life and of the chief source by which they derived revenue from their people.

At the same time the ordinary Native, by his contact with the European economic system, learned the meaning of thrift and of personal property; new wants were created, and so were the means of satisfying them; and as the range of personal possessions increased the Natives began to grow reluctant to part with individual gains. Instead of working for their chief they now worked for themselves: the accumulation of wealth became a motive in the life of every Native. Travel and the absence for longer or shorter periods from their home environment widened the breach between the chief and his subjects. The economic reciprocity which entered so strongly into the relations between chief and subjects, and which formed one of the vital features of the native economic system, has broken down almost completely. The chief no longer plays the part of tribal banker: his function as the holder and distributor of all the surplus wealth has been obliterated by the new economic forces.

Another highly important factor in the breakdown of native economic life was the restriction upon territorial expansion. Under the tribal system there was no effective check upon tribal or individual movements, and it was always a basic assumption in native life that there was an abundant supply of land. A tribe which desired new territory would either oust its neighbours or simply move on and take up vacant territory; while similarly any Native whose fields were no longer productive could always find new lands. The enforcing of the Fish River boundary by the colonial government was the first real suggestion of territorial enclosure to reach the Native. Then after a time followed the expansion of the Colony towards the east, and more and more of the Kafir territory came to be absorbed by the Europeans. Moreover under European administration all unoccupied land was made Crown land, and thus a further check was put upon native extension. The main immediate effect of annexation upon the native land system was the transfer of the administration of the land from the chief to the government. This was a direct blow to the power of the chief, who, by losing his right of allotting land to tribesmen except under the direction of the new paramount power, was deprived of one of his important functions in native life. At the same time white farmers occupied large tracts of country in parts of which the Natives had previously been settled, and the native population was confined more and more to lands specially reserved for them. As the European population increased, the movement for the enclosure of the farms was commenced, and the Native began to find himself more and more cramped for space, hemmed in on all sides by fences, and confined to a limited area.

Following upon this restriction of territorial expansion, there has been a profound change in the nature of land tenure. The colonial administration began by adopting the communal system of occupation observed by the Natives in their independent state, and by gradually adapting it to the changing conditions of life attendant upon the march of civilization, prepared the way for the recognition by the people of the advantages of an individual system tending towards the assimilation of European methods. From about 1830 onwards, various attempts were made in the Ciskei to induce Natives to take up land in this way. At first the attempts did not meet with much success, partly because the Native was too attached to the tribal system, partly because of the complexities presented to the native mind by the European laws of transfer. But the spread of education and the increasing disadvantages of the communal system led to a certain amount of land being taken up on individual tenure. The whole movement was accelerated by the Glen Grey Act of 1894, in which provision was made for the settlement of the Natives of Glen Grey district upon the land, allotments being made to individual applicants. The success of this scheme led to its extension by proclamation to the Transkei territories, the measure being made permissive and applicable only to such districts as voluntarily desired to have it. The movement thus initiated proceeded very slowly at first, but is now making steady progress. The way is being prepared for the extension of the system, and in time, no doubt, the whole of the territories will be included under it.

The general effect both of the restrictions upon territorial expansion and of the introduction of individual land tenure has been to create a definite shortage of land among the Natives. The encroachment of the Europeans and the steady increase in the native population has brought about a situation owing to which the existing native areas cannot support all the Natives. The improvement in agricultural methods has not kept pace with the spread of individual land tenure. The native districts are over-stocked with cattle, while methods of cultivation are not yet sufficiently advanced to enable the Native to make the best of his holdings. More and more Natives are being forced from the land. A definite class of landless Natives has consequently come into being, who depend solely on their labour for a living, and reside permanently in the industrial centres. The drift away from the kraals to the towns, to which reference has already been made, derives most of its impetus from this shortage of land.

Finally there must be mentioned the effects which education has had. The education of the Natives has always been one of the objects of missionary enterprise, and has also been increasingly supported by the administration. Education has led in the first place to an increase in the wants of the Native, and thus forms one of the factors inducing him to seek work in order to obtain the means of satisfying these wants. But of more importance, perhaps, is the fact that it has been one of the most powerful agencies in creating a new class of Natives. Whereas formerly all the Natives were agriculturists and herdsmen, there have now come into being definite artisan and professional classes. Many Natives are learning trades at various institutions, and are beginning to specialize as artisans; a number are employed as police-men and interpreters, and as intermediate and subordinate officials in various government departments; many have become ministers or teachers, and there are a few native editors of newspapers; while medicine and law are also slowly proving attractive.

IV

Brief and inadequate as this survey has necessarily been, it has perhaps made clear the main lines along which the modification of the native economic system has taken place as the result of its contact with European civilization. The introduction of the Native to the economic system of the Europeans, the restrictions upon territorial expansion, and the spread of education have combined to weaken the old tribal system and to destroy the vital economic functions of the chieftainship. There has been a considerable change in the habits of many of the Natives. Their methods of agriculture have markedly improved, and their ideas about stock and stock-raising are slowly being influenced for the better. On the other hand some of their kraal handicrafts have been destroyed, and others injured. Moreover the Natives have been introduced to an economic system which was entirely alien to them. They have learned something of the white man's economic motives, and these have modified their habits and outlook.

Most important and perhaps as the result of all these changes, the Natives have been differentiated into a number of classes. There is in the first place the relatively small class of Natives who still live under the same conditions as prior to the advent of the Europeans, and do not go out to work at all. They do not come into the economic system of the white man, except in so far as they pay taxes and buy goods and perhaps sell a few of their crops. Then there are those kraal Natives who form the great mass of the unskilled labourers of the country, who leave their kraals to work for short periods, and then return home again. This class is still by far the largest in the native population, and includes the great majority of the able-bodied males and more recently also a number of women. Both these classes still live under the communal system of land tenure. Then there are a small number of independent native farmers who own farms of their own. This is a new class which has come into existence fairly recently, under the system of individual land tenure. Another class consists of those Natives who have no land of their own, but live permanently on European-owned farms, either as tenants, labourers, or squatters. They do not come into the general labour market, but render service for a certain period of each year in lieu of rent to the owners of the farms on which they reside. There is also the growing class of Natives who have become detached from their land, and who now live permanently in urban areas. This class has increased during the last decade, very largely indeed owing to the influence of the Native Lands Act of 1913. Finally there is the class of Natives who are neither agriculturists nor unskilled industrial labourers, but are permanently engaged in various trades or professional occupations.

It will be seen, therefore, that the Natives are now differentiated to such an extent that it is impossible to generalize about their habits and characteristics as a whole. Some are living very much as they did under the old tribal system, others have changed very materially indeed, and approximate to the Europeans both in mode of life, economic occupations, outlook on life generally, and individualism. Between these two extremes there are the great majority who are now in a transitional stage. Any attempt to deal with all these different classes as a single unity is doomed to failure. We must recognize their differences, and approach the particular problems they each present, with no illusion about the uniformity of the native question.

11 THE DEVELOPMENT OF SUBSISTENCE AND PEASANT ECONOMIES IN AFRICA[1]

George Dalton

To understand the social implications of rural African develop-ment one must first understand the relation between traditional social organization and economic structure in primitive and peasant communities. Case studies show that unsuccessful de-velopment occurs where an increase in production for sale is un-accompanied by technological and cultural innovations: traditional economy and society are forced to change without new modes of integration being formed, and without sustained growth in income forthcoming. Successful development requires mutually reinforcing innovations in economy, technology, and culture which induce sus-tained growth in income over successive generations, and integrate the local community with the region, the nation, and the world.

This article will be addressed to several specific questions: How do the traditional social and economic structures of rural African subsistence economies influence their receptivity to mea-sures necessary for successful development? What constitutes "successful" social and economic development? What are some connections between technological and economic change? How far is it possible to generalize from studies of particular cases in rural Africa? What policies for development are suggested by the matters considered?

FROM George Dalton, "The Development of Subsistence and Peasant Economies in Africa," *International Social Science Journal,* Vol. XVI, No. 3 (1964), pp. 378–389. Reprinted by permission of the author and pub-lisher.

[1] I am grateful to Paul Bohannan, Ronald Cohen, and Elizabeth Colson for their critical comments and suggestions.

It is necessary at the outset to make a distinction between primitive or subsistence economies, and peasant economies. In primitive economies market exchange transactions are entirely absent, or only of minor importance to livelihood. In marketless economies, no appreciable quantities of labour or land are hired or sold—there are no resource markets—nor are there market sites for the buying and selling of produce. In primitive economies with peripheral markets only, small quantities of produce are sold in face-to-face transactions at market sites; but most people do not depend for livelihood on such sales, and the market-place prices do not affect the production decisions of subsistence producers. We shall include two other features as defining such subsistence economies: modern machine technology and applied science are not used in production processes; and traditional social organization and cultural practices remain in force.

What I shall mean by "peasant" economy differs primarily in one respect: most people have come to depend on production for sale as their primary source of livelihood. Market exchange has become the dominant mode of transaction; commercial production has become more important than subsistence production. In peasant economies appreciable quantities of labour and land as well as produce are bought and sold; money prices and money incomes are familiar. However, with regard to technology, social organization and cultural practice, peasant economies more nearly resemble the primitive than the modern. Machine technology is seldom found and, on the whole, traditional social organization and culture are retained. One must speak in terms of degree here because it is common in peasant communities in Africa for there to be some elements of Western culture grafted on to indigenous practice; for example, a slight ability to speak a European language. It is also common to find within peasant communities a range of technologies, variation in adherence to traditional forms, and different degrees of reliance on production for sale (Cohen 1961).

The distinction between primitive and peasant allows us to attach some well-defined meaning to "subsistence" economy, and to suggest that the social implications of rural African development are sometimes different for primitive as compared to peasant economies, a matter that we shall take up later.

THE STRUCTURE OF PRIMITIVE (SUBSISTENCE) ECONOMIES

Any planned growth is embedded in a set of institutions and attitudes which come from the past. (Keyfitz 1959)

Subsistence economies are usually described in negative terms: they are not exchange economies or money economies. But neither do they consist of self-contained and self-sufficient households each producing and consuming independently of others in the community. In all subsistence economies there is a network of labour, land, and product transactions—a local and contained economic system which integrates community life. It is their positive economic characteristics as these relate to social organization and cultural practice which must be appreciated if we are to understand why social malaise sometimes accompanies economic change.

Distinguishing features of primitive economies are the pervasive social control of production and distribution, and the guarantee of subsistence livelihood through resource allocation and social right to receive aid in time of need. This essential point has frequently been phrased in general terms: for Tönnies, primitive economies are *Gemeinschaft* rather than *Gessellschaft;* for Maine they are characterized by status rather than contract; for Weber and MacIver they are communities rather than associations; Karl Polanyi sees the economy as embedded in the society; Raymond Firth's formula is "from each according to his status obligations in the social system, to each according to his rights in that system."

Specifically, these primitive social economies are so organized that the allocation of labour and land, work organization within production processes, and the disposition of goods and services —in short, production and distribution—are expressions of underlying kinship obligation, tribal affiliation, and religious and moral duty. There is no separate economic system to be analysed independently of social organization. Labour, land, services and produced goods are allocated, exchanged, or appropriated through transactional modes of reciprocity and redistribution (rather than the familiar commercial mode of market exchange)

(Bohannan and Dalton 1962; Polanyi 1944, 1947, 1957).[2]

Reciprocity is obligatory gift-giving and counter gift-giving dictated by obligations of kinship, friendship, neighborhood, tribal affiliation, or some other social relationship. Similarly, redistribution consists of socially obligatory payments of material goods, monetary objects, or labour services to a central political or religious authority which uses the material receipts for its own maintenance, to provide community services (such as defence or feasts), to reward those who have rendered specific services, and as an emergency source of subsistence in time of personal or community disaster (Schapera 1928). Frequently the central authority is also endowed with the right to allocate unused land or hunting sites.[3]

Three points emerge:

1. It is the absence of Western technological and market constraints which allows Africans to organize subsistence production and distribution as an expression of social relationships. As long as labour, land, and other resource ingredients of production are not purchased, and products not disposed of through market sale, the input and output decisions of local producers are not dictated by resource and product prices as they are in Western commercial production.

2. Modern machine technology and applied science (tractors, irrigation equipment, chemical fertilizers) cannot be introduced into primitive subsistence economies unless the production

[2] There is a kernel of truth in the notion of "primitive communism." It is that kind of statement which is right for the wrong reasons. Socialism and communism are children of large-scale, industrial capitalism. Primitive economies are neither large-scale, industrial, nor capitalistic (i.e., integrated by market exchange). The local face-to-face communal ties of family, neighborhood, common ancestry, and language—together, frequently, with isolation from other groups—account for the organization of production and distribution being controlled by social institutions. To those who define things in such a way that if a system is not capitalist, it must be communist, primitive economies appear communistic. If so, they more nearly resemble the communalism of small Utopian communities with a cohesive ethos, than the kinds of socialism we associate with modern Russia and the Welfare States.

[3] In primitive communities economic practices and devices are found (e.g., market-places, external trade, special kinds of money) which bear a superficial resemblance to practices and devices familiar to us in developed economies of the West. However, in primitive economies these practices are organized differently and carry out somewhat different functions from their Western counterparts (Bohannan and Dalton 1962; Dalton 1961, 1965; Polanyi 1944, 1947, 1957).

lines they enter are first commercialized: like hired labour or any other purchased ingredient of production, machines require a cash outlay which is recouped from the monetary sales proceeds of the goods produced with the machines. For primitive economies, the introduction of Western techniques always means economic change—e.g., expanded production of cash crops for market sale.

3. Knowledge of primitive economic and social structure coupled with an appreciation of the economic requisites for using Western technology enable us to understand why social and cultural change inevitably accompanies economic development in rural Africa: the allocation of labour and land, the organization of work, and the disposition of products become rearranged in accordance with market criteria of production at minimum money cost, and the need to earn cash income for livelihood. There must therefore be social disturbances when "subsistence" production is transformed into commercial production. "In primitive communities, the individual as an economic factor is personalized, not anonymous. He tends to hold his economic position in virtue of his social position. Hence to displace him economically means a social disturbance" (Firth 1951).

However, we must not equate social change or disturbance with social malaise or anomie (Beattie 1961). "For the sting of change lies not in change itself but in change which is devoid of social meaning" (Frankel 1955).

We must disentangle several questions and try to answer them in the light of the evidence provided by case studies of rural African change: What constitutes successful socio-economic development? Under what conditions does the traditional structure of primitive and peasant economies prevent successful social and economic change? Is it ever the case in fact that successful economic development is accompanied by unsuccessful social change—personal anomie and social malaise—or, is serious social malaise itself a symptom of unsuccessful economic development?

Economists gauge economic improvement by criteria which have little to do with the questions at issue. The economist's concern is with impersonal growth of a national economy as measured by accretions to aggregate output over time. A national economy may be growing satisfactorily while regional inequalities of income within the country are widening (Myrdal 1957, 1960), and local communities disintegrating socially, as witness the effects of extensive labour migration in East and South Africa (Jaspan 1953).

Liberia is a case of growth without development. From 1950 to 1960 it experienced an average annual growth of gross national product of 11 percent (among the highest in the world), due to enormous expansion in a dozen foreign concessions producing rubber and iron ore (Walters 1962). But in large part output continues to consist of primary products for export; little fabrication, processing, manufacturing or commercial agriculture is undertaken by Liberians. In 1960 about two-thirds of all Liberians still derived the bulk of their livelihood from subsistence activities; the other third depended upon wage employment but supplied mostly unskilled labour. Here, the impressive rate of national economic growth is unaccompanied by successful national economic development or local community development. It remains an enclave economy.

The questions that concern us cannot be answered by reference to impersonal studies of aggregate economic growth. Our concern is with community change—what happens to identifiable groups of people in the course of national economic growth.

Studies of primitive and peasant groups in rural Africa include cases of socio-economic change forced upon communities by the pressing need to earn a livelihood in new ways (Gulliver 1962, 1961); and cases of voluntary change, where the attraction of higher income alone was sufficient to induce change to production activities yielding higher returns (Vansina 1962; White 1959). Sometimes communities reject higher productivity techniques and higher income earning activities (Cohen 1961; Douglas 1958). There are cases of socio-economic change not deliberately planned by anyone (Bohannan 1959); and cases where change is community-planned (Gaitskell 1959). Certain communities have incorporated new commercial activities without disruption of traditional community organization (Watson 1958); and in others fairly extensive social malaise may accompany economic change (Jaspan 1953; Sadie 1960; Schapera 1928). It is with the empirical information provided by case studies and the theoretical insights provided by analysis of socio-economic change that we turn to the questions posed earlier.

WHAT CONSTITUTES SUCCESSFUL COMMUNITY DEVELOPMENT?

Material improvement without social disaster does not necessarily mean successful community development. Enlarged earnings from production for sale may simply mean that more people in the community are engaged in unskilled wage earning or cash cropping. Successful development requires continual increases in *per capita* income, which in turn requires the application of improved technology to whatever enlarged commercial lines of production are undertaken (agriculture, herding). Development also requires wider cultural achievement (literacy, new aspirations for children) than is dictated by the practices and values of primitive and peasant traditional societies. The point is to make successive generations different in specified ways.

Successful development of rural African communities may be regarded as cumulative change over time in the organization of production, the application of technology, and cultural practice. Local development is not a state once-and-for-all achieved; it means a process of continual income growth for a community of people whose successive generations have increased alternatives within a larger society.

I shall suggest that the case studies show the following: that the several changes required for development are not only necessary conditions for continual growth of income, but are also necessary conditions for the avoidance of serious social malaise; that there is no such thing as economically successful local development accompanied by traumatic social malaise: that the social disintegration of local communities is itself an indicator of incomplete and unsuccessful economic development.

Of the three sets of changes which comprise development—economic, technological, and cultural—only the economic has displaced indigenous practice to a significant extent in rural Africa: communities relying upon subsistence production have enlarged their commercial activities, but have not seriously begun to change otherwise (Bohannan 1959). Primitive economies are changing into peasant economies, but frequently peasant communities fail to change into modern communities. To earn cash by selling labour or crops is much less difficult than to learn modern farming techniques, English or French, double entry book-keeping, and to prepare one's children for a different life.

Community malaise is caused by partial change which is not meaningful to persons in terms of their traditional culture (Frankel 1955); persons who in the recently expanded pursuit of commercial income must give up activities which are integrative to traditional social organization (Steiner 1957), and who have lost the material, emotional, and social security given by the primary ties of traditional economy and society, without acquiring a much higher income, or substitute sources of gratification from commitment to modern economic and cultural activities (Fromm 1941; 1955; Polanyi 1944). They have neither unlearned the traditional culture which accompanied subsistence economy, nor are they learning the new culture which accompanies money, commerce, machinery and literacy.[4]

"What is required is that the emergent individual find in the New Society some of what he has lost from the old. This requires . . . that the individual be given those opportunities whereby he can re-establish some communion with his surroundings, find a status in his new position as a wage earner. . . . Social policy has, therefore, to assure that the individual in losing both the benefits and the burdens of the old society acquire no weightier burdens and at least as many benefits as he had in his previous station" (Okigbo 1956).

It is too little change, not too much, which causes personal malaise and community disintegration. It is change from subsistence production to production for sale without further change in technology and culture which dissolves traditional community organization without introducing new forms of integration. Newly acquired dependence on production for sale divorces the economy from traditional society: labour and land allocation, work arrangement, and the choice of the goods to be produced must now be organized in accordance with market criteria rather than

---

[4] To suggest that primitive economy and society provide material and psychological security is to risk being accused of ethnic nostalgia—the modern equivalent of belief in the noble savage. Frequently in primitive societies, material life is poor and physical life is nasty and short: poverty, disease, death, and pain are the common lot. But social life is meaningful, and social relationships immediate and crucial to one's well-being. Undoubtedly, the facts of illiteracy and of isolation contribute to the intensity and the inwardness of personal relations within community life.

as expressions of traditional social obligations (Dalton 1962a). This creates a peasant economy but not a developing community.

That enlarged commercial activities are frequently unaccompanied by the technological and cultural change necessary for development leads Western observers to regard many African communities as "transitional" (Herskovits and Harwitz 1964). The increased numbers of wage labourers, commercial traders, and producers of cash crops have taken a step away from traditional subsistence economy. But "transition" suggests a temporary stage intermediate between the old society and the new. The danger is that the transition becomes semi-permanent, because there is little reason to believe that any automatic progression into the machine-using society of built-in growth and new cultural achievement is inevitable once commercial activities have become necessary to livelihood (Frankel 1955; Redfield 1953; United Nations 1954). It is here that the distinction between primitive and peasant economies is of use, and the record of case studies provides a guide to matters of analysis and policy.

But first a caution. Assessment of the success or failure of community development in rural Africa depends to some extent on expectations. Modest improvement looks like failure to those who expect quick development. In matters of socio-economic change, a reasonable time dimension is several generations: we should be concerned with initiating with the current adult generation policies of which the cumulative effects will be experienced by the next generation. To expect quicker community development is to be disappointed, because what has to develop is not simply production techniques, but organic ways of life.

UNSUCCESSFUL DEVELOPMENT

Case studies of primitive and peasant economies provide us with representative examples of unsuccessful social and economic development from which it may be possible to draw more general conclusions. We shall cite two such cases and then give a composite picture drawn from several others.

The Mambwe of Rhodesia (Watson 1958) have accommodated themselves to cash earnings by institutionalizing wage labour tours in European industry. Upon reaching the traditional age of warriors, young men go off for several years to work in mines with the firm expectation of returning to home villages to claim their rights to land and to resume traditional activities. In their absence, subsistence agriculture is carried on by women in co-operation with the remaining men. When the wage labourers return, they disburse their cash savings in ways which ease their acceptance into traditional organization (e.g., on bridewealth), with the result that traditional "tribal cohesion" is actually strengthened by the labour tour. Material income within the home villages is discernibly larger because of the labour tours, but no dynamic process of development—cultural, economic, or technological—is thus introduced into the home villages. Indeed, the practice has persisted for several generations and can continue indefinitely unless population pressure on the land becomes more intense. There is no community malaise, but neither is there community development.

The Lele of the Congo (Leopoldville) (Douglas 1958, 1962, 1963) are one of the clearest examples on record of how mutually reinforcing elements of traditional social organization and subsistence economy, together with a poor natural environment, inhibit economic and technological development. The example is all the more forceful because the Lele are aware that a neighboring tribe (the Bushong) use superior techniques and earn higher incomes than themselves (Vansina 1962).

It is easier to generalize about the reasons for unsuccessful community development than to provide a formula for success. But even the negative cases yield lessons which are suggestive for policy formulation.

A composite sequence of failure of primitive economies to develop is the following. We start with a traditional subsistence economy in which commercial exchange was either absent or negligible, or perhaps, where commerce is tainted because early commercial contact was with slave traders (Richards 1939); the traditional path to affluence was the achievement of high social status or rank which brought a stream of material receipts (Douglas 1958, 1962). Then the group is forced into commercial activities by a land shortage or some other curtailment of traditional livelihood (Gulliver 1962, 1961), this forced entrance into wage labour or cash cropping being a piecemeal change—unaccompanied by technological change, education, or other innovations. Social malaise then takes the form of violation of obligations stemming from traditional kinship and tribal affiliations. Malaise is expressed in specific stituations of conflict and strained social relations: economic activities which were socially integrative in traditional society are not carried out (e.g., reciprocal work parties to clear fields) (Steiner 1957); land becomes a marketable commodity and litigations over land rights follow in profusion (Hill 1961); Western money displaces such traditional items as bridewealth payments, injecting a commercial element into social relationships with a consequent violation of traditional norms of morality (Bohannan 1959). Young men who formerly depended on relatives to provide bridewealth in kind now provide their own bridewealth out of cash earnings, thus weakening social cohesion. Young men can buy European goods while older men of higher rank cannot (Jaspan 1953). Chiefs try to extend old prerogatives into new cash earning activities (e.g., Liberian chiefs who earn 10 cents per head for recruited labourers sent to rubber plantations), arousing a sense of injustice among the commoners and the feeling that they are being exploited because the chief's new monetary prerogatives or commercial advantages are not matched by commensurate duties and obligations towards the community (Cole 1962; Jaspan 1953).[5]

The lesson to be learned is that undirected piecemeal change in primitive societies is often unsuccessful, economically and socially (Dalton 1962); that merely enlarging cash earning activities while little else is changing causes social disruption which is not ameliorated by the large increases in income, improvement of educational and health services, and the learning of new skills and values which are necessary for sustained community develop-

[5] In traditional societies the material prerogatives of political and lineage leadership—allocation of unused land, receipts of first fruits, tithes, *corvée* labour, fines, and fees—were matched by material obligations of chiefs and leaders to provide emergency subsistence to the unfortunate, reward the service of warriors, provide community feasts, defence, etc. Typically, the rank and file did not begrudge the material payments and services because the chief was merely a funnel to provide community services, and the common people identified the chief's affluence with community affluence (Little 1957; Schapera 1928; Watson 1958). However, when the leaders use their traditional power to share in new cash earnings solely to acquire purchased Western goods for themselves, a socially divisive situation is created: the commoners feel exploited, i.e., unjustly taxed.

ment. Where indigenous social and economic institutions are radically different from those of the West, we cannot expect entrance into market activities automatically to induce technological and cultural change of the necessary kinds. Case studies of unsuccessful rural change are stories of the social backwash effects of economic growth elsewhere (Myrdal 1957).

The problem of inducing successful development of primitive communities has economic, technological, social, and cultural dimensions. To some observers it is traditional social organization (e.g., kinship obligations) and cultural practice (e.g., the treatment of cattle as sacred) which present impediments to successful change (Sadie 1960); they thereby deduce the need for social and cultural change as necessary preconditions for economic and technological improvement. But social organization and cultural practice constitute intangible rules and ingrained values which are not directly amenable to deliberate change by policy measures.[6] The levers of change are primarily economic and technological. Those that are cultural consist not in undoing old practices (teaching people not to hold cattle sacred), but attracting people to new cultural values (e.g., the advantages of literacy). American, European, Japanese, and Russian experience teaches us that traditional ethnic values and social norms are not only tenacious, but that many are compatible with commercial organization and machine technology. Those that are not will disappear in the course of development. But to induce development with the least social hardship, the point surely is to attract people to the new ways; and if the attractions are sufficiently strong, those features of traditional society and culture which are incompatible with the new will be sloughed off.

"The real task is not to force change but to induce it in a manner which will be meaningful to the members of the societies it affects" (Frankel 1955).

[6] Where European political conquest and missionary activities seriously undermined indigenous social organization and culture long before economic improvement was attempted, serious social malaise ensued (Jaspan 1953; Schapera 1928).

My colleague Ronald Cohen cautions me that there is a complicated aspect of rural African development I leave out: the relations between the emerging national government and the traditional form of local government in the primitive and peasant community, and that these relations bear importantly on the receptivity of the local community to developmental schemes initiated from above.

Even in peasant economies, where commercial activities are already important and familiar, technological and economic innovations are sometimes resisted because past experience has taught a community to be suspicious of governmental actions on their behalf. Where traditionally government has been a tax gatherer and little else, local communities come to regard improvement schemes as measures to increase their tax bill (Cohen 1961; Cole 1962; Jaspan 1953; Linton 1952). It must be demonstrated to a community that it will be allowed to keep substantial portions of the higher income resulting from innovations. It would be well to solicit the advice, consent and active participation of community leaders in the formation of development schemes as well as in the execution of specific policies (Little 1953).

An innovation is sometimes resisted because in improving aggregate community income it would diminish the material well-being of some segment of the community. In 1951–52, Ibo women demonstrated violently against the introduction of a processing mill for palm kernels, because, by displacing hand presses, it would deprive them of their traditional right to an independent source of income (Okigbo 1956).

Community development schemes, then, must be addressed to past experience and present socio-economic organization: improvement is always change of what is; and what is, always is affected by what has been. The developers must know the people and their past. But they must know more than this.

Development programmes—especially for primitive economies —should contain several wedges for reasons that have been cogently explained by Myrdal (1953, 1957, 1960). Since sustained development requires change in technology, economic organization and cultural practices, community programmes should contain innovations in each sphere: improved techniques of agricultural production, the provision of education and vocational training, health services, access to Western commodities, and local employment opportunities for trained and educated men. A mutually reinforcing package of improvements is more likely to be economically and socially successful than any one of them introduced separately. Community innovations should be clustered, and (if possible) programmes first initiated where already commercial activities exist and production for sale is under way, and where the people have come to believe that they may retain a large share of expanded income (Fogg 1963).

Development of peasant economies is a slightly different case.[7] Here we are one step closer to what is familiar from European economic history. The problems of developing peasant communities are to increase the productivity of farming, fishing, herding, and manufacturing processes which already depend on commercial transaction, and to introduce the necessary elements of Western culture (e.g., literacy, vocational training) which will equip the next generation to undertake a variety of more productive employments. In changing the folk-culture and traditional technology, the innovations reduce cultural and economic differences between rural communities and the urban centres.[8]

[7] One must qualify because frequently "peasant" economies in the sense in which we use the term are by no means homogeneous. Within a single community one may find a range of practices: some households have become completely specialized in growing cash crops, while others grow little or none; some land may be available for purchase, while other pieces may not be, and yet others hedged about with traditional restrictions on commercial land transfers; some farmers will use modern techniques while others do not. So too with literacy and cultural matters (Cohen 1961; Vansina 1962).

[8] Fallers (1961) has correctly pointed out that traditional peasant societies in Africa are in some ways different in social organization and cultural practice from those of mediaeval Europe and contemporary Asia and Latin America. See Mair (1957, 1963) and Redfield (1953).

III OCEANIA

12 *KULA:* THE CIRCULATING EXCHANGE OF VALUABLES IN THE ARCHIPELAGOES OF EASTERN NEW GUINEA[1]

B. Malinowski

In this article is described a special system of trade, obtaining over a widespread area and possessing several features remarkable in their bearing upon questions of primitive economics, as well as throwing some new light on native mentality.

The distant and perilous trading expeditions of the South Sea islanders are a well-known feature of their tribal life. We possess especially good descriptions of such voyages in Dr. Seligman's *Melanesians.* In that book, the *Hiri,* the seasonal voyage of the Montu to the Gulf of Papua, is treated in a brilliant monograph by Captain Barton, and Dr. Seligman himself gives an excellent analysis of the trading routes between the various islands of the East End of New Guinea (Seligman 1910: Chapters VIII and XL).[2]

All these trading systems are based upon the exchange of indispensable or highly useful utilities, such as pottery, sago, canoes, dried fish, and yams, the food being sometimes imported into islands or districts which are too small or too infertile to be self-supporting. The trading system, however, which will be described in this paper, differs in this and many other respects from the usual Oceanic forms of exchange. It is based primarily upon the circulation of two articles of high value, but of no real use.

FROM B. Malinowski, "Kula; the Circulating Exchange of Valuables in the Archipelagoes of Eastern New Guinea," *Man* (1920), no. 51, pp. 97–105. Reprinted by permission of the Royal Anthropological Institute.

[1] Some results of the Robert Mond Ethnological Research work in British New Guinea.

[2] For the trading system of the Mailu, a tribe living midway between Port Moresby and the East End of New Guinea, Malinowski (1915).

These are armshells made of the *Conus millepunctatus,* and necklets of red shell-discs, both intended for ornaments but hardly ever used, even for this purpose. These two articles travel, in a manner to be described later in detail, on a circular route which covers many miles and extends over many islands. On this circuit, the necklaces travel in the direction of the clock hands and the armshells in the opposite direction. Both articles never stop for any length of time in the hands of any owner; they constantly move, constantly meeting and being exchanged.

This trading system, the *Kula,* embraces, with its ramifications, not only the islands off the East End of New Guinea, but also the Lousiades, Woodlark Island, the Loughlans, the Trobriand Archipelago and the d'Entrecasteaux Group. It touches the continent of New Guinea and extends its indirect influence over several outlying districts, such as Sud-Est Island, Rossell Island, and stretches of the northern and southern coast of the mainland.

A glance at the map will show the enormous geographical extent of the trading system, and the statement may here be anticipated that the *Kula* looms paramount in the tribal life of all the peoples, who participate in it. These peoples belong to that branch of the Papuo-Melanesians whom Dr. Seligman calls the Massim, and whom he has characterised in the above-mentioned work (Seligman 1910: Introduction and Chapters XXXIII–LV). Some of them, living on big islands, have a very highly developed agriculture, and they harvest each year a crop amply sufficient for their needs and with a good deal to spare. Such are the natives of Woodlark Islands, of the Trobriands, of the d'Entrecasteaux Group. Others, again, who live on very small islands, like the volcanic Amphlett Rocks, Wari (Teste Island), Tubetube (Engineer Group), and some of the Marshall Bennett Islands, are not self-supporting as far as food goes. They are, on the other hand, specialised in certain industries, notably pottery and canoe-building, and they are monopolists in intermediary trade. Thus it is evident that exchange of goods had to occur between them. The important point about it, however, is that with them, and notably according to their own ideas, the exchange of utilities is a subsidiary trade, carried on as an incident in the *Kula.*

The *Kula* has been called above "a form of trade." The usual a priori notion of savage trade would be that of an exchange of indispensable, or, at least, useful things, done under pressure of need by direct barter, or casual give and take of presents, without much ceremony and regulation. Such a conception would almost reverse all the essential features of the *Kula*. Thus, first, the objects of exchange—the armshells and strings of shell-discs —are not "utilities" in any sense of the word; as said above, they are hardly ever used as ornaments, for which purpose they could serve. Nevertheless, they are extremely highly valued; nowadays a native will give up to £20 for a good article, and in olden days their value was an equivalent of this sum, if we take as a common measure such utilities as basketfuls of yams, pigs, and other such commodities. Secondly, the exchange, far from being casual or surreptitious, is carried on according to very definite and very complex rules. Thus it cannot be performed between members of these tribes taken at random. A firm and lifelong relationship is always established between any participant in the *Kula,* and a number of other men, some of whom belong to his own community, and others to oversea communities. Such men call one another *karayta'u* ("partner," as we shall designate them), and they are under mutual obligations to trade with each other, to offer protection, hospitality, and assistance whenever needed.[3]

Let us imagine that we look at the whole system from one definite point, choosing the large village of Sinaketa in the Trobriand Islands. An old chief in that village would have, say, some hundred partners southwards, and about as many again to the north and east, while a young commoner would have only a few on both sides. It must be remembered that not all men in a village take part in the *Kula,* and some villages are out of it altogether.

Now another definite rule is that the armshells must always be traded to the south, and the necklets of shell-beads to the north. The word "traded" is, of course, only a rough approximation. Let us suppose that I, a Sinaketa man, am in possession of a pair of big armshells. An oversea expedition from Dobu in the

[3] *Karayta'u* is the word for "partner" in the language of Kiriwina, in the Trobriand Islands. All the terminology in this paper will be given in the language of the Trobriands, from which district the *Kula* has been studied.

d'Entrecasteaux Archipelago, arrives at my village. Blowing a conch shell, I take my armshell pair and I offer it to my overseas partner, with some such words, "This is a *vaga* (initial gift)— in due time, thou returnest to me a big *soulava* (necklace) for it!" Next year, when I visit my partner's village, he either is in possession of an *equivalent* necklace, and this he gives to me as *yotile* (restoration gift), or he has not a necklace good enough to repay my last gift. In this case he will give me a smaller necklace—avowedly not equivalent to my gift—and will give it to me as *basi* (intermediary gift). This means that the main gift has to be repaid on a future occasion and the *basi* is given in token of good faith—but it, in turn, must be repaid by me in the meantime by a gift of small armshells. The final gift, which will be given to me to clinch the whole transaction, would be then called *kudu* (equivalent gift) in contrast to *basi*.

This does not exhaust the subtleties and distinctions of *Kula* gifts. If I, an inhabitant of Sinaketa, happen to be in possession of a pair of armshells more than usually good, the fame of it spreads. It must be noted that each one of the first-class armshells and necklaces has a personal name and a history of its own, and as they all circulate around the big ring of the *Kula*, they are all well-known, and their appearance in a given district always creates a sensation. Now all my partners—whether from overseas or from within the district—compete for the favour of receiving this particular article of mine, and those who are specially keen try to obtain it by giving me *pokala* (offerings) and *kaributu* (solicitory gifts). The former (*pokala*) consists, as a rule, of pigs—especially fine bananas and yams or taro; the latter (*kaributu*) are of greater value: the valuable "ceremonial" axe blades (called *beku*) or lime-spoons of whale's bone are given. There are further complications as to the repayment of these solicitory gifts, into which we cannot enter here, and the *termini technici* of the transactions are by no means exhausted by the words so far given.

But this is sufficient to make clear that the *Kula* involves a complicated system of gifts and countergifts, in which the social side (partnership), as well as the rules of give and take, are definitely established and regulated by custom. It must also be emphasized that all these natives, and more especially the Trobrianders, have both a word for, and a clear idea of, barter (*gimwali*), and that they are fully aware of the difference between the transactions at the *Kula* and common barter. The *Kula* involves the elements of trust and of a sort of commercial honour, as the equivalence between gift and countergift cannot be strictly enforced. As in many other native transactions, the main corrective force is supplied by the deeply engrained idea that liberality is the most important and the most honourable virtue, whereas meanness brings shame and opprobrium upon the miser. This, of course, does not completely exclude many squabbles, deep resentments and even feuds over real or imaginary grievances in the *Kula* exchange.

As said already, the armshells and shell-strings always travel in their own respective directions on the ring, and they are never, under any circumstances, traded back in the wrong direction. Also they never stop. It seems almost incredible at first, but it is the fact, nevertheless, that no one ever keeps any of the *Kula* valuables for any length of time. Indeed, in the whole of the Trobriands there are perhaps only one or two specially fine armshells and shell necklaces permanently owned as heirlooms, and these are set apart as a special class, and are once and for all out of the *Kula*. "Ownership," therefore, in *Kula* is quite a special economic relation. A man who is in the *Kula* never keeps any article for longer than, say, a year or two. Even this exposes him to the reproach of being niggardly, and certain districts have the bad reputation of being "slow" and "hard" in the *Kula*. On the other hand, each man has an enormous number of articles passing through his hands during his lifetime, of which he enjoys a temporary possession, and which he keeps in trust for a time. This possession hardly ever makes him use the articles, and he remains under the obligation soon again to hand them on to one of his partners. But the temporary ownership allows him to draw a great deal of renown, to exhibit his article, to tell how he obtained it and to plan to whom he is going to give it. And all this forms one of the favourite subjects of tribal conversation and gossip, in which the feats and the glory in *Kula* of chiefs or commoners are constantly discussed and rediscussed.

But the tradition of the *Kula* is not limited to the recounting of recent or historical exploits. There is a rich mythology of the *Kula*, in which stories are told about far-off times when mythical ancestors sailed on distant and daring expeditions. Owing to their magical knowledge—how they came to it no one knows distinctly —they were able to escape dangers, to conquer their enemies, to surmount obstacles, and by their feats they established many a precedent which is now closely followed by tribal custom. But their importance for their descendants lies mainly in the fact that they handed on their magic, and this made the *Kula* possible for the following generation.

The belief in the efficiency of magic dominates the *Kula,* as it does ever so many other tribal activities of the natives. Magical rites must be performed over the seagoing canoe, when it is built, in order to make it swift, steady, and safe; also magic is done over a canoe to make it lucky in the *Kula.* Another system of magical rites is done in order to avert the dangers of sailing. The third system of magic connected with overseas expeditions is the *mwasila* or the *Kula* magic proper. This system consists in numerous rites and spells, all of which act directly on the mind (*nanola*) of one's partner and make him soft, somewhat unsteady in mind, and eager to give *Kula* gifts.

In order to form a better idea of how the magic is woven into the many practical activities incidental to the *Kula,* it will be necessary to give a concrete outline of a trading expedition, and thus to supplement the set of rules and features enumerated above somewhat *in abstracto.* It will be best again to adopt a definite starting-point in our geographical orientation and to imagine ourselves again in Sinaketa, one of the main industrial and trading centres of the Trobriands.

Glancing at the map we see a number of circles, each of which represents a certain sociological unit which we shall call a *Kula* community. A *Kula* community consists of a village or a number of villages, who go out together on big overseas expeditions and who act as a body in the *Kula* transactions—perform their magic in common, have common leaders, and have the same outer and inner social sphere, within which they exchange their valuables. The *Kula* consists, therefore, first of the small, inner trade within a *Kula* community or contiguous communities, and secondly of the big overseas expeditions in which the annual exchange of articles takes place between two communities, divided by sea. In the first, there is a chronic, permanent trickling of articles from one village to another, and even within the village. In the second, a whole lot of valuables, amount-

SKETCH MAP OF *KULA*

showing the area, trade routes and communities of the circular exchange. The dotted circles represent the *Kula* communities, the dotted squares represent the districts indirectly affected by the *Kula.*

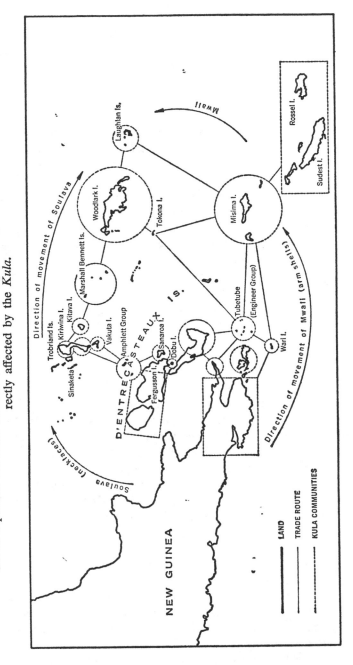

ing to over a thousand articles at a time, are exchanged in one enormous transaction, or, more correctly in ever so many transactions taking place simultaneously.

I will describe the normal and typical course of such a big overseas expedition as it takes place between the *Kula* community of Sinaketa with its surrounding villages and the Amphlett Group and Dobu districts to the south. Such an expedition would take place about once a year, but only every second or third year would it be carried out on a really big scale. On such occasions big preparations take place. First of all the large seagoing canoes must be made ready. As a rule a few new ones have to be built to replace those worn out and unseaworthy, and then those in good order have to be overhauled and re-decorated. The building of a canoe, which cannot be described in this place in detail, is a big tribal affair. A series of magical rites have to be performed by a specialist or specialists, who are versed in the art of constructing and carving—the magic being considered indispensable to both arts. The magical rites aim successively at the expulsion of a wood spirit (*tokway*) from the tree to be felled; at the imparting of stability, swiftness and good luck to the canoe, and at the counteracting of evil influences cast on the canoe by direct sorcery or by the un-witting breaking of taboos. The rites—some performed in a simple manner by a magician alone, some ceremonially with the attendance of the whole community—are carried out in a series, associated with the various activities, inaugurating some, accompanying others. The magic is always interwoven with the technical operations and is to the native mind absolutely indispensable to the successful accomplishment of the task. Another important feature of canoe-building is the communal labour, which is always used at certain stages and for certain tasks, as for sail-making, the piecing together and lashing, caulking and painting of the canoe. The owner of the canoe has to pay for the work by gifts of *vaygu'a* (valuables) and distribution of food, and the expert magician-constructor directs the work.

The building and overhauling of canoes lasts for about six months, for it is done slowly in the intervals of other work. As the expeditions take place usually in February–April, the canoe work begins some time in August or September. When all the canoes are ready, there is a big gathering from the whole district, and the canoes are launched ceremonially, and races and general festivities take place. Some days later all the canoes start on a preliminary trip to the neighbouring districts, that is, in the case of Sinaketa, to the northern half of the island, to Kiriwina proper. There is a custom, called *kabigidoya,* of ceremonially presenting a canoe, and the owner receives gifts, which form part of the subsidiary trade, to be used on the big expedition. More subsidiary trade is obtained by barter (*gimwali*), especially from the manufacturing districts on the north shore of the lagoon. Wooden combs, fibre armlets, baskets, mussel shells, and other articles, abundant here and rare in the Amphletts and in Dobu, are thus acquired in great quantities. On this preliminary trip the Sinaketans also obtain a number of armshells from Kiriwina by inland *Kula,* and with their wealth thus replenished return to Sinaketa.

A period of taboos and initial magic now obtains as the immediate preliminary to main departure. The owner of each canoe is subject to the most stringent restrictions—mainly referring to sexual relations—and he also performs all the magic. On an evening he goes into a garden and uttering a spell he plucks a spray of aromatic mint, which he brings home. Then he prepares some cocoanut oil, anoints the mint with it, and, putting some oil and the mint into a vessel, he medicates it all with another spell. The vessel—in olden days a contrivance of roasted and thus toughened banana leaves, now a small glass bottle—is then attached to the prow of the canoe. This magic aims at the softening of the Dobuan's mind, so that he may be unable to resist any appeal made to his generosity. This aim is explicitly stated by all natives, and an analysis of the magical spells reveals it also as their leading idea. But the magic is full of mythological allusions, of side ideas and of references to animals and birds, and it contains interesting metaphorical circumlocutions of the aims to be attained.

Other spells, all expressing more or less the same ideas, are used in the magical rite performed over a special bundle of valuables and goods, called *lilava,* which is placed in the centre of the canoe and must not be opened before the arrival in Dobu; also in the rite over the cocoanut leaves lining the canoe. Again, in the rite over the provisions of food taken on the journey, the main aim is to make it last long.

After the rites are finished and the expedition is ready, many people from the neighbouring villages assemble, the departing chiefs enjoin chastity to their wives and warn all the neighbouring male villagers to keep off Sinaketa, and prognosticate a speedy arrival with much *vaygu'a* (valuables). They are assured that they can depart in safety as no one will visit their village surreptitiously. Indeed, during their absence, the village should be kept tabooed, and if a man is found loitering about the place, especially at night, he is likely to be punished (by sorcery, as a rule) on the chief's return.

The fleet now sails south; but the first stage of the journey is short, as the natives halt on a sandbank some ten miles off Sinaketa, where they have a ceremonial distribution of food, which imposes an obligation on the *usagelu* (members of the crews) towards the *toliwaga* (owners of canoes) to carry out the expedition even in the face of contrary winds and bad weather. Next morning several rites are performed over the canoes to undo all evil magic and to make them swift and steady.

The open sea now lies before the fleet with the high, distant peaks of the d'Entrecasteaux mountains floating above the haze. In very clear weather the nearer Amphletts can be seen—small steep rocks, scattered over the horizon, misty, but more material against the faint blue of the distant land. These far-off views must have inspired generation after generation of Kiriwinian sailors with zest for adventure, wonder and desire to see the much-praised marvels of foreign lands, with awe and with superstitious fear. Mixed with it all—associated in the native mind with the allurement of the distant *koya* (mountains)—there was the ambition to return with plenty of *vaygu'a*. In myths, in traditional legends, in real stories and in songs, *Kula* expeditions were and are described and praised and there is a definite complex of *Kula* tradition and mythology, governed perhaps by two dominating emotions: the desire to obtain the *vaygu'a* and the dread of the dangers to be encountered.

These latter are real enough, as the wind in the N.W. season, when the expeditions take place, is changeable, and violent squalls obtain, and the sea is full of reefs and sandbanks. But the natives have added to that from their store of myth-making imagination, and have surrounded the real dangers with a fabric of imaginary perils and modes of escape. There exist for them big, live stones, lying in wait for a canoe—they jump up when they see one, and smash it to pieces and destroy the sailors. There is a giant octopus, which will take hold of a canoe and never let it go, unless a sacrifice is made of a small boy, adorned and anointed, who is thrown overboard to the *kwita* (octopus). There may come a big rain, which smashes and submerges the canoe. But the greatest danger comes from flying witches, who, whenever they hear that a canoe is drowning—and they possess the capacity of hearing it at enormous distances—assemble and wait till the men are in the water, and then fall on them. There is a deep belief that shipwreck in itself would not be fatal— the men would float ashore, carried by the *débris* of the canoe— unless the flying witches were to attack them. A whole cycle of beliefs centres round this main idea, and there is a system of rites which are always practised in shipwreck, and which, if carried out properly, would ensure safety to those shipwrecked.

One part of this magic is directed towards the flying witches; it blinds and bewilders them and they cannot attack the men in the waves. Another part is chanted by the *toliwaga* (master of the canoe) whilst he and his companions are drifting, suspended on the float of the outrigger, and it attracts a giant fish (*iraveaka*). This beneficent animal arrives and pulls the float and the men ashore. This is not the end; the shipwrecked party have to go through a series of ceremonies intended to make them immune from the flying witches, and only after that may they return to their village. This interesting account of a potential ship-wreck and the magical rites referring to it I have obtained from several sets of independent informants. There are also a few definite traditions about actual salvage from death by drowning, through the carrying out of the magic.

The normal expedition, however, sails in one day with good following wind, or in several days if the wind is weak or shifting, and arrives at its first stage, in the Amphletts. Some exchange is done here, as well as on the further two intermediate halts in Tewara and Sanaroa and the concomitant magic has to be performed here. There are also several mythologically famed spots in these islands: some rocks from which magic originated—how, the myths do not relate distinctly—and other rocks, formerly human beings, who travelled to their present

sites from very far, and to whom the natives offer *pokala*
(offerings in order to have a propitious *Kula*). The island of
Gumasila in the Amphletts, that of Tewara, and places on
Fergusson Island, are important mythological centres.

But the main aim of the expedition is the district of Dobu,
more especially the north-east corner of Fergusson Island, where
on the flat and fertile foreshore, among groves of cocoanut,
betel-palms, mangoes, and bread-fruit trees, there stretch for
miles the populous settlements of Tautauna, Bwayowa, Deidei,
and Begasi.

Before approaching them, the whole fleet stops on a beach
called *Sarubwoyna,* not far away from the two rocks, *Atu'a'ine*
and *Aturamo'a,* which are the most important, perhaps, of the
rocks to whom *pokala* offering is given. Here the final magic
is performed. All the *usagelu* (members of the crew) go ashore
and collect leaves for magic. Spells are pronounced over them by
the members of each canoe and everyone washes with sea-water
and dries his skin with the medicated leaves. Then spells are
uttered over cocoanut oil, red paint, and aromatic herbs—and
the natives anoint and adorn themselves, the magic making them
beautiful and irresistible. A spell is uttered into the mouth of a
conchshell and the canoes get under way. The last distance, a
few miles only, is traversed by paddling; and powerful spells
are uttered by several men in each canoe, who recite them
simultaneously, and the medicated conchshell is blown. These
spells have to "shake the mountain"—that is, to produce a deep
agitation in the minds of the Dobuans, and impress them with
the arrival of the newcomers. One more important rite is uttered
to prevent the Dobuans from becoming fierce and angry and to
suppress any attempt at attacking the visitors.

Finally the party arrive, and it is the custom for the Dobuans
to meet them with *soulava* (shell-disc necklaces) in their hands.
The conchshells are blown and the necklaces are ceremonially
offered by the Dobuans to the newcomers. Then the party go
ashore, every man going to the house of his main partner. There
the visitors receive gifts of food, and they again give some of
their minor trade as *pari* (visitors' gifts) to the Dobuans. Then,
during a several days' stay, many more *soulava* are given to the
visitors. Often it is necessary for a Kiriwinian to woo his partner
by gifts, solicitations, and magical rites, transparently performed,

if the latter possesses a specially good and desirable article. All the transactions are carried out according to the rules set forth above.

Side by side with the *Kula,* the subsidiary trade goes on, the visitors acquiring a great number of articles of minor value, but of great utility, some of them unprocurable in Kiriwina, as, for instance, rattan, fibre belts, cassowary feathers, certain kinds of spear wood, obsidian, red ochre, and many other articles. This subsidiary trade is carried on by means of gifts and counter-gifts with one's own partners; by means of barter (*gimwali*) with other people; whereas certain articles are procured directly. Among the latter, the most important is the Spondylus shell, fished by Sinaketans in the lagoon of Sanaroa, again under the observance of many taboos, and with the aid of magic, private and collective, simple and ceremonial. The shell called *kaloma* is, on their return home, worked out into the red shell-discs, which serve for making the *Soulava* necklaces.

All the transactions in Dobu concluded, the party receive their parting gifts (*talo'i*) and sail back, doing the spondylus fishing just mentioned in Sanaroa, trading for pots with the Amphletts, and receiving additional *Kula* gifts and *talo'i* (parting gifts) in all the places where they go ashore on their return journey.

In due time, after a year or so, the Dobuans will make their return expedition to Sinaketa, with exactly the same ceremonial, magic, and sociology. On this expedition they will receive some armshells in exchange for the necklets previously given, and others, as advance gifts towards the next *Kula* transaction.

The *Kula* trade consists of a series of such periodical overseas expeditions, which link together the various island groups, and annually bring over big quantities of *vaygu'a* and of subsidiary trade from one district to another. The trade is used and used up, but the *vaygu'a*—the armshells and necklets—go round and round the ring.

We have here a very interesting form of tribal enterprises. In a sense they are *economic,* for the natives carry out their organised purposeful work under the stimulus of a desire for wealth, for ownership. The conception of value and the form of ownership revealed through the *Kula,* are different from those current among us, and this shows how necessary it is to apply a more detailed analysis to their economic ideas.

Again, the *Kula* presents a type of intertribal relationship of unprecedented magnitude, the standing partnership linking together thousands of people scattered over an immense area.

In this short preliminary account I have been able barely to touch upon the essentials of the *Kula*, and to give a summary account of one of its typical concrete manifestations—the expeditions from Sinaketa to Dobu. A more detailed and thorough description, which I trust will soon be forthcoming, will allow me to show many more of its important features.

13 TRIBAL ECONOMICS IN THE TROBRIANDS

Bronislaw Malinowski

II

Before we proceed to the next stage, we must pause in following the events of a Kula expedition, and consider one or two points of more general importance. I have touched in the narrative, but not dwelt upon, certain problems of the sociology of work. At the outset of the preceding chapter it was mentioned that canoe-building requires a definite organisation of work, and in fact we saw that in the course of construction, various kinds of labour were employed, and more especially towards the end, much use was made of communal labour. Again, we saw that during the launching ceremony payment was given by the owner to the expert and his helpers. These two points therefore, the organisation of labour and communal labour in particular, and the system of payment for experts' work must be here developed.

Organisation of Labour. First of all, it is important to realise that a Kiriwinian is capable of working well, efficiently, and in a continuous manner. But he must work under an effective incentive: he must be prompted by some duty imposed by tribal standards, or he must be lured by ambitions and values also dictated by custom and tradition. Gain, such as is often the stimulus for work in more civilised communities, never acts as an impulse to work under the original native conditions. It succeeds

FROM Bronislaw Malinowski, *Argonauts of the Western Pacific,* London, Routledge and Kegan Paul, Ltd., (1922), Chapter VI, Divisions II–VII, pp. 156–194. Reprinted by permission of the English publisher, Routledge and Kegan Paul, Ltd., and of the American publisher, E. P. Dutton.

very badly, therefore, when a white man tries to use this incentive to make a native work.

This is the reason why the traditional view of the lazy and indolent native is not only a constant refrain of the average white settler, but finds its way into good books of travel, and even serious ethnographic records. With us, labour is, or was till fairly recently, a commodity sold as any other, in the open market. A man accustomed to think in terms of current economic theory will naturally apply the conceptions of supply and demand to labour, and he applies them therefore to native labour. The untrained person does the same, though in less sophisticated terms, and as they see that the native will not work well for the white man, even if tempted by considerable payment and treated fairly well, they conclude that his capacity for labour is very small. This error is due to the same cause which lies at the bottom of all our misconceptions about people of different cultures. If you remove a man from his social milieu, you *eo ipso* deprive him of almost all his stimuli to moral steadfastness and economic efficiency and even of interest in life. If then you measure him by moral, legal, or economic standards, also essentially foreign to him, you cannot but obtain a caricature in your estimate.

But the natives are not only capable of energetic, continuous and skilful work; their social conditions also make it possible for them to employ organised labour. At the beginning of Chapter IV, the sociology of canoe-building was given in outline, and now, after the details of its successive stages have been filled in, it is possible to confirm what has been said there, and draw some conclusions as to this organisation of labour. And first, as we are using this expression so often, I must insist again on the fact that the natives are capable of it, and that this contention is not a truism, as the following considerations should show. The just mentioned view of the lazy, individualistic, and selfish savage, who lives on the bounties of nature as they fall ripe and ready for him, implicitly precludes the possibility of his doing effective work, *integrated into an organised effort by social forces*. Again, the view, almost universally accepted by specialists, is that the lowest savages are in the pre-economic stage of individualistic search for food, whereas the more developed ones, such as the Trobrianders, for instance, live at the stage of isolated household economy. This view also ignores, when it does not deny explicitly, the possibility of socially organised labour.

The view generally held is that, in native communities each individual works for himself, or members of a household work so as to provide each family with the necessities of life. Of course, a canoe, even a *masawa,* could obviously be made by the members of a household, though with less efficiency and in a longer time. So that there is *a priori* nothing to foretell whether organised labour, or the unaided efforts of an individual or a small group of people should be used in the work. As a matter of fact, we have seen in canoe-building a number of men engaged in performing each a definite and difficult task, though united to one purpose. The tasks were differentiated in their sociological setting; some of the workers were actually to own the canoe; others belonged to a different community, and did it only as an act of service to the chief. Some worked in order to derive direct benefit from the use of the canoe, others were to be paid. We saw also that the work of felling, of scooping, of decorating, would in some cases be performed by various men, or it might be performed by one only. Certainly the minute tasks of lashing, caulking and painting, as well as sail-making, were done by communal labour as opposed to individual. And all these different tasks were directed towards one aim: the providing the chief or headman with the title of ownership of a canoe, and his whole community with its use.

It is clear that this differentiation of tasks, co-ordinated to a general purpose, requires a well developed social apparatus to back it up, and that on the other hand, this social mechanism must be associated and permeated with economic elements. There must be a chief, regarded as representative of a group; he must have certain formal rights and privileges, and a certain amount of authority, and also he must dispose of part of the wealth of the community. There must also be a man or men with knowledge sufficient to direct and co-ordinate the technical operations. All this is obvious. But it must be clearly set forth that the real force which binds all the people and ties them down in their tasks is obedience to custom, to tradition.

Every man knows what is expected from him, in virtue of his position, and he does it, whether it means the obtaining of a privilege, the performance of a task, or the acquiescence in a *status quo.* He knows that it always has been thus, and thus it is all around him, and thus it always must remain. The chief's authority, his privileges, the customary give and take which exist between him and the community, all that is merely, so to speak, the mechanism through which the force of tradition acts. For there is no organised physical means by which those in authority could enforce their will in a case like this. Order is kept by direct force of everybody's adhesion to custom, rules and laws, by the same psychological influences which in our society prevent a man of the world doing something which is not "the right thing." The expression "might is right" would certainly not apply to Trobriand society. "Tradition is right, and what is right *has* might"—this rather is the rule governing the social forces in Boyowa, and I dare say in almost all native communities at this stage of culture.

All the details of custom, all the magical formulæ, the whole fringe of ceremonial and rite which accompany canoe-building, all these things add weight to the social scheme of duties. The importance of magical ideas and rites as integrating forces has been indicated at the outset of this description. It is easy to see how all the appurtenances of ceremony, that is, magic, decoration, and public attendance welded together into one whole with labour, serve to put order and organisation into it.

Another point must be enlarged upon somewhat more. I have spoken of *organised labour,* and of *communal labour.* These two conceptions are not synonymous, and it is well to keep them apart. As already defined, organised labour implies the co-operation of several socially and economically different elements. It is quite another thing, however, when a number of people are engaged side by side, performing the same work, without any technical division of labour, or social differentiation of function. Thus, the whole enterprise of canoe-building is, in Kiriwina, the result of *organised labour.* But the work of some twenty to thirty men, who side by side do the lashing or caulking of the canoe, is *communal labour.* This latter form of work has a great psychological advantage. It is much more stimulating and more interesting, and it allows of emulation, and therefore of a better quality of work. For one or two men, it would require about a month to do the work which twenty to thirty men can do in a day. In certain cases, as in the pulling of the heavy log from the jungle to the village, the joining of forces is almost indispensable. True, the canoe could be scooped out in the *raybwag*, and then a few might be able to pull it along, applying some skill. But it would entail great hardships. Thus, in some cases, communal labour is of extreme importance, and in all cases it furthers the course of work considerably. Sociologically, it is important, because it implies mutual help, exchange of services, and solidarity in work within a wide range.

Communal labour is an important factor in the tribal economy of the Trobriand natives. They resort to it in the building of living-huts and storehouses, in certain forms of industrial work, and in the transport of things, especially at harvest time, when great quantities of produce have to be shifted from one village to another, often over a great distance. In fishing, when several canoes go out together and fish each for itself, then we cannot speak of communal labour. When on the other hand, they fish in one band, each canoe having an appointed task, as is sometimes done, then we have to do with organised labour. Communal labour is also based upon the duties of *urigubu*, or relatives-in-law. That is, a man's relatives-in-law have to assist him, whenever he needs their co-operation. In the case of a chief, there is an assistance on a grand scale, and whole villages will turn out. In the case of a commoner, only a few people will help. There is always a distribution of food after the work has been done, but this can hardly be considered as payment, for it is not proportional to the work each individual does.

By far the most important part communal labour has to play, is in gardening. There are as many as five different forms of communal labour in the gardens, each called by a different name, and each distinct in its sociological nature. When a chief or headman summons the members of a village community, and they agree to do their gardens communally, it is called *tamgogula*. When this is decided upon, and the time grows near for cutting the scrub for new gardens, a festive eating is held on the central place, and there all men go, and *takayva* (cut down) the scrub on the chief's plot. After that, they cut in turn the garden plots of everyone, all men working on the one plot during a day, and getting on that day food from the owner. This procedure is reproduced at each successive stage of gardening; at the fencing, planting of yams, bringing in supports, and finally, at the weeding, which is done by women. At certain stages, the gardening is often done by each one working for himself, namely at the clearing of the gardens after they are burnt, at the cleaning of the roots of yams when they begin to produce tubers, and at harvesting.

There are, as a rule, several communal feasts during the progress, and one at the end of a *tamgogula* period. Gardens are generally worked in this fashion, in years when big ceremonial dancing or some other tribal festivity is held. This usually makes the work very late, and it has then to be done quickly and energetically, and communal labour has evidently been found suitable for this purpose.

When several villages agree to work their gardens by communal labour, this is called *lubalabisa*. The two forms do not differ very much except by name, and also by the fact that, in the latter form, more than one chief or headman has to direct the process. The *lubalabisa* would only be held when there are several small villages, clustered together, as is the case in the village compounds of Sinaketa, Kavataria, Kabwaku, or Yalaka.

When a chief or headman, or man of wealth and influence summons his dependents or his relatives-in-law to work for him, the name *kabutu* is given to the proceedings. The owner has to give food to all those co-operating. A *kabutu* may be instituted for one bit of gardening, for example, a headman may invite his villagers to do his cutting for him, or his planting or his fencing. It is clear that whenever communal labour is required by one man in the construction of his house or yam store, the labour is of the *kabutu* type, and it is thus called by the natives.

The fourth form of communal labour is called *ta'ula,* and takes place whenever a number of villagers agree to do one stage of gardening in common, on the basis of reciprocity. No great or special payments take place. The same sort of communal labour extending over all stages of gardening, is called *kari'ula,* and it may be counted as the fifth form of communal labour in the gardens. Finally, a special word, *tavile'i,* is used when they wish to say that the gardens are done by individual labour, and that everyone works on his own plot. It is a rule, however, that the chief's plots, especially those of an influential chief of high rank, are always gardened by communal labour, and this latter is also used with regard to certain privileged plots, on which, in a given year, the garden magic is performed first, and with the greatest display.

Thus there is a number of distinct forms of communal labour, and they show many more interesting features which cannot be mentioned in this short outline. The communal labour used in canoe-building is obviously of the *kabutu* type. In having a canoe made, the chief is able to summon big numbers of the inhabitants of a whole district, the headman of an important village receives the assistance of his whole community, whereas a man of small importance, such as one of the smaller headmen of Sinaketa or Vakuta, would have to rely on his fellow villagers and relations-in-law. In all these cases, it would be the call of duty, laid down by custom, which would make them work. The payment would be of secondary importance, though in certain circumstances, it would be a considerable one. The distribution of food during launching forms such a payment, as we have seen in Division I of this chapter. In olden days, a meal of pigs, an abundance of betel-nut and coco-nut and sugar cane would have made a veritable feast for the natives.

Another point of importance from the economic aspect is the payment given by the chief to the builder of the canoe. The canoe of Omarakana was made, as we saw, for To'uluwa by a specialist from Kitava, who was well paid with a quantity of food, pigs and *vaygua* (native valuables). Nowadays, when the power of the chiefs is broken, when they have much less wealth than formerly to back up their position, and cannot use even the little force they ever did and when the general breaking up of custom has undermined the traditional deference and loyalty of their subjects, the production of canoes and other forms of wealth by the specialist for the chief is only a vestige of what it once was. In olden days it was, economically, one of the most important features of the Trobriand tribal life. In the construction of the canoe, which a chief in olden days would never build himself, we meet with an example of this.

Here it will be enough to say that whenever a canoe is built for a chief or headman by a builder, this has to be paid for by an initial gift of food. Then, as long as the man is at work, provisional gifts of food are given him. If he lives away from home, like the Kitavan builder on the beach of Omarakana, he is fed by the *toliwaga* and supplied with dainties such as coco-nut, betel-nut, pigs' flesh, fish, and fruits. When he works in his own home, the *toliwaga* will bring him choice food at frequent intervals, inspecting, as he does so, the progress of the work. This feeding of the worker or bringing him extra choice food is called *vakapula*. After the canoe is finished, a substantial gift is given to the master-builder during the ceremonial distribution of food. The proper amount would be a few hundred basketfuls of yams, a pig or two, bunches of betel-nut, and a great number of coco-nuts; also, a large stone blade or a pig, or a belt of red shell discs, and some smaller *vaygua* of the non-Kula type.

In Vakuta, where chieftainship is not very distinct, and the difference in wealth less great, a *toliwaga* also has to feed the workers during the time of hollowing out, preparing, and building a canoe. Then, after the caulking, some fifty basketsful are given to the builder. After the launching and trial run, this builder gives a rope, symbol of the canoe, to his wife, who, blowing the conch shell, presents the rope to the *toliwaga*. He, on the spot, gives her a bunch of betel or bananas. Next day, a considerable present of food, known as *yomelu*, is given by the chief, and then at the next harvest, another fifty or sixty basketsful of yams as *karibudaboda* or closing up gift.

I have chosen the data from two concrete cases, one noted in Kiriwina, the other in Vakuta—that is, in the district where the chief's power is greatest, and in that where there never has been more than a rudimentary distance in rank and wealth between chief and commoner. In both cases there is a payment, but in Kiriwina the payment is greater. In Vakuta, it is obviously rather an exchange of services, whereas in Kiriwina the chief maintains, as well as rewards his builder. In both cases we have the exchange of skilled services against maintenance by supply of food.

III

We shall pass now to the next ceremonial and customary performance in the succession of Kula events, to the display of a new canoe to the friends and relatives of the *toliwaga*. This custom is called *kabigidoya*. The *tasasoria* (launching and trial run) is obviously at the same time the last act of shipbuilding, and by its associated magical rite, by the foretaste of sailing, it is also one of the beginning stages of the Kula. The *kabigidoya* being a presentation of the new canoe, belongs to the series of building ceremonials; but in so far as it is a provisioning trip, it belongs to the Kula.

The canoe is manned with the usual crew, it is rigged and fitted out with all its paraphernalia, such as paddles, baler, and conch shell, and it sets out on a short trip to the beaches of the neighbouring villages. When the canoe belongs to a compound settlement like Sinaketa, then it will stop at every beach of the sister villages. The conch shell is blown, and people in the village will know "The *kabigidoya* men have arrived." The crew remains in the canoe, the *toliwaga* goes ashore, taking one paddle with him. He goes to the house of his fellow-headman, and thrusts the paddle into the frame of the house, with the words: "I offer thee thy *bisila* (pandanus streamer); take a *vaygua* (valuable), catch a pig and break the head of my new canoe." To which the local headman will answer—giving a present: "This is the *katuvisala dabala* (the breaking of the head) of thy new canoe!" This is an example of the quaint, customary wording used in the exchange of gifts, and in other ceremonial transactions. The *bisila* (pandanus streamer) is often used as a symbol for the canoe, in magical spells, in customary expressions, and in idiomatic terms of speech. Bleached pandanus streamers are tied to the mast, rigging and sail; a specially medicated strip is often attached to the prow of the canoe to give it speed, and there is also other *bisila* magic to make a district partner inclined for Kula.

The gifts given are not always up to the standard of those mentioned in the above customary phrase. The *kabigidoya*, especially from the neighbouring villages, often brings only a few mats, a few dozen coco-nuts, some betel-nut, a couple of paddles, and such articles of minor value. And even in these trifles there is not much gain from the short *kabigidoya*. For as we know, at the beginning of the Kula all the canoes of, say, Sinaketa or Kiriwina are either rebuilt or renewed. What therefore one canoe receives on its *kabigidoya* round, from all the others, will have to be more or less returned to them, when they in their turn *kabigidoya* one after the other. Soon afterwards,

however, on an appointed day, all the canoes sail together on
a visit to the other districts, and on this *kabigidoya,* they receive
as a rule much more substantial presents, and these they will
only have to return much later, after a year or two, when the
visited district will come back to them on their own *kabigidoya.*
Thus, when the canoes of Kiriwina are built and renovated for
a big Kula expedition, they will sail South along the coast, and
stop first in Olivilevi, receiving presents from the chief there,
and walking on a round of the inland villages of Luba. Then
they will proceed to the next sea village, that of Wawela,
leaving their canoes there, and going from there across to Sinaketa.
Thence they proceed still further South, to Vakuta. The villages
on the Lagoon, such as Sinaketa and Vakuta, will return these
visits, sailing North along the Western shore on the Lagoon
side. Then they stop at Tukwaukwa or Kavataria, and from there
walk inland to Kiriwina, where they receive presents.

The *kabigidoya* trips of the Vakutans and Sinaketans are
more important than those of the Northern or Eastern districts,
because they are combined with a preliminary trade, in which
the visitors replenish their stock of goods, which they will need
presently on their trip South to Dobu. The reader will remember
that Kuboma is the industrial district of the Trobriands, where
are manufactured most of the useful articles, for which these
islands are renowned in the whole of Eastern New Guinea. It
lies in the Northern half of the island, and from Kiriwina it
is only a few miles walk, but to reach it from Sinaketa or
Vakuta it is necessary to sail North. The Southern villages therefore go to Kavataria, and from there walk inland to Bwoytalu,
Luya, Yalaka, and Kadukwaykela, where they make their purchases. The inhabitants of these villages also when they hear
that the Sinaketans are anchored in Kavataria, bring their wares
to the canoes.

A brisk trade is carried on during the day or two that the
Sinaketans remain in Kavataria. The natives of Kuboma are
always eager to buy yams, as they live in an unfertile district,
and devote themselves more to industrial productions than to
gardening. And they are still more eager to acquire coco-nuts
and betel-nut, of which they have a great scarcity. They desire
besides to receive in exchange for their produce the red shell
discs manufactured in Sinaketa and Vakuta, and the turtle-

shell rings. For objects of great value, the Sinaketans would give the big clay pots which they receive directly from the Amphletts. For that they obtain different articles according to the villages with which they are exchanging. From Bwoytalu, they get the wonderfully fashioned and decorated wooden dishes of various sizes, depths, and finish, made out of either hard or soft wood; from Bwaytelu, Wabutuma, and Buduwaylaka, armlets of plaited fern fibre, and wooden combs; from Buduwaylaka, Yalaka, and Kadukwaykela, lime pots of different qualities and sizes. From the villages of Tilataula, the district North-east of Kuboma, the polished axe blades used to be acquired in olden days.

I shall not enter into the technicalities of this exchange, nor shall I give here the approximate list of prices which obtain. We shall have to follow the traded goods further on to Dobu, and there we shall see how they change hands again, and under what conditions. This will allow us to compare the prices and thus to gauge the nature of the transaction as a whole. It will be better therefore to defer all details till then.

IV

Here, however, it seems necessary to make another digression from the straight narrative of the Kula, and give an outline of the various forms of trade and exchange as we find them in the Trobriands. Indeed, the main theme of this volume is the Kula, a form of exchange, and I would be untrue to my chief principle of method, were I to give the description of one form of exchange torn out of its most intimate context; that is, were I to give an account of the Kula without giving at least a general outline of the forms of Kiriwinian payments and gifts and barter.

In Chapter II, speaking of some features of Trobriand tribal life, I was led to criticise the current views of primitive economic man. They depict him as a being indolent, independent, happy-go-lucky, yet at the same time governed exclusively by strictly rational and utilitarian motives, and logical and consistent in his behaviour. In this chapter again, in Division II, I pointed out another fallacy implied in this conception, a fallacy which declares that a savage is capable only of very simple, unorganised and unsystematic forms of labour. Another error more or less explicitly expressed in all writings on primitive economics, is that the natives possess only rudimentary forms of trade and exchange; that these forms play no essential part in the tribal life, are carried on only spasmodically and at rare intervals, and as necessity dictates.

Whether we have to deal with the wide-spread fallacy of the primitive Golden Age, characterised mainly by the absence of any distinction between *mine* and *thine;* or whether we take the more sophisticated view, which postulates stages of individual search for food, and of isolated household catering; or if we consider for the moment the numerous theories which see nothing in primitive economics but simple pursuits for the maintenance of existence—in none of these can we find reflected even a hint of the real state of affairs as found in the Trobriands; namely, that *the whole tribal life is permeated by a constant give and take;* that every ceremony, every legal and customary act is done to the accompaniment of material gift and counter gift; that wealth, given and taken, is one of the main instruments of social organisation, of the power of the chief, of the bonds of kinship, and of relationship in law.[1]

[1] I am adducing these views not for any controversial purposes, but to justify and make clear why I stress certain general features of Trobriand Economic Sociology. My contentions might run the danger of appearing as gratuitous truisms if not thus justified. The opinion that primitive humanity and savages have no individual property is an old prejudice shared by many modern writers, especially in support of communistic theories, and the so-called materialistic view of history. The "communism of savages" is a phrase very often read, and needs no special quotation. The views of individual search for food and household economy are those of Karl Bücher, and they have directly influenced all the best modern writings on Primitive Economics. Finally, the view that we have done with Primitive Economics if we have described the way in which the natives procure their food, is obviously a fundamental premise of all the naïve, evolutionary theories which construct the successive stages of economic development. This view is summarised in the following sentence: ". . . In many simple communities, the actual food quest, and operations immediately arising from it, occupy by far the greater part of the people's time and energy, leaving little opportunity for the satisfaction of any lesser needs." This sentence, quoted out of "Notes and Queries on Anthropology," p. 160, article on the "Economics of the Social Group," represents what may be called the official view of contemporary Ethnology on the subject, and in perusing the rest of the article, it can be easily seen that all the manifold economic problems, with which we are dealing in this book, have been so far more or less neglected.

These views on primitive trade, prevalent though erroneous, appear no doubt quite consistent, that is, if we grant certain premises. Now these premises seem plausible, and yet they are false, and it will be good to have a careful look at them so that we can discard them once and for all. They are based on some sort of reasoning, such as the following one: If, in tropical conditions, there is a plenty of all utilities, why trouble about exchanging them? Then, why attach any value to them? Is there any reason for striving after wealth, where everyone can have as much as he wants without much effort? Is there indeed any room for value, if this latter is the result of scarcity as well as utility, in a community, in which all the useful things are plentiful? On the other hand, in those savage communities where the necessities of life are scarce, there is obviously no possibility of accumulating them, and thus creating wealth.

Again, since, in savage communities, whether bountifully or badly provided for by nature, everyone has the same free access to all the necessities, is there any need to exchange them? Why give a basketful of fruit or vegetables, if everybody has practically the same quantity and the same means of procuring it? Why make a present of it, if it cannot be returned except in the same form?[2]

There are two main sources of error at the bottom of this faulty reasoning. The first is that the relation of the savage to material goods is a purely rational one, and that consequently, in his conditions, there is no room for wealth or value. The second erroneous assumption is that there can be no need for exchange if anyone and everyone can, by industry and skill, produce all that represents value through its quantity or its quality.

As regards the first proposition, it is not true either with re-

[2] These views had to be adduced at length, although touched upon already in Chapter II, Division IV, because they imply a serious error with regard to human nature in one of its most fundamental aspects. We can show up their fallacy on one example only, that of the Trobriand Society, but even this is enough to shatter their universal validity and show that the problem must be re-stated. The criticised views contain very general propositions, which, however, can be answered only empirically. And it is the duty of the field Ethnographer to answer and correct them. Because a statement is very general, it can none the less be a statement of empirical fact. General views must not be mixed up with hypothetical ones. The latter must be banished from field work: the former cannot receive too much attention.

gard to what may be called primary wealth, that is, food-stuffs, nor with regard to articles of luxury, which are by no means absent in Trobriand society. First as to food-stuffs, they are not merely regarded by the natives as nourishment, not merely valued because of their utility. They accumulate them not so much because they know that yams can be stored and used for a future date, but also because they like to display their possessions in food. Their yam houses are built so that the quantity of the food can be gauged, and its quality ascertained through the wide interstices between the beams. The yams are so arranged that the best specimens come to the outside and are well visible. Special varieties of yams, which grow up to two metres in length, and weigh as much as several kilograms each, are framed in wood and decorated with paint, and hung on the outside of the yam houses. That the right to display food is highly valued can be seen from the fact that in villages where a chief of high rank resides, the commoners' storehouses have to be closed up with coco-nut leaves, so as not to compete with his.

All this shows that the accumulation of food is not only the result of economic foresight, but also prompted by the desire of display and enhancement of social prestige through possession of wealth.

When I speak about ideas underlying accumulation of food-stuffs in the Trobriands, I refer to the present, actual psychology of the natives, and I must emphatically declare that I am not offering here any conjectures about the "origins" or about the "history" of the customs and their psychology, leaving this to theoretical and comparative research.

Another institution which illuminates the native ideas about food storage is the magic called *vilamalya,* performed over the crops after harvest, and at one or two other stages. This magic is intended to make the food last long. Before the storehouse is filled with yams, the magician places a special kind of heavy stone on the floor, and recites a long magical spell. On the evening of the same day, after the food houses have been filled, he spits over them with medicated ginger root, and he also performs a rite over all the roads entering into the village, and over the central place. All this will make food plentiful in that village, and will make the supplies last long. But, and this is the important point for us, this magic is conceived to act, not on the food, but on the inhabitants of the village. It makes their appetites poor, it makes them, as the natives put it, inclined to eat wild fruit of the bush, the mango and bread fruit of the village grove, and refuse to eat yams, or at least be satisfied with very little. They will boast that when this magic is performed well, half of the yams will rot away in the storehouses, and be thrown on the *wawa,* the rubbish heap at the back of the houses, to make room for the new harvest. Here again we meet the typical idea that the main aim of accumulating food is to keep it exhibited in the yam houses till it rots, and then can be replaced by a new étalage.

The filling of the storehouses involves a double display of food, and a good deal of ceremonial handling. When the tubers are taken out of the ground they are first displayed in the gardens. A shed of poles is erected, and covered with *taitu* vine, which is thrown thickly over it. In such arbours, a circle is pegged out on the ground, and within this the *taitu* (the ordinary small yams of the Trobriands which form the staple harvest) are carefully piled up into a conical heap. A great deal of care is lavished on this task, the biggest are selected, scrupulously cleaned, and put on the outside of the heap. After a fortnight or more of keeping the yams in the garden, where they are much admired by visiting parties, the owner of the garden plot summons a party of friends or relatives-in-law, and these transport them into a village. As we know already, from Chapter II, such yams will be offered to the owner's sister's husband. It is to his village that they are brought, where again they are displayed in conical heaps, placed before his yam house. Only after they have thus remained for several days—sometimes up to a fortnight—are they put into the storehouse.

Indeed, it would be enough for anyone to see how the natives handle the yams, how they admire big tubers, how they pick out freaks and sports and exhibit them, to realise that there is a deep, socially standardised sentiment centring round this staple product of their gardens. In many phases of their ceremonial life, big displays of food form the central feature. Extensive mortuary distributions called *sagali,* are, in one of their aspects, enormous exhibitions of food, connected with their re-apportionment. At harvest of the early yams (*kuvi*) there is an offering of first fruits to the memory of the recently dead. At the later, main

harvest of *taitu* (small yams), the first tubers are dug out, ceremonially brought into the village and admired by the whole community. Food contests between two villages at harvest, in olden
days often followed by actual fighting, are also one of the characteristic features which throw light on the natives' attitude towards edible wealth. In fact, one could almost speak of a "cult
of food" among these natives, in so far as food is the central
object of most of their public ceremonies.

In the preparation of food, it must be noted that many taboos
are associated with cooking, and especially with the cooking pots.
The wooden dishes on which the natives serve their food are
called *kaboma,* which means "tabooed wood." The act of eating
is as a rule strictly individual. People eat within their family
circles, and even when there is public ceremonial cooking of the
taro pudding (*mona*) in the big clay pots, especially tabooed
for this purpose, they do not eat in one body, but in small groups.
A clay pot is carried into the different parts of the village, and
men from that part squat round it and eat, followed afterwards
by the women. Sometimes again the pudding is taken out, placed
on wooden dishes, and eaten within the family.

I cannot enter here into the many details of what could be
called the social psychology of eating, but it is important to note
that the centre of gravity of the feast lies, not in the eating, but
in the display and ceremonial preparation of the food. When a
pig is to be killed, which is a great culinary and festive event, it
will be first carried about, and shown perhaps in one or two villages; then roasted alive, the whole village and neighbours en-
joying the spectacle and the squeals of the animal. It is then
ceremonially, and with a definite ritual, cut into pieces and distributed. But the eating of it is a casual affair; it will take place
either within a hut, or else people will just cook a piece of flesh
and eat it on the road, or walking about in the village. The relics
of a feast such as pigs' jaws and fish tails, however, are often
collected and displayed in houses or yam stores.[3]

The quantity of food eaten, whether in prospect or retrospect,
is what matters most. "We shall eat, and eat till we vomit," is a
stock phrase, often heard at feasts, intended to express enjoy-

[3] As a matter of fact, this custom is not so prominent in the Trobriands
as in other Massim districts and all over the Papuo-Melanesian world, cf.
for instance Seligman (1910:56).

ment of the occasion, a close parallel to the pleasure felt at the idea of stores rotting away in the yam house. All this shows that the social act of eating and the associated conviviality are not present in the minds or customs of the Trobrianders, and what is socially enjoyed is the common admiration of fine and plentiful food, and the knowledge of its abundance. Naturally, like all animals, human or otherwise, civilised or savage, the Trobrianders enjoy their eating as one of the chief pleasures of life, but this remains an individual act, and neither its performance nor the sentiments attached to it have been socialised.

It is this indirect sentiment, rooted of course in reality in the pleasures of eating, which makes for the value of food in the eyes of the natives. This value again makes accumulated food a symbol, and a vehicle of power. Hence the need for storing and displaying it. Value is not the result of utility and rarity, intellectually compounded, but is the result of a sentiment grown round things, which, through satisfying human needs, are capable of evoking emotions.

The value of manufactured objects of use must also be explained through man's emotional nature, and not by reference to his logical construction of utilitarian views. Here, however, I think that the explanation must take into account, not so much the user of these objects, as the workman who produces them. These natives are industrious, and keen workers. They do not work under the spur of necessity, or to gain their living, but on the impulse of talent and fancy, with a high sense and enjoyment of their art, which they often conceive as the result of magical inspiration. This refers especially to those who produce objects of high value, and who are always good craftsmen and are fond of their workmanship. Now these native artists have a keen appreciation of good material, and of perfection in craft. When they find a specially good piece of material it lures them on to lavish on it an excess of labour, and to produce things too good to be used, but only so much the more desirable for possession.

The careful manner of working, the perfection of craftmanship, the discrimination in material, the inexhaustible patience in giving the final touches, have been often noted by those who have seen natives at work. These observations have also come under the notice of some theoretical economists, but it is necessary to see these facts in their bearing upon the theory of value.

That is, namely, that this loving attitude towards material and work must produce a sentiment of attachment to rare materials and well-worked objects, and that this must result in their being valued. Value will be attached to rare forms of such materials as the craftsman generally uses: classes of shell which are scarce, lending themselves especially to fashioning and polishing; kinds of wood which are also rare, like ebony; and more particularly, special varieties of that stone out of which implements are made.[4]

We can now compare our results with the fallacious views on Primitive Economic Man, sketched out at the beginning of this Division. We see that value and wealth exist, in spite of abundance of things, that indeed this abundance is valued for its own sake. Great quantities are produced beyond any possible utility they could possess, out of mere love of accumulation for its own sake; food is allowed to rot, and though they have all they could desire in necessities, yet the natives want always more, to serve in its character of wealth. Again, in manufactured objects, and more especially in objects of the *vaygu'a* type (comp. Chapter III, Div. III), it is not rarity within utility which creates value, but a rarity sought out by human skill within the workable materials. In other words, not those things are valued, which being useful or even indispensable are hard to get, since all the necessities of life are within easy reach of the Trobriand Islander. But such an article is valued where the workman, having found specially fine or sportive material, has been induced to spend a disproportionate amount of labour on it. By doing so, he creates an object which is a kind of economic monstrosity, too good, too big, too frail, or too overcharged with ornament to be used, yet just because of that, highly valued.

V

Thus the first assumption is exploded, "that there is no room for wealth or value in native societies." What about the other assumption, namely, "That there is no need to exchange if anyone

---

[4] Again, in explaining value, I do not wish to trace its possible origins, but I try simply to show what are the actual and observable elements into which the natives' attitude towards the object valued can be analysed.

can by industry and skill, produce all that represents value through its quantity or its quality?" This assumption is confuted by realising a fundamental fact of native usage and psychology: the love of give and take for its own sake; the active enjoyment in possession of wealth, through handing it over.

In studying any sociological questions in the Trobriands, in describing the ceremonial side of tribal life, or religion and magic, we constantly meet with this give and take, with exchange of gifts and payments. I had occasion several times to mention this general feature, and in the short outline of the Trobriand sociology in Chapter II, I gave some examples of it. Even a walk across the island, such as we imagined in that chapter, would reveal to an open-eyed Ethnographer this economic truth. He would see visiting parties—women carrying big food baskets on their head, men with loads on their shoulders—and on inquiring he would learn that these were gifts to be presented under one of the many names they bear, in fulfilment of some social obligation. Offerings of first fruits are given to the chief or to relatives-in-law, when the mango or bread fruit or sugar cane are ripe. Big quantities of sugar cane being borne to a chief, carried by some twenty to thirty men running along the road, produce the impressions of a tropical Birnam Wood moving through the jungle. At harvest time all the roads are full of big parties of men carrying food, or returning with empty baskets. From the far North of Kiriwina a party will have to run for some twelve miles to the creek of Tukwa'ukwa, get into canoes, punt for miles along the shallow Lagoon, and have another good walk inland from Sinaketa; and all this is in order to fill the yam house of a man who could do it quite well for himself, if it were not that he is under obligation to give all the harvest to his sister's husband! Displays of gifts associated with marriage, with *sagali* (food distributions), with payments for magic, all these are some of the most picturesque characteristics of the Trobriand garden, road, and village, and must impress themselves upon even a superficial observer.

The second fallacy, that man keeps all he needs and never spontaneously gives it away, must therefore be completely discarded. Not that the natives do not possess a strongly retentive tendency. To imagine that they differ from other human beings in this, would be to fall out of one fallacy into the opposite one also already mentioned, namely that there is a sort of primitive communism among the natives. On the contrary, just because they think so much of giving, the distinction between mine and thine is not obliterated but enhanced; for the presents are by no means given haphazardly, but practically always in fulfilment of definite obligations, and with a great deal of formal punctilio. The very fundamental motive of giving, the vanity of a display of possession and power, *a limine* rules out any assumption of communistic tendencies or institutions. Not in all cases, but in many of them, the handing over of wealth is the expression of the superiority of the giver over the recipient. In others, it represents subordination to a chief, or a kinship relation or relationship-in-law. And it is important to realise that in almost all forms of exchange in the Trobriands, there is not even a trace of gain, nor is there any reason for looking at it from the purely utilitarian and economic standpoint, since there is no enhancement of mutual utility through the exchange.

Thus, it is quite a usual thing in the Trobriands for a type of transaction to take place in which A gives twenty baskets of yams to B, receiving for it a small polished blade, only to have the whole transaction reversed in a few weeks' time. Again, at a certain stage of mortuary ritual, a present of valuables is given, and on the same day later on, the identical articles are returned to the giver. Cases like that described in the *kabigidoya* custom (Div. III of this chapter), where each owner of a new canoe made a round of all the others, each thus giving away again what he receives, are typical. In the *wasi*—exchange of fish for yams, to be described presently—through a practically useless gift, a burdensome obligation is imposed, and one might speak of an increase of burdens rather than an increase of utilities.

The view that the native can live in a state of individual search for food, or catering for his own household only, in isolation from any interchange of goods, implies a calculating, cold egotism, the possibility of enjoyment by man of utilities for their sake. This view, and all the previously criticised assumptions, ignore the fundamental human impulse to display, to share, to bestow. They ignore the deep tendency to create social ties through exchange of gifts. Apart from any consideration as to whether the gifts are necessary or even useful, giving for the sake of giving is one of the most important features of Trobriand sociology, and, from its very general and fundamental nature, I submit that it is a universal feature of all primitive societies.

I have dwelt at length on economic facts which on the surface are not directly connected with the Kula. But if we realise that in these facts we may be able to read the native's attitude towards wealth and value, their importance for the main theme becomes obvious. The Kula is the highest and the most dramatic expression of the native's conception of value, and if we want to understand all the customs and actions of the Kula in their real bearings we must, first and foremost, grasp the psychology that lies at its basis.

VI

I have on purpose spoken of forms of exchange, of gifts and counter-gifts, rather than of barter or trade, because, although there exist forms of barter pure and simple, there are so many transitions and gradations between that and simple gift, that it is impossible to draw any fixed line between trade on the one hand, and exchange of gifts on the other. Indeed, the drawing of any lines to suit our own terminology and our own distinctions is contrary to sound method. In order to deal with these facts correctly it is necessary to give a complete survey of all forms of payment or present. In this survey there will be at one end the extreme case of pure gift, that is an offering for which nothing is given in return. Then, through many customary forms of gift or payment, partially or conditionally returned, which shade into each other, there come forms of exchange, where more or less strict equivalence is observed, arriving finally at real barter. In the following survey I shall roughly classify each transaction according to the principle of its equivalence.

Such tabularised accounts cannot give the same clear vision of facts as a concrete description might do, and they even produce the impression of artificiality, but, and this must be emphatically stated, I shall not introduce here artificial categories, foreign to the native mind. Nothing is so misleading in ethnographic accounts as the description of facts of native civilisations in terms of our own. This, however, shall not be done here. The principles of arrangement, although quite beyond the comprehension of the natives, are nevertheless contained in their social organisation, customs, and even in their linguistic terminology. This latter always affords the simplest and surest means of approach towards the understanding of native distinctions and classifications. But it also must be remembered that, though important as a clue to native ideas, the knowledge of terminology is not a miraculous short-cut into the native's mind. As a matter of fact, there exist many salient and extremely important features of Trobriand sociology and social psychology, which are not covered by any term, whereas their language distinguishes subdivisions and subtleties which are quite irrelevant with regard to actual conditions. Thus, a survey of terminology must always be supplemented by a direct analysis of ethnographic fact and inquiry into the native's ideas, that is, by collecting a body of opinions, typical expressions, and customary phrases by direct cross-questioning. The most conclusive and deepest insight, however, must always be obtained by a study of behaviour, by analysis of ethnographic custom and concrete cases of traditional rules.

LIST OF GIFTS, PAYMENTS, AND COMMERCIAL TRANSACTIONS

1. *Pure Gifts.* By this, as just mentioned, we understand an act, in which an individual gives an object or renders a service without expecting or getting any return. This is not a type of transaction very frequently met in Trobriand tribal life. It must be remembered that accidental or spontaneous gifts, such as alms or charities, do not exist, since everybody in need would be maintained by his or her family. Again, there are so many well-defined economic obligations, connected with kinship and relationship-in-law, that anyone wanting a thing or a service would know where to go and ask for it. And then, of course, it would not be a free gift, but one imposed by some social obligation. Moreover, since gifts in the Trobriands are conceived as definite acts with a social meaning, rather than transmissions of objects, it results that where social duties do not directly impose them, gifts are very rare.

The most important type of free gift are the presents characteristic of relations between husband and wife,[5] and parents and children. Among the Trobrianders, husband and wife own their things separately. There are man's and woman's possessions, and each of the two partners has a special part of the household goods under control. When one of them dies, his or her relations inherit the things. But though the possessions are not joint, they very often give presents to one another, more especially a husband to his wife.

As to the parents' gifts to the children, it is clear that in a matrilineal society, where the mother is the nearest of kin to her children in a sense quite different to that in our society, they share in and inherit from her all her possessions. It is more remarkable that the father, who, according to native belief and law, is only the mother's husband, and not the kinsman of the children, is the only relation from whom free gifts are expected.[6] The father will give freely of his valuables to a son, and he will transmit to him his relationships in the Kula, according to the definite rules by which it is done (see Chapter XI, Division II). Also, one of the most valuable and valued possessions, the knowledge of magic, is handed over willingly, and free of any counter-gift, from father to son. The ownership of trees in the village grove and ownership in garden plots is ceded by the father to his son during the lifetime of the former. At his death, it often has to be returned to the man's rightful heirs, that is, his sister's children. All the objects of use embraced by the term *gugua* will be shared with him as a matter of course by a man's children. Also, any special luxuries in food, or such things as betel-nut or tobacco, he will share with his children as well as with his wife. In all such small articles of indulgence,

[5] [Malinowski (1926:40–41) changed his mind about "pure gifts": "When . . . I describe a category of offerings as 'Pure Gifts' and place under this heading the gifts of husband to wife and of father to children, I am obviously committing a mistake. I have fallen . . . into the error . . . of tearing the act out of its context, of not taking a sufficiently long view of the chain of transactions. In the same paragraph I have supplied, however, an implicit rectification of my mistake in stating that 'a gift given by the father to his son is said [by the natives] to be a repayment for the man's relationship to the mother' (1922:179). I have also pointed out there that the 'free gifts' to the wife are also based on the same idea." ED.]

[6] These natives have no idea of physiological fatherhood. See Chapter II, Division VI.

free distribution will also obtain between the chief or the headman and his vassals, though not in such a generous spirit, as
within the family. In fact, everyone who possesses betel-nut or
tobacco in excess of what he can actually consume on the spot,
would be expected to give it away. This very special rule, which
also happens to apply to such articles as are generally used by
white men for trade, has largely contributed to the tenacity of
the idea of the communistic native. In fact, many a man will
carefully conceal any surplus so as to avoid the obligation of
sharing it and yet escape the opprobrium attaching to meanness.

There is no comprehensive name for this class of free gifts
in native terminology. The verb "to give" (*sayki*) would simply
be used, and on inquiry as to whether there was repayment
for such a gift, the natives would directly answer that this was
a gift without repayment; *mapula* being the general term for
return gifts, and retributions, economic as well as otherwise. The
natives undoubtedly would not think of free gifts as forming one
class, as being all of the same nature. The acts of liberality on
the part of the chief, the sharing of tobacco and betel-nut by
anybody who has some to spare, would be taken as a matter of
course. Gifts by a husband to a wife are considered also as
rooted in the nature of this relationship. They have as a matter
of fact a very coarse and direct way of formulating that such
gifts are the *mapula* (payment) for matrimonial relations, a conception in harmony with the ideas underlying another type of
gift, of which I shall speak presently, that given in return for
sexual intercourse. Economically the two are entirely different,
since those of husband to wife are casual gifts within a permanent relationship, whereas the others are definite payment for
favours given on special occasions.

The most remarkable fact, however, is that the same explanation is given for the free gifts given by the father to his children;
that is to say, a gift given by a father to his son is said to be
a repayment for the man's relationship to the son's mother. According to the matrilineal set of ideas about kinship, mother and
son are one, but the father is a stranger (*tomakava*) to his son,
an expression often used when these matters are discussed. There
is no doubt, however, that the state of affairs is much more complex, for there is a very strong direct emotional attitude between
father and child. The father wants always to give things to his

child, as I have said, (compare Chapter II, Division VI), and this is very well realised by the natives themselves.

As a matter of fact, the psychology underlying these conditions is this: normally a man is emotionally attached to his wife, and has a very strong personal affection towards his children, and expresses these feelings by gifts, and more especially by trying to endow his children with as much of his wealth and position as he can. This, however, runs counter to the matrilineal principle as well as to the general rule that all gifts require repayment, and so these gifts are explained away by the natives in a manner that agrees with these rules. The above crude explanation of the natives by reference to sex payment is a document, which in a very illuminating manner shows up the conflict between the matrilineal theory and the actual sentiments of the natives, and also how necessary it is to check the explicit statements of natives, and the views contained in their terms and phraseology by direct observation of full-blooded life, in which we see man not only laying down rules and theories, but behaving under the impulse of instinct and emotion.

2. *Customary payments, re-paid irregularly, and without strict equivalence*. The most important of these are the annual payments received at harvest time by a man from his wife's brothers (cf. Chapter II, Divisions IV and V). These regular and unfailing gifts are so substantial, that they form the bulk of a man's income in food. Sociologically, they are perhaps the strongest strand in the fabric of the Trobriands tribal constitution. They entail a life-long obligation of every man to work for his kinswomen and their families. When a boy begins to garden, he does it for his mother. When his sisters grow up and marry, he works for them. If he has neither mother nor sisters, his nearest female blood relation will claim the proceeds of his labour.

The reciprocity in these gifts never amounts to their full value, but the recipient is supposed to give a valuable (*vaygu'a*) or a pig to his wife's brother from time to time. Again if he summons his wife's kinsmen to do communal work for him, according to the *kabutu* system, he pays them in food. In this case also the payments are not the full equivalent of the services rendered. Thus we see that the relationship between a man and his wife's kinsmen is full of mutual gifts and services, in which repayment, however, by the husband, is not equivalent and regular, but spasmodic and smaller in value than his own share; and even if for some reason or other it ever fails, this does not relieve the others from their obligations. In the case of a chief, the duties of his numerous relatives-in-law have to be much more stringently observed; that is, they have to give him much bigger harvest gifts, and they also have to keep pigs, and grow betel- and coco-nut palms for him. For all this, they are rewarded by correspondingly large presents of valuables, which again, how- ever, do not fully repay them for their contributions.

The tributes given by vassal village communities to a chief and usually repaid by small counter-gifts, also belong to this class. Besides these, there are the contributions given by one kinsman to another, when this latter has to carry out a mortuary distribution (*sagali*). Such contributions are sometimes, but ir- regularly and spasmodically, repaid by objects of small value.

The natives do not embrace this class under one term, but the word *urigubu,* which designates harvest gifts from the wife's brothers, stands for one of the most important conceptions of native sociology and economics. They have quite a clear idea about the many characteristics of the *urigubu* duties, which have been described here, and about their far-reaching importance. The occasional counter-gifts given by the husband to his wife's kinsmen are called *youlo.* The chief's tributes which we have put in this category are called *pokala.* The placing of these two types of payment in one category is justified both by the similar mechanism, and by the close resemblance between the *urigubu* gifts, when given to a chief, and the *pokala* received by him. There are even resemblances in the actual ceremonial, which, however, would require too much of a detailed description to be more than mentioned here. The word *pokala* is a general term for the chief's tributes, and there are several other expres- sions which cover gifts of first fruit, gifts at the main harvest, and some other sub-divisions. There are also terms describing the various counter-gifts given by a chief to those who pay him tribute, according to whether they consist of pig's flesh or yams or fruit. I am not mentioning all these native words, in order not to overload the account with details, which would be irrelevant here.

3. *Payment for services rendered.* This class differs from the foregoing one in that here the payment is within limits defined

by custom. It has to be given each time the service is performed, but we cannot speak here of direct economic equivalence, since one of the terms of the equation consists of a service, the value of which cannot be assessed, except by conventional estimates. All services done by specialists for individuals or for the community, belong here. The most important of these are undoubtedly the services of the magician. The garden magician, for instance, receives definite gifts from the community and from certain individuals. The sorcerer is paid by the man who asks him to kill or who desires to be healed. The presents given for magic of rain and fair weather are very considerable. I have already described the payments given to a canoe-builder. I shall have to speak later on of those received by the specialists who make the various types of *vaygu'a*.

Here also belong the payments, always associated with love intrigues. Disinterested love is quite unknown among these people of great sexual laxity. Every time a girl favours her lover, some small gift has to be given immediately. This is the case in the normal intrigues, going on every night in the village between unmarried girls and boys, and also in more ceremonial cases of indulgence, like the *katuyausi* custom, or the mortuary consolations, mentioned in Chapter II, Division II. A few areca-nuts, some betel pepper, a bit of tobacco, some turtle-shell rings, or spondylus discs, such are the small tokens of gratitude and appreciation never omitted by the youth. An attractive girl need never go unprovided with the small luxuries of life.

The big mortuary distributions of food, *sagali*, have already been mentioned several times. On their economic side, these distributions are payments for funerary services. The deceased man's nearest maternal kinsman has to give food gifts to all the villagers for their assuming mourning, that is to say, for blackening their faces and cutting their hair. He pays some other special people for wailing and grave digging; a still smaller group for cutting out the dead man's ulna and using it as a lime spoon; and the widow or widower for the prolonged and scrupulously to be observed period of strict mourning.

All these details show how universal and strict is the idea that every social obligation or duty, though it may not on any account be evaded, has yet to be re-paid by a ceremonial gift. The function of these ceremonial re-payments is, on the surface of it, to thicken the social ties from which arise the obligations.

The similarity of the gifts and payments which we have put into this category is expressed by the native use of the word *mapula* (repayment, equivalent) in connection with all these gifts. Thus in giving the reason why a certain present is made to a magician, or why a share is allotted to a man at the *sagali* (distribution), or why some valuable object is given to a specialist, they would say: "This is the *mapula* for what he has done." Another interesting identification contained in linguistic usage is the calling of both magical payments and payments to specialists: a "restorative," or, literally, a "poultice." Certain extra fees given to a magician are described as *katuwarina kay-kela* or "poultice for his leg"; as the magician, especially he of the garden or the sorcerer, has to take long walks in connection with his magic. The expression "poultice of my back," will be used by a canoe-builder who has been bending over his work, or "poultice of my hand" by a carver or stone-polisher. But the identity of these gifts is not in any way expressed in the detailed terminology. In fact, there is a list of words describing the various payments for magic, the gifts given to specialists, love payments, and the numerous types of gifts distinguished at the *sagali*. Thus a magical payment, of which a small part would be offered to ancestral spirits, is called *ula'ula;* a substantial magical gift is called *sousula;* a gift to a sorcerer is described by the verb *ibudipeta,* and there are many more special names. The gifts to the specialists are called *vewoulo*—the initial gift; *yomelu*—a gift of food given after the object has been ceremonially handed over to the owner; *karibudaboda*—a substantial gift of yams given at the next harvest. The gifts of food, made while the work is in progress are called *vakapula;* but this latter term has much wider application, as it covers all the presents of cooked or raw food given to workers by the man, for whom they work. The sexual gifts are called *buwana* or *sebuwana*. I shall not enumerate the various terminological distinctions of *sagali* gifts, as this would be impossible to do, without entering upon the enormous subject of mortuary duties and distributions.

The classification of love gifts and *sagali* gifts in the same category with gifts to magicians and specialists, is a generalisation in which the natives would not be able to follow us. For them, the gifts given at *sagali* form a class in themselves and so do the love gifts. We may say that, from the economic point of view, we were correct in classing all these gifts together, because they all represent a definite type of equivalence; also they correspond to the native idea that every service has to be paid for, an idea documented by the linguistic use of the word *mapula*. But within this class, the sub-divisions corresponding to native terminology represent important distinctions made by the natives between the three sub-classes; love gifts, *sagali* gifts, and gifts for magical and professional services.

4. *Gifts returned in economically equivalent form.* We are enumerating the various types of exchange, as they gradually assume the appearance of trade. In this fourth class have been put such gifts as must be re-paid with almost strict equivalence. But it must be stressed that strict equivalence of two gifts does not assimilate them to trade altogether. There can be no more perfect equivalence between gift and counter-gift, than when A gives to B an object, and B on the same day returns the very same object to A. At a certain stage of the mortuary proceedings, such a gift is given and received back again by a deceased man's kinsmen and his widow's brothers. Yet it is obvious at once that no transaction could be further removed from trade. The above described gifts at the presentation of new canoes (*kabigidoya*) belong to this class. So do also numerous presents given to one community by another, on visits which are going to be returned soon. Payments for the lease of a garden plot are at least in certain districts of the Trobriands returned by a gift of equivalent value.

Sociologically, this class of gifts is characteristic of the relationship between friends (*luba'i*). Thus the *kabigidoya* takes place between friends, the Kula takes place between overseas partners and inland friends, but of course relations-in-law also belong *par excellence* to this category.

Other types of equivalent gifts which have to be mentioned here shortly, are the presents given by one household to another, at the *milamala,* the festive period associated with the return of the ancestral spirits to their villages. Offerings of cooked food are ceremonially exposed in houses for the use of the spirits, and after these have consumed the spiritual substance, the material one is given to a neighbouring household. These gifts are always reciprocal.

Again, a series of mutual gifts exchanged immediately after marriage between a man and his wife's father (not matrilineal kinsman in this case), have to be put into this category.

The economic similarity of these gifts is not expressed in terminology or even in linguistic use. All the gifts I have enumerated have their own special names, which I shall not adduce here, so as not to multiply irrelevant details of information. The natives have no comprehensive idea that such a class as I have spoken of exists. My generalisation is based upon the very interesting fact, that all through the tribal life we find scattered cases of direct exchange of equivalent gifts. Nothing perhaps could show up so clearly how much the natives value the give and take of presents for its own sake.

5. *Exchange of material goods against privileges, titles, and non-material possessions.* Under this heading, I class transactions which approach trade, in so far as two owners, each possessing something they value highly, exchange it for something they value still more. The equivalence here is not so strict, at any rate not so measurable, as in the previous class, because in this one, one of the terms is usually a non-material possession, such as the knowledge of magic, the privilege to execute a dance, or the title to a garden plot, which latter very often is a mere title only. But in spite of this smaller measure of equivalence, their character of trade is more marked, just because of the element of mutual desire to carry out the transaction and of the mutual advantage.

Two important types of transaction belong to this class. One of them is the acquisition by a man of the goods or privileges which are due to him by inheritance from his maternal uncle or elder brother, but which he wishes to acquire before the elder's death. If a maternal uncle is to give up in his life time a garden, or to teach and hand over a system of magic, he has to be paid for that. As a rule several payments, and very substantial ones, have to be given to him, and he gradually relinquishes his rights, giving the garden land, bit by bit, teaching the magic in instalments. After the final payment, the title of ownership is definitely handed over to the younger man.

I have drawn attention already in the general description of the Trobriand Sociology (Chapter II, Division VI) to the remarkable contrast between matrilineal inheritance and that between father and son. It is noteworthy that what is considered by the natives rightful inheritance has yet to be paid for, and that a man who knows that in any case he would obtain a privilege sooner or later, if he wants it at once, must pay for it, and that heavily. None the less, this transaction takes place only when it appears desirable to both parties. There is no customary obligation on either of the two to enter on the exchange, and it has to be considered advantageous to both before it can be completed. The acquisition of magic is of course different, because that must naturally always be taught by the elder man to the younger in his life time.

The other type of transaction belonging to this class is the payment for dances. Dances are "owned"; that is, the original inventor has the right of "producing" his dance and song in his village community. If another village takes a fancy to this song and dance, it has to purchase the right to perform it. This is done by handing ceremonially to the original village a substantial payment of food and valuables, after which the dance is taught to the new possessors.

In some rare cases, the title to garden-lands would pass from one community to another. For this again, the members and headman of the acquiring community would have to pay substantially to those who hand over their rights.

Another transaction which has to be mentioned here is the hire of a canoe, where a temporary transference of ownership takes place in return for a payment.

The generalisation by which this class has been formed, although it does not run counter to native terminology and ideas, is beyond their own grasp, and contains several of their subdivisions, differentiated by distinct native terms. The name for the ceremonial purchase of a task or for the transfer of a garden plot is *laga*. This term denotes a very big and important transaction. For example, when a small pig is purchased by food or minor objects of value, they call this barter (*gimwali*) but when a more valuable pig is exchanged for *vaygu'a*, they call it *laga*.

The important conception of gradual acquisition in advance of matrilineal inheritance, is designated by the term *pokala*, a word which we have already met as signifying the tributes to the chief. It is a homonym, because its two meanings are distinct, and are clearly distinguished by the natives. There can

be no doubt that these two meanings have developed out of
a common one by gradual differentiation, but I have no data
even to indicate this linguistic process. At present, it would be
incorrect to strain after any connection between them, and indeed this is an example how necessary it is to be careful not
to rely too much on native terminology for purposes of classification.

The term for the hire of a canoe is *toguna waga*.

6. *Ceremonial barter with deferred payment*. In this class we
have to describe payments which are ceremonially offered, and
must be received and re-paid later on. The exchange is based
on a permanent partnership, and the articles have to be roughly
equivalent in value. Remembering the definition of the Kula in
Chapter III, it is easy to see that this big, ceremonial, circulating exchange belongs to this class. It is ceremonial barter
based on permanent partnership, where a gift offered is always
accepted, and after a time has to be re-paid by an equivalent
counter-gift.

There is also a ceremonial form of exchange of vegetable food
for fish, based on a standing partnership, and on the obligation
to accept and return an initial gift. This is called *wasi*. The
members of an inland village, where yams and taro are plentiful
have partners in a Lagoon village, where much fishing is done
but garden produce is scarce. Each man has his partner, and
at times, when new food is harvested and also during the
main harvest, he and his fellow villagers will bring a big quantity
of vegetable food into the Lagoon village, each man putting
his share before his partner's house. This is an invitation, which
never can be rejected, to return the gift by its fixed equivalent
in fish.

As soon as weather and previous engagements allow, the fishermen go out to sea and notice is given to the inland village of
the fact. The inlanders arrive on the beach, awaiting the fishermen, who come back in a body, and their haul of fish is taken
directly from the canoes and carried to the inland village. Such
large quantities of fish are always acquired only in connection
with big distributions of food (*sagali*). It is remarkable that in
the inland villages these distributions must be carried out in fish,
whereas in the Lagoon villages, fish never can be used for ceremonial purposes, vegetables being the only article considered

proper. Thus the motive for exchange here is not to get food in order to satisfy the primary want of eating, but in order to satisfy the social need of displaying large quantities of conventionally sanctioned eatables. Often when such a big fishing takes place, great quantities of fish perish by becoming rotten before they reach the man for whom they are finally destined. But being rotten in no way detracts from the value of fish in a *sagali*.

The equivalence of fish, given in return for vegetable food, is measured only roughly. A standard sized bunch of taro, or one of the ordinary baskets of *taytu* (small yams) will be repaid by a bundle of fish, some three to five kilograms in weight. The equivalence of the two payments, as well as the advantage obtained by one party at least, make this exchange approach barter.[7] But the element of trust enters into it largely, in the fact that the equivalence is left to the repayer; and again, the initial gift which as a rule is always given by the inlanders, cannot be refused. And all these features distinguish this exchange from barter.

Similar to this ceremonial exchange are certain arrangements in which food is brought by individuals to the industrial villages of Kuboma, and the natives of that place return it by manufactured objects when these are made. In certain cases of production of *vaygu'a* (valuables) it is difficult to judge whether we have to do with the payment for services rendered (Class 3), or with the type of ceremonial barter belonging to this class. There is hardly any need to add that the two types of exchange contained in this class, the Kula and the *wasi* (fish barter) are kept very distinct in the minds of the natives. Indeed, the ceremonial exchange of valuables, the Kula, stands out as such a remarkable form of trade that in all respects, not only by the natives, but also by ourselves, it must be put into a class by itself. There is no doubt, however, that the technique of the *wasi* must

[7] This advantage was probably in olden days a mutual one. Nowadays when the fishermen can earn about ten or twenty times more by diving for pearls than by performing their share of the *wasi*, the exchange is as a rule a great burden on them. It is one of the most conspicuous examples of the tenacity of native custom that in spite of all the temptation which pearling offers them and in spite of the great pressure exercised upon them by the white traders, the fishermen never try to evade a *wasi*, and when they have received the inaugurating gift, the first calm day is always given to fishing, and not to pearling.

have been influenced by the ideas and usages of the Kula, which is by far the more important and widespread of the two. The natives, when explaining one of these trades, often draw parallels to the other. And the existence of social partnership, of ceremonial sequence of gift, of the free yet unevadable equivalence, all these features appear in both forms. This shows that the natives have a definite mental attitude towards what they consider an honourable, ceremonial type of barter. The rigid exclusion of haggling, the formalities observed in handing over the gift, the obligation of accepting the initial gift and of returning it later on, all these express this attitude.

7. *Trade, pure and simple.* The main characteristic of this form of exchange is found in the element of mutual advantage: each side acquires what is needed, and gives away a less useful article. Also we find here the equivalence between the articles adjusted during the transaction by haggling or bargaining.

This bartering, pure and simple, takes place mainly between the industrial communities of the interior, which manufacture on a large scale the wooden dishes, combs, lime pots, armlets, and baskets and the agricultural districts of Kiriwina, the fishing communities of the West, and the sailing and trading communities of the South. The industrials, who are regarded as pariahs and treated with contumely, are nevertheless allowed to hawk their goods throughout the other districts. When they have plenty of articles on hand, they go to the other places, and ask for yams, coco-nuts, fish, and betel-nut, and for some ornaments, such as turtle shell, earrings and spondylus beads. They sit in groups and display their wares, saying, "You have plenty of coco-nuts, and we have none. We have made fine wooden dishes. This one is worth forty nuts, and some betel-nut, and some betel pepper." The others then may answer, "Oh, no, I do not want it. You ask too much." "What will you give us?" An offer may be made, and rejected by the pedlars, and so on, till a bargain is struck.

Again, at certain times, people from other villages may need some of the objects made in Kuboma, and will go there, and try to purchase some manufactured goods. People of rank as a rule will do it in the manner described in the previous paragraph, by giving an initial gift, and expecting a repayment. Others simply go and barter. As we saw in the description of the *kabigidoya,* the Sinaketans and Vakutans go there and purchase goods before each Kula expedition to serve for the subsidiary trade.

Thus the conception of pure barter (*gimwali*) stands out very clearly, and the natives make a definite distinction between this and other forms of exchange. Embodied in a word, this distinction is made more poignant still by the manner in which the word is used. When scornfully criticising bad conduct in Kula, or an improper manner of giving gifts, a native will say that "it was done like a *gimwali.*" When asked about a transaction, whether it belongs to one class or another, they will reply with an accent of depreciation, "That was only a *gimwali*—(*gimwali wala!*)" In the course of ethnographic investigation, they give clear descriptions, almost definitions of *gimwali*, its lack of ceremony, the permissibility of haggling, the free manner in which it can be done between any two strangers. They state correctly and clearly its general conditions, and they tell readily which articles may be exchanged by *gimwali*.

Of course certain characteristics of pure barter, which we can perceive clearly as inherent in the facts, are quite beyond their theoretical grasp. Thus for instance, that the element of mutual advantage is prominent in *gimwali;* that it refers exclusively to newly manufactured goods, because second-hand things are never *gimwali*, etc., etc. Such generalisations the ethnographer has to make for himself. Other properties of the *gimwali* embodied in custom are: absence of ceremonial, absence of magic, absence of special partnership—all these already mentioned above. In carrying out the transaction, the natives also behave quite differently here than in the other transactions. In all ceremonial forms of give and take, it is considered very undignified and against all etiquette, for the receiver to show any interest in the gift or any eagerness to take it. In ceremonial distributions as well as in the Kula, the present is thrown down by the giver, sometimes actually, sometimes only given in an abrupt manner, and often it is not even picked up by the receiver, but by some insignificant person in his following. In the *gimwali*, on the contrary, there is a pronounced interest shown in the exchange.

There is one instance of *gimwali* which deserves special attention. It is a barter of fish for vegetables, and stands out in sharp contrast therefore to the *wasi*, the ceremonial fish and yam exchange. It is called *vava*, and takes place between villages which have no standing *wasi* partnership and therefore simply *gimwali* their produce when necessary.

This ends the short survey of the different types of exchange. It was necessary to give it, even though in a condensed form, in order to provide a background for the Kula. It gives us an idea of the great range and variety of the material give and take associated with the Trobriand tribal life. We see also that the rules of equivalence, as well as the formalities accompanying each transaction, are very well defined.

VII

It is easy to see that almost all the categories of gifts, which I have classified according to economic principles, are also based on some sociological relationship. Thus the first type of gifts, that is, the free gifts, take place in the relationship between husband and wife, and in that between parents and children. Again, the second class of gifts, that is, the obligatory ones, given without systematic repayment, are associated with relationship-in-law, mainly, though the chief's tributes also belong to this class.

If we drew up a scheme of sociological relations, each type of them would be defined by a special class of economic duties. There would be some parallelism between such a sociological classification of payments and presents, and the one given above. But such parallelism is only approximate. It will be therefore interesting to draw up a scheme of exchanges, classified according to the social relationship, to which they correspond. This will give us good insight into the economics of Trobriand sociology, as well as another view of the subject of payments and presents.

Going over the sociological outline in Chapter II, Divisions V and VI, we see that the family, the clan and sub-clan, the village community, the district and the tribe are the main social divisions of the Trobriands. To these groupings correspond definite bonds of social relationship. Thus, to the family, there correspond no less than three distinct types of relationship, according to native ideas. First of all there is the matrilineal kinship (*veyola*) which embraces people, who can trace common descent through their mothers. This is, to the natives, the blood relationship, the identity of flesh, and the real kinship. The marriage relation comprises that between husband and wife, and father and children. Finally, the relationship between the husband and the wife's matrilineal kinsmen forms the third class of personal ties corresponding to family. These three types of personal bonds are clearly distinguished in terminology, in the current linguistic usage, in custom, and in explicitly formulated ideas.

To the grouping into clans and sub-clans, there pertain the ties existing between clansmen and more especially between members of the same sub-clan, and on the other hand, the relationship between a man and members of different clans. Membership in the same sub-clan is a kind of extended kinship. The relationship to other clans is most important, where it assumes the form of special friendship called *luba'i*. The grouping into village communities results in the very important feature of fellow membership in the same village community. The distinction of rank associated with clanship, the division into village communities and districts, result, in the manner sketched out in Chapter II, in the subordination of commoners to chiefs. Finally, the general fact of membership in the tribe creates the bonds which unite every tribesman with another and which in olden days allowed of a free though not unlimited intercourse, and therefore of commercial relations. We have, therefore, eight types of personal relationship to distinguish. In the following table we see them enumerated with a short survey of their economic characteristics.

1. *Matrilineal Kinship.* The underlying idea that this means identity of blood and of substance is by no means forcibly expressed on its economic side. The right of inheritance, the common participation in certain titles of ownership, and a limited right to use one another's implements and objects of daily use are often restricted in practice by private jealousies and animosities. In economic gifts more especially, we find here the remarkable custom of purchasing during lifetime, by instalments, the titles to garden plots and trees and the knowledge of magic, which by right ought to pass at death from the older to the younger generation of matrilineal kinsmen. The economic identity of matrilineal kinsmen comes into prominence at the tribal

distributions—*sagali*—where all of them have to share in the responsibilities of providing food.

2. *Marriage Ties.* (Husband and wife; and derived from that, father and children.) It is enough to tabulate this type of relationship here, and to remind the reader that it is characterised by free gifts, as has been minutely described in the foregoing classification of gifts, under (1).

3. *Relationship-in-law.* These ties are in their economic aspect not reciprocal or symmetrical. That is, one side in it, the husband of the woman, is the economically favoured recipient, while the wife's brothers receive from him gifts of smaller value in the aggregate. As we know, this relationship is economically defined by the regular and substantial harvest gifts, by which the husband's storehouse is filled every year by his wife's brothers. They also have to perform certain services for him. For all this, they receive a gift of *vaygu'a* (valuables) from time to time, and some food in payment for services rendered.

4. *Clanship.* The main economic identification of this group takes place during the *sagali,* although the responsibility for the food rests only with those actually related by blood with the deceased man. All the members of the sub-clan, and to a smaller extent members of the same clan within a village community, have to contribute by small presents given to the organisers of the *sagali.*

5. *The Relationship of Personal Friendship.* Two men thus bound as a rule will carry on Kula between themselves, and, if they belong to an inland and Lagoon village respectively, they will be partners in the exchange of fish and vegetables (*wasi*).

6. *Fellow-citizenship in a Village Community.* There are many types of presents given by one community to another. And, economically, the bonds of fellow-citizenship mean the obligation to contribute one's share to such a present. Again, at the mortuary divisions, *sagali,* the fellow-villagers of clans, differing from the deceased man's, receive a series of presents for the performance of mortuary duties.

7. *Relationship between Chiefs and Commoners.* The tributes and services given to a chief by his vassals on the one hand, and the small but frequent gifts which he gives them, and the big and important contribution which he makes to all tribal enterprises are characteristic of this relationship.

8. *Relationship between Any Two Tribesmen.* This is charac-terised by payments and presents, by occasional trade between two individuals, and by the sporadic free gifts of tobacco or betel-nut which no man would refuse to another unless they were on terms of hostility.

With this, the survey of gifts and presents is finished. The general importance of give and take to the social fabric of Boyowan society, the great amount of distinctions and sub-divi-sions of the various gifts can leave no doubt as to the paramount rôle which economic acts and motives play in the life of these natives.

14 PIGS AND CURRENCY IN BUIN: OBSERVATIONS ABOUT PRIMITIVE STANDARDS OF VALUE AND ECONOMICS[1]

Richard C. Thurnwald

A visitor's first impression of life in a Melanesian- or Papuan-speaking community may not encourage his studies in economics. Conditions seem almost too simple. When I met the Buin[2] people for the first time[3] I did not expect much from such investigations, although some features of exchange began to puzzle me.

FROM Richard C. Thurnwald, "Pigs and Currency in Buin: Observations about Primitive Standards of Value and Economics." *Oceania*, Vol. V, No. 2 (1934), pp. 119–141. Reprinted by permission of A. P. Elkin, editor of *Oceania*.

[1] This is a preliminary account resulting from ten months' research work in Buin (Island of Bougainville, Mandated Territory of New Guinea), which was made possible by the liberal provisions of the Australian National Research Council to both Mrs. Thurnwald and myself. We take this opportunity to express our sincere gratitude to the body mentioned. We must also thank His Honour the Administrator of the Territory, General Griffiths, for the effective support he gave to our studies. In particular are we obliged for the help received from the Fathers, and my wife from the Sisters, of the Marist Mission in Bougainville under the patronage of His Lordship its Bishop.

[2] "Buin" is the name of the plains sloping down from the central range of mountains (1–3000 feet high), the backbone of the island of Bougainville (north-western Solomon Islands). It is inhabited by a population of 7,000–8,000, and is today divided into four main districts with "No. I, chiefs," each one controlled 15 to 20 sub-chiefs ("kukurai") for purposes of administration. The Buin language is non-Melanesian.

[3] The author carried on research work in Buin in 1908–1909 (cf. *Forchungen auf den Salomo-Inseln,* etc., Vols. I and III, Berlin, 1912). Consequently, he was able to perceive the changes in social structure and mentality, and notice the loss in tradition that has taken place today (1934).

WORK

Husbandry Within the Family Unit. Men can be observed clearing patches in the forest, setting fire to the big logs, and fencing the garden. The women burn timber and small branches, and plant shoots of various sorts of taro, yams, banana, some sugar cane, tobacco, etc. The harvest of the crops is expected nine or ten months later, and carried home by the women. Every two, three, or four months this clearing and planting work is resumed, either extending the garden under cultivation, or opening up a new field. In the latter case a former plantation is generally used, which has been allowed to lie fallow for several years, and where bushes and small trees have grown in the meantime. Generally there are about three patches under cultivation, in different stages of ripening. A busy woman plants new shoots every two or three weeks in order to be continuously provided with fresh crops for consumption. In the old times (of my first visit) the women made it a point of honour not to ask for or buy taro (the principal food) from others. If a garden is cleared by several heads of families together with their sons, the ground is divided up among the women and boundaries made with logs for each woman's part. The men, with their sons, will often be seen repairing the fence that prevents pigs from devastating the plantation. Individual activity and diligence, however, vary, and hence so too do the qualities of the plantations. Some families do not even have a garden, but rely for existence upon the support of their relatives. Apart from such exceptional cases of *ibaci* (loafers), the religious tabu upon eating taro and pork after a near kinsman's death unsettles the regular rhythm in garden work. It would be considered shameful should smoke be seen going up in a garden within three months of a close relative's cremation. Less provident people neglect plantation work for too long a time, and suffer from the consequences next year. Food may become scarce in a region if a few men with a wide circle of kinsfolk and high social standing have died recently.

The activities are strictly divided up between the sexes. The cutting and washing of sago is exclusively men's work. Puddings of sago and coconut, or sago and "galip" nut (*moi*), of taro and coconut, or taro and "galip,"[4] etc., which are made for feasts and are generally combined with the cooking of pigs, are exclusively prepared by men. But the daily cooking, the carrying of heavy loads of firewood, and the providing of water are performed by the women. They also collect herbs, roots, and berries, and fish for crabs and shrimps, while men as well as women catch fish in hand-nets. The special task and ambitious duty of women is the feeding of the pigs. Every girl is carefully trained in this task before marriage by her own mother, and after betrothal by that of her future husband. The number and quality of pigs is a family's pride. Occasionally men will be found planting a coconut tree, an areca or a sago palm, a bread-fruit or a nut (galip) tree, although some of these grow wild. Ownership of a wild tree is established by making it "tabu" through fastening a band of leaves around it. One sees men in the chief's hall sitting and plaiting baskets, knitting a net or a bag, carving a bamboo case or a gourd for lime, dressing and ornamenting coconut shells as water-bottles or, in the old times, cutting spears, bows and arrows, while chattering with the others who are lounging about on the big drums. The product of such work in general is devoted to each man's own use. A hunting excursion of a few men or even of a single one is a stimulating affair most of which is rather a pleasant sport than an activity of economic importance. The hunters rove about in the forest, sometimes considerable distances away, to catch *"laga"* (kusu and kuskus), some kind of so-called "opossum," bush-fowl, iguanas, and other delicacies. They may be away for a few days, and even for some weeks. The party sleeps under bushes and enjoys the hunter's and gatherer's life for a while. Sometimes they bring home some stems of a parasitic plant which grows on big trees in the mountains, and from the dyed fibres of which they plait armbands and ornaments for their weapons. In such cases the men share in each other's prey, he who gives being sure to receive an equivalent from his friend the next time.

The economic activities of the family unit, such as those which have been outlined above, have been responsible for indiscriminate generalizations which imply that "primitive economics" are

[4] The word for this kind of nut has been taken from the Rabaul speech and adopted into pidgin English.

concerned only with self-supporting and self-sufficient families.

Friendly Help. It is not only when out on hunting expeditions that people give one another help. The sister or co-wife of a woman may assist her by caring for the babies or fetching firewood when the other is ill or busy with particular work. Men and women enjoy working in the company of others of their own sex, chiefly for mutual stimulus when resting together and talking with each other. When a heavy log or large wooden drum is transported, the co-operation of men amounts to team work. But the most outstanding example of reciprocity is the friendly help given by members of the different sexes to each other, both in their work and in the fruits of their labour. The wife enjoys the protection of her husband. This was particularly important in the old times. The splendour of his fame as a fighter was demonstrated concretely in the form of valuables and ornaments, of wealth in pigs and shell money, of co-wives who were sometimes regarded as assistants to the first wife. The man prepares the ground for planting; he does the fencing; he procures pots for cooking; while the woman prepares the daily food, rears the children, and feeds the pigs. When building a house, mutual assistance is freely granted, in the expectation of receiving reciprocal help next time from the man whose house is now being built. The feasting with pigs on such an occasion is regarded more as a stimulus than as a regular payment. Utensils and instruments, hoes, baskets, nets, ornaments are liberally given and received by near relatives according to wish and need. A man will get help from his kinsmen and chief to obtain a suitable wife. They all contribute to collect the bride-price, whereas on the girl's side the corresponding persons share in its distribution (H. Thurnwald 1934:149). A large proportion of the money earned by a man who has worked for three years on a plantation is claimed by his kinsmen and chief to be divided among them. Complete solidarity is exhibited by the blood feuds, although today they are checked to a large extent. The death of a man is usually interpreted as the consequence of black magic, and therefore as requiring vengeance, inciting blood feuds. The idea of friendly help is even extended to the relation between ruler and ruled, as will be explained later on.

The idea of reciprocity as manifested among near kin and those of the same settlement who are related to one another has led some scientists astray into imagining that primitive economics are based upon collectivism. The guiding principle, however, is the same between persons of the same social unit and between members of different groups.

BARTER

Barter is instituted by expanding the circle of reciprocal relations to other groups with which friendship has been established. Therefore *"commercium"* is always a symbol of good will. The extension of reciprocity to other groups produces, however, conditions diametrically opposed to the tendencies towards collectivism discussed above.

Let us first observe some more features of Buin economic life. After a short stay you hear of feasts being held here or there, and of pigs bought for these occasions with the usual "shell money," *ábuta*. It is counted in fathoms (*lagáropi*), one fathom being equal to the length from the tip of the middle finger of one hand to that of the other held over the chest. A pig may be considered to be worth 10, 20, etc., fathoms up to 100. Prices of 12, 25, 37, etc., fathoms are not paid, but always round units of tens. The feast may be connected with providing sacrifices for a dead person; for services rendered in garden work; for paying an ally for his assistance in battle; for doctoring diseases; for magical devices, remedies, or incantations; it may terminate a minor dispute or seal the peace after a serious conflict; or it may be the public expression of an alliance (*unu*) concluded or affirmed between two chiefs. When a girl is married (H. Thurnwald 1934: 148, 150), gifts of pigs and *ábuta* are exchanged constantly between the bride's and the bridegroom's families. After the birth of a baby all the stages of growth are marked by feasts for which pigs are killed. Through these feasts the child is brought into contact with the world, with the supernatural powers and with his community. In the life of the Buin people there is no incident which cannot serve as an occasion for feasting upon pigs and pudding.

At first glance it seems that a man's own pigs may be used for his feasts. It will be noticed, however, that the owner of numerous pigs tells you how much currency he paid for a pig offered at a feast. In fact, at one time a fat pig or an old boar is needed (on which the ghosts of ancestors, the *óliga,* may ride); at another time a small animal will do, worth 20 or 30 fathoms, but it may be that the giver of the feast has not got an animal of just the right value in his own stock. Often certain pigs are ear-marked for a feast to be held one or more years hence. Moreover, the natives will tell you that a man is loath to kill and eat his own pig, to which the family have become attached, "he all the same brother." He would be "sorry" for his pig, and its ghost might cause him mischief. It is different with another man's pig.

The consequence of such sentiments, however, might be a simple exchange of pigs such as is practised by the hill tribes of Nagavisi (a neighbouring people speaking a language related to that of Buin). In Buin the process of exchange is complicated by the intervention of the "shell money."

Closer observation reveals that the interests of the men centre around three foci: women, pigs, and "money." All affairs revolve around these "objects of value." But one other factor may complicate the interplay between them; this is the ever-present dread of being "poisoned," injured by sorcery, at the hands of an enemy. In the old times this fear led to actual murder.

Reviewing briefly what has been written above, we can distinguish three kinds of "economics" running side by side: (1) the husbandry within the family, in which the part played by women in the garden, in the house and in the feeding of the pigs predominates; (2) the inter-individual and inter-familial help among the near relatives and among the members of a settlement united under a chief; (3) the inter-communal relations manifested by barter between individuals belonging to different communities or strata of society.

We must, indeed, realize that economics are intimately bound up with social standing and prestige. It is necessary, therefore, to consider these subjects briefly.

Social Order

We cannot help noticing that the dealings of the chiefs' families cause a break in the equilibrium of reciprocity. These families are inter-related among each other, and constitute an aristocracy.

It is true that complete reciprocity prevails between these families as well as among their "bondsmen" (*kítere*). The *múmira*, members of the chief's stratum, claim the ownership of pigs and *ábuta* for their class, just as the pastoral tribes in Africa do with regard to cattle. They treat the "bondsman" as the warden of the domestic animal. In Africa it is certain that cattle had been introduced by the pastoral tribes. Are we justified in suggesting that in the region in question pigs and shell money were introduced by the people who claim their ownership?

There are some differences in our area. The cultural and racial distinction between the "aristocracy" and the "bondsmen" seems on the whole to be less pronounced here than in Africa. The chief is housed, dressed, and fed exactly like his bondsman. It may be that the fusion between the two is more advanced here. The stratification, therefore, can only be discovered by close observation of the behaviour and customs, and by obtaining confidential information.

The relations between *múmira* and *kítere* are not exactly the same in each region of Buin. Nevertheless general principles can be ascertained for the whole area. The *múmira* family claims all the land of the district. This land is divided up for usufruct among its adult male members and is inalienable. Moreover, each *múmira* owns a number of *kítere* families; a big chief several dozens, a smaller one (second or third line) perhaps half a dozen, or one or two dozen. The head of each *kítere* family has received part of the land belonging to his *múmira*, transmitted perhaps from his ancestors. The *kítere* may sell the land if his *múmira* agrees. If a *kítere* family should die out, the land reverts to the *múmira* to be disposed of as he wishes.

The main obligation of the *kítere* in the old times was to support his *múmira*'s enterprises in warfare, and particularly in head-hunting to offer the skulls to the personal war-god (*orómrui*) of his chief, as his "ghost *kítere*." On the other hand the bondsman was protected by his *múmira*, who also would avenge him in case of any assault or black magic. Today, since the feuds have become obsolete, the raising of pigs is left as the main obligation of the *kítere*. Even in olden days the *kítere* received some reward for a pig given to the *múmira*, although then it was somewhat less than it is today. The amount varied according to local circumstances. The *kítere* could not kill or eat his pig without the consent of his *múmira*, still less could he sell it to someone else. He may dispose of his pigs only after consultation with his chief. But, if he gives a pig to his *múmira*, or to someone else, with his consent, he is paid for it. In the latter case the *múmira* claims part of the payment. The *kítere* is bound to assist his chief in clearing his plantation, repairing his fences, and in house building, particularly in the erection of the chief's hall (*abácio*). The *kítere*'s daughters will help the *mumiána* (chief's wife) in garden and house work, and they are chosen to contribute to the men's pleasures when a big feast is going on. All these services, however, including the last, are remunerated, either by meals of pig or by *ábuta*.

The *kítere* must show respect for his *múmira*, and in particular he must avoid looking upon the chief's wives and daughters. Consequently he was strictly prohibited from walking along the tracks which the *mumiána* took on their way to their gardens. If he were met there he was instantly killed. Discipline in the old times was kept rigidly and sometimes cruelly. On the other hand, a chief would not wantonly deprive himself of the source of his revenue and prestige. If a chief killed the *kítere* of another chief he had to pay the latter 100 fathoms of *ábuta*. For this sum a *kítere* was also treacherously sold for a sacrifice to provide a skull when a new sumptuous hall was erected by a big *múmira tútoberu*.

This "*jus vitæ necisque*" was checked by the right which the *kítere* claimed to leave his *múmira* and seek the tutelage of another chief. A *kítere* would not, however, do this unless a quarrel arose or he was afraid of being killed. In the event of his doing so, he had to leave his house, his pigs, and his *ábuta*, and hide in the bush. In the old times it was a risky affair if he were not sure of the other chief's mind and if he were not intimately related to him or a man of good renown, i.e., a killer of fame (*burúrugaci*). Even if he were accepted by the other chief, he had to make a new start at the new place. If the old chief does not care a *kítere* may in peace transfer himself, e.g., from one brother to another.

But the *múmira* would never antagonize his *kítere*, since he relied on their help as his henchmen as well as raisers of pigs and cultivators of soil. His discipline and authority had therefore always to be tempered with diplomacy, unless he was one of the unusually terroristic rulers like old Cíbelau-Máugoci. The average chief did not forget to reward his *kítere* adequately, in particular by means of frequent feasts, to insure the good will of his people and increase his popularity and prestige. Today the increased ability of the *kítere* to move from place to place and to put themselves under the authority of other chiefs has done much to check the power of the *múmira* and to increase the rewards which they give to their bondsmen.

The head of a *múmira* family is the *"múmira tútoberu,"* the others are simply called *"múmira."* It may be appropriate here to say something of the laws of inheritance and succession. The family is the real owner of the land; its head acts as its trustee. If that head dies, the next senior male succeeds: the eldest son, or if there be none, the next eldest brother. Should the head of the family die and his eldest son be still a child, then the brother next to him in age will take over the position, and will retain it until his death, after which it will devolve upon the son of the elder brother. If, however, the latter has died in the meanwhile, it passes to his own son. If there be no son or brother, a brother's son, or a father's brother's son succeeds. If there are several equally nearly related to the deceased, the man who lives in the place is considered to have the best claim to succeed. It is also possible for a daughter's son to succeed if he live in the place and if he were designated by his grandfather to be his successor. In spite of the law of seniority in the paternal line, allowance is made for special cases and for the reasonable wish of the dead man. If there be no other heir, it is permissible for a half brother (the son of a *kítere* wife) or a *mínei* (to be explained later on) to succeed if he be considered suitable. This indicates how, with the passage of time, men who were not pure blooded members of the aristocracy, attained to positions of authority. Today many claim to be *"múmira"* who indeed are of very mixed ancestry (as the pedigrees which we have collected show). At the present time the aristocracy is in a few places still more or less preserved, but in many others it is undoubtedly completely disintegrated. Although the process of disintegration had begun long before the advent of the whites, it was undoubtedly accelerated by them. The nomination of government chiefs ("kúkurai"—a nickname originally, meaning rooster) who were not selected from the *múmira* families contributed, of course, to a further deterioration of the chief's position and a shattering of authority of the *múmira*.

Daughters do not inherit. If they have been married before their father's death they have got their part of *"tómbu"* (women's shell money, to be explained later on), *ónu, mímíci,* etc., as family valuables. A proportionate part of them is reserved for the unmarried daughter. They generally do not get *ábuta,* except in the western region of Buin, where they receive a limited amount. If the daughter is married to a man of her own community, her husband may claim a part of the forest for hunting and planting.

It is the heir's duty to arrange the cremation and the feasts connected with it. The distribution of the inheritance is partly combined with the ceremonies connected with the feasts. The heir assigns a number of *kítere* to his brothers or other near relatives. Of 100 *kítere,* for example, he will retain 50 for himself, 30 he will give to his brother next to him in age, and 20 to his youngest brother. In a similar proportion he will dispose of a part of the *ábuta* and of the pigs, the trees, the hunting grounds, etc. But the disposition of the pigs and the *ábuta* is complicated by a ceremonial exchange. If the dead chief had left 400 fathoms of *ábuta,* the heir will take 200 to put into his own net-bag (*búkai*) and retain them as his personal property, and on this bag the *óliga* (ghosts of ancestors) will dwell. The other 200 will be divided up among his *kítere,* in portions of 20 or 30, for example. Each *kítere* who received *ábuta* will reciprocate the gift by the donation of a pig of somewhat higher value. A portion of 50 fathoms of *ábuta* may go to a *mínei* or a *búrepi* (to be explained later on), and each one of them will take pride in giving a pig of a correspondingly higher value in return. The heir, consequently, makes a good bargain. To receive *ábuta* from the deceased chief is a special honour, and requires a display of wealth which will be spoken about and which will give prestige. The pigs, on the other hand, are turned into *ábuta.* By handing the pigs over to the *kítere* the heir obtains their good will and keeps them attached to the community, which otherwise they might leave. Some pigs go to the heir's relatives and *múmira* friends. For all the pigs distributed in this way the heir receives ample recompense, more *ábuta* than the pig's normal value. With the *ábuta* received, other pigs are bought to be killed for the feasts connected with the funeral ceremonies.

As remarked at the beginning of this article, garden work is neglected by the nearest kinsfolk of a dead man on account of the rule which prohibits them from eating taro and pork during the whole of the mourning period. During this time the parents, children, brothers and sisters of the deceased live on bananas, sago, yams, and sweet potatoes. Distant relatives or wives of relatives will look after the plantation if need be. The reason given for the prohibition in the old times was the belief that eating taro would interfere with the growth of the shoots which had been cremated with the body and planted by the *úra* (image of man reflected in the water of a coconut shell) in the world beyond, in Rúroru. The ghosts of the pigs consumed at the funeral ceremonies are supposed to go to Rúroru to serve as food there for the *úra* (image souls) and *mára* (demons).

The feasts may be reviewed briefly. The pattern is taken from those held after a chief's death. If a man who is not a chief dies, it depends upon his wealth and that of his kinsmen and friends how sumptuous the feasts will be. Essentially, there is no difference between the social strata. (1) The logs for the pyre have been brought by distant relatives from the neighbourhood, and after a month or so they are recompensed with a few small pigs. This feast is the *kuínke*. It marks the time for some resumption of the work in the gardens. Hunting parties for *laga* (kusu) and fishing should, however, not be taken up before the *améi*. (2) An important feast immediately after cremation is the *tábe,* the "breaking of the spears." Relatives and friends of the deceased rush into the place where the cremation has been carried out, with shouts, jumping and dancing in a spiral and a circle, swinging their spears, and finally throwing them into the centre. The man or men whose spear point breaks is destined to avenge the dead man. If no one can be definitely held responsible for the death, the people resort to ritual means to discover who is guilty of making the sorcery by means of which the dead man was killed. Pork and taro are lavishly distributed at this important ceremony which today, of course, cannot be carried out to its logical conclusion. (3) Three months after the death of a chief his *kítere* are released from the tabu on eating pig and taro, by a meal of pork and taro pudding, to which the heir contributes. This feast is the *améi*. (4) The feast which releases the near kinsmen of the deceased from the tabu on pork and taro, which is also the last feast in his honour, is the *kába*. After the death of a man of no importance, it is held four months after the cremation. The period of mourning is extended and, consequently, the *kába* arranged later and with more display of luxury if a chief or a rich *mínei* has died. The usual term is nine months, by which time the taro planted in Rúroru when the corpse was cremated has begun to ripen. After the death of a *múmira tútoberu* of great power, however, two, three, or four years are allowed to elapse before the *kába*. This means a prolongation of the mourning, an ampler stock of food for the dead in Rúroru, and an accumulation of more pigs (which have been raised expressly for that purpose) and taro (specially planted for the *kába*) for the feast. On this occasion the avengers appear just as they did at the *tábe* festival, dancing and shouting as before, but now they show in pantomime how they wrought vengeance on the dead man's murderer. This feast is the occasion for rewarding these men. The deceased is glorified by a display of some thirty, fifty, or even more pigs. A large number of friends and distant relatives are liberally entertained with cooked pork, which is distributed among them without any obligation on their part to make a return gift.

These feasts have been mentioned in order to show how intricately objects of value are bound up with food and with the obligations of the heir in regard to the exchange of certain parts of the goods which he has inherited. The way in which pig's flesh is distributed is different. Generally, the pig, after being slaughtered, is cut up by the *múmira*. On some occasions he asserts his relationship to the ancestors, who are supposed to ride on the big pigs, by taking his stand on the animal before it is killed, and swinging his club, while uttering a few words addressed to the *óliga* (ghosts of ancestors). The meat is distributed in strips, each of which has a distinctive name. Guests from other districts take the strips and leave immediately for home. There they sit down in their own chief's hall and eat it. Only those of the dead man's community cook the meat in their *abácio,* where the distribution took place. For this reason the gathering of people for the feast never lasts long. At feasts like the *kába,* when the meat is cooked beforehand and thus distributed, the guests disperse even sooner, for they depart immediately after having received their share, and often sit down somewhere in the forest on their way home to eat it. This is probably because of the mutual distrust, the frequent quarrels, and the ever-present disposition to fight. The only exception was the *únu* ceremony, by means of which friendship between two big chiefs was established. Then the men of both sides spent some days together and participated in pleasures with the women of the respective *kítere*.

Only the feasting after a man's death has been outlined. It would take too long to give an account of the *únu,* the feasts connected with marriage, and with the growth of children, etc. What has already been said will be sufficient to demonstrate the inter-relation of religious conceptions and social agencies with even sometimes rationalistic and economic calculations. It has been shown (1) that wealth is bound up with prestige; (2) that wealth requires the participation of the kinsmen and the community to be enjoyed; (3) that it is the display of wealth which is the source of prestige, not its mere possession; (4) that wealth is, moreover, a socializing force through the constant exchange imposed upon it, in spreading good will among the persons involved in the exchanges and in supporting social solidarity.

It should be borne in mind that people promote their acquisition of wealth by using rational calculations of an economic nature. They do it consciously and intentionally, incited thereto by the desire to improve their social position. This process, by which the influence of the hereditary aristocracy was countered by the influence of wealth, began long ago. This is shown by the existence of classes of people who, although they are not *múmira,* are important in virtue of their wealth, arising out of their skill in carrying on exchanges with profit and success. On the other hand a *múmira* who has failed in his enterprise of raising pigs (perhaps on account of an inefficient wife, obstinate *kítere* or bad luck) and of acquiring enough *ábuta* to finance feasts, loses his authority over his *kítere* and his social prestige. In this way the established stratification of society has, in the lapse of time, become disturbed and the principle upon which it was founded has shifted.

The intermediate classes are the *mínei* and the *búrepi.* The word *"mínei"* designates the main pillar in the chief's hall. Used with reference to these men it could be translated by "pillar of the state," thus expressing the services which they are supposed to render to the chief and to the community. Their obligations consist mainly in contributing *ábuta* and pigs for the feasts of the chief and, in the old times, in helping to assemble allies either by personal relations or by contributing shell money for this purpose. Some of them were *"burúrugaci,"* i.e., keen fighters and killers, and were esteemed on this account. The *mínei* are men of mixed descent. The second and third sons of a *múmira* often took daughters of *kítere;* the widows of *mumiána* rank were allowed to marry *kítere* as second husbands. After his elder brother's death the younger one succeeds and becomes head of the *múmira* family. If the elder brother had no male offspring the son of a *kítere* mother may therefore become heir after his father's death. Although even today a *múmira* is considered to be genuine only if he is descended in both the paternal and maternal line from *múmira* stock, it is more and more considered obsolete to take notice of descent through the mother, whereas the paternal line has risen to paramount importance. The chief's attitude towards his *mínei* is distinguished by more confidence than towards the *kítere;* and the *mínei* on his side, being generally a kinsman of the chief, exercises more influence upon him than does the ordinary bondsman. The *mínei,* consequently, is allowed to keep more pigs and *ábuta* for himself. On account of his family relations he is enabled to acquire more wealth and prestige and thus gain an important position in the community. In fact, he may become a "pillar" of the chief's power. The same holds true for the *búrepi,* with the exception that they are of *kítere* descent. They do not constitute a class like the *mínei* who are kinsmen of the *múmira* aristocracy. A man of means among the *kítere* is just called a *búrepi,* a rich man. His position, particularly in the old times, was the result of a shrewd participation in his *múmira's* troubles, both as regards wars and feasts. As mentioned above, a chief, if he were wise, kept his subjects in a good temper in order to be sure of their support. This could be achieved mainly by the help of his *mínei* and *búrepi.*

The importance of these intermediate groups of people has increased today in proportion as that of the *múmira* has decreased. Originally the *múmira* belonged to a stock that swept over Buin from the Alu and Mono Islands.[5] Probably enterprising persons by head-hunting, successful fighting and feasts attracted followers among the "aborigines." As they took wives and settled

[5] A black-skinned, tall race, in some features unlike the rest of the Melanesians or "Papuans."

among the indigenous population, racial and cultural fusion gradually advanced, although the progeny of the invaders reserved privileges for their kinsfolk, thus establishing a kind of feudal regime. In these communities several families were welded together which were better organized than those of the neighbouring tribes, e.g., the Nagavisi, Koromida, Nasioi people in the mountains. The chiefdoms, however, vied with each other, and even within the same *múmira* families sometimes sanguinary conflicts sprang up (as between the brothers Móntai and Mágatu in Boréburu, which involved the neighbouring communities for more than a decade). Sometimes brutal and shrewd persons like the old Cîbelau-Máugoci were able to extend their power over a number of *múmira tútoberu*. Personal talents and particular situations were instrumental in bringing confusion into the traditional ethnic stratification. First of all, however, the possession of objects of value—pigs and *ábuta*—introduced a new cleavage into the old order, although the wealth was of a transitory nature and depended particularly on the wife's competence in raising pigs and on the man's in disposing of it in his fulfilment of all kinds of social obligations. Nevertheless there are not any poor people in the sense in which this term is used in our own societies. The lazy or inefficient couple will be fed by their kinsfolk. Wealth, on the other hand, is concerned with a limited number of performances, as already indicated.

Modern conditions accelerate the process of disintegration of the aristocratic order. The great number of youths recruited for labour in the plantations return home with a new kind of prestige derived from individual possession of European money with its wide range of convertibility (and withhold it as far as possible from their relatives and chiefs by all kinds of tricks), from their knowledge of new devices, and personal relations with the white man.

We can, then, draw the following conclusions: (1) the stratification of society fostered patriarchy; (2) political patriarchy involved reckoning descent in the patrilineal line; (3) the patriarchal chiefs rivalled each other by the display of their power and prestige; (4) this could be manifested directly by fighting, indirectly by feasts; (5) both these means to attain power and prestige necessitated the ownership of resources with which to satisfy their respective henchmen; (6) these followers could be

mustered by playing upon their propensities and instincts, through
the stimulus of feasts and luxuries of life consistent with their
civilization; (7) it became an important affair to procure these
resources, pigs and taro; (8) by a way which has yet to be
considered, they were equated with "shell money."

<h2>CURRENCY</h2>

Payments are distinguished by special terms, according to the
position of the persons concerned and the occasion on which they
are made. The reward of a bondsman by his chief is called
mámoko. It is considered an act of liberality for which there is no
obligation. Any gift of friendship is described by the same name.
A surplus payment over the price agreed is also called *mámoko*.
Tótokai is the excess payment of a *kítere* to his *múmira* for
ensuring his good will and his willingness to credit him with
ábuta on another occasion. *Dákai* designates a payment for reconciliation or reparation between men of equal position. The price
to be paid for a pig sold for a feast is the *dacínke*. A drum
signal is interpreted as saying this word. Currency is also paid
for weregild [bloodwealth], 100 fathoms for a *kítere,* 200 for
a *múmira*. Injuries are settled by minor sums, and *ábuta* is
paid also in cases of adultery. In the latter cases actual fighting
or sham fights often precede the payment. The rain maker, doc-
tor-magician (*mékai*), sorcerer and dealer in special "poisons"
(*mara*) and medicines are recompensed with 10, 20 or 40
fathoms of *ábuta* according to circumstances. Often pigs are required in addition for particular magic. The pursuit of these
"liberal vocations" makes the accumulation of objects of value
possible, and it is facilitated by modern conditions which add
sticks of trade tobacco, calico and coins (shillings) to the wealth
of these practitioners.

In the old times stone blades for axes, spears, arrows, bows,
arm-rings of tridacna were sometimes traded for *ábuta*. Even
today pots, arm-bands (*cíbata*), fishing nets, knitted bags
(*búkai*), plaited bags (*taíne*), specially painted hats, strings of
native tobacco, bamboo cases for lime, baskets, combs with feathers, and modern products such as iron blades, knives, calico, etc.,
are bought and sold for currency. There are no markets. A bargain over pots, for example, is agreed upon at a feast held by

the chiefs, and after some weeks the potters appear with their wares at the hall (*abácio*) of the chief who arranged for their purchase. His men are informed, and come from their hamlets to buy the pots for their wives. The prices of the pots are fixed according to size (I observed four sizes). Pots from different places, however, differ in quality. Other objects are traded at casual meetings, the price being often paid later, though some token is given in advance. All these bargains are carried on between individuals.

One fathom *ábuta* is usually valued at one shilling. The various kinds of shell money differ, however, in worth. The "women's money," "*bum*" or "*tómbu*," is twice the value of *ábuta*. One fathom of *mímici* (red *ónu*), small polished discs obtained from Alu or Roviana, is worth 20 fathoms of *ábuta* (£1); white *ónu* is equated to only 10 fathoms of *ábuta*. *Ábuta* is arranged in bundles of 10 fathom lengths, which are arranged in six strings with one quarter of a string overhanging, and terminated with a small shell of an inland snail. This embodies a curious combination of the decimal system with the sexagesimal system, as evinced in the terms for the numbers in their language.[6] Ten bunches of *ábuta*, i.e., one hundred fathoms, are packed in a netted bag and deposited in the sleeping house; on this bag the ghosts of the ancestors (*óliga*) are supposed to take up their abode.

The currency seems to have been originally used as a token acknowledging the receipt of a pig (in the same way as are boar tusks in New Guinea or dog's teeth in Manus, tridacna rings in Choiseul, etc.). It may be that the *ábuta* has replaced *ónu* or *mímici*. At any rate it was worked (by women) in Alu and Mono from sea shells, and traded at an early time into Buin. The fact that the *múmira* claim all the *ábuta* is a further indication of their origin from the Shortland Islands. The demand for these tokens probably dates back to the beginnings of the contact between the "aborigines" of Buin and the Alu-Mono tribe, a contact which was marked, as in later days, by the barter of pigs, sago, taro, nuts, etc., growing in the swampy region of the hinterland of the

[6] The numbers 1 to 6 are expressed by plain numeration, while 7 and 8 are expressed by deducting respectively 3 and 2 from 10. The counting of further numbers is effected by repeating the set of 1 to 10 within each unit of ten.

coast. The raping of women and children, perhaps, inaugurated the contact. Buin slaves have spread all over the Shortland Islands, and have contributed to a blending of that population. Returning mothers and their offspring brought the necklaces home, as they did all sorts of other things, up to the modern times. The Buin people considered the Alu-Mono natives to be superior to them, and consequently accepted their valuations, just as they do with regard to European wares. The *ábuta* manufactured in Alu represented a crude imitation of the good *ónu* and *mímici,* just as the European pottery arm-rings, which have been sold successfully to the natives, counterfeit the tridacna arm-shells. The returning serfs probably brought the *ábuta* home with pride. Eventually the *ábuta* was set aside to serve only as a token or currency, just as were the money knives of old China, and arrow-heads, etc., in Africa. The form had been preserved from which the symbol of value had developed, but its practical purpose as a necklace had been lost. It is worth noting that in the speech made by the chief at the *únu* festival a promise is expressly made to return the *ábuta* received individually, and to care for its preservation up to that moment. At marriages in Borobere an exchange of an equal number of bunches of *ábuta* takes place. These facts prove that the strings of *ábuta* are still regarded as individual family valuables. But the importation of masses of these strings of shell necklaces reduced their individuality and emphasized their function as currency. Since for a decade or so the communications with the Shortland Islands have been discontinued in order to check the export of labourers from Buin to the British Solomon Islands, the supplies of *ábuta* have become stationary. They have indeed been reduced, owing to the practice of cremating some *ábuta* with the corpse of the owner. The manufacture of *ábuta* on a small island off the Buin coast scarcely makes up for the losses thus incurred. *Tómbu* and *mímici,* some of which are also cremated, are rising in value.

BANKING AND PROFITING

The use of these necklaces as currency made further developments possible along this line. While serving the individual purposes of exchange *ábuta* is also accumulated by important *múmira* families in the interest of their community to form a fund which can be drawn upon in cases of emergency as, for instance, when allies must be won, indemnities paid for men killed among the allies or among his own people, or peace settled with the enemy. Special treasure houses are built concealed in the virgin forest. These *rúbobo* or *dúni* are respected in minor fights, but in bitter warfare it happens that they are attacked and burnt down.

In addition to this, the chief is himself the principal owner of private *ábuta*. This involves him in lending and crediting transactions with his subjects. Moreover, he is the only man who carries on "foreign" business beyond his community. Both these conditions are apt to increase his power if he is a clever man. His *kítere* may approach him for money or pigs with which to buy a wife for himself or his son, either within the community or from abroad. If a girl is given in marriage the chief shares in the return gift. The chief helps a man with *ábuta* or pig for funeral feasts or for any other purpose.

For this reason the men are prone to give something additional, a *tótokai,* when they settle their debts. They are sure to be soon in need of new loans from the chief. A bondsman may pay 10, 20, 30, or even 50 fathoms of *ábuta* when he returns 100 lent to him perhaps three years previously. They are ready to recompense their chief by services such as feeding a pig either for no return or for a purely nominal one (*kórai*), or by presenting him with a pig which has been fattened inside an enclosure (*kúmeke-omi*). But a *tótokai* is paid also between *múmira,* and recompensed by *mámoko,* the one anxious to flatter the other's self esteem. In this merry-go-round of payments each one strives to display his glory and increase his renown. But a clever man never fails to take advantage of the situation. The *mínei* and *búrepi* gained influence by an intelligent use of these exchanges. Some *múmira,* however, like Cíbelau-Máugoci, by spreading terror restricted the amount they paid for pigs to merely formal sums: he gave 10 fathoms for a pig worth 100 fathoms, and that even to other *múmira tútoberu.*

Although it would be wrong to exaggerate this profit making and the rationalistic side of bargaining, it should be noted that it existed even in the pre-European epoch. It has, of course, been strengthened by modern contact. One chief of *mínei* descent who has worked with the whites for some length of time explained carefully his hopes of the profit he could make by juggling *ábuta* and pigs with dexterity. Another one refused to continue the ceremonial exchanges on the occasion of a marriage because they were too expensive from an economic point of view.

The constant transference of pigs and tokens discloses commercial leanings. Although the tokens contain "intrinsic" value to a certain degree, their importance is derived from their ability to be converted into pigs, pigs being the fundamental element of a feast, and a feast standing for a man's social position. We may, then, fairly speak of a pig standard of currency.

MAGIC

Some reference has been made to the part played by magical or religious ideas. Such ideas and the belief in supernatural influences are active in every society, though the details vary. In every society the influence of this aspect of culture upon economic enterprise is considerable. The rites themselves affect, however, the technical side and the aims of production or exchange rather than the foundations of the economic activities.

It has been mentioned that feasts are associated with the growth of children, with marriage and death; that skulls, the spoils of head-hunting, are devoted to the personal war god of the chief, to *Orómrui;* and that the ghosts of the slain are believed to serve as *kítere* to the demon imagined so tall that his head reaches up to the clouds. The close of a successful war expedition gave occasion for a feast to be held, and furthermore feasts sometimes gave occasion for fighting, as for example the *únu* ceremony in the preparation for which the men indulged in the sport of head-hunting. It has been pointed out that a man's death was followed by a number of feasts which were believed to help the soul in the other world, although these feasts were held not only for the sake of the deceased, but often more to enhance his heir's renown.

It must also be borne in mind that a man's economic success is considered to be due to the help of his *óliga* (the ghosts of his ancestors). Without their aid his pigs will die and his garden be devastated by insects. They give him advice concerning his bargains and all his enterprises. If he is not able to confer with them personally he will ask a *mékai,* a magician, to assist him. On the other hand, a man's economic success is considered to be a result of his *óliga's* protection, somewhat in the same way that the Puritans interpreted success in business.

There are innumerable occasions on which "sacrifices" are given to "feed" *Orómrui,* the *óliga,* the *mára,* etc., for food is believed to invigorate members of the spirit world, just as it does man; and like mortals, ghosts and demons are also anxious to maintain their renown.

Conclusion

Summing up, it may be said that these communities of Buin consist of an agricultural population, which also engages in some hunting, fishing, and collecting. The natives are an essentially sedentary people, although dwellings were sometimes moved as a result of warfare and personal quarrels. The communities are kept together by feudal chiefs, each of whom is the representative senior of his family in the district. As pointed out above, there are various layers in the economic system. The social stratification relies on an ethnic patriarchialism that, however, is more and more blurred by the importance of material objects of value. In this way individual wealth allied to democratic tendencies is disintegrating the old order. This process had begun before the advent of the Europeans, but is being accelerated by modern agencies.

Exchange is not indispensable in this society for mere sustenance. The chief motives for exchange are the desire for the luxuries of life, for expensive feasts, and for self-glorification. The process of converting one kind of object of value into another, of pigs into *ábuta,* and *vice versa,* upon the basis of reciprocity is a means of intensifying and adding complexity to the social texture of the community and the intercommunal life.

The usual catchwords for designating primitive economics are insufficient in face of the picture which has been sketched of the Buin economics. From it we can guess at the germs from which more complicated forms of economic organization are able to develop. Several features of Buin economics hint at bridges leading to economic forms such as existed in the ancient Oriental societies of Sumer or Egypt. I am referring to barter with foreigners through the chief, to the tendencies towards individualism, to the making of profits, to the chief as banker, to the growth of a class of rich men, to the profit which can be derived from the rearing of pigs and exchanging them for money. If we want to give a name to this type of economic life which has been described, we might call it tentatively: "early feudal precapitalism," but in a state of decay.

It is an advantage that in this society the symbols of value are closely connected with the fundamental needs of life, and that they are constantly revived by their translation into terms of the enjoyment of life. They have not become abstract and isolated values as they have with us.

15 ROSSEL ISLAND MONEY: A UNIQUE MONETARY SYSTEM

W. E. Armstrong

The island of Rossel lies about 200 miles south-eastward of New Guinea. Approximately 100 square miles in area, it is inhabited by a primitive population numbering about 1000 in all. The Rossel Islanders have characteristics and customs which differentiate them from the Melanesian-speaking peoples of the neighbouring archipelago, but none are so striking as the unique currency system, by the aid of which they carry on their mutual trafficking in pigs and concubines, in canoes and wives.

The outstanding features of the Rossel Island money are that, of each grade of the tokens in use, there is a virtually unchanging stock that has come down to the present generation from time immemorial, and that into the grading of the tokens— their value-relationships to one another—there enters the novel principle of a time-element or interest-element, in place of the more familiar principle of simple proportionality.

The articles which it is here proposed to call money are made from shell, and are of two kinds, named Dap and Kö respectively. A single piece of Dap money, which we may conveniently designate a coin, is a polished bit of shell a few millimetres thick, with flat or slightly curved surfaces, having an area varying from 2 to 20 sq. cms., and of almost any shape, though usually roughly triangular with rounded corners. In colour the coins vary from white through shades of orange and red, especially on the outer more polished surface. The coloration is generally uneven. The shapes and colours suggest

FROM W. E. Armstrong, "Rossel Island Money: a Unique Monetary System," *The Economic Journal,* Vol. XXXIV, September (1924), pp. 423–429. Reprinted by permission of the author and publisher.

that these coins were made from a mollusc allied to the Spondylus, from which the well-known sapi-sapi beads are made. Every coin is perforated within a few millimetres of one of its edges and generally at a corner. A single coin of Kö money consists of ten discs roughly shaped out of some shell, possibly that of the giant clam, each disc of the ten having approximately the same diameter and thickness. The individual discs are not money, for a set of ten discs is only exchanged as a whole.

There are twenty-two main values of Dap money, having separate names, but these names are not descriptive of the values. Certain of these values are subdivided into two or three classes, so that there are about forty distinctions of value altogether in the case of Dap money. For the purposes of the present account these sub-values (which seem to be of little importance) will be ignored, and only the twenty-two main values will be considered. As the names given to them are somewhat clumsy it seems simplest to use here the numbers 1 to 22 to designate them, taking 1 for the lowest, and 22 for the highest value.

Although any piece of Dap is generally at once recognised by the native as being a 1 or an *x,* it is difficult to obtain any definite characterisation of these classes. Very roughly, one can say that the lower values are white or dark red and rather clumsier in shape, while the higher values are lighter red to yellow and more delicate in shape—certainly the higher the value the more pleasing to the eye. This lack of a serial arrangement of attributes to mark value would be almost impossible if additions were continually made to the stock of money; but the money of Rossel is peculiar in that it is not replenished by fresh additions, except in the case of Nos. 1 to 6 or 7; but such money, although bearing the appropriate value-names and obeying the same laws of exchange as the money regarded as original, is recognised as belonging to a different order. In the case of Kö money (the second of the two varieties), it is believed that there have been no additions to the original stock, which was made in a remote past by Wonajö, the supreme god of Rossel (as also was the main stock of Dap money). The shell for the Dap was obtained from a bay at the east end of Rossel; the shell for Kö from a bay on the north side of the island. Both these places are classed with the "yaba," or sacred places, which occur throughout the island, the rites in connection with which serve to preserve the uniform and beneficial order of the universe. If the money on the island be non-renewable and there be not too great an amount of it, it would, of course, be possible for every coin to be individually known; in this case, there might be no general distinguishing marks of the 22 classes, for, in the case at least of Dap, every coin has its perceptible individual characteristics. In the case of Nos. 13 to 22 there is little doubt that all the coins belonging to these classes are individually known by all natives of any consequence in the financial world. Moreover, each coin belonging to Classes 15 to 22 has an individual name in addition to its class-name. It is, therefore, clear that in the case at least of these there need be no defining character of the class other than enumeration of its members. It was possible to ascertain the quantity of Dap on the island of values 15 to 22, which gave a total of 81 coins all distinguished by individual names.

Of Kö money the distinctions of value are fewer, there being a total of sixteen values. The names of these are the Dap names with suffix "kagnö." For instance, the lowest value Kö is called "Tebuda kagnö," Tebuda being the name of No. 7 of the Dap series. The remaining fifteen values of Kö, which may be designated by the numbers 8 to 22, are denoted by means of the names of the remaining higher values of Dap. Thus the name of No. 22, the highest value Dap, with suffix "kagnö," denotes the highest value Kö. Unlike the Dap money, the values of Kö money vary with the variation of one simple character, namely, size of the discs. These discs vary in diameter from about 1½ cms. in the case of the lowest values, to about 3 cms. in the case of the highest.

To pass on to the consideration of how these values are interrelated; in the first place, the same principle of value-relationship applies within each of the two monetary systems, the Dap and Kö, but no member of the one series has any recognised exchange-value in terms of any member of the other, though there is an equivalence for certain purposes between Dap and Kö bearing the same name. Generally speaking, wherever payments of Kö are made, payments of Dap also form part of the transaction—a service or commodity is priced in terms of so much Dap and so much Kö. There are, however, a number of commodities which are priced in terms of Dap only, mostly commodities of low price. It is possible, also, that there are some commodities priced in terms of Kö only—which is most likely to be the case with commodities which pass mainly between women, for it is said that Dap is essentially men's money, while Kö is essentially women's money, though the latter idea seems to be merely a traditional fiction. In the present account only the Dap side of payments will be considered, even though similar important payments of Kö may also be involved.

In nearly all instances of real money throughout the world, where there are coins of different values, a higher value coin is generally regarded as equivalent to so many of the lowest value coins or at least as being composed of so many recognised units of value. This is not the case on Rossel; the value of a coin x in terms of a coin y is expressed by the length of time y would have to be let out on loan in order that x be repayable. If the thought of the islanders were sufficiently systematic, then all the twenty-two values of Dap could be expressed in terms of No. 1 and time; No. 2 would be No. 1 at interest for a few days—No. 22 would be No. 1 at compound interest for several years. Their ideas, however, are not fully systematised to this extent, but the native does systematically apply the principle that a No. x if lent for a few days requires the return of a No. $(x+1)$—if lent for a rather longer period the borrower will be required to repay a No. $(x+2)$, and so on.

Now, if a large number of commodities are priced in terms of a small number of commodities, it will hardly be legitimate to call these latter commodities money, unless they also are systematically related to each other. This type of pseudo-money is all that occurs in the neighbouring Massim area, where, except by a complicated and forced process of calculation, no single commodity can be said to be worth, for instance, x sapi-sapi beads of best quality. The Massim are far removed from having any commodity whose main function is to act as a standard of value and medium of exchange. A statement of this kind can, however, be made with far more directness in the case of Rossel Island, even though in this case commodities are priced in terms of particular Dap and Kö, and not in terms of any Dap and Kö which add up to the required figure. (This, of course, would require a knowledge of the number of units of value in each number

Dap and Kö, which is lacking.) The way this comes about is as follows.

Suppose an individual A wishes to buy a commodity whose price is Dap No. x. A may possess Dap coins, more or less in value than No. x, but not any No. x. He, therefore, borrows a No. x from B and pays for the commodity with this. During the time which elapses before repaying B, he becomes successively liable to No. $(x+1)$, No. $(x+2)$, and so on. If he has one of these values he repays B and all is square. Whether he borrows for a long or a short period does not really make any difference to A so long as he has at the time of borrowing at least as much money as he borrows, either in his possession or preferably lent out with interest, for A's opportunities for lending are presumably as great as B's opportunities—that which makes it necessary for A to borrow from B equally makes it necessary for X to borrow from A in the long run. Owing to the peculiar value-relationships of the Rossel money, money must change hands very many more times in order to effect a single purchase than is necessitated by any of the more usual monetary systems. Given this mobility then we can say that a commodity which is priced in terms of a particular value of Dap is indirectly priced in terms of any Number of the series.

It would be well to elaborate further my earlier implication that there can be said to be a unit of value in the case of Dap and Kö, even though it be impossible to say that a No. x is k times a No. y. If we assume that time is priced, then, of course, the problem is simple—if the interest for unit time, *i.e.* for x to become $x+1$, is taken as 5 percent, for example, then, in terms of No. 1, No. 2 is No. $1+1/20$ No. 2, No. 3 is No. $1+1/10$ No. $1+1/400$ No. 1, and so on, in the compound interest series. But, on the whole, it distorts the facts to say that there is a definite rate of interest. It is better, therefore, to substitute for the statement that x is k times a No. 1 the statement that x is a No. 1 of so many months ago, which brings in a second unit value, time. The common denomination being understood, then the price of any commodity or service might be put in terms of time, *e.g.* "a wife costs a year, a house two years, a basket of taro a week, and so on." This does, I believe, express the native point of view more clearly than to imagine a more or less evaluated rate of interest.

Since there are very few of the high-value coins on the island, and since there are important commodities and services that must be paid for by means of these high-value coins, they move about a good deal (though there is an exception in the case of the highest two or three values). The borrowing and lending of coins is, in fact, so important that there exists a special class of persons who act as agents for these transactions; they are denoted by a special name, which may be translated by the term "broker" without much change of sense. These brokers derive their income by keeping their capital in motion and by a process somewhat analogous to the activities of a London bill-broker—by borrowing at a lower rate of interest and discounting at a higher— and practise a magic by means of which they claim to act on the minds of their debtors, making them repay within the customary time, while the minds of their creditors are effected in the reverse direction.

Since the series of values is finite, the question naturally arises as to what happens in the case of the loan of a high-value coin. Since there are only a few of these coins—seven each of the three highest values—many loans are liable to overreach, by the ordinary mechanism, repayment-value No. 22. It is found that the normal method of repayment of loans of Nos. 18 and above is of a special kind. If, for instance, a No. 18 be borrowed, security is given, generally a stone axe of the type used as money on Sudest. This security is returned on repayment of the loan; but instead of the repayment of a higher value Dap at the end of the required period, a payment of low-value Dap, known as "Döndap," is made at the beginning of the period of the loan, and the Original No. 18 is repaid at the end of the period instead of a No. 19 or higher value. The Döndap for a short-period loan of a No. 18 is generally a series of one each of Nos. 1 to 10; for a longer period there will be two or three each perhaps of Nos. 7 to 9 or 10. For a No. 19 the Döndap will end at No. 11 or perhaps No. 12. If the loan be for several years, as it is occasionally, there will be three or four repetitions of these interest-payments. A good deal of ceremonial attends such payments of interest and it is generally the occasion for some feasting and dancing. An important part of such interest-feasts, or "Dogo," as they are called, is the handling of the money by a number of people, this apparently confirming the transaction. Such feasts are also the occasion for other monetary transactions; for, even when a single low-value coin is borrowed, it must be touched by a number of people, who, as witnesses, act as a safeguard to the lender.

Security was referred to above, which generally takes the form of a ceremonial stone axe of the Massim type; sometimes, however, and this seems rather anomalous, security takes the form of a higher value Dap than that for which it is acting as security. This may be because there is little use for values 19 to 22 at the present day; it seems to be very rare now for there to be any transactions involving payments greater than No. 18. A few years ago, however, No. 20 had an important use as compensation for ritual murder. The death of a chief used to involve the eating of at least one victim, frequently drawn from a neighbouring friendly village. The compensation of the relatives of these victims involved payments whose ramifications are said to have extended over ten years or more. At the present day, No. 18, of which there are twenty coins on the island, is involved in payments for wives, for "ptyilibi" (polyandric wives) and pigs. When a No. 18 passes from person to person, it is handled with great reverence, and a crouching attitude is maintained. Nos. 19 to 22 are so sacred that they are always kept enclosed and are not supposed to see the light of day. Apparently they have little or no work to do now, except as security, and are owned only by chiefs. No. 22, of which there are seven coins, is inherited in the male line; and, apparently, the chiefs who own these are the most important on the island.

It would be impossible within the limits of this paper to describe the details of the financial ritual in connection with payments for wives and pigs, as they are very complicated. In the case of a polyandric wife, bought by five or six men, the method of payment of the No. 18 is ingenious. If there are five husbands, A pays the girl's father a No. 18, B pays A a No. 17, C pays B a No. 16, D pays C a No. 15, and E pays D a No. 14; but, apparently, A does not pay E a No. 13, and B A a No. 12, and so on, as we should expect. It is, of course, an unequal division of the cost, for D pays less than C, B and A, and E pays the most, provided No. 14 is more valuable than the difference between No. 18 and No. 17.

In conclusion, it may be pointed out that Rossel Island money is money in the strict sense of the term. It serves as a medium of exchange and a standard of value, and it is not desired for its utility for other purposes, even for ornament or display. Indeed it is even considered "bad form" to make any sort of display of one's wealth of Dap and Kö. How such a peculiar monetary system came into being it is difficult even to conjecture. The conception of "interest" is rare in Melanesia and New Guinea, though it occurs in simple form in parts of the Bismarck Archipelago. This would point to some exceptional cultural influence which reached the island of Rossel but no other part of this extensive region, unless we suppose that a "higher" culture, containing the germs of the peculiar features of Rossel, once extended over a large area, throughout which it has since degenerated, leaving a vestige on Rossel in the shape of its present fantastic monetary system.

16 PRIMITIVE MONEY[1]

George Dalton

> In a subject where there is no agreed procedure for knocking
> out errors, doctrines have a long life.   JOAN ROBINSON

Primitive money is a complicated subject for several reasons.
There is not in common use a set of analytical categories designed to reveal distinguishing characteristics of markedly different systems: economies without markets and machines still tend
to be viewed through the theoretical spectacles designed for
Western economy (Arensberg 1957:99). Second, francs, sterling,
and dollars are only the most recent of a long series of foreign
monies introduced into primitive economies. Earlier, Arabs,
Portuguese, Dutch, English, and others introduced cowrie, manil-
las, beads, etc., with varying permeation and varying disruption
of indigenous monetary systems. Only rarely do anthropologists
succeed in disentangling the foreign from the indigenous in a way
which reveals the nature of the old money and the consequences
of the new.

Moreover, if one asks what is "primitive" about a particular
money, one may come away with two answers: the money-*stuff*
—woodpecker scalps, sea shells, goats, dogs' teeth—is primitive

FROM George Dalton, "Primitive Money," *American Anthropologist*
(1965), Vol. 67, pp. 44–65. Reprinted by permission of the author and
The American Anthropological Association.

[1] M. L. Burstein, Robert Clower, Ronald Cohen, George Delehanty,
Mitchell Harwitz, Sidney Mintz, and A. A. Walters made critical comments on an earlier draft. I am grateful to these anthropologists and
economists, and to Heyward Ehrlich who suggested changes in style and
presentation. I must acknowledge separately the kindness of Paul Bohannan and Karl Polanyi, both of whom read several drafts and insisted on
improvement. Much of the paper is an elaboration of ideas contained in
Polanyi's lectures and writings.

(i.e., different from our own); and the *uses* to which the money-stuff is sometimes put—mortuary payments, bloodwealth, bride-wealth—are primitive (i.e., different from our own).

Primitive money performs some of the functions of our own money, but rarely all; the conditions under which supplies are forthcoming are usually different; primitive money is used in some ways ours is not; our money is impersonal and commercial, while primitive money frequently has pedigree and personality, sacred uses, or moral and emotional connotations. Our governmental authorities control the quantity of money, but rarely is this so in primitive economies.

Failure to understand the reasons for such differences leads to disputes about bridewealth versus brideprice, to arguments about whether cows, pig tusks, and potlatch coppers are "really" money, to the assumption that modern coinage merely "replaces" indigenous forms of money, and to disagreement of authorities over minimal definitions of money. In these disputes the characteristics of American or European money are too often used as a model.

Some of the most respected comparisons between primitive and Western money fail to go deeply enough into comparative economic and social structure. Even Malinowski and Firth do not explain that it is nationally integrated market organization which accounts for those Western monetary traits they use as a model of "real" money: "The tokens of wealth [*vaygua:* ceremonial axe blades, necklaces of red shell discs, and arm bracelets of shells] have often been called 'money.' It is at first sight evident that 'money' in our sense cannot exist among the Trobrianders. . . . Any article which can be classed as 'money' or 'currency' must fulfill certain essential conditions; it must function as a medium of exchange and as a common measure of value, it must be the instrument of condensing wealth, the means by which value can be accumulated. Money also, as a rule, serves as the standard of deferred payments . . . we cannot think of *vaygua* in terms of 'money'" (Malinowski 1921:13–14).

Firth registers his agreement: "But according to precise terminology, such objects [strings of shell discs] can hardly be correctly described as currency or money. In any economic system, however primitive, an article can only be regarded as true money when it acts as a definite and common medium of exchange, as a convenient stepping stone in obtaining one type of goods for

another. Moreover in so doing it serves as a measure of values.
. . . Again, it is a standard of value . . ." (Firth 1929:881).

Malinowski and Firth use the bundle of attributes money has
in Western market economy to comprise a model of *true* money.
They then judge whether or not money-like stuff in primitive
economies is really money by how closely the uses of the primitive stuff resemble our own—a strange procedure for anthropologists who would never use the bundle of attributes of the Western family, religion, or political organization in such a way.
Quoting from Lienhardt—". . . most anthropologists have ceased
to take their bearings in the study of religion from any religion
practiced in their own society" (1956:310). And Gluckman and
Cunnison write, concerning political organizations: "One important discovery made in . . . [*African Political Systems*] was that
the institutions through which a society organized politically need
not necessarily look like the kinds of political institutions with
which we have long been familiar in the Western world, and in
the great nations of Asia" (1962:vi).

Dollars have that set of uses called medium of exchange,
means of payment, standard of value, etc., precisely because our
economy is commercially organized. Where economies are organized differently, non-commercial uses of monetary objects become important, and "money" takes on different characteristics.
The question is not—as it is conventionally put—are shells,
woodpecker scalps, cattle, goats, dog teeth, or *kula* valuables
"really" "money"? It is, rather, how are the similarities and the
differences between such items and dollars related to similarities
and differences in socio-economic structure?

We shall show below the connections between Western money
and economy, then go on to make some points about primitive
money and economy, and finally will examine the case of Rossel
Island money in detail.

CAPITALISM: MARKET INTEGRATION
DETERMINES ALL MONEY USES

In the economies for which the English monetary vocabulary
was created, there is one dominant transactional mode, market
exchange, to which *all* money uses relate. By contrast, in many
primitive economies before Western incursion, market exchange

transactions are either absent (as with Nuer) or peripheral (as in the Trobriands), but non-commercial uses of money do exist. Seeing non-commercial uses of money through the blinders of commercial money causes difficulty in understanding primitive monies. We must first be made aware of the blinders.

U.S. dollars may be called general purpose money (Polanyi 1957a; 1957b). They are a single monetary instrument to perform all the money uses. Moreover, the same dollars enter modes of transaction to be called redistribution and reciprocity, as enter into market exchange. These features of U.S. money are consequences of economy-wide market integration and require explanation in an anthropological context.

That U.S. economy is integrated by market exchange is explained by the wide range of natural resources, labor, goods, and services transacted by purchase and sale at market-determined prices, and by the extent to which people in our national economy depend for livelihood on wage, profit, interest, and rental income got from market sale. Natural resources and capital goods (land, labor, machines, and buildings of all varieties), consumption goods (food, automobiles), personal and impersonal services (dentistry, electricity), are all purchasable "on the market." Goods and services which are ceremonial and religious, or which serve as prestige indicators, are purchasable in the same way and with the same money as subsistence goods. In market-integrated economy very different items and services are directly comparable, because all are available at prices stated in the same money. The subject of price determination of products and resources under varying conditions of supply and demand (price and distribution theory) is an important field of economics because market exchange is our dominant transactional mode.[2]

[2] For purposes of this paper we simply characterize the dominant transactional mode of Western economy as "market exchange." Price and distribution theory distinguish among many kinds of market exchange, pure competition, monopolistic competition, pure and differentiated oligopoly, etc. These distinctions do not concern us. Similarly, for our purposes we regard U.S. dollars as a single kind of money. For monetary problems in our own economy it is necessary to distinguish among currency, check deposits, and savings deposits, and sometimes between legal tender and money which is not legal tender; but for the matters of contrast that concern us, it is not necessary to make these distinctions. For a discussion of the fine points of money variations within Western economy, see Burstein (1963: Chapter 1).

COMMERCIAL USES OF MONEY IN A
MARKET-INTEGRATED NATIONAL ECONOMY

Except for economic historians, most economists and all economic theory were (until recently) concerned exclusively with
European and American types of economy. Economists do not
find it necessary to distinguish among the transactional modes of
market exchange, reciprocity, and redistribution, because market
exchange is so overwhelmingly important. For the same reason
economists do not find it necessary to describe at length the
different uses of money in our own economy: with only a few
exceptions they all express market exchange transactions.

To make this point clear I will attach to each of the money
uses an adjective describing the transactional mode, thereby
pointing up how they all serve commercial transactions: medium
of (commercial) exchange; means of (commercial) payment;
unit of (commercial) account; standard for deferred (commercial) payment.

The medium of (commercial) exchange function of money
in our economy is its dominant function, and all other commercial uses of money are dependently linked—derived from—the
use of dollars as media of (commercial) exchange. For example,
dollars are also used as a means of (commercial) payment of
debt *arising from* market transactions. It is purchase and sale of
resources, goods, and services which create the money functions
of means of (commercial) payment and standard for deferred
(commercial) payment.[3] All the commercial uses of money are

[3] We can generalize the point by showing how all the commercial uses
of money are brought into play as the result of a single purchase: I buy
a house for $20,000 paying $5,000 down and borrowing $15,000 from a
bank to be repaid in future installments: (1) I acquire rights to a house;
the former owner acquires $20,000. The money is used as a medium of
(commercial) exchange. (2) Dollars here are used also as a measure or
standard of (commercial) value, i.e., as a measuring device to compare
the house with any other commodity priced in dollars. (3) The bank
uses dollars as a unit of (commercial) account in recording my indebtedness to it. (4) My debt to the bank also means that dollars are used
as a standard for deferred (commercial) payments, i.e., as a device to
measure commercial debt. (5) If I save money currently in anticipation
of repaying debt, dollars are used as a store of (commercial) value or
wealth. (6) When I begin to repay the bank, dollars are then used as a
means of (commercial) payment of indebtedness incurred by the past
market purchase.

consequences of market integration, simply reflecting the highly organized credit and accounting arrangements that facilitate market purchases. This is why economists in writing about our economy need not attach the qualifier "commercial" to the money uses. Indeed, we in our market-integrated national economy sometimes regard the terms "money" and "medium of exchange" as interchangeable. But for primitive communities where market transactions are absent or infrequent, it would be distorting to identify money with medium of (commercial) exchange, as Einzig warns us: "Since, however, money has also other functions and since in many instances [of money used in primitive economies] those functions are more important than that of the medium of exchange, it seems to be unjustified to use the term as a mere synonym for 'medium of exchange'" (1948:321).

NON-COMMERCIAL USES OF MONEY

Dollars are also used as a means of non-commercial payment: traffic fines paid to local government and taxes to all levels of government. A structural characteristic of Western economy is that redistributive transactions—obligatory payments to political authority which uses the receipts to provide community services—are made with the same money used as medium of (commercial) exchange in private transactions. The consequences are important and far-reaching.

In all societies having specialized political authority, there must be some institutionalized arrangement for the governing authorities to acquire goods and services for their own maintenance and to provide social services (defense, justice) to the community. In this sense, we may regard the redistributive function (acquiring and disbursing such goods and services) as an "economic" component of political organization. Exactly how the arrangements vary for political authority to acquire and disburse goods and services is one way of differentiating between the organization of Soviet, American, and (say) Bantu economies.

In U.S. economy the government makes use of the market in the process of redistribution: medium of (commercial) exchange money earned as private income is used by households and firms as means of (redistributive) payment of politically incurred obligation (taxes). The government then buys on the market the services and products it requires—civil servants, guns, roads—to provide community services.

In our system, the same can be said for another mode of transaction, reciprocity, or gift-giving between kin and friends. The same money serves the different transactional modes: in purchasing a gift, the money paid is used as medium of (commercial) exchange; giving the gift is part of a reciprocal transaction (a material or service transfer induced by social obligation between the gift partners). If cash is given as a gift, it is a means of (reciprocal) payment of the social obligation discharged by the gift-giving.

Here is yet another reason why economists in dealing with our own economy need not distinguish among transactional modes: redistribution and reciprocity make use of market exchange and make use of the same money used in market exchange. In Western economy, therefore, tax and gift transactions appear as simple variations from the private market norm—special types of expenditure or outlay—which present no theoretical difficulties.

American reliance upon market sale for livelihood and upon the price mechanism for allocating resources to production lines does the following: it makes the medium of (commercial) exchange use of money its dominant attribute, it makes other money uses serve market transactions, and it confers that peculiar *bundle* of traits on our general purpose money which mark off dollars from non-monetary objects. It is our market integration which makes it necessary to institutionalize all uses of money in the same money instrument. As with Malinowski and Firth, we thereby come to think of "money-ness" as this *set* of uses conferred on the single monetary object. And because ours is a market economy, we come to think of medium of (commercial) exchange as the single most important attribute of "money-ness."

LIMITED-PURPOSE MONIES

In primitive economies—i.e., small-scale economies not integrated by market exchange—different uses of money may be institutionalized separately in different monetary objects to carry out reciprocal and redistributive transactions. These money objects used in non-commercial ways are usually distinct from any that enter market-place transactions. And the items which perform non-commercial money uses need not be full-time money, so to speak; they have uses and characteristics apart from their ability to serve as a special kind of money.

In U.S. economy, objects such as jewelry, stocks, and bonds are not thought of as money because (like cattle among the Bantu) these come into existence for reasons other than their "money-ness." Each is capable of one or two money uses, but not the full range which distinguishes dollars, and particularly not the medium of (commercial) exchange use of dollars. It is worth examining these because, we shall argue, primitive monies used in reciprocal and redistributive transactions are the counterparts of these limited or special purpose monies, and not of dollars as media of (commercial) exchange; they resemble dollars only in non-commercial uses (paying taxes and fines, and gift-giving).

Dollars serve as a store of (commercial and non-commercial) value because dollars can be held idle for future use. But this is true also for jewelry, stocks and bonds, and other marketable assets. However, in U.S. economy jewelry is not a medium of (commercial) exchange because one cannot spend it directly, and it is not a means of (commercial or non-commercial) payment because it is not acceptable in payment of debt or taxes.[4]

As a measuring device (rather than as tangible objects) dollars are used as unit of account and standard for deferred payment of debts. Now consider the accounting and payment procedures used by a baby-sitting cooperative in which a number of households club together to draw on each other for hours of baby-sitting time. Family A uses four hours of sitting time supplied by family B. Family A thereby incurs a debt of four hours it owes the co-op; family B acquires a credit of four hours that it may draw upon in future from some member of the co-op. Here, baby-sitting labor time is a unit of (reciprocal) account and a standard for deferred (reciprocal) payments—a limited purpose money in the sense that it performs two of the subsidiary uses of dollars. Other examples (trading stamps, blood banks) could be given. The point is that even where dollars

---

[4] Common stocks may be used as a medium of (commercial) exchange or payment, as when a company is purchased for stock, but it is nevertheless dollars that are used as the (commercial) standard of value.

perform all the money uses for all modes of transaction, there are situations in which a limited range of money uses are performed by objects not thought of as money. These limited purpose monies become important in small-scale communities without market integration and, therefore, without a general purpose money.

CONTROL OVER THE QUANTITY OF MONEY; ABSENCE OF STATUS REQUISITES

In national market economies, governments deliberately control the quantity of general purpose money because dollars (francs, sterling) carry out market sales which the populace depends on for livelihood. Roughly speaking, if the authorities allow too much money to come into use as medium of (market) purchase, the result is inflation. If the authorities allow too little money to come into use, the result is deflation and unemployment (a contraction in the rate of market purchasing below the full employment capacity rate of production). The need to deliberately vary the quantity of money is a direct result of economy-wide market integration.

It has often been noted (e.g., Herskovits 1952:238) that in primitive societies there is seldom any conscious control by political authority over money objects. Such is not merely a difference between primitive *monetary* systems and our own, but one that reflects differences between their *economic* systems and ours. In economies not integrated by market exchange, non-commercial monetary transactions are only occasional events (e.g., blood-wealth, bridewealth), and non-commercial money is not usually connected with production and daily livelihood. That the non-commercial money-stuff may be fixed in quantity for all time (Yap stones), or increase in quantity only through natural growth (cows, pig tusks) does not affect production and daily livelihood (as would be the case with us if dollars were fixed in quantity).

What is also true of our market economy based on contract rather than status, is that having the money price is a sufficient condition for buying most goods. Not only is Western money anonymous, so to speak, but money users are also anonymous: the market sells to whoever has the purchase price and only rarely imposes status prerequisites on the use of money as medium of (commercial) exchange.[5] In contrast, there usually are status prerequisites in non-commercial uses of primitive money. For example, in the use of cattle as means of (reciprocal) payment of bridewealth, status requisites such as lineage, age, rank of the persons, must be complied with. The money users are not anonymous, and a special kind of limited purpose money is necessary to the transaction.

PRIMITIVE MONEY AND SOCIO-ECONOMIC ORGANIZATION

Einzig (1948:323) points out that: "The overwhelming importance of unilateral non-commercial payments in primitive life as compared with payments arising from [commercial] trade is altogether overlooked by practically all definitions [of primitive money]. It is assumed that money must be essentially commercial in character and that any object which serves the purposes of non-commercial payments may safely be disregarded even if its use is of first-rate importance in the economic, p litical, and social life of primitive communities."

When anthropologists employ Western monetary terms to describe uses of money-stuff in non-commercial transactions, a crucial misunderstanding may result: when cattle or seashells perform some money uses in ways unrelated to market purchase and sale, they are not media of (commercial) exchange, or means of (commercial) payment.

The uncritical use of our general purpose money as the model of true money obscures the point that special purpose monies used for non-commercial transactions express salient features of underlying socio-economic structure. When we consider money in communities not integrated by market exchange—the Nuer, the Trobriands, the Tiv—it becomes essential to distinguish among the several transactional modes and among the several money uses: *primitive money-stuff does not have that bundle of related uses which in our economy is conferred on dollars by market*

---

[5] The qualifications necessary are not due to the structure of market economy, but to cultural practices which differ among market societies: in U.S. society (but not, say, in French) Negroes cannot buy housing at will (but they can buy automobiles); people under 18 cannot legally buy liquor; sale of some firearms is controlled by license. But for most people and for most goods and services, there are no status requisites imposed.

integration and by the use of dollars in both commercial and non-commercial transactions. The differences between cattle-money or shell-money and dollars are traceable to the differences in the transactional modes which call forth money uses. When Malinowski says that *kula* valuables are different from Western currency, he is really pointing out that reciprocal gift-giving is different from market purchase and sale (1922). Indeed, anthropologists use Western monetary terms ambiguously whenever they fail to distinguish between the market and the non-commercial modes of transaction. Reining, for example, states: "There seems to have been little exchange among households although iron tools and spears made from locally smelted ore had a limited application as a medium of exchange, being used primarily for marriage payments" (1959:39).

If Western monetary terms are to be used by anthropologists in the meanings they convey for our own economy, the unqualified phrase "medium of exchange" must mean medium of market (or commercial) exchange. Since brides are not acquired through impersonal market transactions by random buyers and sellers, the iron tools are not used as media of (market) exchange, but as media of (reciprocal) exchange: as part of a non-commercial transaction in which a man acquires a bundle of rights in a woman and her children in return for iron tools and other indemnification payments to her kin.

It seems useful to regard the bridewealth items as special purpose "money" because the iron tools and spears—or in other societies, cows or goats—are the *required* items, and because they carry out money uses which do have counterparts in our own society. Whether one calls them special purpose monies or highly ranked treasure items necessary to the transaction for which one may not substitute other items only matters when the subject of money uses in primitive compared to Western economies is raised. Then we can show that cows and armbands of shells do perform some of the uses of dollars but in non-commercial situations. The goal is always to state the role of bridewealth or kula items, or other limited purpose money, from the viewpoint of the analyst concerned with comparative economy, but without distorting the folk-meaning of the items and the transactions they enter.

MONEY USES IN PRIMITIVE AND PEASANT ECONOMIES

Because money and money uses in market-dominated economies differ sharply from money in other economies it is useful to classify economies in accordance with the importance of market exchange transactions (Bohannan and Dalton 1962).

UNDERDEVELOPED COMMUNITIES

Primitive (or Subsistence) Economies		Peasant Economies
Type I	Type II	Type III
Marketless	*Peripheral Markets Only*	*Market-Dominated*
Sonjo	Trobriand Islanders	Malay Fishermen
Nuer	Tiv	Jamaica
Lele	Rossel Islanders	Haiti
Arnhemlanders		Kipsigis
Bemba		Cantel ⎫ Guatemala
Kwakiutl (1840)		Panajachel ⎰
		Kwakiutl (1890)

Type I: Marketless. In marketless communities, land and labor are not transacted by purchase and sale but are allocated as expressions of kinship right or tribal affiliation. There are no formal market-place sites where indigenously produced items are bought and sold. These are "subsistence" economies in the sense that livelihood does not depend on production for sale. The transactional modes to allocate resources and labor as well as produced items and services are reciprocity and redistribution (Polanyi 1944: Chapter 4; 1957a; Dalton 1962). In marketless economies, then, transactions of labor, resources, material goods, and services are of non-commercial sorts—obligatory gifts to kin and friends, obligatory payments to chiefs and priests, bridewealth, bloodwealth, fees for entering secret societies, corvée labor, mortuary payments, etc.—which immediately marks off as different from our own any money-stuff used. Items such as cattle, goats, spears, Yap stones, and pig tusks take on roles as special purpose money in non-commercial transactions: they become means of (reciprocal or redistributive) payment, as is the case with bloodwealth and mortuary payments; or media of (reciprocal) exchange, as is the case with bridewealth.

Type II: Peripheral Markets Only. Everything said above

about marketless economies holds true for those with only peripheral markets, with one exception: market-place sites exist in which a narrow range of produce is bought and sold, either with some money-stuff used as medium of (commercial) exchange, or via barter in the economist's sense (moneyless market exchange). We call these market exchanges "peripheral" because land and labor are not bought and sold and because most people do not get the bulk of their income from market sales. In such small-scale subsistence economies market-place prices do not function —as they do in our national economy—as an integrative mechanism to allocate resources to production lines: labor and land use do not respond to changes in the prices of products transacted in peripheral market places. Malinowski's *gimwali* are peripheral market transactions of an occasional sort without the formal trappings found in African market places.

Type III: Market-Dominated (Peasant) Economies. Small-scale market-dominated communities share with our own nationally integrated market economy the following features: (i) a large proportion of land and labor as well as goods and services are transacted by market purchase and sale; (ii) most people depend upon market sale of labor or products for livelihood; (iii) market prices integrate production. Labor and land move into and out of different production lines in response to profit (and other income) alternatives, as indicated by market prices. In such economies, the medium of (commercial) exchange function of money is the most important; the other commercial uses of money facilitate market transactions, and the same money is used for non-commercial transactions.

Peasant economies (Firth 1946), differ from primitive (subsistence) economies in that peasant producers depend upon production for sale. However, both peasant and primitive communities differ from large-scale, developed, nationally integrated Western economies on two counts: modern machine technology is largely absent, and traditional social organization and cultural practices are largely retained (Dalton 1964).[6]

---

[6] Marketless economies and those with peripheral markets only, refer to descriptions in the literature of situations before serious European incursion. The term "primitive economy" is downright misleading when it is used to include all three types. I prefer to use it to mean only types I and II (Dalton 1964). In type III, where market exchange dominates, economic structure differs markedly, and so too do the uses of money. Firth (1946) is

ROSSEL ISLAND MONEY

Rossel Island money is famous in anthropological literature as something of an enigma. Although it was reported at an early date, and by an economist (Armstrong 1924; 1928) who was in the field for only two months, re-analysis in the light of points made earlier in this paper allows a different interpretation of Rossel Island money and economy.

ARMSTRONG'S THEORETICAL PRESENTATION

Armstrong asserts that Rossel Island money is a rough equivalent of our own (1924:429): that it is a medium of exchange used to purchase a wide range of goods and services, and that it is a standard of value for stating prices. He uses Western monetary and economic terms throughout to describe the Rossel system—medium of exchange, standard of value, buy, sell, price (1928:59).

The Rossel Islanders use two types of shell money, *ndap* and *nko*.[7] Ndap money consists of individual shells (Armstrong calls

---

right to call the market-dominated Malayan economies "pei ant" rather than "primitive" to indicate that a distinction should be made. A useful distinction between peasant and primitive economies is the following: by a peasant economy we mean one in which, (i) most people depend upon market sale of resources or products for livelihood; (ii) modern machine technology is largely absent; (iii) traditional social organization and cultural practices are retained in significant degree. A primitive economy differs primarily on the first point: most people do not depend on market sale of resources or products for livelihood. One might also say that the organizational component of community economic development consists in transforming economies of types I and II into type III.

Failure to distinguish among the three types is responsible for needless dispute in the literature, as when writers generalize from what is true in market-integrated economy, to all economies. Jones (1960) and Miracle (1962) argue the case for "economic man" in Africa: that Africans respond to material incentives and choose among economic alternatives just as we do. But note that *all* their examples come from type III economies, where Africans—like us—have come to depend for livelihood on market sale (of labor or cash crops). What is true for a Rhodesian copper miner is one thing; what is true for a Nuer or a Lele, is another.

[7] Following Armstrong, our treatment will concern ndap shells only. He said too little about strings of nko shells to allow anything more than guesses about how they functioned.

them coins), each of which belongs to one of 22 named classes or denominations, which Armstrong ranks from 1–22, a higher numbered class indicating a higher valued shell.

Armstrong's numbering system for classes of nadp shell money (1928:62)	Number of individual ndap shells in each class
22	7
21	10
20	10
19	10
18	20
17	7
16	7
15	10
14	30
13	30–40

Total in classes 13–22 ≅ 146

Armstrong could not determine the number of ndap shells in each class below 13, but he guesses there are fewer than 1,000 in all (1928:63), which would mean 800 or so in classes 1–12.

Armstrong's theoretical concern is with the value relationships among the ranked shells. He tells us that (as in Western economy) all goods and services on Rossel bear a money price stated as a piece (coin) of a specific class (1–22) of ndap, so that a big house costs a No. 20 ndap shell, and a pig a No. 18 (1928:88). But the shells are not quite like dollar bills numbered 1–22 with a No. 20 (say), bearing twice the value of a No. 10, or an item priced at No. 20 purchasable with two shells of No. 10 variety. In Armstrong's view it is merely an aberration due to custom, and, perhaps, to unsystematic thinking (1924: 426) that the Rossel Islanders insist that something priced at No. 20 must be paid for with a No. 20 shell, rather than with lower denomination pieces adding up to 20. He sees this as an inefficiency in their system as compared to ours—in which all bills and coins are directly convertible into each other. He therefore shows that the Rossel system requires elaborate borrowing to allow a person who does not happen to own a piece of No. 20 money to acquire an item "priced" at 20, and argues that it is the borrowing system that reveals the value relationships among the ranked coins (1924:425 and 423). This is a cumbersome equivalent of our own system—a model T, so to speak—which does the same job as our own media of exchange, but with more work and fuss because one cannot substitute two $10 bills for something priced at $20. Armstrong writes: ". . . the necessity for continual loans is largely the result of the peculiar nature of the system. The same 'amount' of money, where the values are simply related and 'change' can always be given, could perform the same amount of real service (i.e., effect the same number of purchases) with perhaps a tenth or less of the amount of lending necessitated by the Rossel system" (1928:65).

If one borrows a No. 12 for a short time, he will have to repay a No. 13; but for a longer time he will have to repay a No. 14, 15, etc. Therefore, he says, the value relationships among the denominations 1–22 conform roughly to compound interest, which shows the relationship of an initial sum lent to its repayment equivalent, depending upon the rate of interest and the time the initial sum is outstanding. Theoretically, a No. 1 shell is related to any other number, 2–22, by the length of time a No. 1 loan is outstanding before repayment must be made in any higher number (Armstrong 1928:63, 64).

Armstrong's analytical interpretation may be summarized: ndap shell money functions like dollars in that it is a medium of exchange, standard of value, standard for deferred payments, etc. Debts are calculated and goods and services priced in shells of stated denomination. The peculiar (different from our own) feature of the system is that the shell denominations are not freely convertible into one another, which makes necessary frequent borrowing at interest to acquire the exact denomination shell needed for a given purchase.

CONTRADICTORY EVIDENCE

There are two faults in Armstrong's analysis from which stem the subsidiary difficulties in his interpretation of the Rossel monetary system.

(1) He assumes all ndap shells function as media of (commercial) exchange. He does not distinguish among modes of transaction (reciprocity, redistribution, market exchange), but regards all transactions as commercial purchases (1924:427); brides cost a No. 18 shell, just as baskets costs a No. 4 shell. He writes: ". . . any commodity or service may be more or less directly priced in terms of them [*ndap* shells]" [1928:59]. Arm-

strong never doubts that Rossel Island money is essentially like our own media of (commercial) exchange. One could sum up his ethnocentric theorizing in a syllogism: ndap shells are "money"; money is a commercial instrument; therefore Rossel Island is a market economy.

(2) This market preconception leads him to do what the Rossel Islanders do *not* do: to number the ndap classes 1–22. By so doing he can assume that convertibility via borrowing and repayment is practiced throughout the *entire* range, so that one could start by lending a No. 1 shell, and by continual loans at interest, wind up eventually with a No. 22 shell. For example, "Any [*ndap* shell] value can thus be regarded as any lower value plus compound interest for the number of time units equal to the number of values by which the two are separated, so that No. 22, for example, is No. 1 plus compound interest for 21 units of time" (Armstrong 1928:64).

By ranking them 1–22 Armstrong implies that the differences between ndap shell classes are cardinal differences: that a No. 22 is 22 times more *valuable* than a No. 1, in the sense that a $20 bill is 20 times more valuable than a $1 bill. There are no such cardinal differences among ndap shells. To number them 1–22 is to give a false impression of similarity between ndap shell classes and Western money denominations and a false impression about the commensurability or the "purchasing power" relationship between lower and higher numbered ndap shells.

The characteristics of monetary transactions on Rossel that lead us to doubt Armstrong's interpretation may be set out with the following provisos kept in mind: Rossel Island economy is not integrated by market exchange; ndap shells (except for the lowest few classes) are not media of (commercial) exchange; and convertibility throughout the entire range could not be practiced.

There are (on the basis of Armstrong's own data) at least three groups of ndap shells, the shells in each group being necessary for a different range of transactions, and convertibility via borrowing and repayment being possible *within* the lowest two groups, but not *within* the highest group, and not between groups.

The shells Armstrong classes 1–8 or 9 are the only ones capable of increase in quantity (1924:424; 1928:60). The individual shells in each of these classes do not bear separate names, and some of them, at least, enter low echelon transactions, casual market exchange between individuals. In one of the rare descriptions of how shells below class No. 18 are actually used, Armstrong tells us that one may buy a basket, a lime stick, or a lime pot with a No. 4 shell (1928:85).[8] However, the question, "what goods and services will *each* shell class 1, 2, 3, . . . 22 'buy,' or what transactions does each enter?" is not answered except for ndap shells Nos. 4, 18, 20, and 21. What is clear, however, is that shell classes 18–22 are used for a very special range of important transactions which mark them off sharply from lower echelon shells, and that shells below No. 18 are not convertible into shells 18–22 by borrowing and repayment. One cannot start with a No. 1 or 17, and by lending, work it up to a No. 18–22.

Armstrong writes: "Nos. 18–22 seem to be in a somewhat different position from the lower values and one would imagine that they are not related to each other and the lower values in the precise manner set out in generalized form above [i.e., according to the compound interest formula linking the entire series, 1–22]" (1928:68). Convertibility via borrowing and repaying a higher class shell most certainly breaks down between Nos. 17 and 18. I suspect but cannot so readily document from the data that it does so, between Nos. 10 and 11 as well. If such is the case, convertibility is possible among Nos. 1–10, and among Nos. 11–17, but not between the two sets, and not among Nos. 18–22. It is very clear that the entire series is not linked because the uses to which shells 18–22 are put are of an entirely different order from the uses of lower shells. "As a matter of fact, a peculiarity enters as soon as we reach No. 18, which is not, as a rule [when borrowed] repaid by a coin of higher value" (Armstrong 1928:66).

Nos. 18–22 (of which there are fewer than 60 shells in all), are obviously treasure items like especially venerated kula bracelets and potlatch coppers, items with individual names and histories, which must be used to validate important social events and transactions in the same sense that bridewealth items validate a marriage. The folk-view toward these shells helps to explain

---

[8] Armstrong says that No. 4 ndap is the commonest on the island, there being at least 200 of them (1928:63). Note also that each ndap shell in classes 12–22, some 150 shells in all, had individual names, as did some at least, in classes 8–11 (1928:62).

their role as limited purpose money in reciprocal and redistributive transactions. "Nos. 18–22 are peculiar in one other respect. They have a certain sacred character. No. 18, as it passes from person to person, is handled with great apparent reverence, and a crouching attitude is maintained. Nos. 19 to 22 are proportionately more sacred, are almost always kept enclosed, and are not supposed to see the light of day, and particularly the sun . . . I am inclined to think that there may be a real gap [in sacredness and prestige] . . . between Nos. 17 and 18 . . . [No. 22 shells] are said to be inherited in the male line and to be owned by the most powerful chiefs on the island" (Armstrong 1928:68).

To have regarded Nos. 18–22 as especially valuable media of (commercial) exchange—high denomination bills—with which to buy especially high-priced merchandise, is the most telling error Armstrong makes. Nos. 18–22 cannot be acquired by any amount of lower class shells, and there is no way of gauging how many times more valuable a No. 18 is compared to a No. 6 because they enter entirely different transactions.

Without exception, Nos. 18–22 enter non-commercial transactions exclusively: they are used as means of (reciprocal or redistributive) payment or exchange in transactions induced by social obligation. Payments of a No. 18 are a necessary part of ordinary bridewealth, as well as necessary payment for shared wives, and for sponsoring a pig or dog feast, or a feast initiating the use of a special kind of canoe. No. 20 is a necessary indemnity payment to the relatives of a man ritually murdered and eaten, a transaction which is part of mortuary rites for the death of a chief (Armstrong 1928:67, 1924:428). Moreover, there is a connection between shells 18–22 and lineage affiliation which Armstrong notes but makes nothing of. ". . . Nos. 18 to 22 are regarded as property peculiar to chiefs, though continually lent by the latter to their subjects" (1928:66).

The implication throughout is that there exists (as with us) an impersonal money market in which anyone may borrow from anyone else at the going interest rate (1924:426). This is doubtful. Unfortunately, Armstrong is silent on the question, "who may borrow from whom, and with what penalties for failure to repay?"

As with special purpose money for non-commercial transactions elsewhere, there are status requisites involved in the acquisition and use of the high echelon shells on Rossel. Just as marriage is not a market purchase of a wife by anyone who acquires a No. 18 ndap, but rather a reciprocal transaction between two lineage groups (the ndap payment being one of the several necessary conditions within the social situation), so too with pig feasts on Rossel. Only persons of correct status may sponsor the feast and pay the ndap shell. In this case Armstrong notes that social requisites determine who may use upper ndap shells; but he does not see this as a symptomatic difference between Rossel and Western money, i.e., between non-commercial means of (redistributive) payment, and our Western media of impersonal (commercial) exchange. What Armstrong says of pig feasts is equally true of marriage, and all the other *social events* which require payment of high echelon ndap shells:

> There are . . . complex social factors determining who shall have a pig to sell, [sic] and who shall be in a position to buy, [sic] and the buying and selling is not a simple economic occurrence, but a much more significant and complex social occurrence. We must suppose a complexity of social facts, which I am not in a position to define, that determine most of the general relations of a particular pig feast. . . . A particular individual provides a particular *ndap*. . . . A certain readjustment of social relations thus results from the holding of the feast . . . though we abandon the view that the monetary operations at a feast of this nature are to be regarded merely as a collective buying from a collective seller, it still remains that this is a useful way of describing these operations. (1928:82, 83)

It is about as useful to describe a pig feast on Rossel as buying a pig with a No. 18 ndap as it is to describe marriage in America as buying a wife with a wedding ring. To describe the pig feast as a market purchase one must ignore the social requirements of the transaction and the folk-view of the event, both of which differentiate this redistributive transaction from market exchange. Armstrong is forced to use market terms, purchase and sale, to describe pig feasts and bridewealth, because he regards ndap shells as media of (commercial) exchange in a market system.

One bizarre feature of the Rossel system, that a transaction requires a single shell of a specifically named class, and neither a shell from a higher class nor several from lower classes would do, may be examined in the light of what has been said above.

"A man may have to borrow, even though he has money of a higher value in his possession than he requires at the moment. He may have Nos. 11 and 13, but not No. 12 which he requires at the moment. He cannot get change as a rule, for No. 13 is not a simple product of any lower value" (Armstrong 1928:64–65).

The higher values have nothing to do with commercial purchase and sale. One could not use five petty shells, like No. 4 (which buys a pot), to perform a transaction such as bloodwealth (which requires that special treasure Armstrong numbers 20), for much the same reasons that in the Trobriands, one cannot "buy" a renowned kula valuable with the pots bought from hawkers in a gimwali.

One final point. In comparing primitive money with our own, it is important that the writer describe the frequency of different kinds of monetary transactions. Only so can one gauge what role, if any, the money item(s) play in the production system. Armstrong concerns himself with social and ritual events—marriage, death, redistributive feasts, fines—and says almost nothing about production, subsistence goods, natural resource and labor transactions, and all the other ordinary concerns of money and pricing in our own economy. That he nevertheless asserts that Rossel money is much like our own, should make one wary. Einzig is properly suspicious: "It is a pity that there is not enough evidence to show to what extent, if at all, *ndap* and *nko* are used as a medium of exchange in everyday transactions, apart from the purchase [sic] of pigs" (Einzig 1948:75).

If all the ndap shell transactions which Armstrong describes were abolished, subsistence livelihood of Rossel Islanders would remain unimpaired. It is a pity he did not hit upon that distinction which is useful to analyze economies not integrated by market exchange. DuBois (1936:50) writes concerning this: ". . . I should like to make a distinction between subsistence and prestige economy. By subsistence economy is meant the exploitation of the . . . natural resources available to any industrious individual. By prestige economy on the other hand, is meant a series of social prerogatives and status values. They include a large range of phenomena from wives to formulae for supernatural compulsion."

The upper values of ndap shells (and probably the middle values as well—Armstrong is silent here) enter prestige spheres in non-commercial uses. From the Westerner's viewpoint these transactions are outside the production system and subsistence livelihood. Despite Armstrong's assertion to the contrary, there is no evidence that one could opt out of the social and ritual games (through which upper ndap shells are paid and received) by converting upper shells into land, labor, or products, except perhaps as occasional events in emergency situations (Bohannan and Dalton 1962).

ROSSEL ISLAND MONEY: A CASE OF RED HERRINGS[9]

"The study of economics in simple communities should properly speaking be a job for economists. But so far few economists have tackled it, and most of the investigation has perforce been done by anthropologists" (Royal Anthropological Institute 1949:158).

All social scientists are either Sherlock or Mycroft Holmes. Anthropologists are Sherlock: they go to the scene, observe minutely, gather their threads of evidence from what they observe, and—like Sherlock—sometimes reach Paddington before reaching conclusions. Economic theorists are Mycroft: they do not go to the scene to observe minutely. They have no equivalent

[9] Armstrong's short stay on Rossel, his inability to speak the language, his dependence upon informants rather than direct observation, together with his preconception that Rossel money must be essentially like our own media of (commercial) exchange, prevented him from relating those aspects of Rossel money which differed from our own to their different socio-economic structure. Armstrong does not give enough information to make complete sense of the system.
The unresolved problems are many. To understand the system fully we should have to know about the following: what transactions does each kind of ndap shell enter? What is the nko system all about: Why do certain transactions require a sorting of both ndap and nko? Armstrong tells us that there are really more than 22 classes of ndap shells because some of them are subdivided and given separate names, making about 40 distinctions in all; what are the shells in these subdivided classes used for? Who may borrow from whom, and with what penalties for failure to repay? How do rank and lineage affect borrowing and repayment? Are the high echelon ndap shells related to kinship or political organization, in some such fashion as potlatch coppers are? Who are the "brokers" who act as intermediaries between borrowers and lenders, and for what kinds of transactions and between whom do they intermediate? Specific ndap values are identified with specific parts of pigs and men (Armstrong 1928:79), a matter the people regard as important, but which remains unexplained. So too with the number ten, which appears repeatedly: several transactions require payment of a linked series of ten shells, e.g., one each of the ten ndap classes 20–11 is paid as compensation for ritual murder.

to fieldwork because economists are not concerned with social organization or human behavior, but rather with the behavior of prices, income determinants, capital-output ratios, and other impersonal matters relating to the performance of nationally integrated, industrialized, market economies (for which fieldwork is unnecessary). Institutional matters, personal roles, and the social implications of economic organization have long since been consigned to the limbo of sociology. Neither the problems of interest nor the methods of analysis are the same in economics and economic anthropology.

Armstrong is an economist who played at anthropology. His mistake was to bring Mycroft's tools to Sherlock's subject (and without realizing he was doing so). The result—to mix my metaphors—was to create a sort of Piltdown Economic Man, Melanesians with monetary denominations which fit the formula for compound interest. Armstrong's pioneer work is not a hoax, but a red herring; and the lesson to be learned is not analytical—what primitive money is all about—but methodological: how not to do anthropology.

CONCLUSIONS

The distinctions spelled out in this paper may be used to answer questions of interest to economic anthropology, comparative economy, and economic development.

(1) Anthropologists do not hesitate to contrive special terms for special actions and institutions when to use terms from their own society would be misleading. They do not talk about *the* family, but about nuclear, extended, and matrilineal families. The same should be done with economic matters.

Those aspects of primitive economy which are unrelated to market exchange can only be understood by employing socio-economic terms: ceremonial-prestige and subsistence goods; reciprocity and redistribution; spheres and conversions; limited purpose money. Such terms contain a social dimension and so allow us to relate economic matters to social organization, and to express the folk-view toward the items, services, persons, and situations involved. The economist dealing with monetary transactions in Western economy need not concern himself with per-

sonal roles and social situations because of the peculiarly impersonal nature of market exchange. The anthropologist dealing
with marketless transactions cannot ignore personal roles and
social situations and still make sense of what transpires.

Kula armbands, potlatch coppers, cows, pig tusks, Yap stones,
etc., are variously described as money of renown, treasure items,
wealth, valuables, and heirlooms. Malinowski says kula valuables
are regarded like crown jewels or sports trophies in Western
societies. Writers on East Africa say that cows are regarded
like revered pets. Such treasures can take on special roles as
non-commercial money: their acquisition and disposition are carefully structured and regarded as extremely important events;
they change hands in specified ways, in transactions which have
strong moral implications. Often they are used to create social
relationships (marriage; entrance into secret societies), prevent
a break in social relationships (bloodwealth; mortuary payments), or to keep or elevate one's social position (potlatch).
Their "money-ness" consists in their being required means of
(reciprocal or redistributive) payment.

(2) Subsidiary characteristics of Western money-stuff, such as
portability and divisibility, are actually requirements for media
of (commercial) exchange. In peasant and national economies
integrated by market exchange, purchases of goods and services
are a daily occurrence, and so money must be portable; market
purchases are carried out at widely varying price, so the medium
of (commercial) exchange must be finely divisible.

Yap stones, cows, kula armbands, and Rossel Island shells
are not divisible, and some are not conveniently portable. But
neither are they media of (commercial) exchange; they are not
used for daily purchases of varying amount. Their use as non-
commercial money makes their lack of divisibility and portability
unimportant. Here we see one way primitive money-*stuff* is related to primitive money *usage*. As means of (reciprocal or
redistributive) payment used infrequently to discharge social obligations, it does not matter that the money-stuff lacks those
characteristics required of a medium of (commercial) exchange.

(3) Economics textbooks (e.g., Samuelson 1961:54; Reynolds 1963:475) err in citing primitive monies *indiscriminately* as
equivalents of Western media of (commercial) exchange, for
the same reason that Armstrong errs in treating Rossel Island

monies as a single type and as a crude equivalent of our own. By giving the impression that *all* primitive monies perform the same primary function as dollars, they quite wrongly imply that all primitive economies may be regarded as crude market systems.

Economists are correct in saying that some unusual money-stuffs have functioned as media of (commercial) exchange. They have in mind situations such as Colonial America (Quiggin 1949:316ff.) where "primitive money-stuffs" (commodity money such as tobacco and cotton) functioned just as dollars do today, or Prisoner of War camps where cigarettes (primitive money-stuff) became used as media of (market) exchange.

But to conclude that because some primitive money-*stuffs* do perform the primary function of dollars, *all* primitive monies may be regarded as crude media of (commercial) exchange, is an important error. As we have seen in the case of Rossel Island, this market preconception impedes our understanding of market-less economies and those with peripheral markets only. It implies that market exchange is the only transactional mode ever to exist, and so—as economists do in our own economy—one may ignore the social situations in which monetary transactions occur and the folk-view toward the persons, events, and items involved. It is precisely this sort of ethnocentrism that regards all "exchanges" as commercial transactions, and equates all money payments with market purchases, with the result that brides and murder are said to have a price, just as pots and yams in the market place have a price.

(4) A situation of special interest is one where cowrie (in times past), or sterling or francs (in recent times), acquired initially in external market exchange, became used internally for commercial and non-commercial transactions.[10] Such cases of monetary incursion deserve examination for reasons which are of interest to students of community economic development as well as economic anthropology.

[10] In Africa, at least, the impact of cowrie on indigenous economies and indigenous money, varied widely. In some instances, as with sterling and francs, cowrie came to be general purpose money which linked spheres of goods and services formerly kept separate, and which serviced several transactional modes within one society (see Vansina 1962:198); such was the case where cowrie came to be used in market-place exchanges as well as bridewealth. In other cases cowrie were incorporated as just another special purpose money with limited usage within the indigenous system (see Quiggin 1949: Chapter IV).

Cowrie inflation, wampum inflation, and bridewealth inflation are related cases. Cowrie and wampum became used as media of (commercial) exchange through external trade with Europeans in situations where the quantity of money-stuff was uncontrolled and increased rapidly in supply. Similarly, where bridewealth comes to be paid in sterling or francs, the sum increases when earnings of Western money through market sale of labor or produce increase faster than the number of marriageable females (Bohannan 1959; Mayer 1951:22). What might be called "potlatch copper inflation" is a similar case: when the Kwakiutl became increasingly enmeshed in Canadian market economy, they used their market earnings to increase the stakes in the potlatch. The limited number of coppers (like the limited number of brides, elsewhere) fetched a larger bundle of market-purchased goods. All such cases may be described as "upward conversions": newly expanded market earnings are used to acquire treasure items and brides which indigenously were not transacted through market exchange.[11]

Western money does much more than merely displace primitive

[11] The very early date at which Canadian market exchange permeated Kwakiutl life is important to understand how and why potlatches changed over time: before serious Canadian market incursion, potlatches were given infrequently, were the prerogative of nobles, and were necessary to affirm one's rank (Codere 1951). Having the traditional potlatch goods was not a sufficient condition for giving a potlatch because one had to have the rank as well. (As in many primitive societies, only those of high rank could accumulate the necessary goods.)

The nature of the potlatch changed radically with (i) the population decimation around 1840—the population fell from an estimated 23,000 in 1840 to fewer than 3,000 in 1880, and under 2,000 in 1890 (Codere 1951:52). Note that the 600 rank positions remained fixed. (ii) The second important change was the increasing use in the potlatch of items purchased on the Canadian market. Now the opportunity for upward conversions—the use of Canadian goods bought with cash to acquire internal rank and prestige positions—became unlimited. With a shrunken population, practically everyone had one of the 600 rank positions, which was not the case earlier, and everyone had access to Canadian goods (by simply earning cash), which certainly was not the case earlier. Potlatches then came to be given frequently, by anyone (even women and children), and for all kinds of reasons; and, no doubt, even a commercial element entered.

The trouble with the literature is that even the early anthropologists (Boas first wrote in 1887) were describing Western market incursion well under way, without fully appreciating the radical difference it made to the potlatch when everyone had rank positions and access to purchased goods. Any generalization made about the nature of the potlatch should bear a date. See Drucker (1939:56, footnote 3, 63 footnote 22).

monies where the latter were not media of (commercial) exchange indigenously. It allows non-commercial payments and obligations of traditional sorts (such as bridewealth) to be discharged with general purpose money earned in market transactions—instead of with traditional items of special-purpose money. In economies which formerly were marketless or had peripheral markets only, a structural link—Western cash—now exists between spheres of exchange which formerly were separate. Western money therefore has inevitable repercussions on traditional social organization and cultural practices (Schapera 1928; Bohannan 1959; Gulliver 1962; Dalton 1964). In brief, market earnings can now be used for reciprocal and redistributive payments (just as in Western economy goods purchased on the market enter gift-giving, and money earnings are used to pay taxes and tithes).

(5) One source of ambiguity in the literature is the quest for a single, all-purpose definition of money that would include our own kind (and presumably Soviet money), as well as the welter of types in use in primitive and peasant economies differing widely in organization. Einzig writes: "It must be the ultimate goal of the study of primitive money to try to find the common denominator—in so far as it exists—in terms of which both the well-established rules of modern money and the apparently conflicting conclusions on primitive money can be explained" (1948: 19).

To concentrate attention on what all monies have in common is to discard those clues—how monies differ—which are surface expressions of different social and economic organization. Money is not an isolated case. Much the same can be said for external trade and market places, which (like money) also are made use of in economies differing markedly in organization (say, the U.S., the Soviet, and the Tiv economies). Money traits differ where socio-economic organization differs. To concentrate attention on money traits independently of underlying organization leads writers to use the traits of Western money as a model of the real thing (while ignoring the structure of Western economy which accounts for the money traits). Then any primitive money which does not have all the traits of the Western model money is simply ruled out by definition—it is not money.

This does not get us very far towards understanding primitive and peasant economies.

Two distinctions which allow us to contrast primitive and Western money are the distinctions between commercial and non-commercial uses of money, and between marketless economies, those with peripheral markets only, and market-integrated economies. In sum, money has no definable essence apart from the uses money objects serve, and these depend upon the transactional modes that characterize each economy: as tangible item as well as abstract measure, "money is what money does" (Reynolds 1963:474).

IV ASIA

17 TOWARD A MODEL
OF THE HINDU *JAJMANI* SYSTEM

Pauline Mahar Kolenda

Over the past dozen years, Indian, British, and American social anthropologists have studied more than a score of Hindu villages in India.[1] Their reports have been descriptions of caste, leadership, government, factionalism, economic and social change.[2] There have been a few studies also of village religion, family life, kinship, and personality.[3]

As yet, however, there has been little careful, systematic comparison of these many village studies. Redfield and Singer, Mandelbaum, Dube, Srinivas, Mayer, and Gough have all voiced the social anthropologist's commitment to eventual comparison and generalization, especially between villages in different regions of India.[4]

There have been a few attempts to identify all-India social structures and processes, generalizations useful for comparative purposes. M. N. Srinivas suggests that broad similarities are to be

FROM Pauline Mahar Kolenda, "Toward a Model of the Hindu *Jajmani* System," *Human Organization*, Vol. XXII, No. 1, 1963, pp. 11–31. Reprinted by permission of the author and the Society for Applied Anthropology. The author wishes to thank the following for having read an earlier version of this paper and for making suggestions for its improvement: Gerald Berreman, Bernard Cohn, Edward Harper, Walter Neale, Edward Norbeck, and William Rowe.

[1] Book-length contributions include: Lewis (1958), Mayer (1960), Majumdar (1955), Marriott (1955), Singer (1958), Srinivas (1955).

[2] See Bailey (1957); Cohn (1958); Carstairs (1957); Gough (1955; 1960); Majumdar (1958); Srinivas (1952); Dhillon (1955); Park and Tinker (1959); Thorner (1953); Pocock (1957); Lewis (1954); Dube (1955); Mayer (1956; 1957); Opler and Singh (1952).

[3] See Harper (1957; 1959); McCormack (1948); Opler (1958; 1959); Gough (1956); Hitchcock (1960).

[4] See Dube (1955a:6); Gough (1960:11); Mayer (1960:4); Redfield and Singer (1955); Srinivas (1955a:1).

found among the villages of the many regions because of elements of a shared Sanskritic tradition.[5]

S. C. Dube specified some "features" that "characterize a very large number of villages." These include: (1) the distinctiveness of the village as an economic, social, and ritual entity, with (2) a population composed of many interdependent occupational caste groups that are (3) bound . . . by ties of mutual and reciprocal obligations (and) governed by an established usage and social ethics.

These usages are (4) sanctioned by "village elders or by a village council" (Dube 55:7–8). David Mandelbaum compared the eight villages described in *Village India*. Redfield and Singer summarized Mandelbaum's analysis as follows:

> . . . the comparisons begin to show some of the things that are widespread: the balance of caste separation and intercaste dependence; the relations of land tenure to social structure; the importance of maintaining status relationships as between castes and as between individuals, and the possibilities of change in status of groups or individuals; the anxieties and quarrels that have to do with status; the influence of ancient codes or ideas— aggressive protection of honor for "warriors," ascetic withdrawal for others. Widespread also are general processes of change: the disintegration of social systems based on group or corporate relations of status; the decline of occupational specialties; increasing use of money, growth of factionalism; changes in the interdependence of castes and a tendency for the depressed to find common cause in economic or political interests; the double process of Sanskritization and Westernization.[6]

Although focusing upon only one aspect of village life, *A Comparative Analysis of the Jajmani System* by Thomas O. Beidelman represents an attempt at comparison. Shortly before its appearance, in 1959, Lewis and Barnouw pointed out that in the

> . . . literature about the caste system of India, very little attention has been paid to its economic aspects. (Lewis 1958:55)

About the time of its appearance, two other anthropologists, Harold Gould and E. R. Leach, published papers on the eco-

---

[5] Srinivas (1952; 1956). Many earlier writers have spoken of the process of "Hinduization"—for example Crooke (1926); Weber (1958:9–21); Ibbetson (1916:268).

[6] "Foreword," in M. Marriott (1955:iii). Mandelbaum's comparative analysis appears on pages 230–253.

nomic interdependence of castes in village India (Gould 1958; Leach 1960).

These three papers serve as points of departure for this one. Here I shall discuss Beidelman's, Gould's, and Leach's "models" of the *jajmani* system in relation to each other, and in relation to other descriptions of the system, most particularly that of W. H. Wiser (1936). My purpose is to contribute to the development of a more general model of the Hindu *jajmani* system that may be useful in future research and analysis.

Briefly, the *jajmani* system is a system of distribution in Indian villages whereby high-caste landowning families called *jajmans* are provided services and products by various lower castes such as carpenters, potters, blacksmiths, watercarriers, sweepers, and laundrymen. Purely ritual services may be provided by Brahman priests and various sectarian castes, and almost all serving castes have ceremonial and ritual duties at their *jajman's* births, marriages, funerals, and at some of the religious festivals. Important in the latter duties is the lower castes' capacity to absorb pollution by handling clothing and other things defiled by birth or death pollution, gathering up banquet dishes after the feasts, and administering various bodily attentions to new mother, bride or groom.

The landowning *jajmans* pay the serving castes in kind, with grain, clothing, sugar, fodder, and animal products like butter and milk. Payment may amount to a little of everything produced on the land, in the pastures, and in the kitchen. Sometimes land is granted to servants, especially as charity to Brahman priests. In this system, the middle and lower castes either subscribe to each other's services in return for compensations and payments, or exchange services with one another.

When the first full description of this multi-caste village exchange system was written, the author, W. H. Wiser, declined to venture,

> . . . just how general this *jajmani* relationship is in the villages of India. (Wiser 1936:3)

Beidelman found it to exist in many localities. His bibliography includes over one hundred references, most of them dating before 1950 and most contributing information about local varieties of the *jajmani* system.

He concluded:

> The system occurs in most of India. (Beidelman 1959:7)

Hocart's discussion of caste in Ceylon and papers appearing in
E. R. Leach's *Aspects of Caste in South India, Ceylon and
Northwest Pakistan* show that the *jajmani* system is to be found
beyond the boundaries of India as well (Hocart 1950).

There is now some evidence also that there are regions of
South Asia where the *jajmani* system is not present. Edward
Harper reports that in Malnad of South India, a region substantially dependent upon cash crops, the *jajmani* system does
not now operate, nor is there evidence that it was ever present.
McKim Marriott reports that in the largely Muslim Bengal Delta
of Pakistan the *jajmani* system seems to be almost completely
absent (Harper 1959a:760–778; Marriott 1960:50). An important part of work on the *jajmani* system is the specification
of the conditions necessary for its occurrence.

The four papers by Wiser, Leach, Beidelman, and Gould all
present basic principles of the *jajmani* system, and they consequently lend themselves to consideration as descriptive models.
By model, I shall mean a simplified abstract description of a set
of interrelationships. S. F. Nadel has said that the profit from
trying to define descriptive models of social structures comes in
the insights derived in the process (Nadel 1957:154). The
attempt to outline the main variables or factors in the system may
lead to greater understanding and possibly to a sequel of models
of increasingly better fit. A model of the *jajmani* system may
be useful in future comparison of variants of the *jajmani* system
as it occurs in different regions of India.

The sociologist, inspired by Parsons, Nadel, Homans, Williams
(Parsons 1951; Nadel 1957; Homans 1950; Williams 1960),
may ask a standard set of questions about any social system
or partial social system. The questions may be arranged as
follows:

(1) What are the functions of the social system for the
society?

(2) In the system, what are the cultural roles, each made
up of a set of norms guiding rights and privileges, obligations
and duties, and expectations for the reciprocal roles? What are
the role relationships, the reciprocal interacting roles? What are
the groupings within the social system?

(3) How is authority and power distributed among the roles,

both with respect to command over resources and with respect to command over people's actions? What is the distribution of the same powers among groups in the system?

(4) What is the ranking of roles and groups in the system?

(5) What are the motivations of the personnel in the system inducing them to fulfill roles?

(6) What are the general norms of the social system, the rules for expected behavior agreed upon by the members, rules that are shared, enduring, and believed to be right?

(7) What are the general cultural values involved in and legitimizing the social system?

(8) What are the sanctions, both positive and negative, ensuring conformity to the norms of the system? Are there roles for sanctioning agents? How are sanctioning functions integrated into other roles?

(9) What are the relationships between this social system and other social systems?

(10) What are the processes of change in the system, both internal change inherent in the system and changes of the system in its essential form?

(11) What are the points of strain in the system, strain in roles or strain between groups?

We may look at the *jajmani* system as an institution or social system within Indian villages made up of a network of roles and of norms integrated into the roles and into the system as a whole, and legitimized and supported by general cultural values. We may apply to the *jajmani* system the questions above.

In this article, I shall review four models of the *jajmani* system and consider how completely the questions above have been answered and hence how close we are to a reasonably complete model of the *jajmani* system as a social system.

WISER'S MODEL

Wiser's analysis of the Hindu *jajmani* system has influenced many students of Indian villages including Gould and Beidelman whose models will be considered later in this paper (Wiser 1956; Gould 1958; Beidelman 1959). Wiser was the first to delimit and label the system, and to recognize that the occupational division of labor in an Indian village with distribution of services and products was a system of network of role relationships.

His views will be summarized in terms of the social system questions listed above.

(1) FUNCTION OF THE SYSTEM

By providing all necessary products and services, the *jajmani* system functions to maintain the Indian village as "a self-sufficing community" (Wiser 1956:16). The multiplicity of such self-sufficient localities has served historically as the units of the Indian polity.

(2) ROLES

Wiser's description of the duties of the twenty-four castes in village Karimpur and the payments and concessions to which these castes have "rights" is still the most thorough and detailed available.

In what can only be considered Wiser's idealized conception of the *jajmani* system he says,

> . . . each caste in the village at some time during the year is expected to render a fixed type of service to each other caste . . . Each in turn is master. Each in turn is servant. (Wiser 1956:6, 10)

As Beidelman points out, Wiser's own data show that, in fact, the higher castes do not render services to the lower castes in Karimpur (Beidelman 1959:5; Wiser 1956:16–30). We might add also, that only a portion of the village is participating in the *jajmani* system.

With respect to the duration of *jajman-kamin* relationships and norms of job security, Wiser reports that a *kamin's* clientele

> . . . continues from generation to generation, . . . [and] cannot be broken except by the (*kamin*) himself who may choose to sell his rights to another (*kamin*). (Wiser 1956:5)

The *kamin's* clientele may be entirely within one village, or it may extend to a number of villages in a locality.

About the *jajman's* payments or reciprocal obligations for services or products, Wiser says,

> In return for the various services rendered, there are payments in cash and in kind made daily, monthly, bi-yearly per piece of work, and on special occasions, depending on the type of service rendered and in part on the good will of the *jajman*. *The strength of the system depends, however, not on the actual payments made but on the concessions granted to the different occupational groups.* These may be listed as free residence site, free food for family, free clothing, free food for animals, free timber, free dung, rent-free land, credit facilities, opportunities for supplementary employment, free use of tools, implements and draft animals, free use of raw materials, free hides, free funeral pyre plot, casual leave, aid in litigation, variety in diet, healthful location. These concessions do not apply equally to all, but vary according to custom. (Wiser 1956:10–11) [Author's italics.]

For Wiser, groupings within the system are castes, rather than families, factions, or blocks of castes.

(3) DISTRIBUTION OF AUTHORITY AND POWER

Wiser points out that the *jajmani* system is ". . . built on inequality rather than equality."

Only a few of the intercaste relationships, those between the barber, grain parcher, potter, and washerman are equal exchanges. He speaks of the "lordly position of the Brahman," especially with respect to the untouchable Chamar. He says that the Chamar is not a slave because of his freedom of movement, but

> . . . in social attitudes, [the relationship is] little better than that of . . . master and slave. (Wiser 1956:164)

Even when low caste persons are *jajmans* for higher caste *kamins,* the lower caste person is subordinate and displays a "slave-mentality" attitude, according to Wiser.

While one may infer Wiser's position concerning the distribution of power in the *jajmani* system, it is not salient in his presentation. He does not attribute power to any castes except the Brahmans. The successful functioning of the system over time Wiser attributes to the Brahmans' fulfillment of *noblesse oblige* values in their roles as *jajmans.*

Other castes have some power due to the necessity of their caste functions, but as castes differ in their bargaining power,

> . . . No generalization can be made as to these compensations and rights, because each occupational group has acquired its own individual status. No attempt has been made to equalize them, and no one dares to criticise the status of another. The *jajmani* status of each group is inherent in its occupational function, which is governed by birth and established by custom. (Wiser 1956:61)

(4) RANK

Wiser presents a ranking of castes in Karimpur ". . . in their order of social precedence and traditional occupation," but he does not discuss the bases for their ranking, nor how he discovered such a ranking.

The inequality in *jajman-kamin* relationships was discussed above in section 3.

(5) MOTIVATION

The value of the concessions listed under section 2 on roles is sufficient, Wiser says, to prevent the servant from taking a factory job with a fixed cash income. Another motivation for the servant is the sense of security he experiences in the village. This is made possible in part by the Brahman's sense of responsibility for the livelihood of all members of the village.

Despite the security for the servants in the village, most are not too well-off, according to Wiser, since two-thirds have a "poor economic status" (Wiser 1956:149).

(6) NORMS OF THE SYSTEM

Norms include the following:

a. Different occupational groups have legitimate claims to the earnings of the whole village.

b. The *jajman* should not think in terms of payment for the task done, but in terms of sufficient payments with concessions to ensure the servant's living.

c. There is a series of norms concerning rights, duties, payments, and concessions for the *jajman* and the various *kamins*. (Section 2 above.)

(7) GENERAL CULTURAL VALUES

The idea that,

> . . . functional abilities are fixed and transmitted from generation to generation [and that God] assigned separate duties and occupations to each individual from birth

is important (Wiser 1956:175). Inequality in caste ranking is God-given.

The belief in the religious merit of generosity and charity reinforces attitudes of responsibility on the part of the *jajmans.* The general Hindu emphasis upon spiritual power for Brahmans rather than wealth is important, Wiser feels, in the balance of the system, so that the Brahmans' spiritual goal brakes striving for power.

(8) SANCTIONS

In general summary, Wiser says,

> The *jajmani* compensations and rights in Karimpur are maintained and supported by custom and the beliefs of the people themselves, the influence of the village elders, the Sacred Books of the Hindus and the Laws of the State. (Wiser 1956:118)

Wiser frequently cites passages from the *Laws of Manu* describing caste duties, payments, and punishments for failure of duty. He says,

> The *jajmani* system receives its greatest support from Hindu Sacred Books . . . (Wiser 1956:126) The Hindu *Jajmani* system has philosophical and religious sanction in the *Laws of Manu* which served as guide for the Hindu social and economic organization for almost 2000 years. (Wiser 1956:11)

Wiser does qualify this generalization by saying that the Karimpur system

> . . . is ancient in that it recognizes the claims of the different occupational groups to a share of the earnings of the village as a whole, but is not ancient in its detailed form. . . . (Wiser 1956:136)

Written custom in the *wajib-ul-arz,* which details the concessions to which servants have rights, the British law courts' support of traditional law, and the influence of the village elders' council for sanctioning erring *jajmans* and servants are all important.

(9) RELATIONSHIP TO OTHER SOCIAL SYSTEMS

Wiser calls the *jajmani* system a religio-socio-economic system. The importance of the general social structure of caste and the religious sanctions for caste are important to the *jajmani* system.

(10) CHANGES

The possibility of taking disputes to the British courts seemed to have undermined the authority of the village council of elders, and while they could still influence servants effectively, they seemed to be powerless to control erring *jajmans*. Further, the law courts gave an advantage to *jajmans* in cases. Wiser said,

> . . . the court records seem to show that the Brahman through appeals to the Higher Courts are continually strengthening their *jajmani* rights. The lower caste groups on the other hand, because of the lack of finance, the weakness of the Panchayat, or absence of friends to represent their cause, are steadily allowing their rights to disintegrate. (Wiser 1956:179)

Economic competition with the products of factories sold in market towns has weakened several castes. In the late 1920's only half of the Karimpur families participated in the *jajmani* system, and of these eighty families, only fourteen were able to support themselves from their *jajmani* clientele. The other sixty-six supplemented their work with agriculture.

A further disintegrating factor was the introduction of new ideas by teachers in the government-sponsored school. When, in addition, many *jajmans* no longer met the fixed standardized rates customary or recorded in the *wajib-ul-arz,* and the village council was unable to control the *jajmans,* belief in the system was weakened.

Many of the important principles specified in later models of the *jajmani* system are not mentioned by Wiser. For one thing, he has very little to say about ritual pollution and untouchability. He labels a category of castes as "outcastes" and mentions in passing various customs related to pollution, but he does not analyze the *jajmani* system as closely related to this Hindu idea.

He tells almost nothing about land ownership in Karimpur. One passage states that the village is owned by two landlords whose estates are forty and one hundred and ten miles away (Wiser 1956:184). On the first page of his book, he suggests that the village is possessed by, or influenced by Brahmans, but he never says that the Brahmans' power rests on land ownership; instead, he finds it to be based on ancient Hindu law. This emphasis on ancient Hindu law is almost completely ignored by later scholars.

Wiser has little to say about kinship, either fictive kin relations between *jajmans* and servants, or extra-village kinship. He does not present the Brahmans as a strong political power. Although the Brahmans make up one-quarter of the village population, Wiser never mentions their strength through numbers. That the council of elders may be dominated by Brahmans is never suggested by Wiser. In other words, the factors for a dominant caste, emphasized by more recent work, are not mentioned in Wiser's *Hindu Jajmani System*.

He has nothing to say about the "trade-unionism" of the servant castes, nor does he mention caste councils or the power of the strike or boycott by the servants. He does mention that a pan-village boycott on an erring *jajman* was a traditional practice; that is all. He says nothing about intra- or inter-caste competition, nor anything about factionalism in the village. He never uses the term "caste monopoly."

Wiser was interested in the *jajmani* system as an enactment of ancient law.[7] He saw its success as due to the responsible *noblesse oblige* attitudes of Brahmans who took for granted, as did the lower castes, the God-given hierarchy of caste functions. This system was rooted in an extraordinary elaboration of rules for payments, concessions, and services.

[7] Wiser's study could even be considered a first groping attempt to bring together in an Indian research both Hindu text and context. See Singer (1961).

GOULD'S MODEL

If we apply the social system questions to Harold Gould's
model of the *jajmani* system, we may proceed as follows:

(1) FUNCTIONS OF THE SYSTEM

Over-all, the *jajmani* system, Gould says, functions so that
the community can survive.

> . . . in a manner which preserves its Hindu moral premises.
> (Gould 1958:429)

Gould, unlike the other three scholars, sees the Hindu attitudes
concerning ritual pollution as basic to the *jajmani* system; they
". . . underlie and perpetuate that division of labor" (Gould
1958:428).

The lower castes in their servant roles

> . . . absorb the onus or ritual contamination associated with
> the tasks they perform and facilitate the ritual purity and con-
> sequent moral apotheosis of the ["high castes"]. (Gould 1958:
> 431)

The system also functions to distribute agricultural produce in
exchange for menial and craft services. Some servants operate
effectively for the *jajmans* in interfactional communication, including "marital reconnaissance," looking for potential brides or
grooms.

(2) ROLES

Basic to the division of labor in Indian villages are castes
defined by Gould as

> . . . compound patrifamilies . . . ritually subdivided into endog-
> amous clusters in accordance with the moral valuation which
> the Hindu religion places upon their occupational activities.
> (Gould 1958:428)

The units of the *jajmani* system are relationships between families
of different caste.

The castes, Gould divides into two types, the clean Twice Born and the unclean low castes. This division coincides with the division between the

> . . . land-owning, cultivating castes . . . who are subordinate within it. (Gould 1958:429)

Unclean castes have contact with

> . . . "blood, death, and dirt" and must avoid connubial, commensal and many other forms of social contacts with those clusters of patrifamilies who are "clean." (Gould 1958:428– 429)

Gould sketches out the duties of the barber *purjan,* but he is not concerned with recording the detailed descriptions of duties as Wiser was. He describes the system of payments and concessions as ". . . only remotely pecuniary in its basis" (Gould 1950:431).

He indicates three types of payments: "formal," that is the set grain payments after harvests, the considerations (what Wiser called "concessions"), and "informal emoluments," such as extra amounts of grain, sweetmeats and so on. He also suggests the dimensions of distribution of goods by calculating the formal grain payments for seven *purjans* servants in Sherapur, a village of U.P.

Gould's main emphasis is upon the diffuse, kin-like quality of *jajman-purjan* relations. He sees the *jajmani* system as a resolution of a "social structural dilemma," a reconciliation of two opposing principles, the centripetal principles of family and caste and the centrifugal principle of intercaste and intervillage relations. The higher castes avoid the lower castes for fear of ritual contamination, but at the same time they must contact them to hire them for defiling work and other labor. The dilemma is solved by projecting kinship values on to *jajmani* relationships. Gould says:

> A *purjan* must defer to, respect and defend his *jajman* (ideally, of course) as well as serve him, in a way strongly analogous to the manner in which a son of a corporate family is expected to orient himself to his father. (Gould 1958:431)

By extending kin-like behavior and attitudes into intercaste service relations, the fear or avoidance orientation of the higher caste person is overridden. This is Gould's chief point.

While he does not put a great deal of emphasis upon some other role relationships he mentions, they are worthy of note for our purposes. The first is the tendency of a *jajman* and his *purjan*

. . . to compromise a close system of socio-economic interaction in many respects.

Thus the *purjans* of the same *jajman* will exchange services.

Gould suggests the importance of such systems in factional rivalries. He also says that *purjans,* since they have several *jajmans,* have "interfactional mobility." In passing he mentions that such interfactional mobility may be used for "marital reconnaissance" (Gould 1958:434).

(3) POWER DISTRIBUTION

Gould sees the essential relationship as follows:

. . . it is a matter of land-owning, wealth- and power-controlling high castes providing a structurally fixed share of their agricultural produce, along with numerous "considerations," in exchange for craft and menial services rendered by the mainly landless, impoverished, politically weak lower castes. (Gould 1958:431)

Unlike Wiser who saw the system resting upon acceptance of Hindu ideals supporting Brahman superiority, Gould sees power stemming from land ownership and wealth. Like Wiser, however, Gould mentions nothing about the reciprocal powers on the part of the *purjans* except for their indispensability to the "orthodox Hindu Home."

(4) RANK

For Gould, ranking rests upon land ownership and "the configuration of caste functions" with respect to the degree of defilement. He does not present a ranking of the castes in village Sherapur.

(5) MOTIVATION FOR PERSONNEL

Gould feels that the crucial factor in motivation is the diffuse quality of the relationship between *jajman* and *kamin.* The concessions that Wiser claimed were the important things, Gould sees as symbolizing the familistic quality of the system. Higher castes are motivated by their need for lower caste labor and defiling services.

(6) NORMS OF THE SYSTEM

One may infer the following from Gould's analysis: (a) One must not be defiled. (b) One must subscribe to the services of lower castes to prevent defilement. (c) A *jajman* should be paternalistic toward a *purjan* and fulfill his demands. (d) A *purjan* should behave like a son to the father. (e) A *purjan* should support his *jajman* in factional disputes.

(7) GENERAL VALUE-ORIENTATIONS

The pervasive Hindu kinship values are important supports to these economic-ritual relationships of the *jajmani* system.

(8) SANCTIONS

Gould is unconcerned with the sanctions of the system other than the carrot of paternalism and the stick of defilement. He does not mention caste *panchayats* or caste "trade unionism." He says nothing about cases and law courts.

(9) RELATIONS WITH OTHER SYSTEMS

Jajmani relationships tie in closely with the system of land ownership, with factionalism, and with religion, in ceremonies and special occasions.

(10) CHANGES IN SYSTEM

Gould is not concerned with the processes of disintegration in the system. He does mention that of forty-three families in Sherapur, only nineteen actually are *jajmans*. It is not possible to determine whether the other twenty-four families could be *jajmans* or whether they were in the past.

(11) GOULD IS UNCONCERNED WITH STRAINS IN THE SYSTEM

DISCUSSION OF GOULD'S MODEL

Gould's contribution to a general model of the *jajmani* system is his recognition that it integrates beliefs about pollutions. The division of labor and indispensability of the *purjans* themselves rests upon these ideas.

Gould largely ignores caste differences in capacity to pollute, however, he seems to suggest that all lower castes defile higher castes by physical contact or "touch." Actually, such extreme capacity to pollute is usually limited to the very lowest castes or "untouchables." Most *kamin* castes are not untouchables, but even for untouchable *kamins,* rules facilitating contact have been developed.

Rules of pollution, like the rules for duties and payments in the *jajmani* system, are elaborated and institutionalized. They concern not only touch of a higher caste person but also touching his possessions, food, and water. Many more castes can pollute a higher caste by having touched food or water that is then ingested by him, than by touching the person or possessions of the higher caste person. The rules include the idea of degrees of capacity to pollute varying by caste rank.[8]

As far as *kamins* are concerned, it appears that each is accorded a ritual rank high enough not to inconvenience the performance of his services for higher castes. Beidelman has noted this (Beidelman 1959:24). Sometimes exemptions or legal fictions are introduced to make this possible.

With respect to pollution, the roles of *jajman* and *kamin* are coordinated not so much by the fictive kinship Gould speaks of, but by a series of rules facilitating the interaction of castes differing in degree of defilement.

Many observers, besides Gould, have characterized *jajman-kamin* relationships as paternalistic.[9] One may, however, question his argument that it is the quality of the interpersonal relationships which integrates the system rather than the rights and concessions, the services and privileges themselves.

[8] See Blunt (1931); Mahar (1960; 1960a); Stevenson (1954).
[9] See Dube (1955:61); Hocart (1950:7, 10); Opler and Singh (1952: 490); Srinivas (1955:28).

Besides Wiser, a number of writers, Dube, Opler, and Singh, Lewis and Barnouw, and Mayer, have presented detailed accounts of the duties and compensations of the *kamins*.[10] Mayer and Wiser speak of the *kamins'* rights or *hak* to payments, concessions, and clientele. The word "right" suggests the normative quality of these compensations.

These rights, duties, payments, and concessions are myriad. They include most of the essentials of living. The considerable elaboration and definition of the rights and duties in the system suggest that the system itself is dependent upon acceptance and adherence to these rules, not alone upon the diffuse quality of the relationships between *jajman* and *kamin* suggested by Gould. The system is not coordinated only by the voluntary generosity and paternalistic affection of the *jajman* toward his particular *kamin*. Such generosity and affection may often be present, may usually be present, but the norms of the system help ensure that the *kamin* is not dependent upon the personality of the *jajman*.

BEIDELMAN'S MODEL

Although the title of his book, *A Comparative Analysis of the Jajmani System,* suggests both similarities and differences between local varieties of the system in different parts of India, actually Beidelman presents only broad similarities; and although sources are carefully footnoted, so time and place may be checked, there is no systematic consideration of differences in the system under varying conditions. Beidelman explains,

> . . . that in the face of the paucity of material available, one is justified in combining such material which is at hand,

hence to treat the data as though from the same place. Since many of the studies are recent and changes over time have not been great, Beidelman explains, the reports also have been synchronized into an "ethnographic present" (Beidelman 1959: 14).

We may apply to Beidelman's material the same social system questions.

[10] Lewis (1958:60–63); Dube (1955:62–69, 86–87); Mayer (1956:64–71).

(1) FUNCTION OF THE SYSTEM

For Beidelman the *jajmani* system is the "economic aspect of caste." It is the

> . . . distribution of some produce to all in the local area . . . [through] traditional dependence of non-landholders on land-holders. (Beidelman 1959:6)

Beidelman also discusses the importance of the *jajmani* system for the maintenance of the higher castes' prestige expressed in the ritual restrictions they follow and in ceremonial display.

(2) ROLES

Beidelman defines the *jajmani* system as

> . . . a feudalistic system of prescribed, hereditary obligations of payment and of occupational and ceremonial duties between two or more specific families of different castes in the same locality. (Beidelman 1959:6)

While his examples, taken from several studies, include much information about duties and payments, Beidelman is not concerned with description, but with the relative power of the two interacting groups, high caste *jajmans* and lower caste *kamins*. He recognizes that *kamin* duties are both secular and ritual, but he is especially concerned with both kinds of duties as they relate to superordination and subordination in the role relationship of *jajman* and *kamin*.

He is especially nettled by the "idyllic mutuality" interpretation of the *jajmani* system which he attributes to William H. Wiser, the view of the system as a network of more or less equal mutual interchange of services. Contrary to the view attributed to Wiser suggesting that participants in the system play both *kamin* and *jajman* roles, Beidelman holds that members of the dominant land-owning castes are almost always *jajmans,* members of the landless castes, the *kamins*. Beidelman says,

> The village studies show that only a few or none of the higher castes perform caste occupations There are *jajmans,* but they are not *kamins*. (Beidelman 1959:17)

Interchange of services between castes is of minor importance compared to the unilateral service provided the dominant caste.

The landed *jajmans* and the landless *kamins* may be differentiated further in terms of ritual status. Higher caste families have greater prestige to maintain than lower castes and require ritual services of *kamins* and their participation in ceremonial display. These function as manifestations of, and reinforcements to the lower caste *kamins'* subordination. Semi-public ceremonials where the *jajman* presents his *kamins* with gifts both subordinate the *kamin* and glorify the *jajman*. Etiquette showing the inferiors' deference to the superior *jajman* is also important. Beidelman interprets the use of kinship terms between *jajman* and *kamin* as a symbol of subordination, and mentions instances of extreme subordination where a low caste servant is known simply as "so-and-so's Chamar."

Besides ceremonial tasks, the *kamin* role includes menial, craft, and field work. These roles are ranked according to criteria for evaluating occupations held by Hindus.

> Contact with certain wastes, blood and death are polluting. [Beidelman points out.] "In some cases the roles of the *kamins* are almost completely ceremonial, their roles being particularly to remove pollution. (Beidelman 1959:22, 27)

While the *jajmans'* high rank must be reinforced by economic and political power, the *kamins'* varying ranks are largely functions, one may infer from Beidelman's presentation, of Hindu ideas about cleanliness and uncleanliness of occupation, dietary practices, and living habits.

Beidelman is not concerned with the whole network of relationships in the *jajmani* system but with the relations between the dominant caste *jajmans* and lower caste servants (*kamins*). He does cite Dube's division of the *jajmani-kamin* relationships into three types varying according to land ownership and artisan versus menial chores. He mentions in passing that servants may serve each other, thus indicating his recognition that exchange of services between *kamins* does take place.

He does point out also in passing—for it does not influence his over-all analysis—that different dominant castes may have different degrees of ceremonial and ritual requirements. Thus, Rajputs and Brahmans put more emphasis on ceremonial display and prestige than do Jats. The implications of these differences between different dominant castes deserve more systematic and thorough consideration.

Beidelman makes two important points about the system of role relationships as a whole. First, he emphasizes the integration of the system on the local level. He criticizes most works on the caste system for failing to recognize its operation on a local basis.[11] He points out that this local integration is also local insularity. The lack of opportunities outside the system is important. Beidelman reminds us that both Marx and Weber pointed out the importance for the *jajmani* system of the lack of outside markets for labor or products.

Secondly, for the system as a whole, Beidelman is very much concerned with the rather delicate adjustment necessary between numbers of *jajmans* and numbers of *kamins*. How can supply and demand for labor be always in perfect alignment? He suggests that this has always been a problem. Now with the great increase of population he holds that there is an excess of *kamins*, and with the sub-division in landholdings among the landholding castes the economic support for ceremonials and rituals is undermined. Many *jajmans* simply cannot afford the elaborate *kamin* services of the past. The adjustment between numbers of *kamins* and *jajmans* is of course very important for the power distribution of the two power groups.

(3) DISTRIBUTION OF POWER

Beidelman's major proposal was to examine the *jajmani* system critically

> . . . in the light of recent studies in order to determine the locus of power within this system and thus to throw some new light on the controversial question of whether or not it is an exploitative system . . . [He asks] whether there is an equal distribution of power between the two interacting groups,

the dominant caste *jajmans* and the lower caste servants.

The bases of the *jajmani* system, Beidelman says, are land and caste duties (Beidelman 1959:6). Land ownership is almost exclusively in one dominant caste. The dominant caste *jajmans* usually supplement the power derived from land ownership with political power from large numbers. There are usually more in

---

[11] Beidelman (1959:51–52, 12). Some social scientists have recognized this. Bernard Barber said "The localistic character of the Indian stratification system is one of its essential characteristics" (1957:81).

the dominant caste than in any other caste of a village. Given a situation in which there is no other effective police force, the dominant caste *jajmans* have the greater potential physical force.

Beidelman says, "Any integration possible is of a coercive nature" (Beidelman 1959:68). The key factor in the power situation is land tenure. Given the presence of a caste system and a strong family system, Beidelman aims to

> show the methods by which land tenure determines the locus of power in the village system. (Beidelman 1959:33)

In a country where the overwhelming majority of people are dependent upon agriculture, land ownership means control over a large number of items such as

> . . . debts, loans, bribery, employment, water for fields, distribution of tenancy, funds for litigation, advantages in education, control of wood, fuel, pasturage, etc. (Beidelman 1959:41)

Given the importance of land and the wealth stemming from it, Beidelman says that bigger or wealthier landlords are always served by *kamins* first. Low caste *kamins* have to pay more for the same service. High castes are paid more for their services.

Ritual purity and pollution are not an important determinant of power in this system, according to Beidelman. Ritual rankings of castes tend to correlate with politico-economic power, and changes in rank may, in fact, be functions of economic and political power. Once a caste has established dominant economic and political power, high ritual rank as well is likely to be granted readily by the dominated castes in a locality.

The *jajman* has the final political sanction over the *kamin*. Village *panchayats,* law courts, and police all favor the *jajmans* in any disputes, because the *jajmans* tend to be more educated and have more resources to finance bribes, witnesses, and long waiting periods. Beidelman says:

> I contend that one of the major sources of conflict within this system is a lack of any formal and equitable means of settlement. Any integration possible is of a coercive nature. (Beidelman 1959:68)

The coercion here is economic power and the potential physical force of large numbers.

The power of the *kamins* lies in the ritual system and occupational division of labor. Inherited clientele, and monopolies over essential services, supported by trade-unionism within *kamin* castes, support from kin in surrounding villages, and the safety in a multiplicity of *jajmans* are their main bases of power.

Beidelman discounts the reciprocal power of the *kamins*. His shrewd analysis of the sources of their power is interlarded with statements of condition negating and weakening such power. This protestation weakens his over-all presentation.

Beidelman, like Leach, sees the *kamins'* power in caste monopolies, and like Wiser, he sees these as based upon Hindu values, but he discounts the *kamins'* power in caste monopolies by his suggestion that the condition for the monopolies, acceptance of certain social and religious values, has declined or is inoperative.

Caste cohesion is reinforced by kinship ties. Beidelman sees that the

> . . . dispersion of a caste over a wide area may increase its power, [so it is] less dependent upon one family or locale. (Beidelman 1959:42)

Again he counters this strength by suggesting that

> . . . endogamy makes internal caste tensions and competition all the more severe so that dispersion may have a weakening as well as a strengthening effect. (Beidelman 1959:42–43)

The multiplicity of *jajmans,* Beidelman also sees as a source of *kamin* strength. He says:

> Just as having many kin in many villages gives strength to a *kamin's* position, so having several *jajmans,* especially in more than one village, allows for greater freedom to the *kamin.* (Beidelman 1959:46)

Kamins presumably could play *jajmans* off one against the other, but again Beidelman suggests that this is unlikely, because higher castes readily close ranks against the lower castes. In crises, it would seem possible for either caste or both to solidify.

Further, caste solidarity among *kamins* is undermined by one *kamin's* having to side in feuds with his *jajman,* sometimes against *jajmans* supported by his own caste brothers. *Jajmans* also encourage litigation and disputes among their *kamins.*

While *jajmani* rights to a clientele may be inherited, an element in the system contributing to *kamin* security, Beidelman discounts this by saying that *jajmani* rights ". . . may be subdivided [to] a point of usefulness" (Beidelman 1959:51).

This latter subdivision is connected with the population pressure that Beidelman sees contributing to an undermining of the *jajmani* system. (See discussion under Section 2 on Roles above.)

On the whole, Beidelman holds that the *kamins'* reciprocal powers are puny against the economic power of the *jajmans* who own the land and wield the political power through their greater numbers.

The relationship of numbers to power is of great interest to Beidelman. While high numbers of land-owning dominant caste members reinforce both their political and economic power, large numbers of a *kamin* caste appear to have contradictory effects. High numbers make them more of a threat in terms of physical force, but undermine their economic status, since many of them will be unemployed, and their physical threat will mean that *jajmans* will be less generous with concessions. If large numbers are not employed in their caste work, this tends to encourage intra-caste competition and may undermine caste solidarity by numbers of them going to the city.

A last point that Beidelman makes about power has to do with the arbitrariness of the system. He claims that the interpretation of the local *wajib-ul-arz* or written set of rules for *jajmani* rights and duties is flexible, that there is in fact a good deal of leeway in its interpretation, and hence arbitrariness in payments even by traditional rules. He says:

> Despite the supposed fixity of these traditional relationships, they are interpreted varyingly. Such differences in interpretation are a source of conflict since their enactment ultimately rests on coercive measures. The undefined nature of some parts of a local *wajib-ul-arz* facilitates exploitation although economic and numerical power would undoubtedly accomplish this in any case. Many of the tensions in the system may be the result of a difference in expectations and demands due to the actual arbitrariness of the system, despite its traditional basis. (Beidelman 1959:52)

In addition, as caste values and demands are declining, *jajmans* may begin to perform the services themselves. This is quite possible, since most of them involve little investment in training or any high degree of skill.

(4) RANK

Beidelman sees the whole system operating to subordinate the *kamin*.

In the section under Roles, I have discussed the relationship between rank, ritual, and ceremonial, and in the section under Power, the requisite of land ownership for power and high rank in the *jajmani* system.

(5) MOTIVATION

Beidelman, like many other scholars, sees the main advantages for the *kamins* to be security, dependable access to food, and other requirements for living. The *jajmans,* on the other hand, are motivated by their need for cheap, dependable and handy labor, and servants in ceremonial and ritual.

(6) NORMS

Beidelman says that "theoretically" the *kamin* is supposed to do all that a *jajman* asks him to do within his occupational realm and the *jajman* is required to employ only his *kamin's* service; actual practice deviates from this ideal.

(7) GENERAL CULTURAL VALUES

Caste and family values concerning prestige, caste values of pollution and occupational division of labor, and the general cultural emphasis upon hierarchy and inequality, are all tightly involved in the *jajmani* system.

(8) SANCTIONS

The potential coercive power of the dominant caste *jajmans* stemming from land ownership and numerical force are important negative sanctions. The land-owning *jajmans* can take away land rented or granted a *kamin*. Through wealth, education, and influence, the police, law courts, and village *panchayats* favor dominant caste members. Payments are positive sanctions.

The *kamins'* power lies in withdrawal of required services. Such power is increasingly ineffective. This has been discussed above in the section on Beidelman's model.

(9) RELATIONSHIP WITH OTHER SOCIAL SYSTEMS

The *jajmani* system is closely related to kinship, caste, faction-alism, economy, and political structure of the village. Such relationships have been sketched above.

(10) CHANGES

While Beidelman is primarily interested in the distribution of power in the *jajmani* system, he is also interested in factors

. . . disruptive and contradictory to its traditional role relation-ships. (Beidelman 1959:1)

He indicates that some of these factors of change have probably been influencing the *jajmani* system for a long historical period, such factors as

. . . strong central government, influence from outside markets, fluctuations in grain prices, money, population pressures, etc. (Beidelman 1959:13)

While the *jajmani* system has survived such influences during the past, changes now are of such scope that it is doubtful if the *jajmani* system itself will survive.

Population pressure is leading to sub-division of land and agricultural inefficiency as well as an increased demand on a fixed land supply and food. *Jajmani* rights may also be sub-divided among heirs to a point of being almost worthless as a means of support.

For centuries the local basis for Indian economy has been shifting to a national level. Such outside markets affect the value and supply of grain. Employment outside villages has become available. Changes in land-tenure laws have disturbed relations between landed and landless.

Caste values are being discarded. *Jajmans* are becoming willing to do various menial tasks themselves. Some *kamins* have been technologically unemployed as they compete with factory-made goods or more efficient appliances (like pumps and chaff-cutters). *Jajmans* are less able to afford *kamins* and are more interested in cash and profit than service and prestige.

(11) STRAINS

Beidelman suggests that the *jajmani* system must have required continual readjustment due to the disproportion in numbers of *jajmans* and *kamins*. This, he suggests, required adjustment in payments as well.

Another strain in the system according to Beidelman was the vagueness of certain rights and obligations. Currently, the willingness to deviate from traditions makes for even greater conflict and insecurity.

The agricultural outlet probably made the system flexible in the past, but shortage of land makes such adjustment increasingly impossible.

DISCUSSION OF BEIDELMAN

Beidelman's emphasis upon the differential requirements for ritual and ceremony between high castes and low castes as an important value support for the *jajmani* system is close to Gould's view of the high castes as needing the lower castes to absorb pollution for them. Beidelman extends these requirements from pollution alone to requirements of prestige including ceremonial display, celebration of holy days, and so on. Gould and Beidelman together are close to Hocart who caught the flavor of the kingly style of life. It has also been referred to by some as martial (Hitchcock 1958:216–223), semi-feudal (Blunt 1931; Hutton 1951), and feudal.[12] We may expect this especially of a dominant Kshatriya caste. In such a life, the "king" requires the services of lower castes. Like Leach, Hocart saw the local caste interdependence as the heart of the caste system, but he did not

[12] Beidelman (1959). According to Strayer and Coulborn, a feudal society must, by definition, be one based upon *fiefs,* a condition not present universally in India. See Rushton Coulborn and Joseph R. Strayer (1956: 6). They say that the lord-retainer relationship may be important in non-feudal societies.

interpret it as an economic institution only, but as a ritual or sacrificial organization as well (Hocart 1950). He saw the *jajmani*-type system of Ceylon as a degradation of the royal sacrificial organization.

> The king's state is reproduced in miniature by his vassals: a farmer has his court consisting of the personages most essential to the ritual, and so present even in the smallest community, the barber, the washerman, the drummers, and so forth . . . The god in his temple has his court like the king in his palace: smith, carpenters, potters, all work for him. This ritual organization has spread downward to such an extent that the poor cultivators in the jungle have their retainers to play the part which they alone are qualified by heredity to play at births, weddings, and funerals, but these retainers are retainers of the community, the village, not of one lord. (Hocart 1950:68)

Basic to the *jajmani* system is commitment to a royal or lordly way of life as an ideal. This commitment is suggested by Hocart when he says:

> . . . Now Sinhalese society cannot carry on without washerman or barber, not because they do not know how to wash or shave, but because they can no more be born, married or die properly without washerman or barber than a Roman Catholic can without a priest. (Hocart 1950:48–49)

The higher castes depend upon the lower castes to absorb pollution accompanying births, sex relations, and deaths, and all bodily *exuviae*. Hocart emphasized this function of the lower castes.

Beidelman's evaluation of Wiser seems upon appraisal to be rather biased. It is unfair to suggest that Wiser did not recognize the inequality of the relationship between *jajman* and *kamin*. As I have indicated in the section on Wiser, he did emphasize this inequality.

Beidelman's view of the system as two power groups, dominant caste *jajmans* and dominated caste *kamins*, is a rather narrow role frame. In most villages, the *jajmani* system is not a set of relationships between a single *jajman* and his set of servants, but it is a system of many *jajmans* in many relationships, many *kamins* with many *jajmans*. And almost invariably, each *kamin* serves *jajmans* of several different castes.

Mayer reports for Ramkheri, a village of nine hundred persons and twenty-seven castes, that the *kamin* castes of carpenter and blacksmith serve all other castes, and the barber and potter serve all castes except the untouchables. The untouchable tanner serves all who have clovenfooted livestock (Mayer 1956:64–66). Kathleen Gough reported that barbers, carpenters, potters and the village temple priest in the Tanjore village she studied, served the village as a whole (Gough 1960:23). In Rampur, Delhi, a village of twelve castes, seven served all the other castes or all the castes except untouchables (Lewis 1958:62).

The number of *jajmans* in a *kamin's* clientele varies. In Karimpur, U.P., studied by the Wisers, the number of *jajmans* varied from three or four for each watercarrier family up to the whole village of 754 persons for the one florist. For the sixteen *kamin* castes, the mean number of other castes served was 17.5. The range was from one other caste for a seamstress up to twenty-four other castes for the oil-presser.[13] For Sherapur, U.P., studied by Gould, the number of *jajmans* ranged from eleven each for the priest and plowman, up to forty-three for the washerman (Gould 1958:436).

A number of writers, Wiser, Lewis, Opler and Singh, and Srinivas, speak of equal exchange of services and products between various *kamins*. Lewis and Barnouw report that in Rampur there is equal interchange of services among the carpenter, barber, washerman, and potter. For Wiser the counterpart castes are barber, grainparcher, potter, and washerman (Wiser 1956:61; O. Lewis 1958:66, 62; Opler and Singh 1952:495; Srinivas 1955a:13).

There seems to be no question that there are many *jajman-kamin* relationships between members of the non-dominant castes. Beidelman's point that high caste land-owning dominant caste persons play *jajman* roles, but not *kamin* roles is difficult to argue, because the caste function of Kshatriyas is to lead and protect the village, and with conquest to manage their conquered lands.[14] The Kshatriyas do perform these functions today to the extent possible, by distributing food as payments to *kamins* and providing leadership. Perhaps the word *kamin* is inappropriate for them, but they are not just on the receiving end of these relation-

[13] Wiser (1956:12–13). I calculated the arithmetic mean from Wiser's data.

[14] Wiser presents selections from the Hindu law book, the Laws of Manu, Muller (1886). See Wiser (1956:26).

ships. Where there are Brahmans in the position of the dominant caste, it would be necessary to investigate how many clients they have for their priestly services, as well as the number of *kamins* they supply with food and other needs.

Wiser's interpretation of the *jajmani* system as an exchange between specialized castes is not inappropriate. Beidelman's distress with such an interpretation is that it does not emphasize adequately power differentials between castes. Beidelman is more interested in the power distribution in the village context than Wiser.

This criticism of Beidelman is not to deny that exploitation of *kamins* does take place. A perusal of the village reports, however, leads one to suspect that the castes most likely to be exploited are the untouchable agricultural workers—the Chamars in U.P., the Madigas in Hyderabad, the Pallans in Mysore.[15] Possibly the type of *kamin* of whom Beidelman was thinking—for his model does not differentiate within the role of *kamin* different types— was the untouchable Chamar. The ill treatment of these castes may be due to their untouchable status or to their low bargaining power in the economy.

Beidelman points out that the balancing in numbers of *kamins* and *jajmans* to fit the supply and demand for services would seem to require continuous adjustments (Beidelman 1959:53). Leach's model assumes that the high caste *jajmans* are numerically higher than the lower caste *kamins*—thus, that demand is in excess of supply (Leach 1960:6). The model of equal interchange, attributed by Beidelman to Wiser, would suggest a perfect adjustment in numbers. Supply and demand are ideally fitted (Beidelman 1959:4–6). In fact, Beidelman says maladjustments must be usual and activities to put supply and demand into balance must be going on all the time.

Lewis, Srinivas, and Gough, among others, have spoken of the problem of the adjustment of demand for services to numbers present in a caste (Lewis 1958:59–60; Srinivas 1955a:16; Gough 1960:26). Where numbers are excessive there are various methods to relieve the intra-caste pressure and potential competition. Individuals moved to other villages, probably where they

15 See Wiser (1956:51); Opler and Singh (1952:489–490); Lewis (1958: 72, 81); Cohn (1954); Dube (1955:68). For Pallans of Mysore see Gough (1960:23).

had relatives, or they turned to agriculture or other occupations. As one compares village complements of services, it is striking that where a specialist caste is absent, the caste's function is often provided by some other caste. Where drummers are not present, drumming will be done by some other low caste, such as sweepers or Chamars (Opler and Singh 1952:490). A. M. Hocart also mentioned that this kind of substitution took place (Hocart 1950:2–3). It is interesting that in the nineteenth century, B. H. Baden-Powell saw that the village system owed some of its strength to access to wasteland (Wiser 1956:157–159).

Many observers have mentioned the fact that various *kamins* serve more than one village or hamlet to supplement their clientele. Oscar Lewis has asked if mobility of *kamins* between villages in an area is not necessary for the operation of the *jajmani* system (Lewis 1958:59). The excess numbers of *kamin* castes go to localities where demand for their specialties is not being met, or leave the competition by taking up new occupations in cities or other places. In some cases the adjustments may be made by the *kamins* taking up new work. In situations where demand outruns supply, the dominant caste leadership makes efforts to invite more of the *kamin* caste to settle in the locality.

Such draining off of excess *kamins* from a local *jajmani* system strengthens the bargaining power of the *kamin* caste although, as Beidelman's analysis suggests, their political power is weakened by their reduced numbers. In the *jajmani* system fewer numbers of a *kamin* caste may strengthen its economic bargaining power, but weaken its potential political coercive power.

Gerald D. Berreman has recently presented convincing evidence of the importance for the *kamins* of this draining off of excess members (Berreman 1962). In a Himalayan village, population increase of the serving castes seems to have taken place at the same time that access to appealing bazaar-made goods became possible. Supply of servants was increasing at the time that demands for services and goods was decreasing. Members of serving castes who owned land gave up their caste occupations, but the others had no alternative available to them. Agricultural labor in this area is done by impoverished high caste Rajputs or Brahmans. Difficulty of access between mountain villages pre-

vents reliance on clients in other villages. Work, in the city, although not mentioned, is perhaps prohibitive, because of the
considerable cultural differences between the mountains and the
plains where the cities are located. Intra-caste competition is
rampant among the serving castes in this village; there is little
caste cohesion among them. Monopolies on caste occupations
are not respected. In this situation, Berreman reports, the serving
castes ". . . subsist at the discretion of their high caste patrons."
In this village, the servant castes, all untouchables, are in fact
exploited not only because of their untouchability, it appears,
but because of their extraordinarily weak bargaining power.

Beidelman's analysis of the sources of *kamin* power is in-
sightful. In showing that the system is exploitative, he discounts
these reciprocal powers by suggesting conditions under which
they fail to operate. However, we may ask if *kamins* do not have
power in the system because of the safety of a multiplicity of
jajmans. One might also ask what real strength *kamin* castes have
because of relatives in other villages. I have known instances of
whole local caste groupings leaving a village, the various families
scattering to join relatives in various other villages.

Can the distribution of power for any particular locality be
studied empirically? Whether the balance of power is so heavily
on the side of the *jajmans* that the system may be said to be
exploitative of the lower caste servants, or whether the reciprocal
power of the lower castes' indispensability is sufficient to ensure
decent treatment, is not just a matter of different anthropologists' opinions. Empirical power structures need to be assessed
validly and systematically.

In discussing the distribution of power in the *jajmani* system,
Beidelman explicitly limited himself to the single dyadic relationship of *jajman* and *kamin*. To assess power adequately, a more
complicated role frame is necessary. The role of *kamin* may be
differentiated in terms of varying bargaining power in the *jajmani*
system. The role of *jajman* may be differentiated by rank,
whether a high or low caste, whether in the dominant or non-
dominant castes.

Especially important, however, are the implications of the
multiplicity of *jajmans* and *kamins*. And lastly, to understand
the power allocation of the *jajmani* system, it is necessary to

trace its relationships with other aspects of the culture, relationships involving other kinds of transactions.

Beidelman points out that *kamins* may have to participate in their *jajmans'* factional disputes, thus undermining the power of the *kamin* caste (Beidelman 1959:48–49). He also speaks of the fact that a *jajman* prefers to consolidate his hold on a man by having him also as a tenant or debtor (Beidelman 1959:37). Beidelman's insights suggest some further elaboration. Relationship of the *jajmani* system to factionalism and role summation will appear below.

A number of writers have suggested that Indian villagers are preoccupied with maintenance and defense of personal and caste status. These include David Mandelbaum, John Hitchcock, G. Morris Carstairs, E. M. Forster and Alan Beals. Beals has spoken of the Indian village as characterized by "pervasive factionalism."[16]

The factionalism and status rivalries among, especially the dominant caste of a village, can have implications for *kamins*. If a *kamin* has *jajmans* belonging to different factions, he has a potential power against one or another of his *jajmans,* it would appear. Srinivas suggested that something like this happened in a village in Mysore. He speaks of the circles of patrons and clients:

> . . . a rich man is able to put many persons under his obligation. Every rich man tries to "invest in people" so that he can on occasion turn his following to political or economic advantage . . . Only the hard core of a patron's following is willing clearly to declare its allegiance to one patron, while many clients have a marginal affiliation to more than one patron. Marginal clients give fluidity to the followings of the various patrons as they shift their allegiance from one to another over a period of time. (Srinivas 1955a:30–31)

We may use Nadel's term summation for the idea that two persons may play different sets of roles reciprocally (Nadel 1957:63–72). If the summation of roles is a combination of *kamin* role with that of follower or supporter in a faction, played opposite a person playing both a *jajman* role and that of dominant caste faction leader or lieutenant, this may considerably strengthen the *kamin's* power in the reciprocal relationship, some-

---

[16] Mandelbaum (1955:238–239); Hitchcock (1958); Carstairs (1957:39–62); Forster (1953:41–42); Siegel and Beals (1960:394–417).

thing Nadel calls "linked incentives" (Nadel 1957:71). This power may be especially great if the *kamin* is a marginal member of more than one faction.

A *jajman* may have greater power over a *kamin* if the two persons combine the role relationships of *jajman-kamin,* landlord-tenant, debtor-debtee, religious preceptor-disciple and so on. Srinivas said:

> . . . a rich man has many devices: he can oblige others by lending them money, by letting them land, by speaking to an official or big man on their behalf, or by performing acts of generosity. (Srinivas 1955a:28)

Another aspect of factionalism and concern with prestige involves what Nadel calls *triadization* (Nadel 1957:86). This includes the idea that a person plays his role not only vis-à-vis the reciprocal role, but also vis-à-vis the public, or other roles or sub-groups. Thus, the *jajman* plays his role not only with the *kamin,* but also before the audience of caste fellows. In the same way, relationships between caste brothers are judged by those in the *kamin* roles. They form an audience for kin or caste role relationships.

Gough suggests some effects of triadization in the following:

> In recent years a few suits against kinsmen, concerning land disputes, have been filed in Tanjore by Brahmans, but all of these were withdrawn, because the parties felt that to go to court would involve loss of dignity in the eyes of their kin and their villagers. In general, fear of losing dignity before the lower castes, coupled with the belief in *ahimsa,* chiefly toward peers and elders, prevents Brahman quarrels from ending in physical combat. (Gough 1955:44)

The concept of triadization also involves the idea that if A and B are incumbents of a reciprocal role relationship, A will react to and have some interest in B's other role relationships. This approaches another aspect of the power distribution in a community. For example, *jajmans* may support their *kamins* in their disputes with their kin or other castes in the village, so taking an interest in the *kamins'* other relationships. Gough says

> Pallans, as the personal laborers of Brahmans in their own unleased fields have in many ways a closer bond with them than have Non-Brahmans, and are a caste jealous of Non-Brahman power in the village. Non-Brahmans, on the other hand, make efforts to crush Pallans . . . (Gough 1955:44)

In this case, the untouchables attached to the hated Brahmans would suffer because of their attachment, from the Non-Brahmans. Pallans (A) support Brahmans (B) against Non-Brahmans (C, B's other role relationship).

Another example of triadization is given by Srinivas.

> The master is, in certain circumstances, regarded as responsible for the acts and omissions of the servant, though there is no clear and explicit formulation of the doctrine of vicarious responsibility. (Srinivas 1955a:28)

An aspect of the village power structure involving this idea of triadization about which we have very little information, is the relationship between the non-dominant castes, and the response to such relationships on the part of the dominant caste. It is sometimes said that the Hindu pollution concept results in keeping separate the various castes and prevents them from uniting for common cause, say, with respect to the dominant landowning caste. An investigation of the middle and lower castes in relationships with one another has not been done, with the exception of some reports on village elections. The relationships between non-dominant castes should be included in any analysis of the village power structure.

Blocks of castes called by single names and considered to be related, like the Panch Brahman castes, the left-handed castes, and so on, might be analyzed for the meaning of their bond and its influence on the village scene. Blocks of castes including the dominant caste are also of importance, of course. Mayer reports for Ramkheri a block of castes called the Allied Castes, made up of the dominant caste and its *kamin* castes (Mayer 1956:46–47). Berreman also speaks of a "dominant pair" of castes, the Rajputs and Brahmans, in Village Sirkanda, in the Himalayas (Berreman 1962:387).

The balance between the *kamin's* relationships to his *jajmans* and his relationships to his caste brothers, and the balance between the *jajman's* relationships to his *kamins* as compared to those with his caste fellows are important in the analysis of power in the Indian village (Srinivas 1952:214, 1957:529–530; Beidelman 1959:66, 37, 44–49). Some writers have said that the stronger tie with the *jajman* has prevented the lower castes from developing strong counteractive solidarity.

Gough stated that the dyadic relationships between *jajman*

and *kamin* families of different castes are by far the more important set of integrating relations in her Tanjore village. She says:

> Because the highest caste controlled all the land, the most important economic relationships consisted of the rendering of goods and services by lower-caste household upwards to one or more Brahman households in return for food, clothing and shelter . . . because these transactions were dyadic and mutually separate, they did not provide a basis for co-operative bargaining on the part of blocks of lower castes in relation to the landlords. (Gough 1960:27)

Gough suggests that these vertical ties not only undermined intra-caste unity within a lower caste, but also within the dominant caste.

> Sometimes, indeed, a Brahman required his servants to fight on his behalf against the retainers of another Brahman family temporarily at odds with his own. So strong were these inter-household ties, cross-cutting caste loyalties, that a landlord was often found pleading for his own servant and trying to push off the blame on the servants of others, when a collective punishment of lower-caste persons was being meted out. (Gough 1960:50)

Some other writers, Gould among them, have said that the chain of *jajmans* and *kamins* operate as social units of importance in the power structure (Gould 1958:434). Only in one study, however, does the author suggest that the network of relations between a single *jajman* and his various servants is the important social unit. Barth in writing of Swat, North Pakistan, speaks of

> . . . productive teams, in many ways analogous to the European medieval manor. (Barth 1960:120)

Such seem to exist, because the *kamins* do not have multiple *jajmans* in the usual manner.

Where a village is dominated by a single family, or one or two dominant families, or a dominant lineage, then the *kamins'* relationships to these among all the other *jajmans* is especially important. This is another aspect of the differentiation of the *jajman* role.

In the section above, I have tried to suggest some of the ways in which the *jajman-kamin* role may be viewed in terms of a network of role relationships in the village context: its place in

factionalism and status struggles, in the summation or combination of roles combined by the same persons, in terms of third
party responses, in terms of balance between vertical relationships and horizontal relationships, in lower caste inter-caste relations, and with respect to a single dominant family or lineage.

LEACH'S MODEL

E. R. Leach's essay, "What Should We Mean by Caste?," is
relevant to our discussion (Leach 1960:1–10). Although he is
not concerned with the *jajmani* system per se, his ideas about
caste monopoly and competition in the caste system are important for a model of the *jajmani* system.

Leach sees the caste system as a system of interrelationships
between castes,

> . . . a network of economic, political, and ritual relationships
> . . . [It should be seen as] an organic system with each particular
> caste and subcaste filling a distinctive functional role. It is a
> system of labour division from which the element of competi-
> tion among workers has been largely excluded.

He feels that the economic interdependence between castes is
"far more fundamental" than the kind of sociological analysis
which

> . . . puts all the stress upon hierarchy and upon the exclusive-
> ness of caste separation. (Leach 1960:5)

The numerical scarcity of the lower castes and their occupational monopolies are the factors differentiating the caste system
from a class system, according to Leach. He says:

> It is a characteristic of *class*-organized societies that rights of
> ownership are the prerogative of minority groups which form
> privileged elites. The capacity of the upper-class minority to
> "exploit" the services of the lower-class majority is critically de-
> pendent upon the fact that the members of the underprivileged
> group must compete among themselves for the favours of the
> elite. It is the specific nature of a *caste* society that this position
> is reversed. Economic roles are allocated by right to closed
> minority groups of low social status; members of the high-status
> "dominant caste," to whom the low-status groups are bound,
> generally form a numerical majority and must compete among
> themselves for the services of individual members of the lower
> "castes." (Leach 1960:5–6)

Leach's model contrasts with Beidelman's. Leach sees the members of the dominant caste competing among themselves for the services of the lower servant castes; Beidelman sees the dominant caste exploiting the lower servant castes. If Leach's competition is present, the exploitative activity of any single *jajman* would be limited. An aggrieved *kamin* could end his misery by switching to a new *jajman*—what Beidelman called playing one *jajman* off against the other.

Part of the inconsistency of the two models appears to rest on different assumptions about the supply of *kamins* available. Beidelman's model implies the presence of an adequate number —even a surplus of *kamins;* Leach explicitly assumes a shortage —even a scarcity—of *kamins*. If, however, both conditions are in fact present, competition for *kamins'* services and exploitation of the *kamins,* some other factors must be introduced to explain this anomaly.

Evidence for Leach's model of a numerically larger high caste competing for lower caste *kamins* is very slight. As we have seen in the discussion of Beidelman's model above, writers concerned with the adjustment of numbers of *kamins* and *jajmans* have discussed the shift of excess labor into other occupations and other localities, not the problem of recruitment of sufficient labor.

Leach seems to assume that the dominant caste does not close ranks against the lower castes, but that the members compete among themselves. Beidelman, on the other hand, suggests that both upper and lower castes may solidify in disputes or conflicts with the other, but that the upper castes are more likely to be effective and successful in inter-caste disputes.

Leach explicitly generalizes about dominant caste factionalism. He says:

> In any caste system the factional rivalries among members of the locally privileged caste or castes are likely to be acute, but taken together these local "twice born" form a high-status corporation for whose benefit the whole of the rest of the system appears to be organized. (Leach 1960:9)

If one assumes such factionalism in the dominant caste, one might assume that they compete among themselves for *kamin* services; evidence for this needs to be collected.

Leach also suggests that each caste has a monopoly on a needed product or service, and he states that each caste is made up of

... members of some closely organized kinship group who regard it as their privileged right to carry out a task from which
all other members of the total society are rigorously excluded.
(Leach 1960:6)

Further, he points out that

... every caste in a caste system has its special privileges. (Leach
1960:10)

Leach's view suggests that castes, at least traditionally, had
monopolies over occupational functions for which a large patron
caste competed. Dube, Srinivas, and others have also spoken of
the security of the lower castes in their caste monopolies (Dube
1955:57; Srinivas 1952:15). Beidelman, in contrast, leaves the
impression that the need for these services is limited, so that caste
monopolies are worth little in the way of power or protection.

DISCUSSION OF LEACH

Beidelman points out that three conditions must be present for
a local caste-grouping to have the kind of economic security that
Leach speaks of, where a large high caste is competing for the
services of the lower smaller caste. First, the caste must have a
monopoly on a service or product that is indispensable to the
higher castes and/or other villagers. Secondly, the caste must not
be so large that the supply of the service far outruns the demand
for it, and, third, the lower caste members must not compete
among themselves unduly, but must have reasonable unity and
effective caste discipline (Beidelman 1959:43).

Within the *jajmani* style of life, the demand for various services
and products associated with caste differs considerably. We may,
in fact, speak of degrees of dispensability of the various caste
services. While these vary over time and in different places,
studies show surprisingly that the carpenters and blacksmiths are
consistently important. From Opler and Singh's account of the
jajmani system in village Senapur, it is possible to compare the
degree of dispensability of the various *kamins*. Most necessary
are the barber, and carpenter. Their importance is greater than
that of the potter and watercarrier, whose importance is greater
than that of betal leaf distributors, bangle sellers, or sweepers
(Opler and Singh 1952:480, 482, 483, 492, 493).

Others, besides Opler and Singh, have compared degrees of importance among *kamins*. Wiser pronounced the watercarriers "chief among household menials," the barber "chief among local menials," the blacksmith "chief among essential artisans" (Wiser 1956:40, 37, 34). About demand for services, Wiser said:

> The village community is prepared to accept in its organization any caste that performs a necessary function. Where the demand is slight no encouragement is given to the caste to settle. Representatives of two such castes, the *Tamboli* (seller of betal leaf) and the *Ahir* (cattle raiser) formerly lived in the village. When they left, no effort was made by the village to invite others of their caste to take their place. They were not essential to the village economy. (Wiser 1956:161)

Another means of measuring dispensability is to count the number of villages in which a particular functional caste is included in the *jajmani* system. Adrian Mayer found in a survey of eighteen villages in Madhya Bharat that thirteen villages had from four to seven of the following seven *kamin* castes: blacksmith, carpenter, barber, potter, drummer, and tanner. Least important, as suggested by most frequent absence, were the sweeper and drummer (Mayer 1956:77–78).

In most villages the *jajmani* system involves relatively few of the castes present in the village. Most of the villages studied have between five and seven castes in the *jajmani* network.[17] The small number of castes in the system may be a result of recent changes in the village economy. An early study by H. H. Mann showed that the *baluta* or grain-share *jajmani*-type system in a village in Maharashtra included all non-dominant castes.[18] Of more recent studies, the sixteen out of a total of twenty-four castes in Wiser's Karimpur is the highest number of castes included (Wiser 1956:13).

The alternate economic relationships between castes such as share-cropping, slavery, and serfdom in Indian villages should

[17] For example, Shamirpet, Telangana studied by S. C. Dube; Ramkheri, Madhya Bharat, studied by A. Mayer; Rampur, Delhi, studied by Oscar Lewis; Sherapur, U.P., studied by Gould; Khalapur, U.P., studied by Hitchcock, Mayer, Gumperz, and others.

[18] Mann (1916:122). Mann said, "The whole of the non-Maratha population are, in fact, official village servants and entitled to some share in the *baluta* or charge against all the crops grown, for services rendered each in his separate sphere."

be examined and codified. Beidelman points out the importance of precise definition of different systems or relationships (Beidelman 1959:10–11). Dube, Opler and Singh, Srinivas, and Berreman have specified the different types of economic relationships in the villages they knew well (Dube 1955:58–59; Opler and Singh 1952; Berreman 1962:388–389; Srinivas 1955a:1–35). Degrees of dispensability of castes and caste monopolies may be considered with respect to these systems as with the *jajmani* arrangement.

To turn from the condition of dispensability to the condition of monopoly necessary for economic security of the lower castes, we find from a perusal of descriptions that villages vary in the integrity of caste monopolies. Dube reported that in Shamirpet, Hyderabad, only the trader's caste monopoly had been broken (Dube 1955:63). Kathleen Gough reported for a Tanjore village that caste monopolies still held; at least, no caste had as yet taken over another caste's traditional work (Gough 1960:34). In other villages, there are not such strong monopolies. In Ramkheri, Madhya Bharat, studied by Mayer, the occupation of carpenter had been taken over by the blacksmith and other castes (Mayer 1956:70). In Rampur, Delhi, studied by Lewis, caste monopolies of the carpenters and barbers seem to have been rather thoroughly broken. A number of castes do other castes' work in the Himalayan village studied by Berreman (O. Lewis 1958:68, 63; Berreman 1962:390).

Besides competition between different castes doing the same work or taking over each other's work, there is the question of competition within a caste. Whether a *kamin* family's right to a clientele of particular *jajmani* families is respected seems to depend upon the strength of the caste *panchayat* (council) which enforces caste cooperation. At its best, such caste discipline means that a *jajman* cannot change *kamins* easily; he must negotiate with the elders of the *kamin* caste and show just cause for dismissal before a substitute *kamin* will be supplied.

In Dube's Shamirpet, caste councils seem able still to control intra-caste competition. He says:

Each of these castes has its own inter-village council. Occupational castes have a developed trade unionism, and their code of professional ethics and etiquette too is very rigid. The dismissed person will be protected by this professional etiquette. No one else would be willing to act as a substitute, for fear of being penalized by the caste *panchayat.* (Dube 1955:60)

Security of the lower castes depends in part upon the strength of their *panchayats.* In Dube's Shamirpet and Opler and Singh's Senapur, some castes had strong *panchayats.* Opler and Singh also describe effective boycotts of *jajmans* (Opler and Singh 1952:486). In other villages such as Rampur, studied by Lewis, strikes have failed. Caste cohesion among serving castes was largely lacking in the Himalayan village studied by Berreman (O. Lewis 1958:63, 67, 82; Berreman 1962:390–393).

In contrast to the stable situation reported by Dube, Mayer reported a good deal of turnover in employment of servants in Ramkheri, "perhaps even cyclical." The *jajman-kamin* relationship may break if a craftsman or servant lives too far away and a new one comes to live closer, if there are disputes over the quality of work, if service is not prompt enough in emergencies, if there are disputes over wages, or if there is some scandal with respect to either the client's or the craftsman's private life (Mayer 1956:68–69).

Intra-caste competition in Ramkheri varies with differences in the right of inheritance of clients. Mayer explains:

For many village craftsmen have the right (*hak*) to work in Ramkheri, and if there is nobody to carry on, will call on a kinsman to come to the village. The strength of these rights varies from craft to craft. It finds its clearest expression amongst sweepers, where the rights to work and its perquisites in a village are exclusive and can be bought and sold. Other people (e.g., potter, drummer, barber) say that they would resist the attempt by anyone else to come and work in the village, but would not have a case to lay before the caste council unless the newcomer had inveigled clients away from them in the middle of the annual contract period. Their strength would rather lie in the fact that such competition would exist only among fellow-caste mates and so would be tempered by the desire of both parties to avoid quarrels which might spread to other spheres (e.g., a reputation for quarrelsomeness might affect the supply of spouses for a disputant's children). In these cases then, changes in clientele are generally made by agreement. But these rights are not the "property" of the incumbent, as for the sweeper. In contrast, carpentry is an example of a craft which is now open to many castes, and here the work "rights" is almost too strong. (Mayer 1956:70)

M. N. Srinivas also reports considerable turnover in his Mysore village (Srinivas 1955a:15–16).

This is not to say that in the villages where stable conditions appear to exist, the *kamins* have equal bargaining power in the *jajmani* system with the *jajmans*. However, the differences between villages and between castes in these factors would seem to be important in any evaluation of either the power distribution among castes in the village social structure or more narrowly in the *jajmani* system (Beidelman 1959:42).

In this section, we have been concerned with the *jajmani* system from the point of view of labor economics. Is there great demand for the services and products of the *kamin* castes? We suggested that there is much greater demand for some services than for others. This variation in the importance of different castes' services and products in a village's way of life would seem to be true in all villages.

Are caste monopolies over a traditional occupation respected? Is there job security? Is there intra-caste and inter-caste competition for the same work? Are the caste "unions" effective? Are they well-organized and sufficiently disciplined to stage strikes? To all these questions, we must answer that in some places monopolies are respected, *jajman-kamin* relationships are of long duration, caste *panchayats* are effective, and castes are cohesive. In other places, none of these features of a "traditional" *jajmani* system can be said to be entirely true. Villages reported upon can be ordered as more or less traditional in these ways. Karimpur, U.P., reported on by Wiser; Shamirpet, Hyderabad, of Dube; Senapur, U.P., of Opler and Singh, are at one extreme. They are highly traditional. Mayer's Ramkheri, Madhya Pradesh, Lewis's Rampur, U.P., and Berreman's Sirkanda in the Himalayas are toward the opposite extreme.

In our concern with labor economics, we have said little about payments for *kamin* labor. In papers relating to the *jajmani* system, both Edward Harper and Walter Neale have emphasized the importance of payments in grain and the absence of bargaining over wages or payments in the *jajmani* system (Harper 1959a:760–778; Neale 1957:218–236).

Edward Harper developed a brief compact model of the

jajmani system[19] in order to compare it with the employment relations of an areca nut-growing village in Mysore. He concluded that the latter represented a different system of exchange. His comparison of this, the Malnad system, with the *jajmani* system illustrates the usefulness of a model in analysis, for he specifies crucial features of the *jajmani* system not emphasized by others.

Essential for the *jajmani* system, Harper finds, are fixed wages based upon a medium of exchange that has constant purchasing power. Such a medium is grain as it circulates in a closed, traditional, self-sufficient village. In contrast, the Malnad system is substantially based upon cash crops, the values for which fluctuate in response to regional, national, and world markets. Wages for labor are paid in cash, and since the value of cash and cash crops fluctuates, there is continual bargaining over wages, and few enduring employment relationships. Harper assumes two features to be characteristic of *jajmani* systems: enduring, even inherited, *jajman-kamin* relationships, and ". . . little bargaining over wages and prices . . ." The latter point he must assume, since he points out,

> Nowhere in the literature is there any analysis of precisely how payments (in the *jajmani* system) are determined. (Harper 1959a: 764)

The presence of these two features is dependent upon grain as a constant medium of exchange.

M. N. Srinivas has also reported that grain payments are preferred in the Mysore village he studied. He says:

> Such payment is more highly valued than money, as the food-buying power of money varies. (Srinivas 1955a:14)

Two observations about Harper's discussion are these. First, with respect to the Malnad system, the bargaining over wages,

[19] Harper avoided many of the exaggerations of other analysts. He sees the exchange of services in the *jajmani* system but recognizes the importance of the land-owning castes; sees that all or only some of the castes of a village may be involved; sees that the system is dependent upon needs for the *kamin* services, especially needs related to pollution; and sees that the social units of the system are families, but that the rights of the servant castes are "maintained and enforced" at the "caste level." (A boycott of an aberrant *jajman* requires the cooperation of all members of the *kamin's* caste; the *kamin* family of this *jajman* cannot be effective alone.)

whether based on cash or not, would also seem to depend upon, at least periodic, shortages of labor. Second, with respect to the *jajmani* system, if payments are fixed traditionally or for long periods, this limits the conception of the servant castes' *panchayats* as trade-unions; they could have power only concerning job security, not wages.

Beidelman has suggested that payments varied by the numbers of servants available (Beidelman 1959:32). Harper has suggested that much more information is needed about the processes for determining payments in the *jajmani* system. The relationships between payments and occupational skill, ritual caste rank, and importance of an occupation in the village life all need consideration. A direct relationship between demand and compensation is suggested by Opler and Singh when they say that due to

> . . . a lively demand for their service, [the carpenters were] better off economically than most of the *jatis* of the village (Senapur, U.P.). (Opler and Singh 1952:482)

Percival Spear, writing about early nineteenth century villages in Delhi State, suggested that payment was related to importance, not ritual caste rank. He says:

> The extent of their allowances, therefore, depended not upon their caste or social status, but upon the necessary nature of their duties. Thus, the lowly Chamar, the cobbler and dresser of unclean leather, received the highest allowance of all, while the priest or Brahmin was given by these hard-headed people the least . . . The barbers and the water-carriers, two other despised occupations, were also rated highly. (Spear 1951:121)

Spear's report contrasts with Beidelman's generalization, that higher caste *kamins* are paid more. Bernard Cohn has observed that seeming low payments to Brahmans may often occur, because the Brahmans have grants of land as well (Beidelman 1959:40; Cohn, personal communication).

Describing a *jajmani*-type system in Conda District, U.P., Walter Neale states that payments were not economically rational.

> Some rough approximation to work rendered is indicated in the carpenters' and blacksmiths' shares based upon number and size of ploughs, which were also related to the area protected by the watchmen, but this cannot be said of basing the washerman's and barber's shares on the same criteria. (Neale 1957:226)

Like Harper, Neale has emphasized the payments in grain in *jajmani*-type systems. Neale, in fact, sees

> . . . the basis of the whole society [as] the grain heap, in which each constituent rank had its definite interest.[20]

An economic historian, unacquainted with either the work of Wiser or the few anthropological reports then available, Neale drew his model from W. C. Bennett's *Final Settlement Report on District Gonda,* published in 1878.[21] The Gonda system, Neale says, was one of redistribution of grain and reciprocity of services between castes. He reports that village servants received some absolute payments and some proportional payments from the common village grain heap after harvest. The absolute payments gave the village servants

> . . . a basic minimum even if the harvest was so small that their proportional shares would not support them. (Neale 1957:226)

The proportional payments made it possible for them to benefit in prosperous years.

Important in the Gonda system were no bargaining over payments, no payment for specific services, and the norm that each contributor to the life of the village had a claim on its produce.

As a last part to this section, I have tried to suggest some of the problems about payments in the *jajmani* system about which more information is needed—the negotiation and bases of payments, the relationships between caste rank, skill, demand, and payments, the meaning of grain payments.

CONCLUSIONS

It would be unfair to accuse the four analysts of presenting only partial descriptive models of the *jajmani* system since to varying extents the models are constructs I have developed by abstracting the "essentials" from their analyses. While all four of these scholars whose models have been used as *foci,* recognize many important factors, each tends to give his "votes" to one or a very few crucial factors; for Wiser, the representation in living

---

[20] Neale (1957:224); quoting from W. C. Bennett (1878:49).
[21] Bennett (1878:48–49). District Gonda is in Uttar Pradesh.

society of the Hindu law; for Gould, the emphasis upon the coordination of the system through fictive kinship; for Beidelman, the hierarchical dyadic role relationships, backed by the threat of economic and physical coercion; and for Leach, the importance of small lower castes' monopolies upon services and crafts.

While the four do not agree in emphases, they do agree on a number of principles and features of the *jajmani* system. The combination of the four makes possible the development of a useful and detailed guide to the study of any particular *jajmani* system. I must leave it to the researcher to develop the guide, since I have already written an article exasperatingly long.

As a conclusion, however, let me state some directives for drawing up such a guide.

(1) FUNCTIONS OF THE SYSTEM

The *jajmani* system is not merely an economic arrangement for distributing produce and exchanging services between castes, and providing labor. The functions include important contributions to life cycle and festival rites, as well as a set of relationships revolving around beliefs about pollution. The *jajmani* system operates to support superordination of high castes and subordination of lower castes; the prestige of higher castes is reinforced through rites in which servants participate. *Jajmans* and *kamins* may be allies in factional activities and in marriage arrangement.

(2) ROLES

All four students agree that ritual duties are important among the obligations in the *jajmani* system. They all agree that the system is integrated on a local basis, and that most role relationships in the system are hierarchical. Beidelman and Gould, as well as some others, have emphasized the fact that the *jajman-kamin* relationship is one between two families of different caste, not just two persons, nor two *jatis* or local caste groupings.

There has been a tendency for students to analyze the *jajmani* system in terms of a single dyadic relationship, between a high dominant caste *jajman* and an unspecified *kamin*. A much more elaborate role-frame is necessary. It includes multiple *jajmans* of various castes and multiple *kamins; kamins* related to caste brothers, both within the village and outside the village; relationships between non-dominant castes, between *kamin* castes; roles in caste and village *panchayats* as they relate to the *jajmani* relations; roles in factional disputes; roles of lender, politician, and counselor. Role descriptions for *kamins* must include the ritual, menial, craft, and field duties, their rights, payments, concessions, the duration of their relationships with *jajmans,* the quality of these relationships, in-village and out-village clientele.

Concern with roles must include the network of relationships that are part of, or influence the *jajmani* system. The combination or summation of roles, where two people play a number of different reciprocal roles; the triadization of role-play, where third party reactions are important for the role-playing pair; the balance between hierarchical and equal role relationships; the presence of allied castes or *jajman-kamin* chains; the individual's priorities in loyalties to role partners—all these may be considered.

(3) POWER IN ROLES

Jajman and *kamin* sources of power have been discussed at length in this paper. It is especially important in new research to take a labor economics view and consider supply, demand, and bargaining powers.

(4) MOTIVATION

It is especially important to interview villagers for their explanations of motivation.

(5) & (6) NORMS AND SANCTIONS

Codifications of the *jajmani* system in various forms should be collected—whether in ancient law, British, pre-British law, local codes, or strong traditions. The style of life of the dominant caste may be especially important and may vary according to the *varna* of the dominant caste, whether Brahman, Warrior, or Peasant. Is there a conception of a kingly or a spiritual style of life of which the servants are a part? Sanctions for conformity should be explored carefully.

(7) INTERRELATIONSHIP WITH OTHER ASPECTS OF CULTURE

These, especially, should be considered in new studies of the *jajmani* system. The power in the system is drawn largely from other spheres, it would appear.

FINAL WORD

A consideration of the *jajmani* system suggests four views of caste in India. Castes can be seen as classes—using Weber's term, social categories of persons sharing similar relationships to property, income and market, the basic division being the propertied and propertyless. Castes can be seen as "status groups," communities sharing a given degree of social honor, style of life, usually endogamous. Castes within and among themselves may also be seen as "parties," organizations influencing community action, their will contending with that of other parties in establishing programs for the community or attaining personal power goals. Lastly, we may add that castes have to be seen as strata, since these groups are ranked in hierarchies (Weber 1946:180–195). Perhaps the real importance for the students of the Hindu *jajmani* system lies in the possibility of developing a theory of social stratification concerning the interplay of "status," "class," "party," and "stratum."

18 THE FAMILY AS A
PRIMARY ECONOMIC GROUP [CHINA]

Martin C. Yang

Continuing the family line is the main concern of a Chinese farmer, but it is easier to produce progeny than to bring them up. When a man marries, his parents and the spirits of his ancestors are made happy at the thought of the new generation, but the man himself, if he is old enough, feels that a great burden has been put on his shoulders. He is no longer a "free" man but one who has to work for his wife's and his future children's livelihood. His parents also know that the hope of having progeny requires facing the important problem of how to feed, clothe, shelter, and educate the children, and that this problem can only be solved by working hard and living frugally. His wife sees it the same way. Sometimes a young husband may forget his responsibility and be idle or spend money. Then his parents and his wife warn him by reminding him that he is going to have children to take care of. If he does not give heed, his parents will worry and his wife will talk tearfully about the livelihood of the entire family, and that of the children. On the other hand, if the husband is aware of his responsibility, all the others feel very secure.

The old parents share the responsibility, and though they can no longer work as hard as they did, they save as much as they can of what they have. The parents of many families live more frugally than their children, for they are constantly anxious lest their children face poverty or starvation.

A young wife works harder than anybody else in the family

FROM Martin C. Yang, *A Chinese Village*, Chapter 7, pp. 73–85. New York, Columbia University Press (1945). Reprinted by permission of the publisher. [The author describes a peasant family of the 1920s. ED.]

and she lives more thriftily. She does not speak of it, but to her
nothing is more important than the security of the family. Her
most important role is to see that her husband lives cheerfully
and works well, and she advises him on the management of the
farm. Further, she must see that her children are properly trained
to do their share toward building up the family's economy.

When a boy, or girl, is about fifteen years old, he gradually
becomes aware of his responsibility. He is frequently warned by
his parents that the family may not have enough to eat if he
does not work hard, and told that if he wants his family to have
a big ox, a strong mule, two donkeys, three or four good houses,
and many large and good pieces of land, such as a P'an family
of the *tung hu-tung* has, he must learn to work hard. I have
seen many sons of poor families who, though still young and unmarried, were quite mature in this respect.

All three generations have a common interest in the family's
economic security. It is a source of happiness to all; when it is
imperiled, all feel the disaster. This is obvious to anyone who
sees a family at a time when their important crops are threatened
by drought or flood. Not only the older generation manifest great
concern, but the young too share the anxiety. If, on the other
hand, the harvest of the year is especially abundant and there is
a good possibility of having some savings at the year's end, then
everybody, old and young, is happy. When a piece of land is
bought, even if it be a very small piece, it occasions happiness
in the heart of every member of the family. In such a year the
family's New Year Festival will be celebrated with great cheer
and color.

A farm family is a unit unto itself in production. The family
members produce collectively and they produce for the family
as a whole, not for any individual member. This holds true for
everything.

The work, in the field, on the threshing ground, in the vegetable garden, and at home, is divided among persons according to
experience and physical ability. For example, the father is assigned to plant the sweet potato vines, since he is the experienced
one. He knows which is the upper end and which the bottom
end of the vines and can put them in the right positions. He
knows how deep the vines should be planted and also the proper
distance between every two plants. Others may also know these

things but as yet cannot put them into practice as efficiently. The elder son is asked to carry water from a distant place because he is the strongest in the family. The younger brother and sister are put to pouring water into the small holes because this does not require much experience or strength. Finally, the work of covering the vines and of accumulating earth to support the young plants needs some experience but not much physical strength, and that is why the mother and the elder sister are assigned to these tasks.

We must bear in mind that this organization is not elaborately planned beforehand, but happens very naturally. When the family arrives at the field, the members simply begin their proper tasks, neither the father nor the mother has to give any orders. Needless to say there is flexibility in the arrangement. When there is enough water for a while, the elder son may pick up his father's work for practice. At another time the second son may ask permission to carry water for at least one trip in order to show that he, also, is strong. Or, the elder daughter may insist that she exchange positions with her younger sister on the pretext that the latter should learn a grown-up's work.

This organization also depends upon cooperation. The children may sometimes quarrel, but that is a small matter. Let us still use the cultivation of sweet potatoes as an example. When all is ready in the field, the father begins work and simultaneously the elder son goes for water. By this time the two younger children are ready with their implements. When the water arrives, they immediately pour it into the holes and then the mother and the elder daughter begin their tasks. There is no gap or overlapping in the whole process. In harvesting the potatoes the cooperation shown is even more impressive. In the early morning the younger son is sent to cut and remove the vines from the field, while other members are busy putting all things in order at home and on the threshing ground. By the time the young lad has cleared up a considerable section of the field, the father and the elder son arrive and the digging begins. When all the vines have been cut, the young boy begins collecting the sweet potatoes on the ground into the baskets tied on the wheelbarrow. The elder son, the donkey, the wheelbarrow, and the boy form a team to transport the harvest to the place where it is to be processed.

As this progresses, the mother and daughters arrive there and start cleaning and cutting the sweet potatoes.

The intricate cooperation and division of labor is just as evident in domestic work. When *chiao-tze* are made for the New Year, for example, all the members of the family eat an early breakfast and get the dishwashing done. Then under the mother's supervision someone is assigned to fetch the cabbages from the storage place; another is ordered to wash and chop them. One member takes out the big piece of pork and chops it while the mother herself carefully seasons the mixture. Then the whole group sits at a long desk or on the mother's warm brick bed and begin the hardest part, which is to shape the round pieces for wrapping. Since not all can do this job, the one who takes care of it is generally regarded as the most important in the group. The role he or she plays is strategic because all the others must wait for the round pieces of dough before they can themselves begin. Wrapping is also skilled work. Some merely fold the piece of dough, while others make very fancy forms which receive a great deal of admiration. A newly married daughter-in-law who is adept at this art is very likely to win approval from her mother-in-law. Actually there is a certain amount of competition among the young people, but it is an enjoyable occupation. With the New Year just ahead, the sisters and brothers tease each other more freely than at any other time. The mother says nothing except occasionally to scold them laughingly which only makes the youngsters more mischievous. This is one reason why it is best for the father not to participate in this work, for his presence would kill all the laughter and jokes.

In an old-fashioned family, the kind which predominates in Taitou, everyone works or produces for the family as a whole, be he a farmer, a mason, a cloth weaver, a merchant or what not. It goes without saying that those who work on the family's farm work for the whole family. Any earnings made in special trades also belong to the family. If someone keeps a part of his wages, he will be condemned by the family head and suspected by all the other members of the family as being untrustworthy. A merchant who has to do his business outside may spend what he has made for his living expenses and according to his own judgment, but he must turn over all the rest and report what he has spent to the family head. If some of his expenses are found to have been unnecessary, he will be questioned about them in detail. Only when satisfactory reasons are given will his account be closed. If he is already middle-aged and has a prominent position, he may have more freedom in spending his money and the family head may not restrict him too much. But even so, he must know the limits of his freedom and must give the family the lion's share, or the others will complain and the unity of the family will be threatened. When a son goes to work on another family's farm as a hired laborer, his wages are given directly to his father or to his family. He may ask his father to give him a few dollars from his wages, or he may keep or spend the small money given to him by his employer for attending an opera or the local fair, but he is not working for himself but for the family of which he is a member.

An unmarried girl can make money for herself, if there is any work for her to do. If she gleans the peanut fields, her father will sell her gatherings and give the money to her. She might also work for the local oil-pressing shops and then the wages belong to her. Some grown-up girls gather seashells and sell them in the market town. A girl might have ten or twenty dollars saved by the time she is fifteen or seventeen. With this as capital her mother will buy her cotton and thus help her start a home industry of cloth weaving. Or she may lend it to a fellow villager and thus make it grow. By the time she marries, the girl may have accumulated thirty to fifty dollars of her own.

A family of the Yang clan has three sons, one of whom is a very popular mason in this district. The family was terribly poor two decades ago but because the sons worked very hard and saved as much as they could, the family's condition gradually improved. It was really the efforts of the eldest that contributed most to this. His trade brought in about one hundred dollars every year besides his own maintenance. A great part of this money was saved to buy land or repair houses. Recently he helped his two younger brothers to get married, though he has not married himself because he thinks he is too old and his health is not good enough. He still works as a mason and gives all he earns to the family. Their father died years ago and their mother is nominally head of the family, but it is he who manages a great part of the family's affairs.

Another family, a member of the P'ans, has four sons. They are primarily a farm family, but in addition run a small foundry in the village, and the first son teaches in the village school. One son usually works in the foundry while the others work on the farm, though when the exigencies of the season demand it, they all work together. The proceeds from work on the farm, teaching in school, and the foundry are all turned over to the family as a whole, that is to the family head. Neither the foundry worker nor the teacher would claim that a greater part of the money is earned by him. As a result of this cooperation the family is now one of the most prosperous in the village. Thus, in each of the four clans in the village there are a number of families whose recent prosperity was created or developed by the genuine cooperation and unity among brothers who were working in different fields.

Since the members of the same family work together, wear the same clothes, live in the same quarters and participate in the same social sphere, their needs are relatively the same. The family always eats together and shares what is on the table and each enjoys the same food. If the father or mother eats better food, it is not because he or she has the privilege of claiming it but because the children want to favor the parent in this way. If the younger children get more food, it is because the parents feel they need it to grow strong and the older children concur in this. It is true that women, especially young women, usually have less choice food than their men have, but the difference is by no means significant, and the women usually take it for granted. "Men's work is heavy, they must eat better; men are the family's pillars, we depend for our lives on them, so they must be fed well." It is frequently reported in other parts of the country that women as a whole are maltreated at home, that they are always overworked and underfed, and that they are almost slaves of their men. This is not true in Taitou; if it occurs at all, it is a very unusual case. When special food is served, the parents always try to gather the whole family together and are regretful if some member of the family must be absent from the feast. Special food is important to a farm family, but family spirit is most important of all. It is not simply a matter of eating good food; it is the shared enjoyment of the results of common toil. Thus, all the family members who are temporarily absent are urged to come home for the *Ching-ming, Tuan-wu, Chung-chiu* and other festivals. The New Year Festival, which is the most important, makes this almost imperative, and if someone fails to come home for it, an empty seat is kept for him and a place set at table so that the places represent the total number of family members. It is very common to hear a mother say at *Ching-ming* or *Chung-chiu* feast: "I wish Lien-erh could be home with us. Since it is impossible, I hope he enjoys the same food as we do now." One also frequently hears an absentee son saying, while he is eating a good meal on a special occasion: "This is good; I know those at home would like it too."

The joy of a good harvest is also shared with the family's ancestors. After the winter wheat is harvested, there is the festival of *Tuan-wu* at which the spirits are invited home or sacrifices are offered in the graveyard. When millet and several other kinds of cereal have been harvested there comes the *Chi Yueh Shih Wu* feast, specially designed for dead relatives, and when the most important fall harvest is in sight there is the *Chung-chiu* festival. Although this is primarily a feast for the living members, the dead are invited with the same sincerity. Finally, the New Year celebration is the most important feast at which both living and dead enjoy the total result of the year's hard work.

Except for personal belongings, everything in a farm family is owned in common, or by the family as a whole. A member who earns more for the family is honored by the others and he may even enjoy some prestige which does not accrue to them, but he cannot claim ownership of the family's property any more than they can. On the other hand, a member who produces or earns less but is doing his best is on equal terms of ownership with the others. There may be someone who produces or earns nothing, and indeed wastes money every day but, as long as he is a member of the family, he is not only entitled to his living but can also claim ownership of the family's property. Should someone work outside permanently but maintain his membership in his family, he is the owner of the family's property on the same basis with those at home and the family owns his earnings.

Personal belongings are negligible. An unmarried boy has only his own clothes, and even these can be shared by his younger brothers when the parents deem it necessary. After he is married, he has absolute ownership of his clothing. No man can have any money as his own except what he has saved from his allowance, since he is provided for out of the general fund. There are very few occasions on which a boy or an adult would need money. At the time of the New Year Festival, or when there is a fair in the market town or an opera in a neighboring village, the father or the family head will give to everyone a small sum which becomes his individual property. He can use it or save it according to his own decision. If someone has to make a trip to a distant place, the family will supply him with the needed money, but when he returns he must report his expenses to the family and return what is left to the family head. A young man may do some trading in off seasons. If he borrows money on his own credit and takes all responsibility for whatever risks are involved, the profit he makes will be his own and he can spend it as he wills. Anything like this, however, would be a most unusual occurrence.

The daughters are given a dowry at the time of their marriage, to which they add any money they may have earned and saved while in their parents' home. The young wife can either invest this sum in small home industries or lend it at interest to fellow villagers. When the sum is sufficient, she can buy land with it and this land will belong to the small family unit including herself, her husband and children, and not to the large family of her husband. Her husband's family may cultivate her land and get the harvest. Sometimes the wife may lend her money to the large family, in which case the family would pay it back with interest. This kind of property is called *hsiao hueh* and it is legally recognized but not encouraged by the family at large. When young wives manage to make money, they become selfish and, as a result, quarrels arise which threaten the unity of the large family.

Wives often think of how many *mow* of land and how many *gien* of house each unit will have when the family has separated. They are happy when a new piece of land is added to the common property but their happiness is different from the joy of the primary family group. It is not only shallow but each of the wives secretly wishes that the land will become the property of her own group. She may think that the piece of land is largely the result of her own husband's effort and feel it is unfair to make it common property and have it divided equally among the brothers. She may persuade her husband to accumulate personal property by hiding a part of his earnings, if he has any, or by grabbing from the family's income. Because a wife can buy land with her own money which will not be divided among the sons, she can use her husband's secret money to buy land for her own small unit. The small family will come to differentiate between its own land and that of the large family, and its members will do everything possible to increase the former at the expense of the latter. If one unit acts this way, the others will follow without hesitation.

The distribution of family goods may foster rivalry. Special food or fruit must be evenly divided among the small family units, who then retire to their own room to eat it. Thus, the household splits into several units. A son's wife can receive gifts from her own parents or kinsmen and keep whatever is not clearly intended for her parents-in-law or for the household as a whole. What she keeps will be enjoyed by herself, her children, and her husband in their own room. This menaces the communal spirit. The covetous eyes of the children of the one brother see that the children of another brother have cakes to eat. The depressed ones will certainly go back to their mother and complain that they have no cakes. If the mother is narrow-minded, and unfortunately she usually is, she will shout, "How can you complain? You haven't got rich grandparents like they have, have you? Don't you know that you are poor seeds?" These bitter words are shouted so that they can be heard by the other mother, and she will certainly take it as an insult and swear to pay it back at the first opportunity. Thus, when the other brother's children have some special thing to eat, the same complaining and shouting will be repeated. Of course, not all young wives act in this fashion. Many of them divide what they have among all the children in the family without discrimination, or, else submit the gift to the grandmother and let her distribute it. If the other wives follow her example, it may become the general rule.

When the family is small, everyone is willing to live frugally so money can be saved to buy more land or build a new house. Even the youngsters, who are longing for better meals, rejoice with their parents when new property is bought. In a large family, however, the situation is different. The brothers may still be eager to save, but this is not true for the women or the children who, though they also would like to see land or a new house added to the household, would nevertheless not raise any objection to better meals, more cloth, or to some luxury. Wives do prefer individual benefit. Their primary allegiance is to their immediate families and they look forward to the eventual division of the large household. Thus the small units are, through them, brought into comparative competition. Small households have a better chance of survival.

The continuity of a family line depends not only on having generation follow generation, but also upon the uninterrupted transmission of the family's common property. Thus, inheritance becomes an important matter in a Chinese family. As we have noted, to the Chinese mind, a family is not merely a group of related people, but also the land, the houses, the livestock, and the family reputation. A prosperous family is one which is increasing in members and in property. In a declining family both are disappearing. This idea is indicated in the common saying, *Chia pai jen wang*—"family property depleted and members perished." For this reason, when a dying father realizes that he has no property left, he feels guilty toward his ancestors and ashamed before his offspring, because he has only half accomplished the continuity of the family line. This is not only because property is the most dependable insurance for the next generation, but also because the family is an economic unit, so that family property is one of the primary interests which holds them together. As long as the property is intact the family exists. When the property is sold, the individual members may still remain, but the family is gone.

A Chinese family is made up not only of living persons but also of the dead of past generations and the prospective children of the future, and all share in the ownership of the property. If the property of the living generation is inherited from the previous one, then the present members are merely the stewards who keep it intact and hand it down to a new generation. Family ethics give a son the right to the property but also assign to him an obligation. If a man has his inherited property intact when he is old, he can die peacefully. He triumphantly summons his sons to his side and tells them that he feels no guilt toward his ancestors and no shame toward his children. Some Chinese parents have said: "Do not be oxen or horses for your children; poor or rich, they must take care of themselves," but they only say this when they have been disappointed in their sons or daughters. And even then, they only say it and do not really mean it.

If a man has inherited nothing from his parents but has accumulated all that he possesses through the efforts of himself and his wife, he will feel the same obligation toward his ancestors and his children. The need to leave property to his sons to continue the family line is just as great for him as it is for others, but he will be proud of himself. He may tell his children: "Your grandfather did not leave anything to me. What we now have is all the result of your mother's and my hard work." There is hidden bitterness in this, and it is bitterness toward his dead parents. Then the father will add: "But we want to leave this to you, children. We hope you will keep it intact forever." In these words there certainly is a feeling of pride. The fact that he did not inherit from his parents is their fault, but this does not exempt him from his obligations. It gives him no freedom to dispose of what he has, for his relations to his ancestors and to his children remain the same. Though his parents did not leave him property, they did give him life and it is from this life that he has given life to his children. There are other reasons for emphasizing inheritance.

If it is true, as the farmers believe, that after one dies one's spirit still needs things in the next world, and if it is true that these necessities must be supplied by one's own children who remain in this world, then one must leave some property to one's children, so they will have the means to care for the dead. Thus, for the fortune of one's own spirit, the transmission of property is a necessity. To the common people, leaving property is the most important way of being remembered after death. Parents who leave nothing to their children will either be blamed for a long time after or be forgotten immediately. Parents who added something to the property, or who restored the original fortune of a family, are inscribed on the family record. They are celebrated by their descendants, and are talked about with pride as long as the family exists.

In this part of the country inheritance is patrilineal, though daughters in some cases have a certain share. Sons have exclusive and definite claims on what the father has left. In spite of the new government law which gives a person the legal right to dispose of his property at will, except for a certain percent which must go to his sons and daughters, it remains true that no father, or son, had any thought but that his sons have an absolute right to their father's property.

The inheritance of the parents' movable belongings takes various forms, though the major part also goes to the sons. The equal division of movable property depends largely upon whether or not the family is well-to-do. In principle, it is supposed to be equally divided. A mother's personal belongings usually go to the unmarried daughters. A married daughter may or may not claim them. If there is no daughter, they are passed on to the daughters-in-law, or sometimes to the father's sister.

Immovable property constitutes by far the most important kind of property. It is the main item over which sharp family controversies occur. The witnesses and helpers called in to attend the division of the estate mainly concern themselves with the equal and just division of the immovable property.

The principle of division of land and houses is that an equal share goes to each son. If the division takes place while the parents are still alive, they may prefer to keep a larger share than is given to any of the sons. Whether or not they succeed depends upon their ability to exercise their authority, the opinion of the witnesses, the attitude of the sons, and the size of the total property. Daughters, if unmarried, have a certain amount of money put aside for their dowries. Unmarried sons also have an extra amount for future marriage expenses. Indebtedness is shared equally by the different parties. If one of the parents is dead, the division may be made in one of several ways. The mother or the father may have a share either larger, equal to, or smaller than that of any of the sons. The mother can choose which son she wishes to live with permanently. She can also choose to live independently, if her portion is adequate for that purpose. Or, she may live with each of the sons in turn for periods of a month or so. In such an arrangement she retains no independent property. An important feature is that the youngest son, although not expressly favored, in reality has certain advantages. The mother, or the parents usually choose to live with him, sometimes because he needs further tutelage and protection. In such instances, the parents invariably specify in the contract of division that after their death, their property must be given to the son who has served them. In this way, a further share of the inheritance is given the youngest son. But if the parent or parents live independently after the division of property, their share will be redivided equally among the sons after their death.

Adoption is closely related to inheritance. As long as the deceased has a son, the problem of adoption does not arise, but if a man has no son, the adoption of an heir is imperative. The male line must be continued. The adopted heir is always the next of kin, or the father's brother's son. There is no definite rule as to which brother's son is to be taken in the case of several brothers. If a man dies without having provided an heir, the brother's son who is next in line and who is the first to put on a son's mourning gown, or to perform the ceremony which is designed for a proper heir, will inherit. The decision on the part of the adopting parents depends upon their personal relationship with the brother and the brother's son. They may adopt the son just before their death or long before it. They usually make known their intention by taking great interest in the prospective son's behavior. This state of suspense, if the future father is well-to-do, induces the prospective heir to be very kind, generous, and obedient to his uncle.

When a brother's son is not available, the choice falls on the next nearest kin in the patrilineal line. Adopting a member from the matrilineal line, such as a wife's brother's son, is unknown, but custom allows a son-in-law to take a real son's place in continuing the family line. In such a case, the daughter of the family will marry her husband at her parents' home. The husband and their children will take her family's name.

In discussing inheritance we must not neglect the seeming contradiction between the desire of keeping a family's property intact and the desire for more progeny. Once a Western friend told the writer that since the Chinese inheritance system is to divide the family's property equally among the sons he could not understand why Chinese parents want so many sons. Though apparently a reasonable observation, this is not the way Chinese see it. When a son is born even to a poor family, he is not looked upon as someone who will further divide the family's land, but as one who will add to it. When a second son is born, the parents do not worry that their small piece of land will be divided into two parts. Instead, they begin to hope that when their sons are grown up, one will be a hired laborer, another a mason, and they will earn not only their own living but add fifty dollars or so to the family every year. In two or three years, they can buy one more *mow* of land with their savings. Thus, when the parents are old, they will be better off than they now are. This expectation increases with each son born. A son, unlike a daughter, is always looked upon as an economic asset.

It is true that when the time comes to divide a house, a self-seeking wife may secretly wish that her husband did not have so many brothers. But at the same moment she may also proudly look at her three or four sons and say in her heart: "Why should I worry? I have four sons. Land and houses? They will earn them." When she looks at her second sister-in-law, she secretly has pity on her: "Poor Second Sister-in-law, she has only one son but three daughters. What can those daughters do? They are only money-losers."

19 THE DISINTEGRATION OF THE OLD
FAMILY SYSTEM [FEUDAL JAPAN]

Matsuyo Takizawa

In an analysis of the family system of feudal Japan, it must be kept in mind throughout that the samurai class and the peasant class lived in entirely different worlds politically, socially, and economically. The nature of the family system in the two classes is thus so different that the subject seems best considered in two sections, in which the samurais and the peasants are treated separately.

First, let us take the samurai class. In the Tokugawa period there were about two hundred and sixty daimyos, who held their fiefs on the condition that they should remain loyal vassals to the Shogun. Each of these daimyos had as his retainers numerous samurais, who received either land or rice stipends from their respective daimyos for their faithful services. The family of a samurai or a daimyo consisted of his wife and children and any number of relatives who were living in his house. A strict order prevailed in the positions of the members of the family. The head of the family, i.e., the daimyo or the samurai himself, had absolute authority in his family; but when the retired father of the head of the house was still living, his will must be done first. Next to the head of the house came his oldest son, who was the heir to the entire family property. He was seated above all other sons, and he was brought up to become the worthy successor to his honorable father. All the other members of the family were ranked according to their age; many duties and

FROM Matsuyo Takizawa, "The Disintegration of the Old Family System," Chapter VII, pp. 108–131, in *The Penetration of Money Economy in Japan and Its Effects upon Social and Political Institutions*. New York, Columbia University Press, 1927. Reprinted by permission of the publisher.

forms of etiquette of the samurai family being strictly observed as between the members. Since all the inheritance of the family went to one successor of the family line, the younger sons had to seek their fortunes independently. Some of them found favor with the daimyos and were granted fiefs or rice stipends, thus establishing themselves as the heads of independent families. Many of them were adopted by heirless families and succeeded to their family names and property, while others stayed on in the houses of their eldest brothers.

In the samurai family, the wife was held to have only one function, the raising of offspring. Sterility was, therefore, legitimate ground on which a husband could divorce his wife or take a concubine; occasionally the wife even advised her husband to bring a concubine into the family. The first son born to the concubine was treated most respectfully as the heir of the house, but the position of his mother was no higher than that of a servant. Shortly after birth, the son was taken away from the mother and placed in the hands of a specially appointed nurse in order that he might be brought up with all the dignity pertaining to an heir of a samurai family; while the mother continued to be a household servant, and was even required to address her own son with all the formalities that pertained to relations between master and servant.

The provisions for adoption did not exist at the beginning of the Tokugawa period; therefore if an heirless samurai would not take a concubine or if his concubine failed to give him a son, the samurai family forfeited its land and family name to the overlord. This sort of forfeiture was practised quite freely by the earlier Shoguns so that they might increase land under their direct control and thereby increase their power. According to Dr. Nakamura, between Keicho VI (1601) and Keian IV (1651), about sixty-one feudal families lost their fiefs due to the lack of heirs, a loss amounting to 5,179,000 *koku,* and six houses lost a greater part of their fiefs, amounting to 84,000 *koku* (Nakamura 1924:39). In 1615, however, it was made possible for a feudal lord to adopt an heir from among his relatives of the same family name, and this law and the prohibition of "death-bed adoption," i.e., the adoption of an heir at the death-bed of the head of a house, was strictly enforced (Hozumi 1912:158). But this enforcement had many undesirable effects from the point of view of the feudal lords. In the first place, the adoption of an heir was impossible in case there was no suitable man among those who bore the same family name; and in the second place, the prohibition of death-bed adoption caused much distress when the head of the house was attacked with a sudden illness before he had chosen his heir. In this event, the heirless family lost its feudal stipend, and all the dependents of the house, including many attendant samurais, were deprived of their livelihood and swelled the class of gentleman-wanderers, called *ronin* (literally, men of waves). They had no longer a particular lord to serve; there was no economic security in their life; yet they were too proud to earn their living by manual labor. Thus they lost their place in the social structure and were constantly watching for an opportunity to turn the world upside down in order to realize a better day for themselves. The attitude of the Tokugawa government toward these *ronins* was that of strict suppression. They made no attempt to get at the root of the difficulty, and as a result the atmosphere of unrest grew thicker and thicker until it finally led to a serious conspiracy. Toward the middle of the seventeenth century, Yui Shosetsu headed a group of *ronins* in an attempt to overthrow the Shogunate. Their plot was discovered and they were promptly and ruthlessly punished. This incident made such a deep impression upon the Tokugawas as well as upon the public that in Keian IV (1651) an important modification was made in the law of adoption. According to the amended law, it was made permissible to adopt a son of a different family name in case there was no suitable person of the same name. This amendment is said to have been justified on the ground that all Japanese were of kindred blood, but the real meaning of the amendment was that it was a concession of the Tokugawa Shogun to those vassals who had been resentful about the Tokugawas' despotic policy of concentration of land. An amendment was also made to the law against death-bed adoption. Although this was prohibited ordinarily, the adoption of an heir at the last moment was made permissible if the dying man was under fifty years of age—the validity of such adoption to be determined according to the circumstances of each case (Nakamura 1924:39). When such an adopted heir was a near relative of the family, he took in a wife from outside. In cases where there was a daughter in a family with no male heir, it was

provided that she might take in a husband, who later was converted into a legal son to inherit the house. This method of
adoption was called *muko-yoshi,* or the adoption of the son-in-
law as heir. These laws of adoption remained substantially the
same for more than two hundred years; that is, until the end of
the Tokugawa régime.

To a samurai nothing was so threatening as the loss of his
fief. So long as he had a fief, he had all the social prestige connected with his family name, but once he lost it, he became a
wandering samurai, and his family was deprived of means of
subsistence. The daimyos were therefore very careful to avoid
everything that was offensive to the Shogun. The Shogun, on the
other hand, used every means to weaken the daimyos and
watched for every opportunity to increase his own power. One of
the means that he used was to make the whole family responsible
for the guilt of one of its members. If the head of a family had
committed a crime, the members of his family were punished according to the degrees of relationship to the head. If one of the
sons had committed a crime, all the other members of the family,
including the head of the house, were punished. And in all such
cases, their feudal stipends or fiefs were wholly or partially
forfeited. It was, therefore, most important to protect and safeguard the house by eliminating any member who might endanger
it. Hence the institution of *kwando* (disinheritance) and *kyuri*
(alienation), through which the entire relationship of the disinherited or the alienated was cut away, no matter how closely
connected he might be in blood. The outlaw was reported to the
officer of the feudal court and his name was taken out of his
family registry forever. This was so freely practised during the
Tokugawa period that Yamakata Hoshu attributed to it the increasing number of highway robbers and indolent people, and
he advocated that the disinherited or the alienated should be
marked either by having their thumbs cut or having their fore-
heads tattooed (Hoshu *circa* 1820:299). It is not known whether
his suggestion was actually carried out or not, but it at least
shows the prevalence of such dissociated elements in society.

While this rigid family system prevailed among the samurai
class, there was no systematized code of family relations among
the peasants. In those days, law was never clearly differentiated
from ethics, and the feudal government issued various proclama-

tions concerning the social affairs of the people, in which the penalties of law were stated together with moral teachings. It is through such proclamations as well as through the contemporary writings of various kinds that one may study the condition of the peasant family in feudal Japan.

The peasant family was not always limited to a man and wife and their children, but might include any number of relatives besides the immediate family. Makabe Yoshu explained that according to *Den-en* one peasant house meant a family of six persons, i.e., a man who supported five persons was considered as a full house owner (Yoshu 1759:180). Miyazaki Antei also spoke of an average family as composed of five or seven (Antei 1696:99). Again, we find in *Ichiwa Ichigen* a few descriptions of families composed of a man and his wife and their children (Nampo 1800–1823:41). But more often, a family included, besides the wife and children of the head of the house, his widowed mother, his unmarried sisters and brothers, and sometimes even married brothers and uncles together with their respective wives and children. Moreover, if the head of the family succeeded to the headship on account of the abdication (*inkyo*) of his father, the house might include the father and even the grandfather. Thus the constitution of a peasant family varied greatly, and there was no statute that decided who should be included in a house; only it was customary to recognize as one family a group of relatives represented by one peasant who was registered as a regular tenant of the Shogun or a daimyo.

The economic basis of each family was land, as in the case of the samurai family. Each peasant family was attached to a piece of land, which was cultivated from one generation to another. Since it was the lord who had the right to the produce of the land, each peasant family subsisted on whatever was left after the lord collected all the tax due from the land. Each peasant family was an organic part of a village community. A village community of feudal Japan constituted a unit of taxation, and to the eyes of the ruler, it was little more than a tax-producing organism, of which each family was only a part. Not only in paying taxes, but also for criminal offenses committed by the villagers, there was communal responsibility, so that the conduct of each family had vital consequences in regard to the village community as a whole. It was natural, therefore, that the company of five and the entire village community should have had a considerable degree of control over the domestic affairs of individual families. Quarrels between husband and wife were often settled by the intervention of the company of five. An abused wife often found a refuge among her neighbors; and when her husband came to claim her, the company returned her to him on the condition that he would be gentle to her. But if the offense was repeated, the man was reported to the chief of the companies or else he was threatened with ostracism, which usually brought him to terms (Wigmore n.d.).

Succession to the headship of a family and disposition of the family property were interfered with not only by the relatives but by the company of five or sometimes by the whole village. Succession to the headship had to be recognized not only by the relatives, but by the company of five to which the family belonged. Since primogeniture was of minor consideration compared with the fitness of a man to maintain the economic status of the family and to contribute to the welfare of the village community, the head of a house usually chose an heir through the consultation with the relatives and the company of five. When a man died without an appointed heir, the council of relatives appointed one upon the approval of the company of five; but even if a man had left a will it might or might not be recognized by the relatives and the company. For the transfer of the title of headship, application was made to the feudal lord under the joint signature of the family concerned and the company chief. It was often the case, furthermore, that if the head of a house offended the whole village for any reason, the village officials had a right to force him to abdicate.

The distribution of patrimony also required the approval of the relatives and the company. Although a man had a right to make a will with regard to the distribution of inheritance, when the provisions of the will were ambiguous or unjust the relatives and the company had a right to disregard the will and make a proper distribution. In general, a will was not valid unless it was opened in the presence of the relatives, the company and the beneficiaries, and was publicly announced. When a man wished to portion off his land to his daughter or to a younger brother or son, thereby establishing a branch house, he was expected to consult the relatives and the company. In some villages the consent

of all the villagers was required in such a case, and a new house-
holder was obliged to pay three to five *yen* to the village as
"face money" or *menkin,* which was applied to community expenses. Very often, however, a peasant divided his land among
several sons without setting them up as separate houses. In this
case, the younger sons were called *junzuke hyakusho* (apportioned
peasants); that is to say, they had their own pieces of land to
work on, but they were not registered as independent peasants.
They had their private households so far as their daily living was
concerned, but they paid their taxes under the name of their
oldest brother, who was registered as the head of a regular
peasant family. A peasant who possessed less than ten *koku*
worth of land was absolutely prohibited from establishing a
branch house by portioning off a part of his land to a relative.
This was frequently evaded, but both the government and the
village community endeavored to enforce the prohibition strictly.
A proclamation of Kyoho VII (1722) states:

> A peasant who has less than ten *koku* or one *chobu*[1] is pro-
> hibited from portioning off his land. This law was proclaimed
> several times in the past, but there have been many transactions
> secretly carried on. From now on, only the surplus of the house
> property over ten *koku* may be portioned off. A peasant who
> has less than ten *koku* is strictly prohibited from dividing up
> his land under any circumstances. Those dependent on him,
> therefore, should work with him on the farm or should be sent
> out to serve others. (Hisanori 1791–1794)

Man-o Tokiharu, a scholar in the province of the lord of Tamba,
taught:

> The farmer who has less than ten *koku* should not divide up his
> land among his sons. . . . If the land should be divided up, each
> portion would produce so little that each son would suffer from
> scanty provisions, and they would all be reduced to the status of
> water-drinking farm laborers. It is for this reason that the division
> of land into too small portions has come to connote foolishness.
> (Tokiharu 1725:16)

In a society whose unit was a family instead of an individual,
it was natural that individuals were controlled by ethical teachings that were conducive to the prosperity and perpetuity of the

---

[1] One *chobu* (=2.45 acres) is an area that was estimated to produce ten
koku of rice; one *koku* equals 5.12 bushels.

family, upon which the subsistence of individuals so inevitably depended. "Be loyal to thy lord and be filial to thy parents" is the commandment of the Japanese ethical code; but at no time was it emphasized so strongly as in the Tokugawa period. The Chinese philosophy of ancestor worship, too, never gained such an overwhelming popularity as in this period. In ancient Japan, ancestor worship was mystical rather than ethical, having its origin in the foundation of the empire by Amaterasu Omikami; it was the great unifying force in the life of the Japanese. But when the institution of private property was securely established, ancestor worship began to have an ethical and philosophical meaning. It is true that even in the feudal age there persisted the idea that the entire land in the country was the sacred inheritance of the Mikado, who was the direct descendant of Amaterasu Omikami; but so long as a man was faithful to his overlord, his land remained his exclusive possession for all practical purposes, a possession which he could hand down to his descendants. The justification for the perpetuation of his property came to be sought in the belief that it was the will of his illustrious ancestor to perpetuate his family and also the duty of his descendants to obey him. Hence the teaching that the son ought to be filial to his father as the father to the grandfather, and so on to the ancestor. Scholars of Chinese classics wrote many books during the Tokugawa period, exalting the virtue of filial piety. Indeed, as Miyazaki Antei taught, filial piety was the foundation of all knowledge, without which one could never discern the deep meaning of humanity (Antei 1696:1).

The feudal government found the teachings of the scholars to be very useful and generously listened to their advice with regard to administration and social legislation. From time to time, the government issued proclamations with regard to the right conduct of their subjects, and these were read to the congregations of peasants on festival occasions or posted on the intersections of the fields. As an example, let us take the proclamation of February 26, Keian II (1649). It runs as follows:

> Be filial to thy parents. The first precept of filial piety is to keep thyself healthy. It is especially pleasing to parents if thou refrain from drinking and quarrelling, and love thy younger brother and obey thy elder brother. If thou hold to the above principle, blessings of gods and Buddha will be upon thee, and thou mayst walk

in the right path and thy land shall bring forth good harvests. On the other hand, if thou become indulgent and lazy, thou wilt become poor and broken, and finally resort to stealing. Then the law shall overtake thee and bind thee with rope and put thee in a cage, and perhaps hang thee. If such a thing happens, how heart-broken thy parents must be! Moreover, thy wife and children and brothers must all suffer punishment because of thy crime.[2] It is, therefore, very important that thou keep thyself straight and industrious day and night. If thou become well-to-do, thou canst build a good house and dress and eat as thou wilt. Even if thou become wealthy the officials shall not be exacting, as this is a peaceful time, nor shall anybody snatch away thy possession. So thy offsprings will live comfortably even in famine years, for thou canst give them thy stored grain. Indeed, the farmer has the securest kind of life if only he pays his tax regularly. Keep, therefore, the above precept always in thy mind and teach thy sons and grandsons to be ever industrious. (Anonymous 1908:196–7)

While filial piety was the religion of the family, solidarity and cooperation was the creed of its members. In those days, the property of individual members was not recognized, for the land was the communal possession of the family. The members contributed their labor for the cultivation of the land and what they produced jointly they enjoyed together. Hence it was most essential that the members of the family should keep together and cooperate with one another in order to secure the means of subsistence. Since t' : family produced most of the necessaries themselves, some task was allotted to each member of the family except the very aged or the invalid or the infant. Even the child could help by pulling the weeds out of the rice-field, collecting eggs, etc. It was the task of the young daughter to plant the rice seedlings in the spring. Besides helping in the fields, the women span and wove in order to clothe the whole family. A filial son was never supposed to go away from his home, when he could help his father. Even the religious aspiration of individuals was crushed when it was injurious to the welfare and solidarity of the family group. The radical exponents of the Chinese sage, to whom the present life was more real than the future, attacked the pious devotion of the people to Buddha, denying all the teachings of Buddha as the illusions of barbarians. They argued that it was the foremost duty of man to worship

[2] A family was made responsible for a criminal offense of any of its members.

the parents who had actually given him his flesh and blood, and to work hard with his brothers in order to increase the inheritance of the family.[3] Filial piety, family solidarity and family cooperation, then, were the categorical imperatives of family life, which were destined to hold a firm grip upon the consciences of every person born into a family group during the feudal period.

But even this time-honored family system began to show signs of disintegration in the later Tokugawa period. The legislators and moral philosophers of the time thought it an unpardonable sin for the people to slight or disturb the order of the family, which was the sacred heritage of their ancestors. Their desperate efforts, however, to preserve the family system were of little avail against the great forces that were transforming the whole economic and social system.

In commercial towns, which were rapidly developing, the demand for labor was limitless. The poor agricultural people, who were finding it harder and harder to support large families, began to send their children to be apprentices or servants in the houses of thriving merchants. The term of apprenticeship was generally ten years, during which they were fed and clothed by the masters, while their parents received small sums of money for the contract. When they had finished the term of apprenticeship, they might return to their parents or might continue to serve their masters for money wages; but the majority of them chose the latter plan and never went back to their native villages, where they would have to toil in the fields—a prospect which did not seem very bright. If they stayed in town they could live on their money wages and might hope to make a fortune. In big commercial houses, it was the custom to institute a faithful servant, who had served ten or fifteen years, as the head of a new branch of the master's firm. He was then allowed to use the trademark of his master, who had already established his reputation, and

[3] "There is no such thing as paradise. This is a false belief and it has no foundation whatsoever. But foolish people believe it and imagine that there is a real paradise in the western part of the universe. They are charmed to hear of the exquisite and beautiful life of tranquility and comfort, and in order to be born in that country next time they give up all their possessions and vocations. They even desert their families and native places, and they become disciples of Buddha. What a deplorable thing this is!" (Hoshu 1820:438–439)

thus got a good start in his business. A kind master sometimes gave a share of his capital to his servant, and even procured a wife for him. But even those men who did not succeed in becoming regular merchants or tradesmen preferred to be day-laborers in town rather than to remain in the village like beasts of burden. For these unskilled laborers in Yedo, there was established toward the end of the seventeenth century an employment office consisting of four townsmen appointed by the town-magistrate. All the day-laborers were required to receive a license at the office and were placed at various temporary tasks such as transportation and road repairing. Although the wages of these unskilled laborers are not known at present, the fact that they could pay the thank-money of twenty-four *mon* (later thirty *mon*) of copper money per month to the employment office shows that they could get along comfortably on their wages except at times when there was a sudden jump in the price of rice. Thus masses of young people in the villages were driven into the towns. They no more regretted breaking away from their families than throwing away old shoes, as Dazai Shundai expressed it (Shundai 1729:243). This tendency was regretted deeply by the moral philosophers and legislators as a menace to the family system. They tried to check the townward drift by various teachings and legislations such as exalting filial piety and decreeing the return of town laborers to their native villages, but such efforts were in vain.

As more and more avenues of work opened up for those who left their village homes, the family became less and less significant as an economic unit. Many of the industries of the home were taken over by the artisans, who now produced for the market. In olden times, women span and wove cloth for the use of their own families. In some districts, women were engaged in the textile industry in winter when there was little to do in the fields. The product was sold in markets and fairs which were held in the vicinity of their villages. In the later Tokugawa period, however, spinning and weaving became a distinct industry. On account of accessibility to raw materials and geographical advantages, the silk industry was localized in Kyoto, Kiryu, Isezaki, Hino, Fukushima, etc., while the cotton industry was localized in Satsuma, Iyo, Kurume, Kokura, Echigo, etc. In these places, women were hired by clothiers for money wages. Already in the later Tokugawa period, there was in Kyoto a group of what might be called factory girls. They were termed *oriko,* or "weaving girls." But in most places the women were hired to do the work in their own homes. They were supplied with materials and brought back the finished product to the clothiers in exchange for wages. The exact wages they received are not known, but they were considered very high compared with the returns the workers got from farm labor, as may be judged from the following proclamation of the government:

> Recently farm laborers have become very scarce and therefore very costly. Especially the so-called weaving women get extraordinarily high wages. This is going the wrong way. It is a great mistake for a peasant to take up such an occupation and neglect the fundamental one. It is the strict order of the government, therefore, that the peasants should understand that their calling is very different from that of the traders, who aim at temporary gains, and that they should have no other thought than caring for their respective fields with all their might. (Anonymous 1908:Vol. VI, 9)

The development of the textile industry made it less and less necessary for most women to learn how to spin and weave—an ability which used to be a primary requisite for a good wife. The first Shogun, Iyeyasu, had taught his subjects to choose wives who were expert weavers. In those early days a bride was expected to show her skill in weaving. In some provinces it was the custom for a bride to be returned to her home with a load of cotton thread. When she came back to her husband's house a fortnight or so later, she had to present him with a dress made out of the thread that she had taken with her. When it became easier to buy cloth from traders, most women were freed from such a standard; although many social thinkers regretted the change, saying that women were getting so lazy that they would not even weave.

Not only spinning and weaving but dying also had been a woman's occupation before the penetration of the money economy. Toward the beginning of the eighteenth century, however, the industry passed out of the hands of the women almost completely. Guilds of dyers arose in towns. Moreover, many kinds of dyes were invented by the new artisans, and many new patterns were put on the market. Even sewing was no longer held to be an occupation of women exclusively, as there appeared expert tailors in the towns, of which Ota Nampo remarked: "Now-a-days, a man can buy his belt ready made out of a heavy material. Just as there are now very few women who make coats at home, so very soon the time will come when no more women will sew men's belts in their homes" (Nampo 1800–1823:5).

During this period, the artisan class was being differentiated into many groups. Already in the Genroku period (1688–1703), there were more than a hundred and thirty kinds of handicrafts, and various craft guilds had arisen in the large towns. As men came to identify their economic interests with such guilds, they became less and less attached to their ancestral homes. In olden times, the family land was the sole source of income and support for the family. But now the members of the family were able to choose their own occupations and so to support themselves, and hence they were growing more indifferent toward the system of adoption. In case there was no son in a family to inherit the family name, the members of the family divided the property among themselves. This tendency was slow to appear in the villages, where land was still the main property of the family; and yet the increasing transactions in land in the later Tokugawa period show that the peasants were parting with their ancestral land more and more willingly. In towns, where the family property consisted chiefly of money, the people were certainly growing indifferent toward the perpetuation of the family line. Their property, unlike land, was of the owner's own making and so had no family tradition. The members of the family had no such reverent and mystical attitude toward money as had prevailed toward land. Moreover, the commercial world was so unstable that it tended to make the perpetuation of family property a matter of chance. One family might keep its line through many generations by successful management of its business; but it was just as likely that the family would lose all its money through wrong speculation, in which case there was nothing left for the successor to inherit. "It is very rare for a merchant family to last for many generations," observed Tsutsumi Masatoshi, "but there are many families in the villages that are several hundred years old" (Masatoshi n.d.:535). "There is no evil greater than the lack of an heir to the family," said Shoji Koki, "but now-a-days there is only one in ten families among the masses that adopts an heir, although among the samurai class more than half of the childless families adopt their heirs" (Koki 1841:151). On the other hand, the younger sons were getting less and less inclined to be adopted. In olden times, when most of the family property went down to the successor in the family line and when agriculture was practically the only occupation, the younger sons could never become richer than their oldest brother who was the head of the ancestral family, unless they were adopted by childless families which were more wealthy than their own families. Hence it was considered a better fortune for a younger son to become an adopted heir than to stay in his brother's home as a dependent. But now opportunities were being opened up for younger sons to build up their own fortunes, for they no longer needed land or even houses of their own in order to earn their living and live respectably. Around 1840, Shoji Koki tells us (Koki 1841:485), there were in Osaka more than 122,000 families, of which only 18,000 owned their own houses; and yet they were engaged in all other types of occupations and could support their families comfortably. Yamakata Hoshu also tells us that in the towns there sprang up many families which were much more prosperous than their ancestral houses. Hence the economic significance of the main family often became so diminished that the younger sons came to detest being adopted (Hoshu 1820:280).

As the family property came to consist of money, the division of inheritance became easier. Even in the feudal period, the division of patrimony was allowed with some limitations, as explained above. The division of land, however, was not so easy as that of money. Furthermore, since land was used only for agriculture, it was more profitable for the several sons to stay with their main family and take communal responsibility over the property than to become independent peasants with small pieces of land. The matter became quite different when money came to constitute the essential part of family property. Unlike the case of land, not all members of a family wanted to use money in the same way, because the differentiation of occupations afforded many ways of investing money profitably. Thus in towns, the division of inheritance came to be practised quite freely. "In the night of mourning, one eye weeps for the departed, while the other eye stealthily glances over the property of the deceased," runs a famous satirical *hokku* (a seventeen-syllabled poem of the period) sharply disclosing the psychology of the money-mad townspeople at that time. Men came to quarrel more and more over the division of inheritance. As Raku-o Ko observed:

> In the present age, there are few families which have not appealed to the court as the result of dispute over the shares of inheritance. Even among those families which have not gone into court, there are very few in which the relatives enjoy harmonious relations. This is due to the loosening of customary relations in the family and the increase of selfishness and avarice. (Sadanobu 1891)

When men took up different lines of work and earned money incomes, they acquired a consciousness of personal possessions apart from their families. They no longer identified their economic interest with that of their relatives, as each family pursued its own interest. "They are too stingy to spend even half a *sen* [=ten *mon* of copper money] for their poor relatives," said Tsutsumi Masatoshi (Masatoshi n.d.:482). "People are getting so avaricious," Shoji Koki also wrote, "that relatives and friends quarrel over such a trifle as ten *sen*. A man refuses to buy anything from his brother's store, if he can get it even three *mon* cheaper in other stores" (Koki 1841:47). Since communal responsibility in regard to land did not apply to money, individuals could not only spend their money as they wanted but could even contract debts in their own names. Even the courts inclined to treat as individuals those who brought up money actions. When the plaintiff asked the court to make the relatives of the defendant responsible for the debt, the court generally refused to do so.

When the economic condition of the time necessitated the breaking-up of the family into several lines of occupation and the scattering of its members to various places, the teaching of filial piety became less and less practicable. Many sons and daughters left their aged parents in the village despite the teaching that a filial son should never travel far while his parents were still living. The tendency of the young people towards the pursuit of their own personal interests regardless of their parents made Shiba Kokan utter the desperate words, "Ah, it is altogether better not to have children at all in the modern age!" (Kokan 1811:306). The teaching of solidarity among brothers could not keep its firm grip upon those who had different interests to pursue, and hence many lawsuits were brought before the magistrates as the result of family quarrels. All these evils, most ethical teachers believed, were due to the slackening of moral teachings and the lack of incentive for right living. They proposed, therefore, that the government should give rewards to filial sons and daughters, obedient daughters-in-law, etc. In fact, many feudal lords and the Shogun actually gave rewards to such worthy people. A farmer was sometimes awarded a name of distinction and the privilege of wearing a sword as a reward for his great filial piety (Hisanori 1791–1794). Kamizawa Teikan tells us that in Yedo, on the seventeenth of March, 1791, one man was awarded seven sheets of silver, and twenty-seven men and three women were awarded five sheets of silver each because of their filial piety. Ota Nampo's (Teikan 1776:8) *Ichiwa Ichigen* also abounds with examples of filial sons and daughters who were publicly rewarded. Yet all the endeavors of the government and the moralists were quite fruitless. The family could not be restored to its state of filial piety and solidarity. It was not the slackening of moral teachings that produced the condition so lamented by the ethical leaders of the time; rather, the invasion of money into the family called forth new attitudes and brought new opportunities which undermined the old system at its very roots—the family.

Another reflection of the tendency of the family to disintegrate was the growth of prostitution in all commercial towns. Men financially distressed sold their daughters, or sometimes even their wives, into prostitution. "Formerly, women were greatly ashamed of selling themselves to houses of ill-fame, and parents thought it a gross disgrace to sell their daughters on account of poverty," writes Shoji Koki. "But now in all places where there are houses of prostitution, people sell their daughters, and if their new-born babies are fair daughters, they are a cause for rejoicing as the blessing of the gods. In Nagasaki, I have heard that all the present prostitutes are natives of the town" (Koki 1841:241). The Tokugawa government legalized the institution, and allowed the business to be carried on within certain licensed districts. In Yedo, there were over 2,500 prostitutes in 1788 (Nampo 1800–1823:12). Besides this group, there arose also a class of dancing girls, whose business it was to entertain men åt their feasts. As time went on, the number of houses of prostitution increased so much that many people began to open new houses outside the licensed districts. According to Professor Takegoshi, there were toward the beginning of the nineteenth century over 4,180 unlicensed prostitutes in a district of twenty-three streets (Takegoshi 1921:687). "There are more houses of prostitution, questionable inns and tea-rooms than I can count!" declared Yamakata Hoshu; and he added, "Ah, shame on us! What would foreigners say if they saw such conditions?" (Hoshu 1820:346). Thereupon, the government began a strict censorship of illegal prostitution. When the town magistrate discovered an inn or a tea-room keeping unlicensed prostitutes, he ordered the place to be shut down. Sometimes a more severe magistrate punished a whole street in which an illegal house had been discovered. In June, 1790, there was a city-wide hunt for unlicensed prostitutes in Kyoto, and within one night over two thousand women were arrested (Teikan 1776:56–59). Sometimes the proprietors of illegal houses were imprisoned with their hands chained together, and all their property was confiscated. But at other times the government officials were easily bribed and the law was not strictly enforced. It was, moreover, too great a temptation for the financially distressed government to refuse the thank-money which such houses were constantly offering in order to be allowed to go on with their business. At the beginning of the nineteenth century, therefore, the prevalence of illegal prostitution was so great in all large towns that it became impossible to remove the evil all at once. Hence some indirect methods were proposed to abolish the system. Yamakata Hoshu suggested as a reform measure that houses of prostitution should be taxed very heavily and the revenue used to help any proprietor of an illegal house who wanted to go out of the business and start over again in a decent occupation. The amount of the tax he had been paying was to be borne by the remaining men until the burden of taxation should become so heavy that finally the owners of such houses could no longer maintain themselves in the business (Hoshu 1820:343). But unfortunately such a measure was not practicable in an age when the profits of the business were as great as they were at that time, even heavy taxation and occasional punishment were powerless to prevent the carrying-on of such a fruitful enterprise.

Compared with the family system among the masses, the family system in the samurai class was much slower to show signs of disintegration. In spite of the fact that the samurais realized that the economic value of their land was diminishing year by year, their ideas and actions in regard to other callings proved much less flexible than those of the peasants. Consequently, the loosening of the family bonds came much more gradually than in the peasant class—when it came at all. This certainly was a great check to the disintegration of the family system.[4] Nevertheless, it cannot be denied that the character of the samurai family was greatly deteriorated by the invasion of a new source of power—money. Samurai families who were economically ruined began to seek alliances with rich merchants who craved social distinctions. Thus arrangements for adoption and marriage began to be made between samurai families and merchant families on the basis of large dowries from the latter. Matsudaira Sadanobu regretted this tendency as a source of disintegration of the family system, on the grounds that a wife with a large dowry was apt to be so proud that she became unmanageable and might even domineer over her husband (Sadanobu 1891). He discussed various social evils that resulted from the institution of dowry. First of all, the arrangement of marriage between a samurai and a daughter from a lower rank with a great deal of money is detrimental to the samurai family, because a wife without samurai culture would tend to spoil the noble tradition of the samurai; second, a samurai of small means cannot marry his daughter into a good family, in which case, the daughter is obliged to remain unmarried—a situation which degrades sex morality; third, a younger son of a family, who might be adopted into an heirless family, cannot do so unless he has a dowry—and consequently he remains unmarried and resorts to houses of prostitution. As the remedy for these evils, the author suggested that the custom of taking husbands or wives on the basis of the dowry should be prohibited by law, in order that men and women should not miss the right time for marriage. Such suggestions bore no fruit, however, and the practice of marrying for the dowry became more and more prevalent as time went on.

After the Meiji revolution, with the abolition of feudalism, the privileges of the samurai class—such as wearing swords and re-

[4] ". . . now-a-days, there is only one in ten families among the masses that adopts an heir, although among the samurai class, more than half of the childless families adopt heirs." (Koki 1841)

ceiving feudal bounties—were taken away. The samurais were placed on the same social plane as the commoners and were expected to earn their living by whatever occupations they could find. Consequently the process of disintegration that had been going on in the family system of the masses now repeated itself in that of the samurai class. And as the classes merged, the individual came to take the place of the family as the important unit in the new society reared on the basis of money exchange and valuation.

20 SOCIAL CHANGE AND ECONOMIC MODERNIZATION IN TWO INDONESIAN TOWNS: A CASE IN POINT

Clifford Geertz

The two towns I shall compare are Modjokuto (a pseudonym), in eastern central Java, and Tabanan, in southwest Bali. Although they are culturally diverse and show certain important differences in social structure, they stem from a common historical tradition, represent approximately the same level of organizational complexity, and are embraced by a single national state and economy. It is this similarity amid difference which gives them their peculiar value for the analysis of Indonesian development. Modjokuto was studied in 1952–54, Tabanan in 1957–58.

MODJOKUTO: A JAVANESE MARKET TOWN

Modjokuto, which is located in the great Brantas River valley, is a typical example of the drab, overcrowded, busily commercial little crossroads which are spaced every 15 or 20 miles apart along the main thoroughfares of the Javanese rice plains. It has a population of 24,000, including some 2,000 Chinese, and is the administrative headquarters for a district of some 170 square miles containing nearly 250,000 people. Its market forms the

FROM Clifford Geertz, "Social Change and Economic Modernization in Two Indonesian Towns: A Case in Point," Chapter 16 of Everett E. Hagen, *On the Theory of Social Change,* Dorsey Press, 1962, pp. 385–407. Reprinted by permission of the author, the Center for International Studies, the Massachusetts Institute of Technology, and the publisher, Dorsey Press, Homewood, Illinois.

hub of a far-flung and intensively active trade network through which a fabulous variety of goods flows and from which perhaps a majority of the town population in one way or another draws its living; and it has a fairly large trade in the export of cash crops and the import of manufactures, carried on by the Chinese. As a community, it reflects the elaboration of modern nationalist political life, with a great many parties, labor unions, youth groups, women's clubs, and so on; and there are probably more than 2,000 students enrolled in the various schools of the town.

Modjokuto was founded in the latter half of the nineteenth century. By the early decades of this century it became a rapidly expanding boom town on the basis of Dutch activities in large-scale commercial agriculture, most particularly in cane sugar, in the surrounding countryside. Though the main economic returns resulting from this period of rapid growth went to the Dutch, there were important effects among the Javanese population as well. Native commerce of all kinds expanded and an incipient middle class of traders and landholders appeared, as did a proletarian class of landless workers employed on the plantations and in the mills.

In the early thirties, as a result of the world-wide depression, expansion ceased rather suddenly and rapid contraction occurred. Peasants who now had no income from renting their land to the mills turned to cash crops. The market was flooded with hundreds of very small-scale traders eking out a marginal living where a few large merchants had prospered before. And a certain amount of putting-out, cottage, and small industry appeared as an effort to take up the slack. Paradoxically, though income fell, the town experienced an intensification rather than a slowing down of human effort in economic activity. The overall trend toward the conversion of the bulk of Modjokuto's inhabitants into small-scale businessmen continued unabated through the Japanese occupation period into the postwar era.

In the pre-1930 boom period the town was composed of four main status groups: the gentry (*prijaji*), consisting of the government civil servants and some of the higher white collar workers from the mills; the traders (*wong dagang*), who were dealers in cloth, tobacco, hardware, and so on; the "little people" (*wong tjilik*), consisting of landless laborers, small peasants, and petty craftsmen; and the Chinese (*wong tjina*), who, although they were almost without exception traders, actually stood largely outside the Javanese social system as a foreign, self-contained, and disliked minority.

The gentry represented the cultural and political elite of the town. They were rather less numerous than in most contemporary towns of equal size because Modjokuto was only a district capital while most of the otherwise comparable towns were regency capitals with consequently much larger civil servant contingents.

However, as an effect of the plantation economy, the commercial, trader class was much larger than normal for a town of its size. The leading figures in this group, the more substantial merchants, were strongly pious Moslems migrant from Java's north coast, for centuries the center of Javanese commercial life and Islamic learning. Thrifty, industrious, moralistically pious, they infused the town with the atmosphere of the bazaar, giving it an almost Levantine tone. And despite the greater cultural prestige of the gentry, the traders were, in this period, the most dynamic element in the society.

There were also probably more "little people" than in neighboring towns of comparable size, but this group played a mainly passive role. For their part, the Chinese lived in a separate quarter, devoted themselves almost solely to business, and maintained an uneasy but nevertheless workable relationship with the mass of the population.

After 1930, and particularly during the Japanese occupation and the immediate postwar period, the lines between the three Javanese groups began to blur. Depression, forced labor, guerrilla warfare, and runaway inflation, following one upon the other over a 15-year period, fundamentally disturbed the entire social system. By the time of the transfer of sovereignty from Holland to Indonesia in 1950, the process of dislocation of the traditional social structure had been accelerated to the point where the need for new patterns of organization was very keenly felt, a need only partially satisfied by the proliferation of political parties and other nationalist organizations after independence.

As a result, the most outstanding characteristic of contemporary Modjokuto social life is its provisional, in-between, "neither-fish-nor-fowl" quality. From a town composed of self-contained sub-cultural status groups having no more contact with one another than was absolutely necessary, Modjokuto has more and more come to consist of a melange of mass organizations engaged in competitive interaction.[1] Yet not only have the more traditional social loyalties not wholly dissolved and the more modern ones not wholly crystallized; the general economic structure of the town also remains peculiarly poised between the past and the future. The reconstruction of Modjokuto's economic life, like the reconstruction of her social structure generally, is so far but half-begun; it remains tentative, ill-defined, seemingly unable to complete itself. Bustling, fluid, forward-looking, and yet for all that basically undynamic, the town seems stranded between the heritage of yesterday and the possibilities of tomorrow.

TABANAN: A BALINESE COURT TOWN

Tabanan, located in the southwest quarter of the island of Bali, has a population of 12,000, including about 800 Chinese. According to tradition, the Tabanan royal line was founded in 1350. In 1906, 18 generations of theoretically unbroken succession later, the ruling king of Tabanan, tricked into captivity by the Dutch, cut his throat, and the 500-year reign was interrupted. In the twenties, the closest living relative of the dead king was restored to a cardboard throne as a Dutch gesture toward Balinese self-government. In 1955 the most recent king in the line abdicated for political reasons. Since then there has been no official king, but the role of the nobility still remains central. Here it has not been the bazaar but the palace which has stamped its character upon the town, not the Islamized trader but the Hinduized aristocrat who has been its distinctive figure.

Compared to Modjokuto, Tabanan has much more of a "just beginning" quality about it in terms of social, political, and economic modernization. One index of this is the striking contrast between the occupational structures of the two towns.

[1] These organizations, though of great political importance, cannot be adequately described in this summary. They include political parties, labor unions, youth groups, peasant organizations, women's clubs, and so on.

Percentage of Population

	Modjokuto	Tabanan
Farmer	6	42
Storekeeper, trader, peddler	41	21
Skilled worker, craftsman	12	9
Unskilled worker	34	20
Civil servant, teacher, clerk	7	8

Despite the lesser detraditionalization of Tabanan as compared to Modjokuto, the Balinese town is also beginning to change toward a more modern type of structure. Within the last five years a great number of Balinese-owned businesses have appeared, the local civil service bureaucracy has expanded, and political activity has become more intense and involves an increasing proportion of the population. Though still calm, well-ordered, and in a sense self-contained, the town is not static, and a fundamental transformation of its social and economic structure seems to have at least commenced.

The primary moving force in the transformation is the local nobility. Before 1906 the members of about 15 noble houses, all of them patrilineally related to one another and to the royal family at their head, formed the effective ruling group not only in the town but also in the surrounding countryside. The peasantry was tied to them by customary obligations to render corvée and military service, and looked to them for general leadership in certain supravillage religious matters as well. In addition, though most of the nobles lived in the town, all of them owned land in the villages (which was worked by commoner share tenants), had taxation rights, and exercised judicial powers. Although internally riddled with intrigue, the nobility, which formed an endogamous caste, was unreservedly accepted by the mass of the population as the legitimate bearer of regional political authority.

When the Dutch took over South Bali just after the turn of the century (before this time, the Dutch though nominally sovereign, had permitted the Balinese kings to rule their bailiwicks largely independently), they suppressed the traditional political service tie between lord and peasant and replaced it with a territorialized bureaucratic relationship, transforming the nobles into colonial civil servants. Though they were able to maintain their economic ascendency as landlords and much of their caste-based prestige, the nobles lost a great part of their effective political power.

Since the revolution even this modified pattern of aristocratic pre-eminence has come under attack. Progressive land taxation, laws protecting tenants against displacement and high rents, and the general egalitarian sentiments engendered by nationalist ideology have made landlordism a much less attractive proposition than it was before the war. Further, the opening of administrative posts to talent and to political party patronage has tended to reduce the monopolistic hold of the aristocracy on the civil service.

In such a situation trade and industry, insofar as they can be profitably pursued, become an attractive means to maintain one's threatened status, wealth, and power; so it is perhaps not entirely surprising that it is this group of obsolete princelings which is behind Tabanan's recent economic expansion. The fundamental instability introduced into Tabanan's social system by the Dutch displacement of the indigenous aristocracy from their position at its political center has now begun, 50 years later, to have its effect on the economic structure of the society. The "just starting" quality of the town's modernization is in part misleading, for the sources of the changes now occurring trace back to the reduction of Tabanan in 1906. The suicide of the old king represented in a quite literal sense the death of the old order; and the contemporary movement of his heirs into the yet but partly formed world of trade and industry represents the birth, whether it ultimately proves to be abortive or not, of a new one. In Modjokuto the economic leadership has fallen to the successors of the Islamized commercial elite of the tens and twenties, in Tabanan to the successors of the Hinduized, caste-insulated political elite of the traditional state.

ECONOMIC DEVELOPMENT IN MODJOKUTO

In Modjokuto the problem of economic development presents itself primarily as an organizational one. What the entrepreneurial group of Islamic small businessmen most lacks is not capital, for in terms of the realistic opportunities for innovation which they actually have, their resources are not inadequate. Not drive, for they display the typically "Protestant" virtues of industry, frugality, independence, and determination in almost excessive abundance. Certainly not a sufficient market, for the possibilities for significant expansion of both trade and industry stand apparent in Modjokuto on all sides. What they lack is the ability to mobilize their capital and channel their drive in such a way as to exploit the existing market possibilities. They lack the capacity to form efficient economic institutions. They are entrepreneurs without enterprises.

Progress toward more effective patterns of economic activity in Modjokuto takes the form of a movement away from a bazaar type economy—that is, one in which the total flow of commerce is fragmented into a very great number of small and disconnected person-to-person transactions—toward a firm economy— that is, one in which trade and industry take place mainly within the framework of a set of impersonally defined, corporate social institutions which organize a variety of specialized occupations with respect to some particular productive end. It is the creation of firm-like distributive or productive institutions, of small stores, service shops, and factories, which represents the process of development in the present state of Modjokuto's economy. Out of the diffuse, individualistic, confused tumult of the bazaar a few of the more ambitious of the town's established trading class are attempting to organize their activities in a more systematic manner and conduct them on a larger scale. In the means these men use and in the obstacles they face in their endeavor to move out of the world of the bazaar and into the world of the business establishment they display most clearly the characteristic texture of the problem of economic growth as it appears in contemporary Modjokuto.

THE TRADITIONAL BAZAAR ECONOMY

The traditional bazaar (*pasar*) is at once an economic institution and a way of life, a general mode of commercial activity reaching into all aspects of Modjokuto society and a sociocultural world nearly complete in itself. As agriculture for the peasant, so petty commerce for the trader provides the concrete backdrop against which almost all of his activities are set. It is his environment, as much, from his perspective, a natural phenomenon as a cultural one; and the whole of his life is shaped by it.

To understand the bazaar in this broad sense one needs to look at it from three points of view: as a patterned flow of economic goods and services; as a set of economic mechanisms to sustain and regulate that flow; and as a social and cultural system within which those mechanisms are embedded.

So far as the flow of goods and services is concerned, one of the most salient characteristics of the bazaar is the sort of material with which it deals: unbulky, easily portable, easily storable foodstuffs, textiles, small hardware, and the like whose inventories permit marginal alterations in the scale of trading operations rather than demanding discontinuous major changes in investment levels. A second important characteristic is that, whatever the wares, though volume in any sale is very small, turnover is very high. Goods flow through the bazaar channels at a dizzying rate, not as broad torrents but as hundreds of little trickles, funneled through an enormous number of transactions. And this flow of goods is anything but direct: commodities once injected into the market network tend to move circuitously, passing from trader to trader for a fairly extended period before they come within the reach of a genuine customer. One piece of cloth may have half a dozen or more owners between the time it leaves the Chinese-owned factory in a nearby city and the time it is finally sold to someone who seems likely to use it. And, third, it needs to be emphasized that most of the processing and manufacturing activities which take place in Modjokuto are also included within the bazaar realm. The bazaar is not merely a simple distributive apparatus; it is a productive apparatus as well. The two elements, the movement of goods and their processing, insofar as this is accomplished in Modjokuto, are wholly intertwined.

As for the set of economic mechanisms which sustain and regulate this flow of goods and services, three are of central importance: a sliding price system, a complex balance of carefully managed credit relationships, and an extensive fractionization of risks and, as a corollary, of profit margins.

To a degree, the continual haggling over terms merely reflects the fact that the absence of complex bookkeeping and long-run cost or budgetary accounting make it difficult for either the buyer or the seller to calculate very exactly what, in any particular case, is a reasonable price. The buyer and seller have to explore the matter through a system of offer and counter-offer.

Even more important, the sliding price system tends to create a situation in which the primary competitive stress is between buyer and seller. In a firm economy the fixed-price system, along with standardization, brand names, advertising, and the other economic customs which accompany it, relieves the buyer-seller relation of competitive pressure and places that pressure on the relation between sellers. Lacking fixed prices, in the bazaar the buyer pits his knowledge of the contemporary state of the market, as well as his stubbornness and persistence, against a similar knowledge on the part of the seller and the seller's nerve and stubbornness.

One result of this kind of competition is that it tends to focus all the trader's attention on the individual two-person transaction. The aim is always to get as much out of the deal immediately at hand as possible; and the bazaar trader is perpetually looking for a chance to make a smaller or larger killing, not attempting to build up a stable clientele or a steadily growing business. His aim is not so much to create a market for whatever he has to sell as it is to be present when a chance to sell appears and to make the most of it. The sliding price system provides the flexibility needed in the fluid economic context of the bazaar, but it does so at the cost of encouraging an essentially speculative, *carpe diem* attitude toward commerce.

The second economic mechanism of importance is a complex and ramified network of credit balances binding larger and smaller traders together. This network is the primary integrative factor in the bazaar, for it creates a hierarchic ranking of traders in which larger traders give credit to smaller ones. These credit balances are only half understood if they are seen only as a means by which capital is made available, for they set up and stabilize more or less persisting commercial relationships. If a buyer owes you too small a balance, it is relatively easy for him to shift his business to some other seller; if he owes you too much, he may default. The margin between these two possibilities is carefully calculated. From the financial point of view, the bazaar consists of a complex of debts carefully managed to keep trade active and yet not disrupt it. Most of everyone's time is consumed in pursuing debtors and dunning them, or in trying to wheedle a little more credit from one's creditors. Such an economy can be seen as a sort of hydraulic system in which the balance of credit pressures at hundreds of larger and smaller couplings determines the speed, direction, and volume of the flow of goods through the system.

Third, despite his aim to maximize his trading activities, the bazaar trader has a tendency to spread himself thin over a very wide range of deals rather than plunge deeply on any one. As a result, even moderately large single deals with only two persons involved are very rare even if the traders involved are large enough to handle such deals alone. Both large and small transactions usually involve a multiplicity of people, each making a small contribution and each taking out a small return, thus fractionating both risks and profits. The bazaar traders are individualists in the sense that they operate independently of any persisting economic organizations, make decisions entirely in terms of their own interests as they conceive them, and relate to each other wholly through separate person-to-person agreements; but this does not mean that alliances among traders are not extremely common. The individual trader is the center of a series of rapidly forming and dissolving one-deal, compositely organized trading coalitions. Further, this tendency to spread risks and profits is so much a habitual reaction of bazaar traders that it would persist for a long time even if capital were to become much more readily available.

Lastly, as a sociocultural system the bazaar is characterized by an interstitial position within Javanese society generally; by a highly developed division of labor which, in the absence of firms, guilds, and so on, provides directly the major basis of social-structural organization for the market as a whole; and by a very sharp segregation of specifically economic from diffusely non-economic social ties.

From an historical point of view, the main reason for the interstitial position of the bazaar within Javanese society is that it is primarily not a local growth but was introduced from outside after Java had already achieved very high levels of social, political, and religious development. It was only in the fourteenth and fifteenth centuries, when Madjapahit, the island's greatest kingdom, climaxed more than a thousand years of political and cultural evolution under the aegis of Hinduism, that a comprehensive commercial network was forged. Islam was introduced, and the bazaar pattern took its characteristic historical form. A quality of intrusiveness, of incongruity and alienness, clings to the bazaar trader even today. The Javanese word for "trader" still also means "foreigner," "wanderer," or "tramp." The status of the traditional merchant in the wider society is thus ambiguous at best, pariah-like at worst: the peasant tends to fear the trader as a cheat, the gentleman to despise him as a money grubber.

On the social-structural side the most notable characteristic of the bazaar pattern is the hyperspecialized division of labor, of which the folk caricature is the trader who sells only left shoes. This overdifferentiation reflects more than an oversupply of labor. The fact that in what is otherwise an extremely fluid system there is a strong tendency for individuals to persist in a single kind of trading rather than to shift easily among various sorts is evidence of the fact that trading is a full-time, technically demanding, completely professionalized occupation, not the part-time job of a farmer come to market.

Relationships between traders are highly specific: commercial ties are carefully insulated from general social ties. Friendship, neighborliness, and even kinship are one thing; trade is another. The impersonal approach to economic activity which has sometimes been held to characterize only advanced economies is present in the Modjokuto bazaar in marked degree. It is the one institutional structure in Javanese society where the formalism and status consciousness so characteristic of the culture generally are relatively weak: bargaining, credit balances, and trade coalitions, largely free of the constraints of diffusely defined cultural norms, all respond quite directly to the narrow concerns of material advantage.

In sum, the bazaar economy is traditional in the sense that its functioning is regulated by fixed customs of trade hallowed by centuries of continuous use, but not in the sense that economic behavior is not well differentiated from other sorts of social behavior. What the bazaar economy lacks is not elbow room but organization, not freedom but form.[2]

[2] For a full description and analysis of the Modjokuto market, see Dewey (1962).

THE DEVELOPING FIRM-TYPE ECONOMY

The exact nature of the innovational task facing Modjokuto's would-be entrepreneurial class is conditioned by two main determinants: the general character of the bazaar as an economic institution, and the emerging form of postrevolutionary urban society. From an individualistic, speculative, marvelously intricate trading pattern, the entrepreneurs must move to a systematically yet simply organized firm-based "business" pattern dedicated to long-term economic ends. And from an interstitial, vaguely outcast position within traditional society they must move to an established place as respected shopkeepers and manufacturers, true bourgeois, within the now developing modern type of class structure.

In the light of the theories of Max Weber concerning the role of Protestantism in stimulating the growth of a business community in the West, it is perhaps not surprising that the leaders in the creation of such a community in Modjokuto are for the most part intensely Reformist Moslems, for the intellectual role of Reform in Islam has, at least in some ways, approached that of Protestantism in Christianity. Emphasizing that the systematic and untiring pursuit of worldly ends may be a religiously significant virtue of fundamental importance, Reformism, which swept through the urban trading classes of Java from 1912 to 1920, paved the way for the creation of a genuinely bourgeois ethic. By substituting a progress-oriented self-determinism for classical Islam's ineluctable fatalism it injected into the bazaar context a dynamic which had previously been lacking. Chinese-owned enterprises aside, of the seven well-established stores in Modjokuto, six are run by Reform Moslems; of the two dozen or more small factories of one sort or another, all but three or four are in pious Moslem hands.

Thus, despite marked cultural differences, economic development in Modjokuto is tending to take the classic form we have known in the West. An at least in part religiously motivated, generally disesteemed group of small shopkeepers and petty manufacturers arising out of a traditionalized trading class are attempting to secure an improved status in a changed society through the rational, systematic pursuit of wealth. This sequence of change, occurring several centuries after it occurred in Europe, and taking place in a world which is already partially industrialized, will have a significance and outcome in Java quite different from what it had in Europe, but the general similarities between the two cases are nevertheless quite real.

Leaving aside any detailed descriptions of the enterprises the Javanese pioneers in economic change have in fact created, it is worth noting that they are all either small "Western-type" retail stores or small work-place-type factories, and thus are true firms in the broad sociological sense of well-defined corporate institutions specifically devoted to economic ends. The stores, catering to the modernizing tastes of the new urban classes—school teachers, students, political leaders, civil servants, technicians—are characterized both by a generally better quality of goods, including many that are imported, and a more regularized manner of doing business than is typical of the bazaar. They have fixed (or nearly fixed) prices, a concern with firm reputation and advertising, a steady clientele, and an interest in creating markets rather than merely responding to them. The extreme complications in distributive patterns have been eliminated, and in fact success in such retailing enterprises seems heavily dependent upon the ability of the owner to establish workable relations with stable, reliable distributors (or manufacturers) in one or another of the major cities of the island to complement the growth of sales relationships with the emerging urban public. The factories—cigarette, garment, food processing, furniture—are all small scale (the largest employs about 50 workers), but a number have become at least partly mechanized, follow rigorous work schedules, and produce a cheaper and more reliable product than those of which cottage industry, putting-out arrangements, or individual craftsmen are usually capable. The establishment of these stores and factories is not to be thought of as merely comparable in difficulty with a similar operation by an enterprising American individual. Each involved a set of breaks with tradition which required boldness, judgment, and a certain unconventionality not possible for the traditional bazaar trader. The storekeeper or factory owner is a new type of man. To conceive of the required deviations from traditional purchase, employment, management, and sales practices, and to persuade some of the other parties to the transaction that the new relationships were appropriate and acceptable, required considerable talents. To establish the stores even more than the factories required a set of new relationships each of which would have been more difficult if the conditions permitting the others had not also existed.

A RISING MIDDLE CLASS AND ITS PROBLEMS

Modjokuto's fitful and sporadic movements toward economic change are but part of her more general movement, also fitful and sporadic, toward a whole new pattern of social life. The movement from territorially based traditional political allegiances toward ideologically based modern ones in the nationalist parties and associations, the transformation of the stratification system from a collection of discrete, more or less closed status groups to across-the-board, culturally heterogeneous open classes, and the development of corporate economic firms out of a background of hyperindividuated bazaar trading are all of a piece. Each of these changes demands the others as its environment for it to flourish, and together they both produce and are the results of fundamental alterations in cultural beliefs, attitudes, and values. It is in this sense that such often vaguely employed terms as "modernization," "urbanization," "rationalization," and "economic development" are really equivalent in their basic meaning; they all point, if from somewhat different directions, to an integral pattern of social change.

Nevertheless, Modjokuto's pattern of development has its own specific quality, as indices of which four points may be mentioned.

First, Modjokuto's entrepreneurs are almost all traders or traders' sons; their activities both grow out of the bazaar context and are a rebellion against it. The traditional trading culture of Modjokuto is both facilitative and inhibitory of economic reform; it is both the source of the innovators' methods and aspirations and one of the major barriers against the employment of those methods and the realization of those aspirations.

Second, the immediately limiting factor on entrepreneurial activity is not lack of capital, shortages of skilled or disciplined labor, insufficiency of markets, or lack of technical knowledge (though these all are problems), but the task of organizing diverse activities into unified institutions—stores or small factories. It is the ability and originality to organize a range of different economic activities in a systematic manner that most distinguishes a Modjokuto entrepreneur from his noninnovative bazaar-trader fellows—not wealth, not education, not even drive.

Third, the entrepreneurial group *is* a group, not a random collection of individuals. Innovators are clearly set apart by both their social origins and their religious intensity, and they represent the sort of generally disesteemed, highly serious petty businessmen who have appeared in the early stages of economic revolution in many countries.

And fourth, Modjokuto's economic growth is dependent on an on-going revolution in urban style of life—explicitly in the emergence of the postrevolution pattern of politicosocial organization, the new bases of social ranking which have appeared along with this pattern, and the expansion of the school system which sustains it. Together, these have caused a critical shift in taste in the urban masses as against their prewar counterparts.

On the other side of the ledger, there are two main barriers to the success of the Javanese entrepreneurial group in Modjokuto. One is the presence of the Chinese. In the race to be the town's modern middle class the Chinese have the advantages of possessing more capital and greater business acumen; they have more experience and are better organized than the Javanese shopkeepers and factory owners. But they are Chinese, and resentment against them, always great, has mounted rapidly since the revolution. The recent regulation forbidding the residence of noncitizen Chinese in towns the size of Modjokuto may have greatly reduced their role. It is difficult to say whether for the better or the worse so far as the economy is concerned.

Secondly, a middle class, to be successful, will have to be able to move into industry, and there may be some question whether the Javanese shopkeepers will be able to do so because of the so-called "lumpiness" problem. Some recent economic theory has emphasized the discontinuities in economic change, the quantum jumps which are often required in moving from traditional to modern production methods. Steel mills, automobile plants, or even capital-intensive sugar refineries do not come in all sizes; nor do they arise gradually by incremental changes from obscure beginnings. Some observers feel that in the context of this requirement there is about Modjokuto's "shopkeeper revolution" a peculiar air of irrelevancy.

There are, however, a number of counterarguments to this view. In the first place, without the growth of some sort of sturdy, indigenous business class the Indonesian government is likely to find the task of inducing rapid economic growth an insuperable one. Such a class provides the skills, values, and motivations without which industrial development is as impossible as it is without natural resources; and no more than iron or coal deposits can such resources be created by fiat. It is one thing to stimulate, channel, and supplement the growth of a modern economy; it is quite another to create such an economy *ex nihilo* out of an almost wholly traditional culture. Whatever their shortcomings, Modjokuto's shopkeepers and manufacturers are a human resource for the Indonesian government to work with.

Second, the establishment without prior steps of fairly large industrial units, even if it should be a necessary part of the process of economic development, which is not certain, is only a small part. Multiple and unconnected regional expansions, intermittent and self-contained spurts of this industry or that, largely independent, even contradictory, institutional developments—all these too are characteristic of countries in the initial stages of growth. It is necessary neither that everything be done at once nor that maximum integration be maintained at each and every stage of development. And, in any case, in the sort of jammed and disorganized situation Indonesia finds herself in today, no genuine growing point is so small or so peripheral as to be irrelevant. Modjokuto is not Indonesia, but neither is Djakarta.

ECONOMIC DEVELOPMENT IN TABANAN

In Tabanan the nascent entrepreneurial class of displaced aristocrats is concerned not with reorganizing a bazaar economy but with readjusting an agrarian one. They are not trying to give some articulate form to a fluid, individualistic trading pattern but to adapt the intensely collective and long-established institutions of traditional peasant society to novel economic ends.

By mobilizing habitual sentiments of loyalty, respect, obligation, and trust they hope to make ancient custom serve modern enterprise.

Such modern enterprise does not yet exist in Tabanan; they must create it. Like their Modjokuto counterparts, they must establish autonomous merchandising and manufacturing firms, institutional forms more or less novel to the society; but the social and cultural building blocks available for the task come not from the bazaar but from the village. Enmeshed, as they have always been, in a complex network of traditional ties both with one another and with the great mass of commoners they once ruled, the town-based aristocracy is attempting to manipulate these ties in such a way as to construct and support modern economic enterprises. Thus an analysis of social and economic organization in the Balinese village is prerequisite to an analysis of this urban-based pattern of development.

RURAL SOCIAL STRUCTURE AND ECONOMIC ORGANIZATION

The general organization of the Balinese village is best seen as a set of overlapping and intersecting corporate associations known as *seka*. A *seka* is a more or less enduring social group, formed on the basis of a single criterion of membership and dedicated to some narrowly specified social end. Some *seka* are permanent, others temporary; in some membership is ascribed, in others more or less voluntary; in all, each member has absolutely equal rights and duties regardless of what his general position in the society may be. Every Balinese belongs to from three to four up to a dozen *seka,* and the Balinese do virtually everything except make love in *seka,* for they strongly prefer to act in groups rather than as individuals. This combination of an almost ant-like attack on the performance of important social activities with a tendency to direct any one group to a single end rather than employing the same group for multiple purposes leads to what one might call, paradoxically, a pluralistic collectivism. The crosscutting of social alliances means that almost no one is completely engrossed in any single totally comprehensive institution without alternative loyalties to which he may have recourse against group pressures, and yet no one is ever obliged to operate entirely on his own, independently of some well-defined social aggregation.

There are, speaking roughly, five types of *seka:* temple congregations, residential units, irrigation societies, kinship groups, and voluntary associations.

1. *Temple congregations.* Members of each such group are obliged to worship at a given temple on certain holy days, and to maintain it. The first duty involves elaborate ritual offerings of food, and so on; the second, financial support. Both demands are met by collective economic activity more often than by monetary assessments: harvesting jointly and contributing the harvester's tenth share to the temple; working riceland bought in the name of the temple; dance and drama performances for its benefit; and so on.

2. *Residential units:* hamlets of a dozen to a couple of hundred households centered around a communal meeting house. There are monthly gatherings at which policy decisions (taxes, fines, exiling wrongdoers, public works undertakings) are made, and the hamlet can call on members for public services of various sorts. To earn income the hamlet may form a harvesting group, or sponsor a dance society, or buy riceland. There are also hamlet-owned enterprises such as coffee shops, retail stores, and small brick and tile factories. One hamlet even started its own bus company, financed by selling its riceland, and used the profits to build a school and pay the teachers' salaries. Other hamlets form the basis for co-operatives, one particularly successful consumer-producer co-operative being maintained by 16 hamlets in concert. In addition, some hamlets are craft-specialized, concerned with the manufacture of salt, the forging of musical instruments, weaving, pot making, carpentry, tailoring, or some other occupation.

3. *Irrigation societies.* Members of these *seka* are all those whose land is irrigated from a single watercourse. As land holdings tend to be scattered, one man may be a member of several such societies, and the members of any such society come from perhaps 10 to 15 hamlets. The main functions of an irrigation society are management of water resources, coordination of planting, and the performance of agricultural rituals. Within an irrigation society a water *seka* may undertake to keep dams in repair and canals clean for pay. In rare instances wholly pro-

fessionalized water *seka* composed almost entirely of landless villagers belonging to no irrigation society at all are paid to perform these tasks for three or four irrigation societies.

4. *Kinship groups.* Descent is patrilineal, residence patrilocal, and semiendogamous corporate kin groups play a very important role in village life in some hamlets, often forming the framework for economic enterprise. Thus in one village four such groups were engaged in the competitive manufacture of gamelan orchestra instruments, primarily a smithing job; in others weaving, harvesting, or other activities may be organized in kinship terms.

5. *Voluntary associations.* Membership in such *seka* is through voluntary affiliation, and they often have purely economic functions. They may plant, weed, harvest, carry sheaves from the fields, make house roofing from grasses and palms, transport goods, perform dances, drama, or music, hawk iced drinks or snacks, make tiles and pottery. Sometimes several tasks are performed by a single, well-established, long-persisting voluntary *seka*.

In short, *seka* organization, whether religious, political, irrigation, kinship, or voluntary based, is the heart of Balinese social structure, which can in fact be seen as a set of crosscutting *seka* of various types loosely adjusted to one another. It is on this type of pluralistic collectivism that the aristocratic entrepreneurs of Tabanan town must base their efforts at innovation, reform, and economic growth.

THE TABANAN ARISTOCRACY AND THE FIRM-TYPE ECONOMY

One of the most persistent, most widespread, and most fallacious scholarly stereotypes of Balinese social organization is that it consists, and has for centuries consisted, of almost wholly independent, closed-in peasant communities—socially insulated, self-absorbed "village republics" enduring passively and patiently beneath an equally self-contained and aloof though more unstable gentry ruling class. In this view, kings, dynasties, whole ruling classes have come and gone, but the peasant, the real, original Balinese, for whom such political upheavals merely signify a change of tax collectors, plods on forever in the unchanging paths of uncounted centuries. Between noble and commoner the relations are conceived to have always been ones of pure hostility and a direct opposition of interest.

This view of gentry-peasantry relationships is wholly misconceived. The Balinese gentry were not "outsiders" but, from the very beginning, an integral part of Balinese society. They were not simply tribute takers; they performed altogether crucial interlocal political, religious, and economic functions upon which the supposedly self-subsistent villagers were dependent for their very existence. In traditional times (that is, prior to 1906) nobles gathered commoners into military *seka* for wars. They judged interhamlet legal issues and punished various crimes, such as miscaste marriages. They inherited the ricelands of village decedents without heirs, executed the more serious hamlet-passed punishments, supported exiles from the hamlets; and, of course, they had a very large number of retainer families living in the villages themselves. Further, they conducted important ceremonies, such as cremations and temple consecrations, in which the whole population was involved both as mobilized labor and tribute givers and as audience for the great ritual dramas produced.

The members of the gentry were also landlords maintaining village-dwelling sharecroppers, played a certain role in co-ordinating irrigation societies, monopolized foreign trade, and set up local markets. In politics, religion, art, and economics the rulers and the ruled represented, in traditional Bali, not parallel but intersecting, not independent but complementary, social groups. Though the caste barrier between aristocrat and commoner was almost impermeable, the etiquette of deference extraordinarily well developed, and the lines between local and supralocal concerns very sharply drawn, both the Balinese state and the Balinese village became what they became in great part as the result of the close, multifaceted, long-term, and ever-changing interaction they had with one another, a circumstance too obvious to need special comment were it not so often denied.

It is this heritage of undisputed leadership in supralocal affairs which the Tabanan aristocracy is now attempting to turn to their account in building an urban-based nationally oriented firm economy. In contrast to the Modjokuto small businessmen, whose puristic Islamic piety represents a nonconformist pattern within the local culture, Tabanan entrepreneurs are cultural exemplars.

They symbolize the quintessence of indigenous culture, demonstrate its furthest reaches of complexity, refinement, and sophistication. And today, when many of the specific structural arrangements which supported this role of cultural representative have been either dissolved or drastically reorganized, the sentiments which underlay them persist. Thus in their bid to create a modern economy the aristocrats have at their disposal a quantity of cultural capital in the form of traditionalized social loyalties and expectations which Modjokuto's self-made shopkeepers entirely lack. "We have lost control of the government," these disestablished nobles say, "so we'll capture the economy."

Perhaps the most striking case example of the manner in which modern firm-building in Tabanan reflects and depends upon traditional patterns of organization and loyalty is the development of what is today the town's largest and most important business concern, Gadarata (an abbreviation meaning "The People's Trade Association of Tabanan"). Founded in 1945 by four local noblemen plus a long-resident Javanese market trader, who evidently served as a technical advisor, the association amassed its capital of 100,000 rupiah by levying a "contribution" of five rupiah on every household head in the region, each contributor being awarded a voting share in the projected enterprise. Approximately 10,000 villagers bought a share apiece, and the remaining 50,000 rupiah were raised by selling multiple shares to richer individuals, most of them town aristocrats. The plan was to funnel all export trade of the region through this one well-organized, incorporated, upper-caste-managed concern as well as to launch certain other associated business enterprises. A large two-story warehouse, store, and office building, the town's most imposing edifice, was erected at the main crossroads near the market.

In 1950, after the transfer of sovereignty, the governing board, which by now had had two more strategic members of the ruling family added to it (the Javanese trader had withdrawn), reorganized the firm by changing the value of the shares from five to 100 rupiah each, thereby reducing the total number of shares from about 20,000 to about 1,000 at a single blow. The individual household head shareholders in the villages were thus forced into either selling out their interests to larger holders or banding together into "Gadarata *seka*" of 20 people each and selecting a representative to cast their vote at the annual meeting. Altogether, about 350 such *seka* were formed, covering about 7,000 of the original 10,000 villagers, while the rest of the small owners sold out to the leadership group, which thus consolidated its hold on the firm through this process. By the end of 1957 the enterprise had become worth something more than a half million rupiah and dominated much of the export trade of the area. By almost any measure, Gadarata, which now operates a retail store selling a wide variety of imported goods as well, has been a most successful undertaking.

Overall management and policy making are by now completely in the hands of seven salaried directors, five of whom, including the chairman and vice-chairman, are members of the ruling family. The process of bringing the firm progressively under the sole control of the "palace" group is now almost completed, a fact recognized and for the most part accepted by aristocrats and villagers alike. Despite some grumbling, most of the peasants do not expect to have any particular say in an institution focused around the nobility simply because they have provided capital any more than they expected to influence state policy simply because they contributed work and material to the lord's ceremonies in the old days. The managerial revolution has come quickly to Tabanan mainly because it involves no revolution.

A number of other stores and industries, some of them differently organized, of course, but also all noble led and dominated, could be cited as further examples—another trading concern, a tire recapping factory, several hotels, a weaving factory, a bus line, a bookstore, a garment-making shop, an ice factory. Thus, though there are also some smaller stores run by commoners, at the heart of Tabanan's postrevolutionary economic expansion has been a very small group of displaced traditional rulers. Tabanan's erstwhile ruling family—about 6 percent of its population—overwhelmingly dominates the nascent modern economy of the town.

UPPER CASTE REVOLUTION AND THE LIMITS OF TRADITION

The esential nature of Tabanan's "upper caste revolution" can be summarized, and its longer-run prospects tentatively assessed, by making a fourfold comparison of similarities and differences between development in Tabanan and in Modjokuto.

1. *Business Organization.* The bringing together of hundreds of villagers (as stockholders) into a single firm is not a realistic possibility to a Modjokuto entrepreneur. Not only does he entirely lack the traditional prestige to mobilize people on such a scale, but 300 years of intensive, Western-stimulated social change in Java have eroded the foundations for large-scale collective effort in the villages. And, too, Modjokuto's entrepreneurs emerge directly from a bazaar economy in which individualistic, every-man-for-himself activity is carried almost to an extreme, in contrast to the lineage-like organization of the generally solidary and corporate ruling family from which Tabanan's new men come.

As a result, almost all modern enterprises in Modjokuto are individual or immediate family concerns. Capital must be raised either through personal savings or government loans; selling shares to villagers or large-scale borrowing on the open market is virtually absent. Even partnerships, so easily formed in Tabanan, where strong noneconomic ties of kinship, co-residence, or status deference usually insure their persistence, are almost nonexistent in Modjokuto. When it comes to the organizational problem, the Tabananers have a clear advantage.

Yet there is another side to the coin, which is reflected in the constant complaint of the directors of the popularly based large firms that they are unwieldy and inefficient. In particular, as national political affairs come to have more importance, there is a tendency for the operation of these supposedly specifically economic institutions to reflect them, causing internal disruption, something the individualistic Modjokuto entrepreneur completely avoids. Cast in quasi-political terms to begin with, Tabanan's firms can easily become political in modern terms, a condition which, at least in a democratic, multiparty state, is extremely disfunctional to further growth or even continued solvency.

Second, and perhaps even more important, the popularly based concern has a tendency to behave very uneconomically because of the "social welfare" pressures of its members, who, for the most part, are not basically growth-minded. Not only is there great pressure to divide profits rather than reinvest them but there is also a tendency to employ overly large staffs in an attempt by the directorate to appease the rank and file.

Both Tabanan's group-centered approach to change and Modjokuto's individual-centered approach have defects and virtues. Tabanan's method smooths the way to the formation of larger-scale concerns; but traditional values supporting collective benefits as against individual enrichment induce a strong resistance to the rationalization of these concerns once they are formed. Modjokuto's method avoids this problem; but, although bold and rugged, not to say ruthless, individualism has advantages in stimulating creativity and destroying traditional constraints on enterprise, it also imposes severe limitations on the capacity to grow by limiting the effective range of collective organization. Modjokuto firms seem to grow so large and then no larger, because the next step means widening the social base of the enterprise beyond the immediate family connections to which, given that lack of trust which is the obverse of individualism, they are limited. Where Tabanan's approach tends to expand firms beyond their most efficient organizational base, Modjokuto's tends to confine them to too narrow a one.

2. *Religious and Ideological Dynamics.* In Modjokuto the entrepreneur mainly follows a discordant, rationalized, and self-consciously critical Islamic modernism—which sets him apart from his much less devout and zealous fellows and which in its very nature makes economic achievement ethically significant. His countertraditional ideological orientation puts him in the position of being not only an economic but also a religious and ethical innovator. Tabanan's economic leaders, on the other hand, are committed to religious beliefs and values which, far from clashing with those of the general society, are the most elaborate, developed, and systematic expression of the culture's traditionally institutionalized ethos.

Thus both marked deviation from the main stream of traditional religious thought and complete conformity to it seem able to provide an ideological context suitable to growth. What is important as a stimulus to economic enterprise is not whether a creed is revisionist or restorationist, but whether the state of affairs the creed celebrates differs significantly from the entrepreneurs' perception of the actual situation. In both Java and Bali there yawns a gap between the vision of the way things ought to be and the way they seem to be. In Modjokuto the pious shopkeepers see themselves as the vanguard of a truly Islamic Indonesia which must be created out of a community whose religion is now heterodox and outmoded. In Tabanan the nobility sees itself as wrongfully displaced from its true position as cultural cynosure, and as fighting to maintain the traditional patterns of deference, respect, and reverence upon which it feels the intrinsic value of Balinese culture rests.

3. *Political- versus Economic-Based Development.* The Javanese entrepreneurs want mainly to get rich, the Balinese to get (or remain) powerful. Tabanan's entrepreneurs, in contrast to Modjokuto's, have come from a class long used to wielding power; they have not lost the sense of confidence that comes with the effective exercise of political power on a broad scale. The comparable class in Modjokuto—the civil servant *prijaji* —has over 150 years been reduced to a group of nonpolicy-making petty bureaucrats, and has long since lost its original sense of playing a decisive role in its society. Thus in Tabanan the taste of the individual entrepreneur for economic innovation grows out of an aristocratic, even arrogant sense of being a man born to lead, while in Modjokuto it grows out of his sense of his superior shrewdness, toughness, flexibility, and ambition as contrasted to the passive, acceptant traditionalism of the mass of the population.

Again, each movement has its strength and weakness. Modjokuto's is apparently more apt to lead to democratic liberalism and the protection of individual political freedom; but it may be unable to cope with the need for large-scale enterprises which now seems to be faced by latecomer backward nations. The Tabanan entrepreneurs can set up larger enterprises by virtue of their ability to corral larger amounts of capital and also by virtue of being able to get the protection of monopoly situations or other special privileges from the government. But their developmental pattern skates fairly close to totalitarianism, and the development of this politically based sort of pattern into a Japanese-type industrial feudalism, a semitraditional, semimodern capitalism in which a small elite gains most of the advantages of modernization, is a very possible even if not necessary outcome. A traditional elite can make a more integral attack on the multiple problems of economic modernization than can a foot-loose bourgeoisie, which must go at its task haphazardly and piecemeal, but there is the danger of that intense domination of political concerns over all other concerns which is the hallmark of modernized totalitarian states.

4. *Urbanization.* As noted, Modjokuto is much more urbanized than Tabanan. The Balinese town, several centuries older, is only now losing the outlines of a traditional court center. Urbanization, which the growth of the plantations stimulated in Modjokuto, brings a mingling of individuals from all walks of life, greater personal anonymity (and hence greater freedom from traditional constraints and prejudices), a more variegated life. The brisk disorder of Modjokuto, compared to the sedate deliberateness of Tabanan, is certainly conducive to change, flexibility, and aggressiveness, if only because it is impossible for everyone to stand still very long and continue to survive.

Yet urbanization, particularly when it occurs within a wider society which is economically stagnant, also breeds malaise, discouragement, and aimlessness; and so, though urbanization may be a necessary condition for economic takeoff, it is hardly a sufficient one. Tabanan lacks a large commercial class, a developed proletariat, a strong office clerk and schoolteacher intelligentsia comparable to that of Modjokuto, but on the other hand it may be fortunate in starting the whole process of modernization at a time when it may prove possible to avoid the sort of change without progress characteristic of the Javanese town since the middle thirties. Everything depends upon what happens in Indonesia as a whole. If over the next decade or so economic opportunities expand significantly, Tabanan's lack of a history of boom, bust, and stagnation may prove advantageous; half an urbanization may prove to have been worse than none.

CONCLUSIONS

Indonesia as a nation is not the village or the small town writ large. One cannot generalize in any direct way from Modjokuto or Tabanan to the country as a whole. What then can be learned from a study of the two towns? The following six propositions are intended as tentative summary hypotheses derived from the above comparative analysis, designed only to point out some possible leads for future research:

1. *Innovative economic leadership (entrepreneurship) occurs in a fairly defined and homogeneous group.*

In both towns the entrepreneurs come neither from the general population in a more or less random way nor from several distinct social groups at once; in both they come almost entirely from a single quite clearly demarcated, set-apart group, the pious Islamic traders in Modjokuto, the ruling family in Tabanan.

2. *This innovative group has crystallized out of a larger traditional group which has a very long history of extravillage status and interlocal orientation.*

In neither area are the peasants leaders in economic change; both leadership groups are primarily interlocal in their outlook, some of their most important ties being with groups and individuals in areas other than their own. In Modjokuto this horizontal orientation originated out of contact with the all-Indonesia trading network which grew out of the internationally based bazaar culture of the fifteenth and sixteenth centuries. In Tabanan horizontality was an aspect of the sophisticated "great tradition" court culture associated with the indigenous Indonesian state structure, which was carried forward through the whole of the colonial period as well.

3. *The larger group out of which the innovating group is emerging is one which is at present experiencing fairly radical change in its relationships with the wider society of which it is a part.*

In prewar Modjokuto the town's traders were a self-contained, set-apart, rather despised group; today they are becoming integrated into a broad and generalized middle class within an uncertainly urbanizing structure. In prewar Tabanan the aristocrats were the unquestioned political and cultural elite of the region; today their position is increasingly threatened by the growth of a universalistic civil bureaucracy and the populist sentiments of nationalist ideology. It is thus neither upward nor downward class mobility or a blockage of these which is necessarily crucial but any kind of decisive change in intergroup relations which, by throwing accepted status demarcations into disarray, stimulates active efforts to anchor social positions to new moorings.

4. *Ideologically the innovative group conceives of itself as the*

main vehicle of religious and moral excellence within a generally wayward, unenlightened, or heedless community.

Islamic Reform, a sort of Moslem puritanism, the doctrine of the overwhelming majority of the entrepreneurs in Modjokuto, aims at a radical purification of the prevailing religious and moral syncretism of heterodox elements and is intensely critical of a wide range of established usages of ethics and worship. The ideology of Tabanan's new men, on the other hand, is catholic and restorationist, but they have the same sense of representing the proper against the prevailing. They see abandonment of customary patterns of deference, progressive usurpation of political power by the hereditarily unequipped, and growing failure of the average man to recognize and appreciate the indispensable social and cultural functions performed by those of high status as symptoms of a general cultural decline. Thus both innovative groups tend to see the general cultural level of the whole wider community as almost entirely dependent upon the success of themselves and their activities.

5. *The major innovational problems the entrepreneurs face are organizational rather than technical.*

The specific technical problems so far as development is concerned in the two towns now have mostly been solved; they need only be adopted to local needs. The Indonesian entrepreneur does not have to invent a sugar press, an ice machine, or a tire recapper; he has only to purchase them. It seems likely, therefore, that the organizer will play the central role in stimulating Indonesian takeoff rather than the engineer-inventor as in the English and American experience.

6. *The function of the entrepreneur in such transitional but pretakeoff societies is mainly to adapt customary, established means to novel ends.*

It is their uncommon ability to operate at once in the traditional world of established custom and in the modern world of systematic economic rationality which is the chief resource of the economic innovators of both Modjokuto and Tabanan. In Modjokuto the small shopkeepers and manufacturers capitalize on the knowledge and skills developed in the bazaar economy and attempt to apply them toward the creation of economic institutions better organized and more efficient than the bazaar economy has been able to produce. In Tabanan the businessmen nobles redirect the political loyalties of agrarian society into the support of economic rationalization. Both groups draw much of their strength from this ability to operate on both sides of the line between traditional and modern in economic matters and so form a bridge between the two. As a result, they are able to create transitional economic institutions within which many of the values, beliefs, structure, and skills of a customary trading or peasant culture are integrated with features characteristic of developed and specialized-enterprise (firm) economies.

The degree to which these propositions, or others which might be derived from our two-town comparison, will prove of value to the analysis of development generally remains to be seen. But, in more general terms, perhaps this sort of community-study approach to economic growth will help to turn planning in underdeveloped countries away from the rigid, a priori, hyper-theoretical, almost dogmatic approach which has often been characteristic of it toward a more pragmatic, concrete, and realistic approach—one which uses general principles, economic or sociological, not as axioms from which policies are to be logically deduced but as guides to the interpretation of particular cases upon which policies are to be based.

V EUROPE

21 WEALTH AND LABOR
[ARCHAIC GREECE]

M. I. Finley

In the second book of the *Iliad* the poet catalogues the contending hosts, in the case of the Greeks by the names of their chief
leaders and the number of ships each brought with him. "But
the multitude (i.e., the commoners) I could not relate nor name,
not if I had ten tongues, nor ten mouths" (Iliad 2.488–89). The
list totals 1186 ships, which, at a minimum computation, means
over 60,000 men, a figure as trustworthy as the four hundred
thousand Saracens of *The Song of Roland*. The world of Odysseus was a small one in numbers of people. There are no
statistics and no ways of making good guesses, but the five-acre
sites of the archaeologists, together with what is known from
later centuries, leave no doubt that the populations of the individual communities were to be reckoned in four figures, often
even in three, and that the numbers in the poems, whether of
ships or flocks or slaves or nobles, are unrealistic and invariably
err on the side of exaggeration.

One of the smallest contingents in the catalogue of ships was
led by Odysseus, a mere twelve (Agamemnon had one hundred
and provided sixty others for the inland Arcadians). He is announced as king of the Cephallenians, who inhabit three ad-
jacent islands in the Ionian Sea, Cephallenia, Ithaca, and Zacyn-
thus, together with two sites apparently on the nearby mainland.
But it is with Ithaca specifically that he is always directly identified. And it is on the island of Ithaca, not in the Never-Never

FROM M. I. Finley, *The World of Odysseus*, Chapter III, pp. 46–73. Copyright 1954, © 1965 by M. I. Finley. Reprinted by permission of the author
and The Viking Press, Inc.

Land through which he later wandered, that the world of Odysseus can chiefly be examined.

The island population was dominated by a group of noble families, some of whose men participated in the expedition against Troy, while others remained at home. Among the latter was Mentor, to whose watchful eye Odysseus entrusted his young wife, Penelope, who came from another land, and his only child, his newborn son Telemachus, when he himself went off. For twenty years there was a strange hiatus in the political leadership of Ithaca. Odysseus' father, Laertes, did not resume the throne, though still alive. Penelope could not rule, being a woman. Mentor was no guardian in any legal sense, merely a well-intentioned, ineffectual figure, and he did not function as a regent.

For ten years a similar situation prevailed throughout the Greek world, while the kings, with few exceptions, were at war. With the destruction of Troy and the great homecoming of the heroes, life was resumed in its normal ways. The fallen kings were replaced; some who returned, like Agamemnon, ran into usurpers and assassins; and the others came back to the seats of power and its pursuits. But for Odysseus there was a different fate. Having offended the god Poseidon, he was tossed about for another ten years before he was rescued, largely through the intervention of Athena, and permitted to return to Ithaca. It was this second decade that perplexed the people at home. No one in all Hellas knew what had befallen Odysseus, whether he had died on the return journey from Troy or was still alive somewhere in the outer world. This uncertainty laid the basis for the second theme of the poem, the story of the suitors.

Again there is trouble with numbers. No less than 108 nobles, 56 from Ithaca and the other islands ruled by Odysseus, and 52 from a neighboring mainland kingdom, says the poet, were paying court to Penelope. She was to be forced to choose Odysseus' successor from among them. This was no ordinary wooing, ancient style or modern. Except that they continued to sleep in their own homes, the suitors had literally taken over the household of the absent Odysseus and were steadily eating and drinking their way through his vast stores; "not twenty men together have so much wealth," according to the swineherd Eumaeus (Odyssey 14.98–99). For three years Penelope defended herself by delaying tactics, but her power of resistance was wearing down. The ceaseless carouse in the house, the growing certainty that Odysseus would never return, and the suitors' open threat, made publicly to Telemachus, "to eat up your livelihood and your possessions" (Odyssey 2.123), were having their effect. Just in time Odysseus returned, disguised as a wandering beggar. By employing all his craft and prowess, and a little magic, he succeeded in slaughtering the suitors, and, with the final intervention of Athena, in re-establishing his position as head of his household and king in Ithaca.

Abroad, Odysseus' life was one long series of struggles with witches, giants, and nymphs, but there is none of that in the Ithacan story. On the island we are confronted with human society alone (including the ever-present Athena, to be sure, but in a sense the Greek gods were always a part of human society, working through dreams, prophecies, oracles, and other signs). The same is true of the *Iliad*. For the story of the few days between the insult by Agamemnon and the death of Hector at the hands of Achilles, as for the main plot of the Ithacan theme, the nobility provides all the characters. The *Odyssey* parades other people of the island, but largely as stage props or stock types: Eumaeus the swineherd, the old nurse Eurycleia, Phemius the bard, the nameless "carvers of the meat," the sailors and housemaids and miscellaneous retainers. The poet's meaning is clear: on the field of battle, as in the power struggle which is the Ithacan theme, only the aristocrats had roles.

A deep horizontal cleavage marked the world of the Homeric poems. Above the line were the *aristoi*, literally the "best people," the hereditary nobles who held most of the wealth and all the power, in peace as in war. Below were all the others, for whom there was no collective technical term, the multitude. The gap between the two was rarely crossed, except by the inevitable accidents of wars and raids. The economy was such that the creation of new fortunes, and thereby of new nobles, was out of the question. Marriage was strictly class-bound, so that the other door to social advancement was also securely locked.

Below the main line there were various other divisions, but, unlike the primary distinction between aristocrat and commoner, they seem blurred and they are often indefinable. Not even so simple a contrast as that between slave and free man stands out in sharp clarity. The word *drester,* for example, which means "one who works or serves," is used in the *Odyssey* for the free and the unfree alike. The work they did and the treatment they received, at the hands of their masters as in the psychology of the poet, are often indistinguishable.

Slaves existed in number; they were property, disposable at will. More precisely, there were slave women, for wars and raids were the main source of supply, and there was little ground, economic or moral, for sparing the lives of the defeated men. The heroes as a rule killed the males and carried off the females, regardless of rank. Before offering up his prayer for his son, Hector, who knew his own doom, said to his wife: "But I care not so much for the grief of the Trojans hereafter . . . as for yours, when one of the bronze-clad Achaeans will carry you off in tears; and you will be in Argos, working the loom at another woman's bidding, and you will draw water from Messeis or Hypereia, most unwillingly, and great constraint will be laid upon you" (Iliad 6.450–58).

Hector did not need Apollo's aid in foretelling the future. Never in Greek history was it otherwise; the persons and the property of the vanquished belonged to the victor, to be disposed of as he chose. But Hector showed gentle restraint, for his prophecy was not complete. The place of slave women was in the household, washing, sewing, cleaning, grinding meal, valeting. If they were young, however, their place was also in the master's bed. Of the old nurse Eurycleia, the poet reports that "Laertes bought her with (some of) his possessions when she was still in the prime of youth . . . but he never had intercourse with her in bed, and he avoided the anger of his wife" (Odyssey 1.430–33). It was the rarity of Laertes' behavior, and the promise of his wife's wrath, that warranted the special comment. Neither custom nor morality demanded such abstinence.

It is idle to seek for numbers here. Odysseus is reported to have had fifty female slaves, but that is surely a convenient round figure, used for the household of King Alcinous of the Phaeacians too. A few men were also in bondage, such as the swineherd Eumaeus, an aristocrat by birth, who had been kidnaped when a child by Phoenician traders and sold into slavery.

Like the women, the male slaves worked in the home, and in the fields and vineyards, never abroad as servants or orderlies.

Of the Ithacans who were not slaves, the free population who were the bulk of the community, some were surely independent householders, free herders and peasants with their own holdings (although the poet tells us nothing about them). Others were specialists, carpenters and metal workers, soothsayers, bards, and physicians. Because they supplied certain essential needs in a way that neither the lords nor the non-specialists among their followers could match, these men, a handful in numbers, floated in mid-air in the social hierarchy. Seers and physicians might even be nobles, but the others, though they were close to the aristocratic class and even shared its life in many respects, were decidedly not of the aristocracy, as the treatment and behavior of the bard Phemius attest.

Eumaeus, we remember, called these specialists *demioergoi,* literally "those who work for the people" (and once Penelope attached the same classificatory label to the heralds). From the word, used in the Homeric poems only in these two passages, it has been suggested that the *demioergoi* operated in a way well known among primitive and archaic groups, the Kabyle of Algiers, for instance: "Another specialist is the blacksmith, who is also an outsider. The villagers lend him a house, and each family pays him a fixed portion of his yearly salary in grain and other produce" (Coon 1951:305). Unfortunately the evidence for the world of Odysseus is far from clear or decisive. Once when Nestor, at home, wished to make sacrifice, he ordered his servants, "'Bid the goldsmith Laerces come here, that he may gild the horns of the cow.' . . . And the smith came, with the smith's tools in his hands, the instruments of his craft, anvil and hammer and well-made fire-tongs, with which he worked the gold. . . . And the old horseman Nestor gave gold, and the smith then skillfully gilded the horns" (Odyssey 3.425–38). Neither the status of the goldsmith nor even his domicile is indicated here, unlike the passage in the *Iliad* about the great "unwrought mass of iron" which Achilles offered from his booty for a weight-throwing contest. The iron was to be both the test and the prize for the winner. He will have it, said Achilles, "to use for five full years, for neither the shepherd nor the plowman

will have to go into town for lack of iron, but this will furnish it"
(Iliad 23.833–35).

Although nothing is ever said about remuneration, it does not
necessarily follow that each family in the community gave the
smith, or the other *demioergoi,* a fixed annual maintenance
quota. They could have been paid as they worked, provided only
that they were available to the public, to the whole *demos.* That
availability would explain the word well enough.

Eumaeus indicated still another special quality of the *demioergoi* when he asked "who ever summons a stranger from abroad
. . . unless he be one of the *demioergoi"* (again with a parallel
among the Kabyle). Were they, then, traveling tinkers and min-
strels, going from community to community on a more or less
fixed schedule? Actually the logic of Eumaeus's question is that
all invited strangers are craftsmen, not that all craftsmen are
strangers. Probably some were and some were not, and, of those
who were, none need have worked on a circuit at all. The heralds
were certainly permanent, regular, full-scale members of the
community. The bards may have wandered a bit (in the poet's
own day they traveled all the time). Regarding the others, we
are simply not informed.

Indispensable as the *demioergoi* were, their contribution to the
quantity of work performed on an estate was a very small one.
For the basic work of pasturage and tillage in the fields, of stew-
ardship and service in the house, there was no need of specialists:
every man in Ithaca could herd and plow and carve, and those
commoners who had their own holdings worked them themselves. Others made up the permanent staffs of Odysseus and
the nobles, free men like the unnamed "carvers of the meat,"
who were an integral part of the household. Still others, the least
fortunate, were *thetes,* unattached, propertyless laborers who
worked for hire and begged what they could not steal.

"Stranger," said the leading suitor Eurymachus to the beggar
(Odysseus in disguise), "would you be willing to work as a *thes,*
if I should take you in my service, on a farm at the border—
you can be sure of pay—laying walls and planting tall trees?
There I would furnish you ample grain and put clothes on your
back and give you shoes for your feet." Ample grain and clothes
and shoes made up the store of a commoner's goods. But
Eurymachus was mocking, "creating laughter among his compan-

ions," at the direct inspiration of Athena, who "would by no means permit the arrogant suitors to refrain from heartrending scorn, so that the pain might sink still more deeply into the heart of Odysseus son of Laertes" (Odyssey 18.346–61).

A little of the joke lay in the words, "you can be sure of pay." No *thes* could be sure. Poseidon once angrily demanded of Apollo why he of all the gods should be so completely on the side of the Trojans. Have you forgotten, Poseidon asked, how, on order from Zeus, "we worked as *thetes* for one year, for an agreed-upon pay," for Laomedon, king of Troy, building the wall around the city and herding cattle? And how, at the end of the year, Laomedon "deprived us of our pay and sent us off with threats?" (Iliad 21.441–52). The real joke, however, the utter scornfulness of Eurymachus's proposal, lay in the offer itself, not in the hint that the pay would be withheld in the end. To see the whole point, we turn to Achilles in Hades rather than to Poseidon on Olympus. "Do not speak to me lightly of death, glorious Odysseus," said the shade of Achilles. "I would rather be bound down, working as a *thes* for another, by the side of a landless man, whose livelihood was not great, than be ruler over all the dead who have perished" (Odyssey 11.489–91).

A *thes,* not a slave, was the lowest creature on earth that Achilles could think of. The terrible thing about a *thes* was his lack of attachment, his not belonging. The authoritarian household, the *oikos,* was the center around which life was organized, from which flowed not only the satisfaction of material needs, including security, but ethical norms and values, duties, obligations, and responsibilities, social relationships, and relations with the gods. The *oikos* was not merely the family, it was all the people of the household and its goods; hence "economics" (from the Latinized form, *oecus*), the art of managing an *oikos,* meant running a farm, not managing to keep peace in the family.

Just what it meant, in terms of customary or legal obligation and in a man's own familial life, to be a permanent but free member of the *oikos* of another is by no means clear. Negatively it meant considerable loss of freedom of choice and of mobility. Yet these men were neither slaves nor serfs nor bondsmen. They were retainers (*therapontes*), exchanging their service for a proper place in the basic social unit, the household—a vicarious membership, no doubt, but one that gave them both material security and the psychological values and satisfactions that went with belonging. Altogether the chief aristocrats managed, by a combination of slaves, chiefly female, and a whole hierarchy of retainers, supplemented by *thetes,* to build up very imposing and very useful household forces, equipped to do whatever was required of a man of status and power in their world. The hierarchy of retainers, it should be added, reached very high indeed. As a child Patroclus was forced to flee his home. Peleus received him in his palace and "named him retainer" of young Achilles (Iliad 23.90). The analogy that comes to mind at once is that of the noble page in some early modern court, just as "lord Eteoneus, the ready retainer of Menelaus" who met guests at the door and poured the wine for them, might well have been the counterpart of a Lord Chamberlain (Odyssey 4.22–23).

A *thes* in Ithaca might even have been an Ithacan, not an outsider. But he was no part of an *oikos,* and in this respect even the slave was better off. The slave, human but nevertheless a part of the property element of the *oikos,* was altogether a nice symbol of the situation. Only twice does Homer use the word that later became standard in Greek for a slave, *doulos,* which seems etymologically tied to the idea of labor. Otherwise his word is *dmos,* with its obvious link with *doma* or *domos,* a house; and after Homer and Hesiod *dmos* never appears in literature apart from a few instances of deliberate archaizing, as in Sophocles and Euripides. The treatment of the slaves was essentially milder and more humane than the pattern familiar from plantation slavery. Eumaeus, a favorite slave, had even been able to purchase a slave for himself. To be sure, a dozen of the slave girls were hanged in the midst of the carnage of Odysseus' successful return, but it was the method of their execution alone that distinguished them from the lordly suitors, who died by the bow and the spear.

There was little mating of slave with slave because there were so few males among them. Nearly all the children born to the slave women were the progeny of the master or of other free males in the household. Commonly, in many different social systems, as among the Greeks later on, such offspring were slaves like their mothers: "the belly holds the child," say the Tuareg nomads of the Sahara in explanation. Not so in the world of Odysseus, where it was the father's status that was determinative.

Thus, in the fanciful tale with which Odysseus sought to conceal his identity from Eumaeus immediately upon his return to Ithaca, his father was a wealthy Cretan, his mother a "bought concubine." When the father died the legitimate sons divided the property, giving him only a dwelling and a few goods. Later, by his valor, he obtained to wife the daughter of "a man of many estates" (Odyssey 14.199–212). The slave woman's son might sometimes be a second-class member of the family, but even then he was part of that narrower circle within the *oikos* as a whole, free and without even the stigma of bastardy in our sense, let alone the mark of slavery.

Fundamentally the difference between the ordinary landowner and the noble lay in the magnitude of their respective *oikoi,* and therefore in the numbers of retainers they could support, which, translated into practical terms, meant in their power. Superficially the difference was one of birth. At some past point, remote or near in time, either conquest or wealth created the original separation. Then it froze, continued along hereditary lines, was given divine sanction through genealogies that assigned every noble family a god for an ancestor, and was called a blood-distinction.

The nature of the economy served to seal and preserve the class line. Wherever the wealth of the household is so decisive, unless there is a measure of mobility in wealth, unless the opportunity exists to create new fortunes, the structure becomes caste-like in its rigidity. This was the case in Ithaca. The base of the *oikos* was its land, and there was no way, under normal, peaceful conditions, to acquire new land in the settled regions. Hypothetically one might push to the frontier and take up vacant land, but few men actually did anything so absurd and foolhardy, except under the most violent compulsions. It was not out of mere sentiment for the fatherland that banishment was deemed the bitterest of fates. The exile was stripped of all ties that meant life itself; it made no difference in this regard whether one had been compelled to flee or had gone from home in the search for land by free choice.

The primary use of the land was in pasturage. To begin the story of his adventure among the Cyclopes, which he told at the court of Alcinous, Odysseus underscored the primitive savagery of the one-eyed giants. First of all, they had not learned the art of agriculture: "they neither plant anything nor till" (Odyssey 9.108). Nevertheless, Odysseus' own world was one of pasturage, not of tillage (unlike the Greek world at the time of Homer himself and of Hesiod, when agriculture had moved to the fore). Greek soil is poor, rocky and waterless, so that no more than twenty percent of the total surface of the peninsula can be cultivated. In places it once provided excellent pasturage for horses and cattle; virtually all of it is still, in our day, good for the smaller animals, sheep and pigs and goats. The households of the poems carried on a necessary minimum of plowing and planting, especially on orchard and vine-land, but it was their animals on which they depended for clothing, draft, transport, and much of their food.

With their flocks and their labor force, with plentiful stone for building and clay for pots, the great households could almost realize their ideal of absolute self-sufficiency. The *oikos* was above all a unit of consumption. Its activities, insofar as they were concerned with the satisfaction of material wants, were guided by one principle, to meet the consuming needs of the lord and his people; if possible by the products of his estates, supplemented by booty. But there was one thing which prevented full self-sufficiency, a need which could neither be eliminated nor satisfied by substitutes, and that was the need for metal. Scattered deposits existed in Greece, but the main sources of supply were outside, in western Asia and central Europe.

Metal meant tools and weapons, but it also meant something else, perhaps as important. When Telemachus had concluded his visit at the palace of Menelaus in Sparta, in search of news about his father, his host offered him, as a parting gift, "three horses and a chariot-board of polished metal and . . . a fine goblet." The young man demurred. "And whatever gift you would give me, let it be treasure. I will not take horses to Ithaca. . . . In Ithaca there are neither wide courses nor any meadowland" (Odyssey 4.590–605). The Greek word customarily rendered by "treasure" is *keimelion,* literally something that can be laid away. In the poems treasure was of bronze, iron, or gold, less often of silver or fine cloth, and usually it was shaped into goblets, tripods, or caldrons. Such objects had some utilitarian worth and they could provide aesthetic satisfaction too, but neither function was of real moment compared to their value as symbolic wealth or prestige wealth. The twin uses of treasure were in possessing it and in giving it away, paradoxical as that may appear. Until the appropriate occasion for a gift presented itself, most treasure was kept hidden under lock and key. It was not "used" in the narrow sense of that word.

When Agamemnon was finally persuaded that appeasement of Achilles was absolutely essential to prevent the destruction of the Achaean forces, he went about it by offering amends through gifts. His offer included some to be presented at once, others on conditions of victory. And what a catalogue it was: seven cities, a daughter to wife with a great dowry "such as no one ever yet gave with his daughter," the girl Briseis, over whom the quarrel had broken out, seven captive women from Lesbos skilled in crafts, twelve prize-winning racehorses, and his choice of twenty Trojan women when the war was won. These, apart from the horses, were the utilitarian gifts. But Agamemnon began with none of them; first came "seven tripods that have never been on the fire and ten talents of gold and twenty glittering caldrons," and further on, from the anticipated Trojan spoils, as much gold and bronze as his ship would hold (Iliad 9.121–56).[1] That was treasure, and its high importance is marked by the care with which it is enumerated here and again later in the poem. Menelaus's gift to Telemachus, all treasure, reappears four more times in the *Odyssey,* in three different books.

Whatever its purpose or its source, metal created for the individual *oikos* a special problem in the distribution of goods. For the most part distribution was internal and hence no problem at all. Since there has never been a world of Robinson Crusoes, the simplest human groups perforce have a mechanism, and it is the same one that served, with some extension, even the most elaborate princely *oikos*. All the productive work, the seeding and harvesting and milling and weaving, even the hunting and raiding, though performed by individuals, was carried on in behalf of the household as a whole. The final products, ready for consumption, were gathered and stored centrally, and

---

[1] In Plato's will, preserved by Diogenes Laeritus, *Lives* 3.41–43, the itemized bequest included "three minas of silver, a silver bowl weighing 165 drachmas, a small cup weighing 45 drachmas, a gold ring and gold earrings weighing 4½ drachmas together." This is treasure, now narrowed to gold and silver, and, like Agamemnon's, it is made up indifferently of metal and metal objects.

from the center they were redistributed—in the authoritarian household, by its head at a time and in a measure he deemed appropriate.

It made no difference in essence whether the family members within the household were no more than a husband, wife, and child, or whether the *oikos* was that of King Priam of Troy, with his fifty sons and their wives, twelve daughters and their husbands, and his uncounted grandchildren; or the more reasonable example of Nestor at Pylos, with six sons and some sons-in-law. The sons possessed arms and treasure of their own, from gifts and booty, as the wives and daughters had their fine garments and jewels. But unless the males left the paternal household and established their own *oikoi,* their personal property was an essentially insignificant factor. Normally, the poems seem to say, although the evidence is not altogether clear and consistent, the sons remained with their father in his lifetime.

Architecturally the heart of the system was the storeroom. Preparing for his journey to Pylos, Telemachus "went down to his father's spacious, high-ceilinged storeroom, where gold and copper lay piled up, and clothing in chests, and fragrant oil in plenty; and there stood jars of wine, old and sweet, filled with the unmixed divine drink, close together in a row along the wall" (Odyssey 2.337–42). And of course it contained arms and grain in quantity. More than three hundred years after Homer the Athenian Xenophon, a gentleman farmer and no tribal chieftain or king, still placed proper care of the storeroom high on the list of wifely virtues.

It was when distribution had to cross *oikos* lines that the creation of new and special devices became necessary. Wars and raids for booty, indistinguishable in the eyes of Odysseus' world, were organized affairs, often involving a combination of families, occasionally even of communities. Invariably there was a captain, one of whose functions was to act as the head and distribute the booty, all of which was first brought to a central storage point. Division was by lot, much like the division of an inheritance when there were several heirs. For example, not all of Odysseus' homecoming , adventures were tragic. Two or three times he and his men had the pleasant opportunity to raid. "From Ilion," he began the account of his wanderings, "the wind bore me near to the Cicones, to Ismarus. There I sacked the city and killed the men; taking the women and many goods, we divided them, so that no one might go cheated of his share through me" (Odyssey 9.39–42).[2]

Forcible seizure, followed by distribution in this fashion, was one way to acquire metal or other goods from an outside source. Some scholars think that the kernel of historical truth in the tale of the Trojan War is precisely such a mass raid for iron supplies. Whether they are right or not, there were surely many smaller Trojan wars to such a purpose, against Greeks as well as against barbarians. But the violent solution was neither always feasible nor even always desirable; if the aggrieved party were strong enough it invited retaliation, and there were times and conditions when even the fiercest of the heroes preferred peace. An exchange mechanism was then the only alternative, and the basic one was gift-exchange. This was no Greek invention. On the contrary, it is the basic organizing mechanism among many primitive peoples, as in the Trobriand Islands, where "most if not all economic acts are found to belong to some chain of reciprocal gifts and counter-gifts" (Malinowski 1952:40).

The word "gift" is not to be misconstrued. It may be stated as a flat rule of both primitive and archaic society that no one ever gave anything, whether goods or services or honors, without proper recompense, real or wishful, immediate or years away, to himself or to his kin. The act of giving was, therefore, in an essential sense always the first half of a reciprocal action, the other half of which was a counter-gift.

Not even the parting gift was an exception, although in this one instance there was an element of risk. The last of the recognition scenes in the *Odyssey,* between the hero and his aged father, began in the customary fashion, with Odysseus claiming to be someone else, a stranger from another land in search of information about "Odysseus." Your son, he said to Laertes, visited me about five years ago and received the proper gifts. "Of well-wrought gold I gave him seven talents, and I gave him a bowl with flower designs, all of silver, and twelve single cloaks and as many carpets and as many fine mantles, and as many tunics besides, and in addition four pretty women skilled in excellent work." Laertes wept, for he had long been satisfied that

---

[2] The final line also appears in the *Iliad,* 11.705.

his son had perished, and he could think of no better way to reveal that fact to the stranger than by commenting on the gift situation. "The countless gifts which you gave, you bestowed in vain. For if you had found that man still alive in the land of Ithaca, he would have sent you on your way well provided with gifts in return" (Odyssey 24.274–85).

Then there is the interesting scene in the opening book of the *Odyssey,* in which the goddess Athena appeared to Telemachus in the shape of Mentes, a Taphian chieftain. When she was ready to part, the young man followed the expected custom: "Go to your ship happy in your heart, bearing a gift, valuable and very beautiful, which will be your treasure from me, such as dear guest-friends give to guest-friends."[3] This created a very delicate situation for the goddess. One did not refuse a proffered gift, yet she could not accept it under the false pretense of her human disguise. (Gods as gods not only accepted gifts from mortals, they expected and demanded them.) Being the cleverest of the gods, Athena unhesitatingly found the perfect solution. "Do not detain me any longer as I am eager to be on my way. The gift, which the heart of a friend prompts you to give me, give it to me on my return journey that I may carry it home; choose a very beautiful one, that will bring you a worthy one in exchange" (Odyssey 1.311–18).

Telemachus had said nothing about a counter-gift. Yet he and "Mentes" understood each other perfectly: the counter-gift was as expected as the original gift at parting. That was what gift-giving was in this society. The return need not be forthcoming at once, and it might take several forms. But come it normally would. "In a society ruled by respect for the past, a traditional gift is very near indeed to an obligation" (Bloch 1941: 262).[4] No single detail in the life of the heroes receives so much attention in the *Illiad* and the *Odyssey* as gift-giving, and always there is frank reference to adequacy, appropriateness, recompense. "But then Zeus son of Cronus took from Glaucus his wits, in that he exchanged golden armor with Diomedes son of Tydeus for one of bronze, the worth of a hundred oxen for the worth of nine oxen" (Iliad 6.234–36). The poet's editorial comment, so

---

[3] "Guest-friend" is explained in the latter part of Chapter IV.

[4] Bloch is discussing the early Germanic world described by Tacitus.

rare for him, reflects the magnitude of Glaucus's mistake in judgment.

There was scarcely a limit to the situations in which gift-giving was operative. More precisely, the word "gift" was a cover-all for a great variety of actions and transactions which later became differentiated and acquired their own appellations. There were payments for services rendered, desired, or anticipated; what we would call fees, rewards, prizes, and sometimes bribes. The formulaic material was rich in such references, as in the lines with which Telemachus and twice Penelope responded to a stranger's favorable interpretation of a sign from the gods: "Stranger, would that these words be fulfilled! Speedily should you become aware of friendship and many gifts from me, so that whoever met you would congratulate you" (Odyssey 15.536–38, 17.163–65, 19.309–11).

Then there were taxes and other dues to lords and kings, amends with a penal overtone (Agamemnon's gift to Achilles), and even ordinary loans—and again the Homeric word is always "gift." Defending himself for having lent Telemachus a ship with which to sail to Pylos and Sparta seeking information about Odysseus, a young Ithacan noble made this explanation: "What can one do when such a man, troubled in heart, begs? It would be difficult to refuse the gift" (Odyssey 4.649–51). In still another category payment for service was combined with the ceremonialism necessary to an important event. There is much talk in the *Odyssey* about the "gifts of wooing," and the successful suitor, who reminds one of nothing so much as the highest bidder at an auction, in turn received his counter-gift in the dowry, which normally accompanied the bride. The whole of what we call foreign relations and diplomacy, in their peaceful manifestations, was conducted by gift-exchange. And even in war occasions presented themselves, as between Diomedes and Glaucus, for example, or Ajax and Hector, when heroes from the two contending sides stopped, right on the field of combat and before the approving eyes of their fellow heroes, and exchanged armor.

Odyssean trade differed from the various forms of gift-exchange in that the exchange of goods was the end itself. In trade things changed hands because each needed what the other had, and not, or only incidentally, to compensate for a service, seal an alliance, or support a friendship. A need for some specific object was the ground for the transaction; if it could be satisfied by other means, trade was altogether unnecessary. Hence, in modern parlance, imports alone motivated trade, never exports. There was never a need to export as such, only the necessity of having the proper goods for the counter-gift when an import was unavoidable.

Laertes bought Eurycleia "with (some of) his possessions . . . , and he gave the worth of twenty oxen" (Odyssey 1.430–31). Cattle were the measuring stick of worth; in that respect, and only in that sense, cattle were money. Neither cattle, however, nor anything else served for the various other, later uses of money. Above all, there was no circulating medium like a coin, the sole function of which was to make purchase and sale possible by being passed from hand to hand. Almost any useful object served, and it is noteworthy that the measure of value, cattle, did not itself function as a medium of exchange. Laertes bought Eurycleia for unspecified objects worth twenty oxen; he would never have traded the oxen for a slave.

A conventional measuring stick is no more than an artificial language, a symbol like the X, Y, Z of algebra. By itself it cannot decide how much iron is the equivalent of one cow, or how much wine. In Adam Smith's world that determination was made through the supply-and-demand market, a mechanism utterly unknown in Troy or Ithaca. Behind the market lies the profit motive, and if there was one thing that was taboo in Homeric exchanges it was gain in the exchange. Whether in trade or in any other mutual relationship, the abiding principle was equality and mutual benefit. Gain at the expense of another belonged to a different realm, to warfare and raiding, where it was achieved by acts (or threats) of prowess, not by manipulating and bargaining.

The implication that exchange rates were customary and conventional seems unavoidable. That is to say, there was no constituted authority with the power to decree a set of equations—so much of X for so much of Y. Rather the actual practice of exchange over a long period of time had fixed the ratios, and they were commonly known and respected. Even in the distribution of booty, where a central authority, the head of the *oikos* or a king or commander-in-chief, took charge, he was obviously bound by what was generally deemed to be equitable. The circumstance that no one could punish him for flouting custom, as in the conflict between Agamemnon and Achilles, is irrelevant to the issue. For the very fact that just such a situation gave the theme for the *Iliad* illustrates how dangerous the violation could be. In this world custom was as binding upon the individual as the most rigid statutory law of later days. And the participant in an exchange, it may be added, had the advantage over the passive participant in the distribution of booty. He could always refuse to go through with the transaction if the rules were manifestly being upset, or if he merely thought they were.

None of this is to say that no one ever deliberately profited from an exchange. But the exceptional instance is far less noteworthy than the essential point that, in a strict sense, the ethics of the world of Odysseus prohibited the practice of trade as a vocation. The test of what was and what was not acceptable did not lie in the act of trading, but in the status of the trader and in his approach to the transaction. So crucial was the need for metal that even a king could honorably voyage in its search. When Athena appeared to Telemachus as Mentes, the Taphian chieftain, her story was that she was carrying iron to Temesa in quest of copper.[5] That gave no difficulties, and her visit ended with the colloquy regarding costly gifts between guest-friends.

A stranger with a ship was not always so welcome or so free from suspicion. He might have been Odysseus before Ismarus, or Achilles: "Twelve cities of men have I destroyed from shipboard and eleven on foot, I say, in the fertile region of Troy; from all these I took out much good treasure" (Iliad 9.328–31). No wonder that some Greeks eventually objected to Homer as the teacher of the Hellenes. Glorification of piracy, disapproval of theft (seizure of goods by stealth), and encouragement of robbery (seizure of goods and persons by physical prowess)—truly this seemed a world of mixed-up moral standards. "Theft of property is mean," protested Plato, "seizure by force shameless; none of the sons of Zeus delighted in fraud or violence, nor practiced either. Therefore, let no one be falsely persuaded by poets or by some myth-tellers in these matters" (Law 941B).

[5] Neither Taphos nor Temesa is otherwise known as a place name, and the many attempts, all failures, to identify them with one or another mining region illustrate once again the futility of such "historicizing" of the Homeric poems.

Yet there was a pattern and a consistency in the moral code;
and it made sense from the premises. The distinctions rested on
a specific social structure, with strongly entrenched notions regarding the proper ways for a man to behave, with respect to
property, toward other men. Upon his arrival among the Phaeacians, but before he had identified himself and told of his wanderings, Odysseus was entertained by King Alcinous. Following
the feast, the younger nobles competed in athletics. After a time
the king's son Laodamas approached Odysseus and invited him
to participate.

"Come, stranger and father, you enter the games, if perchance
you are skilled in any; you seem to know games. For there is no
greater fame for a man, so long as he is alive, than that which is
made by foot and hand."

Odysseus asked to be excused, pleading the heavy burden of
his sorrows. Another young aristocrat then interposed. "No indeed, stranger, I do not think you are like a man of games, such
as there are many among men; but like one who travels with a
many-benched ship, a master of sailors who traffic, one who re-
members the cargo and is in charge of merchandise and coveted
gains" (Odyssey 8.145–64).

The insult was unbearable under all circumstances, and to
Homer's audience it must have carried an added barb when directed against Odysseus. There was something equivocal about
Odysseus as a hero precisely because of his most famed quality,
his craftiness. There was even a soft spot in his inheritance: his
maternal grandfather, the goodly Autolycus, "surpassed all men
in thievishness and the oath, for that was a gift to him from the
god Hermes" (Odyssey 19.395–97). Later the doubts of many
Greeks turned to open contempt and condemnation. "I know full
well," says Philoctetes in the Sophoclean play, "that he would
attempt with his tongue every evil word and villainy" (Philoctetes
407–408). What saved the Homeric Odysseus was the fact that
his guile was employed in the pursuit of heroic goals; hence
Hermes, the god of tricks and stealth, may have given him the
magic with which to ward off Circe the witch, but it was Athena
who was his protector and his inspiration in his heroic exploits.
To the insult in Phaeacia he first replied with an indignant
speech, but Odysseus, of all men, could not establish his status
with words. Having finished his reply, he leaped up, seized a

weight greater than any the young men had cast, and, without removing his garment, threw it far beyond their best mark.

Possibly there were men, a very few from among those who were not men of games, living in the interstices of society, who traveled in many-benched ships and trafficked. Yet there is no single word in either the *Iliad* or the *Odyssey* that is in fact a synonym for "merchant." By and large, the provisioning of the Greek world with whatever it obtained from the outside by peaceful means was in the hands of non-Greeks, the Phoenicians in particular. They were really a trading people, who sailed from one end of the known world to the other, carrying slaves, metal, jewelry, and fine cloth. If they were motivated by gain—"famed for ships, greedy men" (Odyssey 15.415–16)—that was irrelevant to the Greeks, the passive participants in the operation.

The need for metal, or any similar need, was an *oikos* affair, not an individual matter. Its acquisition, whether by trade or by raid, was therefore a household enterprise, managed by the head. Or it could be larger in scale, involving many households acting cooperatively. Internally, the situation was altogether different. Trade within the household was impossible by definition: the *oikos* was a single, indivisible unit. Because a large sector of the population was enmeshed in the great households, it too was withdrawn from any possibility of trade, external or internal. The *thetes,* finally, were absolutely excluded; having nothing, they had nothing to exchange.

That leaves the non-aristocratic, small-scale herders and peasants. In their households shortages were chronic, if not absolute as a consequence of a crop failure or a disaster to their flocks, then partial because of an imbalance in the yield. Their troubles are not the subject of heroic poetry, and neither the *Iliad* nor the *Odyssey* is informative in this regard. The inference is permissible, however, that some of their difficulties were alleviated by barter, primarily with one another, and without the instrumentality of a market or fair, absolutely unknown in this world. They exchanged necessities, staples, undoubtedly on the same principles of equivalence, ratios fixed by custom, and no gain.

Herders and peasants, including the *thetes,* always had another resource to draw upon. They could work. As with trade, so with labor, the society's moral judgment was directed not to the act itself but to the person and the circumstance. Back in Ithaca, but still disguised as a beggar, Odysseus, in reply to Eurymachus's mocking offer of employment, challenged the suitor to a plowing contest—just as, in his proper guise, he boasted of his superior bowmanship or his weight throwing. But Odysseus was not required to plow in order to live. In fact, it is obvious that, though he knew how to till and herd and build a raft, he rarely did any work on his estate except in sport. That was the great dividing line, between those who were compelled to labor and those who were not. Among the former, the men with the inspired skills, the bards and the metalworkers and the others, were an elite. Above all, the test was this, that "the condition of the free man is that he not live under the constraint of another."[6] Hence there was a sharp line between those who, though they worked, remained their own masters, the independent herders and peasants, and on the other side the *thetes* and the slaves who labored for others, whose livelihood was not in their own hands. The slaves, at least, were usually the victims of chance. The *thes* was in that sense the worst of all: he voluntarily contracted away his control over his own labor, in other words, his true freedom.

Much of the psychology of labor, with its ambivalence between admiration of skill and craft and its rejection of the laborer as essentially and irretrievably an inferior being, found its symbol on Olympus. Having humanized the gods, the bard was consistent enough to include labor among the heavenly pursuits. But that entailed a certain difficulty. Zeus the insatiable philanderer, Apollo the archer who was also a minstrel, Ares the god of battle—these were all embodiments of noble attributes and activities, easily re-created in man's image. But how could the artisan who built their palaces and made their weapons and their plate and their ornaments be placed on equal footing with them, without casting a shadow over the hierarchy of values and status on which society rested? Only a god could make swords for gods, yet somehow he must be a being apart from the other gods.

The solution was neatly turned, very neatly indeed. The divine craftsman was Hephaestus, son of Hera. His skill was truly fabulous, and the poet never tired of it, lingering over his forge and his productions as he never sang of the smith in Ithaca. That was the positive side of the ambivalence. The other was this: of

[6] Aristotle, *Rhetoric* 1.9, 1367a32, writing with specific reference to labor.

all the gods, Hephaestus alone was "a huge limping monster" with "a sturdy neck and hairy chest" (Iliad 18.410–15). Hephaestus was born lame, and he carried the mark of his shame on his whole personality. The other gods would have been less than human, in consequence, were Hephaestus not to be their perennial source of humor. Once, when Zeus and Hera were having a fearful quarrel, the limping god attempted the role of peacemaker, filling the cups with nectar for all the assemblage. "And unquenchable laughter was stirred up among the blessed gods as they watched Hephaestus bustling about the palace" (Iliad 1.599–600). And the social fabric of the world of Odysseus was saved.

In fact, the mirror-image on Olympus was still more subtle. In art and craftsmanship, Athena was frequently linked with Hephaestus, as in the simile in which a comparison is drawn with a goldsmith, "a skillful man whom Hephaestus and Pallas Athena taught all kinds of craft (*techne*)" (Odyssey 6.232–34). But there was absolutely nothing deformed or the least bit comical about Athena, deservedly her father's favorite among the gods. It was unnecessary to apologize for Athena's skill with her hands, for the pattern with respect to work differed somewhat for women. Denied the right to a heroic way of life, to feats of prowess, competitive games, and leadership in organized activity of any kind, women worked, regardless of class. With her maids, Nausicaa, daughter of the Phaeacian king, did the household laundry. Queen Penelope found in her weaving the trick with which to hold off the suitors. Her stratagem, however, of undoing at night what she had woven in the day, repeated without detection for three full years until one of her maids revealed the secret, suggests that her labor was not exactly indispensable. The women of the aristocracy, like their men, possessed all the necessary work skills, and they used them more often. Nevertheless, their real role was managerial. The house was their domain, the cooking and the washing, the cleaning and the clothesmaking. The dividing line for them was rather in the degree to which they performed the chores themselves—between those who supervised, working only to pass the time, and those whom circumstances compelled to cook and sew in earnest.

22 ASPECTS OF MEDIEVAL EUROPEAN ECONOMY

Henri Pirenne

INTRODUCTION

It is quite plain, from such evidence as we possess, that from the end of the eighth century Western Europe had sunk back into a purely agricultural state. Land was the sole source of subsistence and the sole condition of wealth. All classes of the population, from the Emperor, who had no other revenues than those derived from his landed property, down to the humblest serf, lived directly or indirectly on the products of the soil, whether they raised them by their labour, or confined themselves to collecting and consuming them. Movable wealth no longer played any part in economic life. All social existence was founded on property or on the possession of land. Hence it was impossible for the State to keep up a military system and an administration which were not based on it. The army was now recruited only from among the holders of fiefs and the officials from among the great landowners. In these circumstances, it became impossible to safeguard the sovereignty of the head of the State. If it existed in principle, it disappeared in practice. The feudal system simply represents the disintegration of public authority in the hands of its agents, who, by reason of the very fact that each one of them held a portion of the soil, had become independent and considered the authority with which they were invested as a part of their patrimony. In fact, the appearance of feudalism in Western Europe in the course of the ninth century

FROM Henri Pirenne, *Economic and Social History of Medieval Europe,* pp. 7–15, 58–67, and 97–103. Reprinted by permission of the English publisher Routledge & Kegan Paul, Ltd., and of the American publisher, Harcourt, Brace, & World, Inc.

was nothing but the repercussion in the political sphere of the return of society to a purely rural civilisation.

From the economic point of view the most striking and characteristic institution of this civilisation is the great estate. Its origin is, of course, much more ancient and it is easy to establish its affiliation with a very remote past. There were great landowners in Gaul long before Caesar, just as there were in Germany long before the invasions. The Roman Empire allowed the great Gallic estates to stand and they very rapidly adapted themselves to the organisation which prevailed on the estates of the conquerors. The Gallic *villa* of the imperial era, with its reserve set apart for the proprietor and numerous holdings of *coloni,* represents the same type of exploitation as that described by the Italian agronomists in the time of Cato. It went through the period of the Germanic invasions with hardly a change, Merovingian France preserved it and the Church introduced it beyond the Rhine, step by step as the lands there were converted to Christianity.[1]

Thus the organisation of the great estate was not, in any respect, a new fact. But what was new was the way in which it functioned from the moment of the disappearance of commerce and the towns. So long as the former had been capable of transporting its products and the latter of furnishing it with a market, the great estate had commanded and consequently profited by a regular sale outside. It participated in the general economic activity as a producer of foodstuffs and a consumer of manufactured articles. In other words, it carried on a reciprocal exchange with the outside world. But now it ceased to do this, because there were no more merchants and townsmen. To whom could it sell, when there were no longer any buyers, and where was it to dispose of a produce for which there was no demand, because it was no longer needed? Now that everyone lived off his own land, no one bothered to buy food from outside, and for sheer want of demand, the landowner was obliged to consume his own produce. Thus, each estate devoted itself to the kind of economy which has been described rather inexactly as the "closed estate economy," and which was really simply an economy without markets. It did so not from choice but from necessity, not because it did not want to sell, but because buyers no longer came

---

[1] For all this I am content to refer the reader to the excellent account by M. Bloch, *Les charactères originaux de l'histoire rurale française,* p. 67 et seq.

within its range. The lord made arrangements not only to live on his demesne and the dues of his peasants, but also to produce at home, since he could not procure them elsewhere, the tools and garments which he needed for the cultivation of his lands and the clothing of his servants. Hence the establishment of those workshops or "gynaeceas," so characteristic of the estate organisation of the early Middle Ages, which were simply designed to make up for the absence of commerce and industry.

It is obvious that such a state of things inevitably exposed men to all the hazards of climate. If the harvest chanced to fail, the supplies laid up against a scarcity were soon exhausted and it was necessary to tax all one's wits to get the indispensable grain. Then serfs were sent round the countryside to get it from some more fortunate neighbour, or in some region where abundance reigned. In order to provide them with money the lord caused his plate to be melted down at the nearest mint, or ran into debt with the abbot of a neighbouring monastery. Thus, under the influence of atmospheric phenomena, a spasmodic and occasional commerce existed and kept up an intermittent traffic on the roads and waterways. Similarly, in years of prosperity people sought to sell the surplus of their vintage or their harvest in the same way. Finally salt, a condiment necessary to life, was found only in certain regions, where they had perforce to go and get it. But there is nothing in all this that can be regarded as commercial activity, in the specific and professional sense. The merchant was, so to speak, improvised at the will of circumstances. Sale and purchase were not the normal occupation of anyone; they were expedients to which people had recourse when obliged by necessity. Commerce had so completely ceased to be one of the branches of social activity that each estate aimed at supplying all its own needs. This is why we see abbeys situated in regions without vineyards, such as the Low Countries, leaving no stone unturned in their efforts to obtain the gift of estates in the Seine basin, or in the valleys of the Rhine and the Moselle, so as to be sure each year of replenishing their wine-cellars.[2]

The large number of markets might seem at first sight to contradict the commercial paralysis of the age, for from the beginning of the ninth century they increased rapidly and new ones

---

[2] H. Van Werveke, *Comment les établissements religieux belges se procuraient-ils du vin au haut Moyen Age?* in Revue belge de phiol. et d'hist., t. II (1923), p. 643 et seq.

were continually being founded. But their number is itself proof of their insignificance. Only the fair of St. Denys, near Paris (the fair of Lendit), attracted once a year, among its pilgrims, occasional sellers and buyers from a distance. Apart from it there were only innumerable small weekly markets, where the peasants of the district offered for sale a few eggs, chickens, pounds of wool, or ells of coarse cloth woven at home. The nature of the business transacted appears quite clearly from the fact that people sold *per deneratas,* that is to say, by quantities not exceeding a few pence in value.[3] In short, the utility of these small assemblies was limited to satisfying the household needs of the surrounding population, and also, no doubt, as among the Kabyles to-day, to satisfying that instinct of sociability which is inherent in all men. They constituted the sole distraction offered by a society settled in work on the land. Charlemagne's order to the serfs on his estates not to "run about to markets" shows that they were attracted much more by the desire to enjoy themselves than by considerations of trade.[4]

Thus we seek in vain for professional merchants. None existed, or rather none but the Jews, who alone, from the beginning of the Carolingian era, carried on a regular commerce, so much so that the words *Judaeus* and *mercator* appear almost synonymous. A certain number of them were settled in the south, but the majority came from the Moslem countries of the Mediterranean and reached Western and Northern Europe through Spain. They were the Radanites, perpetual travellers who still kept up a superficial contact with Oriental countries.[5] The commerce in which they engaged was, moreover, exclusively that of spices and precious stuffs, which they laboriously transported from Syria, Egypt, and Byzantium to the Carolingian Empire. Through them, a church could procure the incense indispensable to the celebration of the divine offices, and, at long intervals, those rich fabrics of which cathedral treasuries have preserved occasional specimens down to our own day. They imported pepper, a condiment which had become so rare and dear that it was sometimes used instead of money, and enamels or ivories of oriental manufacture, which formed the luxuries of the aristocracy. Thus the Jewish merchants addressed themselves to a very limited clientèle. The

---

[3] *Edictum Pistense,* 20. Boretius, *Capitularia,* t. II, p. 319.

[4] *Capitulaire de Villis,* 54. *Ibid.,* t. I, p. 88.

[5] On the Jews see the *Livre des routes et des pays* of Ibn Khordadbeh (about 850), translated by Barbier de Maynard, *Journal asiatique,* 1865.

profits which they realised must have been substantial, but when full allowance is made for this, their economic rôle cannot be considered as anything but that of accessories. Society lost nothing essential by their disappearance.

Thus, from every point of view, Western Europe, from the ninth century onwards, appears in the light of an essentially rural society, in which exchange and the movement of goods had sunk to the lowest possible ebb. The merchant class had disappeared. A man's condition was now determined by his relation to the land, which was owned by a minority of lay and ecclesiastical proprietors, below whom a multitude of tenants were distributed within the framework of the great estates. To possess land was at the same time to possess freedom and power; thus the landowner was also a lord. To be deprived of it, was to be reduced to serfdom; thus the word *vilain* was used both for the peasant living on a domain (*villa*) and for the serf. It is of no importance that here and there among the rural population a few individuals happened to preserve their land and consequently their personal liberty. As a general rule serfdom was the normal condition of the agricultural masses, that is to say, of all the masses. There were, of course, many gradations in this serfdom, for, side by side with men who were still not far removed from the slavery of antiquity, there were to be found descendants of small dispossessed proprietors who had voluntarily commended themselves to the protection of the great. The essential fact was not their legal but their social condition, and socially all who lived on seigneurial soil were now dependents, at once exploited and protected.

In this strictly hierarchical society, the first place, and the most important, belonged to the Church, which possessed at once economic and moral ascendancy. Its innumerable estates were as superior in extent to those of the nobility, as it was itself superior to them in learning. The Church alone, moreover, thanks to the gifts of the faithful and the alms of pilgrims, had at its disposal financial resources which allowed it, in times of scarcity, to lend to necessitous laymen. Furthermore, in a society which had relapsed into general ignorance, it alone still retained those two indispensable instruments of culture, reading and writing, and it was from churchmen that kings and princes had necessarily to recruit their chancellors, their secretaries, their "notaries," in short, the whole lettered personnel without which it was impossible for them to function. From the ninth to the eleventh century the whole business of government was, in fact, in the hands of the church, which was supreme here, as in the arts. The organisation of its estates was a model which the estates of the nobility sought in vain to equal, for only in the Church were there men capable of drawing up *polyptycha,* keeping registers of accounts, reckoning up receipts and expenditure, and, consequently, balancing them. Thus, the Church was not only the great moral authority of the age, but also the great financial power.

Moreover, the Church's conception of the world was admirably adapted to the economic conditions of an age in which land was the sole foundation of the social order. Land had been given by God to men in order to enable them to live here below with a view to their eternal salvation. The object of labour was not to grow wealthy but to maintain oneself in the position in which one was born, until mortal life should pass into life eternal. The monk's renunciation was the ideal on which the whole of society should fix its gaze. To seek riches was to fall into the sin of avarice. Poverty was of divine origin and ordained by Providence, but it behoved the rich to relieve it by charity, of which the monasteries gave them an example. Let the surplus of their harvests, then, be garnered and distributed freely, just as the abbeys themselves advanced freely sums borrowed from them in cases of need.

"Mutuum date nihil inde sperantes." Lending at interest, or "usury" (to employ the technical term used for it, which now took on the derogatory meaning which it has retained down to our own day), was an abomination. It had been forbidden from the very beginning to the clergy, and from the ninth century the Church succeeded in prohibiting it also to the laity and in reserving it for the jurisdiction of ecclesiastical courts. Moreover, commerce in general was hardly less disreputable than commerce in money, for it too was dangerous to the soul, which it turned away from the contemplation of its latter end. *"Homo mercator vix aut nunquam potest Deo placere."*[6]

It is easy to see how well these principles harmonised with the facts and how easily the ecclesiastical ideal adapted itself to reality. It provided the justification for a state of things by which

---

[6] K. Goldschmidt, *Universalgeschichte des Handelsrechts,* t. I, p. 139 (Stuttgart, 1891).

the Church itself was the first to benefit. What was more natural than the reprobation of usury, commerce, and profit for profit's sake, in those centuries when each estate was self-supporting and normally constituted a little world of its own? And what could have been more beneficent, when we remember that famine alone compelled men to borrow from their neighbours and hence would at once have opened the door to every abuse of speculation, usury and monopoly, to the irresistible temptation to exploit necessity, if these very abuses had not been condemned by religious morality? Of course, theory and practice are miles apart and the monasteries themselves very often transgressed the Church's order. But, for all that, so deeply did it impress its spirit upon the world, that it took men centuries to grow used to the new practices demanded by the economic revival of the future and to learn to accept as legitimate, without too great a mental reservation, commercial profits, the employment of capital, and loans at interest.

The Land and the Rural Classes

I. MANORIAL ORGANISATION AND SERFDOM[7]

The influence of the bourgeoisie in every period of the Middle Ages, is all the more surprising because it is in strong contrast

[7] Bibliography: To the works by Inama-Sternegg, Lamprecht, H. Sée and M. Bloch, mentioned in the general bibliography, should be added K. Lamprecht, *Étude sur l'état économique de la France pendant la première partie du Moyen Age*, trans. Marignan, Paris, 1889.—L. Delisle, *Études sur la condition de la classe agricole et l'état de l'agriculture en Normandie au Moyen Age*, Paris, 2nd ed., 1903.—A. Hansay, *Étude sur la formation et l'organisation économique du domaine de Saint-Trond jusqu'à la fin du XIII⁰ siècle*, Gand, 1899.—L. Verriest, *Le Servage dans la comte de Hainaut. Les sainteurs. Le meilleur catel*, Brussels, 1910 (Mém. de L'Académie de Belgique).—G. des Marez, *Note sur le manse brabançon au Moyen Age*, in *Mélanges Pirenne*, Brussels, 1926.—F. Seebohm, *The English Village Community*, London, 1883.—P. Vinogradoff, *The Growth of the Manor*, London, 1905.—*Id.*, *English Society in the Eleventh Century*, Oxford, 1908.—G. G. Coulton, *The Medieval Village*, Cambridge, 1925.— G. F. Knapp, *Grundherrschaft und Rittergut*, Leipzig, 1897.—W. Wittich, *Die Grundherrschaft in Nordwestdeutschland*, Leipzig, 1896.—O. Siebock, *Der Frondienst als Arbeitssystem*, Tübingen, 1904.—R. Gaggese, *Classi e communi rurali nel medio den boerenstand en den landbouw in Nederland*, Groningen, 1902–4, 2 vols.—G. Roupnel, *Histoire de la campagne française*, Paris, 1932.—M. Bloch, *Liberté et servitude personnelles au Moyen Age, particulièrement en France*, in *Annario de Historia del Derecho Español*, 1933.—C. E. Perrin, *Recherches sur la seigneurie rurale en Lorraine*, Paris, 1935.

with its numerical importance. The towns contained a minority, sometimes even a very small minority of the population. In the absence of statistical data prior to the fifteenth century no precise numerical estimate can, of course, be formed, but we shall probably not be far wrong in supposing that in the whole of Europe between the twelfth and the fifteenth centuries the urban population never comprised more than a tenth part of the total number of inhabitants.[8] It was only in a few districts, such as the Low Countries, Lombardy or Tuscany, that this proportion was exceeded to any large extent. In any case, it is an undoubted fact that from the demographic point of view, medieval society was essentially agricultural.

Upon this rural society the great estate set so deep a mark that in many countries its traces did not disappear until the first half of the nineteenth century. We need not here go back to the origin of this institution, which the Middle Ages inherited from antiquity. All that is necessary is to describe it as it existed at its height in the course of the twelfth century, that is to say, at a time when it had not yet begun to change owing to the influence of the towns.[9] It is, perhaps, unnecessary to add that the manorial organisation was not imposed on all the rural population. It spared a certain number of small free proprietors, and in isolated districts we meet with villages which more or less escaped its control. But those are only exceptions which need not be considered in a broad outline of the general evolution of Western Europe.

From the point of view of size, the great medieval estates amply justified the name. They seem to have contained on an average three hundred farms (*mansi*), or about 10,000 acres, and many of them were undoubtedly considerably larger. But their lands were never all together. They were always scattered. The "villas" of the same landowner were separated by greater

---

[8] F. Lot, *L'État des pariosses et des feux de 1328*, in the *Bibliothèque de l'École des Chartes*, t. XC (1929), p. 301, holds that at the beginning of the fourteenth century the urban population of France constituted between one-tenth and one-seventh of the total population. But, for Brabant, J. Cuvelier, *Les denombrements de foyers en Brabant*, p. cxxxv, states that in 1437 two-thirds of the houses in the whole duchy were to be found in the countryside.

[9] It is hardly necessary to call attention to the fact that since manorial organisation differed in different parts of Europe, it can only be described here in a very general way, only the main and typical features being outlined.

and greater distances, the further they lay from the manorial centre. The monastery of Saint-Trond, for example, was the lord of a vast property, the bulk of which was grouped around it, but which had distant annexes, as far north as the environs of Nimwegen and as far south as those of Trier.[10] This scattering naturally resulted in a considerable interweaving of manors, to such an extent that the same village often owed allegiance to two or three lords. The situation was still further complicated when an estate extended, as frequently happened, to regions under the rule of several princes, or to territories speaking different languages. This situation was the result of the building up of territorial agglomerations by means of successive gifts from a multitude of benefactors, in the case of the Church, or by the accident of matrimonial alliances or of inheritance, in that of the nobility. No uniform design had brought about the formation of the large estate; it was what history had made it, independent of all economic considerations.

Scattered though it was, it nevertheless possessed a powerful organisation, which in essentials seems to have been the same in all countries. The centre of the estate was the customary residence of the landowner, whether it was cathedral, church, abbey or fortified castle. The whole of the land was parcelled out into a number of divisions, each of which contained one or more villages (*villae*) and was under the jurisdiction of a *curtis* (*cour* in the countries of the Romance tongue, *hof* in those of the German, and *manor* in England). Here were grouped the farm buildings, barns, cattle-sheds, stables, etc., as well as the domestic serfs (*servi quotidiani, dagescalci*) employed in looking after them. Here also lived the agent in charge of the administration, the *villicus* or *major* (*maire, mayeur* on the Continent; *seneschal, steward,* or *bailiff* in England), chosen from among the *ministeriales,* that is to say, the serfs attached as confidential men to the house of the lord. By virtue of the general evolution peculiar to the agricultural period of the Middle Ages, this agent, who in the beginning was liable to dismissal, soon came to have an hereditary right to his office.

The whole of the soil under the jurisdiction of a *cour* or manor was divided into three parts: the demesne, the tenants'

[10] See the map of this estate in the thirteenth century in Pirenne (1896).

holdings and the commons. The *demesne* (*terra indominicata, mansus indominicatus*) constituted the seigneurial reserve, and consisted of all the lands set apart for the exclusive use of the lord. It is impossible to determine exactly their proportional importance, which varied considerably in the different manors. As a general rule, they consisted of scattered strips lying among those of the tenants. The size of the tenants' holdings, on the other hand, showed a remarkable fixity in each *villa,* though they often differed very considerably in different regions. They comprised, in fact, the amount of land sufficient for the support of a family, with the result that they varied in size with the fertility of the soil.[11] They were known by the name of *mancus* (*manse, mas*), in Latin, *hufe* in German and *virgate* or *yardland* in English. All were burdened with labour services and dues (usually in kind) for the profit of the lord. All gave their occupant common rights of usage over the natural meadows, marshes, heath or forest which surrounded the cultivated soil and which are called *communia* or *warescapia* in the documents. Efforts have been made without success to find traces of so-called collective ownership in these common lands. In reality their ownership was vested in the lord.

With the exception of the lord, all who lived on the territory of a manor were either serfs or, so to speak, quasi-serfs. Though the slavery of the ancient world had disappeared, traces of it still remained in the status of the *servi quotidiani* and *mancipia,* whose very persons belonged to the lord, and who were attached to his service and kept by him. It was from among them that he recruited the labourers on his demesne, herdsmen, shepherds and the workpeople of both sexes whom he employed in the "gynaecea," under which name were indiscriminately grouped the workshops of the manorial *curtis,* where the flax and wool produced on the estate were woven, and where wheelwrights, blacksmiths, ale brewers and other artisans were also set to work. Personal serfdom was less marked among the tenants established, or (to use an expression general down to the twelfth century)

[11] According to the work of Des Marez, cited in the bibliography, the *manse* in Brabant consisted ordinarily of 10 to 12 *bonniers,* which, given the varying size of the *bonniers,* was equivalent to about 8 to 15 hectares (i.e., about 20 to 37½ acres). According to Mark Bloch (1935:159) the area of the forms in France fluctuated between 5 and 30 hectares, the average being about 13 hectares.

casati, on the holdings, though there were still a large number of
nuances. But in reality all in the end had acquired hereditary
possession of the land they cultivated, although many had held it
in the beginning by a very precarious title. Among them were
even to be found former freemen, whose liberty was very much
curtailed by the obligation to pay the labour services and dues
which weighed heavily on their holdings. On the monastic manors a privileged class had grown up in the midst of the manorial
population, *cerocensuales,* the descendants for the most part of
widowed women of free origin who had placed themselves under
the protection of an abbey, granting it the ownership of their
estates on condition that they themselves enjoyed the revenues,
in return for a payment of wax at the big annual church festivals.[12] Slightly different from the tenants, properly so-called,
were the cotters or bordars (*cotarii, bordarii*), serfs holding a
mere patch of ground, who were employed as agricultural labourers in the service of the lord or of the virgaters.

The dependence of the manorial population upon the lord was
still further increased by the fact that the latter exercised jurisdiction over them. All serfs were, without exception, amenable to
it, while the other tenants were not infrequently subject to the
common law courts, in the matter of crimes and misdemeanours.
The competence of seigneurial jurisdiction varied in the different
countries according to the extent of feudal encroachments on the
sovereignty of the king. It attained its maximum in France and
its minimum in England. But everywhere it extended at least to
all questions concerning holdings, labour services, dues and the
cultivation of the soil. Each manor had its court, composed of
peasants, presided over by the bailiff or *villicus* and giving judgment according to "the custom of the manor," that is to say, the
traditional usages which at long intervals the population, consulted by the lord, declared and set down in the custumals or
Weistümer.

Just as each manor formed a jurisdictional unity, so also it
formed a religious one. The lords had built near their principal
seat a chapel or a church, endowed with land, the incumbent of
which they themselves nominated. This was the origin of a very
large number of rural parishes, so that ecclesiastical organisation,

[12] In Hainault and the neighbouring regions they were called *sainteurs.*

whose dioceses have preserved for so long the boundaries of Roman "cities," sometimes still perpetuates to-day in the outline of its parishes, that of many a lordship of the early Middle Ages.

Thus the manor was not only an economic but a social institution. It imposed itself upon the whole life of its inhabitants. They were a good deal more than merely tenants of their lord; they were his men in every sense of the word, and it has been justly observed that seigneurial authority rested more on the attributes of chieftainship which it conferred on its possessor than on his attributes as a landed proprietor. The manorial organisation was essentially patriarchal. Language itself bears testimony to this. What was the *seigneur* (senior) if not the elder, whose authority extended over the *familia* whom he protected? For, unquestionably, he did protect them. In times of war he defended them against the enemy and sheltered them within the walls of his fortress, and it was clearly to his own advantage to do so, since he lived by their labour. The idea we are accustomed to form of seigneurial exploitation is perhaps a little summary. The exploitation of man implies the wish to make use of him as a tool to obtain the maximum of production. The rural slavery of the ancient world, that of the negroes in the colonies in the seventeenth and eighteenth centuries, or the condition of the workers in the great industry in the first half of the nineteenth century, furnish us with familiar examples. But all this is very different from the medieval manors, where all-powerful custom determined every man's rights and obligations. This fact alone was enough to prevent the pitiless severity to which the free exercise of economic supremacy gives rise under the spur of profit. Moreover, the whole idea of profit, and indeed the possibility of profit, was incompatible with the position occupied by the great medieval landowner. Unable to produce for sale owing to the want of a market, he had no need to tax his ingenuity in order to wring from his men and his land a surplus which would merely be an encumbrance, and as he was forced to consume his own produce, he was content to limit it to his needs. His means of existence was assured by the traditional functioning of an organisation which he did not try to improve. Before the middle of the twelfth century, the greater part of the soil belonging to him was given over to heaths, forests, and marshes. Nowhere do we

perceive the least effort to break with the age-old system of rotation, to suit the crops cultivated to the properties of the soil, or
to improve agricultural implements. Considering its potential capacity, the enormous landed capital at the disposal of the Church
and the nobility produced in the main no more than an insignificant return.

It would be interesting, though it is impossible, to discover
how much the peasants made on these manors which their
holders did not farm for profit, after working for a whole year
from one to three days a week on the lord's demesne and after
paying on the customary dates the dues in kind which burdened
their land. It must have been little, if anything. But this little
sufficed for men whose sole object, like that of their lord, was
to produce enough for their own needs. Free from all fear of
expulsion, since his land was hereditary, the *vilain* enjoyed the
advantage of security, but on the other hand the agrarian system
gave him neither the opportunity nor the desire for individual
exploitation. The system, indeed, of necessity entailed work in
common. This was the case with the two great methods of cultivation whose origin undoubtedly dates back to prehistoric times,
long strips or irregular fields. In both the rotation of cultivation,
whether the two-field or the three-field system was in use (that
is to say, whether one-half or one-third of the cultivable surface
lay fallow each year), imposed collective cultivation on all alike.
The same patches of the same *shot,* or *quartier,* or *gewann*
had to be ploughed together, sown, or given over to common
of shack after the harvest. The fact that they were intermingled
meant that they had to remain open up to the moment the corn
began to come up, when they were enclosed by a temporary
fence. After the harvest, the community did not lose its rights.
All the animals in the village were driven in a single herd to
pasture on the stubble of the ploughed fields, from which the
corn had been garnered and the fences removed.

In such a state of things, the activity of each depended
upon the activity of all and as long as it lasted economic
equality must have been the general rule among the peasant-
farmers. In case of illness or invalidism, neighbours would come
to the rescue. Certainly, the taste for saving, which was later to
become characteristic of the peasant, had no opportunity of
manifesting itself. If a family were too numerous, the younger

sons entered the group of cotters (*cotarii*), or went to increase the crowds of vagrants who drifted through the country.

Again, the rights of the lord fettered individual activity, in divers degrees, according to persons. The serfs, properly so-called, could not marry without paying a tax, nor *formarier,* i.e., marry a woman outside the manor, without permission. At their death, the lord received all or part of their inheritance (*corimedis, mortmain, heriot*). Labour services and dues in kind weighed heavily on all tenants, or, rather, on all holdings, for in the course of time they had been transformed from personal into real charges. In this connection there were various distinct categories of *mansi;* some were *ingenuiles,* some *serviles,* some *lidiles,* and their obligations differed according to whether they had originally been occupied by a "body serf," a *lite* (half-free) or a freeman. The tallage which the lord also required from his men in case of need was unquestionably the heaviest and the most odious burden to which they were submitted. It subjected them to a levy which was not only gratuitous, but arbitrary, and was thus capable of grave abuse. It was otherwise with the "banalities" which obliged the *vilains* to grind their grain in the lord's mill, to brew their ale in his brewery, or to press their grapes in his wine-press. The taxes which had to be paid for all this were at least compensated for by the use of plant which had been set up at the lord's expense.

In conclusion it should be observed that the lord did not profit by all the dues collected on the manor. It frequently happened that his lands were encumbered by "justiciary" rights, that is to say, rights emanating not from property but from sovereignty. This was very often the case, for instance, with the *champart* or *medem,* which may be considered as a remote survival, incorporated in the land, of the Roman public tax. Many landowners had confiscated it for their own benefit, but sometimes also it was collected for the benefit of the territorial prince, or for someone else entitled thereto. Very different in kind, the tithe constituted a much severer and, above all, a much more general charge. Theoretically, it should have been collected by the Church; actually, many lords had possessed themselves of it. In any case, the origin of all these dues mattered little to the peasant, since, whatever their nature, it was on him that all alike were piled.

II. THE FAIRS[13]

One of the most striking features of the economic organisation of the Middle Ages was the important rôle played by the fairs, more especially down to the end of the thirteenth century. They abounded in all countries, and everywhere had the same fundamental character, so that they may be considered an international phenomenon, inherent in the very conditions of European society. They were at their height in the era of peripatetic commerce; in proportion as the merchants became sedentary, they dwindled. Those which were created at the end of the Middle Ages were of an altogether different type and, all things considered, their importance in economic life was not comparable with that of their predecessors.

It would be fruitless to seek the origin of the fairs (*nundinae*) in those small local markets, which by the beginning of the ninth century were appearing in ever-increasing numbers over the whole of Europe. Though the fairs were subsequent to the markets, they were not connected with them by any link and indeed present the most complete contrast to them. The aim of the local markets was to supply the provisions necessary for daily life to the population settled in the district. This explains their being held weekly, their very limited circle of attraction and the restriction of their activity to small retail operations. The fairs, on the contrary, were periodical meeting-places for professional merchants. They were centres of exchange and especially of wholesale exchange, and set out to attract the greatest possible number of people and of goods, independent of all local consideration. They may perhaps be compared with international exhibitions, for they excluded nothing and nobody; every in-

[13] BIBLIOGRAPHY.—F. Bourquelot, *Étude sur les foires de Champagne*, Paris, 1865, 2 vols.—C. Bassermann, *Die Champagnermessen, Ein Beitrag zur Geschichte des Kredits*, Leipzig, 1911.—G. Des Marez, *La lettre de foire à Ypres au XIIIe siècle*, Brussels, 1901 (Mém. Acad. Belgique).—H. Laurent, *Documents relatifs à la procédure en foire de Champagne contre des débiteurs défaillants*, in *Bulletin de la Commission des anciennes lois et ordonnances de Belgique*, t. XIII (1929).—H. Pirenne, *Un conflit entre le magistrat yprois et les gardes des foires de Champagne*, in *Bulletin de la Commission royale d'histoire de Belgique*, t. LXXXVI (1922).—A. Sayous, *Les opérations des banquiers italiens en Italie et aux foires de Champagne pendant le XIIIe siècle*, in *Revue historique*, t. CLXX (1932).

dividual, no matter what his country, every article which could be bought or sold, whatever its nature, was assured of a welcome. Moreover, it was impossible to hold them more than once, or at most twice a year in the same place, so great was the necessary preparation involved. It is true that the radius of most of the fairs was limited to a more or less extensive region. Only the Champagne fairs in the twelfth and thirteenth centuries attracted merchants from the whole of Europe. But the important thing is that in theory each fair was open to all trade, just as each seaport was open to all shipping. Between the fair and the local market the contrast was not simply a difference in size, but a difference in kind.

With the exception of the fair at Saint Denis, near Paris, which dates back to the Merovingian era and which, during the agricultural period of the Middle Ages, merely vegetated and found no imitators, the fairs date from the revival of trade. The oldest amongst them were in existence in the eleventh century; in the twelfth their number was already large and it continued to increase further during the thirteenth. Their sites were naturally determined by the great movements of commerce. They increased in number, in proportion as trade in each country became more active and more important. Only the territorial prince had the right to found them. Very often he granted them to towns, but by no means all great urban centres possessed them; some towns of the first importance, like Milan and Venice, had none; in Flanders, although there were fairs at Bruges, Ypres, and Lille, there were none in so active a centre as Ghent, while they are to be found at Thourout and Messines, which were never more than small market-towns. It was the same in Champagne as regards places like Lagny and Bar-sur-Aube, which were as insignificant as the fairs held in them were famous.

Thus the importance of a fair was independent of the place where it was set up, and this is easily understood, since the fair was nothing more than a periodic meeting-place for a distant clientèle and attendance at it did not depend on the density of the local population. It was only in the second half of the Middle Ages that fairs were founded for the mere purpose of furnishing certain towns with supplementary resources, by attracting a temporary throng of people. But it is clear that in these cases considerations of local trade were paramount and that the institution was turned from its original and essential object.

The law gave the fairs a privileged position. The ground on which they were held was protected by a special peace, carrying with it particularly severe punishments in case of infringement. All who went there were under the *conduit,* that is to say, the protection, of the territorial prince. "Guards of the fairs" (*custodes nundinarum*) maintained order and exercised a special jurisdiction there. Letters of obligation sealed with their seal were recognised as specially binding, and a number of privileges were designed to attract the greatest possible number of participants. At Cambrai, for example, special permission was given to throw dice and play cards during the fair of Saint Simon and Saint Jude. "Feasts and plays were the chief attractions."[14] But the most effective advantages consisted in the "franchise," which exempted merchants going to the fair from the right of reprisal for crimes committed or debts contracted outside it, and from the right of escheat, and which suspended lawsuits and measures of execution as long as the peace of the fair lasted. Most precious of all was the suspension of the canonical prohibition of usury (i.e., loans at interest) and the fixing of a maximum rate of interest.

If we examine the geographical distribution of the fairs, it is at once apparent that the busiest among them were grouped almost half-way along the great trade route, which ran from Italy and Provence to the coast of Flanders. These were the famous "fairs of Champagne and Brie" which followed each other through the whole course of the year. First came the fair of Lagny-on-the-Marne in January, next on the Tuesday before mid-Lent that of Bar, in May the first fair of Provins, called the fair of Saint Quiriace, in June the "warm fair" of Troyes, in September the second fair of Provins or the fair of Saint Ayoul, and finally, in October, to end the cycle, the "cold fair" of Troyes. In the twelfth century, these assemblies continued for about six weeks, leaving only the necessary interval for the removal of wares. The most important, because of the season in which they took place, were the fairs of Provins and the

14 Huvelin, *op. cit.,* p. 438.

warm fair of Troyes. The success of these fairs was undoubtedly
due to their excellent position. It seems clear that as early as
the ninth century the rare merchants of the time frequented
the plain of Champagne if, as everything appears to indicate,
the *sedem negotiatorum Cappas* mentioned in a letter of Loup
de Ferrières[15] is to be placed at Chappas, in the department
of Aube. As soon as trade revived, the increasing passage through
Champagne induced its counts to secure the maximum advantage for their country by offering the merchants the convenience
of fairs set up at places near together. In 1114 those of Bar
and Troyes had already been in existence for some time and
undoubtedly it was the same with those of Lagny and Provins,
near which others (which did not, however, enjoy the same
success) were to be found at Bar-on-the-Seine, Châlons-on-the-
Marne, Château-Thierry, Nogent-on-the-Seine, etc. Corresponding to these Champagne fairs, at the end of the line which led
from them to the North Sea, were the five Flemish fairs of
Bruges, Ypres, Lille, Thourout and Messines.

The twelfth century saw an extraordinarily rapid growth
in the prosperity of this commercial system. There is no doubt
that already in 1127 a very active intercourse was going on
between the fairs of Flanders and those of Champagne, for
Galbert has described the terrified flight of the Lombard merchants from the fair of Ypres, on the news of the assassination
of Count Charles the Good. On their part the Flemings found
in Champagne a permanent market for their cloth, which was
despatched from there either by themselves, or by their Italian
and Provençal buyers, to the port of Genoa, and thence exported
to the seaports of the Levant. From Champagne, in return, the
Flemings imported woven silk-stuffs, gold and silver goods and
especially spices, with which the sailors of the North supplied
themselves at Bruges at the same time as Flemish cloth and
French wines. In the thirteenth century, commercial relations
reached the height of their development. At each of the Champagne fairs the Flemish drapers had their "tents," grouped according to towns, where they exhibited their cloth, and "Clerks
of the fairs" rode without interruption between Champagne and

---

[15] A. Giry, *Études carolingiennes*, in *Études d'histoire du Moyen Age
dédiées à Gabriel Monod,* p. 118 (Paris, 1896).

Flanders, carrying the merchants' correspondence.[16] But if the Champagne fairs certainly owed much of their importance to the contact which they early established between Italian commerce and Flemish industry, their influence radiated over all parts of the West. "At the fairs of Troyes there was a German house, and markets and inns belonging to merchants from Montpellier, Barcelona, Valencia, Lérida, Rouen, Montauban, Provins, Auvergne, Burgundy, Picardy, Geneva, Clermont, Ypres, Douai, and Saint-Omer." At Provins, the Lombards had their special lodgings, and one of the quarters of the town was called *Vicus Allemannorum,* just as there was a *Vicus Angliae* at Lagny.[17]

Nor was it only trade in merchandise which attracted people from afar to the Champagne fairs. So numerous and important were the settlements of accounts which took place there, that they soon became, to use a happy phrase, "the money market of Europe."[18] At every fair, after a preliminary period devoted to sales, there followed one of payments. These payments not only involved the clearing of debts contracted at the fair itself, but often settled credits contracted at preceding fairs. From the twelfth century onwards this practice led to the establishment of an organisation of credit, in which we must apparently seek the origin of bills of exchange. In this the Italians, who were more advanced than the continentals in the matter of commercial usages, doubtless took the initiative. As yet the bills were nothing more than simple written promises to pay a sum of money in a place other than that in which the debt was contracted, i.e., in legal terminology, "paper payable to order at a specified place." The signatory, in fact, undertook to make payment in another place to the obligee or to his *nuntius,* i.e., his representative (active order clause), and sometimes also himself to pay these through a *nuntius* acting for him (passive order clause). The Champagne fairs were so widely frequented that most debts were made payable at one or other of them, no matter where contracted. This was the case not only with commercial debts, but with simple loans contracted by individuals, princes, or religious

[16] G. Espinas gives lively details regarding these clerks in *Une guerre sociale inter-urbaine dans la Flandre wallonne au XIII*[e] *siècle,* pp. 24, 35, 72, 82, 83, etc. (Paris-Lille, 1930).

[17] Huvelin, *op. cit.,* p. 505.

[18] L. Goldschmidt, *Universalgeschichte des Handelsrechts,* p. 226.

houses. Furthermore, the fact that all the marts of Europe were in contact with the fairs of Champagne brought about the introduction there, in the thirteenth century, of the practice of settling debts by *"compensation,"* i.e., by clearing arrangements. Thus in the Europe of that day the fairs played the part of an embryonic clearing house. When it is remembered that people flocked there from all parts of the Continent, it is easy to realise how they must have initiated their clients into the perfected credit processes in use among the Florentines and Sienese, whose influence was preponderant in the trade in money.

The Champagne fairs may be considered to have reached their height in the second half of the thirteenth century. The beginning of the following century saw their decline. The essential cause was undoubtedly the substitution for peripatetic commerce of more sedentary practices, at the same time as the development of direct shipping from the Italian ports to those of Flanders and England. No doubt, too, the long war which set the County of Flanders and the kings of France by the ears from 1302 to 1320 also contributed to their decay, in depriving them of the most active group of their northern customers. A little later the Hundred Years' War dealt them the decisive blow. Henceforth those great business centres, to which for two centuries all the merchants of Europe had bent their steps, were no more. But the practices learned there now opened the way to an economic life, in which the general use of correspondence and the operations of credit enabled the business world to give up its journeys to Champagne.

23 THE MEANING AND PRESUPPOSITIONS
OF MODERN CAPITALISM

Max Weber

Capitalism is present wherever the industrial provision for the needs of a human group is carried out by the method of enterprise, irrespective of what need is involved. More specifically, a rational capitalistic establishment is one with capital accounting, that is, an establishment which determines its income yielding power by calculation according to the methods of modern bookkeeping and the striking of a balance. The device of the balance was first insisted upon by the Dutch theorist Simon Stevin in the year 1698.

It goes without saying that an individual economy may be conducted along capitalistic lines to the most widely varying extent; parts of the economic provision may be organized capitalistically and other parts on the handicraft or the manorial pattern. Thus at a very early time the city of Genoa had a part of its political needs, namely those for the prosecution of war, provided in capitalistic fashion, through stock companies. In the Roman empire, the supply of the population of the capital city with grain was carried out by officials, who however for this purpose, besides control over their subalterns, had the right to command the services of transport organizations; thus the leiturgical or forced contribution type of organization was combined with administration of public resources. Today, in contrast with the greater part of the past, our everyday needs are supplied capitalistically, our political needs however through compulsory contributions, that is, by the performance of political duties of

FROM Max Weber, *General Economic History,* Chapter XXII, pp. 275–278. Reprinted by permission of The Free Press. Copyright 1927, Greenberg, Publisher, Inc., reprinted 1950. Translated by Frank H. Knight from the German edition of 1923.

citizenship such as the obligation to military service, jury duty, etc. A whole epoch can be designated as typically capitalistic only as the provision for wants is capitalistically organized to such a predominant degree that if we imagine this form of organization taken away the whole economic system must collapse.

While capitalism of various forms is met with in all periods of history, the provision of the everyday wants by capitalistic methods is characteristic of the occident alone and even here has been the inevitable method only since the middle of the nineteenth century. Such capitalistic beginnings as are found in earlier centuries were merely anticipatory, and even the somewhat capitalistic establishments of the sixteenth century may be removed in thought from the economic life of the time without introducing any overwhelming change.

The most general presupposition for the existence of this present-day capitalism is that of rational capital accounting as the norm for all large industrial undertakings which are concerned with provision for everyday wants. Such accounting involves, again, first, the appropriation of all physical means of production—land, apparatus, machinery, tools, etc. as disposable property of autonomous private industrial enterprises. This is a phenomenon known only to our time, when the army alone forms a universal exception to it. In the second place, it involves freedom of the market, that is, the absence of irrational limitations on trading in the market. Such limitations might be of a class character, if a certain mode of life were prescribed for a certain class or consumption were standardized along class lines, or if class monopoly existed, as for example if the townsman were not allowed to own an estate or the knight or peasant to carry on industry; in such cases neither a free labor market nor a commodity market exists. Third, capitalistic accounting presupposes rational technology, that is, one reduced to calculation to the largest possible degree, which implies mechanization. This applies to both production and commerce, the outlays for preparing as well as moving goods.

The fourth characteristic is that of calculable law. The capitalistic form of industrial organization, if it is to operate rationally, must be able to depend upon calculable adjudication and administration. Neither in the age of the Greek city-state (polis) nor in the patrimonial state of Asia nor in western countries down to the Stuarts was this condition fulfilled. The royal "cheap justice" with its remissions by royal grace introduced continual disturbances into the calculations of economic life. The proposition that the Bank of England was suited only to a republic, not to a monarchy (Weber 1950:265), was related in this way to the conditions of the time. The fifth feature is free labor. Persons must be present who are not only legally in the position, but are also economically compelled, to sell their labor on the market without restriction. It is in contradiction to the essence of capitalism, and the development of capitalism is impossible, if such a propertyless stratum is absent, a class compelled to sell its labor services to live; and it is likewise impossible if only unfree labor is at hand. Rational capitalistic calculation is possible only on the basis of free labor; only where in consequence of the existence of workers who in the formal sense voluntarily, but actually under the compulsion of the whip of hunger, offer themselves, the costs of products may be unambiguously determined by agreement in advance. The sixth and final condition is the commercialization of economic life. By this we mean the general use of commercial instruments to represent share rights in enterprise, and also in property ownership.

To sum up, it must be possible to conduct the provision for needs exclusively on the basis of market opportunities and the calculation of net income. The addition of this commercialization to the other characteristics of capitalism involves intensification of the significance of another factor not yet mentioned, namely speculation. Speculation reaches its full significance only from the moment when property takes on the form of negotiable paper.

24 THE EVOLUTION OF THE CAPITALISTIC SPIRIT

Max Weber

It is widespread error that the increase of population is to be included as a really crucial agent in the evolution of western capitalism. In opposition to this view, Karl Marx made the assertion that every economic epoch has its own law of population, and although this proposition is untenable in so general a form, it is justified in the present case. The growth of population in the west made most rapid progress from the beginning of the eighteenth century to the end of the nineteenth. In the same period China experienced a population growth of at least equal extent—from 60 or 70 to 400 millions, allowing for the inevitable exaggerations; this corresponds approximately with the increase in the west. In spite of this fact, capitalism went backward in China and not forward. The increase in the population took place there in different strata than with us. It made China the seat of a swarming mass of small peasants; the increase of a class corresponding to our proletariat was involved only to the extent that a foreign market made possible the employment of coolies ("coolie" is originally an Indian expression, and signifies neighbor or fellow member of a clan). The growth of population in Europe did indeed favor the development of capitalism, to the extent that in a small population the system would have been unable to secure the necessary labor force, but in itself it never called forth that development.

Nor can the inflow of precious metals be regarded, as Sombart suggests, as the primary cause of the appearance of capitalism.

FROM Max Weber, *General Economic History,* Chapter XXX, pp. 352–369. Reprinted by permission of The Free Press. Copyright 1927, Greenberg, Publisher, Inc., reprinted 1950. Translated by Frank H. Knight from the German edition of 1923.

It is certainly true that in a given situation an increase in the supply of precious metals may give rise to price revolutions, such as that which took place after 1530 in Europe, and when other favorable conditions are present, as when a certain form of labor organization is in process of development, the progress may be stimulated by the fact that large stocks of cash come into the hands of certain groups. But the case of India proves that such an importation of precious metal will not alone bring about capitalism. In India in the period of the Roman power, an enormous mass of precious metal—some twenty-five million *sestertii* annually—came in in exchange for domestic goods, but this inflow gave rise to commercial capitalism to only a slight extent. The greater part of the precious metal disappeared in the hoards of the rajahs instead of being converted into cash and applied in the establishment of enterprises of a rational capitalistic character. This fact proves that it depends entirely upon the nature of the labor system what tendency will result from an inflow of precious metal. The gold and silver from America, after the discovery, flowed in the first place to Spain; but in that country a recession of capitalistic development took place parallel with the importation. There followed, on the one hand, the suppression of the *communeros* and the destruction of the commercial interests of the Spanish grandees, and, on the other hand, the employment of the money for military ends. Consequently, the stream of precious metal flowed through Spain, scarcely touching it, and fertilized other countries, which in the 15th century were already undergoing a process of transformation in labor relations which was favorable to capitalism.

Hence neither the growth of population nor the importation of precious metal called forth western capitalism. The external conditions for the development of capitalism are rather, first, geographical in character. In China and India the enormous costs of transportation, connected with the decisively inland commerce of the regions, necessarily formed serious obstructions for the classes who were in a position to make profits through trade and to use trading capital in the construction of a capitalistic system, while in the west the position of the Mediterranean as an inland sea, and the abundant interconnections through the rivers, favored the opposite development of international commerce. But this factor in its turn must not be overestimated. The civilization of antiquity was distinctively coastal. Here the opportunities for commerce were very favorable (thanks to the character of the Mediterranean Sea), in contrast with the Chinese waters with their typhoons, and yet no capitalism arose in antiquity. Even in the modern period the capitalistic development was much more intense in Florence than in Genoa or in Venice. Capitalism in the west was born in the industrial cities of the interior, not in the cities which were centers of sea trade.

Military requirements were also favorable, though not as such but because of the special nature of the particular needs of the western armies. Favorable also was the luxury demand, though again not in itself. In many cases rather it led to the development of irrational forms, such as small work shops in France and compulsory settlements of workers in connection with the courts of many German princes. In the last resort the factor which produced capitalism is the rational permanent enterprise, rational accounting, rational technology, and rational law, but again not these alone. Necessary complementary factors were the rational spirit, the rationalization of the conduct of life in general, and a rationalistic economic ethic (Weber 1909:30ff.).

At the beginning of all ethics and the economic relations which result, is traditionalism, the sanctity of tradition, the exclusive reliance upon such trade and industry as have come down from the fathers. This traditionalism survives far down into the present; only a human lifetime in the past it was futile to double the wages of an agricultural laborer in Silesia who mowed a certain tract of land on a contract, in the hope of inducing him to increase his exertions. He would simply have reduced by half the work expended because with this half he would have been able to earn twice as much as before (sic). This general incapacity and indisposition to depart from the beaten paths is the motive for the maintenance of tradition.

Primitive traditionalism may, however, undergo essential intensification through two circumstances. In the first place, material interests may be tied up with the maintenance of the tradition. When for example in China, the attempt was made to change certain roads or to introduce more rational means or routes of transportation, the perquisites of certain officials were threatened; and the same was the case in the middle ages in the west, and in modern times when railroads were introduced. Such special interests of officials, landholders, and merchants assisted decisively in restricting a tendency toward rationalization. Stronger still is the effect of the stereotyping of trade on magical grounds, the deep repugnance to undertaking any change in the established conduct of life because supernatural evils are feared. Generally some injury to economic privilege is concealed in this opposition, but its effectiveness depends on a general belief in the potency of the magical processes which are feared.

Traditional obstructions are not overcome by the economic impulse alone. The notion that our rationalistic and capitalistic age is characterized by a stronger economic interest than other periods is childish; the moving spirits of modern capitalism are not possessed of a stronger economic impulse than, for example, an oriental trader. The unchaining of the economic interest merely as such has produced only irrational results; such men as Cortez and Pizarro, who were perhaps its strongest embodiment, were far from having an idea of a rationalistic economic life. If the economic impulse in itself is universal, it is an interesting question as to the relations under which it becomes rationalized and rationally tempered in such fashion as to produce rational institutions of the character of capitalistic enterprise.

Originally, two opposite attitudes toward the pursuit of gain exist in combination. Internally, there is attachment to tradition and to the pietistic relations of fellow members of tribe, clan, and house-community, with the exclusion of the unrestricted quest of gain within the circle of those bound together by religious ties; externally, there is absolutely unrestricted play of the gain spirit in economic relations, every foreigner being originally an enemy in relation to whom no ethical restrictions apply; that is, the ethics of internal and external relations are categorically distinct. The course of development involves on the one hand the bringing in of calculation into the traditional brotherhood, displacing the old religious relationship. As soon as accountability is established within the family community, and economic relations are no longer strictly communistic, there is an end of the naïve piety and its repression of the economic impulse. This side of the development is especially characteristic in the west. At the same time there is a tempering of the unrestricted quest of gain with the adoption of the economic principle into the internal economy. The result is a regulated economic life with the economic impulse functioning within bounds.

In detail, the course of development has been varied. In India, the restrictions upon gain-seeking apply only to the two uppermost strata, the Brahmins and the Rajputs. A member of these castes is forbidden to practice certain callings. A Brahmin may conduct an eating house, as he alone has clean hands; but he, like the Rajput, would be unclassed if he were to lend money for interest. The latter, however, is permitted to the mercantile castes, and within it we find a degree of unscrupulousness in trade which is unmatched anywhere in the world. Finally, antiquity had only legal limitations on interest, and the proposition *caveat emptor* characterizes Roman economic ethics. Nevertheless no modern capitalism developed there.

The final result is the peculiar fact that the germs of modern capitalism must be sought in a region where officially a theory was dominant which was distinct from that of the east and of classical antiquity and in principle strongly hostile to capitalism. The *ethos* of the classical economic morality is summed up in the old judgment passed on the merchant, which was probably taken from primitive Arianism: *homo mercator vix aut numquam potest Deo placere;* he may conduct himself without sin but cannot be pleasing to God. This proposition was valid down to the fifteenth century, and the first attempt to modify it slowly matured in Florence under pressure of the shift in economic relations.

The typical antipathy of Catholic ethics, and following that the Lutheran, to every capitalistic tendency, rests essentially on the repugnance of the impersonality of relations within a capitalist economy. It is this fact of impersonal relations which places certain human affairs outside the church and its influence, and prevents the latter from penetrating them and transforming them along ethical lines. The relations between master and slave could be subjected to immediate ethical regulation; but the relations between the mortgage creditor and the property which was pledged for the debt, or between an endorser and the bill of exchange, would at least be exceedingly difficult if not impossible to moralize (Weber 1909:544). The final consequence of the resulting position assumed by the church was that medieval economic ethics excluded higgling, overpricing, and free compe-

tition, and were based on the principle of just price and the assurance to everyone of a chance to live.

For the breaking up of this circle of ideas the Jews cannot be
made responsible as Sombart asserts (Sombart 1913). The position of the Jews during the middle ages may be compared
sociologically with that of an Indian caste in a world otherwise
free from castes; they were an outcast people. However, there
is the distinction that according to the promise of the Indian
religion the caste system is valid for eternity. The individual may
in the course of time reach heaven through a course of rein-
carnations, the time depending upon his deserts; but this is
possible only within the caste system. The caste organization is
eternal, and one who attempted to leave it would be accursed
and condemned to pass in hell into the bowels of a dog. The
Jewish promise, on the contrary, points toward a reversal of
caste relations in the future world as compared with this. In the
present world the Jews are stamped as an outcast people, either
as punishment for the sins of their fathers, as Deutero-Isaiah
holds, or for the salvation of the world, which is the presupposition of the mission of Jesus of Nazareth; from this position they
are to be released by a social revolution. In the middle ages the
Jews were a guest-people standing outside of political society;
they could not be received into any town citizenship group because they could not participate in the communion of the Lord's
Supper, and hence could not belong to the *coniuratio*.

The Jews were not the only guest-people (Weber 1950:196,
217); besides them the Caursines, for example, occupied a similar
position. These were Christian merchants who dealt in money
and in consequence were, like the Jews, under the protection of
the princes and on consideration of a payment enjoyed the privilege of carrying on monetary dealings. What distinguished the
Jews in a striking way from the Christian guest-peoples was
the impossibility in their case of entering into *commercium* and
conubium with the Christians. Originally the Christians did not
hesitate to accept Jewish hospitality, in contrast with the Jews
themselves who feared that their ritualistic prescriptions as to
food would not be observed by their hosts. On the occasion of
the first outbreak of medieval anti-semitism the faithful were
warned by the synods not to conduct themselves unworthily and
hence not to accept entertainment from the Jews who on their

side despised the hospitality of the Christians. Marriage with Christians was strictly impossible, going back to Ezra and Nehemiah.

A further ground for the outcast position of the Jews arose from the fact that Jewish craftsmen existed; in Syria there had even been a Jewish knightly class, though only exceptionally Jewish peasants, for the conduct of agriculture was not to be reconciled with the requirements of the ritual. Ritualistic considerations were responsible for the concentration of Jewish economic life in monetary dealings (Weber 1950:196). Jewish piety set a premium on the knowledge of the law and continuous study was very much easier to combine with exchange dealings than with other occupations. In addition, the prohibition against usury on the part of the church condemned exchange dealings, yet the trade was indispensable and the Jews were not subject to the ecclesiastical law.

Finally, Judaism had maintained the originally universal dualism of internal and external moral attitudes, under which it was permissible to accept interest from foreigners who did not belong to the brotherhood or established association. Out of this dualism followed the sanctioning of other irrational economic affairs, especially tax farming and political financing of all sorts. In the course of the centuries the Jews acquired a special skill in these matters which made them useful and in demand. But all this was pariah capitalism, not rational capitalism such as originated in the west. In consequence, hardly a Jew is found among the creators of the modern economic situation, the large entrepreneurs; this type was Christian and only conceivable in the field of Christianity. The Jewish manufacturer, on the contrary, is a modern phenomenon. If for no other reason, it was impossible for the Jews to have a part in the establishment of rational capitalism because they were outside the craft organizations. But even alongside the guilds they could hardly maintain themselves, even where, as in Poland, they had command over a numerous proletariat which they might have organized in the capacity of entrepreneurs in domestic industry or as manufacturers. After all, the genuine Jewish ethic is specifically traditionalism, as the Talmud shows. The horror of the pious Jew in the face of any innovation is quite as great as that of an individual among any primitive people with institutions fixed by the belief in magic.

However, Judaism was none the less of notable significance for modern rational capitalism, insofar as it transmitted to Christianity the latter's hostility to magic. Apart from Judaism and Christianity, and two or three oriental sects (one of which is in Japan), there is no religion with the character of outspoken hostility to magic. Probably this hostility arose through the circumstance that what the Israelites found in Canaan was the magic of the agricultural god Baal, while Jahveh was a god of volcanoes, earthquakes, and pestilences. The hostility between the two priesthoods and the victory of the priests of Jahveh discredited the fertility magic of the priests of Baal and stigmatized it with a character of decadence and godlessness. Since Judaism made Christianity possible and gave it the character of a religion essentially free from magic, it rendered an important service from the point of view of economic history. For the dominance of magic outside the sphere in which Christianity has prevailed is one of the most serious obstructions to the rationalization of economic life. Magic involves a stereotyping of technology and economic relations. When attempts were made in China to inaugurate the building of railroads and factories a conflict with geomancy ensued. The latter demanded that in the location of structures on certain mountains, forests, rivers, and cemetery hills, foresight should be exercised in order not to disturb the rest of the spirits.[1]

Similar is the relation to capitalism of the castes in India. Every new technical process which an Indian employs signifies for him first of all that he leaves his caste and falls into another, necessarily lower. Since he believes in the transmigration of souls, the immediate significance of this is that his chance of purification is put off until another rebirth. He will hardly consent to such a change. An additional fact is that every caste makes every other impure. In consequence, workmen who dare not accept a vessel filled with water from each other's hands, cannot be employed together in the same factory room. Not until the present

[1] As soon as the Mandarins realized the chances for gain open to them, these difficulties suddenly ceased to be insuperable; today they are the leading stockholders in the railways. In the long run, no religious-ethical conviction is capable of barring the way to the entry of capitalism, when it stands in full armor before the gate; but the fact that it is able to leap over magical barriers does not prove that genuine capitalism could have originated in circumstances where magic played such a role.

time, after the possession of the country by the English for almost a century, could this obstacle be overcome. Obviously, capitalism could not develop in an economic group thus bound hand and foot by magical beliefs.

In all times there has been but one means of breaking down the power of magic and establishing a rational conduct of life; this means is great rational prophecy. Not every prophecy by any means destroys the power of magic; but it is possible for a prophet who furnishes credentials in the shape of miracles and otherwise, to break down the traditional sacred rules. Prophecies have released the world from magic and in doing so have created the basis for our modern science and technology, and for capitalism. In China such prophecy has been wanting. What prophecy there was has come from the outside as in the case of Lao-Tse and Taoism. India, however, produced a religion of salvation; in contrast with China it has known great prophetic missions. But they were prophecies by example; that is, the typical Hindu prophet, such as Buddha, lives before the world the life which leads to salvation, but does not regard himself as one sent from God to insist upon the obligation to lead it; he takes the position that whoever wishes salvation, as an end freely chosen, should lead the life. However, one may reject salvation, as it is not the destiny of everyone to enter at death into Nirvana, and only philosophers in the strictest sense are prepared by hatred of this world to adopt the stoical resolution and withdraw from life.

The result was that Hindu prophecy was of immediate significance for the intellectual classes. These became forest dwellers and poor monks. For the masses, however, the significance of the founding of a Buddhistic sect was quite different, namely the opportunity of praying to the saints. There came to be holy men who were believed to work miracles, who must be well fed so that they would repay this good deed by guaranteeing a better reincarnation or through granting wealth, long life, and the like, that is, this world's goods. Hence Buddhism in its pure form was restricted to a thin stratum of monks. The laity found no ethical precepts according to which life should be molded; Buddhism indeed had its decalogue, but in distinction from that of the Jews it gave no binding commands but only recommendations. The most important act of service was and remained the physical maintenance of the monks. Such a religious spirit could never be in a position to displace magic but at best could only put another magic in its place.

In contrast with the ascetic religion of salvation of India and its defective action upon the masses, are Judaism and Christianity, which from the beginning have been plebeian religions and have deliberately remained such. The struggle of the ancient church against the Gnostics was nothing else than a struggle against the aristocracy of the intellectuals, such as is common to ascetic religions, with the object of preventing their seizing the leadership in the church. This struggle was crucial for the success of Christianity among the masses, and hence for the fact that magic was suppressed among the general population to the greatest possible extent. True, it has not been possible even down to today to overcome it entirely, but it was reduced to the character of something unholy, something diabolic.

The germ of this development as regards magic is found far back in ancient Jewish ethics, which is much concerned with views such as we also meet with in the proverbs and the so-called prophetic texts of the Egyptians. But the most important prescriptions of Egyptian ethics were futile when by laying a scarab on the region of the heart one could prepare the dead man to successfully conceal the sins committed, deceive the judge of the dead, and thus get into paradise. The Jewish ethics knows no such sophisticated subterfuges and as little does Christianity. In the Eucharist the latter has indeed sublimated magic into the form of a sacrament, but it gave its adherents no such means for evading the final judgment as were contained in Egyptian religion. If one wishes to study at all the influence of a religion on life one must distinguish between its official teachings and this sort of actual procedure upon which in reality, perhaps against its own will, it places a premium, in this world or the next.

It is also necessary to distinguish between the virtuoso religion of adepts and the religion of the masses. Virtuoso religion is significant for everyday life only as a pattern; its claims are of the highest, but they fail to determine everyday ethics. The relation between the two is different in different religions. In Catholicism, they are brought into harmonious union insofar as the claims of the religious virtuoso are held up alongside the duties of the laymen as *consilia evangelica*. The really complete Christian is the monk; but his mode of life is not required of everyone, although some of his virtues in a qualified form are held up as ideals. The advantage of this combination was that ethics was not split asunder as in Buddhism. After all the distinction between monk ethics and mass ethics meant that the most worthy individuals in the religious sense withdrew from the world and established a separate community.

Christianity was not alone in this phenomenon, which rather recurs frequently in the history of religions, as is shown by the powerful influence of asceticism, which signifies the carrying out of a definite, methodical conduct of life. Asceticism has always worked in this sense. The enormous achievements possible to such an ascetically determined methodical conduct of life are demonstrated by the example of Tibet. The country seems condemned by nature to be an eternal desert; but a community of celibate ascetics has carried out colossal construction works in Lhasa and saturated the country with the religious doctrines of Buddhism. An analogous phenomenon is present in the middle ages in the west. In that epoch the monk is the first human being who lives rationally, who works methodically and by rational means toward a goal, namely the future life. Only for him did the clock strike, only for him were the hours of the day divided—for prayer. The economic life of the monastic communities was also rational. The monks in part furnished the officialdom for the early middle ages; the power of the doges of Venice collapsed when the investiture struggle deprived them of the possibility of employing churchmen for oversea enterprises.

But the rational mode of life remained restricted to the monastic circles. The Franciscan movement indeed attempted through the institution of the tertiaries to extend it to the laity, but the institution of the confessional was a barrier to such an extension. The church domesticated medieval Europe by means of its system of confession and penance, but for the men of the middle ages the possibility of unburdening themselves through the channel of the confessional, when they had rendered themselves liable to punishment, meant a release from the consciousness of sin which the teachings of the church had called into being. The unity and strength of the methodical conduct of life were thus in fact broken up. In its knowledge of human nature the church did not reckon with the fact that the individual is a closed unitary ethical personality, but steadfastly held to the view that in spite of the warnings of the confessional and of penances, however strong, he would again fall away morally; that is, it shed its grace on the just and the unjust.

The Reformation made a decisive break with this system. The dropping of the *concilia evangelica* by the Lutheran Reformation meant the disappearance of the dualistic ethics, of the distinction between a universally binding morality and a specifically advantageous code for virtuosi. The other-worldly asceticism came to an end. The stern religious characters who had previously gone into monasteries had now to practice their religion in the life of the world. For such an asceticism within the world the ascetic dogmas of Protestantism created an adequate ethics. Celibacy was not required, marriage being viewed simply as an institution for the rational bringing up of children. Poverty was not required, but the pursuit of riches must not lead one astray into reckless enjoyment. Thus Sebastian Franck was correct in summing up the spirit of the Reformation in the words, "you think you have escaped from the monastery, but everyone must now be a monk throughout his life."

The wide significance of this transformation of the ascetic ideal can be followed down to the present in the classical lands of Protestant ascetic religiosity. It is especially discernible in the import of the religious denominations in America. Although state and church are separated, still, as late as fifteen or twenty years ago no banker or physician took up a residence or established connections without being asked to what religious community he belonged, and his prospects were good or bad according to the character of his answer. Acceptance into a sect was conditioned upon a strict inquiry into one's ethical conduct. Membership in a sect which did not recognize the Jewish distinction between internal and external moral codes guaranteed one's business honor and reliability and this in turn guaranteed success. Hence the principle "honesty is the best policy" and hence among Quakers, Baptists, and Methodists the ceaseless repetition of the proposition based on experience that God would take care of his own. "The Godless cannot trust each other across the road; they turn to us when they want to do business; piety is the surest road to wealth." This is by no means "cant," but a combination of religiosity with consequences which were originally unknown to it and which were never intended.

It is true that the acquisition of wealth, attributed to piety, led to a dilemma, in all respects similar to that into which the medieval monasteries constantly fell; the religious guild led to wealth, wealth to fall from grace, and this again to the necessity of reconstitution. Calvinism sought to avoid this difficulty through the idea that man was only an administrator of what God had given him; it condemned enjoyment, yet permitted no flight from the world but rather regarded working together, with its rational discipline, as the religious task of the individual. Out of this system of thought came our word "calling," which is known only to the languages influenced by the Protestant translations of the Bible (Weber 1909:63ff., 163ff., 207ff.). It expresses the value placed upon rational activity carried on according to the rational capitalistic principle, as the fulfillment of a God-given task. Here lay also in the last analysis the basis of the contrast between the Puritans and the Stuarts. The ideas of both were capitalistically directed; but in a characteristic way the Jew was for the Puritan the embodiment of everything repugnant because he devoted himself to irrational and illegal occupations such as war loans, tax farming, and leasing of offices, in the fashion of the court favorite.[2]

This development of the concept of the calling quickly gave to the modern entrepreneur a fabulously clear conscience—and also industrious workers; he gave to his employees as the wages of their ascetic devotion to the calling and of co-operation in his ruthless exploitation of them through capitalism the prospect of eternal salvation, which in an age when ecclesiastical discipline took control of the whole of life to an extent inconceivable to us now, represented a reality quite different from any it has today. The Catholic and Lutheran churches also recognized and practiced ecclesiastical discipline. But in the Protestant ascetic communities admission to the Lord's Supper was conditioned on ethical fitness, which again was identified with business honor, while into the content of one's faith no one inquired. Such a powerful, unconsciously refined organization for the production of capitalistic individuals has never existed in any other church

---

[2] In a general way, though with necessary reservations, the contrast may be formulated by saying that Jewish capitalism was speculative pariah-capitalism, while Puritan capitalism consisted in the organization of citizen labor. See Weber, 1920:181ff., Note 2.

or religion, and in comparison with it what the Renaissance did for capitalism shrinks into insignificance. Its practitioners occupied themselves with technical problems and were experimenters of the first rank. From art and mining, experimentation was taken over into science.

The world-view of the Renaissance, however, determined the policy of rulers in a large measure, though it did not transform the soul of man as did the innovations of the Reformation. Almost all the great scientific discoveries of the sixteenth and even the beginning of the seventeenth century were made against the background of Catholicism. Copernicus was a Catholic, while Luther and Melanchthon repudiated his discoveries. Scientific progress and Protestantism must not at all be unquestioningly identified. The Catholic church has indeed occasionally obstructed scientific progress; but the ascetic sects of Protestantism have also been disposed to have nothing to do with science, except in a situation where material requirements of everyday life were involved. On the other hand it is its specific contribution to have placed science in the service of technology and economics.[3]

The religious root of modern economic humanity is dead; today the concept of the calling is a *caput mortuum* in the world. Ascetic religiosity has been displaced by a pessimistic though by no means ascetic view of the world, such as that portrayed in Mandeville's Fable of the Bees, which teaches that private vices may under certain conditions be for the good of the public. With the complete disappearance of all the remains of the original enormous religious pathos of the sects, the optimism of the Enlightenment which believed in the harmony of interests, appeared as the heir of Protestant asceticism in the field of economic ideas; it guided the hands of the princes, statesmen, and writers of the later eighteenth and early nineteenth century. Economic ethics arose against the background of the ascetic ideal; now it has been stripped of its religious import. It was possible for the working class to accept its lot as long as the promise of eternal happiness could be held out to it. When this consolation fell

[3] See also E. Troeltsch (1913). Among the opponents of the above conceptions of Max Weber regarding the significance of Calvinism should be mentioned L. Brentano, (1916:117ff.) and G. Brodnitz (n.d.:282ff.). Another exposition in English of Weber's theories in this field may be found in two articles by P. T. Forsyth (1910). Cf. also R. H. Tawney (1926). [Tr.]

away it was inevitable that those strains and stresses should appear in economic society which since then have grown so rapidly. This point had been reached at the end of the early period of capitalism, at the beginning of the age of iron, in the nineteenth century.

Oscar E. Handlin

The immigrant movement started in the peasant heart of Europe. Ponderously balanced in a solid equilibrium for centuries, the old structure of an old society began to crumble at the opening of the modern era. One by one, rude shocks weakened the aged foundations until some climactic blow suddenly tumbled the whole into ruins. The mighty collapse left without homes millions of helpless, bewildered people. These were the army of emigrants [to the United States].

The impact was so much the greater because there had earlier been an enormous stability in peasant society. A granite-like quality in the ancient ways of life had yielded only slowly to the forces of time. From the westernmost reaches of Europe, in Ireland, to Russia in the east, the peasant masses had maintained an imperturbable sameness; for fifteen centuries they were the backbone of a continent, unchanging while all about them radical changes again and again recast the civilization in which they lived.

Stability, the deep, cushiony ability to take blows, and yet to keep things as they were, came from the special place of these people on the land. The peasants were agriculturists; their livelihood sprang from the earth. Americans they met later would have called them "farmers," but that word had a different meaning in Europe. The bonds that held these men to their acres were not simply the personal ones of the husbandman who temporarily mixes his sweat with the soil. The ties were deeper,

FROM Oscar E. Handlin, *The Uprooted,* Chapter 1, pp. 7–36. Copyright 1951 by Oscar Handlin. Reprinted by permission of the author and Atlantic-Little, Brown and Co.

more intimate. For the peasant was part of a community and the community was held to the land as a whole.

Always, the start was the village. "I was born in such a village in such a parish"—so the peasant invariably began the account of himself. Thereby he indicated the importance of the village in his being; this was the fixed point by which he knew his position in the world and his relationship with all humanity.

The village was a place. It could be seen, it could be marked out in boundaries, pinned down on a map, described in all its physical attributes. Here was a road along which men and beasts would pass, reverence the saint's figure at the crossing. There was a church, larger or smaller, but larger than the other structures about it. The burial ground was not far away, and the smithy, the mill, perhaps an inn. There were so many houses of wood or thatch, and so built, scattered among the fields as in Ireland and Norway, or, as almost everywhere else, huddled together with their backs to the road. The fields were round about, located in terms of river, brook, rocks, or trees. All these could be perceived; the eye could grasp, the senses apprehend the feel, the sound, the smell, of them. These objects, real, authentic, true, could come back in memories, be summoned up to rouse the curiosity and stir the wonder of children born in distant lands.

Yet the village was still more. The aggregate of huts housed a community. Later, much later, and very far away, the Old Countrymen also had this in mind when they thought of the village. They spoke of relationships, of ties, of family, of kinship, of many rights and obligations. And these duties, privileges, connections, links, had each their special flavor, somehow a unique value, a meaning in terms of the life of the whole.

They would say then, if they considered it in looking backward, that the village was so much of their lives because the village *was* a whole. There were no loose, disorderly ends; everything was knotted into a firm relationship with every other thing. And all things had meaning in terms of their relatedness to the whole community.

In their daily affairs, these people took account of the relationships among themselves through a reckoning of degrees of kinship. The villagers regarded themselves as a clan connected within itself by ties of blood, more or less remote. That they did so may have been in recollection of the fact that the village was anciently the form the nomadic tribe took when it settled down to a stable agricultural existence. Or it may have been a reflection of the extent of intermarriage in a place where contact with outsiders was rare. In any case, considerations of kinship had heavy weight in the village, were among the most important determinants of men's actions.

But the ties of blood that were knotted into all the relationships of communal life were not merely sentimental. They were also functional; they determined or reflected the role of individuals in the society.

No man, for instance, could live alone in the village. Marriage was the normal expected state of all but the physically deformed. If death deprived a person of his marriage partner, all the forces of community pressure came into play to supply a new helpmate. For it was right and proper that each should have his household, his place in a family.

The family, being functional, varied somewhat to suit the order of local conditions. But always the unit revolved about the husband and wife. The man was head of the household and of its enterprises. He controlled all its goods, made the vital decisions that determined its well-being, had charge of the work in the fields, and was the source of authority and discipline within the home. His wife was mother, her domain the house and all that went on in and about it. She was concerned with the garden and the livestock, with domestic economy in its widest sense—the provision of food, shelter, and clothing for all. The children had each their task, as befitted their age and condition. Now they herded the cattle or assisted in the chores of cleaning and cookery; later they would labor by the side of mother and father, and prepare to set up families of their own. Other members too had their allotted and recognized roles. Grandparents, aunts and uncles, sometimes cousins up to the fourth degree with no establishments of their own, found a place and a job. The family felt the obligation of caring for all, but also knew that no one could expect food and a corner in which to sleep while doing nothing to earn it. In this respect such collateral relatives did not differ in condition from the hired servants, where they existed, who were also counted members of the family.

The family was then the operating economic unit. In a sense

that was always recognized and respected, the land on which it worked was its own. The head of the household, it was true, held and controlled it; legally, no doubt, he had certain powers to waste or dispose of it. But he was subject to an overwhelming moral compulsion to keep it intact, in trust for those who lived from it and for their descendants who would take a place upon it.

The family's land was rarely marked out in a well-defined plot. The house, the garden, and the barnyard with its buildings were its own, but the bulk of agricultural lands were enmeshed in a wide net of relationships that comprehended the whole community.

Once, it seems, the village had held and used all the land communally; until very recent times recognizable vestiges of that condition persisted. The pastures and meadows, the waste, the bogs and woodlands, existed for the use of all. It hardly mattered at first that the nobility or other interlopers asserted a claim to ownership. The peasants' rights to graze their cattle, to gather wood for building and peat for fire, in practice remained undisturbed. In some parts of Europe, even the arable lands rested in the hands of the whole village, redivided on occasions among its families according to their rights and condition.

Even where particular pieces of land were permanently held, it was rarely in such consolidated plots as the peasants might later see on American farms. A holding consisted rather of numerous tiny strips that patched the slopes of the countryside in a bewildering, variegated design. A Polish peasant, rich in land, could work his nine acres in forty different places.

Agriculture conformed to the pattern of landholding. By long usage, the fields almost everywhere were divided into thirds, a part for winter crops—wheat, rye; another for summer crops—barley, oats, and potatoes; and another to lie fallow. Since no man's lands were completely apart from his neighbor's, there was no room for individuality in working the soil. Every family labored on its own and kept the fruit of its own labors. Yet all labor had to be directed toward the same ends, in the same way, at the same time.

Many important aspects of agriculture, moreover, were altogether communal. The pastures were open to all villagers; in the common fields, the boys tended the cattle together or a hired herdsman had their oversight. Women, working in groups at the wearisome indoor tasks, spinning or plucking cabbage leaves, could turn chores into festive occasions, lighten their labors with sociable gossip. The men were accustomed to give aid to each other, to lend or exchange as an expression of solidarity. After all, folk must live with each other.

So the peasants held together, lived together, together drew the stuff of life from an unwilling earth. Simple neighborliness, mutual assistance, were obligations inherent in the conditions of things, obligations which none could shirk without fear of cutting himself off from the whole. And that was the community, that the village—the capacity to do these things together, the relationships that regulated all.

Their all-embracing quality gave peasant ways a persistent quality, forced each generation to retrace the steps of its predecessors. Family and land in the village were locked in an unyielding knot. And the heart of the bond was the marriage system.

Marriage affected not only the two individuals most directly involved; it affected deeply the lives and the lands of all those related to them. Marriage destroyed the integrity of two old productive units and created a new one. The consummation of the union could be successful only with provisions for the prosperity of both the new and the old families, and that involved allocation of the land among the contracting parties in a proper and fitting manner.

Long-standing custom that had the respect and usually the effect of law regulated these arrangements, and also determined the modes of inheritance. Almost everywhere the land descended within the family through the male line, with the holding passing as a whole to a single son. But provision was also made for the other children. The brothers had portions in money or goods, while substantial amounts were set aside as dowries for the sisters.

The marriage of the oldest son was the critical point in the history of the family. The bride came to live in her father-in-law's home in anticipation of the time when the old man would retire and her husband become the head of the household. In a proper marriage, she brought with her a dowry profitable enough to set up the younger brothers in the style to which they were accustomed and to add to the dowries of the daughters of the family.

No marriage was therefore isolated; the property and the future welfare of the whole family hung in the balance each time an alliance was negotiated. And not only the family's; the whole community was directly concerned. Naturally matters of such importance could not be left to the whim of individuals; they rested instead in the hands of experienced, often of professional, matchmakers who could conduct negotiations with decorum and ceremony, who could guarantee the fitness of the contracting families and the compatibility in rank of the individuals involved.

The whole family structure rested on the premise of stability, on the assumption that there would be no radical change in the amount of available land, in the size of the population, or in the net of relationships that held the village together. Were there daughters without dowries or sons without portions, were no lands made vacant to be bought with dowry and portion, then a part of the community would face the prospect of economic degradation and perhaps, even more important, of serious loss in status.

Not within the village, but beside it, were mushrooming treacherous growths that would jeopardize all that assumed stability.

The village loomed so large in the peasants' consciousness that they were tempted to think it the whole of their society, to behave as if it were entirely self-sufficient and self-contained. The family worked to cover its own needs and expected to subsist by consuming what it produced. But the actual functioning of village life contradicted that assumption and the strain of that contradiction weakened the peasants' whole place on the land.

It was true that the peasant could adjust his consumption to the level of his productivity, eat more in good times, less in poor. But in practice he found himself compelled to produce a disquieting surplus upon which he could not reckon and which regularly upset his scheme of life. To create that surplus he had either to raise his productivity or to divert a part of his produce away from his own consumption. Neither alternative was easy or pleasant.

After all, much as he disliked to consider the fact, the peasant was not alone in his society. Superimposed upon the ranks of the husbandmen was a formidable array of groups that lived by his labors. Beside the village and the village lands were the manor house and the manor lands. That imposing structure, those extensive tracts bespoke the power and wealth of the landlords, nobility or gentry, in peasant eyes equally lords. He who lived within the manor gates was not a part of the village; but his will had a profound effect upon it. The lord owned all about him, land and water and even wind (for only he could build a mill). The lord was strong. On horse, with sword, he wielded power.

The sword of the lord protected the peasant, gave him peace against hostile strangers. The sword of the lord did justice among peasants, interceded in quarrels, and supported right against wrong. But the sword of the lord also took days' work from the peasant, collected rents and dues from the tillers of the soil. These payments constituted a first charge against the income of every household in the village; failure to pay entailed the danger of losing the land. The peasant could meet these charges only by deductions from his own consumption or by producing a surplus.

Apart from the village was also the priest's house. Its occupant, the church over which he presided, and the essential services he performed, were also supported by the peasant. Almost everywhere compulsory dues of some sort recurred year after year and special contributions marked the critical points of every man's life. In kind or in cash there were gifts to bring at holidays and festivals and fees at birth, marriage, and death. It was the good peasant's duty to pay as well for memorials for his dead, for thanksgiving at special good fortune, or for prayers against particular calamities. Those who labored in the fields sometimes grumbled that it was easier to grow rich by plowing with a pen, but they dutifully provided such unavoidable expenses out of a surplus laid by for the purpose.

Yet these were not all the peasant bore on his back. Some tasks he could not perform for himself or even with the aid of his fellows. His work often brought him to the point at which he needed the paid services of a specialist endowed with unusual skill or possessed of unusual equipment; such were the smith's work, the miller's work, and the weaver's. Or there were things—butchery, for instance—not reckoned proper for a man to do, obnoxious, loathsome tasks undertaken by someone else for a fee.

There were also services the peasants were obligated to perform for each other without charge, but services so expensive that fulfillment of the obligation would be ruinous to the conscientious individual. Conventionally such services were transferred to an outsider who could take payment. Peasant solidarity thus demanded that loans be without interest and hospitality without cost; "Am I a Jewess or a trader, to take money for a little fire and water?" asked the goodwife.

Yet nothing in this world, she knew, was given for nothing and the burden of the obligation could only rarely be suffered by any man. Hence the resort to moneylenders and innkeepers, neutral outsiders not expected to conform to the peasant requirements of solidarity. These too drew support from the peasant's surplus.

Furthermore, the village ideal of self-sufficiency could not protect it against the temptation of dealing in the markets of the outside world. Some things it had to buy: always salt, but later also some luxuries became necessities, as tea. From time to time peddlers passed the peasant's door, tantalized his women with offerings of cloth and ribbons, teased away coin, egg, or fowl. Peddlers of another sort bought and sold horses, bartered livestock. Wandering tinkers periodically made the circuit of the villages, willing for a consideration to sell or repair utensils of kitchen or field. All brought to his very threshold wares tempting enough to induce the peasant to accumulate a surplus.

And that was not all. Seasonally there were fairs, booths crammed into the market place, spilling over with attractions. Who was so dull as to stay away from these festive occasions, or to leave at home the pig, cow, and handful of accumulated silver? And who was so stern, once there, to resist the pleas of women and children, of his own longings for some indulgence away from the necessities of his everyday life?

In the sober reckonings of the morrow, there was a double significance to all these demands upon the peasant's surplus. In the first place, they tempted him to expand his production in the hope that the ever-growing populations of the towns would take off his hands ever larger quantities of agricultural goods. At the same time, the dealing in surpluses made room for many strangers, people who were not peasants, yet who lived side by side with the peasants and played an important part in the peasant world. The nobility and clergy had long been there. But there were, as well, Jews to carry on the functions of trade, to act as innkeepers and moneylenders, to serve as middlemen between lords and peasants. Gypsies dealt in horses and livestock, worked as blacksmiths and tinsmiths. There were places where outlandish Italian masons, Slovak besombinders, Hungarian bricklayers, made each their appointed appearance to do their appointed tasks. Of these groups, some were of necessity itinerant; no single village could support them the year round. Others settled in the village, though not part of it, or lived in the little towns in close proximity to it. And not distant in miles, though worlds removed, were the cities, regions of total strangeness into which the peasant never ventured, where not the people alone, but the very aspect of the earth was unfamiliar.

The peasant, as an individual, welcomed the strangers. These were not wild men of the woods, but for generations planted in his midst, and in an immediate way, they made his life easier. But as a member of the community the peasant disapproved, knowing that these outsiders were a threat to the stability of the village. The myth of the gypsies who ran off with the child had a literal and a figurative meaning. The wanderers brought with them the heady smell of wonderful distances, now and then lured to city or to the open road those impatient with family burdens or with the stolid peasant ways.

The figurative snatching was more dangerous. More often than the gypsy stole the child, he stole the birthright. For in these strangers was incarnated the temptation to acquire a surplus beyond the needs of the peasants' livelihood and that temptation was feared lest it some day destroy the delicate balances by which the village held together.

The drive for a surplus was dangerous because it was difficult to expand the volume of production without an enormous strain upon the whole village. Only with difficulty could the peasant, later in America, describe the smallness of his holdings, not only because size varied so much in time and place, but because the scale of things was so inconceivably different. Anywhere at any time, in the Old World, a family that held twelve acres was incredibly well off. In areas particularly poor, in nineteenth-century Galicia for instance, a plot as large as five acres was not usual; and nowhere would that have been reckoned too small. From such tiny acreage the peasant had to draw the sustenance of all the souls dependent upon him. It was certainly difficult to draw from it also enough to leave a surplus.

Furthermore, the techniques of production were inefficient and it was difficult to make changes. Since so much of the work of the fields was communal, innovations had to wait upon the conversion to the new idea of the whole village, and that meant indefinite postponement. Radical departures from traditional, that is, from safe, ways of acting were not introduced without long, acrimonious debate. Naturally there was no room for risky experimentation. The gamble was too great, for failure meant starvation, not for an individual alone, but for his whole family, and perhaps for the whole village.

A large part of the productive land lay idle; who would give up the fallow year on the guess that there were other means of restoring fertility? Who would venture to turn woodland and pasture into arable land for the possibility of gains necessarily remote? The scrawny peasant animals could never grow fat. There were neither enough acres in the fields nor enough hands in the family to raise fodder to feed them. The beasts were allowed to fare for themselves as best they could in the meadows and, in winter, were either slaughtered or grew lean—visible evidence of the peasants' inability to lay aside a surplus.

In every phase of their labor the peasants ran headlong into the same difficulty. They could never get together capital, turn accumulations into further production. Every fragment of income, long before they had it, was dedicated to some specific end and was not to be used for any other purpose. Indeed money, when they laid hands on it, was never regarded as capital. It made no peasant sense to think of gold and silver, even of tools, as themselves productive. The precious metals could be hoarded up against the expected needs, against the recurrent disasters that were not long absent in their lives; they had no other use, were merely provisional substitutes for the goods or services they would ultimately buy—rent money, shoe money, salt money, funeral money. So many previous immediate claims ate up the little extras good fortune occasionally left that nothing could be laid aside. These people could not plan for the proximate future; it would be foolish to give the grass time to grow while the steed starved. This was their plight, always to be eating up their seed corn.

It was against these rigid limits of production that the demands for a surplus pushed. There was the danger. Squeezed by the pressure of rising charges and fixed income, the peasant could see in the offing the greatest disaster of all, loss of his land, the sole measure of his worth in the community.

For the peasant loss of the land was a total calamity. The land was not an isolated thing in his life. It was a part of the family and of the village, pivot of a complex circle of relationships, the primary index of his own, his family's status. What was a man without land? He was like a man without legs who crawls about and cannot get anywhere. Land was the only natural, productive good in this society.

Within the village economy there was little the landless could do. Paid labor was degrading. The demand for any kind of work for others was slight. Those who sought such labor had to enter service—in a measure, they surrendered their freedom, their individuality, the hope of establishing families of their own. They lost thereby the quality and rank of peasants. That was why the peasant feared to encumber his land with mortgages, preferred to pay high interest for personal loans. That was why he hesitated to divide his holding, felt threatened by every new charge against it.

Yet time in its changes had made it difficult for some men to assume the position and maintain the station of peasants. Son after son found that modifications in the pattern of land ownership prevented him from taking the place his father had held.

By the beginning of the nineteenth century the effects were noticeable in almost every part of Europe. As landlords, eager to consolidate holdings, combined the old strips into contiguous plots, the peasant suffered. Whether he emerged with the same or lesser acreage, the creation of larger productive units put him at a competitive disadvantage in the market place. He could thrive only if he managed to become a farmer, that is, managed to rent a large plot under a long-term lease, perhaps for life, or for several lifetimes, or without limit of term. (Some indeed were fortunate enough to become proprietors.)

Consolidation widened the differences among peasants. A few grew wealthy as they rose to the status of farmers (*gospodarze,* the Poles called them; *bøndar,* the Norwegians). Many more became poor, were completely edged off the land, and sank helplessly into the growing class of landless peasants, ironic contradiction in terms. Cottiers they were named where English was spoken, *husmaend* in Norwegian, *Häusler* in German, *komorniki* in Polish. The designation described their condition. Their only right was to rent the cottage in which they lived. By sufferance they used the common fields. But their livelihood they earned by day labor for others or by renting small plots under short-term leases or from year to year.

Their livelihood! Such huts they lived in as they themselves in a few days could build. Such clothes they wore as their wives alone could make. Food was what the paid rent left. In Ireland the annual expenditures of a family of cottiers ran not above thirty-two shillings a year. Calculate a shilling how you will, that is still a grim standard of living.

Could anything be worse? Indeed it could—the times disaster struck, broke in upon the even tenor of these plowmen's ways. Within the rigid, improvident system of production, no reserve absorbed the shock of crop failures. No savings tided him over whose roots rotted in the hostile ground. The very idea was a mockery; if he had had those coins, to what market would he turn? Trade took food from the village, never brought it back. When the parched earth yielded only the withered leaves of famine, then, alas, conditions were somewhat equalized. Farmer and cottier looked to their larders, already depleted since the last year's harvest, and, reconciled, delayed the day the last measured morsel would disappear. Many then reached in vain, found starvation in the empty barrels. No power could help them.

Calamity was familiar. If not the ill-favor of nature, then the caprice of human beings could give her entree to the peasant household. The whims, the incomprehensible needs and interests of landlords created crises for whole villages. Wars came, taxes, laws. The roll of drums desolated fields. Resentful, silent eyes watched the men in uniform drive off the beasts, enlist sons who might never come back, pour out the winter's stored-up grain in heedless waste.

Disaster chained the peasant to his place. The harshness of these burdens immobilized those upon whom they fell, made the poor also poor in spirit. Revolt, escape, were not the stuff their dreams were made of as they paused in the sickle's swing or leaned back in the shadows of the long winter evening. It was for an end to all striving that their tired hearts longed.

While there was no surcease, they would hold on. Peasant wisdom knew well the fate of the rolling stone, knew that if it remained fixed, even a rock might share in growth. The unwillingness to move reflected, in part, a stubborn attachment to that fierce mistress, the land. It expressed also a lethargic passivity in which each man acquiesced in the condition of his life as it was.

Long habit, the seeming changelessness of things, stifled the impulse to self-improvement. In the country round (the parish, *okolica*) each village had a reputation, a pack of thieves, a crew of liars, a lot of drunkards, fools, or good husbandmen, thrifty, prosperous. Within the village, each family had its place, and in the family each individual. Precisely because the peasant thought only in terms of the whole, he defined his own station always by his status within the larger units. The virtue of one brought benefits, his sin, shame to the whole.

The efforts of man were directed not toward individual improvement but toward maintenance of status. It was fitting and proper to exact one's due rights, to fulfill one's due obligations. It was not fitting to thrust oneself ahead, to aspire to a life above one's rank, to rebel against one's status; that was to argue against the whole order of things.

The deep differences among peasants and between the peasants and the other groups were not a cause for envy. This was the accepted configuration of society. The lord was expected to be proud and luxurious, but humane and generous, just as the peasant was expected to be thrifty and respectful. Even bitterly burdensome privileges were not open to dispute. All knew that to him that can pay, the musicians play. The peasant did not begrudge the magnates the pleasures of their manor houses; let *them* at least draw enjoyment from life.

Acceptance of status stifled any inclination toward rebelliousness. There were occasional peasant outbursts when the nobility deviated from their expected role or when they tried to alter traditional modes of action. The Jacquerie then or Whiteboys, the followers of Wat Tyler or of Pugachev, savagely redressed their own grievances. But apart from such spasmodic acts of vengeance there were no uprisings against the order within which peasant and noble lived. The same docility blocked off the alternative of secession through emigration. If disaster befell the individual, that was not itself a cause for breaking away. It did not become so until some external blow destroyed the whole peasant order.

The seeds of ultimate change were not native to this stable society. They were implanted from without. For centuries the size of the population, the amount of available land, the quantity of productive surplus, and the pressure of family stability, achieved together a steady balance that preserved the village way of life. Only slowly and in a few places were there signs of unsteadiness in the seventeenth century; then more distinctly and in more places in the eighteenth. After 1800, everywhere, the elements of the old equilibrium disintegrated. The old social structure tottered; gathering momentum from its own fall, it was unable to right itself, and under the impact of successive shocks collapsed. Then the peasants could no longer hang on; when even to stay meant to change, they had to leave.

Earliest harbinger of the transformations to come was a radical new trend in the population of Europe. For a thousand years, the number of people on the continent had remained constant. From time to time there had been shifts in the areas of heaviest density. In some centuries famine, plague, and war had temporarily lowered the total; in others, freedom from famine, plague, and war had temporarily raised it. But taken all in all these fluctuations canceled each other out.

Then in the eighteenth century came a precipitous rise, unprecedented and, as it proved, cataclysmic. For a hundred years growth continued unabated, if anything at an accelerating rate. Between 1750 and 1850 the population of the continent leaped from about one hundred and forty million to about two hundred and sixty, and by the time of the First World War to almost four hundred million. In addition, by 1915 some two hundred and fifty million Europeans and their descendants lived outside the continent. Even taking account of the relief from emigration, the pressure on social institutions of this increase was enormous. The reckoning is simple: where one man stood in 1750, one hundred and sixty-five years later there were three.

This revolutionary change came under the beneficent guise of

a gradual decline in the death rate, particularly in that of children
under the age of two. Why infants, everywhere in Europe, should
now more often survive is not altogether clear. But the consequences were unmistakable; the happy facility with which the
newborn lived to maturity put a totally unexpected strain upon
the whole family system and upon the village organization. The
new situation called into question the old peasant assumption
that all sons would be able to find farms capable of maintaining
them at the status their fathers had held. As events demonstrated
the falsity of that assumption, stability disappeared from peasant
life.

The eldest sons waited for their inheritance. They married,
brought children into the world, and still had only a place in the
parental home. Until the old men died the middle-aged heirs
could not assume the station of householders. Impatient, weary
of being commanded, the sons saw the years of their best powers
go by and themselves, with no land of their own, deprived of the
dignity and authority of the head of a family. Tense in the fear
of unfulfillment, they urged the fathers to retire, to surrender
possession, to make room.

Against the claims of a crowding new generation, the elders
stubbornly held to their own. If they were to yield, move off to a
corner, learn to take orders, cease to be productive, could they
count on respect to leave them more than the crumbs of family
income when already the grandchildren were there to be provided
for? Turn over the property, and to what rights could they lay
claim—to a rope with which to hang themselves, to a stone to tie
around their necks!

Then too, a father's obligations were more onerous now. It
was more difficult to provide for the younger sons and for the
daughters. An ironic providence had, in the old days, made sure
that not too many boys would reach an age to claim a man's
estate. The same kind fate that kept more children alive complicated the problem of their settlement. Few holdings fell vacant
through want of heirs; few peasants had so much land they would
willingly part with some of it. Dowries were increasingly inadequate to settle the young bridegrooms. A class of men grew up
for whom there was no longer room within the constricted acreage of the village. Dissatisfied and unhappy, peasants' sons

looked ahead to a bleak degradation, to a final loss of status in the community.

The available expedients were pitifully inadequate to meet the needs of the desperate situation. Only a few found hired work or learned to draw an income from other than agricultural pursuits. More delayed marriage to an unseasonable age, not having the means to undertake it properly.

But the presence in the village of unmarried adults was itself a danger. Most often, the seeming solution was subdivision of the old plots, the creation of two holdings from one to serve the more numerous families. Within a single man's lifetime, in Poland, the fifteen farms of one village grew to twoscore; in another place two hundred and ninety-four households came to work the land that had fifty years earlier held forty-two. Land was then indeed scarce, divided again and again; its price rose steadily whether for purchase or rent, and each rise diminished further the margin left for the peasant's subsistence. Now, whether the harvest be rich or poor, the folk found themselves always poorer.

So the peasants learned that poverty was a dog whose teeth sank deep. The struggle for existence grew fiercer; yet there was no halt to the steady recession in standard of living. The mark of that deterioration was the uninterrupted advance across Europe of the cultivation of the potato, the cheapest of foods, the slimmest sustenance to keep bodies alive. In place after place, the tillers of the soil came to rely for their own nourishment upon this one crop, while their more valuable products went to markets to pay rents, to maintain the hold upon the soil. The peasant diet became monotonously the same—potatoes and milk. Meat was a rare luxury, and even tea. The housewife found there was never enough for the mouths to be fed; and those whom the constricted acreage condemned to idleness were not likely to be left a share. Often the old folk were sent out in winter to beg for the bread of God's giving, only to come home like the birds to their nests in the spring.

To hold to the land, those strong in arm would also sometimes venture away, roam the countryside in search of a hirer, move in ever-wider circles away from the home, for which they still labored and to which they seasonally returned. In time these migratory workers became familiar to every part of Europe.

The Irish spalpeen made somehow his way to the sea, crossed

to Liverpool, to toil for a spell in the fertile English Midlands.
On the same errand, Italian peasants drifted across the border to
Austria, France, and Switzerland, then moved still deeper into
Germany. Polish peasants became known in the wheat fields of
Prussia, in the beet fields of the Ukraine, or as drivers on the
barges that moved down the river to Danzig. Thus they bent
their backs over alien soil, tended the crops of strangers, to the
end that enough would be paid them, while the family got on at
home, to hold their own dear land which alone could no longer
sustain them and meet as well the other charges against it.

Of these migrants, some sought refuge in the growing cities,
perhaps like the others, with the intention of making the stay
temporary. For to accept permanent residence there was truly
the last resort; only those thought of it who gave up entirely the
struggle for the land, who surrendered ancestral ways and the
hope of maintaining status. Every instinct spoke against that
course; the peasant knew well that he "who rides away from his
lands on a stallion will come back on foot a tatterdemalion."

Much safer at any cost to hold on! So the whole peasant order
came to live under the sense of a desperate tension to retain a
grip on the land. As against that predominant consideration all
other problems receded in importance. With every energy mobilized against this one overwhelming strain, men regarded every
other attendant difficulty with apathy—the wretched diet, occasional periods of starvation, squalid quarters, blank future.
Within the closed horizons of this perspective was not much
scope for aggressive venturesome action, only a plodding determination to resist further changes; for all that changed changed
for the worse.

But already a far-reaching transformation in the organization
of European agriculture and industry was beginning to turn these
strains into the causes for emigration.

The calls on the land for its produce grew more insistent as
the eighteenth century drew to a close and continued as the
nineteenth century advanced toward its middle. It was not only
that the population as a whole grew, but particularly that the
urban population grew. The peasants could not know it, but
those who went to the cities, in effect, increased the pressures on
those who stayed behind. Townsfolk could not raise their own

food; more numerous at the market place, they multiplied the demands upon agriculture.

You cannot make the land to stretch, the peasants said; and that was true enough in their own experience. But others witnessed with impatience the multitude of buyers, calculated the advance in prices and the prospect of profit, and disagreed. What if the land could be made to stretch under a more efficient organization of production? In the more advanced, that is, the more densely settled, areas of the continent there were significant attempts to answer that question. In the Netherlands and in England experiments tested the utility of new crops. Perhaps there were ways of eliminating the fallow year that had kept one third of the land annually out of production. Perhaps it was possible to bring more meat to the butcher not only by increasing the number of beasts, but also by increasing the weight of each through scientific breeding.

Landlords everywhere were quick to sense the potentialities. In region after region, England, Ireland, France, the Rhineland, Italy, Prussia, Hungary, Poland, Russia, there were excited speculations, eager efforts to apply the new developments.

But everywhere the old wasteful peasant village stood in the way. In these minuscule plots too many men followed stubbornly their traditional communal ways. As long as they remained, there could be no innovations. Sometimes the landlords tried to introduce the changes on their own lands, using outsiders as intermediaries, English farmers in Ireland, for instance, or Germans in Poland. But such compromises left untouched the great common meadows and forests, to say nothing of the arable lands in the grip of the peasants themselves. The ultimate solution, from the viewpoint of efficient exploitation, was consolidation of all the tiny plots into unified holdings and the liquidation of the common fields.

Only the power of government could effect the transition, for the dissolution of vested rights, centuries old, called for the sanctions of law. From England to Russia, in the century or so after 1750, a series of enactments destroyed the old agricultural order. The forms were varied; there were statutes by parliament, decrees from the Crown. The terms varied—enclosure, reform, liberation. But the effect did not vary.

Men drove into the village. They had the appearance of officers and the support of law. They were heavy with documents and quick in reckoning. They asked questions, wished to see papers, tried to learn what had been in time beyond the memory of man. There came with them also surveyors to measure the land. Then the peasants were told: they were now to be land-owners, each to have his own farm proportionate to his former share and in one piece. The communal holdings were to disappear; every plot would be individual property, could be fenced around and dealt with by each as he liked.

Whether or not strict justice was done the peasant depended upon local circumstances and the conscience of the executing officials; it was not always possible to supply precise legal proof for property traditionally held. But in every case, the change undermined the whole peasant position. They were indeed now owners of their own farms; but they were less able than ever to maintain their self-sufficiency. The cost of the proceedings, in some places the requirement of fencing, left them in debt; they would have to find cash to pay. When the wastes disappeared there disappeared also the free wood for fire or building; there would have to be cash now to buy. If there were no longer common meadows, where would the cows graze?

All now found themselves compelled to raise crops that could be offered for sale. Confined to their own few acres and burdened with obligations, the peasants had no other recourse. The necessity was cruel for these were in no position to compete on the traders' market with the old landlords whose great holdings operated with the efficiency of the new methods and ultimately of the new machinery. Steadily the chill of mounting debt blanketed the village. Like the chill of winter, it extinguished growth and hope, only worse, for there seemed no prospect of a spring ahead.

The change, which weakened all, desolated those whose situation was already marginal. The cottiers, the cropsharers, the tenants on short-term leases of any kind could be edged out at any time. They had left only the slimmest hopes of remaining where they were.

Some early gave up and joined the drift to the towns, where, as in England, they supplied the proletariat that manned the factories of the Industrial Revolution. Others swelled the ranks of the agricultural labor force that wandered seasonally to the great estates in search of hire. Still others remained, working the land on less and less favorable terms, slaving to hold on.

A few emigrated. Those who still had some resources but feared a loss of status learned with hope of the New World where land, so scarce in the Old, was abundantly available. Younger sons learned with hope that the portions which at home would not buy them the space for a garden, in America would make them owners of hundreds of acres. Tempted by the prospect of princely rewards for their efforts, they ventured to tear themselves away from the ancestral village, to undertake the unknown risks of transplantation. The movement of such men was the first phase of what would be a cataclysmic transfer of population.

But this phase was limited, involved few peasants. A far greater number were still determined to hold on; mounting adversities only deepened that determination. In addition, the costs of emigration were high, the difficulties ominous; few had the energy and power of will to surmount such obstacles. And though the landlords were anxious to evict as many as possible, there was no point in doing so without the assurance that the evicted would depart. Otherwise the destitute would simply remain, supported by parish charity, in one way or another continue to be a drain upon the landlords' incomes.

Soon enough disaster resolved the dilemma. There was no slack to the peasant situation. Without reserves of any kind these people were helpless in the face of the first crisis. The year the crops failed there was famine. Then the alternative to flight was death by starvation. In awe the peasant saw his fields barren, yielding nothing to sell, nothing to eat. He looked up and saw the emptiness of his neighbors' lands, of the whole village. In all the country round his startled eyes fell upon the same desolation. Who would now help? The empty weeks went by, marked by the burial of the first victims; at the workhouse door the gentry began to ladle out the thin soup of charity; and a heartsick weariness settled down over the stricken cottages. So much striving had come to no end.

Now the count was mounting. The endless tolling of the sexton's bell, the narrowing family circle, were shaping an edge of resolution. The tumbled huts, no longer home to anyone, were urging it. The empty road was pointing out its form. It was time.

He would leave now, escape; give up this abusive land his fathers had never really mastered. He would take up what remained and never see the sight of home again. He would become a stranger on the way, pack on back, lead wife and children toward some other destiny. For all about was evidence of the consequences of staying. Any alternative was better.

What sum the sale of goods and land would bring would pay the cost. And if nothing remained, then aid would come from the gentry or the parish, now compassionate in the eagerness to rid the place of extra hands, now generous in the desire to ease the burden on local charity. So, in the hundreds of thousands, peasants came to migrate. This was the second phase in the transfer of a continent's population.

It was not the end. Years of discontent followed. The burdens of those who stayed grew no lighter with the going of those who went. Grievances fed on the letters from America of the departed. From outposts in the New World came advice and assistance. Across the Atlantic the accumulation of immigrants created a magnetic pole that would for decades continue to draw relatives and friends in a mighty procession. This was the third phase.

With the peasants went a host of other people who found their own lives disrupted by the dislocation of the village. The empty inn now rarely heard the joy of wedding celebrations. The lonely church ministered to a handful of communicants. The tavernkeeper and priest, and with them smith and miller, followed in the train of those they once had served. There was less need now for the petty trade of Jews, for the labor of wandering artisans, for the tinkering of gypsies. These too joined the migration.

And toward the end, the flow of peoples received additions as well from the factories and mines. Often these were peasants or the sons of peasants whose first remove had been to the nearby city, men who had not yet found security or stability and who, at last, thought it better to go the way their cousins had earlier gone.

So Europe watched them go—in less than a century and a half, well over thirty-five million of them from every part of the continent. In this common flow were gathered up people of the most diverse qualities, people whose rulers had for centuries been enemies, people who had not even known of each other's existence. Now they would share each other's future.

Westward from Ireland went four and a half million. On that crowded island a remorselessly rising population, avaricious absentee landlords, and English policy that discouraged the growth of industry early stimulated emigration. Until 1846 this had been largely a movement of younger sons, of ambitious farmers and artisans. In that year rot destroyed the potato crop and left the cottiers without the means of subsistence. Half a million died and three million more lived on only with the aid of charity. No thought then of paying rent, of holding on to the land; the evicted saw their huts pulled down and with bitter gratitude accepted from calculating poor-law officials the price of passage away from home. For decades after, till the end of the nineteenth century and beyond, these peasants continued to leave, some victims of later agricultural disasters, some sent for by relatives already across, some simply unable to continue a way of life already thoroughly disrupted.

Westward from Great Britain went well over four million. There enclosure and displacement had begun back in the eighteenth century, although the first to move generally drifted to the factories of the expanding cities. By 1815, however, farmers and artisans in substantial numbers had emigration in mind; and after midcentury they were joined by a great mass of landless peasants, by operatives from the textile mills, by laborers from the potteries, and by miners from the coal fields. In this number were Scots, Welsh, and Englishmen, and also the sons of some Irishmen, sons whose parents had earlier moved across the Irish Sea.

From the heart of the continent, from the lands that in 1870 became the German Empire, went fully six million. First to leave were the free husbandmen of the southwest, then the emancipated peasants of the north and east. With them moved, in the earlier years, artisans dislocated by the rise of industry, and later some industrial workers.

From the north went two million Scandinavians. Crop failures, as in 1847 in Norway, impelled some to leave. Others found their lots made harsher by the decline in the fisheries and by the loss of the maritime market for timber. And for many more, the growth of commercial agriculture, as in Sweden, was the indication no room would remain for free peasants.

From the south went almost five million Italians. A terrible cholera epidemic in 1887 set them moving. But here, as elsewhere, the stream was fed by the deepr displacement of the peasantry.

From the east went some eight million others—Poles and Jews, Hungarians, Bohemians, Slovaks, Ukrainians, Ruthenians—as agriculture took new forms in the Austrian and Russian Empires after 1880.

And before the century was out perhaps three million more were on the way from the Balkans and Asia Minor: Greeks and Macedonians, Croatians and Albanians, Syrians and Armenians.

In all, thirty-five million for whom home had no place fled to Europe's shores and looked across the Atlantic.

What manner of refuge lay there?

VI AMERICA

26 THE POTLATCH

Philip Drucker

The word "potlatch" comes from Chinook Jargon, a widespread trade language, and means simply "giving," in the sense of giving a gift. In each native language there were special terms to designate the institution. The potlatch was common to all groups except those at the southern extreme, and while there were numerous minor differences in details, the basic pattern of the potlatch and its function were uniform.

A potlatch was a ceremonial given by a chief and his group, as hosts, to guests composed of another chief or chiefs with their respective groups, at which the guests were given wealth goods. Essential to a potlatch was the guest-host relation, although the exact composition of the groups might vary. Properly, the local group was the basic unit, both as host group and guest group, but sometimes larger units were involved. Indians distinguished between affairs at which only food was given, to be eaten immediately and to be carried home by the guests, and those at which other forms of goods were distributed. The former may be called "feasts," the latter, "potlatches." The distinction refers to the main event, and a potlatch usually included at least some preliminary feasting.

The overt purpose of both feast and potlatch was the announcement of an event of social significance: marriage of an important person, birth of a potential heir to one of the group's titles, crests, and high statuses, inheritance and formal assump-

FROM Philip Drucker, *Cultures of the North Pacific Coast*, pp. 55–66. Copyright © 1965 by Chandler Publishing Company. Reprinted by permission of the publisher.

tion of one of these titles or crests and its corresponding position, and rescue or ransom and restoration to free status of a war
captive. These announcements were not made perfunctorily.
When a title was concerned, the announcement included an
account of its origin, how it had been acquired by an ancestor,
whether bestowed by a supernatural being or captured in warfare, how it had been transmitted down the family line to the
person on whom it was being bestowed. Much of the legendary
history of the group was recited to prove the right to use the
name or privilege. Then the gifts were distributed in the name
of the recipient of the title or crest. The first and largest gift
went to the highest-ranking guest, the second and next largest
to the second in precedence, and so on down the line. Recital
of the history of the privilege and the distribution of wealth
served to validate its use. The guests were witnesses to the fact
that the privilege was rightfully owned and rightfully transmitted
to its new bearer. This sanction was the essence of the potlatch
and the prime purpose of the wealth. The effect of the procedure
may be compared to that of notarizing a document or of
registering a deed.

A person might be recognized as the only proper heir to the
highest-ranking status, but until a potlatch had been given at
which he formally claimed the position and its privileges, he had
no right to use them. Nor was he entitled to the deference and
honors of the status. For example, he was not invited to potlatches
of others nor given gifts. The myriad of rights in North Pacific
Coast culture had to be validated in this manner. The rights
included those to names and titles, not only names of persons but
traditionally owned names for houses and other property, the
right to use specific masks and symbols in rituals, the right to
perform the rituals themselves, to use carvings, feast dishes, and
the ownership of places of economic and ritual importance. Feasts
had a similar function. It was usual to announce to guests, for
example, that they were invited to eat sockeye salmon from
such-and-such a stream, which had been discovered, given to, or
captured in war by an ancestor and transmitted to the incumbent
head of the group. The public announcement and tacit recognition of the fact by the guest group, so to speak, legalized the
claim.

THE FORMALITIES OF THE POTLATCH

Actual procedure of the potlatch was both complex and highly formal. The first step after plans and preparations was the dispatching of an invitation party to the village of the guests. This party was ceremoniously treated, and was given a feast where they could deliver the invitation orally to the assembled group, setting the date on which the guests would be expected. If the villages were distant and the weather uncertain, guests usually arrived by canoeloads a day or two ahead of time and camped nearby or were quartered informally among the hosts; but if so, on the appointed day they reembarked to make a mass arrival. If there were preliminary feasts or ceremonials, these were begun; if not, the guests were ushered into the potlatch house.

Among many groups, guests of high rank were called in order of precedence, each in turn being escorted by ushers to a place of honor corresponding to his rank. When more than one group of guests had been invited, an elaborate protocol had to be worked out, the chief of the highest-ranking group being seated first, and chief of the second-highest group next, then that of the third group, and so on. Then those of second rank were seated. The problem was as complex as that of seating admirals of various navies at a formal banquet in Washington. Men of lower rank and commoners were seated as a group. Just where the line was drawn between the guests individually seated and the rest depended partly on local custom and partly on the elaborateness of the potlatch. When large amounts of riches were to be distributed, more guests were individually seated than at small-scale distributions. Speeches of welcome were made and replied to, supplementing those made on the formal arrival. Men thoroughly versed in the etiquette of the potlatch, the precedence order of the guests, and the family traditions, did the speechmaking for many chiefs, just as researchers and writers assist modern public figures in preparing their public addresses.

The next step was usually the display of crests and performance of dances and songs, not just for entertainment but because these referred to the privileges about to be bestowed. In the northern portion of the area, where major potlatches were strongly commemorative, revolving about the theme of the death of a chief and the inheritance of his title and status, dirges were sung and offerings to the deceased chief and his predecessors were made by burning food and other articles. The new holder of the title was presented, the gifts were distributed, the quantity or nature of each gift was announced by the speaker, and the tallymen busily counted bundles of mnemonic sticks to keep accounts of the presents and the recipients. (Recently chiefs have used secretaries, literate young men with notebooks and fountain pens, instead of the prehistoric tallyman.) Thanks were given by the recipient of each gift, and at the conclusion of the distribution the ranking guest or his speaker made a speech of thanks for all his group not only for the gifts, but for having been shown the prized privileges and having had the new holder of the privileges presented to them.

The foregoing is a synthesized outline of typical potlatch procedure, but there were numerous local differences in detail. For example, groups of the central portion normally potlatched outdoors, rather than in a house. Some Coast Salish were fond of the "scramble" as a method of distributing goods to commoners, but never to chiefs. Goat-wool robes were torn into strips that were tossed into the crowd rather than distributed in more orderly fashion, and contests of various sorts were part of the preliminary entertainment during a potlatch given on the occasion of a marriage. A common form of these contests consisted in a scramble for a wooden ball; the winner was given a prize, apart from the gift he might receive in the formal distribution of presents.

The minor deviations from the basic pattern do not obscure the fact that the potlatch was a formal function with a rigid etiquette, given for a serious purpose, that of validating the assumption of hereditary rights and thereby the whole system of rank. It also validated the social rank of the guest group, whose social precedence was recognized in the seating arrangements, in the use of guests' formal titles, and in the order in which the gifts were given. Reciprocity was expressed in this aspect of the institution. When the roles were reversed and the guests in their turn potlatched, they demonstrated their approval of the ex-hosts' claims by using the titles they had witnessed and by recognizing the order of rank associated with these titles.

Another function of the potlatch is its effect as a force contributing to the social solidarity of the basic social unit, the extended family-local group, which was also the potlatch unit, whether as host or guest. In some areas there were confederations of local groups into "tribes," although the constituent local groups retained their identity and many of their functions. These tribes occasionally acted as units in potlatching, but this fact does not negate the primary importance of the local group.

The chief of the group was the nominal host and played the most prominent single role because of his position as administrator of the extended family's properties. However, everyone recognized that the whole group—nobles and commoners, whether closely or distantly related to the chief—were hosts. The entire host group assembled on the beach to greet the guests on their formal arrival. All assisted in the preparations, including the assembling of the goods for the distribution. All were identified with their group during the proceedings, if not as stellar performers, as speakers, tallykeepers, ushers, dancers, or singers.

During the potlatch, individuals of lesser rank, including commoners, also received names or other privileges from the group store according to their status. The contributions of parents (of maternal uncles in matrilineal societies) sponsoring low-rank recipients of privileges were often announced, further emphasizing identification as group members. The guests similarly were invited as members of their social unit and treated as a group even though the amount of the potlatch goods given to a commoner guest might be inconsequential. In short, at a potlatch every member of both host and guest groups participated with his social unit and thereby publicly identified himself as a member of it.

Some ethnographic literature on the economics of the potlatch, unfortunately, has confused the potlatch with two other phenomena: the loans at interest and the spectacular rivalry potlatch. For example, it has been asserted that among the Southern Kwakiutl every potlatch gift had to be returned at 100 percent interest. According to this interpretation, if Chief A invited ten other chiefs—B, C, D, E, F, G, H, I, J, and K—to a potlatch at which he presented each with 100 cheap trade blankets, he would thus distribute 1,000 blankets. Chiefs B, C, D, and so forth would be obligated, when they potlatched, to invite Chief A and give him 200 blankets in return. This would mean that if all ten chiefs were punctilious, A would eventually receive 2,000 blankets. But, according to this erroneous view, the obligation did not stop here; it was endless, a sort of commercial chain letter. Chief A would have to repay each of the 200 gifts at 100 percent interest, or in other words to distribute ten gifts of 400, or 4,000 blankets. It is unnecessary to continue this example to the 64,000-blanket level. It is evident that a system in which debts increased endlessly by geometric progression is impossible.

In addition to the fact that a single sequence of potlatches would soon involve tremendous amounts of valuables, as illustrated, Chief A would be invited to other potlatches besides those of B to K, and theoretically each would result in a similar progression. It has been suggested that the quantities of blankets were fictitious, the whole system operating on credit, but there are accounts of eyewitnesses who observed bales of trade blankets and other valuables being distributed.

Internal evidence from detailed descriptions of potlatches and data from informants of groups who potlatched until recent days agree that the loans at interest were quite apart from the potlatch gifts. The amount of each potlatch gift had no relation to any previous gift, except in the general sense that a potlatch gift should be adequate, not niggardly. The amount given each guest depended upon the total amount distributed, modified by the relative rank of the recipient. Guests of noble rank who participated in the potlatch were expected sooner or later to potlatch, "returning" the gifts they had received in much the same way that a modern host expects his dinner invitations to be "returned." There was no requirement that each successive distribution had to be twice as large as the preceding one, or in any exact relation to previous potlatch gifts. Validation of social rank, through formally assuming hereditary privileges, was the purpose of the institution.

It is patent that the potlatch pattern before the introduction of trade goods differed from the pattern after white contact, in frequency and splendor but not in function. During the period for which fullest ethnographic data are available, trade blankets were introduced mainly by Hudson's Bay Company and sold for $1.50 apiece. They became almost an equivalent of currency and were the principal articles distributed in potlatches, where they were used by the hundreds. Before the advent of bales of blankets and other mass-produced trade articles, native wealth was used. These items were scarce, for one of several possible reasons. They were rare in nature, like the nuggets of pure copper from which "coppers" were made. Or they were a long time in the making, like the laboriously manufactured canoes and robes. Or they were difficult to take, like the peltries of the shy sea otter and the marmot. Consequently, even a populous and industrious group would need years to assemble enough wealth articles for a potlatch. Well-informed Indians from groups famous in recent times for their numerous and opulent potlatches often told me of the traditional statement that in prewhite times feasts were common, but potlatches were infrequent. This does not mean that the potlatch is merely an historical phenomenon. It means that the abundance of trade goods gave a new exuberance to the potlatch in the distribution of spectacular quantities of articles. However, even in the epoch of the plethora of imported goods, the Tlingit, Haida, and Tsimshian of the northern part of the area preserved an aspect of the ancient pattern. Of their numerous potlatches the only one considered major was on the death of the chief to honor his memory and to transmit his status and position to his heir. Thus, each chief gave only one major potlatch in his career—that in which he formally assumed his title. If, as seems reasonable, in aboriginal times potlatches were infrequent and could utilize only a relatively limited store of wealth goods, no endless chain of double repayment could have prevailed.

The Potlatch and Loans at Interest

In spite of its limited practice, the loan at interest is another factor contributing to the misunderstanding of the operation of the potlatch. Simple loans had a somewhat wider distribution. In a number of groups kinsmen *outside* the social unit of the potlatch might lend valuables for the distribution. These loans were repaid, after an indefinite period, in the amount given. Some informants aver that it was in good taste to return a little more than the amount of the original loan to demonstrate gratitude and solvency, but there was no fixed rate of increase. However, loans at interest were strictly commercial transactions, the rate being agreed upon at the time of the loan. The ruinous 100 percent rate was usual for a long-term loan, that is, for several years. Loans for shorter periods called for lower, but still usurious rates: 50 percent for a year or so, and 20 to 25 percent for a few months.

The only connection between these loans and the potlatch was that a creditor could demand repayment of principal and interest only when he was about to give a potlatch, in other words, when he needed the surplus. There are no exact data on the origin of the custom, but there is reason to suspect it may not be aboriginal in origin, particularly because of the differential in rates according to duration of the loan. It is probably significant that loans at interest consisted of trade blankets or money, not of aboriginal value items.

THE RIVALRY POTLATCH

The spectacular rivalry potlatches came to a peak in the latter decades of the nineteenth century and the opening years of the twentieth. In these affairs, great quantities of valuables were given away or destroyed—coppers were broken, canoes were smashed, money was thrown in the fire, and in the days before the white man's law was enforced, slaves were slain—all to humiliate a rival. The serene, super-polite, and occasionally jovial air of the common potlatch was replaced by an atmosphere of bitterness. Insults were flung and guests were made uncomfortable, as when olachen oil was poured on the fire both to destroy the oil and to force the guests to abandon their seats near it.

Competition between two men for a specific status resulted in the rivalry potlatch. It involved two rivals who were potential heirs for a position, for primacy in the protocol or precedence, or for a particular title with its attendant privileges and prerogatives. First, one would give a potlatch to announce his claims, more or less in the normal manner. Then, the rival would potlatch to the same group of guests, or to additional groups as well. He would deny and belittle the claims of his rival and emphasize his own claims to the status. The first claimant was obliged thereby to give another potlatch to reiterate his pretensions, the challenger replied in kind, and the competition went on and on.

Each rival attempted to outdo his opponent's latest effort, giving away and destroying more wealth to demonstrate his economic superiority. The contests were not merely to see which rival had the most wealth; the specific goal was to obtain validation of the claim to the rights in question. The motive for outdoing the rival was to mold the opinion of the chiefs whose places in the potlatch were recognized without dispute, for they were the court of final appeal who recognized or disregarded a claim.

A hypothetical example, assuming alphabetical Indians A to K, may clarify the reasoning. Let us assume that A and B were distant relatives of Chief X who died without direct heirs, that is, brothers or sons. Both A and B desired the position, which included the highest rank among the chiefs who assembled in the potlatch as demonstrated by the right to receive the first gift. Both potlatched, claiming the inheritance, before Chiefs C to K. After a time, Chief G gave a potlatch at which he had claimant B seated in the contested place, addressed him by the title of the deceased X, and gave him the first gift. Claimant A might protest by giving away or destroying valuables, and continue his competition with B. If he did so, however, he invited conflict with Chief G. G could either assist B in assembling potlatch valuables to reassert his claims or himself potlatch again, repeating his approval of B's claim. If the other chiefs supported G's stand, either at once or over a period of time as they gave potlatches, it became useless for A to continue his efforts to gain the title.

If one of the contestants went bankrupt, that is, could not assemble enough riches to equal or surpass the last effort of his opponent, he could no longer press his claim, losing it by default. The claim of the winner was regarded as justified, as in medieval Europe the victor in trial by combat was regarded to have proved his case. This special variety of potlatch was limited in distribution, and its origins are not known. However, several cultural and culture-historical factors contributed to its development.

Among groups that practiced the potlatch, there was also the face-saving presentation, which took place after any public indignity involving a person of high status. If he tripped and fell on a formal occasion, if he were shown to an inferior seat at a feast or potlatch, or if he were captured in war, his only recourse was to wipe away the affront by public announcement of his title and status and by giving away valuables. The elaborateness of the gift giving depended on the circumstances of the loss of dignity: if they were regarded as accidental, due to natural causes, a brief speech and a small gift were adequate to dispose of the matter. However, a deliberate insult—and a clumsy fall in public might be the result of magical machinations by persons of ill will—required a larger distribution of wealth or a full-dress potlatch. This was the *raison-d'être* for the potlatch on the occasion of the ransom or escape of a war captive. His liberation from slavery was celebrated by a reaffirmation of his status and titles, accompanied by a distribution of wealth. Then, as after all face-saving procedures, the disgrace was considered removed and was never again to be mentioned. The rivalry potlatch can be regarded as an application of the face-saving technique: it was the standard procedure when dignity had been injured, in this case, when claim to a status had been challenged.

A variant of the rivalry potlatch involved the status of groups rather than that of individuals. The rivalry might develop when two groups were invited to an occasion where previous custom dictated only one guest group be invited. The addition of guests might be associated with increase in prosperity, as when the introduction of trade goods in abundance stimulated an increase in frequency and scale of potlatching. Inviting new groups immediately raised questions of precedence that could well lead to conflicting claims.

Another factor contributed to rivalry: the confederation of several neighboring local groups into something approaching tribal organization, in which the originally autonomous local groups, although retaining their identities and most of their properties and rights, united in a common village during the winter season. In every such "tribe," the constituent local groups and their chiefs came to be ranked in a graded series, first, second, third, and so forth. Furthermore, there were mergers of tribes into still larger loose confederacies in which all local groups and chiefs were assigned places in a single precedence scale. Such mergers were patently made to order to produce conflict situations and competitive claims. The rivalry potlatch reached its maximum at two sites of early Hudson's Bay Company trading posts, where a number of tribes came to assemble for winter residence.

A third factor that set the stage for bitter rivalries was the sharp decrease in Indian population during the nineteenth century. Decrease was due chiefly to epidemics of diseases such as smallpox and venereal infections, introduced by Europeans, and to the greater efficiency of native warfare following the introduction of firearms. As a result, when the holder of an important title died, there was often no direct heir according to the rules of succession—younger brother, or son, or sister's son among matrilineal groups—and two distant relatives might emerge as competitors for the prestigeful inheritance. It would have been considered ridiculous for a distant kinsman (second or third cousin) to try to assert priority of right over a younger brother or a son. But when the only claimants were both about equally distant genealogically, they became potential rivals. The competitive potlatch afforded them a technique for the resolution of their conflict.

Nearly all specific accounts of potlatch rivalries fall into one of two conflict situations: the attempt to establish or to alter the order of precedence of groups, and the attempt to claim a vacant title and status. One additional category must be noted—the feigned rivalry. Where the rivalry potlatch was common, the people apparently enjoyed the excitement of its bickering, lavish giving, destruction of wealth, and constant threat of open violence. Hence, now and then two chiefs planning to potlatch would arrange in secret to pretend conflict. A common pretext was to allege that their ancestors had been rivals. They gave their potlatches with all the apparent furor and anger that characterized true rivalry, but carefully controlled the spectacles to come out a draw, thus entertaining the public and damaging no one's prestige. On the other hand, many coastal divisions who did not practice the rivalry potlatch regarded such affairs, true or feigned, as ridiculous or in bad taste, not in keeping with the dignified formality of the normal potlatch.

COPPERS

Important items in the potlatch were plaques called "coppers." Placer copper was beaten into a plaque, the upper portion resembling in outline the keystone of an arch, the lower portion a rectangle. The two forms were set apart by the horizontal element of a T-shaped ridge, the vertical stem of which bisected the rectangle. In examples of aboriginal manufacture, the T-shaped ridge is formed of solid metal; in recent specimens of mill-made sheet copper imported by white traders, the ridge is repoussé, visible on the back of the piece as a concavity. Coppers varied from about a foot and a half to three feet in length.

Something of a mystery surrounds the making of the aboriginal coppers. Apparently they came already shaped from the Copper River region, but such metallurgical skill seems beyond the scope of the peoples of that area. The possibility remains that they were archaeological pieces. As they were traded southward, many were decorated with engraving or shallow carving by artists of the northern portion of the coast, as the style of the design attests.

These objects were invariably related to the potlatch complex. When a copper was sold, the transaction had implications beyond that of an ordinary commercial deal in the inherent obligation to use the proceeds of the sale in a potlatch. Among northern groups, the coppers were displayed, then broken during the memorial potlatch for a deceased chief and the assumption of his position by the heir. The copper fragments, referred to as the "bones of the deceased," were given to high-ranking guests. The value of the coppers increased as they were traded from group to group southward, and at the southern margin of their distribution unbroken coppers attained great worth. The price was at least double that of the previous sale.

As coppers lost their association with mortuary rites, they became closely associated with marriage payments and were often given as part of the bride-price and bride-price repayment: they were supposed to be sold to augment the wealth distributed in the potlatches made with the bride-price and its repayment. In rivalry potlatches the objects were boastfully displayed, then hacked to pieces in order to compel the rival to sacrifice a copper of as great or greater value.

Individual coppers were named, and their histories were well known. In the 1880's when Canadian law made potlatching illegal, police authorities confiscated coppers and other ceremonial appurtenances, which were presented to the National Museum of Canada. However, the Indians regarded the confiscation as unjustified and continued to recognize Indian title to the wealth.

Certain splendid specimens of coppers in the museum continued to figure in marriage presentations and potlatch transactions for many years. Particular items came to have fabulous value, for they were safe from the normal destiny of coppers: they could not be broken, but title to them continued to be transferable.

27 POMO TRADE FEASTS[1]

Andrew P. Vayda

Largely on account of the perishability of primitive consumption goods, the capacity to postpone consumption tends to be low in primitive societies. Indeed, the limitations on this capacity have been emphasized by Forde (1956:340–342) and other students of economic anthropology (e.g., Gluckman 1943:35; Worsley 1956:71–72) as the mark of a primitive economy. My first object in this paper is to suggest how the capacity to postpone consumption may be augmented through the intercourse of local groups in regions where the production and availability of subsistence goods significantly varies from one place to another and from one time to another. A second object is to show a particular way in which the intercourse of local groups can contribute to the spreading out or equalization of subsistence not only through time but also in space and not only between communities but also within communities. The data used in the paper are drawn from ethnographic accounts of intervillage trade among the Pomo Indians of central California. Although the data have been published previously (see especially Loeb 1926 and Barrett 1952), they have not received the attention that I think they deserve.

FROM Andrew P. Vayda, "Pomo Trade Feasts," *Humanités, Cahiers de l'Institut de Science Économique Appliquée* (1966). Reprinted by permission of the author and publisher.

[1] An earlier version of this paper was mimeographed in March 1954 as Memorandum 8 of the Columbia University Interdisciplinary Project on "Economic Aspects of Institutional Growth," directed by Professors K. Polanyi and C. M. Arensberg.

THE BACKGROUND OF POMO INTERVILLAGE TRADE

The Russian River drainage in the Coast Range north of the San Francisco area was the heart of the territory of the Pomo Indians. Aboriginally, the region was among the most densely peopled areas north of the Rio Grande. Total Pomo population has been estimated at some 7 or 8 thousand, distributed among thirty-four "tribelets" or village communities (Kroeber 1925: 237–238; 1953:96). In pre-white days, there was complete dependence on wild foods, and these occurred in great variety and usually in abundance (Barrett 1952:47; Kniffen 1939), although occasionally there were famines (Barrett 1952:112–113; cf. Aginsky 1939:209–210). Each community relied mainly on its immediate environs for its subsistence, but some foods had to be obtained from distant points, since there were geographical differences in the availability of such foods as lake fish, salmon, sea food, acorns, game, etc. Thus, for example, the people living in the interior journeyed to the coast for sea foods once or twice every year, and the coast residents made journeys inland to get foods not common to their region. Permission to harvest what they wanted was usually granted to visitors. There was also a custom by which other communities would be invited over to share in a superabundance of some particular kind of food. The visitors brought a considerable amount of beads for their hosts if they accepted the invitation to the feast. Sometimes, the local over-supply of some given product (x) would be made the occasion not only of feasting by a host people and a guest people but also of a regular beads-for-x trade. This trade, well described by E. M. Loeb, is the feature of Pomo economic practices which has particular relevance for us.

Before, however, we consider this, attention must be given to the use of beads by the Pomo, since this figures importantly in the trade.

For both magnesite and shell beads, but especially the shell ones, there were many uses. In gift-giving, which had to be reciprocated (and with great liberality if prestige was to be attained), the standard of value, according to S. A. Barrett, always was beads, especially the clam-shell discs. Payments of beads were sometimes the means of settling intervillage feuds, such as those occasioned by trespassing (Barrett 1952:289).

At times, beads were used for buying such valued products as salt cakes at fixed rates from better supplied communities. No community, however, held a monopoly of any such product. If they made proper presentation of gifts to the local inhabitants, any Pomo Indians could have access to the salt deposits, the clam shells and magnesite, the stones for arrow heads and the materials for paints—all of which were procured from definite localities that usually were neutral ground by virtue of general Pomo custom.

In funerary and other offerings and in the discharging of blood-revenge debts, the beads had perhaps their greatest use (Barrett 1952:289; cf. Loeb 1926:201, 203–205, 209, 283, 287, 292, 294, 297, 311, 312, 327, 383). Funeral customs, including the burning of the greater part of one's material possessions at death, contributed to preventing the growth of significant inequalities of fortune (Loeb 1926:195, 199). Barrett does note that some "well-to-do persons . . . hired their work done," the payment often being made in beads. However, the greater the liberality of payment, the greater was the resultant prestige (Barrett 1952:290).

DESCRIPTION OF THE TRADE

The following account of Pomo trade feasts is a compilation from the descriptions by Loeb (1926:192–194) and Barrett (1952:352–353, 416).

Suppose, says Loeb, that the Lake people had an over-supply of fish. The Yokaia people might then be asked to come over for a feast. A good runner among the Lake people would be dispatched as a messenger with a special "invitation string" to the Yokaia. The invitation string consisted of short sticks of willow or wormwood, tied, each separately, into a string. The number of sticks used equalled the number of days, usually between two and eight, intervening before the feast was to commence. A fish-tail was attached to the invitation string to indicate that the invitation was to share fish. (If it were to share acorns, an acorn would be attached.) The "big" chief of the Yokaia village received the invitation string, along with any accompanying message, and then made the announcement to his people. If the Yokaia chiefs decided to accept the fish feast invitation, they asked the men of the village each to contribute as many beads as he could to a common fund. A single stick was broken off the invitation string for each day that passed. The Yokaia Indians moved, in a body, to the Lake village so as to arrive when the last stick had been broken off. At the Lake village, the Yokaia chiefs' spokesman presented the beads to the Lake chiefs' spokesman, saying, "Here are a few beads with which to help yourself." Then he told how pleased the Yokaia people were with the Lake people's invitation and friendship.

After this, there were several days of festivities prior to completion of the trade. The Lake chiefs freely fed the Yokaia visitors during their stay, apparently from stores that had been assembled especially for the occasion. The men visitors made free use of the sweat-houses; they gambled and sweated there.

In finally consummating the deal, the host chief divided the presented beads into strings of hundreds. The Lake chiefs then determined in council how much produce they would give for each string of beads. After the beads had been laid upon the ground at some prearranged spot, the several family representatives of the Lake people went to their respective stores and each returned with measures of produce to the value of one string. The giver of the fish, after he had left a measure of produce on a common pile, went to where the strings of beads had been placed and took the string of a hundred beads to which he was entitled. This transaction of piling up the fish and taking the beads was kept up by the fish givers as long as they continued to desire to make the trade, or else as long as the beads held out.

When the fish were all piled up, the chief of the guests took possession. Up to this point, the Yokaia people had not been involved in the transaction but had merely waited to take what was offered without making any effort to haggle. The Yokaia chief now allotted to each family a basketful or other equal portion of fish, going around as many times as the pile afforded. He kept for himself whatever remained when there was no longer enough to go around once more in the same proportion.

Some variations on these trading practices are reported from

Morgan Valley, where the Lower Lake visitors traded beads not directly for fish but rather for the right, following a great feast, to go fishing in the creek belonging to the Morgan Valley hosts. This creek contained certain species of fish not found in the waters of the Lower Lake. Each of the Morgan Valley people is said to have had a certain section of the creek allotted to him, and all the fish caught in it were his. After the Lower Lake people had gone home, the beads and other presents which they had brought were distributed by the Morgan Valley chief to each of his people in accordance with the amount of fish caught from his section of the creek.

Pomo trade feasts resulted commonly from fish invitations and acorn invitations and occasionally from seed invitations. The Sherwood people annually took bows and arrows to the East Lake Pomo and accepted beads in exchange. However, it was more common for the Lake people to procure arrow heads or bows by traveling uninvited in parties of nine or ten north to the Sherwood people.

DISCUSSION

What are some of the implications of variations in the production and availability of subsistence goods from one place to another and from one time to another? They can mean that community A at some given time would be able to get more food than it could consume by itself while community B at the same time might be short of food supplies; at some other time, community B might have the "superabundance," while there would be shortage in community A. Where there are these contingencies, it is advantageous to have some mechanism whereby members of a community can temporarily "bank" a surplus of food with members of other communities. The Pomo trade feasts seem to have been such a mechanism. By accepting an invitation to a trade feast, the Pomo Indians who had previously "banked" food would be getting food back, and they might be doing this at a time when the food would be more needed by them for consumption than had been the case with the goods that they had traded earlier to other communities. In other words, the trade feasts apparently served to augment the people's capacity to postpone the consumption of subsistence goods.

It needs to be noted that the trade feasts apparently promoted the spreading out and equalization of consumption in space as well as in time. For the trade feasts Pomo Indians not well supplied at a given time with particular foods journeyed to a village having a superabundance of those products. The food was traded for beads. Thus, whereas prior to the trading there was inequality in the two peoples' resources of particular foods, it may be presumed that the operations of the trade transferred at least the major part of that inequality to the amount of beads possessed by each group.

These beads were prized mainly for the prestige which their possession and, even more, their generous expenditure bestowed. When the chiefs of a village accepted an invitation to a trade feast they called on the men of the village each to give as many beads to the common fund as he could spare. Every man must have given as liberally as possible, since therein lay prestige; therefore, a community that had received a "superabundance" of beads through its trading may be expected to have disposed of that superabundance when it in turn was invited to a trade feast. It should also be recalled that the chief of the host village arranged for distribution of the beads according to the amount of food that each of his people contributed, but the visitors' chief allotted the food with no regard for the amount of beads furnished by the several members of his community. Thus it seems that the Pomo trade feasts served to convert inequalities in subsistence into more or less temporary inequalities in the possession of beads not only between communities but also within communities. Accordingly the feasts may be regarded comparable in function to mechanisms operating in other systems to reduce either intercommunity or intracommunity inequalities in subsistence goods. Among such mechanisms that may be instanced from various parts of the world are the potlatches of the Northwest Coast Indians (Suttles 1960; Vayda 1961); the ceremonial slaughtering and distributing of cattle or pigs in certain African, Asian, and Oceanian societies (Fürer-Haimendorf 1962:117–118; Schneider 1957; Vayda, Leeds, and Smith 1961); and the prescribed distributions of consumption goods by holders of ritual offices in Latin American peasant communities (Nash 1961:190; Wolf 1955:458).

We may, in concluding, note that some students have looked at systems in which such mechanisms operate and have decided that the importance of the systems lies primarily either in establishing or maintaining social bonds among people (e.g., Colson 1955:77ff.; Deacon 1934:16–17, 202; Leslie 1960:73–74) or in satisfying the desires of individuals for prestige and status (e.g., Firth 1951:145; Herskovits 1952:476). Even Loeb, whose description of Pomo trade feasts is so valuable, has written elsewhere that primitive trade is "essentially of social rather than economic significance" (Loeb 1936:154). The analysis of Pomo trade feasts presented here suggests to me that the effects which particular kinds of trading or feasting practices have upon the distribution of subsistence goods need probably to be re-examined carefully before we can be justified in concluding that the primary function of those practices is something other than economic.

28 TYPES OF LATIN AMERICAN
PEASANTRY: A PRELIMINARY
DISCUSSION[1]

Eric R. Wolf

As anthropology has become increasingly concerned with the study of modern communities, anthropologists have paid increasing attention to the social and cultural characteristics of the peasantry. It will be the purpose of this article to draw up a tentative typology of peasant groups for Latin America, as a basis for further field work and discussion. Such a typology will of necessity raise more questions than can be answered easily at the present time. To date, anthropologists working in Latin America have dealt mainly with groups with "Indian" cultures, and available anthropological literature reflects this major interest. Any projected reorientation of inquiry from typologies based mainly on characteristics of culture content to typologies based on similarities or dissimilarities of structure has implications with which no single writer could expect to cope. This article is therefore provisional in character, and its statements wholly open to discussion.

There have been several recent attempts to draw a line between primitives and peasants. Redfield, for example, has discussed the distinction in the following words (1953:31):

> There were no peasants before the first cities. And those surviving primitive peoples who do not live in terms of the city are not peasants. . . . The peasant is a rural native whose long-established order of life takes important account of the city.

FROM Eric R. Wolf, "Types of Latin American Peasantry: A Preliminary Discussion." *American Anthropologist,* Vol. 57 (1955), pp. 452–471. Reprinted by permission of the author and publisher.

[1] The writer would like to thank Morton H. Fried, Sidney W. Mintz, Robert F. Murphy, Robert Redfield, Julian H. Steward, and Ben Zimmerman for helpful criticisms and suggestions.

Kroeber has also emphasized the relation between the peasant and the city (1948:284):

> Peasants are definitely rural—yet live in relation to market towns; they form a class segment of a larger population which usually contains also urban centers, sometimes metropolitan capitals. They constitute part-societies with part-cultures.

Peasants thus form "horizontal sociocultural segments," as this term has been defined by Steward (1950:115).

Redfield further states that the city was made "possible" through the labor of its peasants (1953), and both definitions imply—though they do not state outright—that the city consumes a large part of what the peasant produces. Urban life is impossible without production of an agricultural surplus in the countryside.

Since we are interested less in the generic peasant type than in discriminating between different types of peasants, we must go on to draw distinctions between groups of peasants involved in divergent types of urban culture (for a discussion of differences in urban centers, cf. Beals 1951:8–9; Hoselitz 1953). It is especially important to recognize the effects of the industrial revolution and the growing world market on peasant segments the world over. These have changed both the cultural characteristics of such segments and the character of their relations with other segments. Peasants everywhere have become involved in market relations of a vastly different order of magnitude than those which prevailed before the advent of industrial culture. Nor can this expansion be understood as a purely unilineal phenomenon. There have been different types of industry and markets, different types of industrial expansion and market growth. These have affected different parts of the world in very different ways. The peasantries found in the world today are the multiple products of such multilineal growth. At the same time, peasants are no longer the primary producers of wealth. Industry and trade rather than agriculture now produce the bulk of the surpluses needed to support segments not directly involved in the processes of production. Various kinds of large-scale agricultural enterprises have grown up to compete with the peasant for economic resources and opportunities. This has produced a world-wide "crisis of the peasantry" (Firth 1952:12), related to the increasingly marginal role of the peasantry within the prevalent economic system.

In choosing a definition of the peasant which would be adequate for our present purpose, we must remember that definitions are tools of thought, and not eternal verities. Firth, for example, defines the term as widely as possible, including not only agriculturists but also fishermen and rural craftsmen (1952:87). Others might be tempted to add independent rubber gatherers and strip miners. For the sake of initial analysis, this writer has found it convenient to consider each of these various kinds of enterprise separately and thus to define the term "peasant" as strictly as possible. Three distinctions may serve as the basis for such a definition. All three are chosen with a view to Latin American conditions, and all seem flexible enough to include varieties which we may discover in the course of our inquiry.

First, let us deal with the peasant only as an agricultural producer. This means that for the purposes of the present article we shall draw a line between peasants, on the one hand, and fishermen, strip miners, rubber gatherers, and livestock keepers, on the other. The economic and cultural implications of livestock keeping, for example, are sufficiently different from those of agriculture to warrant separate treatment. This is especially true in Latin America, where livestock keeping has been carried on mainly on large estates rather than on small holdings.

Second, we should—for our present purpose—distinguish between the peasant who retains effective control of land and the tenant whose control of land is subject to an outside authority. This distinction has some importance in Latin America. Effective control of land by the peasant is generally insured through direct ownership, through undisputed squatter rights, or through customary arrangements governing the rental and use of land. He does not have to pay dues to an outside landowner. Tenants, on the other hand, tend to seek security primarily through acceptance of outside controls over the arrangements of production and distribution, and thus often accept subordinate roles within hierarchically organized networks of relationships. The peasants generally retain much greater control of their processes of production. Outside controls become manifest primarily when they sell their goods on the market. Consideration of tenant segments belongs properly with a discussion of *haciendas* and plantations rather than with a discussion of the peasantry. This does not mean that in dealing with Latin America we can afford to forget for a moment that large estates overshadowed other forms of landholding for many centuries, or that tenant segments may exert greater ultimate influence on the total sociocultural whole than peasants.

Third, the peasant aims at subsistence, not at reinvestment. The starting point of the peasant is the needs which are defined by his culture. His answer, the production of cash crops for a market, is prompted largely by his inability to meet these needs within the sociocultural segment of which he is a part. He sells cash crops to get money, but this money is used in turn to buy goods and services which he requires to subsist and to maintain his social status, rather than to enlarge his scale of operations. We may thus draw a line between the peasant and another agricultural type whom we call the "farmer." The farmer views agriculture as a business enterprise. He begins his operations with a sum of money which he invests in a farm. The crops produced are sold not only to provide goods and services for the farm operator but to permit amortization and expansion of his business. The aim of the peasant is subsistence. The aim of the farmer is reinvestment (Wolf 1951:60–61). . . .

In setting up a typology of peasant segments we immediately face the difficulty that peasants are not primitives, that is, the culture of a peasant segment cannot be understood in terms of itself but is a part-culture, related to some larger integral whole. Certain relationships among the features of peasant culture are tied to bodies of relationships outside the peasant culture, yet help determine both its character and continuity. The higher the level of integration of such part-cultures, the greater the weight of such outside determinants.

> In complex societies certain components of the social super-structure rather than ecology seem increasingly to be determinants of further developments. (Steward 1938:262)

This is especially true when we reach the organization level of the capitalist market, where the relationship of technology and environment is mediated through complicated mechanisms of credit or political control which may originate wholly outside the part-culture under investigation.

We must not only be cognizant of outside factors which affect the culture of the part-culture. We must also account for the manner in which the part-culture is organized into the larger sociocultural whole. Unlike other horizontal sociocultural segments, like traders or businessmen, peasants function primarily within a local setting rather than on an interlocal or nonlocal basis. This produces considerable local variation within a given peasant segment. It means also that the peasantry is integrated into the sociocultural whole primarily through the structure of the community. We must therefore do more than define different kinds of peasants. We must also analyze the manner in which they are integrated with the outside world. In other words, a typology of peasants must include a typology of the kinds of communities in which they live.

The notion of type also implies a notion of history. The functioning of a particular segment depends on the historical interplay of factors which affect it. This point is especially important where we deal with part-cultures which must adapt their internal organization to changes in the total social field of which they are a part. Integration into a larger sociocultural whole is a historical process. We must be able to place part-cultures on the growth curve of the totality of which they form a part. In building a typology, we must take into account the growth curve of our cultural types.

Here we may summarize briefly our several criteria for the construction of a typology of peasant groups. First, it would seem to be advisable to define our subject matter as narrowly as possible. Second, we shall be interested in structure, rather than in culture content. Third, the initial criteria for our types can be primarily economic or sociopolitical, but should of course include as many other features as possible. Fourth, the types should be seen as component parts of larger wholes. The typical phenomena with which we are dealing are probably produced principally by the impact of outside forces on pre-existing local cultures. Fifth, some notion of historical trajectory should be included in the formulation of a type.

Two Types of Peasant Part-cultures

To make our discussion more concrete, let us turn to an analysis of two types of peasant segments. The first type comprises certain groups in the high highlands of Latin America; the second covers peasant groups found in humid low highlands and tropical lowlands. While these types are based on available field reports, they should be interpreted as provisional models for the construction of a typology, and thus subject to future revision.

Our first type (1) comprises peasants practicing intensive cultivation in the high highlands of Nuclear America. While some production is carried on to cover immediate subsistence needs, these peasants must sell a little cash produce to buy goods produced elsewhere (Pozas 1952:311). Production is largely unsupported by fluid capital. It flows into a system of village markets which is highly congruent with such a marginal economy.

The geographical area in which this type of peasant prevails formed the core area of Spanish colonial America. It supported the bulk of Spanish settlement, furnished the labor force required by Spanish enterprises, and provided the mineral wealth which served as the driving force of Spanish colonization. Integration of this peasantry into the colonial structure was achieved typically through the formation of communities which inhibited direct contact between the individual and the outside world but interposed between them an organized communal structure. This structure we shall call here the "corporate" community. It has shown a high degree of persistence, which has been challenged successfully only in recent years when alternative structures are encroaching upon it. Anthropologists have studied a number of such communities in highland Peru and Mexico.

The reader will be tempted immediately to characterize this type of community as "Indian" and perhaps to ask if we are not dealing here with a survival from pre-Columbian times. Since structure rather than culture content is our main concern here, we shall emphasize the features of organization which may make this type of community like corporate communities elsewhere, rather than characterize it in purely ethnographic terms. Moreover, it is necessary to explain the persistence of any survival over a period of three hundred years. As we hope to show below, persistence of "Indian" culture content seems to have depended primarily on maintenance of this structure. Where the structure collapsed, traditional cultural forms quickly gave way to new alternatives of outside derivation.

The distinctive characteristic of the corporate peasant community is that it represents a bounded social system with clear-cut limits, in relations to both outsiders and insiders. It has structural identity over time. Seen from the outside, the community as a whole carries on a series of activities and upholds certain "collective representations." Seen from within, it defines the rights and duties of its members and prescribes large segments of their behavior.

Fortes recently analyzed groupings of a corporate character based on kinship (1953:25–29). The corporate peasant community resembles these other units in its corporate character but is no longer held together by kinship. It may once have been based on kinship units of a peculiar type (see Kirchhoff 1949: 293), and features of kinship organization persist, such as a tendency toward local endogamy (for Mesoamerica, cf. Redfield and Tax 1952:31; for the Quechua, cf. Mishkin 1946:453) or in occasionally differential rights of old and new settlers. Nevertheless, the corporate community in Latin America represents the end product of a long process of reorganization which began in pre-Columbian times and was carried through under Spanish rule. As a result of the conquest any kinship feature which this type of community may have had was relegated to secondary importance. Members of the community were made co-owners of a landholding corporation (García 1948:269), a co-ownership which implied systematic participation in communal political and religious affairs.

Several considerations may have prompted Crown policy toward such communities. First, the corporate community performing joint labor services for an overlord was a widespread characteristic of European economic feudalism. In trying to curtail the political power of a potential new landholding class in the Spanish colonies the Crown took over management of Indian communities in order to deny the conquerors direct managerial control over labor. The Crown attempted to act as a go-between and labor contractor for both peasant community and landowner. Second, the corporate community fitted well into the political structure of the Spanish dynastic state, which attempted to incorporate each subcultural group and to define its radius of activity by law (Wolf 1953:100–1). This enabled the Crown to marshal the resources of such a group as an organized unit, and to impose its economic, social, and religious controls by a type of indirect rule. Third, the corporate structure of the peasant communities permitted the imposition of communal as well as of individual burdens of forced labor and taxation. This was especially important in view of the heavy loss of labor power through flight or disease. The imposition of the burden on a community rather than on individuals favored maintenance of a steady level of production.

Given this general historical background, what is the distinctive set of relationships characteristic of the corporate peasant community?

The first of these is location on *marginal land*. Needs within the larger society which might compel the absorption and exploitation of this land are weak or absent, and the existing level of technology and transportation may make such absorption difficult. In other words, the amount of energy required to destroy the existing structure of the corporate community and to reorganize it at present outweighs the capacity of the larger society.

In the corporate peasant community marginal land tends to be exploited by means of a *traditional technology* involving the members of the community in the continuous physical effort of manual labor.

Marginal location and traditional technology together limit the production power of the community, and thus its ability to produce cash crops for the market. This in turn limits the number of goods brought in from the outside which the community can afford to consume. The community is *poor*.

Within this economic setting, the corporate structure of the community is retained by community *jurisdiction over the free disposal of land*. Needless to say, community controls tend to be strongest where land is owned in common and re-allocated among members every year. But even where private property in land is the rule within the community, as is common today, the communal taboo on sale of land to outsiders (cf. Aguirre 1952: 149; Lewis 1951:124; Mishkin 1946:443) severely limits the degree to which factors outside the community can affect the structure of private property and related class differences within the community. Land is thus not a complete commodity. The taboo on sale of land to outsiders may be reinforced by other communal rights, such as gleaning rights or the right to graze cattle on any land within the community after the harvest.

The community possesses a system of power which embraces the male members of the community and makes the achievement of power a matter of community decision rather than a matter of individually achieved status (Redfield and Tax 1952:39; Mishkin 1946:459). This system of power is often tied into a religious system or into a series of interlocking religious systems. The *political-religious system* as a whole tends to define the boundaries of the community and acts as a rallying point and symbol of collective unity. Prestige within the community is largely related to rising from religious office to office along a prescribed ladder of achievement. Conspicuous consumption is geared to this communally approved system of power and religion rather than to private individual show. This makes individual conspicuous consumption incidental to communal expenditure. Thus the community at one and the same time levels differences of wealth which might intensify class divisions within the community to the detriment of the corporate structure and symbolically reasserts the strength and integrity of its structure before the eyes of its members (Aguirre 1952:242; Mishkin 1946:468).

The existence of such leveling mechanisms does not mean that class divisions within the corporate community do not exist. But it does mean that the class structure must find expression within the boundaries set by the community. The corporate structure acts to impede the mobilization of capital and wealth within the community in terms of the outside world which employs wealth capitalistically. It thus blunts the impact of the main opening wedge calculated to set up new tensions within the community and thus to hasten its disintegration (cf. Aguirre 1952; Carrasco 1952:48).

While striving to guarantee its members some basic livelihood within the confines of the community, the lack of resources and the very need to sustain the system of religion and power economically force the community to enter the outside market. Any imposition of taxes, any increase in expenditures relative to the productive capacity of the community, or the internal growth of the population on a limited amount of land, must result in *compensatory economic reactions in the field of production*. These may be wage labor, or the development of some specialization which has competitive advantages within the marginal economy of such communities. These may include specializations in trade, as among the Zapotecs, Tarascans, or Collas, or in witchcraft, as among the Killawallas or Kamilis of Bolivia.

In the field of consumption, increases of expenditures relative to the productive capacity of the economic base are met with attempts to decrease expenditure by decreasing consumption. This leads to the establishment of a culturally recognized standard of consumption which consciously excludes cultural alternative (on cultural alternatives, their rejection or acceptance, cf. Linton 1936:282–83). By reducing alternative items of consumption, along with the kinds of behavior and ideal norms which make use of these items of consumption, the community reduces the threat to its integrity. Moore and Tumin have called this kind of reaction ignorance with a "structural function" (1949:788).

In other words, we are dealing here not merely with a lack of knowledge, an absence of information, but with a *defensive ignorance,* an active denial of outside alternatives which, if accepted, might threaten the corporate structure (Beals's "rejection pattern" 1952:229; Mishkin 1946:443). Unwillingness to admit outsiders as competitors for land or as carriers of cultural alternatives may account for the prevalent tendency toward community endogamy (Redfield and Tax 1952:31; Mishkin 1946:453).

Related to the need to maintain a steady state by decreasing expenditures is the conscious effort to eat and consume less by "pulling in one's belt," while working more. This "exploitation of the self" is culturally institutionalized in what might be called a *"cult of poverty."* Hard work and poverty as well as behavior symbolic of these, such as going barefoot or wearing "Indian" clothes (cf. Tumin 1952:85–94), are extolled, and laziness and greed and behavior associated with these vices are denounced (Carrasco 1952:47).

The increase in output and concomitant restriction of consumption is carried out primarily within the *nuclear family.* The family thus acquires special importance in this kind of community, especially in a modern setting (Redfield and Tax 1952:33; Mishkin 1946:449–51). This is primarily because

> on the typical family farm . . . the farmer himself cannot tell you what part of his income comes to him in his capacity as a worker, what in his capacity as a capitalist who has provided tools and implements, or finally what in his capacity as owner of land. In fact, he is not able to tell you how much of his total income stems from his own labors and how much comes from the varied, but important efforts of his wife and children. (Samuelson 1948:76)

The family does not carry on cost-accounting. It does not know how much its labor is worth. Labor is not a commodity for it; it does not sell labor within the family. No money changes hands within the family. It acts as a unit of consumption and it can cut its consumption as a unit. The family is thus the ideal unit for the restriction of consumption and the increase of unpaid work.

The economy of the corporate community is congruent, if not structurally linked, with a marketing system of a peculiar sort. Lack of money resources requires that sales and purchases in the market be small. The highland village markets fit groups with low incomes which can buy only a little at a time (for Mexico, cf. Foster 1948:154; for the Quechua, cf. Mishkin 1946: 436). Such markets bring together a much larger supply of articles than merchants of any one community could afford to keep continuously in their stores (Whetten 1948:359). Most goods in such markets are homemade or locally grown (Whetten 1948:358; Mishkin 1946:437). Local producers thus acquire the needed supplementary income, while the character of the commodities offered for sale reinforces the traditional pattern of consumption. Specialization on the part of villages is evident throughout (Whetten 1948; Foster 1948; Mishkin 1946:434). Regular market days in regional sequence making for a wider exchange of local produce (Whetten 1948; Mishkin 1946:436; Valcarcel 1946:477–79) may be due to the fact that villages producing similar products must find outlets far away, as well as to exchanges of produce between highlands and lowlands. The fact that the goods carried are produced in order to obtain small amounts of needed cash in order to purchase other needed goods is evident in the very high percentage of dealings between producer and ultimate consumer. The market is in fact a means of bringing the two into contact (Whetten 1948:359; Foster 1948; Mishkin 1946). The role of the nuclear family in production and in the "exploitation of the self" is evident in the high percentage of goods in whose production the individual or the nuclear family completes an entire production cycle (Foster 1948).

Paralleling the mechanisms of control which are primarily economic in origin are psychological mechanisms like *institutionalized envy,* which may find expression in various manifestations such as gossip, attacks of the evil eye, or in the fear and practice of witchcraft. The communal organization of the corporate community has often been romanticized; it is sometimes assumed that a communal structure makes for the absence of divisive tensions. Lewis has demonstrated that there is no necessary correlation between communal structure and pervasive good-will among the members of the community (Lewis 1951:428–29). Quite the contrary, it would seem that some form of institutionalized envy plays an important part in such communities (Gillin 1952:208). Kluckhohn has shown that fear of witchcraft acts as an effective leveler in Navaho society (1944:67–68). A similar relationship obtains in the type of community which we are discussing. Here witchcraft, as well as milder forms of institutionalized envy, have an integrative effect in restraining non-traditional behavior, as long as social relationships suffer no serious disruption. It minimizes disruptive phenomena such as economic mobility, abuse of ascribed power, or individual conspicuous show of wealth. On the individual plane, it thus acts to maintain the individual in equilibrium with his neighbors. On the social plane, it reduces the disruptive influences of outside society.

The need to keep social relationships in equilibrium in order to maintain the steady state of the corporate community is internalized in the individual as strong conscious efforts to adhere to the traditional roles, roles which were successful in maintaining the steady state in the past. Hence there appears a strong tendency on the social psychological level to stress "uninterrupted routine practice of traditional patterns" (Gillin 1952:206). Such a psychological emphasis would tend to act against overt expressions of individual autonomy, and set up in individuals strong fears against being thrown out of equilibrium (Gillin 1952:208).

An individual thus carries the culture of such a community, not merely passively as a social inheritance inherited and accepted automatically, but actively. Adherence to the culture validates membership in an existing society and acts as a passport to participation in the life of the community. The particular traits held help the individual remain within the equilibrium of relationships which maintain the community. Corporate communities produce "distinctive cultural, linguistic, and other social attributes," which Beals has aptly called "plural cultures" (1953:333); tenacious defense of this plurality maintains the integrity of such communities.

It is needless to add that any aspect relates to any other, and that changes in one would vitally affect the rest. Thus the employment of traditional technology keeps the land marginal from the point of view of the larger society, keeps the community poor, forces a search for supplementary sources of income, and requires high expenditures of physical labor within the nuclear family. The technology is in turn maintained by the need to adhere to traditional roles in order to validate one's membership in the community, and this adherence is produced by the conscious denial of alternative forms of behavior, by institutionalized envy, and by the fear of being thrown out of equilibrium with one's neighbor. The various aspects enumerated thus exhibit a very high degree of covariance.

The second type (2) which we shall discuss comprises peasants who regularly sell a cash crop constituting probably between 50 and 75 percent of their total production. Geographically, this type of peasant is distributed over humid low highlands and tropical lowlands. Present-day use of their environments has been dictated by a shift in demand on the world market for crops from the American tropics during the latter part of the nineteenth century and the early part of the twentieth. On the whole, production for the market by this type of peasant has been in an ascendant phase, though often threatened by intermittent periods of decline and depression.

In seasonally rainy tropical lowlands, these peasants may raise sugar cane. In chronically rainy lowlands, such as northern Colombia or Venezuela or coastal Ecuador, they have tended to grow cocoa or bananas. The development of this peasant segment has been most impressive in humid low highlands, where the standard crop is coffee (Platt 1943:498). This crop is easily grown on both small and large holdings, as is the case in Colombia, Guatemala, Costa Rica, and parts of the West Indies.

Such cash crop production requires outside capitalization. The amount and kind of capitalization will have important ramifications throughout the particular local adaptation made. Peasants of this type receive such capitalization from the outside, but mainly on a traditional, small-scale, intermittent and speculative basis. Investments are not made either to stabilize the market or to reorganize the apparatus of production and distribution of the peasantry. Few peasant groups of this type have been studied fully by anthropologists, and any discussion of them must to some extent remain conjectural until further work adds to our knowledge. For the construction of this type the writer has relied largely on his own field work in Puerto Rico (Wolf 1951) and on insights gained from studies made in southern Brazil Hermann 1950; Pierson and others 1951).

The typical structure which serves to integrate this type of peasant segment with other segments and with the larger sociocultural whole we shall here call the "open" community. The open community differs from the corporate peasant community in a number of ways. The corporate peasant community is composed primarily of one subculture, the peasantry. The open community comprises a number of subcultures of which the peasantry is only one, although the most important functional segment. The corporate community emphasizes resistance to influences from without which might threaten its integrity. The open community, on the other hand, emphasizes continuous interaction with the outside world and ties its fortunes to outside demands. The corporate community frowns on individual accumulation and display of wealth and strives to reduce the effects of such accumulation on the communal structure. It resists reshaping of relationships; it defends the traditional equilibrium. The open-ended community permits and expects individual accumulation and display of wealth during periods of rising outside demand and allows this new wealth much influence in the periodic reshaping of social ties.

Historically, the open peasant community arose in response to the rising demand for cash crops which accompanied the development of capitalism in Europe. In a sense, it represents the offshoot of a growing type of society which multiplied its wealth by budding off to form new communities to produce new wealth in their turn. Many peasant communities were established in Latin America by settlers who brought to the New World cultural patterns of consumption and production which from the outset involved them in relations with an outside market. Being a Spaniard or Portuguese meant more than merely speaking Spanish or Portuguese or adhering to certain kinds of traditional behavior and ideal norms. It implied participation in a complex system of hierarchical relationships and prestige which required the consumption of goods that could be produced only by means of a complicated division of labor and had to be acquired in the market.

No amount of Indian blankets delivered as tribute could make up for the status gained by the possession of one shirt of Castilian silk, or for a small ruffle of Cambrai lace. Prestige goods as well as necessities like iron could only be bought with money, and the need for money drove people to produce for an outside market. The demand for European goods by Spanish colonists was enormous and in turn caused heavy alterations in the economic structure of the mother country (Sombart 1928, I, Pt. 2:780–81). In the establishment of the open community, therefore, the character of the outside society was a major determinant from the beginning.

It would be a mistake, moreover, to visualize the development of the world market in terms of continuous and even expansion, and to suppose therefore that the line of development of particular peasant communities always leads from lesser involvement in the market to more involvement. This line of reasoning would seem to be especially out of place in the case of Latin America where the isolation and homogeneity of the "folk" are often secondary, that is to say, follow in time after a stage of much contact and heterogeneity. Redfield has recognized aspects of this problem in his recent category of "remade folk" (1953:47). Such a category should cover not only the Yucatecan Indians who fled into the isolation of the bush but also groups of settlers with a culture of basically Iberian derivation which were once in the mainstream of commercial development, only to be left behind on its poverty-stricken margins (cf. e.g., the Spanish settlements at Culiacán, New Galicia, described by Mota 1940:99–102, and Chiapa Real, Chiapas, described by Gage 1929:151–53).

Latin America has been involved in major shifts and fluctuations of the market since the period of initial European conquest. It would appear, for example, that a rapid expansion of commercial development in New Spain during the sixteenth century was followed by a "century of depression" in the seventeenth (cf. Borah 1951; Chevalier 1952:xii, 54). The slack was taken up again in the eighteenth century, with renewed shrinkage and disintegration of the market in the early part of the nineteenth. During the second part of the nineteenth century and the beginning of the twentieth, many Latin American countries were repeatedly caught up in speculative booms of cash crop production for foreign markets, often with disastrous results in the case of market failure.

Entire communities might find their market gone overnight, and revert to the production of subsistence crops for their own use.

Two things seem clear from this discussion. First, in dealing with present-day Latin America it would seem advisable to beware of treating production for subsistence and production for the market as two progressive stages of development. Rather, we must allow for the cyclical alternation of the two kinds of production within the same community and realize that from the point of view of the community both kinds may be alternative responses to changes in conditions of the outside market. This means that a synchronic study of such a community is insufficient, because it cannot reveal how the community can adapt to such seemingly radical changes. Second, we must look for the mechanisms which make such changes possible.

In the corporate peasant community, the relationships of individuals and kin groups within the community are bounded by a common structure. We have seen that the community aims primarily at maintaining an equilibrium of roles within the community in an effort to keep intact its outer boundary. Maintenance of the outer boundary reacts in turn on the stability of the equilibrium within it. The open community lacks such a formalized corporate structure. It neither limits its membership nor insists on a defensive boundary. Quite the contrary, it permits free permeation by outside influences.

In contrast to the corporate peasant community where the community retains the right to review and revise individual decisions, the open community lends itself to rapid shifts in production because it is possible to mobilize the peasant and to orient him rapidly toward the expanding market. Land is usually owned *privately*. Decisions for change can be made by individual families. Property can be mortgaged, or pawned in return for capital. The community *qua* community cannot interfere in such change.

As in the corporate peasant community, land tends to be marginal and technology primitive. Yet functionally both land and technology are elements in a different complex of relationships. The buyers of peasant produce have an interest in the continued "backwardness" of the peasant. Reorganization of his productive apparatus would absorb capital and credit which can be spent better in expanding the market by buying means of transportation, engaging middlemen, etc. Moreover, by keeping the productive apparatus unchanged, the buyer can reduce the risk of having his capital tied up in the means of production of the peasant holding, if and when the bottom drops out of the market. The buyers of peasant produce thus trade increasing productivity per man-hour for the lessened risks of investment. We may say that the *marginality of land* and the *poor technology* are here a function of the speculative market. In the case of need, the investor merely withdraws credit, while the peasant returns to subsistence production by means of his traditional technology.

The fact that cash crop production can be undertaken on peasant holdings without materially reorganizing the productive apparatus implies furthermore that the amount of cash crop produced by each peasant will tend to be *small,* as will be the income which he receives after paying off all obligations. This does not mean that the aggregate amounts of such production cannot reach respectable sums, nor that the amounts of profit accruing to middlemen from involvement in such production need be low.

In this cycle of subsistence crops and cash crops, subsistence crops guarantee a stable minimum livelihood, where cash crops promise higher money returns but involve the family in the hazards of the fluctuating market. The peasant is always concerned with the problem of striking some sort of balance between subsistence production and cash crop production. Preceding cycles of cash crop production have enabled him to buy goods and services which he cannot afford if he produces only for his own subsistence. Yet an all-out effort to increase his ability to buy more goods and services of this kind may spell his end as an independent agricultural producer. His tendency is thus to rely on a basic minimum of subsistence production and to expand his cash purchases only slowly. Usually he can rely on traditional norms of consumption which define a decent standard of living in terms of a fixed number of culturally standardized needs. Such needs are of course not only economic but may include standardized expenditures for religious or recreational purposes, or for hospitality (cf. Wolf 1951:64). Nor are these needs static. Viewing the expansion of the market from the point of view of subsistence, however, permits the peasant to expand his consumption only slowly.

> In cutting down on money expenditures, he defers purchases of new goods, and distributes his purchases over a long period of time. The peasant standard of living is undergoing change but the rate of that change is slow. (Wolf 1951:65)

The cultural yardstick enables him to limit the rate of expansion but also permits him to retrench when he has overextended himself economically. As in the corporate peasant community, the unit within which consumption can best be restricted while output is stepped up is again the *nuclear family*.

This *modus operandi* reacts back on his technology and on his ability to increase his cash income. The buyer of peasant produce knows that the peasant will be slow in expanding his demand for money. He can therefore count on accumulating his largest share of gain during the initial phase of a growing market, a factor which adds to the speculative character of the economy.

Peasants who are forced overnight to reorient their production from the production of subsistence crops for their own use to cash crop production are rarely able to generate the needed capital themselves. It must be pumped into the peasant segment from without, either from another segment within the community, or from outside the community altogether. The result is that when cash crop production grows important, there is a tightening of bonds between town and country. Urban families become concerned with the production and distribution of cash crops and tie their own fate to the fate of the cash crop. In a society subject to frequent fluctuations of the market but possessed of little fluid capital, there are few formal institutional mechanisms for insuring the flow of capital into peasant production. In a more highly capitalized society, the stock market functions as an impersonal governor of relationships between investors. Corporations form, merge, or dissolve according to the dictates of this governor. In a society where capital accumulation is low, the structure of incorporation tends to be weak or lacking. More important are the *informal alliances of families and clients* which polarize wealth and power at any given time. Expansion of the market tends to involve the peasant in one or the other of these blocs of family power in town. These blocs, in turn, permit the rapid diffusion of capital into the countryside, since credit is guaranteed by personal relationships between creditor and debtor. Peasant allegiance then acts further to reinforce the social and political position of a given family bloc within the urban sector.

When the market fails, peasants and urban patrons both tend to be caught in the same downward movement. Open communities of the type we are analyzing here are therefore marked by the repeated "circulation of the elite." Blocs of wealth and power form, only to break up and be replaced by similar blocs coming to the fore. The great *concern with status* is related to this type of mobility. Status on the social plane measures the position in the trajectory of the family on the economic plane. To put it in somewhat oversimplified terms, status in such a society represents the "credit rating" of the family. The economic circulation of the elite thus takes the form of shifts in social status. Such shifts in social and economic position always involve an urban and a rural aspect. If the family cannot find alternate economic supports, it loses prestige within the urban sector, and is sooner or later abandoned by its peasant clientele who must needs seek other urban patrons.

We are thus dealing with a type of community which is continuously faced with alignments, circulation and realignments, both on the socioeconomic and political level. Since social, economic, and political arrangements are based primarily on personal ties, such fluctuations act to redefine personal relationships, and such personal relationships are in turn watched closely for indices of readjustment. Relations between two individuals do not symbolize merely the respective statuses and roles of the two concerned; they involve a whole series of relations which must be evaluated and readjusted if there is any indication of change. This "overloading" of personal relations produces two types of behavior: behavior calculated to retain social status, and a type of behavior which for want of a better term might be called "redefining" behavior, behavior aimed at altering the existing state of personal relationships. Both types will be present in any given social situation, but the dominance of one over the other will be determined by the relative stability or instability of the economic base. Status behavior is loaded with a fierce consciousness of the symbols of status, while "redefining" behavior aims at testing the social limits through such varied mechanisms as humor, invitations to share drinks or meals, visiting, assertions of individual worth, proposals of marriage, and so forth. The most important of these types of behavior, quite absent in the corporate community, consists in the ostentatious exhibition of commodities purchased with money.

This type of redefining behavior ramifies through other aspects of the culture. Wealth is its prerequisite. It is therefore most obvious in the ascendant phases of the economic cycle, rather than when the cycle is leveling off. Such accumulation of goods and the behavior associated with it serves as a challenge to existing relations with kin folk, both real and fictitious, since it is usually associated with a reduction in relations of reciprocal aid and hospitality on which these ties are based.

This disruption of social ties through accumulation is inhibited in the corporate peasant community, but can go on unchecked in the type of community which we are considering. Here forms of envy such as witchcraft are often present, but not institutionalized as in the first type of community. Rather, fear of witchcraft conforms to the hypothesis proposed by Passin (1942:15) that

> in any society where there is a widespread evasion of a cultural obligation which results in the diffusion of tension and hostility between people, and further if this hostility is not expressed in overt physical strife, . . . sorcery or related non-physical techniques will be brought into play.

Fear of witchcraft in such a community may be interpreted as a product of guilt on the part of the individual who is himself disrupting ties which are valued, coupled with a vague anxiety about the loss of stable definitions of situations in terms of clear-cut status. At the same time, the new possessions and their conspicuous show serves not only to redefine status and thus to reduce anxiety but also as a means of expressing hostility against those who do not own the same goods (cf. Kluckhohn 1944:67, fn. 96). The "invidious" comparisons produced by this hostility in turn produce an increase in the rate of accumulation.

SUGGESTIONS FOR FURTHER RESEARCH

The two model types discussed above by no means exhaust the variety of peasant segments to be found in Latin America. They were singled out for consideration because I felt most competent to deal with them in terms of both time and field experience. Pleading greater ignorance and less assurance, I should nevertheless like to take this opportunity to indicate the rough outlines of some other types which may deserve further investigation. These types may seem to resemble the "open" communities just discussed. It is nevertheless important to conceptualize them separately. We may expect them to differ greatly in their basic functional configurations, due to the different manner of their integration with larger sociocultural systems, and to the different histories of their integration.

Thus, it seems that within the same geographical area occupied by the second type, above, there exists a third type of peasant (3) who resembles the second also in that a large percentage of his total production is sold on the market. This percentage is probably higher than that involved in the second case; between 90 and 100 percent of total production may go directly into the market. This peasant segment seems to differ from the second one in the much greater stability of its market and in much more extensive outside capitalization. Much of the market is represented by the very high aggregate demand of the United States, and United States capital flows into such peasant segments through organizations such as the United Fruit Company. In the absence of foreign investment, capital may be supplied by new-style local groups of investors of the kind found in the coffee industry of Antioqueño, Colombia (cf. Parsons 1949:2–9). Anthropologists have paid little attention to this type of peasantry.

(4) A fourth type is perhaps represented by peasants who habitually sell the larger part of their total production in restricted but stable local markets. Such markets are especially apt to occur near former political and religious settlements in the high highlands which play a traditional role in the life of the country but do not show signs of commercial or industrial expansion. Outside capitalization of such production would appear to be local in scale, but a relatively stable market may offer a certain guarantee of small returns. Into this category may fit groups relatively ignored by anthropologists, such as many Mexican *ranchero* communities (cf. Armstrong 1949; Humphrey 1948; Taylor 1933) or the settlers of the Bogotá Basin (cf. Smith and others 1945).

(5) The fifth group is perhaps represented by peasants located in a region which once formed a key area of the developing system of capitalism (Williams 1944:98–107). This region is located in the seasonally rainy tropical lowlands of northeastern Brazil and the West Indies. Here sugar plantations based on slave labor flourished in the sixteenth, seventeenth, and eighteenth centuries. These plantations were weakened by a variety of factors, such as the end of the slave trade and the political independence movement in Latin America, and most of them

were unable to compete with other tropical areas. Where the old plantation system was not replaced by modern "factories in the field," as has been the case in northeastern Brazil (Hutchinson 1952:17) and on parts of the south coast of Puerto Rico (Mintz 1953:244–49), we today find peasant holdings as "residual bits" of former large-scale organizations (Platt 1943:501) which have disintegrated, as in Haiti or Jamaica. The economy of such areas has been contracting since the end of slavery, with the result that this type of peasant seems to lean heavily toward the production of subsistence crops for home use or toward the production and distribution of very small amounts of cash produce.

(6) A sixth group is perhaps represented by the foreign colonists who introduced changes in technology into the forested environment of southern Brazil and southern Chile. These areas seem to show certain similarities. In both areas, the settlers chose the forest rather than the open plain for settlement and colonization. In both areas, colonization was furthered by the respective central governments to create buffers against military pressures from outside and against local movements for autonomy. In both areas, the settlers found themselves located on a cultural ecological frontier. In southern Brazil, they faced cultural pressures from the Pampa (Willems 1944:154–55) and from the surrounding population of casual cash crop producers (Willems 1945:14–15, 26). In southern Chile, they confronted the Araucanians. In both areas, an initial period of deculturation and acculturation would seem to have been followed by increasing integration into the national market through the sale of cash crops.

(7) A seventh type is perhaps made up of peasants who live on the outskirts of the capitalist market, on South America's "pioneer fringe" (Bowman 1931). This would include people who raise crops for the market in order to obtain strategic items of consumption, like clothing, salt, or metal, which they cannot produce themselves. The technological level characterizing this type of peasant seems to be low; his agriculture would appear to be mainly of the slash-and-burn type. His contacts with the market seem to be sporadic rather than persistent, and the regularity with which he produces a cash crop seems to depend both on uncertain outside demand and on his periodic need for an outside product.

Due largely to the requirements of the agricultural system, families live in dispersal, and the family level is probably the chief level of integration. Since there is no steady market, land lacks commercial value, and occupancy is relatively unhampered. A family may occupy land for as long as required and abandon it with decreasing yields. Such circulation through the landscape would require large amounts of land and unrestricted operation. Concepts of fixed private property in land would tend to be absent or nonfunctional. The land may belong to somebody who cannot make effective commercial use of it at the moment, and permits temporary squatting (for the *tolerados* of Santa Cruz, Bolivia, cf. Leonard 1952:132–33; for the *intrusos* of southern Brazil, cf. Willems 1942:376; for the squatters in other parts of Brazil, cf. Smith 1946:459–60; for Paraguay, cf. Service Ms.).

Once again I want to express the caution that the above list represents only suggestions. Further work will undoubtedly lead to the formulation of additional or other types, and to the construction of models to deal with transitional phenomena, such as changes from one type of segment to another. Since segments relate with other segments, further inquiry will also have to take account of the ways in which type segments interrelate with each other and of the variety of community structures which such combinations can produce.

29 THE SOCIAL CONTEXT OF ECONOMIC CHOICE IN A SMALL SOCIETY

Manning Nash

The distinctions between complex, monetized, and civilized societies and the small-scale, non- or partially-monetized peasant and primitive societies in economic life are startling, deeply rooted, and easily apparent. These distinctions have frequently been laid to a special rationale of economic choice in small-scale non-Western societies. Boeke (1947:2) finds a cleavage so deep between the small-scale economy and the capitalistic organization of economic life that a new name is needed, and he suggests "oriental economics" to account for the workings of non-Western economies. Polanyi (1957:46 f.) sees the essential difference in the "absence of a motive of gain" from primitive societies, and of course from Maine onward there is a literature which claims that peasant values subordinate economic activity to social ends. It is the contention of this paper that the rationale of economic choice in peasant society follows the same general rule of maximization as economic activity does anywhere, at any time. What is distinctive about peasant and primitive societies are not the habits of mind about advantage, nor an inability to calculate costs and benefits of a course of action, nor even an absence of a motive of gain; but rather the possession of a set of concrete social organizations which directly channel economic choice, on the one hand, and a set of sanctions which operate to keep economic deviants in physical as well as moral jeopardy on the other. A corollary of this contention is that debate of rules of choice or abstract principles of economic organization will be barren and lead only to a

FROM Manning Nash, "The Social Context of Economic Choice in a Small Society," *Man* (1961), No. 219, pp. 186–191. Reprinted by permission of the author and the Royal Anthropological Institute.

"special dance of bloodless categories," to the profusion of empty boxes of theory; while the emphasis on the stipulation of the economic consequences of concrete social structures will generate an empirically powerful body of middle-range theory.

By an examination of the economy of peasant Indians in the state of Chiapas, Mexico,[1] I hope to show how the structure and membership criteria of production units limit maximization; how the level and rhythm of output are consequences of the ceremonial cycle; and how notions of witchcraft and the supernatural combine to keep wealth from being used for economic ends and thus contribute to the steady state of small, reduplicative, productive units with little interest in, or incentive for, technological or social innovation.

In south-eastern Chiapas, Tzeltal- and Tzotzil-speaking Indians are the predominant population. These Indians live in communities whose general characteristics are familiar from work done with neighbouring highland Maya in Guatemala (Tax 1937). One Tzeltal community is that of Amatenango de Valle. Amatenango is a *municipio* (the administrative unit of Mexico, like a township, but tending to coincide with an Indian society in highland Chiapas and Guatemala) situated just off the Pan-American Highway some 44 kilometres south of the region's largest Mexican city. Amatenango, for an Indian community, has a reputation for wealth and independence. Its people call themselves *Tzontajal;* they wear a distinct costume; their mode of speech is dialectically distinct from neighbouring Tzeltal-speaking communities; they are nearly endogamous; they have economic skills not shared by neighbours; a local civil administration; a local set of sacred officials, and a particular calendar of sacred and secular festivals. They are a corporate community (Wolf 1955), united by blood and custom, living on their own territory, with an ethnic distinctiveness which sets them apart in their minds, and in fact, from their Indian neighbours and the superordinate communities of Mexicans which surround them.

[1] I am indebted to the National Institute of Mental Health, the Department of Anthropology and the Graduate School of Business of the University of Chicago for financing the field work on which this paper is based. June Nash covers in detail the social structure of Amatenango in Social Relations in Amatenango: An Activity Analysis, unpublished Ph.D. thesis, University of Chicago. Miss Joan Ablon aided in some of the data here reported during her field work in the community.

Amatenango makes its living by cultivating the soil, by cattle-raising, and by producing pottery. The technology of agriculture is on a relatively low level. The ox-drawn plough, the machete, the digging stick, the sickle and a net bag make up the tool kit. A simple irrigation system of ditching serves some of the land, and the watered lands are rotated between milpa crops (corn beans, squash) and a wheat cash crop. Fertilizer is not used. Soil-nutrient is added only by the burning of corn or wheat stubble and leaving the ash, or by turning animals loose in the fields after harvest. Seed-selection is not rigorous. And as in most peasant agriculture the vicissitudes of wind, rain, frost and sun make for wide swings in the annual harvest. Famine, or even real hunger, however, is not part of Amatenango experience, except in the days when the warring factions of the Mexican revolution swept through the region and disrupted life and devastated agriculture. The agriculture complex also includes garden plots near house sites, as distinct from field lands. Garden plots are used for some milpa, but their chief economic significance lies in the growing of *chayote,* a squash-like plant, and its root which are sold to other communities. The maguey plants, lima and avocado tree and some fruit trees supply domestically used produce. The agricultural complex is part of a system of regional interdependence based on ecological and traditional differences. Nearby communities specialize in other products, and there is a lively exchange of agricultural products between Amatenango, its neighbours and the nearby coastal "hot" lands. The interpretation of the agricultural complex seems simple enough: ecological specialization on the base of natural resources combined with special agricultural skills and knowledge. The actual distribution of agricultural specialties results from the operation of comparative advantage over a long stretch of time.

Insight into the economic dynamics of the community and of the region may be had more clearly through the industrial rather than the agricultural organization of Amatenango. Agriculture does not, by itself, maintain Amatenango at its expected level of living. The making and selling of pottery is an important component in the meeting of the customary standard of life. Of the 280 households in the town centre of Amatenango (the peripheries of the community were recently settled either by Indians uprooted from other communities, or by poor Mexicans, and pose a special problem for social analysis) only two or three are not engaged in the production of pottery for sale. Pottery-making is a community specialization, not an individual skill. It is part of the socialization process for women in Amatenango. All women who are born and grow up in Amatenango know how to, and do, make pots. The striking nature of the community specialization comes home forcibly when it is observed that an adjoining community with virtually the same natural resources as Amatenango does not produce one single pot, and that in a region nearly 40 miles long and 30 across, there is no other Indian pottery-making community, although a few pottery-makers are scattered elsewhere in the region. In short, in a regionally diversified marketing area, only the people of Amatenango produce salable pottery, and all of the women produce it. The technique does not spread to other Indian communities, whatever the abstract profitability of such diffusion might be, because making pottery is part of a way of life, learned in the informal, intimate setting in which the basic parts of culture are acquired, and not a technique of production to be acquired by whoever sees the main chance.

Although women are the makers of pottery in Amatenango, pottery is not considered, and is not, strictly a woman's product. Men bring most of the firewood necessary for the firing of the pottery, and men take the pottery to the points of sale (now by bus and truck passage, but formerly on horseback), but the packing of pots in grass-padded net bags is still an arduous task. Pottery requires male and female co-operation, and single women make pots only if they live in a household with male members, or have male relatives who are willing to aid in the work.

The technology of pottery-making is simple and inexpensive. As the skills come to the women potters in the process of being socialized (there are, however, some women who do not know how to make the more specialized pottery like incense burners and perforated pots, and "on order" pottery sold exclusively to *Ladinos,* as the non-Indians are called, is made by very few families) and so provide every household with the art, so the technology, in terms of skill and materials, is within the reach of even the poorest household in the community. Pottery is a hand industry. No wheel, no mould, no oven are required. The shaping hand of the female potter, the open street firing of the ware, the slipping and decorating are ingenious skills, but technologically simple. Not even purchased, non-indigenous materials are necessary in pottery-production. The clay, the temper, the pigment, the scraping stone, the wood used in firing, the net bags used in packing, all come from communal resources and are open to every member of Amatenango equally. No payment or special permission is needed to use these resources. Community membership gives free (but not costless, since labour is involved) access to the materials of pottery-making. If one purchases part of the equipment (a steel blade for scraping, a smooth board for resting pot bases, a burlap bag or skirt under the potter's knees, nets, bags) the cost is under three dollars, and every household has that at its disposal.

There exists wide variations in the output of different pottery-making households. Estimating the range of variation in output and finding the reasons for output differences is, in a preliterate culture, a difficult task. In one household a daily record covering the entire annual production was obtained, and in three other households lesser periods, ranging from one to four months, were recorded. This information is supplemented by observations on pottery-making in several dozen households, and was checked against the complete field census of the community, so that the typicality of the sample can be judged. At any rate, the problem of measuring the gross community output of pottery was not the major research interest (though a reasoned and plausible estimate could be constructed from the data in hand). The problem was to assess the limits of output variability and to pin these down to a set of factors which were the determinants of production. The determinants of production would, when checked by micro-comparison between households in the community, indicate the "controlling mechanism" regulating the pottery industry, and by extension the economic life of the community.

Fig. 1 is a composite of the production of one of the most intensive pottery-producing households in the community. An inspection of this figure (the special ware represents pottery made only in a few households, the dash line is commonly but not universally made ware, and the solid is pottery made in all households) shows that pottery-making tends to reach its peak just before the major festive occasions in the community and in surrounding communities. This is explicable in terms of the nature of the ecological market situation. Pottery-making is a cash-raising activity. Ware is sold in an impersonal, free market with prices set by the interaction of supply and demand. The festal occasions are the times when Amatenangueros need money; they are also the periods when the largest demand from visitors to a local fiesta may be expected, so producers reach a maximum of output just prior to the festal times of heavy buying and selling. Production is maximized not at the time of highest prices on the market, but rather in time with the rhythm of sacred and secular celebrations which require cash outlay and provide opportunities for disposal without storage problems.

The peaks reached for fiestas are not of the same height. Two things operate here: the size or local importance of the given fiesta and whether it falls in the rainy or dry seasons. In the rainy months (from June to September, but heaviest from late July to mid September) less pottery is made than in the dry sunny times of the year. However, in January and February, dry sunny months, there is high wind which complicates the drying of pottery (because the pottery must be kept under leaves to keep moisture in it until it is ready for firing) and hence output is reduced. The general pattern of seasonal flux is common to all households, and so is the peak and trough pattern of production along with fiestas.

While Fig. 1 establishes the rhythm of pottery-production common to the society by virtue of its technology and annual cycle, Fig. 2 compares the differences in level of production among three households. Household No. 6 outproduces No. 4, and No. 13 outproduces both No. 6 and No. 14 (the numbers refer to a genealogical map and census of the community which is not here included). Each of the households is differently constituted in numbers of potters in it. Household No. 13 has four potters (two young women, one middle-aged and one old). Household No. 6 has two potters (one young and one middle-aged woman) and No. 14 has two potters (one young and one middle-aged). Therefore the sheer number of hands which can be mustered in No. 13 is greater and helps explain its greater output. Furthermore No. 14 and No. 6 have small children under three years of age in the household, and No. 13 does not. Child care and household maintenance compete with pottery-making for a woman's time, so the small child is a further brake on production in these two households.

Fig. 1. Annual Production in Household 13 (4 Women Producers, No Children)

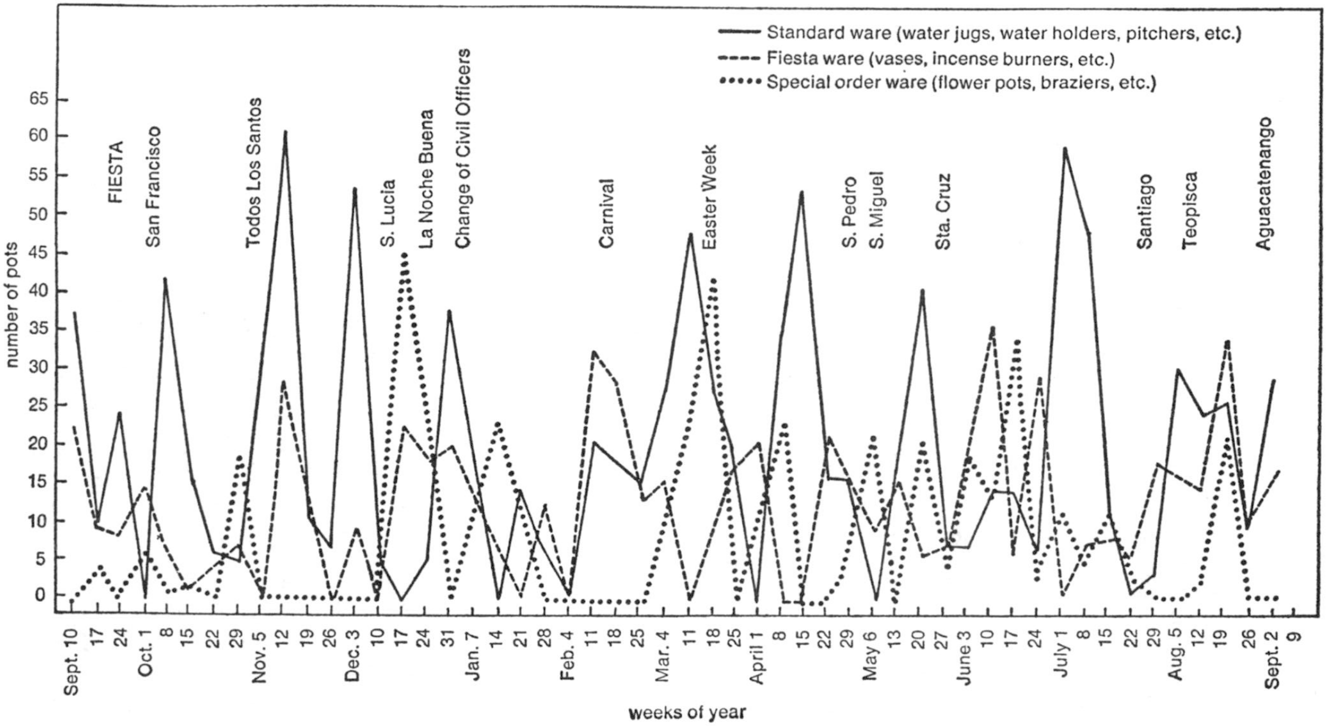

Inspection of Fig. 2 shows that four women produce more than twice as much as do two women (even adjusting for children). Part of this is an "economy of scale." Pottery-production has some assembly-line aspects. Women work on a part of a pot, making bases, then they turn to making bodies, then to making necks, and finally to putting handles on the pot. Between these operations the pots are partially dried. If there are four women, the division of labour is better, and relative efficiency of the producing unit rises. Beyond four, not much increase occurs. But the differences in output between No. 6 and No 14 are such that sheer numbers of hands will not serve as an explanation, and the factors of relative efficiency, or of skill, are so nearly matched in these households, that it does not really enter as a factor in the account of output differences. Explanation must be sought in the wider economic setting of the productive unit.

If all of the households in the community were ranked in terms of the major source of wealth—land at the disposal of the household—an immediate connexion would be noted between the wealth of the household and its level of output. The motivation to work at the top of the bent is stronger in poorer households, because alternative sources of income are less, and more of the family's subsistence must come from pottery-making. Land, of course, needs men to work it, and household No. 13 has but one old man, and he cannot work much land, nor lay claim to government-grant lands (*ejido*) of any considerable size. In richer households (in terms of land and cattle owned) there is sufficient milpa raised to ensure that corn need not be bought, and the need for continuous cash income is not so pressing. This also has a circular effect: richer households tend to be able to keep more children alive; with more children to care for, women devote less time to pottery. Conversely poorer households depend upon pottery income, have fewer living children, and hence have both the opportunity and the need to produce almost continuously.

The rate of output is determined on two levels:

(1) that common to the whole society (technology, resources, seasons and ceremonial cycle);

(2) the organization and wealth differences among producing units (number of women, number of children under three, number of men, and amount of land and cattle owned).

To understand why the second level of determinants of production continues to be operative, involves a move from the micro-structural analysis of producing units, to the macro-structural analysis of the whole social and economic organization of Amatenango. It moves the question from that of incentives and motivations of actors and producers to the plane of the structural sources of and constraints upon incentives and motivation. The units of production are households, and the households are kinship units. As a kinship unit, membership comes only by being born or marrying into the unit. The household unit, with its kinship of recruitment, sets the size of the "labour force" available for pottery-making. No one hires out to do pottery for wages, since pottery-making is only part of a woman's job as a member of a household (and even if a wage were paid it could not cover all activities and still yield anything to an employer). Amatenango's kinship system is one of nearly perfectly balanced bilateralism. A combination of personal tastes and wealth of the household determines whether a married couple will live with his or her parents. Wealthier households can attract either sons-in-law or daughters-in-law to live with them, and have a slightly larger labour force potential. But the absence of wage labour in a household production system limits any given unit's ability to expand pottery activities. Expected, and, of course observed, is the common feature of peasant economic organization, a multiplicity of small reduplicative, productive units, with no tendency toward agglomeration or centralization. Furthermore, since pottery-production is household-organized, many activities compete with it for the time of the same set of personnel. Economic activities are but one field in which maintenance needs are met. Internal family social relations, the socialization of members, sickness and curing, religious activity, social status, and dispute settlement are tasks partly centred in the family, and in household organization. Economic activity, be it in the market, field, or handicraft, is a means to implement and provide facilities for other aspects of household activity. It is not an instance of conflicting standards when a woman with small children stops pottery-making, but rather a case of clear priorities.

This bears on an analogy sometimes used by anthropologists when a household is compared to a firm (Tax 1952). A household may be conceived of as a unit trying to maximize, given its resources and personnel. The analogy is misleading, not on

Fig. 2. Pottery Production of Three Households

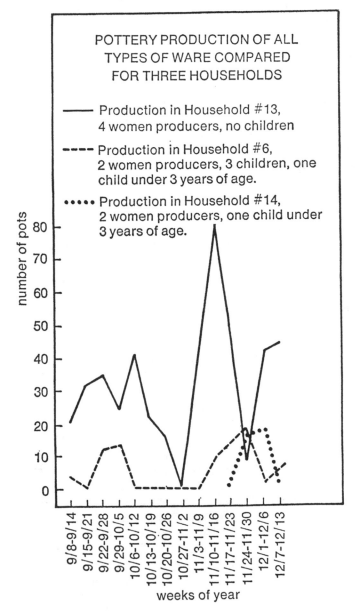

POTTERY PRODUCTION OF ALL
TYPES OF WARE COMPARED
FOR THREE HOUSEHOLDS

—— Production in Household #13,
4 women producers, no children

---- Production in Household #6,
2 women producers, 3 children, one
child under 3 years of age.

••••• Production in Household #14,
2 women producers, one child under
3 years of age.

the grounds of the kind of *rules* of allocation, but on the nature of the social structures involved. Firms are special organizations for economic activity in societies of highly differentiated structure based on complex technology, extensive social division of labour, large numbers of people, and deliberate, continual technical and economic innovation. Firms may or may not follow the rule of income-maximization depending upon the larger social structure (*viz.* the firm in the Soviet economy and the firm in the United States economy). But in peasant and primitive societies like Amatenango the context of economic choice is a multipurposed social organization, which, unlike a firm, cannot liquidate if it makes poor calculations. Households, or more precisely the members of them, in Amatenango are as acutely aware as we are of relative costs and are keenly sensitive to economic gain. When marketing their pottery they go to Las Casas, or Comitán, or Las Rosas, or other points of sale in accord with price differentials. They closely question men returning from the various places as to prevailing prices and act accordingly. Price is on every tongue and is a topic of unending interest. Amatenangueros are "rational" economic actors in the sense of bringing means and ends together, only their ends are values other than (or in addition to) maximization of a given single magnitude. The formal convergence of rules of choice in a household and in a firm does not lead to similar social arrangements or similar social consequences simply because the organization of personnel, resources and methods of role-recruitment form a different social structure.

The households, of course, form a social system. And the social system operates so that households orient to the prevailing value system, on the one hand, and remain fairly equivalent in wealth, on the other. Fig. 3 gives a land-distribution chart based upon the informant's self-reported wealth (it does not include the two *tablones* of government land which most family heads have granted to them). This suffers from underestimation and deliberate concealment of assets, but serves to approximate the *shape* of the real distribution of land. Land is the best index to wealth. The features of social life which account for the shape of the curve, and the position of any given family at a point on the curve can be conceptualized as a levelling mechanism (Nash 1958; 1959). Levelling mechanisms are ubiquitous devices in peasant economies in this region (Wolf 1955). Not only do they ensure a "democracy of poverty" but they serve to inhibit economic expansion of any given unit within the society under the threat of expulsion or sacral retribution. The levelling mechanism rests first on the absolute level of wealth in the community. Amatenango's low-level technology and its restricted land base impose severe limits on the wealth of the society as a whole, and for households and individuals a correspondingly low level. No

FIG. 3. Size of Landholdings

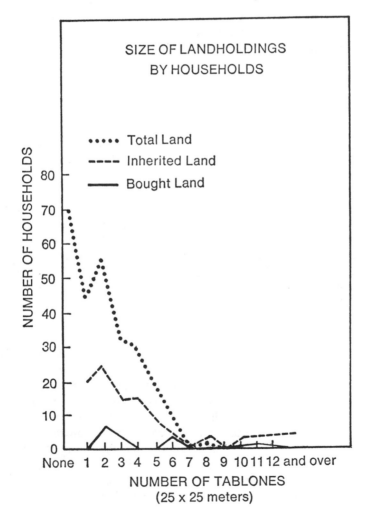

household is so rich that the spectre of poverty is not a real possibility in the wake of long illness or a sustained run of bad luck. Given a relatively low level of absolute wealth, the inheritance mechanism tends to fracture such estates as are accumulated. In Amatenango inheritance is bilateral, with equal inheritance for all the offspring (although there are prerogatives of women in inheriting houses and house sites, and of men in receiving horses and cattle). The process of inheritance scrambles land-holdings among sons and daughters even before death of the head of a household. However, Fig. 3 shows a skewed land-distribution, and this is a necessary part of Amatenango's social organization. The important point is that the rich, or large land-holders, change from generation to generation, and if the technical and economic levelling factors do not inhibit accumulation of wealth or capital, there are social means for ensuring that wealth does not adhere to family lines. There are a series of offices in which a man (as a representative of a family) must serve. This hierarchy of civil and religious offices is a drain on work time and uses up some of the resources of the household. Its offices are unpaid, and since a man must serve in 12 such offices before he is relieved of communal service, they are a continuing cost all through his adult, productive life.

Another social mechanism reducing accumulation is the institution of the *Alférez*. The Alférez office, of which there are four to be filled every year, is a ritual and sacred office filled by a younger man. The cost of this office is, in terms of Amatenango's wealth, exorbitant. An Alférez expends more than the annual income of even the richest Amatenanguero in feasting a group of neighbours, relatives and officers of the hierarchy, in the great consumption of liquor and the renting of the special costumes. Before the Alférez feast weeks of preparation for it occupy the household. Women make pottery to use for the cooking of the larger amounts of special food, as well as pottery for sale. Men of the household spend their time making liquor in the hills near Amatenango, and chopping wood for the firing of pots and cooking of foods. They also make extra trips to sell pottery. Members of the bilateral kindred come in to aid in the pottery-making and liquor-distilling. Undertaking the post of Alférez leaves the family in reduced straits and with depleted assets.

Alfereces are selected by the officials of the civil and religious hierarchy, and the selection is almost strictly on ability to pay.

The eligible households are few in number, and are those on the right-hand side of Fig. 3. Richer households have a levy placed against them in consequence of their prosperity. In a community like Amatenango it is nearly impossible to conceal one's wealth—the cows and horses owned are visible, and the land cultivated is public knowledge, and the health of one's children is a reliable index of it. Strong negative sanctions—witchcraft, gossip and envy—would be consequent on a refusal to accept the post of Alférez when it was proferred. These things together—(1) low level of technology and limited land, (2) fracture of estate by bilateral inheritance, (3) expenditure of time and resources in communal office, (4) forced expenditure in ritual by the wealthy—combine to keep the fortunes of the various households nearly equivalent, and to maintain the shift of family fortunes throughout time. In addition, the business of marrying is expensive and uses household resources. Nobody gains goods in exchanges like marriage payment, or Alférez feasts or payments for dispute-settlement. The use of liquor as the medium of payment—the completely consumable good—precludes accumulation.

Not only are households in a situation where maximization of an output or income dimension is unfeasible because of their social structure, but should a given household decide on the course of maximization or be lucky or exceedingly skilled in its economic operations, the "levelling mechanism" comes into play to minimize differences. In short, Amatenango presents a socio-economy where wealth is not easily turned to technical and economic uses, but is drained by the social and religious constitution of the culture.

Behind, and sanctioning, the social and religious organization of Amatenango is a pervasive system of belief in witchcraft. Witchcraft befalls those who violate the norms of familial and household harmony, who do not get along with neighbours, who are rich but not generous, who refuse communal obligations, who become outstanding in some dimension which violates the corporate nature of the community or upsets its tendency to economic homogeneity. Amatenangueros do not formulate the principles of witchcraft in this manner, but they behave as if their actions were governed by these premises. Witchcraft as a working means of sanctioning behaviour is not an easy thing to live with, and at least one man is killed every two months for being a practitioner of witchcraft. But the tension between economic expansion and social coercion is apparently not so strong that the system appears in immediate or even remote danger of falling under its own weight.

The economy of Amatenango, like the rest of the social structure, shows little dynamism, and change and innovation are not by-products of economic activity, as they are in the "developed" industrial societies. The simple technology, the absence of literary skills, the shortage of capital, the lack of credit all help to explain this fact. But the social and cultural basis of Amatenango's indifference to finding means to economic change depends upon the twin facts of household organization of production and the social and religious system of witchcraft which inhibits accumulation and prevents the discovery or utilization of economic opportunity. No one can run the risks of wide economic differentials, and even if the risks were taken, membership in the community would require investment in social relations, not economic ones. Amatenango presents the paradox of a community whose market economy makes it aware of economic calculation and relative costs and benefits, but a social structure and value system which channels economic choice toward economic stability and social continuity. Communities like Amatenango develop in the face of great economic pressure from the superordinate society, or *via* the extension of economic links with persons and social systems in which the rules of choice and values, and organizations are congruent with sustained ability to seize or make economic opportunity.

In small-scale societies like Amatenango, the facts of interconnexion of economy and society and their reciprocal interaction are open to inspection. They need not be bracketed away in the abstract language of formal economic analysis. Anthropologists do not have to lose the advantages of small scale by following the trend to principle-construction at the level of the skeletal model, universal, beyond time and space, for the dubious benefits of elegance and easy manipulation. The task of understanding a representative series of social structures and their economic consequences and correlates is still to be done. With this intellectual task pursued, the making of "principles" or the fashioning of "models" will be only the happy task of summary and extrapolation.

BIBLIOGRAPHICAL ESSAY

THEORETICAL ISSUES

The issue which causes the most heat in economic anthropology concerns the applicability of conventional economics to the analysis of subsistence economies. Those who stress the similarities between primitive economies and our own use conventional economic terms to describe subsistence economies—capital, surplus, maximizing, supply, demand, (bride) price—and try to put the same questions to primitive economy that economists put to our own. See Raymond Firth, "Capital, Saving and Credit in Peasant Societies: A Viewpoint from Economic Anthropology," in R. Firth and B. S. Yamey, editors, *Capital, Saving and Credit in Peasant Societies,* 1964; Raymond Firth, "The Place of Malinowski in the History of Economic Anthropology," in R. Firth, editor, *Man and Culture,* 1957; Raymond Firth, "Problems of Primitive Economics," Chapter 1 in R. Firth, *Primitive Polynesian Economy,* 1939; Melville J. Herskovits, *Economic Anthropology,* 1952; D. M. Goodfellow, *Principles of Economic Sociology,* 1939; E. E. LeClaire, "Economic Theory and Economic Anthropology," *American Anthropologist,* 1962; H. K. Schneider, "Economics in East African Aboriginal Societies," in M. J. Herskovits and M. Harwitz, editors, *Economic Transition in Africa,* 1964; Richard Salisbury, *From Stone to Steel,* 1962; Leopold Pospisil, *Kapauku Papuan Economy,* 1963; R. Burling, "Maximization Theories and the Study of Economic Anthropology," *American Anthropologist,* 1962; S. Cook, "The Obsolete 'Anti-Market' Mentality: a Critique of the Substantive Approach to Economic Anthropology," *American Anthropologist,* 1966.

Another group of writers stress the differences between primitive economies and our own and the connections between economic and social organization. They use special categories of analysis—gift-giving, reciprocity, redistribution, spheres, conversions, special purpose money—which have no counterparts in conventional economics. Early works along this line, aside from Malinowski, are Marcel Mauss, *The Gift,* 1954 (translated from the French edition of 1925), and Cora DuBois, "The Wealth Concept as an Integrative Factor in Tolowa-Tututni Culture," in *Essays in Anthropology Presented to A. L. Kroeber,* R. H. Lowie, editor, 1936. The more recent work stems from K. Polanyi, C. M. Arensberg, and H. W. Pearson, *Trade and Market in the Early Empires,* 1957 (see especially K. Polanyi, "The Economy as Instituted Process"; Daniel B. Fusfeld, "Economic Theory Misplaced: Livelihood in Primitive Society"; Walter C. Neale, "Reciprocity and Redistribution in the Indian Village," and "The Market in Theory and History"); Marshall D. Sahlins, "Political Power and the Economy in Primitive Society," in Dole and Carneiro, editors, *Essays in the Science of Culture in Honor of Leslie White,* 1960; Marshall D. Sahlins, "On the Sociology of Primitive Exchange," in M. Banton, editor, *The Relevance of Models for Social Anthropology,* 1965; Neil J. Smelser, "A Comparative View of Exchange Systems," *Economic Development and Cultural Change,* 1959; Paul Bohannan and George Dalton, "Introduction," in *Markets in Africa* (rev. ed.), 1965; George Dalton, "Economic Theory and Primitive Society," *American Anthropologist,* 1961; George Dalton, "Primitive, Archaic, and Modern Economies: Karl Polanyi's Contribution to Economic Anthropology and Comparative Economy," in *Proceedings of the Annual Spring Symposium of the American Ethnological Society,* 1965; George Dalton, "Bridewealth versus Brideprice," *American Anthropologist,* 1966. A good summary and critique of recent work in economic anthropology is Maurice Godelier, "Objet et Méthodes de L'Anthropologie Économique," *L'Homme,* 1965.

General Views

There are several good general descriptions of primitive and peasant economies, of chapter length: Raymond Firth, "Work and Wealth," Chapter 3 of *Human Types* (rev. ed.), 1958;

J. H. M. Beattie, "Economic and Property Relations," Chapter 11 of *Other Cultures*, 1964; Godfrey Lienhardt, "Economics and Social Relations," Chapter 4 of *Social Anthropology*, 1964.

There are no general or comparative works on economic anthropology of book length, that I can recommend. Several contain descriptive information and bibliographies of value, but all of them, I think, have serious theoretical defects: Elizabeth E. Hoyt, *Primitive Trade, Its Psychology and Economics*, 1926; Richard Thurnwald, *Economics in Primitive Communities*, 1932; Stephan Viljoen, *The Economics of Primitive Peoples*, 1936; D. M. Goodfellow, *Principles of Economic Sociology*, 1939; Paul Einzig, *Primitive Money*, 1948; A. Hingston Quiggin, *A Survey of Primitive Money*, 1949; Melville J. Herskovits, *Economic Anthropology* (rev. ed.), 1952; Cyril Belshaw, *Traditional Exchange and Modern Markets*, 1965.

ABORIGINAL SUBSISTENCE ECONOMIES

One reason for the disputes over conceptual categories in economic anthropology is the attempt on the part of some writers to lump together all economies studied by anthropologists and make theoretical statements which would apply to them all. I think this is not a fruitful approach because of the wide range of economies included. Conventional economic theory—price, distribution, aggregate income, and growth theory—is really concerned exclusively with our own type of economy, industrial capitalism. If economists were to lump the Soviet economy with our own, they would be able to make many fewer theoretical statements than they do. It is unfortunate that Raymond Firth, the anthropologist above all others who can be said to specialize in economic anthropology, takes the generalizing view. Firth did fieldwork among the Maori and Tikopians, both of whom had subsistence economies, and among Malay fishermen, who were commercially dependent peasant producers. I think the ambivalence which is discernible in some of his methodological and theoretical pronouncements is due to his attempt to generalize about primitive *and* peasant economies, as though they were a single type, together with the inevitable distortion which results from translating primitive economies into market terminology (see the works of Firth cited above in the section on Theoretical

Issues, and Firth's review of Pospisil's "Kapauku Papuan Economy" in the *American Anthropologist,* February 1965).

I will suggest readings for each group separately, because I think the differences between primitive and peasant economies are sufficiently great to warrant separate theoretical analysis (just as the differences between U.S. and Soviet economy are sufficiently great to warrant separate analysis).

The literature on subsistence economies—traditional economies furthest removed from our own—is richest for Africa and Oceania, for small-scale economies rather than kingdoms and empires, and for agriculturalists rather than hunters and gatherers, pastoralists, etc. Malinowski's work is the single best source, especially "The Primitive Economics of the Trobriand Islanders," *The Economic Journal,* 1921; *Argonauts of the Western Pacific,* 1922; *Coral Gardens and Their Magic,* Vol. 1, 1935; *Crime and Custom in Savage Society,* 1926. (See also the very useful work of J. P. Singh-Uberoi, *The Politics of the Kula,* 1962.) Other good ethnographic accounts of subsistence economies are: Raymond Firth, *Economics of the New Zealand Maori* (2nd ed.), 1959; Raymond Firth, *Primitive Polynesian Economy,* 1939; D. F. Thomson, *Economic Structure and the Ceremonial Exchange Cycle in Arnhem Land,* 1949; E. E. Evans-Pritchard, *The Nuer,* 1940; Audrey I. Richards, *Land, Labour and Diet in Northern Rhodesia,* 1939; Mary Douglas, *The Lele of the Kasai,* 1963; Paul and Laura Bohannan, *Tiv Economy,* 1967; P. H. Gulliver, *The Family Herds,* 1955.

On the economies of kingdoms, and other politically centralized societies, the best works are: S. F. Nadel, *A Black Byzantium, the Kingdom of Nupe in Nigeria,* 1942; Karl Polanyi, *Dahomey and the Slave Trade,* 1966; Jaques Maquet, *The Premise of Inequality in Ruanda,* 1961; Max Gluckman, "Essays on Lozi Land and Royal Property," *Rhodes-Livingstone Papers,* No. 10, 1943; Rosemary Arnold, "A Port of Trade: Whydah on the Guinea Coast," Chapter 8 in K. Polanyi, C. M. Arensberg, H. W. Pearson, editors, *Trade and Market in the Early Empires,* 1957.

There is a growing number of symposium volumes which contain valuable information on traditional economic organization: M. Fortes and E. E. Evans-Pritchard, editors, *African Political Systems,* 1940; A. R. Radcliffe-Brown and Daryll Forde, editors,

African Systems of Kinship and Marriage, 1950; Elizabeth Colson and Max Gluckman, editors, *Seven Tribes of British Central Africa*, 1951; Paul Bohannan and George Dalton, editors, *Markets in Africa*, 1962; Daniel Biebuyck, editor, *African Agrarian Systems*, 1963; John Middleton and David Tait, editors, *Tribes without Rulers*, 1958; McKim Marriott, editor, *Village India*, 1955.

A few works on pre-industrial European economic history will be cited: Michel Rostovtzev, *Economic and Social History of the Hellenistic World*, 1932; Karl Polanyi, "Aristotle Discovers the Economy," Chapter 5 in K. Polanyi, C. M. Arensberg, H. W. Pearson, *Trade and Market in the Early Empires*, 1957; on the extremely valuable work of M. I. Finley, see, by Pierre Vidal-Naquet, "Économie et société dans la Grèce ancienne: l'oeuvre de Moses I. Finley," *Archives Européennes de Sociologie*, 1965, and the bibliography cited; Marc Bloch, *Feudal Society*, 1961; Marc Bloch, "European Feudalism," in the *Encyclopaedia of the Social Sciences;* H. S. Bennett, *Life on the English Manor: A Study of Peasant Conditions, 1150–1400*, 1962; Henri Pirenne, *Medieval Cities*, 1948.

TRADITIONAL PEASANT ECONOMIES

There is an enormous literature on peasantry, but unfortunately little of it is analytically concerned with peasant economy as a kind of economy. The emphasis, stemming perhaps from Redfield, is on peasant culture: Robert Redfield, *The Folk Culture of Yucatan*, 1941; Robert Redfield, "The Folk Society," *American Journal of Sociology*, 1947; Robert Redfield, *The Primitive World and Its Transformations*, 1953; Robert Redfield, *Peasant Society and Culture*, 1956.

"Peasantry," like "feudalism," is a conceptual category which arouses dispute in the literature: on feudalism, see John Beattie (7), and Jack Goody, "Feudalism in Africa?" *Journal of African History*, 1963; on peasantry, see Eric Wolf (28), and Lloyd Fallers, "Are African Cultivators to Be Called 'Peasants'?" *Current Anthropology*, 1961. Conceptual disputes over classifying communities as "peasant" arise because of the wide differences among specific communities given the same label.

Briefly, what is true about peasant societies and economies, in contrast to those called primitive and modern, is that most peasant communities contain thorough mixtures of traditional ("primitive") and modern elements of economy, technology, social organization, and culture. One finds frequently in the same small peasant community a range of practices: old technology and new technology; subsistence production and production for sale; illiteracy and literacy; world religion and pagan practices; traditional leaders and the presence of eminent persons from outside (priests, schoolteachers). Good works on peasant *economy* are: Raymond Firth, *Malay Fishermen: Their Peasant Economy,* 1946; M. G. Smith, *The Economy of Hausa Communities of Zaria,* 1955; Sol Tax, *Penny Capitalism,* 1953. On marketing in peasant economies, see the extensive work of Sidney Mintz, e.g., "The Employment of Capital by Market Women in Haiti," in R. Firth and B. S. Yamey, editors, *Capital, Saving and Credit in Peasant Societies,* 1964 (and the bibliography of Mintz cited there); Alice Dewey, *Peasant Marketing in Java,* 1962.

SOCIAL AND ECONOMIC CHANGE IN SUBSISTENCE AND PEASANT ECONOMIES

Both the theoretical literature and the ethnographic case studies on social and economic change and development are very large indeed and growing rapidly as the number of peoples still living in traditional societies diminishes, and the concern of social scientists with the subject increases.

Some good ethnographic case studies are: Raymond Firth, *Social Change in Tikopia,* 1959 (and Beattie's excellent review article, J. H. M. Beattie, "Culture Contact and Social Change," *British Journal of Sociology,* 1961); Cyril S. Belshaw, *Changing Melanesia,* 1954; T. Scarlett Epstein, *Economic Development and Social Change in South India,* 1962; F. C. Bailey, *Caste and the Economic Frontier,* 1957; Clifford Geertz, *Peddlers and Princes,* 1963; L. P. Mair, *Studies in Applied Anthropology,* 1957; Monica Hunter, *Reaction to Conquest,* 2nd ed., 1961; Audrey I. Richards, editor, *Economic Development and Tribal Change,* n.d.; W. Watson, *Tribal Cohesion in a Money Economy,* 1958; Manning Nash, *Machine Age Maya,* 1958; Walter Elkan, *Mi-*

grants and Proletarians, 1960; Polly Hill, *The Migrant Cocoa Farmers of Southern Ghana,* 1963.

Writings of journal article length which are very good are: Mary Douglas, "Lele Economy Compared with the Bushong: a Study of Economic Backwardness," in P. Bohannan and G. Dalton, editors, *Markets in Africa* (rev. ed.) 1965; Ralph Linton, "Cultural and Personality Factors Affecting Economic Growth," in B. F. Hoselitz, editor, *The Progress of Underdeveloped Areas,* 1952; M. A. Jaspan, "A Sociological Case Study: Communal Hostility to Imposed Social Changes in South Africa," in Phillips Ruopp, editor, *Approaches to Community Development,* 1953; M. Yudelman, "Some Aspects of African Agricultural Development," in E. A. G. Robinson, editor, *Economic Development for Africa South of the Sahara,* 1964; Hla Myint, "Social Flexibility, Social Discipline and Economic Growth," *International Social Science Journal,* 1964; for an unusually successful case of community development, see the articles on Vicos, "The Vicos Case: Peasant Society on Transition," *The American Behavioral Scientist,* March 1965.

Several journals frequently publish articles on the social and cultural aspects of economic change, growth, and development: *International Social Science Journal* (UNESCO); *Economic Development and Cultural Change* (University of Chicago); *Development Digest* (National Planning Association, Washington, D.C.); *Comparative Studies in Society and History* (University of Michigan); *Human Organization* (Cornell University).

Symposium volumes which consider a variety of topics relating to social and economic change and development are: B. F. Hoselitz and W. E. Moore, editors, *The Impact of Industry,* 1963; W. E. Moore and A. S. Feldman, editors, *Labor Commitment and Social Change in Developing Areas,* 1960; Phillips Ruopp, editor, *Approaches to Community Development,* 1953; B. F. Hoselitz, editor, *The Progress of Underdeveloped Areas,* 1952; Raymond Firth and B. S. Yamey, editors, *Capital, Saving and Credit in Peasant Societies,* 1964; UNESCO, *Social Implications of Industrialization and Urbanization in Africa South of the Sahara,* 1956; Aidan Southall, editor, *Social Change in Modern Africa,* 1961; M. J. Herskovits and M. Harwitz, editors, *Economic Transition in Africa,* 1964; William H. Friedland and Carl G. Rosberg, Jr., editors, _African Socialism,_ 1964; UNESCO, _Social Aspects of Economic Development in Latin America,_ two volumes, 1963.

Some recent works in applied anthropology which analyze community change and development are: Ward Hunt Goodenough, _Cooperation in Change,_ 1963; George M. Foster, _Traditional Cultures: and the Impact of Technological Change,_ 1962. Charles J. Erasmus, _Man Takes Control,_ 1961.

Among the best works by economists on social and economic change which contain theoretical insights of importance to anthropologists are: Gunnar Myrdal, _Rich Lands and Poor,_ 1957; Everett E. Hagen, _On the Theory of Social Change,_ 1962; W. Arthur Lewis, _The Theory of Economic Growth,_ 1955. A very promising quantitative approach to the political and social aspects of national economic development is the work being done by Irma Adelman and Cynthia Taft Morris, "Factor Analysis of the Interrelationship Between Social and Political Variables and Per Capita Gross National Product," _Quarterly Journal of Economics,_ 1965 (and their forthcoming book on the same subject). Two works by sociologists on social aspects of European and American industrialization which can be highly recommended are: Reinhard Bendix, _Work and Authority in Industry: Ideologies of Management in the Course of Industrialization,_ 1956; and Neil J. Smelser, _Social Change in the Industrial Revolution: an Application of Theory to the Lancashire Cotton Industry 1770–1840,_ 1959.

BIBLIOGRAPHY

Adelman, Irma, and Morris, Cynthia Taft. 1965. "Factor Analysis of the Interrelationship Between Social and Political Variables and Per Capital Gross National Product," *The Quarterly Journal of Economics*, Vol. LXXIX, 555–578.

Aginsky, B. W. 1939. "Population Control in the Shanel (Pomo) Tribe," *American Sociological Review*, 4:209–216.

Aguirre, Beltrán Gonzalo. 1952. "Problemas de la población indigena de la Cuenca del Tepalcatepec," Memorias del Instituto Nacional Indigenista 3, México, D.F.

Almond, G. A., and Coleman, J. S. 1960. *The Politics of Developing Areas*. Princeton: Princeton University Press.

Akiga, B. 1939. *Akiga's Story*. London: International Institute of African Languages and Cultures.

Anonymous. 1908. *Koji Rui-en: a Collection of Historical Data*. Tokyo. (Compiled and edited by a group of scholars under the auspices of the government.)

Antei, Miyazaki, 1696. *Nogyo Zensho*. Vol. xi.

Apter, D. 1956. *The Gold Coast in Transition*. Princeton: Princeton University Press.

Arensberg, Conrad M. 1957. "Anthropology as History," in *Trade and Market in the Early Empires*, K. Polanyi, C. M. Arensberg, H. W. Pearson, eds., Glencoe, Ill.: The Free Press.

Armstrong, John M. 1949. "A Mexican Community: a Study of the Cultural Determinants of Migration," Ph.D. dissertation, New Haven: Yale University.

Armstrong, W. E. 1924. "Rossel Island Money: a Unique Monetary System," *Economic Journal*, 34:423–429.

1928. *Rossel Island*. Cambridge: Cambridge University Press.

Ashton, T. S. 1949. "The Standard of Life of the Workers in England, 1790–1830," *Journal of Economic History*, Supplement IX.

Bailey, F. C. 1957. *Caste and the Economic Frontier.* Manchester: Manchester University Press.

Baker, Sir Samuel. 1895. *Ismailia.* London: The Macmillan Co.

Bales, R. F. 1950. *Interaction Process Analysis.* Cambridge, Mass.: Addison-Wesley Press.

Barber, Bernard. 1957. *Social Stratification.* New York: Harcourt, Brace & World.

Barrett, S. A. 1952. "Material Aspects of Pomo Culture," Bulletin of the Public Museum of the City of Milwaukee, 20, Parts I, II.

Barth, Frederik. 1960. "The System of Social Stratification in Swat, North Pakistan," in E. R. Leach, ed., *Aspects of Caste in South India, Ceylon and Northwest Pakistan,* Cambridge: Cambridge University Press.

Beals, Ralph L. 1951. "Urbanism, Urbanization and Acculturation," *American Anthropologist,* 53:1–10.

1952. "Notes on Acculturation," in Sol Tax, ed., *Heritage of Conquest,* 225–231.

1953. "Social Stratification in Latin America," *American Journal of Sociology,* 58:327–339.

Beattie, J. H. M. 1959. "Rituals of Nyoro Kinship," *Africa,* XXIX: 2:134–145.

1960. "On the Nyoro Concept of Mahano," *African Studies,* XIX: 3:145–150.

1960a. *Bunyoro: an African Kingdom.* New York: Henry Holt & Co.

1961. "Culture Contact and Social Change," *British Journal of Sociology,* XII, 2:165–175.

1961a. "Democratization in Bunyoro," *Civilizations,* XI, 1:8–20.

Beidelman, T. O. 1959. *A Comparative Analysis of the Jajmani System,* Monograph of the Association for Asian Studies VII, Locust Valley, New York: J. J. Augustin.

Belshaw, C. S. 1955. *In Search of Wealth,* Memoir of the American Anthropological Association, No. 80, Washington: American Anthropological Association.

Berliner, J. S. 1962. "The Feet of the Natives Are Large: an Essay on Anthropology by an Economist," *Current Anthropology,* 3:47–61.

Berreman, Gerald D. 1962. "Caste and Economy in the Himalayas," *Economic Development and Cultural Change,* X:386–394.

Bikunya, P. 1927. *Ky'Abakama ba Bunyoro.* London.

Bloch, Marc. 1941. "The Rise of Dependent Cultivation and Seignioral Institutions," in J. H. Clapham and Eileen Power, eds., *The*

Cambridge Economic History, Vol. 1, Cambridge: Cambridge University Press.

Bloch, Marc. 1961. *Feudal Society.* London: Routledge & Kegan Paul.

Blunt, E. A. A. 1931. *Caste System of Northern India.* Madras: Oxford University Press.

Boeke, J. H. 1942. *The Structure of the Netherlands Indian Economy,* New York: International Secretariat, Institute of Pacific Relations.

1947. *Oriental Economics,* New York: Institute of Pacific Relations.

Bohannan, Laura. 1949. "Dahomean Marriage: A Reevaluation," *Africa,* XIX:273–287.

Bohannan, Laura and Paul. 1953. *The Tiv of Central Nigeria,* London: International African Institute.

Bohannan, Paul and Laura. 1958. *Three Source Notebooks in Tiv Ethnography,* New Haven: Human Relations Area Files.

1967. *Tiv Economy.* Evanston: Northwestern University Press.

Bohannan, Paul. 1954. *Tiv Farm and Settlement.* Colonial Office Research Studies 15. London, H.M.S.O.

1955. "Some Principles of Exchange and Investment Among the Tiv," *American Anthropologist,* 57:60–69.

1959. "The Impact of Money on an African Subsistence Economy," *The Journal of Economic History,* 19:491–503.

1960. "Africa's Land," *The Centennial Review,* IV.

Bohannan, Paul, and Dalton, George. 1962. "Introduction," in *Markets in Africa,* Evanston: Northwestern University Press.

Borah, Woodrow. 1951. "New Spain's Century of Depression," *Ibero-Americana 35,* Berkeley: University of California Press.

Bowman, Isaiah. 1931. "The Pioneer Fringe," American Geographical Society Special Publication 13, New York.

Brentano, L. 1916. *Die Anfänge des Modernen Kapitalismus.* Munich.

Brodnitz, G. n.d. *Englische Wirtachaftsgeschichte,* I.

Burstein, M. L. 1963. *Money.* Cambridge, Mass.: Shenkman.

Carrasco Pizana, Pedro. 1952. "Tarascan Folk Religion: an Analysis of Economic, Social and Religious Interactions," Middle American Research Institute Publication, 17:1–64, New Orleans: Tulane University.

Carstairs, G. M. 1957. *The Twice-Born.* London: Hogarth.

Chevalier, François. 1952. "La Formation des Grands Domaines au Mexique: Terre et Société aux XVIe–XVIIe Siècles," *Travaux et Mémoires de l'Institut d'Ethnologie,* 56, Paris.

Cline, Walter. 1937. *Mining and Metallurgy in Negro Africa.* Menasha, Wisconsin: George Banta.

Codere, Helen. 1951. *Fighting with Property.* New York: J. J. Augustin.

Cohn, Bernard. 1954. *The Camars of Senapur*. Ph.D. dissertation, Ithaca, N.Y.: Cornell University.

Cohn, B. S. 1958. "Changing Traditions of a Low Caste," *Journal of American Folklore*, LXXI:413–421.

Cohen, Ronald. 1961. "The Success That Failed: an Experiment in Culture Change in Africa," *Anthropologica*, new series, Vol. III, No. 1, pp. 1–16.

Cole, Johnetta. 1962. "Some Liberian Impressions of Government," in *Northwestern University Economic Survey of Liberia*, mimeograph.

Coleman, J. S. 1957. "Nationalism in Tropical Africa," in L. W. Shannon, *Underdeveloped Areas*, New York: Harper & Row.

Colson, Elizabeth. 1955. "Native Cultural and Social Patterns in Contemporary Africa," in C. Grove Haines, ed., *Africa Today*, Baltimore: Johns Hopkins Press.

Coon, Carleton S. 1951. *The Story of the Middle East*. New York: Henry Holt & Co.

Coulborn, Rushton, and Strayer, Joseph R. 1956. *Feudalism in History*. Princeton: Princeton University Press.

Crazzolara, J. P. 1950. *The Lwoo*. Verona.

Dalton, George. 1961. "Economic Theory and Primitive Society," *American Anthropologist*, 63:1–25.

1962. "Traditional Production in Primitive African Economies," *The Quarterly Journal of Economics*, 76:360–378.

1962a. "The Dilemma of Piecemeal Change in Tribal Life," in *Northwestern University Economic Survey of Liberia*, mimeograph.

1964. "The Development of Subsistence and Peasant Economies in Africa," *International Social Science Journal*, 16:378–389.

1965. "Primitive Money," *American Anthropologist*, 67:44–65.

1965a. *Primitive, Archaic, and Modern Economies: Karl Polanyi's Contribution to Economic Anthropology and Comparative Economy*. American Ethnological Society Symposium.

Davenport, William H. 1961. "Primitive and Civilized Money in the Santa Cruz Islands," in V. E. Garfield, ed., *Patterns of Land Utilization and Other Papers*, Seattle: University of Washington Press.

Davis, K. 1955. "Social and Demographic Aspects of Economic Development in India," in S. Kuznets, W. E. Moore, J. J. Spengler, eds., *Economic Growth: Brazil, India, Japan*, Durham: Duke University Press.

Deacon, A. Bernard. 1934. *Malekula, a Vanishing People in the New*

Hebrides. Camilla H. Wedgwood, ed., London: George Routledge & Sons.

Deane, Phyllis. 1953. *Colonial Social Accounting.* Cambridge: Cambridge University Press.

Dewey, Alice G. 1962. *Peasant Marketing in Java.* New York: The Free Press of Glencoe.

Dhillon, H. 1955. *Leadership and Groups in a South Indian Village.* New Delhi: Planning Commission, Government of India Press.

Douglas, Mary. 1951. "A Form of Polyandri Among the Lele of the Kasai," *Africa,* XXI, No. 1.

    1954. "The Lele of the Kasai," in Daryll Forde, ed., *African Worlds,* London: Oxford University Press.

    1957. "Animals in Lele Religious Symbolism," *Africa.* XXVII, No. 1.

    1958. "Raffia Cloth Distribution in the Lele Economy," *Africa,* XXVIII:109–122.

    1962. "Lele Economy Compared with the Bushong: a Study of Economic Backwardness," in P. Bohannan and G. Dalton, eds., *Markets in Africa,* Evanston: Northwestern University Press.

    1963. *The Lele of the Kasai.* London: Oxford University Press.

Drucker, Philip. 1939. "Rank, Wealth, and Kinship in Northwest Coast Society," *American Anthropologist,* 41:55–65.

Dube, S. C. 1955. *Indian Village.* London: Routledge & Kegan Paul.

    1955a. *India's Changing Villages.* London: Routledge & Kegan Paul.

DuBois, Cora. 1936. "The Wealth Concept as an Integrative Factor in Tolowa-Tututni Culture," in R. H. Lowie, ed., *Essays in Anthropology Presented to A. L. Kroeber,* Berkeley: University of California Press.

Durkheim, Emile. 1949. *The Division of Labor in Society.* Glencoe, Ill.: The Free Press.

Einzig, Paul. 1948. *Primitive Money.* London: Eyre & Spottiswoode.

Eisenstadt, S. N. 1957. "Sociological Aspects of Political Development in Underdeveloped Countries," *Economic Development and Cultural Change,* V, No. 4.

Fallers, L. A. 1961. "Are African Cultivators to Be Called 'Peasants'?" *Current Anthropology,* Vol. 2, No. 2, pp. 108–110.

Firth, Raymond. 1929. "Currency, Primitive," in *Encyclopaedia Britannica,* 14th ed.

    1946. *Malay Fishermen: Their Peasant Economy.* London: Kegan Paul, Trench, Trubner & Co.

    1951. *The Elements of Social Organization.* London: C. A. Watts & Co.

1954. "Money, Work, and Social Change in Indo-Pacific Systems," *International Social Science Bulletin*, 4:400–410.

1958. *Human Types*. New York: Thomas Nelson and Sons.

Fisher, A. B. 1911. *Twilight Tales of the Black Baganda*. London: Marshall Brothers.

Fogg, C. Davis. 1963. "Economic and Social Factors Affecting the Development of Smallholder Agriculture," Conference of M.I.T. Fellows in Africa, mimeograph.

Forde, Daryll, and Douglas, Mary. 1956. "Primitive Economics," in Harry L. Shapiro, ed., *Man, Culture and Society*, New York: Oxford University Press.

Forster, E. M. 1953. *The Hill of Devi*. New York: Harcourt, Brace & Co.

Forsyth, P. T. 1910. "Calvinism and Capitalism," *Contemporary Review*.

Fortes, M., and Evans-Pritchard, E. E. 1940. *African Political Systems*. London: Oxford University Press.

Fortes, M. 1953. "The Structure of Unilineal Descent Groups," *American Anthropologist*, 55:17–41.

Foster, George M. 1948. "The Folk Economy of Rural Mexico with Special Reference to Marketing," *Journal of Marketing*, 12:153–162.

Frankel, S. H. 1955. *The Economic Impact on Under-developed Societies*. Cambridge: Harvard University Press.

Fromm, Erich. 1941. *Escape from Freedom*. New York: Rinehart.

1955. *The Sane Society*. New York: Rinehart.

Fürer-Haimendorf, Christoph von. 1962. *The Apa-Tanis and Their Neighbours: a Primitive Civilization of the Eastern Himalayas*. London: Routledge & Kegan Paul.

Gage, Thomas. 1929 (1648). *A New Survey of the West Indies, the English-American*. Argonaut Series, New York: McBride.

Gaitskell, Arthur. 1959. *Gezira: a Story of Development in the Sudan*. London: Faber & Faber.

García, Antonio. 1948. "Regimenes Indigenas de Salariade," *America Indigena*, 8:249–287.

Gerschenkron, Alexander. 1952. "Economic Backwardness in Historical Perspective," in B. F. Hoselitz, ed., *The Progress of Underdeveloped Areas*, Chicago: University of Chicago Press.

Gillin, John. 1952. "Ethos and Cultural Aspects of Personality," in Sol Tax, ed., *Heritage of Conquest*, pp. 193–212.

Gluckman, Max, and Cunnison, I. G. 1962. "Foreword," in J. P. Singh Uberoi, *Politics of the Kula Ring*, Manchester: Manchester University Press.

Gluckman, Max. 1943. "Essays on Lozi Land and Royal Property," *Rhodes-Livingstone Papers,* No. 10.

1945. "How the Bemba Make Their Living," *Rhodes-Livingstone Institute Journal,* 2:55–67.

Goodenough, Ward H. 1951. *Property, Kin and Community on Truk.* New Haven: Yale University Press.

Goodfellow, D. M. 1939. *Principles of Economic Sociology.* London: George Routledge & Sons.

Goody, Jack. 1963. "Feudalism in Africa?" *Journal of African History,* No. IV, 1, pp. 1–18.

Gough, E. K. 1955. "The Social Structure of a Tanjore Village," in M. Marriott, ed., *Village India,* American Anthropological Association, Memoir No. 83.

1956. "Brahman Kinship in a Tamil Village," *American Anthropologist,* LVII:826–853.

1960. "Caste in a Tanjore Village," in E. R. Leach, ed., *Aspects of Caste in South India, Ceylon and Northwest Pakistan,* Cambridge: Cambridge University Press.

Gould, H. 1958. "The Hindu Jajmani System: a Case of Economic Particularism," *Southwestern Journal of Anthropology,* XIV: 428–437.

Gulliver, P. H. 1961. "Land Shortage, Social Change, and Social Conflict in East Africa," *Journal of Conflict Resolution,* Vol. V, No. 1, pp. 16–26.

1962. "The Evolution of Arusha Trade," in P. Bohannan and G. Dalton, eds., *Markets in Africa,* Evanston: Northwestern University Press.

Hagen, Everett E. 1962. *On the Theory of Social Change.* Homewood, Ill.: Dorsey Press.

Harper, E. B. 1957. "Shamanism in South India," *Southwestern Journal of Anthropology,* XII:267–287.

1959. "A Hindu Village Pantheon," *Southwestern Journal of Anthropology,* V:227–234.

1959a. "Two Systems of Economic Exchange in Village India," *American Anthropologist,* LXI:760–778.

Harrison, S. E. 1960. *India: the Most Dangerous Decades.* Princeton: Princeton University Press.

Hermann, Lucila. 1950. "Classe Media en Guarantigueta," Materiales para el Estudio de la Clase Media en la América Latina, 3:18–59, Publicaciones de la Oficina de Ciencias Sociales, Unión Panaméricana, Washington, D.C.

Herskovits, Melville J., and Harwitz, Mitchell. 1964. *Economic Transition in Africa.* Evanston: Northwestern University Press.

Herskovits, M. J. 1938. *Dahomey, an Ancient West African King-dom.* New York: J. J. Augustin.

—— 1952. *Economic Anthropology.* rev. ed. New York: Alfred A. Knopf.

—— 1952a. "The Problem of Adapting Societies to New Tasks," in B. F. Hoselitz, ed., *The Progress of Underdeveloped Areas,* Chicago: University of Chicago Press.

Hill, Polly. 1961. "The Migrant Cocoa Farmers of Southern Ghana," *Africa,* Vol. XXXI, No. 1, pp. 209–230.

Hisanori, Oishi. 1791–1794. *Jikata Bonrei Roku.* Vol. VII.

Hitchcock, J. 1958. "The Idea of the Marital Rajout," *Journal of American Folklore,* LXXI:216–223.

—— 1960. "Surat Singh, Head Judge," in J. Casagrande, ed., *In the Company of Man,* New York: Harper & Brothers.

Hocart, A. M. 1950. *Caste.* London: Methuen & Co.

Hodgkin, T. 1957. *Nationalism in Colonial Africa.* New York: New York University Press.

Homans, George C. 1950. *The Human Group.* New York: Harcourt, Brace & Co.

Hoselitz, B. F., ed. 1952. *The Progress of Underdeveloped Areas.* Chicago: University of Chicago Press.

—— 1953. "The Role of Cities in the Economic Growth of Underdeveloped Countries," *Journal of Political Economy,* 61:195–208.

—— 1953a. "Non-economic Barriers to Economic Development," *Economic Development and Cultural Change,* I: No. 1.

Hoshu, Yamakata. 1820. *Yume no Shiro.* B.J.A.P., Vol. XXV.

Hoyt, E. 1924. *Primitive Trade.* London: K. Paul, Trench, Trubner & Co.

Hozumi, Nobushige. 1912. *Ancestor Worship and Japanese Law.* Tokyo: Maruzen Kabushiki-Kaisha.

Humphrey, Norman D. 1948. "The Cultural Background of the Mexican Immigrant," *Rural Sociology,* 13:239–255.

Hutchinson, Harry W. 1952. "Race Relations in a Rural Community of the Bahian Reconcave," in Charles Wagley, ed., *Race and Class in Rural Brazil,* pp. 16–46, Paris: UNESCO.

Hutton, J. H. 1951. *Caste in India.* Calcutta: Oxford University Press.

Jacoby, E. H. 1949. *Agrarian Unrest in Southeast Asia.* New York: Columbia University Press.

Jaspan, M. A. 1953. "A Sociological Case Study: Communal Hostility to Imposed Social Changes in South Africa," in Phillips Ruopp, ed., *Approaches to Community Development,* The Hague, W. Van Hoeve.

Jones, William O. 1960. "Economic Man in Africa," *Food Research Institute Studies,* 1:107–134.

1961. "Food and Agricultural Economies of Tropical Africa; A Summary View," *Food Research Institute Studies* (Stanford University), Vol. II, No. 1, pp. 3–20.

K.W. 1937. "The Kings of Bunyoro-Kitara, Part III," *Uganda Journal,* Vol. 2 (1937).

Kenyatta, Jomo. 1938. *Facing Mount Kenya.* London: Secker & Warburg.

Keyfitz, N. 1959. "The Interlocking of Social and Economic Factors in Asian Development," *The Canadian Journal of Economics and Political Science,* XXV:34–46.

Kirchhoff, Paul. 1949. "The Social and Political Organization of the An Peoples," in Julian Steward, ed., *Handbook of South American Indians,* Vol. 5, pp. 293–311.

Kluckhohn, Richard. 1962. "The Konso Economy of Southern Ethiopia," in Bohannan, P., and Dalton, G., eds., *Markets in Africa,* Evanston: Northwestern University Press.

Kniffen, Fred B. 1939. "Pomo Geography," *University of California Publications in American Archaeology and Ethnology,* 36:353–400.

Kokan, Shiba. 1811. *Shumparo Hikki,* Vol. XII, B.J.A.P.

Koki, Shoji. 1841. *Keizai Mondo Hiroku.* Vol. XXI, B.J.A.P.

Kroeber, A. L. 1925. "Handbook of the Indians of California," Bulletin 78, Bureau of American Ethnology, Washington.

1948. *Anthropology.* New York: Harcourt, Brace & Co.

1953. "The Nature of Land-holding in Aboriginal California," in *Aboriginal California: Three Studies in Cultural History,* Berkeley: University of California Press.

Kroeber, Alfred L., and Kluckholn, Clyde. 1952. "Culture," *Papers of the Peabody Museum of American Archaeology and Ethnology,* Harvard University 47, No. 1, Cambridge, Mass.

Kuznets, S. 1955. "International Differences in Income Levels," in S. Kuznets, W. E. Moore, and J. J. Spengler, eds., *Economic Growth: Brazil, India, Japan,* Durham: Duke University Press.

Leach, E. R. 1951. "Structural Implications of Cross-cousin Marriage," *Journal of the Royal Anthropological Institute,* LXXXI.

1960. *Aspects of Caste in South India, Ceylon and Northwest Pakistan.* Cambridge: Cambridge University Press.

Leonard, Olen E. 1952. *Bolivia.* Washington, D.C.: Scarecrow Press.

Leslie, Charles M. 1960. *Now We Are Civilized: a Study of the World View of the Zapotec Indians of Mitla, Oaxaca.* Detroit: Wayne State University Press.

Lewis, Oscar. 1951. *Life in a Mexican Village: Tepoztlan Revisited.* Urbana: University of Illinois Press.

1954. *Group Dynamics in a North Indian Village.* New Delhi: Planning Commission, Government of India Press.

1958. *Village Life in Northern India.* Urbana: University of Illinois Press.

Lewis, W. Arthur. 1955. *The Theory of Economic Growth.* London: Allen & Unwin.

Lienhardt, R. Godfrey. 1956. "Religion," in Harry L. Shapiro, ed., *Man, Culture, and Society,* New York: Oxford University Press.

Linton, Ralph. 1936. *The Study of Man.* New York: Appleton-Century.

1952. "Cultural and Personality Factors Affecting Economic Growth," in B. F. Hoselitz, ed., *The Progress of Underdeveloped Areas,* Chicago: University of Chicago Press.

Lipset, S. M., and Bendix, R. 1959. *Social Mobility in Industrial Society.* Berkeley and Los Angeles: University of California Press.

Little, Kenneth L. 1953. "Social Change in a Non-literate Community," in Phillips Ruopp, ed., *Approaches to Community Development,* The Hague, W. Van Hoeve.

Lloyd, Peter. 1953. "Craft Organization in Yoruba Towns," *Africa,* XXIII.

Loeb, E. M. 1926. "Pomo Folkways," *University of California Publications in American Archaeology and Ethnology,* 19:149–404.

1936. "The Distribution and Function of Money in Early Societies," in R. H. Lowie, ed., *Essays in Anthropology Presented to A. L. Kroeber,* Berkeley: University of California Press.

MacIver, R. M. 1933. *Society, Its Structure and Changes.* New York: R. Long and R. R. Smith.

Mahar, P. M. 1960. "A Ritual Pollution Scale for Ranking Hindu Castes," *Sociometry,* XXIII:292–306.

Mair, L. P. 1957. *Studies in Applied Anthropology.* London: University of London, The Athlone Press.

1963. *New Nations.* London: Weidenfeld & Nicolson.

Majumdar, D. N. 1955. "Rural Profiles," *Ethnographic and Folk Culture Society,* U.P., Lucknow, India.

1958. *Caste and Communication in an Indian Village.* Bombay: Asia Publishing House.

Malinowski, Bronislaw. 1915. "Mailu," in *Proceedings of the Royal Society of South Australia.*

1921. "The Primitive Economics of the Trobriand Islanders," *Economic Journal,* 31:1–15.

1922. *Argonauts of the Western Pacific*. London: George Routledge & Sons.

1926. *Crime and Custom in Savage Society*. New York: Humanities Press, 1952; Ames, Iowa: Littlefield, Adams & Co., 1959.

1935. *Coral Gardens and Their Magic*. Vol. I. New York: American Book Publishing Co.

Mandelbaum, David. 1960. "The World and the World View of the Kota," in M. Marriott, ed., *Caste Ranking and Community Structure in Five Regions of India and Pakistan*, Poona: Deccan College.

Mann, H. H. 1916. "Land and Labour in a Deccan Village," *University of Bombay, Economic Series*, No. 1, London and Bombay: Oxford University Press.

Manners, R. A. 1962. "Land Use, Trade and the Growth of Market Economy in Kipsigis Country," in Paul Bohannan and George Dalton, eds., *Markets in Africa*, Evanston: Northwestern University Press.

Maquet, Jacques. 1961. *The Premise of Inequality in Ruanda*. London: Oxford University Press.

1961a. "Une Hypothèse pour l'Étude des Féodalités Africaines," *Cahiers d'Études Africaines*, II, pp. 292–314.

Marriott, McKim. 1955. *Village India*, American Anthropological Association Memoir, No. 83, LVII.

1960. *Caste Ranking and Community Structure in Five Regions of India and Pakistan*. Poona: Deccan College.

1964. "Social Change in an Indian Village," in A. and E. Etzioni, eds., *Social Change*, New York: Basic Books.

Masatoshi, Tsutsumi. n.d. *Shodo Kyuhen*. B.J.A.P. Vol. XX.

Matossian, M. 1957. "Ideologies of Delayed Industrialization," *Economic Development and Cultural Change*, VI, No. 3.

Mauss, Marcel. 1925. "Essai sur le Don," *L'Année Sociologie*, (n.s.) 1:30–186.

1954. *The Gift*. Translated by I. G. Cunnison from the French edition of 1925. London: Cohen & West, Ltd.; Glencoe, Ill.: The Free Press.

Mayer, A. 1956. "Development Projects in an Indian Village," *Pacific Affairs*, XXIX:37–45.

1957. "An Indian Community Development Block Revisited," *Pacific Affairs*, XXX:34–46.

1960. *Caste and Kinship in Central India*. Berkeley: University of California Press.

Mayer, Philip. 1951. *Two Studies in Applied Anthropology in Kenya*. London: HMSO.

McCormack, W. 1948. "The Forms of Communication in Virasaiva Religion," *Journal of American Folklore*, LXXI:325–335.

Mead, Margaret. 1937. "Interpretive Statement," in Mead, ed., *Cooperation and Competition Among Primitive Peoples*, New York: McGraw-Hill Book Co.

Menger, Carl. 1892. "On the Origin of Money," *Economic Journal*, II, pp. 439–477.

Mintz, Sidney W. 1953. "The Culture History of a Puerto Rican Sugar Cane Plantation, 1876–1949," *Hispanic American Historical Review*, 33:224–251.

——— 1961. "Pratik," in V. E. Garfield, ed., *Patterns of Land Utilization and Other Papers*, Seattle: University of Washington Press.

Miracle, Marvin P. 1962. "African Markets and Trade in the Copperbelt," in P. J. Bohannan and G. Dalton, eds., *Markets in Africa*, Evanston: Northwestern University Press.

Mishkin, Bernard. 1946. "The Contemporary Quechua," in Julian Steward, ed., *Handbook of South American Indians*, Vol. 2, pp. 411–476, Washington D.C.: U. S. Government Printing Office.

Moore, W. E. 1955. "Labor Attitudes Toward Industrialization in Underdeveloped Countries," *American Economic Review*, XLV: 156–165.

Moore, W. E., and Feldman, A. S. 1960. *Labor Commitment and Social Change in Developing Areas*. New York: Social Science Research Council.

Moore, Wilbert E., and Tumin, Melvin M. 1949. "Some Social Functions of Ignorance," *American Sociological Review*, 14: 787–795.

Mota Escobar, Alonso de la. 1940. *1601–31 Descripción Geográfica de los Reines de Nueva Galicia, Nueva Vizcaya y Nueve León*. México, D.F.: Editorial Pedro Robrodo.

Muller, Max. 1886. *Laws of Manu*. London: Oxford University Press.

Murdock, G. P. 1959. *Africa, Its Peoples and Their Culture History*. New York: McGraw-Hill Book Co.

Myrdal, Gunnar. 1953. "The Relation Between Social Theory and Social Policy," *British Journal of Sociology*, Vol. IV, pp. 210–242.

——— 1957. *Rich Lands and Poor*. New York: Harper & Bros.

——— 1960. *Beyond the Welfare State*. New Haven: Yale University Press.

Nadel, S. F. 1942. *A Black Byzantium, the Kingdom of Nupe in Nigeria*. London: Oxford University Press.

——— 1957. *The Theory of Social Structure*. London: Cohen & West, Ltd.

Nakamura, Koya. 1924. *Kokumin Bunka Shi Gairon*. Vol. II. Tokyo.

Nampo, Ota. 1800–1823. *Ichiwa Ichigen*. Vol. VII.

Nash, M. 1954. "Some Notes on Village Industrialization in South and East Asia," *Economic Development and Cultural Change*, III, No. 3.

—— 1958. *Machine Age Maya*. Memoir 87 American Anthropological Association. Glencoe, Ill.: The Free Press.

—— 1959. "Some Social and Cultural Aspects of Economic Development," *Economic Development and Cultural Change*, 7:137–150.

—— 1961. "The Social Context of Economic Choice in a Small Society," *Man*, 61:186–191 (Art. ✗219).

Neale, Walter C. 1957. "Reciprocity and Redistribution in the Indian Village: Sequel to Some Notable Discussions," in Polanyi, Arensberg, and Pearson, eds., *Trade and Market in the Early Empires*, Glencoe, Ill.: The Free Press.

Oberg, K. 1940. "The Kingdom of Ankole in Uganda," in M. Fortes and E. E. Evans-Pritchard, eds., *African Political Systems*, London: Oxford University Press.

Okigbo, Pius. 1956. "Social Consequences of Economic Development in West Africa," *Annals of the American Academy of Political Social Science*, 125–133.

Opler, M. E. 1958. "Spirit Possession in a Rural Area of Northern India," in Lessa and Vogt, eds., *Reader on Comparative Religion*, Evanson, Ill.: Row, Peterson & Co.

—— 1959. "The Place of Religion in a North Indian Village," *Southwestern Journal of Anthropology*, XV:219–226.

Opler, M. E., and Dingh, R. D. 1952. "Economic, Political and Social Change in a Village of North Central India," *Human Organization II*.

Park, R., and Tinker, I. 1959. *Leadership and Political Institutions in India*. Princeton: Princeton University Press.

Parsons, James J. 1949. "Antioqueño Colonization in Western Colombia," *Ibero-American 32*, Berkeley: University of California Press.

Parsons, Talcott. 1951. *The Social System*. Glencoe, Ill.: The Free Press.

Passin, Herbert. 1942. "Sorcery as a Phase of Tarahumara Economic Relations," *Man*, 42:11–15.

Pierson, Donald, and others. 1951. "Cruz das Almas: a Brazilian Village," Institute of Social Anthropology Publication 12, Smithsonian Institution, Washington, D.C.

Platt, Robert. 1943. *Latin America: Countrysides and United Regions*. New York: Whittlesey House.

Pocock, D. 1957. "The Bases of Faction in Gujerat," *British Journal of Sociology*, VII:295–306.

Polanyi, Karl. 1944. *The Great Transformation.* New York: Rinehart & Co.

— 1947. "Our Obsolete Market Mentality," in *Commentary*, February.

— 1957. "Notes on the Place Occupied by Economies in Societies," in *Selected Memoranda on Economic Aspects of Institutional Growth* (mimeo), New York: Columbia University.

— 1957a. "The Economy as Instituted Process," in K. Polanyi, C. M. Arensberg, H. W. Pearson, eds., *Trade and Market in the Early Empires*, Glencoe, Ill.: The Free Press.

— 1966. *Dahomey and the Slave Trade.* Seattle: University of Washington Press for the American Ethnological Society.

Potekhin, I. I. 1960. "On Feudalism of the Ashanti," paper read to Twenty-fifth International Congress of Orientalists, Moscow.

Pozas, Ricardo. 1952. "La Situation Économique et Financière de l'Indien Américain," *Civilization*, 2:309–329.

Quiggin, A. H. 1949. *A Survey of Primitive Money.* London: Methuen & Co.

Redfield, Robert. 1953. *The Primitive World and Its Transformations.* Ithaca, New York: Cornell University Press.

Redfield, R., and Singer, M. 1955. "Foreword," in M. Marriott, ed., *Village India*, American Anthropological Association Memoir No. 83.

Redfield, Robert, and Tax, Sol. 1952. "General Characteristics of Present-day Mesoamerican Indian Society," in Sol Tax, ed., *Heritage of Conquest*, pp. 31–39.

Registre Ethnographique, Basongo. 1924. *Rapport Économique.*

Reining, Conrad C. 1959. "The Role of Money in the Zande Economy," *American Anthropologist*, 61:39–43.

Reynolds, Lloyd G. 1963. *Economics, a General Introduction.* Homewood, Ill.: Richard D. Irwin, Inc.

Richards, Audrey I. 1939. *Land, Labour and Diet in Northern Rhodesia.* London: Oxford University Press.

Roscoe, John. 1923. *The Bakitara or Banyoro.* Cambridge: Cambridge University Press.

Rostow, W. W. 1960. *The Stages of Economic Growth.* Cambridge: Cambridge University Press.

Royal Anthropological Institute of Great Britain and Ireland. 1949. *Notes and Queries on Anthropology.* 6th ed. London: Routledge & Kegan Paul.

Sadanobu, Matsudaira. 1891. *Raku-o ko Isho (The Works of Raku-o ko).*

Sadie, J. L. 1960. "The Social Anthropology of Economic Development," *Economic Journal*, LXX.

Salisbury, R. 1962. *From Stone to Steel.* Cambridge: Cambridge University Press.

Samuelson, Paul Anthony. 1961. *Economics, an Introductory Analysis.* 5th ed. New York: McGraw-Hill Book Co.

Schapera, I. 1928. "Economic Changes in South African Native Life, *Africa*, I:170–188.

Schapera, I., and Goodwin, A. J. H. 1937. "Work and Wealth," in I. Schapera, ed., *The Bantu-speaking Tribes of South Africa,* London: George Routledge & Sons.

Schneider, Harold K. 1957. "The Subsistence Role of Cattle Among the Pakot in East Africa," *American Anthropologist,* 59:278–299.

Seligman, C. G. 1910. *The Melanesians of British New Guinea.* Cambridge: Cambridge University Press.

Service, Elman R. *Tobati: a Paraguayan Community.* (to be published)

Shundai, Dazai. 1729. *Keizai Roku.* B.J.A.P., Vol. VI.

Siegel, J., and Beals, Alan. 1960. "Pervasive Factionalism," *American Anthropologist,* LXII:394–417.

Singer, M. 1958. "Traditional India: Structure and Change," *Journal of American Folklore,* LXXI.

1961. "Text and Context in the Study of Contemporary Hinduism," Adyar Library Bulletin, Parts 1–4, XXV:274–303.

Smelser, Neil J. 1959. "A Comparative View of Exchange Systems," *Economic Development and Culture Change,* 7:173–182.

1959a. *Social Change in the Industrial Revolution.* Chicago: University of Chicago Press.

Smith, T. Lynn, and others. 1945. "Tabio: a Study in Rural Social Organization," Office of Foreign Agricultural Relations, U. S. Department of Agriculture, Washington, D.C.

1946. *Brazil: People and Institutions.* Baton Rouge: Louisiana State University Press.

Sombart, W. 1913. *The Jews and Modern Capitalism.* New York: E. P. Dutton & Co.

1928. *Der Moderne Kapitalismus.* 2 vols. München-Leipzig: Duncker and Humblot.

Southall, A. W. 1956. *Alur Society.* Cambridge: Cambridge University Press.

Spear, Percival. 1951. *Twilight of the Moghuls.* Cambridge: Cambridge University Press.

Srinivas, M. N. 1952. *Religion and Society Among the Coorges of South India.* Oxford: Oxford University Press.

1955. *India's Villages.* West Bengal: West Bengal Government Press.

1955a. *In Village India.* M. Marriott, ed. American Anthropological Association Memoir No. 83.

1956. "A Note on Sanskritization and Westernization," *Far Eastern Quarterly*, XV:481–496.

1957. "Caste in Modern India," *Journal of Asian Studies*, XVI:529–530.

Steiner, Franz. 1954. "Notes on Comparative Economics," *British Journal of Sociology*, V:118–129.

1957. "Towards a Classification of Labor," *Sociologus*, 7:118–119.

Stenton, D. 1955. *English Society in the Middle Ages*. Vol. III. Harmondsworth: Penguin Books.

Stevenson, H. N. C. 1954. "Status Evaluation in the Hindu Caste System," *Journal of the Royal Anthropological Institute*, IV: 45–65.

Steward, Julian H. 1938. "Basin-plateau Aboriginal Sociopolitical Groups," Bureau of American Ethnology Bulletin 120, Smithsonian Institution, Washington, D.C.

1946–51. "Handbook of South American Indians," Bureau of American Ethnology Bulletin 143, Smithsonian Institution, Washington, D.C.

1950. "Area Research: Theory and Practice," Social Science Research Council Bulletin 63, New York.

Suttles, Wayne. 1960. "Affinal Ties, Subsistence, and Prestige Among the Coast Salish," *American Anthropologist*, 62:296–305.

Takegoshi, Yosaburo. 1921. *Nisen-Gohyaku Nen Shi*. Tokyo.

Tawney, R. H. 1926. *Religion and the Rise of Capitalism*. London and New York: Harcourt, Brace & Co.

Tax, Sol. 1937. "The Municipios of the Midwestern Highlands of Guatemala," *American Anthropology*, 39:423–444.

1952. *Heritage of Conquest*. Glencoe, Ill.: The Free Press.

Taylor, Paul S. 1933. "A Spanish-American Peasant Community: Arandas in Jalisco, Mexico," *Ibero-Americana 4*, Berkeley: University of California Press.

Teikan, Kamizawa. 1776. *Okina Gusa*. Vol. XX.

Thorner, D. 1953. "The Village Panchayat as a Vehicle of Change," *Economic Development and Cultural Change*, II.

Thurnwald, Hilde. 1934. "The Status of Women in Buin Society," *Oceania*, V:119–141.

Tokiharu, Man-o. 1725. *Kwan-no Kohonroku*. Vol. II.

Tönnies, Ferdinand. 1955. *Community and Association*. London, Routledge & Kegan Paul.

Troeltsch, E. 1913. *Die Sociallehren der Christlichen Kirchen und Gruppen*. Tuebingen.

Tumin, Melvin M. 1952. *Caste in a Peasant Society*. Princeton: Princeton University Press.

Udy, Stanley H. 1959. *Organization of Work*. New Haven: Human Relations Area Files Press.

United Nations. 1954. *Enlargement of the Exchange Economy in Tropical Africa*. New York: United Nations, Department of Economic Affairs.

Valcarcel, Luis E. 1946. "Indian Markets and Fairs in Peru," in Julian Steward, ed., *Handbook of South American Indians*, Vol. 2, pp. 477–482.

van der Kroef, J. 1955. "Economic Development in Indonesia: Some Social and Cultural Impediments," *Economic Development and Cultural Change*, IV, No. 2.

Vansina, Jan. 1962. "Trade and Markets Among the Kuba," in P. J. Bohannan and G. Dalton, eds., *Markets in Africa*, Evanston: Northwestern University Press.

Vayda, Andrew P. 1961. "A Re-examination of Northwest Coast Economic Systems," Transactions of the New York Academy of Sciences, 2nd Series, 23:618–624.

Vayda, Andrew P., Leeds, A., and Smith, D. B. 1961. "The Place of Pigs in Melanesian Subsistence," Proceedings of the 1961 Annual Spring Meeting of the American Ethnological Society, Viola E. Garfield, ed., pp. 69–77, Seattle: University of Washington Press.

Walters, A. A. 1962. "National Income and Economic Accounts of Liberia, 1950–1960," in *Northwestern University Economic Survey of Liberia*, mimeograph.

Watson, William. 1958. *Tribal Cohesion in a Money Economy*. Manchester: Manchester University Press.

Weber, Max. 1909. "Agrargeschichte, Altertum," in *The Handwörterbuch der staatswissenschaften*, 3rd ed., I, Jena.

1946. "Class Status, Party," in M. Weber, ed., *Essays in Sociology*, New York: Oxford University Press.

1947. *The Theory of Social and Economic Organization*. Glencoe, Ill.: The Free Press.

1949. *The Methodology of the Social Sciences*. Glencoe, Ill.: The Free Press.

Whetten, Nathan L. 1948. *Rural Mexico*. Chicago: University of Chicago Press.

White, C. N. M. 1959. *A Preliminary Survey of Luvale Rural Economy*. The Rhodes-Livingstone Papers No. 29. Manchester: Manchester University Press.

Wigmore, J. H. n.d. "Materials for the Study of Private Law in Old Japan," *Transactions of the Asiatic Society of Japan*, Vol. XX, supplement.

Willems, Emilio. 1942. "Some Aspects of Cultural Conflict and Acculturation in Southern Rural Brazil," *Rural Sociology,* 7:375–384.

——— 1944. "Acculturation and the Horse Complex among German-Brazilians," *American Anthropologist,* 46:153–161.

——— 1945. *El Problema Rural Brasilene desde el Punto de Vista Antropológico.* Jornadas 33. Mexico, D.F.: Colegio de México, Centro de Estudios Sociales.

Williams, Eric. 1944. *Capitalism and Slavery.* Chapel Hill: University of North Carolina Press.

Williams, Robin M., Jr. 1960. *American Society.* New York: Alfred A. Knopf.

Winter, E. H. 1962. "Livestock Markets among the Iraqw of Northern Tanganyika," in P. Bohannan and G. Dalton, eds., *Markets in Africa,* Evanston: Northwestern University Press.

Wiser, W. H. 1936. *The Hindu Jajmani System.* Lucknow, India: Lucknow Publishing House.

Wolf, Eric R. 1951. *Culture Change and Culture Stability in a Puerto Rican Coffee Community.* Ph.D. dissertation, New York: Columbia University.

——— 1953. "La Formación de la Nación: un Ensaye de Formulación," *Ciencias Sociales,* 4:50–62, 98–111, 146–171.

——— 1955. "Types of Latin American Peasantry: A Preliminary Discussion," *American Anthropologist,* 57:452–471.

Worsley, P. M. 1956. "The Kinship System of the Tallensi," *Journal of Royal Anthropological Institute,* 86:37–75.

Yoshu, Makabe. 1759. *Chiri Sairon Shu.* B.J.A.P., Vol. XIV.